**INORGANIC LIFE**

**ECKARDT LINDNER**

**INORGANIC LIFE**
ON POST-VITALISM

DIAPHANES

# TABLE OF CONTENTS

**Introduction** — 11
  The Inexistence of the Inorganic — 13
    *The Lure of the Inorganic 13—The In/Existence of the Inorganic 15– The Disappearance of the Inorganic 17*
  The Critique of Life — 22
    *The Animation of the Inorganic 22—Deleuze's Inorganic Vitalism 28*
  Thinking Inorganic Life — 38
    *A Mineral Deleuze and the Question of Methodology 38—Towards an Inorganic Vitalism 43*

**Sublime Organicism** — 47
  On the Uses and Abuse of Thinking for Life — 49
    *The Intimacy of Thinking and Life 49—Thought in the Service of Life 55*
  Hylozoic Madness — 60
    *Kant's Rejection of the Life of Matter 60—Some Dreams of Life and Thought 61—The Utter Madness of Living 67—Dead Matter 77—Purposiveness and the Insufficiency of Hylozoism 79*
  The Organic Image of Thought — 84
    *Organic Histories and Ends of Thought 84—Noology 86—Organic Representation 90—Tracing the Transcendental 93*
  The Desire for Organic Unity — 97
    *The Possibility of the Discord of the Faculties 97—The Conative Striving Towards Organic Unity, or Life and Lust 99—The Natural Striving Towards Organic Unity, or The Biological Roots of the Categories 103—The Cultural Striving Towards Organic Unity, or The Whole Life 118—The Monstrous Sublime 122—From Aesthetic to Teleological Judgement 127*
  Life and Two Worlds Physics — 131
    *Transcendental Philosophy's Nature: Organic Anti-Physics 131—Relative Anti-Physics: Kantian Phenomenalism and Somatism 133—Absolute Anti-Physics: Fichte's Radicalization of the Primacy of the Practical 137—Less than Nothing 140*

## The Unlivable     145

### The Transcendental Empiricism That Has Never Been     147
*The Judgement of God 147—The Inorganic Life of Passive Synthesis 150— Suspending the Lived Body 169—On Not Being at Home 176*

### The Monstrous Epigenesis of the Transcendental     182
*The Unlivable, or the Transcendental Encounter 182—External and Internal Determination 190—The Idea as Non-Organic Life 193*

### The Inorganic Life of the Ideas     198
*Temporality and Normativity 198—The Problematic and the Law 206— Vitalism and Mathematics 211—Construction and Genesis 216—Desire, Truth and Inorganic Life 223—The Inorganic Life of the Transcendental Field 227*

## Absolute Xenogenesis     239

### Speculative Hylozoism     241
*The Unfathomable Depth of Time 241—The Bergsonian Problem 249— The Anonymity of Affects 263—Deleuzian Platonism 269—The Process of Individuation 275*

### Organs without Bodies     290
*Individuating Monsters 290—Hylozoism as Idealism 302*

## Non-Life     309

### To Have Done with the Transcendental     311
*Getting Caught Up in Life 311—The Transcendental Split in Deleuze 314— What Do Transcendental Arguments Do? 320—The Transcendental Argument and its Discontents 320*

### (Non-)Philosophical Immanence     335
*Two Formulas 335—Decision as Transcendental Auto-Deduction 336— Idealism at the Heart of Philosophy 343*

### Deleuze's Vitalist Idealism     349
*The Deleuzian Decision 349—The Event as the Name of Being 351— The Eternal Return as Transcendental A Priori 355—Thinking Through Ideal Difference 358—Impersonal Dispersion 362*

Life After Idealism ... 366
*Visioning the Real 366—In Defense of Disputatio 369—Singular and Generic Life 371—Vitalism After Idealism, or the Things to Come 374*

**Post-Vitalism** ... 381
Passivity ... 383
*Vitalism, Active and Passive Deleuze Against Flat Ontologies 383—Trapping the Cosmic Animal 395—The Fichtean Organicism of New Materialism 403—The Poverty of Panpsychism 415*
Death ... 428
*This Event, Death 428—The Doctrine of Death 435—The Thanatropic Reason of Unbound Inorganic Life 443—The Demand of Inassimilable Inorganicity 451—Unbinding the Death Drive 460*
Inertia ... 471
*The Speculative Neutral Genesis of Passive Vitalism 471—The Three Fundamental Concepts of Life: Madness, Stupidity and Malevolence 481*

**Conclusion: Failure** ... 505
Deleuze after Vitalism ... 507
Existence and De-Creation ... 514
*The Ethics of Non-Productivity 514—The Aftermath of Exhaustion 537*

*Index* ... 541

"HAMM: […] Use your head, can't you, use your head, you're on earth, there's no cure for that!
[…]
CLOV: I say to myself that the earth is extinguished, though I never saw it lit.
*(Pause.)*
It's easy going.
*(Pause.)*
When I fall I'll weep for happiness."[1]


"Today space is splendid
The mountains have come loose
Let's unmake something"[2]


"It is the Intolerable, and not Evolution,
which ought to be biology's hobbyhorse."[3]

---

1  Samuel Beckett, *Endgame* (New York: Grove Press, 1958), p. 68, 81.
2  Michael Palmer, "Odd-Even," *Boundary* 14, no. 1 (1985), p. 11.
3  E. M. Cioran, *All Gall Is Divided: The Aphorisms of a Legendary Iconoclast* (New York: Arcade Publishing, 1999), p. 32.

# INTRODUCTION

"We must be humble. We are so easily baffled by appearances
And do not realize that these stones are one with the stars.
It makes no difference to them whether they are high or low,
Mountain peak or ocean floor, palace, or pigsty.
There are plenty of ruined buildings in the world but no ruined stones."[4]

---

[4] Hugh MacDiarmid, "On A Raised Beach," in *Selected Poetry of Hugh MacDiarmid* (New York: New Directions, 2008), p. 148.

# THE INEXISTENCE OF THE INORGANIC

## THE LURE OF THE INORGANIC

In the lyrical first chapter of *Pierres Réfléchies,* Roger Caillois follows the traces of a peculiar "Devonian heritage" in man. Neatly arranged or intentionally scattered, "landscaping stones are enclosures for dreams,"[5] they attract us by virtue of being surfaces for projection, for the tendency of the human imagination to construct meaning and myths from their unique yet arbitrary appearance. The same cannot be said of fossils. The petrified remains of once living beings are not organic anymore yet also do not belong to the realm of minerals. Even though they lasted merely for the duration of a flash before returning to the ground, they left a trace. But these archives of life do not invoke dreams. They do not animate the imagination. On the contrary, the preserved shell of the mollusk imposes on the mind the thought of its strict and relentless morphology, of the complete and determinate geometry of its genesis. It is not that the inflexible mechanism of nature is taken as an object in this forced thought. Instead, in a mimetic movement, thinking approximates the power of nature by traversing the multiplication of orders that comprises nature's history. Still legible in the fossil is the struggle of energies which finally gave the creature its form, as if its creation was "the resolution of a confusion."[6] Once life had fled the organism, the "architecture" of its being, as if it were a monument, was preserved by petrification—an ossuary, thorny legs spread out over a carmine ground, protruding from a marble-like jagged fort. A gallery of dispersed symbols, which, after an unfathomable time has passed after the creature's death, humans will gather and connect by force, falsely attributing to the creature the emphatic and vague notion of beauty. The misconception of the fossil's harmonious beauty is a defense mechanism designed to dispel the lure of the

---

5    Roger Caillois, *Pierres Réfléchies* (Paris: Gallimard, 1975), p. 33, my translation.
6    Ibid.

life of the inanimate. The fossil creates a zone of indeterminacy, since it implicates in the living the inanimate time before and after it.

Even though much of Caillois's work is dedicated to the study of the diagonal relations between beings (the various forms of mimesis performed by the octopus and the praying mantis, for example, as described in *Méduse et Cie*), he displays a fundamental indifference towards warm blooded creatures. Instead of projecting the capacities and values of the human into inanimate nature, this petrified thought instantiates an inverse anthropocentrism. Confronted with the lure of the inanimate, man might discover that the order and force operating in the formation of the now fossilized living being is the same as in the genesis of crystals or of humans themselves—a headless creation, without goals. Caillois's disinterest in the fate or nature of a transitory species like ours might at the same time be read as an attempt to trace the ever-elusive genesis of being, not only beyond the human but beyond the advent of life itself, culminating in the mimetic desire "to make oneself a contemporary of the immemorial,"[7] as Cioran writes. And so, minerology supports a certain spiritual exercise that is not tied to the imagination or the joyful contemplation of God. When Caillois detects "anterior" water in a nodule of agate that has been trapped since before the dawn of man, as if he spotted an afterglow of its genesis, he recapitulates the Copernican Revolution at a higher level. The depth of time emanating from the rock gives us pause and, in contemplating this sensation, we appear to ourselves as uninvited guests in this world, with senses far too dull to comprehend what is presented to us. We are not trained to be in the presence of inertia or inanimation and do not recognize the genesis they signal. As Cioran, with reference to Caillois, warns us: "But we got in the habit of attaching ourselves to the future, of putting apocalypse above cosmogony, of idolizing the explosion and the end, of banking to an absurd degree on the Revolution or the Last Judgment."[8] History, even that of nature, has become fully organic in this rush for the end, assimilating every process from the vantage point of the

---

[7] E.M. Cioran, *Anathemas and Admirations* (New York: Arcade Publishing, 1991), p. 207.
[8] Ibid., p. 208.

apocalypse, unable to grasp any genesis that is not yet completed and exhausted. These stones do not animate the mind, they do not give rise to concepts or enliven the imagination, and so they do not appear as an object worthy of thought. Philosophy does not care about the inorganic, in the same way that the inorganic does not concern itself with philosophy. And yet the inorganic remains the unthought and the irretrievable outside of thought right at the heart of philosophy itself—the non-philosophy constituting philosophy.

## THE IN/EXISTENCE OF THE INORGANIC

This book called *Inorganic Life* is concerned with the peculiar in/existence of the inorganic. As a conceptual horizon for this discussion, the course of the argument will follow the largely unchallenged presupposition of zonta-centrism, by which is understood here the assumption that living things (*hōs zōnta*) are different in kind from non-living things, insofar as the former possess a distinct ontological status and this status is in a very specific way superior to that of the latter. From this claim follows the assumption that the organism is the model for, the embodiment of or the pure expression of life itself, because it *demonstrates* certain characteristics of the living, such as self-organization, unity, reproduction, teleology. Conversely, it is only through the organism's demonstration of unique capacities which are irreducible to the general mechanical laws that the living can be conceptually determined. Retroactively, this organo-centrism then justifies the assumption of the ontological elevation of life, insofar as the organism is defined by its distinct capacities for self-relation, which translate into specific epistemological registers (e.g. perceiving, feeling), and at their highest efficiency in the human entail the capacity for autonomous action and cognition. Which means that the organism is the epistemological condition of knowledge and truth, and the ontological locus of freedom and morality. Philosophy, being animated itself by these values (truth and morality), whether implicitly or explicitly, thus relies on the organic as its condition.

This does not mean that philosophy has not thought the inorganic, since it has obsessively (or possessively or possessed by it) contemplated things, forces and geological objects in order to ensure the abyssal border between organized teleological living beings and disorganized mechanical dead beings, and so define the organic at its limits.[9] Philosophy, thus, has thought the inorganic only ever in terms of a mode of in/existence. The formulation "in/existence" invokes both the question of the presence of the inorganic and its curious absence, or even the idea that the mode of existence of the inorganic is a form of double inexistence: as a privative mode of existence in relation to the organic (i.e. as a fundamental lack of organic qualities such as activity, thought or feeling) and as a dialectical inexistence insofar as the inorganic is only for-the-organic or a foreclosed in-itself (even though it is a foreclosure *for* the organic), but is never a for-itself. These two modes of inexistence, however, hint at the promise of another yet unrealized mode of thinking the inorganic or even of thinking with it.

Maybe the distinct "organic chauvinism"[10] of philosophy, resulting in the absence of the inorganic, should not be a surprise to us. There is a minimally vitalist ethics that forms the underlying basis for philosophical thought, a progressive quest for animation. The history of philosophy could be reconstructed as a series of critiques of previous systems of thought, which target the unquestioned assumptions that underlie those systems in order to retrieve an obscured genesis. The promise is that, by dispelling illusion or overturning false reification, by returning to the genesis of things, there might be a revitalization of the mind or of life. "Vitalism," as Claire Colebrook writes, "is not one ethics among others but the way in which ethics is established: always on the basis of life."[11] Nietzsche finds expressions of the Will to Power even in the life-denying philosophies built on ascetic values of truth and morality. To be in the presence of

9   Being a presupposition of philosophy, this organo-centrism is implicitly operative even when not explicit or thematic in the concrete philosophy itself.
10  Richard Iveson, "Being Without Life: On the Trace of Organic Chauvinism with Derrida and DeLanda," in *Philosophy After Nature*, ed. Rosi Braidotti and Rick Dolphijn (London; New York; Lanham: Rowman & Littlefield Publishers, 2017), p. 179. See also Manuel DeLanda, *A Thousand Years of Nonlinear History* (New York: Zone Books, 1997).
11  Claire Colebrook, *Deleuze and the Meaning of Life* (London: Continuum, 2010), p. 44.

this genesis, all spectrality (the trace of an absence disturbing presence), all hints at an outside, must be dispelled. And so, as Jean-Luc Nancy remarks in "The Heart of Things," an essay in *The Birth to Presence*, the inorganic thing, appearing as spectral or opaque resistance, becomes a problem for philosophy itself: "one must not seek the living beat of universal animation in the heart of things"; rather, the "thing is nothing other than the immanent immobility of the fact *that there are* things."[12] No animation or becoming is perceived in the pure "being-there" (*il y a*) of the non-living thing, and thus any engagement with the excessive immobility of the thing in an attempt to penetrate its heavy inert thinking "collapses under its own weight."[13] The noo-centrism of philosophy, assuming an always already available and accessible ability to think (and to think *de jure*), as well as the transparency of thought to itself (i.e. the voluntary ability to engender thought in thought and represent thinking), clashes with the inanimation and opacity that the inorganic thing seems to force on thought.

The distinct lure of the inorganic might be found in this decisive failure of thought, in which "thought finds its true gravity"; "it is there [in its collapse] it recognized itself,"[14] being thrown back onto the unthought within thinking. It might even be the case that, as Mario Perniola claims in *The Sex Appeal of the Inorganic*, this failure leads the human being to consider herself as a thing and desire the thing's own inert and immobile nature.[15] The question of this book will thus be: is it possible to think the inorganic and its peculiar life.

### THE DISAPPEARANCE OF THE INORGANIC

The *problem* of the inorganic, in its intertwined dual expression in science and philosophy, must, as François Jacob notes in his *The Logic of*

---

12  Jean-Luc Nancy, *The Birth to Presence* (Stanford: Stanford University Press, 2009), p. 169.
13  Ibid., p. 171.
14  Ibid.
15  Compare Mario Perniola, *The Sex-Appeal of the Inorganic: Philosophies of Desire in the Modern World* (New York; London: Bloomsbury Academic, 2017), p. 7, 37, 53.

*Life*, be considered in the broader context of the history of the development of the notion of life and the living. In the *epistēmē* of the seventeenth century, mechanism provided universal explanatory grounds for the "automatic" movement of animals, plants and inorganic nature alike, not via analogy between them but by total identification. Thus "the living extended without a break into the inanimate [...] There was as yet no fundamental division between the living and the non-living"[16] Spurred by the discoveries of Newton and Harvey, universal mechanism was accepted as the only explanatory model in line with the uniformity and continuity of nature, presenting the researcher with merely epistemological and no ontological limitations. The thought of Descartes and Hobbes, which worked along these lines, conceiving of organic beings as intricate machines, found more nuanced and differentiated expressions in Buffon's "moule intérieure" and Bonnet's preformist germ theory.[17]

With Lamarck's theory of heredity, which meant that "the living was separated from the inanimate," and which "established biology as a science," the "abyssal"[18] gulf between the organic and the inorganic first appears. In his 1778 study *La Flore Française*, Lamarck outlines the characteristics (along apparently Aristotelean lines) that define living beings and distinguish them from other things. Firstly, every organic being possesses an internal organization wherein every part is able to perform a specific function for the advantage (*jouissent*) of the whole, culminating in the ability to reproduce. Secondly, due to this interior organization, some organic beings are endowed with sensibility, sentiment and the capacity for movement other than that caused by external forces (animals), while others (plants) are restricted to the movement resulting from their internal organization or external forces.[19] The inorganic, for its part, is negatively defined. It has no internal organization (and thus no unity); the in-

---

16   Francois Jacob, *The Logic of Life: A History Of Heredity* (Princeton: Princeton University Press, 1993), p. 33.
17   See section "The Desire for Organic Unity" in this book.
18   Ibid., p. 152.
19   See Jean-Baptiste Lamarck, *La Flore Français* (Paris: Imprimerie Royale, 1778), p. 1f., and David Wills, *Inanimation: Theories of Inorganic Life* (Minneapolis: University of Minnesota Press, 2016), p. 3.

side of the stone and the outside are continuous *in principle*. The inorganic does not possess organs and lacks therefore all the capacities afforded to the organic; in other words, mineral beings cannot reproduce, they have neither sensibility nor sentiment, they can expand or decrease in volume through aggregation but cannot grow, they can be moved by external forces but cannot move with purpose or voluntarily. The inorganic or mineral realm does not know unity or ends. The organism, with its teleological movement, irreducible to mechanics, or, as Derrida calls it, commenting on Jacob's study, the "sovereign automotive," which "moves by itself, spontaneously, sponte sua—this is how the living being in general is defined."[20] The distinction made by Lamarck recapitulates the discussion between Boerhaave and Stahl more than half a century earlier and repeats the latter's emphasis on the connection between interior unity and voluntary locomotion peculiar to the organism. Boerhaave claimed that the composition and actions of and in the human body could be sufficiently explained in Newtonian terms, while Stahl argued that the unity of the parts of the body and their deployment for intentional action necessitated an immaterial supplement (i.e. a soul). Thus, Lamarck's remarks on mineral and organic beings situate themselves in an ongoing debate between, on the one hand, champions of universal mechanism and, on the other, vitalists insisting on the necessary existence of an immaterial force to account for the animation of the inorganic (thus enabling teleology, unity, reproduction and sensibility) or the even stricter distinction that "life is born from life, and of life alone."[21] While the discussion was settled scientifically by the Wöhler synthesis in 1828, which produced urea, the last element that vitalist researchers had claimed could only be produced by a living being's organism, outside of the human body, the philosophical debate continued. Vitalist positions explicitly structured around the mechanism associated with materialism (and thus the inorganic) can still be found in Bergson's notion of the *élan vital*, which is "more than anything

---

20  Jacques Derrida, *The Beast and the Sovereign* (Chicago: University of Chicago Press, 2009), p. 211.
21  Jacob, *The Logic of Life: A History Of Heredity*, p. 126.

else, a tendency to act upon inert matter,"[22] in German *Lebensphilosophie* from Dilthey to Heidegger, or in dualist theories like Schrödinger's or Prigogine's, which insist on a dual tendency within nature towards both the increase of disorder proper to the inorganic (entropy) and the spontaneous creation of order.[23] Even though nominally "materialisms," the spirit of these vitalisms is still embodied by several "New Materialisms."[24]

Kant's approach to the abyssal gulf between the inorganic and the organic in his *Critique of Judgement* relocates this problem from a dichotomy within nature itself to a conflict of the subjective capacities of the mind. He transposes the issue into the antinomy of teleological judgement: the understanding's operation of subsuming phenomena under universal and general (mechanical) laws is in discord with reason's insistence on specific laws, irreducible to general laws, to account for the exceptional activity of organized beings. His solution, which relies on the suprasensible unity of the faculties, and which we will discuss in detail in the section "The Desire for Organic Unity," did not resolve the gulf, but rather reaffirmed the exceptional position of the organic as the locus of truth, freedom and the realization of the unity of nature.[25] Kant's successors generally reiterated the elevation of the living—especially Fichte, whose emphasis on the primacy of the practical, and thus activity, sought to eradicate the inorganic on ethical grounds—but Schelling is a notable exception, insofar as his nature-philosophy (*Naturphilosophie*) emphasized transcendental philosophy's limits with respect to inorganic nature. Given his repeated insistence on the philosophical relevance of geology, one might read his warning about Fichte's philosophy, which "consists of nothing but a moralizing of the entire world that undermines life and hollows it out; a true disgust towards all nature and vitality except that in the subject, and a crude extolling of morality and the doctrine of morals as the one reality

---

22  Henri Bergson, *Creative Evolution* (Lanham: University Press of America, 1983), p. 96.
23  See Erwin Schrödinger, *What is Life?* (Cambridge: Cambridge University Press, 2012), and Ilya Prigogine and Isabelle Stengers, *Order Out of Chaos: Man's New Dialogue with Nature* (London: Bantham Books, 1984); also compare section "Passivity" in this book.
24  See also sections "Hylozoic Madness," "Passivity" and "Death."
25  Compare section "Life and Two Worlds Physics."

in life and science,"[26] as a defense of the vitality of the inorganic against transcendental philosophy. If nature is only considered within the confines of transcendental philosophy, which presupposes the existence of the mind as the absolute condition of thought, no investigation into the genesis of the mind itself is possible. Transcendental philosophy's range only extends to its own organic condition, unable to investigate its genesis from or in the inorganic. It expels the inorganic unthought from organic thought.

As we will see in the course of the book, this elevation of the organic or living over the inanimate or inorganic is still present in numerous contemporary approaches to the living. It will therefore not be the concern of this work to find a possible "in-between" but rather to construct a feasible "beyond" of mechanism and vitalism.

---

[26] Friedrich Wilhelm Schelling, *Sämmtliche Werke. Vol. 7* (Stuttgart: Cotta'scher Verlag, 1859), p. 19. Quoted as translated in: Iain Hamilton Grant, *Philosophies of Nature after Schelling* (London: Continuum, 2008), p. 61.

# THE CRITIQUE OF LIFE

### THE ANIMATION OF THE INORGANIC

Within the contemporary debate on this subject, we can identify three approaches which aim at subverting the ontological or epistemological hierarchy between the living/organic and the inanimate/inorganic. Firstly, while accepting the strict line separating the living from the non-living, some recent approaches, paradigmatically those of Speculative Realism and post-phenomenology, have attempted to highlight being in itself apart from (or before) organic sentience or thought. Secondly, studies methodologically inspired by discourse analysis and deconstruction have questioned the gulf between the animate and inanimate as a historically contingent and "logocentric" demarcation. Thirdly, rejecting the ontological distinction between the organic and the inorganic, New Materialist and other Deleuze-inspired philosophies have proposed materialisms or neo-vitalist theories that attempt to move beyond the incompatibility of mechanism and vitalism.

The first set of approaches insists on the inanimate in itself and its power to resist the organic, providing the former with a positive existence independent from the latter. In the slipstream of the debate on the human/inhuman divide from Lyotard's *The Inhuman* to Haraway's *A Cyborg Manifesto* to, more recently, Wolfe's *What is Posthumanism?*, the critique of anthropocentrism has created a new philosophical interest in that which escapes the grasp or resists the human.[27] In *The Open*, for example, Agamben critiques Heidegger's analysis of and distinction between the "worldless" stone, the lizard "poor in world" and the human who "has a

---

[27] See Jean-François Lyotard, *The Inhuman: Reflections on Time* (Stanford: Stanford University Press, 2005); Donna Haraway, "A Cyborg Manifesto," in *Simians, Cyborgs, and Women: the Reinvention of Nature* (New York: Routledge, 1991), p. 149–181; Cary Wolfe, *What Is Posthumanism?* (Minneapolis: University of Minnesota Press, 2010), and Katherine Hayles, *How We Became Posthuman: Virtual Bodies in Cybernetics, Literature, and Informatics* (Chicago: University of Chicago Press, 1999).

world," not only highlighting the peculiar positionality of the animal, but also the carelessness with which the stone "gets quickly set aside."[28] This Heideggerian disregard for stones does, however, open up the space for further analysis of the specific modes of existence of the inorganic. Drawing more explicitly from the (post-)phenomenological tradition, Nancy's *The Birth to Presence* emphasizes the experience of inertia, opacity and inanimation when confronted with the sterile "being-there"[29] of things, highlighting how the inorganic's immanent immobility asserts itself within dynamic organic thought without being reducible to it. Rereading Blanchot's thoughts on the sterility and inertia of Being in the light of Nancy's phenomenological analysis of the encounter with the inorganic "thing," Kaufman has hinted at a not yet realized "mineralogy of being."[30] Explicitly anti-phenomenological, Meillassoux's speculative materialism in *After Finitude* asks how we can think the existence of an "arche-fossil," which predates the emergence of any sentient organism, or of life as such; i.e. it exists prior to the emergence of organic life, of cognition and of representation. He proposes that since Kant philosophy has succumbed to "correlationism," by which he means "the idea according to which we only ever have access to the correlation between thinking and being, and never to either term considered apart from the other."[31] While a correlationist position (whether transcendental, phenomenological, deconstructive, or otherwise) might posit, he claims, that the fossil can be *represented* as older than life, or is a *trace* of this absence of life, it can always only do so by reducing the material being of the ancestral fossil to the correlation between thinking and being (e.g. the transcendental conditions of experience, the text, structures of power, and so on). If the fossil, however, existed before the conditions of all these correlations obtained, the material

---

[28] Giorgio Agamben, *The Open: Man and Animal* (Stanford: Stanford University Press, 2004), p. 51.
[29] Nancy, *The Birth to Presence*, p. 169.
[30] Eleanor Kaufman, "The Mineralogy of Being," in *Architecture in the Anthropocene: Encounters Among Design, Deep Time, Science and Philosophy*, ed. Etienne Turpin (New York: Open Humanities Press, 2013), p. 153.
[31] Quentin Meillassoux, *After Finitude: An Essay on the Necessity of Contingency* (London; New York: Continuum, 2009), p. 5.

object possesses positive qualities that fall outside of the epistemological regime of transcendental philosophy, or the "noetico-neomatic" correlation. As Eugene Thacker points out, the same correlationism applies if the inorganic in-itself is considered as existing independently from organic cognition by means that either reduce it to a presence for the organism or to an opposition to or absence for the organism.[32] Radicalizing Latour's actor-network-theory, which considered the "agency" of things within interactions, the object-oriented ontology of Harman, on the other hand, picking up the critique of correlationism, insists on the potential of things to interact and change *and* exist non-relationally without the condition of human minds.[33] Common to both the (post-)phenomenological and the speculative realist approaches is the insistence on upholding the distinction between the organic and the inorganic in order to think the latter properly.

The second set of approaches would include work such as Foucault's and Jacob's on the emergence of the concept of life and its historical contingencies, as well as more recent analysis into the discourses and rhetoric of the life sciences, such as Doyle's *On Beyond Living* and *Wetwares*.[34] Under this rubric, we will also include deconstructive approaches to the animate/inanimate divide like Derrida's own study *Life Death*, which argues for a shift away from approaches that begin with the presence of life to an analysis of how the absence that is death has always already contaminated and constituted the living. Against Jacob's logic of reproduction, Derrida highlights the primacy of production, which includes techne, artifice and other inorganic means, in order to enable the organic to repro-

---

32  Compare Eugene Thacker, *After Life* (Chicago: University of Chicago Press, 2010), p. 249.
33  See Bruno Latour, *Reassembling the Social: An Introduction to Actor-Network-Theory* (Oxford: Oxford University Press, 2007); Graham Harman, *Towards Speculative Realism: Essays and Lectures* (Ropley: Zero Books, 2010), and Ian Bogost, *Alien Phenomenology, or, What It's Like to Be a Thing* (Minneapolis: University of Minnesota Press, 2012).
34  Compare Michel Foucault, *The Order of Things: An Archaeology of the Human Sciences* (London: Routledge, 1997), p. 136; Jacob, *The Logic of Life*; Richard Doyle, *On Beyond Living: Rhetorical Transformations of the Life Sciences* (Stanford: Stanford University Press, 1997), and Richard Doyle, *Wetwares: Experiments in Postvital Living* (Minneapolis: University of Minnesota Press, 2003). *The Logic of Life: A History Of Heredity* (Princeton: Princeton University Press, 1993

duce and sustain its presence.[35] Thus, he asks us to reconsider "the limits between the human and the animal, the human and the natural, the human and the technical."[36] This deconstruction of the alleged logocentrism (and physiocentrism) in the assumption of a primacy of the natural before the artificial, hence also of the organic before the inorganic, has inspired investigations into the prosthetic (and artificial) condition of organic life. With respect to the life sciences this thesis can be found expressed in David Wills's *Prosthesis* and *Dorsality*,[37] or, in reference to the technological condition of contemporary life and the inextricable entanglement of inorganic machinery and organic being, in Bernard Stiegler's three volume series *Technics and Time*.[38] While not eradicating the line between the inorganic and the organic entirely, these approaches either focus on the historical contingency of the distinguishing line or attempt to complicate the demarcation by demonstrating how differences begin to multiply once the border separating the two realms is approached.

The third set of approaches subverts the hierarchy between the inorganic and the organic by rejecting the reduction of the processes of life to the organic. These new material vitalisms or vitalist materialisms attempt to move beyond the mechanism/vitalism distinction in the direction of a, in Deleuze and Guattari's terms, "universal machinism."[39] They proceed by supplanting the dualism of inorganic matter and organic life with a Spinozist single Substance for all modes and attributes; on this "plane of Nature" the organic living being is defined by its ability to perform "a transcoding of milieus,"[40] which involves engendering reverse causalities,

---

35 See Jacques Derrida, *Life Death* (Chicago: Chicago University Press, 2020), p. 6–12.
36 Jacques Derrida, "Nietzsche and the Machine," in *Negotiations* (Stanford: Stanford University Press, 2002), p. 241.
37 Compare David Wills, *Dorsality: Thinking Back through Technology and Politics* (Minneapolis: University of Minnesota Press, 2008), and David Wills, *Prosthesis* (Minneapolis: University of Minnesota Press, 2021).
38 See Bernard Stiegler, *Technics and Time, 1: The Fault of Epimetheus* (Stanford: Stanford University Press, 1998); Bernard Stiegler, *Technics and Time, 2: Disorientation* (Stanford: Stanford University Press, 2008), and Bernard Stiegler, *Technics and Time, 3: Cinematic Time and the Question of Malaise* (Stanford: Stanford University Press, 2010).
39 Gilles Deleuze and Félix Guattari, *A Thousand Plateaus: Capitalism and Schizophrenia II* (London; New York: Bloomsbury Publishing, 1988), p. 283.
40 Ibid., p. 266, 336.

the constitution of a stratum and destratification. These operations of stratification and destratification specific to organic life do not, however, exhaust all processes of living or of producing consistency, nor is organic life exclusively constituted by processes attributable to its activity; i.e. even organic life only occurs transversally across various strata. Hence, Deleuze and Guattari claim: "not all Life is confined to the organic strata; rather, the organism is that which life sets against itself in order to limit itself, and there is a life all the more intense, all the more powerful for being anorganic."[41] Already the 1997 *A Thousand Years of Non-Linear History* by Manuel DeLanda proposes a non-organic history of life that is neither centered around the emergence of life nor presupposing organisms as its condition. Recapitulating the nineteenth century debate on the possibility of a "history" of nature itself, the "robot historian" solves the problem by multiplying, interlacing and overlapping various mineral, vegetal and animal histories. Translating Deleuze's vitalism into the field of non-equilibrium thermodynamics and dynamical systems theory, DeLanda's *Intensive Science and Virtual Philosophy* proposes a theory of "morphogenesis" (i.e. the generation of form), wherein processes of formation only differ in degree of intensity between organic and inorganic individuations, but not in kind. The ends of teleological movements, which are supposedly exclusive to the organic, are considered in their genesis and traced back to intensive sub-representational processes of repetition and feedback loops, which create the transcendental illusion of "purposiveness" for representational thought.[42] The diverse field of authors comprising the New Materialism(s) have, with varying proximity or distance to Deleuze's vitalism, proposed different conceptions of "matter" endowed immanently with the capacities formerly only ascribed to the organic (e.g. agency, formation of unity, affectability), without relying on an immaterial animating force. Jane Bennett's *Vibrant Matter*, for example, emphasizes the agency of things within (Deleuzian) assemblages due to their

---

[41] Ibid., p. 503
[42] Manuel DeLanda, *Intensive Science and Virtual Philosophy* (London; New York: Continuum, 2002), p. 156.

capacity to affect and be affected (and thus express a Spinozist "conatus"), regardless of whether these composites contain organic actors or not.[43] The "vibrant" capacity of matter to engender becomings within assemblages hence circumvents the mechanism-vitalism distinction.[44] The formation of an embodied, yet "nomadic" subjectivity in Rosi Braidotti's materialism is characterized by the same intersection of organic and inorganic strata on the deterritorialized plane of immanence: "A piece of meat activated by electric waves of desire, a text written by the unfolding of genetic encoding. [...] a folding-in of external influences and a simultaneous unfolding outwards of affects."[45]

Against the grain of these New Materialisms' attempts to conceptualize affirmative encounters and becomings of the human being, things and forces (i.e. the possibility of a self-furthering relation of the organic and inorganic), the philosophy of Nick Land represents a radical (and idiosyncratic) reading of Deleuze and Guattari's "machinic phylum," which proposes a "de-humanization" of thought. His "libidinal or machinic materialism" dispenses with Bergsonian intuition and proposes instead the intensification of the primary (sub-representational) process of matter's self-differentiation through the disruption of the inhibiting secondary process of structuration, especially the structuration of the organism. In this hyper-vitalism, the "inorganic" does not merely denote a certain form of material organization on the plane of immanence, but the movement of matter itself, which is hindered in its excessive production by the conservative economy of the organism.[46] What Land and the New Materialisms have in common is that they are less interested in the historical con-

---

[43] Jane Bennett, *Vibrant Matter: A Political Ecology of Things* (Durham, N.C.: Duke University Press, 2009), p. 20.

[44] See section "Passivity," compare also Diana Coole, "Rethinking Agency: A Phenomenological Approach to Embodiment and Agentic Capacities," *Political Studies* 53, no. 1 (March 2005), p. 124–142, and Karen Barad, *Meeting the Universe Halfway: Quantum Physics and the Entanglement of Matter and Meaning* (Durham, N.C.: Duke University Press, 2007). *Political Studies* 53, Nr. 1 (March 2005).

[45] Rosi Braidotti, "Teratologies," in *Deleuze and Feminist Theory*, ed. Claire Colebrook and Ian Buchanan (Edinburgh: Edinburgh University Press, 2000), p. 159.

[46] See Nick Land, "Machinic Desire," in *Fanged Noumena: Collected Writings 1987–2007* (Windsor Quarry: Urbanomic, 2014).

tingency of the demarcation between the organic and the inorganic, and more in trying to subvert the gulf between the organic and the inorganic with a univocal and immanent ontology and a non-representational epistemology.

The inorganic vitalism proposed in this book will align itself with this third set of approaches, while also putting emphasis on the merits of the first one and highlighting the limits and weaknesses of the New Materialism(s) as well as Land's libidinal materialism.

## DELEUZE'S INORGANIC VITALISM

*Regarding the Question, Why "Inorganic Life"?*
To date, there has been no comprehensive study on Deleuze's notion of inorganic life. One might give three intersecting explanations for this curious absence: Firstly, the notion of inorganic life appears *explicitly* only a handful of times in Deleuze's whole œuvre, and even when it does, it serves as a placeholder for other concepts. Therefore, due to the lack of material the notion of inorganic life seemingly does not warrant a more extensive investigation. Secondly, Deleuze's univocal ontology is sometimes seen as a "flat" ontology, within which the same life is distributed equally in everything, meaning that inorganic matter is animated with organic properties. If this is the case, then it is not so much inorganic life as the life of the inorganic that is key. And thirdly, even though it has not been investigated as a concept, the spirit of inorganic life is embodied in various works and studies that apply it, i.e. determining the concept by using it in practice, thus rendering theoretical approaches superfluous.

Against the claim of the first explanation, this book will insist that, even when not explicitly mentioned by name, the concept of inorganic life has informed all of Deleuze's major works. It is present, if still only somewhat obscurely foreshadowed, in the early works on Hume, Bergson, Kant and Nietzsche, more clearly expressed (even if only mentioned in passing) in *Difference and Repetition* and *The Logic of Sense*, and transformed but explicit in *A Thousand Plateaus*. The minor works on literature and art, however, especially the *Essays Critical and Clinical* and his study on Francis Bacon, seem to speak of nothing else. Here we see the organism's struggle with being constituted by a life that at the same time tears it apart, the encounter with the impersonal and unlivable grounds of personal life, with organic life's inorganic condition.

The second explanation will be discussed in the section "The Transcendental Empiricism That Has Never Been" and in more detail in the later section "Passivity," but, broadly speaking, it pertains to a tendency prevalent in New Materialism to animate the inorganic by ascribing to matter all the organic capacities that it had formerly been deprived of (e.g. agency, formation of form, sensibility, mind). As we shall see below, this line of inquiry first accepts the divide between the organic and the inorganic, only to then extract the exclusively organic properties which *result* from the animate/inanimate divide and project them back onto inorganic matter. Life in these New Materialisms is still organic in principle, but now even the inorganic partakes in the organic vitality. This misunderstanding of Deleuzian univocity focuses on the specific ways in which the inorganic demonstrates organic vitality, rather than investigating Deleuze's reconceptualization of life and vitality itself. Or, in other words, it focuses on the life of the inorganic at the expense of Deleuze's concept of inorganic life. The chapter "A Life of Metal" from Bennett's *Vibrant Matter*, in which she recapitulates an argument made by DeLanda in his 1992 text "Non-Organic Life," is a good example. The crystal grains of iron, she explains, are organized in regular arrays, but also contain imperfections—loose atoms, for example—not belonging to any individual grain. These radicals existing at the interfaces of grains render them "porous" and thus introduce "intercrystalline spaces."[47] She then goes on to claim: "A metallic *vitality*, a (impersonal) life, can be seen in the quivering of these free atoms at the edges between the grains of the polycrystalline edifice."[48] To elucidate this point, she connects it to the dynamics of the spreading of cracks in metal. Due to the imperfections in the crystalline

---

[47] Bennett, *Vibrant Matter*, p. 59.
[48] Ibid.

structure of metal, the path and the exact dynamic behavior cannot be fully determined in advance of the actual crack, since every interaction of forces in the process expresses an emergent causality influencing the reactions around it. Thus, she claims: "The dynamics of spreading cracks may be an example of what Deleuze and Guattari call the 'nomadism' of matter."[49] It is, however, unclear what establishes the "vitality" of the "quivering atoms" or the "dynamics of spreading cracks," aside from the fact that they seem to display non-mechanical causality and hence non-deterministic movement. The equation of non-mechanical movement and life, however, merely serves to recapitulate the mechanism-vitalism divide and to deepen it. It is thus a concern of this book to provide a reading of Deleuze that avoids these pitfalls.

It is correct, as per the third explanation, that many works embody the spirit or employ the concept of inorganic life without explicitly dedicating a sustained study to the notion itself. Even Deleuze himself alludes to inorganic life in the presupposition of the unlivable condition of the lived, rather than creating a fully consistent concept of it. That means, however, that a thorough conceptualization remains, perhaps begs, to be undertaken. The wager of this investigation into the concept is that, if the constantly imminent danger of failing to create it can be somehow avoided, it might engender other becomings and events in thinking, thus furthering, with a small contribution, the creation of a new (post)-vitalism.

### *The Inorganic Life of the Gothic Line*

The most sustained and explicit treatment of the notion of inorganic life can be found in Deleuze and Guattari's interpretation of Worringer on the expressions of Gothic artistic volition (*Kunstwollen*) in the second volume of *Capitalism and Schizophrenia*. In line with the *Lebensphilosphie* of the early twentieth century, Worringer's *Abstraction and Empathy* is concerned with the formulation of an anti-mimetic model of art history, which investigates the interplay of the psychological needs and drives that are involved in and inform artistic activity, and traces the formal quali-

[49] Ibid.

ties corresponding to this process, which he called "style." Blurring the lines of deduction, induction and hermeneutics, he firstly identifies in a historical analysis the psycho-existential needs or desires of a culture in an attempt to interpret the artistic volition specific to a time, whilst simultaneously analyzing the style of the time to measure the psycho-existential condition of the will that expresses itself in the *Kunstwollen*. This interplay of psycho-existential forces is structured around two opposing needs: empathy and abstraction. While the former is aligned with organic life, rationality and immanence, the latter is aligned with inorganic death, transcendence and instinct. Art history, according to Worringer, should be regarded in its diachronic development and its synchronic phenomena as a shifting constellation and differential coupling of these needs, which are not transparent to the artists of the time itself. Style, the expression of the will to art in the specific constellation of psycho-existential needs, remains thus unintelligible to the artists, appearing to them as a mysterious and powerful, yet obscure force. Detached from any conscious volition, the first abstract artistic productions were instinctual, not rational:

> This urge was bound to find its first satisfaction in pure geometric abstraction, which, set free from all external connections with the world, represents a felicitation whose mysterious transfiguration emanates not from the observer's intellect, but from the deepest roots of his somato-psychic constitution.[50]

By rooting the desire for abstraction not in intellect but in instinct, Worringer reveals that the more one probes the organic body (and its intellect), the more it appears itself only as an instinctual secondary formation (*Weiterbildung*) or a deviation (*Differenzierung*) from its inorganic ground. Abstract art does not speak to and nor does it come from the intellect or the organic body, but is an echo of inorganic nature, which is felt as the longing or painful desire for a primordial, ancestral simplicity. Even

---

[50] Wilhelm Worringer, *Abstraction and Empathy: A Contribution to the Psychology of Style* (New York: International Universities Press, 1953), p. 35.

though the human is irretrievably organic, in artistic volition she can establish an encounter (*Auseinandersetzung*) with her inorganic condition. In his discussion of organic and abstract ornamentation, Worringer alludes to this derivative nature of organic life and the primacy of an inorganic life:

> Both styles, linear as well as vegetal ornament, thus represent at bottom an abstraction, and their diversity is, in this sense, really only one of degree; just as, in the eyes of a monist, organic regularity, in the last analysis, differs only in degree from that of the inorganic-crystalline.[51]

The formerly antithetical terms of the organic and the inorganic are embedded in a deeper continuum, separating them only in degree, but in and on the terms of abstraction; i.e. the organic is reduced to a peculiar, outwardly living expression of an inert and rigid structure, while this dead structure is at the same time endowed with an uncanny "life." It is precisely this overlap of opposites that comprises the mystery of the continuum between them, of the point at which the undead, unconscious, instinctual aspect of the body is connected to, tangled with or mashed into the living, intellectual, conscious mind. It is not in the resolution in the expression of this mystery that inorganic life emerges. Even though unintelligible in principle, this problem of style (i.e. of the will expressed in the dynamics of abstraction and empathy) can, Worringer claims, still be felt by certain artists or people. Northern Europe's Gothic peoples, he claims, were besieged and possessed by this problem, which found constant expression in their art:

> In spite of the purely linear, inorganic basis of this [Gothic] ornamental style, we hesitate to term it abstract. Rather it is impossible to mistake the restless life contained in this tangle of lines. This unrest, this seeking, has no organic life that draws us gently into its movement; but there is life there, a vigorous, urgent life, that compels us joylessly to follow its movements.

---

51  Ibid., p. 60f.

Thus, on an inorganic fundament, there is heightened movement, heightened expression.[52]

The secret of the continuum is thus that the confrontation or encounter of the inorganic need for abstraction and the organic need for empathy are not resolved in the *"expression"* of the art work, but rather that it is a mutual escalation of the conflict that constitutes the Gothic artistic volition. No synthesis, no commensurability is possible. Rather, in the work of art, in the impossible correspondence of the two needs, one does violence to the other: the living is infused with the rigor mortis of abstraction—eternal, inert, rigid—while transience, aliveness and rationality are breathed into the inorganic. This tumult and violence, the constant escalation of the conflict between the organic and the inorganic in the "expression" of art, is inorganic life, an uncanny vitality that for good reason shocked a defender of reason like Lukács to the core.[53]

This notion of expression, understood as oscillation and escalation between organic and inorganic needs, is recast as a methodological tool in *A Thousand Plateaus* to productively approach the movement in-between various oppositional poles (haptic/optic, smooth/striated, nomadic/royal), and is thus detached from art history, realigned and "perverted" in the process. The inorganic vitality of expression thus is translated into the passage between primary poles of interest:

> The abstract, on the contrary, begins only with what Worringer presents as the "Gothic" avatar. It is this nomadic line that he says is mechanical, but in free action and swirling; it is inorganic, yet alive, and all the more alive for being inorganic. It is distinguished both from the geometrical and the organic. It raises "mechanical" relations to the level of intuition [...]. This streaming, spiraling, zigzagging, snaking, feverish line of variation liberates a power of life that human beings had rectified and organisms

---

52 Ibid., p. 76f.
53 Compare Georg Lukács, *The Destruction of Reason*, trans. Peter Palmer (London: Merlin Press, 1980), p. 817.

had confined, and which matter now expresses as the trait, flow or impulse governing it. If everything is alive, it is not because everything is organic or organized but, on the contrary, because the organism is a diversion of life. In short, the life in question is inorganic, germinal, and intensive, a powerful life without organs, a Body that is all the more alive for having no organs.[54]

The spirit of the whole second volume of *Capitalism and Schizophrenia* might be seen to be condensed here, in the call to trace lines of flight, which are the expressions of inorganic life within the seemingly organic, molar, striated manifestations of politics, art, philosophy and life. All production, even of the social order, contains such lines: "there is no social system that does not leak from all directions, even if it makes its segments increasingly rigid in order to seal the lines of flight,"[55] and thus liberation becomes a matter of exacerbating and intensifying them. These nomadic lines, describing the witch's flight, are synonymous with the Gothic lines of Worringer. They are pure passage, not moving from one point to the other, not delineating an inside or outside or circumscribing a contour, but describing only the constant and continuous variation of their movement.[56] Inorganic life is here presented as a means to liberate life wherever it is trapped or confined.

## Towards a Critical Vitalism

Deleuze and Guattari, in occasional moments, are however themselves concerned about the dialectic immanent to this liberation of life by means of life. Quite optimistically, *Essays Critical and Clinical* expresses the goal of the literary line of flight (or the literary style) as the "creation of syntax that gives birth to a foreign language within language," which "is *the outside* of language, but is not outside it."[57] The same structural

---

54 Deleuze and Guattari, *A Thousand Plateaus*, p. 498f.
55 Ibid., p. 204.
56 Ibid., p. 497.
57 Gilles Deleuze, *Essays Critical and Clinical* (Minneapolis: University of Minnesota Press, 1997), p. 112.

relation is repeated in the complex interplay between the war machine and the state apparatus in "1227: Treatise on Nomadology–The War Machine," but this time its goal is not to liberate but to capture or disable resistance. Discussing the minoritarian or proletarian means of resistance, they highlight the ambiguity of the lines of flight subject to the "deepest law of capitalism: it continually sets and then repels its own limits."[58] The revolutionary power of the minority against capitalism would consist, they claim, in the figure of the proletariat. Because, however, the working class derives its own determination from, and can only constitute itself on, the "plane of capital" they cannot leave, even under the condition of a factually overthrown State; the power of the state apparatus would prevail. Even though they insist that "it is by leaving the plan(e) of capital, and never ceasing to leave it, that a mass becomes increasingly revolutionary and destroys the dominant equilibrium of the denumerable sets,"[59] due to the "deepest law of capitalism," the act of detaching from the plane forms *the outside* of capital but does not reach an outside of capital. While this configuration can be read affirmatively as the constant creation of openings—"[a]t the same time as capitalism is effectuated in the denumerable sets serving as its models, it necessarily constitutes nondenumerable sets that cut across and disrupt those models"[60]—it also means that the war machine, the nondenumerable infinite set positioned against the denumerable sets, is itself only the structural effect of the state apparatus. As they confess at the end of the "Treatise," all the propositions presented are "undecidable," not because their outcome is uncertain, but because there is an inseparability, or even a zone of indeterminacy, between the revolutionary lines of flight and those "which the system conjugates."[61] Although undecidability is ultimately affirmed as the germ of revolutionary action in the "Treatise," the conclusion of "1440: The Smooth and The Striated" expresses similar doubts:

---

58  Deleuze and Guattari, *A Thousand Plateaus*, p. 472.
59  Ibid.
60  Ibid.
61  Ibid., p. 473.

> Of course, smooth spaces are not in themselves liberatory. But the struggle is changed or displaced in them, and life reconstitutes its stakes, confronts new obstacles, invents new paces, switches adversaries. Never believe that a smooth space will suffice to save us.[62]

Encompassing the movement of the various passages between two poles of oppositional interests that comprises *A Thousand Plateaus* as a whole, this assertion recontextualizes the means of liberating inorganic life. Neither the nomadic line, nor the rhizome is liberatory in itself; Deleuze and Guattari highlight, for example, the rhizomatic aspect of fascist mass mobilization. Although it might engender life and foster becomings, the creation of a body without organs might also result in a cancerous or a catatonic body. The ambiguity and undecidability involved in following a line of flight, as affirmed by Deleuze and Guattari, should thus also enable, perhaps out of step with the political ambitions of *A Thousand Plateaus*, a revaluation of life or vitalism itself.

There is, it seems, a twofold critique of life implied here. First of all, there is a critique of traditional vitalism, which issues from the demands of inorganic life to rethink the notion that life is exclusive to the conservative economy of the organism. Secondly, there is a critique of the "life" implied in the concept of an inorganic vitality, which would address the ambiguities around the liberation of life and ask whether there is still an organic good will of life implied in inorganic life, i.e. whether a liberation of life is equal to the self-furthering of life because life *naturally* strives for its own maximum of power or perfection. Deleuze's vitalism seems singular in that, though these critiques strike at the core of the affirmative side of his philosophy, they are present in the philosophy as a whole, which is also equipped to answer them with a new or (post-)vitalism.

As Colebrook notes, "In some sense it is quite appropriate to define Deleuze as a vitalist and a philosopher of life, but this is only if his vitalism is qualified to the point where it is almost an inversion of all that vitalism

---

62   Ibid., p. 500.

has come to represent."[63] Deleuze's first "inversion" of vitalism, related to the first part of the twofold critique mentioned above, detaches life from its bondage to the conservative economy of the organism. By tracing individuation to a sub-representational field of pre-personal intensities and by providing a model for the genesis of both organic formation and the organism's capacities from inorganic forces and passive processes, without presupposing organic spontaneity or activity, Deleuze detaches life from the necessary condition of the organism and even demonstrates how the personal life of the organism is constituted by an impersonal life. As well as adhering to notions of the conservative economy of the organism, classical vitalism sought to revitalize life by recovering the genetic grounds that certain forces (e.g. the intellect, reification, technology), which oppose or pervert the self-furthering tendency of life, cover up, a recovery which is supposed to purify life from what renders it impotent. Deleuze's second inversion of vitalism, related to the second part of the critique mentioned above, reintroduces into the heart of vitalism all the aspects that have been expelled (malevolence, stupidity, madness, the unlivable). For Deleuze, life is always out of line with itself, and is not so much naturally self-furthering as self-perverting. This book will attempt to stage this critical engagement of vitalism with itself and shed light on the peculiar inorganic vitalism of Deleuze.

---

[63] Colebrook, *Deleuze and the Meaning of Life*, p. 135.

# THINKING INORGANIC LIFE

### A MINERAL DELEUZE AND THE QUESTION OF METHODOLOGY

*Life, Structure and Systematicity*

At the beginning of "New Ontologies," Andrew Pickering, in order to illustrate the perspective of *The Mangle of Practice*, confronts two notions of abstraction, represented by Mondrian and de Kooning, and their corresponding ontological visions. The instantly recognizable geometrical abstractions of Mondrian's later work, he writes, "speak to me first of a certain dualism of people and things, a clean split between the painter and his work."[64] Situating Mondrian's abstract works in a time-less structural space removed from the dynamics of bodies, he conjectures that "we have to imagine them as products of Mondrian's *mind*."[65] De Kooning's works, on the other hand, are no less abstract, "yet his smeary canvasses speak powerfully of a dense, embodied, material *engagement* with the world."[66] By depicting the temporality involved in the constitution of experience and demonstrating the agency of materiality in the production of his works, a process of active creation and passive discovery, de Kooning's paintings allow for an encounter of human and non-human agents. The ontological visions correlating to their notions of abstraction, as Pickering presents them, are thus different. Mondrian champions the sovereign subject of Western tradition opposed to the world, "both detached from it and dominating it from outside," whereas de Kooning's engagement with the world represents an ontology of constant "joint production of the human and the nonhuman"[67] and thus a more distributed and mobile being. Interestingly, he mentions in relation to the second ontological vision Deleuze and Guattari's outline of a "his-

---

64  Andrew Pickering, "New Ontologies," in *The Mangle of Practice: Science, Society and Becoming* (Durham N.C.: Duke University Press, 2008), p. 1.
65  Ibid.
66  Ibid., p. 2.
67  Ibid.

tory of sciences in the de Kooning style rather than that of Mondrian, which they refer to as 'nomad' or 'minor sciences'."[68]

While it is apparent that Pickering offers a very reductive if not outright incorrect reading of Mondrian's and de Kooning's notions of abstraction, it is his alignment of Deleuze and Guattari with the latter painter *at the expense* of the geometrical abstraction of the former that is the more instructive inaccuracy. It demonstrates the normative core (or even ethical injunction) presupposed in certain readings of Deleuze and Guattari's conceptual apparatus. Recapitulating classical vitalist ethics, such readings position (inorganic) systematicity and structure against (organic) unpredictability and liveliness, proposing mobility and connectivity (the rhizome, nomadism, the molecular, the minority and smooth spaces) as ethical norms. This leads to a peculiar double bind: insisting on "life" itself as a normative concept not only breaks with the aspirations of a philosophy of immanence, since it ascribes a transcendent value to life itself, but also makes "life" unquestionable and immune to critique. At the same time, the embodied and engaged approach Pickering ascribes to de Kooning, while opening the organism up to an encounter with the inhuman, is embedded in the meaningful practices of the active subject, rendering both the passive discovery and the active creatorship *personal* events for the organism.

However, we could read Pickering against himself, to grasp the uncanny inorganic life in the works of Mondrian, for whom "even the usual tenuous connection of looking at the world —the artist gazing at a landscape and somehow representing it in paint—is missing."[69] Could it be that this disengagement from that world constituted by the meaningful practices of the organism, or even the destruction of that world, is a condition of the emergence of a more radical notion of inorganic life beyond the agency of matter?[70] Mondrian presents us with a specific logic of sensation by moving the line away from figurative contour, not abandoning it but making it intensive. Due to the absence of any center, which also

---

68 Ibid., p. 11.
69 Ibid., p. 2.
70 See sections "The Monstrous Epigenesis of the Transcendental" and "Passivity."

cannot be reconstructed through the capacities of the organic onlooker, the structural radicality of the composition destroys extensive (actual) space, to reveal "the strange space of virtuality unleashed when the line is not constrained by the closure of the punctual system."[71] The impersonal production of sense generated by the structural composition and not the personal meaning engendered by the viewer or artist is what is expressed in Mondrian's abstractions. It is not the unceasing mobility of nomads and rhizomes but the immobility of structure which presents us with an uncanny "inorganic life" here.

*Approaching the Organic and the Inorganic Image of Thought*
Understanding the specific way in which the twofold critique of life mentioned above is applied to Deleuze, as well as the way he might answer to this critique, could help us to "isolate a Deleuze of the mobile, indeterminate, rhizomatic vegetable (the Deleuze of Deleuze and Guattari's *A Thousand Plateaus*) from the earlier, hierarchical, structural, mineral Deleuze of *The Logic of Sense*"[72] (and *Difference and Repetition*). The latter Deleuze, supplanting the primacy of the practical with hyper-theory and joyful activity with exhausted passivity, might, we conjecture in this book, provide us with a radical understanding of inorganic life, which not only allows for the life of the inorganic but also the inorganicity of life. The two volumes of *Capitalism and Schizophrenia* possess a more pronounced spatial orientation (assemblages, connectivity, nomadism, smooth spaces, rhizomes, distributions, lines of flight) and thus promote mobility far more than the more overtly temporal orientation of *Difference and Repetition* and *The Logic of Sense* (the synthesis of time, events, time as the paradoxical element of structure, Aion/Chronos). Even though this distinction might appear tenuous at first glance, we will see how Deleuze's earlier works, due to their closer relation to Kant and their thorough discussion and transformation of transcendental philosophy,

---

71    Judy Purdom, *Thinking in Painting: Gilles Deleuze and the Revolution from Representation to Abstraction* (Ph.D. diss., University of Warwick, 2000), p. vii, see also p. 114f.
72    Eleanor Kaufman, *Deleuze, the Dark Precursor: Dialectic, Structure, Being* (Baltimore: The Johns Hopkins University Press, 2012), p. 142.

provide the means for conceiving of a more passive vitalism. Along these lines, even though Deleuze abandons the notion of "structure" for the concept of the "machine" after his encounter and subsequent collaboration with Guattari, we will argue that the notion of structure (or synonymously the problem of the Idea) and its dramatization allows us to grasp life "from the middle" in a manner distinct from the later works. Although *A Thousand Plateaus* doesn't consider inorganic life as a life exclusively constrained by the organic strata, the focus on the earlier works allows us to investigate the largely overlooked connection between the organism and the "image of thought" and thus trace the possibility of an inorganic power of thought excluded from or escaping this image.

Firstly then, in order to determine the object of inquiry, we will take what Deleuze called "noology," i.e. the tracing of the set of normative prescriptions in place in a given "image of thought," and apply it to Kant's critical philosophy in order to show in what way his image of thought is "organic." By tracing the parallel movement of the development of Kant's philosophical system and changes in the understanding of epigenesis and the conception of "life" in eighteenth century biology, the book will attempt to identify the complex, problematic constellation of forces that give birth to the modern understanding of the gulf between the organic and the inorganic (the *Entstehungsherd* in Nietzsche's terms), in order to retrospectively intervene and attempt to find an alternative solution. The movement beyond this image towards another (inorganic) image of thought proper to Deleuze's transcendental empiricism, however, presents us with a methodological problem. Not unlike deconstruction, the transcendental empiricism Deleuze champions might be regarded less as a method and more as an "attitude," which engenders or calls for a plurality of methodologies. With respect to inorganic life, transcendental empiricism forces us to consider the question of methodology more than it provides us with one. It is this question of a methodology able to approach the conceptualization of inorganic life that will occupy a sizable portion of this book. Of particular interest in this discussion will be Deleuze's relationship to the transcendental method, which we will examine through the lens of Laruelle's non-philosophy in the chapter "Non-Life."

The book is neither interested in investigating the discursive conditions of Deleuze's concept of life, nor in a deconstruction of his vitalism; rather, we want to apply the same affirmative and selective reading strategy to Deleuze's works that he employs in his treatment of the history of philosophy. This can be seen in three distinct aspects of our approach. Firstly, in relation to the creation of concepts: "In the end," Deleuze and Guattari ask us in *What is Philosophy?*, "does not every great philosopher lay out a new plane of immanence, introduce a new substance of being and draw up a new image of thought"?[73] There is neither the need, nor the possibility of representing the pre-philosophical plane of immanence and all the concepts a philosopher creates; instead, Deleuze and Guattari urge us to "affiliate" ourselves with the delirium of Hume or the water of Thales, i.e. to read not to know and represent but only to create and become. Similarly, we are not interested in a philological reconstruction of Deleuze's usage of the term "inorganic life" but in the possible creation of a concept. Secondly, in the *Dialogues*, Deleuze identifies one of his strategies for engaging with a philosopher or system of thought as the "pick-up," a means to appropriate an idea or thought without the need for opposition. As de Bolle puts it bluntly, Deleuze does not argue "for the sake of being right, he picks up what is of interest to him and moves on."[74] Rather than treating Deleuze's work as an organism or complete system that can only be opposed as a whole, we will proceed by appropriating and intensifying selected elements of his philosophy. Thirdly, Deleuze's affirmative readings always attempt to portray the philosopher in question not only without malintent, but also, as opposed to a deconstructive reading, in what is, for him, the most consistent version of their thought possible, even going beyond what they themselves said. He investigates the history of philosophy as a series of advances in the direction of immanence followed by retreats in the face of the results; Psychoanalysis, and especially

---

73 Gilles Deleuze and Félix Guattari, *What Is Philosophy?*, trans. Janis Tomlinson and Graham Burchell III (New York: Columbia University Press, 2014), p. 51.
74 Leen de Bolle, "Preface: Desire and Schizophrenia," in *Deleuze and Psychoanalysis: Philosophical Essays on Deleuze's Debate with Psychoanalysis*, ed. Leen de Bolle (Leuven: Leuven University Press, 2010), p. 7.

Jung, knew the becoming-animal of the human being in masochism and fetishism, but they "did not understand, or did not want to understand."[75] By pushing an image of thought to its limits, its transcendent exercise, at the point of its highest consistency, Deleuze unearths in the shadows of philosophies insights and creations that were either obscured by illusions or disavowed by their creators. As we will attempt to show, Deleuze's philosophy of inorganic life suggests the need to reintroduce the notions of madness, malevolence and stupidity into the concept of life, but recoils in the last instance.[76]

## TOWARDS AN INORGANIC VITALISM

The first chapter of this book, "Sublime Organicism," will introduce the problem of the relation of thinking and life from the perspective of Nietzsche and Kant, in order to create a vantage point to understand Kant's rejection of hylozoism. By tracing the functions and underlying values of Kant's organic image of thought, we can then more clearly outline the co-development of Kant's system and theories of epigenesis in the eighteenth century. By investigating the different roles of common sense in aesthetic and teleological judgement in the *Critique of Judgement* we will be able to highlight the organicism which Kant not only proposes but uses to structure his philosophy as such. As a first attempt to subvert the organic image of thought, while staying close to Kant in order not to fall behind him, we consider at the beginning of the second chapter, "The Unlivable," Husserl's discovery of passive synthesis, as well as Deleuze's appropriation of this phenomenological idea. From Husserl's failure to construct a transcendental empiricism, which stems from the problem of the transgressive nature of passive synthesis, we will move to Deleuze's solution to the problem of the genesis of normativity in his notion of the transcendental encounter and his reconceptualization of the

---

75  Deleuze and Guattari, *A Thousand Plateaus*, p. 259.
76  See section "Inertia."

Kantian "Idea." The inorganic life of the Idea will provide a model for the genesis of common sense and the capacities for activity of the organism from pre-personal singularities. Reconsidering the relation of time and ground from the perspective of the inorganic life of ideas outlined thus far, we will then attempt in the third chapter, "Absolute Xenogenesis," to consider this vitality beyond transcendental philosophy's concern with the animation of the mind by providing a reading of Deleuze's notion of individuation. In the fourth chapter, "Non-Life," Laruelle's non-philosophy provides a substantial critique of the foundation of Deleuze's vitalism in transcendental philosophy. He suspects that a fundamental idealism underlies Nietzsche's and Deleuze's vitalism, insofar as all actual existence is judged by an immaterial principal (life or becoming), which therefore means ideality and reality become identical. The expression of this normative perspective of life, according to Laruelle, can be seen in the ethical injunction to intensify thinking, which creates hierarchical differences between thoughts according to thinking's proximity to Being. Against this, he proposes a radical immanence within which all thoughts are equal due to the unilateral relation between the Real and thought. The non-philosophical critique thus presents an attack on the Nietzschean foundations of inorganic life and questions its implicit ethical vision of the world. By orienting the critiques of Brassier and Badiou along the lines of Laruelle's non-philosophical critique, the fifth and last chapter, "Post-Vitalism," attempts to solve the problems posed by these thinkers in relation to vitalism. By distinguishing between two forms of vitalism, one active and one passive, the former being interested in revitalizing life by recovering the genetic grounds covered up by reifying forces, the latter being interested in the genesis of the lived from the unlivable and hence the constant differentiation of life from itself, we can identify tendencies in the various readings of inorganic life presented so far. Applying the critiques of inorganic life by Laruelle, Badiou and Brassier to the Deleuze-inspired New Materialisms, we will use the emerging problems to demonstrate the impasses of the active vitalist approach. Rereading Deleuze's interpretation of Freud's death drive as a temporal structure, we will claim that the pure and empty form of time can be read as the inorganic life of the event itself. Connecting the radical temporality of the event to the account of structural genesis we provided in the second and third chapters, the ending of the fifth will formulate the fundamental concepts of a passive, inorganic vitalism: malevolence, madness and stupidity. The conclusion will provide, with references to Bataille, Agamben and Beckett, a brief evaluation of the possibility of transposing this vitalism into an ethics or politics.

## SUBLIME ORGANICISM

"These stones go through Man, straight to God, if there is one.
What have they not gone through already?
Empires, civilisations, aeons. Only in them
If in anything, can His creations confront Him."[1]

---

[1] McDiarmid, "On a Raised Beach," p. 150.

# ON THE USES AND ABUSE OF THINKING FOR LIFE

## THE INTIMACY OF THINKING AND LIFE

It may well be that thinking only really occurs if life is unbearable; when life is too much or too little, when it has almost nothing left to sustain itself, thinking seeps into the smooth operations of cognition. There are moments in which life and thought become intertwined, when they form a "complex unity: one step for life, one step for thought. Ways of living inspire ways of thinking"[2] not reducible to either personal events or public discourse, neither biography nor bibliography: a pre-Socratic unity of life and thought, richer than the individual, but made finite by constantly coming up against its internal limit (dissolution). In other words, one becomes by means of what one thinks and reconfigures thought by means of what one becomes. But the question of what thinking in the service of life means does not revolve around this, an ultimately moot point. The apartment building manager in Camus's *The Myth of Sisyphus*, having lost his young daughter, deteriorates over the course of the years not simply on account of the loss, but because of the ruminations, the incessant call of his thoughts breaking the chain of everyday gestures, finally brought to a halt by his suicide. Thinking, as Camus puts it, "undermined" him.[3] Whether thinking and life do in fact have or even could have the same interests is still up for debate.

After the first two *Critiques*, which concern the two domains of the concepts of nature and the concepts of freedom respectively, Kant must find a solution to the problem of their mediation. But due to his advanced age his time is running out. It must be a power that enables Kant's systematic approach to explain how both can exercise their legislation in and over the same territory ("the sum total of the objects of all possible expe-

---

2  Gilles Deleuze, *Nietzsche and Philosophy* (New York: Columbia University Press, 1983), p. 18.
3  See Albert Camus, *The Myth of Sisyphus* (New York: Vintage Books, 2018), p. 4.

rience") harmoniously. At the same time, Kant must find the justification for the existence of such a power from *within* the system so far by showing how the systematic unity of the critical project relies on the assumption of an unfamiliar, while not unrelated, element.[4] But "how difficult it is to solve a problem that nature has made so involved [*verwickelt*],"[5] Kant complains. So, he "must gain time, not let the delay accumulate, hurry on toward the doctrine,"[6] as Derrida puts it. Feeling that the completion of his project could narrowly slip his grasp, he must advance quickly, even if the first part of the *Third Critique* might lack some clarity, to the "doctrinal one, in order to snatch from my advancing years what time may yet be somewhat favourable to the task."[7] In just this one instance Kant writes about the entanglement of his age and his thought. His work becomes here a confession or "a kind of involuntary and unconscious memoir."[8] There seems to be "a moment of grace between life and death"[9] in the late work of philosophers and artists, where the forces of life have already begun to tear apart the body's organic-muscular integrity and the consistency of rational cognition fades, but thought leaps once more. One does not recount one's personal experience here, one does not think or write with one's decay, but thinking might open up to new modes and enable becomings when confronted with the singular or impersonal nature of life. In his early study on Nietzsche, Deleuze highlights his subject's distinctive position on illness: while physically debilitating, illness might offer a unique perspective on and of life, insofar as it engenders thoughts that differ from the ones that befall you in good health.[10] Nietzsche's novelty does not consist in romanticizing physical affliction, but in using ill-

---

[4] Compare Immanuel Kant, *Critique of Judgement* (Oxford; New York: Oxford University Press, 2007), p. 174.
[5] Ibid., p. 170.
[6] Jacques Derrida, *The Truth in Painting* (Chicago: University of Chicago Press, 1987), p. 43.
[7] Kant, *Critique of Judgement*, p. 170.
[8] Friedrich Nietzsche, *Beyond Good and Evil: Prelude to a Philosophy of the Future*, trans. Walter Kaufmann (New York: Vintage Books, 1989), p. 19.
[9] Deleuze and Guattari, *What is Philosophy?*, p. 1.
[10] Compare John Marks, *Gilles Deleuze: Vitalism and Multiplicity* (London: Pluto Press, 1998), p. 10.

ness as just another mask for his work, to help create "a new image of the thinker and thought."[11] There is always a multiplicity of thinkers, or an intersubjectivity of thinkers who think, rather than a unified self in Nietzsche: "a psychical polycentricity."[12] If the self in and thought were always the same, then by determining it one would erase it at the same time, since then thinking could be abstracted from and hence divorced from the act. But, since there is never the same thinker who thinks, thinking becomes a singular performance that must be lived.

When conceiving such a convergence of life and thought, at the "secret point where the anecdote of life and the aphorism of thought amount to one and the same thing,"[13] we encounter another problem, as Deleuze remarks: "Actually, there is only one term, Life, that encompasses thought, but conversely this term is encompassed only by thought."[14] If Life is *only* ever grasped (and must be grasped) by thought, how can we conceive of its relation to reason—or, in other words, what would be a thinking *adequate* to Life?

Deleuze's philosophy is (maybe exclusively) concerned with posing and answering this question in various ways by making thinking a vital function, a creative rather than a reproductive act. Thinking of his Nietzschean reading of Spinoza, we could say that proper thought is creation, which marks a "becoming active," i.e. one becoming free by firstly detaching oneself from the passive passions imposed by "the forces on the level of the body"[15] and secondly by inventing one's own law. Deleuze further explains this point by setting Kant against Nietzsche on the question of the relation of life, thinking and reason:

> Rational knowledge sets the same limits to life as reasonable life sets to thought; life is subject to knowledge and at the same time thought is sub-

---

11 Deleuze, *Nietzsche and Philosophy*, p. 17.
12 Graham Parkes, *Composing the Soul: Reaches of Nietzsche's Psychology* (Chicago: University of Chicago Press, 1996), p. 252.1996
13 Gilles Deleuze, *The Logic of Sense* (New York: Columbia University Press, 1990), p. 128.
14 Gilles Deleuze, *Spinoza, Practical Philosophy* (San Francisco: City Lights Books, 1988), p. 14.
15 Joe Hughes, *Philosophy after Deleuze*, Deleuze Encounters (New York: Continuum, 2012), p. 73.

ject to life. Reason sometimes dissuades and sometimes forbids us to cross certain limits: because it is useless (knowledge is there to predict), because it would be evil (life is there to be virtuous), because it is impossible (there is nothing to see or think behind the truth).[16]

Viewed through the lens of the legislative function of reason over life and thought, life gets caught up in the matrix of reason, hence thought determines what is true and in turn gets determined by truth as its (natural) end, while life becomes the pursuit of the good. As such, both are bound by an upper and lower limit and these limits are defined by what is possible, which again reflects the value of truth and the limit of the unity in and through reason of them both. This is what Kant calls a "system": the ultimate unity of practical and theoretical philosophy, without this unity being deduced from a common root. To subject life to legislation by a finite subject, and hence to the finitude of man itself—an idea which we can still find in Heidegger—makes life a desperate warding off and escape from death, rather than an affirmative pursuit of joy. The limits of the finite subject become the limits of life and hence the limits of the subject become its absolute limits. There is no way for life to break through these limits. Thinking becomes an organic structure which only grows from within, limiting its exposure to the outside by means of a membrane of legislation, clinging to its unity at every cost. The organic structure of thinking is ascesis incarnate.

In Nietzsche, Deleuze sees a new image of thought that does away with the primacy of the rational organization of life we find in Kant, but also in Spinoza and Bergson. Deleuze is, however, not denying the intimacy of thought and life, but the modes in which their relationship is effectuated and what thinking therefore means. While in Spinoza, "the different kinds of knowledge are also different ways of living, different modes of existing,"[17] a consequence of the univocity of being, the possibilities of thinking and living are ultimately aligned with *ratio* for their own good,

---

[16] Deleuze, *Nietzsche and Philosophy*, p. 101.
[17] Ibid., p. 103.

since only the rational organization of both guarantees freedom from sadness. But while Nietzsche also invents the different configurations of life and thinking—the ascetic man, the last man, the guilty man etc.—he does not intend to limit life and thinking to a pregiven or proposed structure; rather the analysis of these configurations is done through and discovers "the real forces that *form* thought."[18] This is what Nietzsche ascribes to his new image of the thinker, the artist: not the submission to the rational, which would limit these forces, but a practice of using the excess in them, generating thought to create new ways of thinking and living. Rather than determining the true, which can only, since truth is not created, be measured against what is, Nietzsche's thought is the creation of new ways of living which don't yet exist, which are not yet true but are relentlessly geared towards the future. Unlike in Bergson, where the "fundamental law of life" is "a law of action"[19] which submits life to utility, Nietzsche's creation is not aligned with any end transcending it, since the life that is its goal is itself in the process of determination through thinking. If there is no gap separating life from thinking anymore, no determinable function can be assigned to life and thinking—it becomes, from a standpoint outside of life, useless. From within life, however, the goal of the reciprocal determination of life and thinking is its own function—or means to an end and end itself. By not getting life caught up in either the determinations of rationality or utility, Nietzsche reconstructs what thinking means, and enables a "thought that would go to the limits of what life can do."[20]

Somewhat surprisingly, however, it is not Nietzsche but Fichte who Deleuze, together with Spinoza, sees as his avatar for this new image of thought, involving the creation of "vital concepts," as described in *What is Philosophy?*:

> Ideas can only be associated as images and can only be ordered as abstractions; to arrive at the concept we must go beyond both of these and arrive

---

[18] Ibid.
[19] Henri Bergson, *Matter and Memory* (New York: Zone Books, 1988), p. 150.
[20] Deleuze, *Nietzsche and Philosophy*, p. 101.

*as quickly as possible* at mental objects determinable as real beings. This is what Fichte or Spinoza have already shown: we must make use of fictions and abstractions, but only so far as is necessary to get to a plane where we go from real being to real being and advance through the construction of concepts.[21]

This understanding of Fichte is referencing the shift in his thinking about the relation between life and reason that takes place in his late *Diarium*. While in the early versions of the *Science of Logic* he rejects life as lived in favor of speculation, in the philosophical diaries written in old age he reevaluates the role of life radically.[22] Just months before his death he writes: "I tell you it is thus . . . it is not the I that *sees* itself, but rather life looks upon I: / that it [the I] speaks afterwards: it has seen itself, is the reflex of the perception [of life]."[23] The reflection of life upon itself, which Fichte equates with intuition, gives rise to the "I" as the lawful point of this act. Conversely, the absolute must be "pure life through and through in itself and through itself,"[24] therefore determining itself only through itself, like the divine thought in Spinoza. The intimacy of life and thought is expressed explicitly when the understanding comes to understand itself as a function of life.

Deleuze's friendly attitude towards Fichte, also repeated in "Immanence: A Life ...," hides two distinct idealist traps. Firstly, the I, while being given a genetic dimension, still remains the lawful place of the reflection of life upon itself, and secondly, Fichte still refuses materialism and binds life to idealism. He acknowledges that life is not a *verbum neutrum* but always an active verb and that "[t]hat is indeed the main purpose of Idealism: to cancel out the *verbum neutrum* completely, so that

---

21   Deleuze and Guattari, *What is Philosophy?*, p. 207.
22   See also Günter Zöller, *Fichte's Transcendental Philosophy: The Original Duplicity of Intelligence and Will* (Cambridge; New York: Cambridge University Press, 1998), p. 30.
23   Johann Gottlieb Fichte, *Diarium II* (Stuttgart-Bad Cannstatt: Frommann-Holzboog, 2011), p. 235.
24   Günter Zöller, "Leben und Wissen. Der Stand der Wissenschaftslehre beim letzten Fichte," in *Der transzendentalphilosophische Zugang zur Wirklichkeit: Beiträge aus der aktuellen Fichte-Forschung*, ed. Erich Fuchs, Marco Ivaldo, and Giovanni Moretto (Stuttgart-Bad Cannstatt: Frommann-Holzboog, 2001), p. 322.

everywhere only active verbs remain."[25] This cancelation of the *verbum neutrum* has been Fichte's philosophical goal from the early drafts of the *Science of Knowledge*, where physics is purposefully split in two to achieve this goal, since it is only beings that are organic, living and thinking that are able to embody this cancellation, while the rest of nature remains inert matter. While "Life is to the concept, and the concept is to the understanding, as *natura naturans* is to *natura naturata*,"[26] Fichte finds the expression of these relations through negation of nature as the inert. Paradoxically, even depicting the absolute as life does not prompt a radical materialism because the primacy of the practical incorporates nature (and by extension matter) in its ethical image of the world exactly by expelling it.

Deleuze thus favorably refers to Fichte and shares his focus on the primacy of the active or practical. Furthermore, even though Deleuze might avoid restricting life to the realm of those organic beings capable of voluntary acts, he still reproduces Fichte's ethical subjugation of the world. The problem that the relationship of Deleuze to Fichte poses will permeate this work.

### THOUGHT IN THE SERVICE OF LIFE

The opposition of Nietzsche's new image of thought to Kant's critical philosophy can be understood in terms of the relation between tautological determination and life. Since thought is conceived by Nietzsche and Deleuze as inherently differential or as an interplay of real forces, the determination of essences appears as either paradoxical or impossible. Several fragments of *The Will to Power* discuss the problem of differential tautologies using the denaturalized concepts of "Morality for morality's sake" and "Art for art's sake."[27] While the first, as "impersonal ideal,"

---

[25] Zöller, *Fichte's Transcendental Philosophy*, p. 111.
[26] Frederick Amrine, "'The Magic Formula We All Seek': Spinoza + Fichte = x," in *At the Edges of Thought: Deleuze and Post-Kantian Philosophy*, ed. Craig Lundy and Daniela Voss (Edinburgh: Edinburgh University Press, 2015), p. 186.
[27] Friedrich Nietzsche, *Wrtings from the Late Notebooks* (Cambridge: Cambridge University Press, 2003), p. 206.

severing itself even from lived religion and everyday life, "appears as ultimate value," the second "introduces a false antithesis into things,"[28] defaming the real as the ugly and thus its counterpart. As ideals or essences—Nietzsche specifically mentions the Platonic triad of the Good, the True and the Beautiful—which have their end in themselves, they purify themselves from the flaw of reality, which is necessarily never adequate to be identified with them. But "if one severs an ideal from reality one debases the real, one impoverishes it, one defames it."[29] An ideal folded back on itself is therefore understood as idealism, insofar as Nietzsche understands reality only to be relational and reversible. What is in question however is not the ontological status of art, morality or knowledge, because these exist in one way or the other, but the clouding and covering up of their practical utility for life. They are *"means*: instead of recognizing in them the aim of enhancing life, one has associated them with the antithesis of life, with 'God'."[30] This error of misconstruing the means for enhancing life, the tools for bio-engineering, as self-contained authorities separate from reality is moreover translated into the metaphysical register. Since ideals are neither immersed in the struggle of real existing forces, nor emerge from them, they "betray certain conditions of existence,"[31] i.e. by refusing to participate in the essential war that is reality, they do not properly exist at all. If every individual being that exists does so by struggling as a differential event, a complex of forces in a differential relationship with other forces, then self-identical ideals are at once useless for life and self-contradictory. Contrary to some interpretations, Nietzsche does not reject reason as a useful tool, but given invariable, atemporal status, it necessarily turns against itself, obstructing its own usefulness. We can see this in Nietzsche's dismissal of Kant's term of the "thing-in-itself":

---

28  Friedrich Nietzsche, *The Will to Power*, trans. Walter Arnold Kaufmann and R. J. Hollingdale (New York: Vintage Books, 1968), p. 168.
29  Ibid.
30  Ibid.
31  Ibid.

Incidentally, even in the Kantian concept of the "intelligible character of things" something remains of this lascivious ascetic discord that loves to turn reason against reason: for "intelligible character" signifies in Kant that things are so constituted that the intellect comprehends just enough of them to know that for the intellect they *are utterly incomprehensible*.[32]

The devolution of philosophy to a "theory of knowledge"[33] is in the end not only not useful for life, but left to its own devices and *only* its own devices it engenders a moribund existence. But even this attenuated existence strives to live nonetheless, and hence "the ascetic ideal is an artifice for the preservation of life."[34]

However, we have given Nietzsche the hermeneutic benefit of the doubt and let him formulate the problem of the relation of life, thought and reason in and on his terms, since—again from the Nietzschean perspective—such a perspectivism is unavoidable. It is, however, not right—as Deleuze's tendentious reading of Kant and Nietzsche suggests—that Kant is a philosopher in opposition to vital forces, if we view things from the vantage point of the critical project itself. If we consider the case of the moral life of microbes which Kant relates in *The Conflict of the Faculties*, the proximity and difference to Kant and Deleuze in relation to the primacy of the practical becomes apparent. Following the Stahl-Boerhaave debate, microorganisms held a central position in the eighteenth century natural sciences.[35] The reducibility of the functions of the presumed smallest living creatures to *general* physical laws would substantiate the assumption of an uninterrupted continuum between living and non-living matter held by mechanistic approaches against vitalist theories, which claimed *particular* laws (irreducible to general laws) to be necessary for the study of living beings. The third part of *The Conflict of the Faculties*

---

32    Friedrich Nietzsche, *On the Genealogy of Morals*, trans. Walter Kaufmann (New York: Vintage Books, 2011), p. 135.
33    Nietzsche, *Beyond Good and Evil*, p. 123.
34    Ibid.
35    See Theodor M. Brown, "From Mechanism to Vitalism in Eighteenth-Century English Physiology," *Journal of the History of Biology* 7, no. 2 (1974), p. 179–216.

debates the issue of medicine and health by contrasting the theories of Brown and the corresponding theory of Hufeland's *Microbiotics* on the irritability of microbes and their ability to act in response to stimuli. Kant's interest in Hufeland is, however, not founded in the theoretical proximity to Brown, but rather in the practical or ethical distance between the two. Brown assumed, following his discoveries in the study of the excitability of organisms and his rejection of the humoral pathological tradition, that some excessive behaviors could, through a high intensity of excitation, have a medical, therapeutic and in the end restorative effect. Aptly subtitled *The Art of Prolonging Human Life*, Hufeland's book claims the opposite: due to the nature of the vital force which animates the organism, only a moral and rational lifestyle promotes a healthy life and guarantees the "fortification of the vital force."[36] While Kant remains critical of the metaphysical underpinnings of Hufeland's notion of life, he not only agrees with him on his moral convictions but affirms his medical assertions when reflecting on his own habits, his strict sleeping schedule and regular nasal inhalations, among other things, which allowed him to create his extensive philosophical work, despite being born with a weak physical constitution.[37] This confession, despite Kant's apologies for the "nuisance of telling others about my private feelings,"[38] should not just be taken as a biographical footnote but as the expression of a tension within Kant's conception of life, understood in its double meaning: the moral life according to ideas and the physiological life. To avoid this tension, Mellin, working after Kant, separates these two aspects of life as incommensurable, rejecting Kant's unifying account. There is an inherent struggle between the speculative and practical interests of reason which is reflected in Kant's philosophy of biology and returns in neo-Kantian approaches as a partitioning of the critical project into "an epistemology of scientific

---

36 Christoph Wilhelm Hufeland, *Makrobiotik oder die Kunst menschliche Leben zu verlängern* (Leipzig: Insel Verlag, 1984), p. 24.
37 See Immanuel Kant, "On the Power of the Mind to Master Its Morbid Feelings by Sheer Resolution," in *The Conflict of the Faculties*, trans. Mary Gregory (Lincoln, Neb.: University of Nebraska Press, 1992), p. 185.
38 Ibid., p. 177.

research and a theory of action."[39] Such a separation, however, again begs the question of the relation and mediation of the concepts of nature and freedom. While it is possible to think life as internally split in two, it is one life that ultimately must be lived.

While Brown's account relied on the application of external forces to upset the equilibrium of the organism, hence relying on individual experimentation with one's body and its powers, Hufeland's physiology proposes putting all forces in the service of the fortification of life (vital force) by living morally, which means according to moral ideas. However, against the Nietzschean position, the Kantian position found in Hufeland could be expressed as the necessity of tautological determination, especially in morality, since it is the only way not to weaken one's life, or in other words, the only way to avoid sickness. In the Nietzsche-Deleuzian understanding of life, a body finds its vital potential in the creation of a law, while in the Kantian approach to life and living, a body fortifies its vitality by conforming to the law, which is presumed to be life's law itself. It is therefore fair to say that both Kant *and* Nietzsche are vitalists[40] to a certain extent. But, while Kantian vitalism is based on morality,[41] Nietzsche's and Deleuze's is "a vitalism rooted in aesthetics."[42]

The choice between the critical and the affirmative position hence rests on whether we should think life as constituted by pre-existing boundaries or conceive of boundaries as resulting from life.

---

[39] Alberto Toscano, *The Theatre of Production: Philosophy and Individuation between Kant and Deleuze* (Basingstoke: Palgrave Macmillan, 2006), p. 19.

[40] While this claim is obvious for Nietzsche, for an understanding of Kant's vitalism, his influence on eighteenth- century organic generation theory and nature philosophy, as well as the influences on him, especially Haller, Buffon and Blumenbach, see Timothy Lenoir, "Kant, Blumenbach, and Vital Materialism in German Biology," *Isis* 71, no. 1 (1980), p. 77–108. Lenoir describes Kant in conjunction with Blumenbach as championing a "vital materialism."

[41] This, however, does not mean that Kant's moral philosophy is an anti-aesthetics. He does in fact devote a large portion of the *Third Critique* to the relation of morality, beauty, and the sublime. Conversely, while Deleuze's aesthetics seems to reject pregiven morality, it does express a certain ethics or even a preliminary morality. The question is again one of grounding and primacy, rather than superiority.

[42] Gilles Deleuze, *Negotiations, 1972–1990* (New York: Columbia University Press, 1995), p. 91.

# HYLOZOIC MADNESS

## KANT'S REJECTION OF THE LIFE OF MATTER

The question we return to then is again the question of the boundaries and territories of the legislative function, or more specifically their legality. While many boundaries in Kant become, especially in his later work, disputed, one boundary is always properly upheld and maintained: the boundary between the intelligible and the sensible. The stark defense of the difference in kind between the two not only shapes and structures Kant's work in general, but guides in particular his rejection of hylozoism, i.e. the position that would allow for inorganic life. We will claim in this section that Kant's sensible/intelligible distinction not only provides the basis for his dismissal of hylozoism and of inorganic life, but does so on moral grounds, or based on an organic moral image of thought closer to hylomorphic conceptions of life. The same process of moral grounding is operative in the rejection of hylozoism, "the claim that matter is self-organizing and can generate its own formal principle of organization,"[43] i.e. the power of matter to give itself its own law. This informs the condemnation of any form of aesthetic vitalism, in which (corporeal, physical) life creates its own law. While it is apparent that hylozoism implies the continuity of the sensible and the intelligible, and is even predicated upon it, Kant's moral argument for its rejection will build on the impossibility of such a continuity. The mapping of Kant's argument, its moral foundation as well as its consequences, will be the goal of this section. Questioning the legitimacy of the boundary between the intelligible and the sensible will be the goal of the next one.

A year after Spinoza's death, Ralph Cudworth publishes *The True Intellectual System of the Universe*. In it, he argues against varieties of atheism and certain forms of determinism by depicting them as misconceptions

---

[43] Brent Adkins and Paul Hinlicky, *Rethinking Philosophy and Theology with Deleuze* (London: Bloomsbury, 2014), p. 28.

of the nature of matter, e.g. by portraying Hobbes as the avatar of "hylopathism," a kind of base physicalist materialism. Far less problematic for Cudworth,[44] however, is the philosophical lineage that he, inspired by Aristotle's notion of hylomorphism, dubs "hylozoism," the claim that life can be justifiably attributed to matter. While he traces this position back to Strato of Lampsacus, the emergence of Spinoza's later hylozoistic system reconfigured this lineage, referring it back to Epicurus rather than Strato. While the equation of these three figures will be questioned by Kant's later works and their positions considered in detail, Kant's first struggle with hylozoism in his pre-critical work references none of them, but simply refers to Cudworth's depiction. For Kant, the problem of hylozoism and the materiality of life first becomes virulent through the dreams of the philosopher and the spirit-seers.

## SOME DREAMS OF LIFE AND THOUGHT

Nobody can recount for sure the dream that Herder might have had during Kant's lecture on metaphysics, but he notes with incredible specificity that even "tadpoles" (*Rotzfische*) must possess a principle of life, and this can only be immaterial and internal.[45] In his notes, these dreams are followed by Kant's own fantasies of an army of sophisticated animal slaves, which will build cities and make human labor redundant.[46]

The assumption that life cannot be sufficiently explained in mechanical terms (i.e. from external principles) and must therefore find its expression in an immaterial, i.e. inner, principle already dates back to Kant's

---

[44] This is because hylozoism does not necessarily imply atheism. It does so, according to Cudworth, only if taken together with materialism, i.e. the claim that there is only matter and nothing besides.

[45] Compare Immanuel Kant, *Vorlesungen über Metaphysik und Rationaltheologie*, Akademiausgabe, Vol. XXVIII (Berlin: Preußische Akademie der Wissenschaften, 1968), p. 115 (my translation). Herder explicitly comments on this inner principle, saying that it must be postulated in order to give a reason and not just a cause for movement in animals as opposed to inanimate things.

[46] See Paul Menzer, *Kants Lehre von der Entwicklung in Natur und Geschichte* (Berlin: de Gruyter, 1911), p. 102.

early works. In the *Universal Natural History and Theory of Heaven* he already states that we will fully explain the "development of all the cosmic bodies [...] before we completely and clearly understand the development of a single plant or caterpillar on mechanical principles."[47] Although it is not clear here whether this concern is meant to be taken as an epistemological problem or a problem of ontological categorization, the same line of reasoning is later expressed in Kant's discussion of the assumedly fatal nature of materialism, which "kills everything,"[48] and his rejection of hylozoism, which is the "death of all natural philosophy."[49] This in no way means that life has no relation to the material, but that mere matter (materialism) and animate matter (hylozoism) must be the lower and upper limits of any philosophical notion of life.[50]

There is thus a tension in Kant's pre-critical thought between a concept of immaterial life, necessary for any account of life and at the same time assuring the unique vitality and incommensurability of animals and humans, and the demand of rigorous philosophy not to fall prey to a *pigra ratio* that seeks refuge in a *qualitas occulta*.[51] This tension must at some point be resolved. It therefore seems to be no coincidence that the great silence that precedes Kant's critical project sets in after the *Dreams of a Spirit-Seer*. Here Kant confronts his "twin"[52] in the form of the mystic and scientist Swedenborg. Despite the harsh opposition often portrayed as existing between the two thinkers, Kant's approach to the spirit-seer is far more an auto-critique than just a pure dismissal of Swedenborg's method.

The philosophical stakes of the *Dreams* revolve around Swedenborg's claim to be able to establish a connection with the dead. To communi-

---

47   Immanuel Kant, *Universal History and Theory of the Heavens or an Essay on the Constitution and the Mechanical Origin of the Entire Structure of the Universe Based on Newtonian Principles* (Arlington: Richer Ressources Publications, 2008), p. 18.
48   Immanuel Kant, *Dreams of a Spirit-Seer* (London: Nabu Press, 2010), p. 57.
49   Immanuel Kant, *Metaphysical Foundations of Natural Science*, trans. Michael Friedman (Cambridge; New York: Cambridge University Press, 2004), p. 84.
50   See Adkins and Hinlicky, *Rethinking Philosophy and Theology with Deleuze*, p. 30.
51   Kant constantly, especially in his handwritten notes, attacks his own idea of an immaterial life as lazy philosophy.
52   I borrow this term from Friedemann Stengel, *Kant und Swedenborg: Zugänge zu einem umstrittenen Verhältnis* (Tübingen: Niemeyer, 2008), p. 35.

cate with the deceased, we would have to assume a primitive force that animates the body while living and exists independently of this body as a separate entity after death, while still being able to interact with the living, e.g. by communicating with them. Kant's text is not so much concerned with the claim of these entities' existence, but with the methods of legitimizing their existence *through* experience. We should acknowledge Kant's outright rejection of psychological solutions—that either the spirit-seers are just liars or plain insane—as a genuine philosophical gesture, a gesture of trying to ensure the unity of his own account of experience by viewing these deceptions and illusions as special cases of a regular faculty. The problem of seeing spirits is first and foremost a spatial one. Our perception involves the apperception of the location of objects, real or imaginary.[53] While in the case of the sensation of external objects the lines of our impression meet *outside* the brain, fantasies are produced by the lines of impression meeting *inside* it. In both cases the location of the object is (more or less) clearly apperceived as a *focus imaginarius* of experience. Being deceived by the illusion of seeing spirits could therefore be explained by a failure to register the *focus imaginarius* correctly, mistaking a fantasy for an external object. Most likely such a mistake could be explained by a disturbance in the functional apparatus of the brain, Kant assumes.[54]

Kant could have ended his discussion on Swedenborg right here, having explained the phenomenon of communication with the dead, as well as insanity in general.[55] But he does not do so.[56] The distinct philosophical and auto-critical turn is executed in Kant's rejection of the physiological answer to the problem because it covers up a deeper philosophical one. If he was determined to prove Swedenborg *de facto* wrong, he would need to supply *de jure* grounds for this first. The process of orientation,

---

53  Compare Kant, *Dreams of a Spirit-Seer*, p. 78.
54  Ibid., p. 80.
55  See Monique David-Menard, *La Folie Dans la Raison Pure. Kant Lecteur de Schwedenborg* (Paris: Vrin, 1990), p. 26.
56  See also Monique David-Menard and Alison Ross, "An Essay on the Maladies of the Mind; and Observations on the Feeling of the Beautiful and the Sublime," *Hypatia* 15, no. 4 (2000), p. 20.

i.e. the locating of the *focus imaginarius*, relies on a delicate adjustment of the brain's functions and operations. But there is no difference in kind between the "nerve-vibrations" which are a "copy" of sense-impressions and those which are a "copy"[57] of fantasies, because there is no generality by which we could judge and therefore warrant such a distinction of particular vibrations only differing in degree of physical properties, e.g. amplitude, frequency. The question of the legitimacy of specific experiences, therefore, cannot be resolved by empirical facts about the composition or functioning of the brain, which in turn would be subject to the same question *ad infinitum*.

Kant, then, writes further—and here the argument changes considerably in tone—that one might be tempted to circumvent the problem of the distinction between fantasy and sensation by excluding experience from this justification from the start. This metaphysical approach leads to its own dreams, spatial confusions and justificatory problems. But, unlike the spirit-seer, rather than locating the *focus imaginarius* incorrectly, the metaphysician lets the lines of reason and experience "run alongside each other into infinity without ever meeting."[58] So, the problem "of beginning I don't know where, and of coming I don't know whither"[59] seems to entail a peculiar kind of kinship between the dreams of the philosopher and the dreams of the spirit-seer. In fact, Kant is not entirely sure what the difference is, though he upholds that one cannot deduce the origin of the one kind of dream from the other. But even more than that, they might be complementary, insofar as Kant's accusation against the spirit-seers changes in the course of the text: while at the beginning he holds that the illusion is generated by mistaking fantasy for sensation, later he sees the illusion as an invention of reason, which is then substantiated by false impressions. If Swedenborg becomes a philosopher by proposing an intelligibility of the soul on the basis of his experiences, then philosophers can become spirit-seers when, by virtue of their academic craft, they furnish

---

57 Kant, *Dreams of a Spirit-Seer*, p. 79.
58 Ibid., p. 99.
59 Ibid.

their concepts based on reason with experiences. Or as Kant says about this maneuver of sophisticated metaphysicians: "With this ingenious method several men of merit have caught even secrets of religion by pure reasoning; just as a novelist makes the heroine flee into remote countries that there, by a lucky adventure, she haply may meet her lover."[60] Both, in their own ways, seems to be plagued and vitalized by an *internal* relation of reason and madness.[61]

The affliction that seems to produce false images in both the "reason-dreamer" and the "sensation-dreamer"[62] is therefore not located in the senses itself, but in the inability to make them an object of a judgement that would allow for a distinction between sensation proper and fantasy. The principles of such a judgement can be supplied neither by the understanding nor by reason. The understanding has no principles a priori to supply the faculty of judgement with. And reason cannot remedy the cause of the illusion—the misinterpretation of the *focus imaginarius*—since it is not caused by a logical mistake. One cannot reason away an impression.

Finally, then, Kant applies his auto-critique, when discussing the notion of life. As he seeks to disentangle the knot between body and its animating principle to create a critique of Swedenborg's positing of an autonomous soul, he himself becomes subject to his critique. He confesses that, for reasons that are obscure to himself, he wants to uphold the principle of life as an immaterial "inner capacity to determine oneself by one's own will power."[63]

The essential characteristic of matter is that it fills space by a necessary force which is limited by counteraction. Thus, the state of everything that is material is externally dependent and forced into place. But those enti-

---

60 Ibid., p. 100.
61 Monique David-Ménard, "La Folie Dans la Raison Pure," *Les Cahiers du GRIF* 46, no. 1 (1992), p. 84.
62 Kant, *Dreams of a Spirit-Seer*, p. 75.
63 The whole passage reads: "The reason of this, which appears to myself very obscure, and probably will remain so, concerns at the same time that which sensates in animals. Whatever in the world contains a principle of life, seems to be of immaterial nature. For all life rests on the inner capacity to determine one's self by one's own will power." Kant, *Dreams of a Spirit-Seer*, p. 52.

ties which are said to contain the cause of life, which act from themselves and from inner powers, the intrinsic nature of which, in short, is to be able to change themselves at will, can hardly be said to be material. It cannot in turn, however, reasonably be expected that we understand, in their subdivisions, under their various species, such unknown and immaterial beings, the existence of which we know for the most part only by hypothesis. We can only see that those immaterial beings which contain the cause of animal life (and which establish their drives, inclinations, etc.) are different from those which comprise reason in and as their self-activity, the latter being called spirits.[64]

The consequence of such a characterization is that we have no "data"[65] to think this principle *positively* and must therefore resort to thinking it *negatively*. But even these negations cannot be grounded in experience or deductions, but can only be constructed "upon invention, to which a reason deprived of all other expedients finally resorts."[66] Life, it seems, insofar as it can be thought, cannot be experienced. Thus, the thought of life itself becomes an invention or fabrication of reason. Life becomes a problem not only *in* philosophy, but *for* philosophy itself, insofar as life is a condition for thought. Indeed, it becomes Kant's pre-critical threshold.

The aporia thus presented can, however, according to Kant, be resolved. Even if Kant could have forfeited the immateriality of life, even though this would have turned his philosophy on its head, this would not have solved the underlying problem. Instead, it can only be resolved by resorting to a "trick."[67] Just as we can only detect a merchant's transgressions against civil law by switching the places of weights and goods, we must also change the weighting on the "scales of reason [Verstandeswage]."[68] Therefore, a judgement should not be judged by one's own reason by itself, but as if the reason of another was judging. Therefore, we must use

---

64  Compare ibid., p. 52f.
65  Ibid., p. 89.
66  Ibid.
67  Ibid., p. 85.
68  Ibid.

the inventions of reason as a "*fictio heuristica,*"[69] to then be judged (or be treated as if they were judged) by another member of the community of spirits. Life then can only be thought negatively, although this does not mean through negation but through the inventions of reason, which are then crossed out by the negative understanding using the shift in the scales of reason.[70] Through this, metaphysics transforms from speculation into "the science of the boundaries of human reason."[71] The primary task therefore is to recognize and clarify the limits of our possible knowledge. Although we might acquire knowledge of particular processes of nature, the principles will remain obscure. The investigation of life must shift from the attempt to determine the notion of an immaterial inner principle of life to a method of avoiding reason's attempt to seek refuge in this necessary obscurity. Rather than any positive determination of the living, Kant is more interested in an agnostic, negatively defined notion of life.[72]

**THE UTTER MADNESS OF LIVING**

*Kant, the Hypochondriac*

E. M. Cioran confesses that he turned his back on philosophy when he could not detect "in Kant any human weakness, any authentic melancholy, in Kant and in all the philosophers."[73] His anti-philosophical inclinations are not themselves philosophical, but are rooted in the experiences of the body: the decay, the pain and suffering that philosophy rationalizes and even glorifies in its sublation.[74] It might be self-evident

---

[69] Immanuel Kant, *Briefwechsel 1747–1788* (Berlin: Preußische Akademie der Wissenschaften, 1900), p. 72.
[70] See Kant, *Dreams of a Spirit-Seer*, p. 89.
[71] Ibid., p. 113.
[72] Compare Reinhard Löw, *Philosophie des Lebendigen: Der Begriff des Organischen bei Kant, sein Grund und seine Aktualität* (Frankfurt am Main: Suhrkamp, 1980), p. 160.
[73] E. M. Cioran, *A Short History of Decay*, trans. Eugene Thacker and Richard Howard (New York: Arcade Publishing, 2012), p. 47.
[74] While philosophy's refusal to acknowledge the body in its incommensurability to thought, especially the body's suffering, is a reoccurring theme throughout his work, it is

that a builder of systems cannot afford to show weakness, since the responsibility put on him is too immense. There might also be a non-trivial reason why we find admissions of personal and human weakness in the philosophers that abstained from such architectonic endeavors: Montaigne, Pascal, Kierkegaard, Nietzsche, Bataille. But then there are the mentions of nightmares in Kant's *Anthropology*, his attraction to the sublime nature of "misanthropy" in the *Critique of Judgement*, or his verdict that the whole of life judged in terms of the sum of pleasure and pain always amounts to less than zero. Then there is the letter that, in old age, Kant wrote to his friend Hufeland, who had just sent the philosopher his new work *On the Art of Prolonging Human Life*. In it, the physician claimed that a moral lifestyle promotes good health until old age, an assumption Kant wholeheartedly agreed with. His response to the book, which was published as "On the Power of the Mind to Master its Morbid Feelings by Sheer Resolution" in the *Conflict of the Faculties*, is not a mere review, but offers some practical advice for living longer and enjoying old age, ranging from the way one should breathe, to the side one should sleep on, to what ink to use when the strength of the eyes starts to wane. And in sharing personal experiences and wisdoms, since he can draw "only from what I have experienced in myself," it also serves as a private confession about his ailments and their connection to his philosophy, entailing reflections about the connection of life to thought, especially in relation to his depression and hypochondria.[75]

Kant was prone to nervous maladies on account of his "flat and narrow chest,"[76] which compressed his heart and lungs. Such a physical weakness calls forth a "*fictitious* disease" not located in the body but in the mind, resulting in "brooding about the ills that could befall one, and that one would not be able to withstand if they should come. It is a kind of insanity."[77] By

---

very prominent and pointed in *On the Heights of Despair*. See E.M. Cioran, *On the Heights of Despair* (Chicago: The University of Chicago Press, 1992), p. 48f.
[75] Kant, "On the Power of the Mind to Master Its Morbid Feelings by Sheer Resolution," p. 177.
[76] Ibid., p. 189.
[77] Ibid., p. 187, original emphasis.

naming this inclination *melancholia* or *hypochondria vaga*, Kant seeks to denote the opposite of the mastery over one's melancholic feelings, situating hypochondria and depression intentionally in close proximity to one another.[78] The overactive imagination caused by the misinterpretation of otherwise normal physical processes by a nervous mental disposition might still be mastered, however, by sheer resolution. The *heautontimorumenos*[79] on the other hand flat out refuses to "discipline the play of his thoughts [...], these harassing notions that arise involuntarily,"[80] tormenting himself even if he cannot find the object of his anxiety. Kant's suggestion that one should move on to the "the agenda of the day," despite the inner feelings that suggest it has "nothing to do with me,"[81] amounts to the self-overcoming through reason of the very hypochondria that disabled reason's use. One is urged to perform a certain mental cleansing, to re-establish the mind's vitality by purging from it the negative—a hygienic motif that will reoccur in Nietzsche as well.[82] At this point, Kant defends the long-held belief that, while psychology only studies the mechanisms of the mind, philosophy is the discipline able to establish mental health. Defining the therapeutic function of reason in the *Critique of Judgement*, he distinguishes between philosophy and philosophizing. One does not have be a philosopher to do the latter, anyone can exercise reason which succeeds in "warding off many disagreeable feelings and [is], besides, a stimulant to the mind that introduces an interest in its occupation."[83] Philosophizing is a form of homeostatic regulation, of mental immunization.

---

[78] Melancholia, as we will see, does not denote the Aristotelean appreciative meaning nor the later romantic one, but the tendency to primarily torture oneself with involuntary thoughts.

[79] Also "Heauton Timorumenos" (Εαυτὸν τιμωρούμενος) from Greek is the "self-tormentor."

[80] Kant, "On the Power of the Mind to Master Its Morbid Feelings by Sheer Resolution," p. 188.

[81] Ibid.

[82] Nietzsche recommends a new hygiene on several occasions, in an often familiarly Kantian cadence. Del Caro dedicates many passages to this hygiene of immanence in Nietzsche, see Adrian Del Caro, *Grounding the Nietzsche Rhetoric of Earth* (Berlin: De Gruyter, 2023), p. 126f.

[83] Kant, *Critique of Judgement*, p. 317.

## The Last Judgement

At 72 years old, Kant, faced with mental illness caused by his ailing body, again regains an unbridled confidence in reason's ability to master involuntary thoughts. While noting that nobody would be able to convince a hypochondriac to use his reason properly, if one did he could conquer his anxiety. What, however, if we were to reject such sanitary efforts and pause to bring into view the melancholiac's inner operations? Firstly, we might agree with Cioran, who, having learned from the body, recommends physical inaction as an (anti-)philosophical strategy, since "[s]loth is a somatic scepticism, the way the flesh doubts."[84] And we might recall Kant's earliest insights into the inner connection between insanity and reason, to the point that reason's unrestrained use is seen as a kind of madness. One might even say, paraphrasing Goya, that "the insomnia of reason produces monsters." The hypochondriac, in a way, uses reason *too well* and, by extension, we might say that a certain depression can result from the use of reason: the barrage of involuntary thoughts one surrenders to, caused by the equally compulsive activity of the unbound speculative interest.

Recounting the monstrosity of the sublime portrayed in the *Critique of Judgement* in his late work "The End of All Things," Kant first confronts "the end of all time [...] as a magnitude (*duratio Noumenon*) wholly incomparable with time, of which we are obviously able to form no concept."[85] It is as if one were confronting an infinite abyss, one which "for anyone who sinks into it no return is possible."[86] Or, as Deleuze describes it in *What is Philosophy?*, one returns from the edge of the plane of immanence, where one thinks with infinite speed, with "bloodshot eyes."[87] "[Y]et," Kant continues, "there is something attractive there too: for one cannot cease turning one's terrified gaze back to it again and again."[88] Reason

---

[84] Cioran, *A Short History of Decay*, p. 23.
[85] Immanuel Kant, "The End of All Things," in *Religion and Rational Theology* (Cambridge: Cambridge University Press, 1996), p. 221.
[86] Ibid.
[87] Deleuze and Guattari, *What is Philosophy?*, p. 41.
[88] Kant, "The End of All Things," p. 221.

attempts to go to its limits, and fails. It forms only negative concepts but can nevertheless not restrain itself. We are in the same position with regards to the end of all things. Hence, the end of time is solely the concern of the suprasensible, i.e. the moral. The last day before the end of time still belongs to time since something happens. And because the end can only be conceived in terms of the suprasensible, the end will be the final act or court of morality: judgement day. No fire, no falling stars—simply the last judgement. This is reason's furthest limit, right before the only negatively conceivable end. When considering such an end, we tend to harbor the conviction of it being a terrible one. The "omens of the last day,"[89] Kant says, seem to some to confirm it, from moral degradation, i.e. the mistreatment and oppression of the poor, to the general loss of faith, from bloody wars to natural disasters. Therefore, "it is not without cause that human beings feel their existence a burden, even if they themselves are the cause."[90] At the limits of reason, with judgement day as a vantage point, Kant begins to speculate whether humans actually rule the earth and, if so, whether they deserve their regency. Enlightenment rationality brought to its logical conclusion might break with our anthropocentric convictions and disappoint all hopes of an intimate unity of nature and freedom, men, and the world. The depression that Kant outlines here might not only be spurred by such disillusionment but also by the realization that reason does not naturally master melancholic feelings. In the late writings, one can make out some of the concerns that featured in the pre-critical works about the real limits of reason and its detachment from human beings. Even more, one might be tempted to speculate that thinking, as Brassier writes, "has interests that do not coincide with those of living; indeed, they can and have been pitted against the latter."[91]

---

89    Ibid., p. 225.
90    Ibid.
91    Ray Brassier, *Nihil Unbound: Enlightenment and Extinction* (Basingstoke: Palgrave Macmillan, 2007), p. xi.

## Taming the Madness of Life

In a late note, Kant gives his work a final motto: "No surrender now to panics of darkness."[92] And perhaps Kant's critical project can be understood as a struggle to hold the madness, the *inner* limit of reason, at bay. "I am persuaded," Badiou once remarked, "that the whole of the critical enterprise is set up to shield against the tempting symptom represented by the seer Swedenborg, or against 'diseases of the head', as Kant put it."[93] While in pre-critical thought madness was an external force acting upon the sane mind (demons, angels, spirits, gods), with Kant madness itself becomes humanized and transformed into a power or potentiality of reason's employment itself.[94] While in the Renaissance madness reduces the insane to a less than human status, in Kant's pre-critical writings madness becomes a flaw of the individual all-too-human mind.[95] Critical philosophy seeks to ensure the safe passage to knowledge from what can be thought, or even worse dreamed of. In the *Anthropology*, we find Kant's argument for the exclusion of dreams from philosophy in a condensed form: "When we awake, we have a common world. But when we are asleep each has its own world."[96] Similarly, only if reason can hold up to scrutiny in a public court is its employment legitimate. By taking away the "natural right" of reason that Descartes claimed for it, Kant can now subject it to "natural law."[97]

Philosophy, in a way, has to be protected from itself, folded back on itself to not only cancel out the tendencies towards insane ramblings, but also to make it digestible for academia, which does not operate with the material of the external world, but rather constrains itself to the pieces

---

[92] According to de Quincey, which, of course, is probably a fictional account. Thomas de Quincey, "Last Days of Immanuel Kant," in *De Quincey's Works*, Vol. III (Boston: Shepard and Gill, 1923), p. 142.
[93] Alain Badiou, *Logics of Worlds: Being and Event, Vol. 2* (New York: Bloomsbury Academic, 2018), p. 536.
[94] Compare Adrian Johnston, *Time Driven: Metapsychology and the Splitting of the Drive* (Evanston: Northwestern University Press, 2005), p. 70.
[95] Compare Ben Woodard, "Mad Speculation and Absolute Inhumanism: Lovecraft, Ligotti, and the Weirding of Philosophy," *Continental* 1, no. 1 (2011), p. 7.
[96] Immanuel Kant, *Anthropology from a Pragmatic Point of View*, trans. Robert B. Louden (Cambridge; New York: Cambridge University Press, 2006), p. 190.
[97] Gilles Deleuze, *Difference and Repetition* (New York: Columbia University Press, 1994), p. 136.

and parts that are philosophizable, in short, to the mediocre.[98] This wards off the inherent danger of thinking. As Deleuze remarks, "people will readily agree that intense physical pursuits are dangerous, but thought too is an intense and wayward pursuit. Once you start thinking, you're bound to enter a line of thought where life and death, reason and madness, are at stake, and the line draws you on."[99] Avoiding this line, "Kant's critical philosophy," as Land remarks, "is the most elaborate fit of panic in the history of the earth."[100]

### Banishing the Madness of Hylozoism

Four years after the break with the reliance on spirits in and beyond philosophy for explanations of the natural world, Kant solidifies his new approach in his inaugural dissertation, *On the Form and Principles of the Sensible and the Intelligible World*, the beginning of the critical period. In the dissertation, with reference to Plato, he readopts the notions of and sharp distinction between phenomena and noumena, which remains throughout the undisputed boundary and basic structure of the critical project. Pivotal to this reconfiguration of philosophy is Kant's distinction between the sensed and its form (or the form applied to the sensed), which didn't apply in either the rationalist or the empiricist traditions, since they only claim a difference in degree, not in kind, between the sensible and the intelligible. He prepares this move carefully. Directly preceding the dissertation, in *The Differentiation of Directions in Space*, he had already established this basic principle. He attempts a discussion of Leibniz's idea of an *analysis situs* by showing its conditions of possibility.[101] He does so by insisting on the distinction of position, as determined by the relation of entities to each other, and direction, as defined by the reference to absolute space. This had become necessary, since Leibniz,

---

[98] See Francois Laruelle, *Principles of Non-Philosophy*, trans. Nicola Rubczak and Anthony Paul Smith (London: Bloomsbury, 2017), p. 103.
[99] Deleuze, *Negotiations, 1972–1990*, p. 103.
[100] Nick Land, *The Thirst for Annihilation: Georges Bataille and Virulent Nihilism. An Essay in Atheistic Religion* (London; New York: Routledge, 1992), p. 1.
[101] Henry E. Allison, *Kant's Transcendental Deduction: An Analytical-Historical Commentary* (Oxford: Oxford University Press, 2015), p. 44.

in a critique of Newton's notion of space, had claimed that space was "an order of coexistences, as time is an order of successions,"[102] and hence that absolute space was neither epistemologically nor ontologically prior to phenomena. Kant's rejection of absolute space as merely ideal and his subsequent proof of its reality faced a specific problem. While Euler had proved that absolute space must be real, since the Newtonian laws of motion would otherwise be inexplicable, he could not *show* this application *in concreto*. Due to the fact that space is not an object of outer sensation, the motion of bodies cannot be determined by laws without the relation to a pre-given object, absolute space. To avoid this dead end, Kant therefore transforms space into "a fundamental concept which first of all makes possible all such outer sensation."[103] From this perspective, if we perceive space as the intersection of three spatial planes, the ability to distinguish directions and the ability to determine three-dimensional objects in space "derives from the relation between these intersecting planes and one's body."[104] Taken together with the argument for enantiamorphs—the existence of pairs of objects that while topologically identical are still incongruent, which is inexplicable without reference to real and absolute space—this proves for Kant the reality of absolute space. By demonstrating that space is a function of human sensibility, while still being real, he moves away from the absolute reality of space in Newton or Clarke. These conclusions prepare the bigger shift in the *Dissertation* to making space *merely* a form of intuition.

Following from the "great light" of 1769, Kant proposes to end the deadlock between and within rationalism and empiricism by distinguishing between two cognitive faculties which by working together produce cognition, but only if given that both have their own a priori conditions. This strategy yields cognition, insofar as the sense data given in intuition is brought under concepts, so that objects can be thought. Rationalism and

---

102  Ibid.
103  Immanuel Kant, "Von Dem Ersten Grunde Des Unterschiedes Der Gegenden Im Raume," in *Vorkritische Schriften: 1747–1756* (Berlin: Preußische Akademie der Wissenschaften, 1902), p. 383.
104  Allison, *Kant's Transcendental Deduction*, p. 45.

empiricism, therefore, are both guilty of a simple conflation of the two faculties, either in the identification of an ultimate or grounding cognitive faculty, while the other cognitive power is merely a derivate, a mere difference in degree, or as one being reducible to the other. While in the Leibnizian tradition, hence also for Wolff, the distinction between sensible and intellectual cognition is a cornerstone of epistemology, these two powers are only different in their respective degree of distinctness and clarity. The rejection of this position turns on the understanding of space sketched out above. Kant had demonstrated that representations of space are inseparable from human sensible intuition. Taken together with his proof that space cannot simply be conceived in the purely relational sense, since these relations are already conditioned by the very representations of space they supposedly produce, he concludes that space (and similarly time)[105] are *forms* of human sensibility. Hence, our representations of these forms are *pure* intuitions because the form of sensation cannot be abstracted from or be a product of what is sensed. Kant therefore concludes that the sensible and its form cannot only be different in degree but must be so in kind. While rationalism (namely Wolff) intellectualized the sensible, empiricism (namely Locke) "sensitivized"[106] the intelligible by making cognition a sensation distinct only by its lesser degree in vividness. As a solution, Kant introduces a radical discontinuity between the sensible and the intelligible.

The close of the *Dissertation* defends the newly-introduced discontinuity against three fallacies of "subreption," which would reintroduce a continuity between the sensible and the intelligible. The three principles of harmony established from this map out, at least implicitly, the conse-

---

[105] From his first works, Kant is mostly concerned with space. One can even reconstruct the development of his critical project by following the process of refinement of his argument against Leibniz's topological understanding of space. Time, however, is not a relative concern until later and can only be understood in its homology to space. The structure of the "Transcendental Aesthetic" of the *Critique of Pure Reason* further illustrates this. While the metaphysical exposition and the transcendental deduction are developed before our eyes for space, the following section on time is clearly simply mapped onto this structure.

[106] Locke "sensitivized the concepts of the understanding." Immanuel Kant, *Critique of Pure Reason*, ed. Max Müller, trans. Marcus Weigelt (London: Penguin Books, 2007), A271/B327.

quences of the discontinuity for the concept of matter. The first principle of harmony claims that nothing can happen in violation of the order of nature, thereby also resituating the positions of the *Dreams of the Spirit-Seers* concerning rational psychology and pneumatology. While "miracles, such as the influences of spirits, are carefully excluded from the explanation of phenomena,"[107] the discontinuity wards off positions like the one of the anti-Leibnizian Cruz, which state that everything, including the soul, must be in space and time.[108] This argument is salient, since in the *Critique of Pure Reason* and the *Critique of Practical Reason* it turns into a position threatening the postulate of freedom. The third principle, however, deals with matter proper, insofar as Kant relocates all changes in the world in forms and no longer in matter, since "[n]othing material at all comes into being or passes away."[109] This is, according to Kant,

> because, if you concede that matter itself is in flux and transitory, there would be nothing left at all which is stable and enduring, which would further advance the explanation of phenomena in accordance with universal and constant laws, and which would, therefore, further the advance of the understanding.[110]

The argument, at this stage, is presented as an epistemological one. It is not yet complete but already contains the germs of the final argument. To see the transition from the epistemological to the moral standpoint, we must trace the consequences of the erection and maintenance of a boundary between the sensible and the intelligible for hylozoism further through the critical project. It is not the rejection of the life of matter that prompts the sensible/intelligible distinction, but this must still be rejected because it threatens it. However, it is not the case that the rejec-

---

107 Immanuel Kant, "On the Form and Principles of the Sensible and Intelligible World," in *Theoretical Philosophy, 1755–1770* (Cambridge: Cambridge University Press, 1992), p. 414.
108 See Allison, *Kant's Transcendental Deduction*, p. 47.
109 Kant, "On the Form and Principles of the Sensible and Intelligible World," p. 47.
110 Ibid., p. 419.

tion of living matter is, seen in the context of Kant's entire corpus, first and foremost a consequence of the aforementioned boundary, since Kant had already dismissed it as untenable in the *Dreams*. Rather, there is a common ground for the sensible/intelligible distinction *and* the rejection of hylozoism, not rooted in theoretical, but in practical philosophy.

### DEAD MATTER

It has often been proposed that Kant's dismissal of hylozoism is due to his involvement in eighteenth century natural science and its depiction of matter as inert in contrast with the spontaneity of living creatures. This, however, is not accurate, or at least not Kant's primary argument against the attribution of life to matter. Moreover, Kant seems to actively combat this line of reasoning, calling its judgements illegitimate. The ferocity of Kant's attack on hylozoism in the *Critique of Judgement*—based on the idea that for hylozoism "one must [...] endow matter as mere matter with a property [...] that contradicts its essence"[111]—can, however, temporarily give the impression that the problem is the inert nature of matter. The argument, however, that the hylozoist must claim that matter is both alive and dead at the same time rather begs the question and is therefore secondary in his line of argumentation. As mentioned, Kant does question elsewhere the legitimacy of such attributions, since "inertia" at least implies the possibility that something can move voluntarily or according to one's desires, which is illegitimate to claim for matter.[112] The same goes for the Lockean depiction of matter as "dead": matter does not live and therefore cannot die. This line of reasoning first grants matter organic properties (e.g. will, life) only to then negate them. But

---

111   Kant, *Critique of Judgement*, p. 254.
112   In his earlier *Lectures on Metaphysics*, he still held such a belief, since he held hylozoism only to the standard of the animal desire. "If one assumes that matter as matter thinks, lives, e.g. acts according to representations, then this is above all contrary to physics." Immanuel Kant, *Lectures on Metaphysics*, trans. Karl Ameriks and Steve Naragon (Cambridge: Cambridge University Press, 1997), p. 753.

even the negative claim, then, is a categorical mistake, since it proposes a *qualita occultas*, an *organic* force that would be the same in all organic and inorganic matter, something which necessarily could never be observed. Or, translated into the terms of the *Critique of Judgement*: claiming that matter is "dead" or "inert" would be making a determinative judgement where only a reflective judgement would be permissible. In his confrontation with his student Herder, this criticism becomes the central point. Kant dismisses, not without foundation, Herder's "speculative philosophy of nature," since Herder does not employ any preformistic or epigenetic principles to explain life, but instead posits a single "vital force," which finds different expressions in stones, plants and animals. This is problematic for Kant for at least two reasons. Firstly, Herder claims to have some inferential knowledge of the organic force, which is, according to Kant, "the author's attempt to explain what is not understood in terms of what is understood even less."[113] Secondly, building on this first criticism, Kant states that, insofar as the "organic force is known only from its effects, Herder transcends the limits of possible experience,"[114] and therefore has to postulate the ground of his system and dogmatically incorporate everything in it retroactively, switching the places of *explanans* and *explanandum*.[115]

While it is, however, true that the *Metaphysical Foundations of Natural Science* characterizes matter through the "law of inertia" as "lifeless," this is not yet the refined form of Kant's argument. He claims here that "for a substance to have life is for it to be able to get itself, through its own inner resources, to act."[116] The only cause which is known to us that would satisfy this definition is desire, and the only inner activity known to us is thought. Desire and thought are both absent in matter and hence, matter cannot be said to be alive. But, as Kant vehemently adds, this is *"all* it says," because

---

113 Immanuel Kant, *Kant: Political Writings*, trans. Hans Siegbert Reiss (Cambridge: Cambridge University Press, 1991), p. 209.
114 Beth Lord, "Against the Fanaticism of Forces: Kant's Critique of Herder's Spinozism," *Parallax* 15, no. 2 (April 2009), p. 59.
115 See John Zammito, *The Genesis of Kant's Critique of Judgment* (Chicago: Chicago University Press, 1992), p. 203.
116 Kant, *Metaphysical Foundations of Natural Science*, p. 544.

we could still misunderstand "inertia"[117] in terms of an unwillingness to change to avoid some other state. But "inertia" has no positive meaning here at all. Material change can therefore only be explained in terms of life if we search for the "cause in some other substance that is different from matter although bound up with it."[118] So far, this argument sits flush with earlier considerations in the *Universal Natural History and Theory of the Heavens* and *The Only Possible Argument in Support of a Demonstration of the Existence of God* on the physico-theological argument for the existence of god, which both present a skeptical position on the explicability of organized beings through purely mechanical models. When he turns to hylozoism in the *Metaphysical Foundations of Natural Science*, however, the argument shifts. To attribute life to matter is not "the death of all natural philosophy"[119] because it subjects everything to mechanism—this is the criticism levelled against materialism—but rather because it only gives us either dogmatic or empty explanations. Instead of tracing a concept of life from the observation of living beings, we would be attempting to explain living beings by a principle we do not know anything about, except what we know about our observations of living beings.

### PURPOSIVENESS AND THE INSUFFICIENCY OF HYLOZOISM

Following the skepticism about the possibility of a mechanical explanation for *all* appearances of nature in the *Theory of the Heavens*, which did not yet develop a systematic approach to this problem, *On the Different Races of Man* is the first text of Kant's to introduce the problem of purposiveness. Building on preformistic theories, he claims the common ancestry of all humankind, with climate differentiating the manifestation of the common dispositions. Since such an organized distribution of races could not be explained by blind mechanism alone, "as Kant under-

---

[117] Ibid.
[118] Ibid., p. 555.
[119] Ibid.

stood it, racial differences called for a purposive account."[120] However, at this stage of his work, Kant is a devoted follower of Newtonian physics, which he regards as natural science proper, providing universal laws of nature. The problem that the specific laws of purposiveness seem irreducible to the general laws of mechanics, creates the further problem as to whether a science of purposiveness is possible at all. The problem of the gap in explanation left by merely conceiving of nature in terms of a *nexus effectivus*, but not yet being able to provide an explanation according to a *nexus finalis within* science, forces Kant in 1775 to fall back on an act of divine creation to circumvent the problem.

The *Critique of Judgement*'s "Critique of Teleological Judgement" could be viewed as a reworking and answer to this problem according to and in systematic unity with the principles of the *First* and *Second Critique*. He sets up this discussion with two important restrictions. Firstly, we can "only say that the character of our understanding and of our reason is such that the only way we can conceive of the origin of such [organized] beings is in terms of final causes."[121] This might be regarded as a solution to the deadlock brought on by the conception of purposiveness as *real* teleology in the *Races of Man*. Since it is only a "subjective necessity" to "adduce a teleological basis"[122] where the mechanical principles of Newtonian physics do not suffice to conceive of the self-organization potentialities of organized beings, these judgements do not refer to nor change anything in nature. They inform us only about "the character of our (human) cognitive power,"[123] and hence these judgements are reflective and not determinative. Under this condition the problematic concept of intrinsic purposiveness can be taken up and treated critically, but only "if we consider it only in relation to our cognitive power, and hence in relation to the subjective conditions under which we think it, without venturing to decide anything about its object."[124] The second restriction concerns the kinds of objects

---

120 Robert Bernasconi, *Race* (Malden: Blackwell, 2001), p. 29.
121 Kant, *Critique of Judgement*, p. 416.
122 Ibid., p. 360.
123 Ibid., p. 399.
124 Ibid., p. 395.

of which teleological judgements can be made. As already implicit in the first restriction, intrinsic purposiveness can only be said to be possessed by *organized* beings. This is crucial, since Kant had struggled with the mechanical nature of animals and plants throughout his numerous writings on the matter. While, inspired by Reimarus, he had granted animals an immaterial animal soul, and while he had seemed in adopting Haller's theory of irritability even to bestow a non-mechanical potential on plants, he had still held that a plant is *machina hydraulica* and that animals are very sophisticated automata, in keeping with his Newtonian leanings. Now, his look at the question as part of the critical project does include all organized beings, and even features a tree as his prime example. The term *organized*, however, denotes the fact that such a natural thing "must relate to itself in such a way that it is both cause and effect of itself"[125] and hence calls for a causality different from mechanics. As Ginsborg notes, this implies a twofold mechanical inexplicability. "Organized" denotes the teleological organization of interrelated and, in terms of functionality, interdependent parts, which cannot be understood by reference to blind mechanism, since its complexity is irreducible to chance. In order to satisfy the requirements for an organized being to have a natural cause, then, firstly, "the possibility of its parts (as concerns both their existence and their form) must depend on their relation to the whole."[126] Since this could be said of a clock, as well as of Descartes's teleological or Leibniz's entelechial machines, organized beings are also defined by their ability to maintain their form by replacing defective parts and to reproduce, to create new organized beings, without external cause. The second requirement "is that the parts of the thing combine into the unity of a whole because they are reciprocally cause and effect of their form."[127]

Following the "Antinomy of Teleological Judgement," arising from the equally justified but contradictory maxims that "[a]ll production of material things and their forms must be judged to be possible in terms of

---

125  Ibid., p. 372.
126  Ibid., p. 373, see also Julie Books, *The Supersensible in Kant's Critique of Judgement* (Lausanne: Peter Lang, 2016), p. 73.
127  Kant, *Critique of Judgement*, p. 373.

merely mechanical laws," "while some products of material nature cannot be judged to be possible in terms of merely mechanical laws,"[128] Kant first introduces an exhaustive list of prior attempts by others to solve the problem, before presenting his own solution. He ensures the completeness of his typology by positing that regarding objective purposiveness one can either be an idealist or a realist and regarding the ground of matter either a physicalist or hyper-physicalist, giving us four positions in total: lifeless matter, the lifeless God, living matter and the living God. He rejects the Epicurean (idealist, physicalist) position as outright untenable since its causal model does not have any explanatory power. Spinoza's fatalistic position (idealist, hyper-physicalist), however, appears harder to refute, since the formal ground of matter is not in matter but in substance, and Spinoza therefore seems to be able to provide a principle of organization external to matter. Nevertheless, since the ends of the modes do not follow causally but are entailed in substance, one of two things must be correct: either all the modes follow unintentionally from substance, which would make ends impossible, or every mode is created intentionally, although then purposiveness could not be compared against anything, since there would then be nothing that is not intentional. Hence, both Spinoza's and Epicurus's interpretations do not provide adequate explanations, since Spinoza still champions continuity on the formal side, while Epicurus still champions continuity on the material side.

On the realist side, the option of theism (realist, hyper-physicalist), a position Kant himself still championed in 1775, is simply mentioned and presumed untenable in the critical project. He again considers hylozoism (realist, physicalist), however, at some length. In the *Metaphysics of Morals* he had grappled with the problem that no experience or inference can contain any indication of whether humans possess a soul or "whether life may well be, instead, a property of matter";[129] he now excludes the question as such. Accordingly, he transforms his characterization of hylozo-

---

[128] Ibid., p. 387.
[129] Immanuel Kant, *The Metaphysics of Morals*, trans. Mary J. Gregor (Cambridge: Cambridge University Press, 1996), p. 419.

ism, which now becomes the position that "regards the purposes in nature as based on the analogue of a mental power that acts according to intention."[130] Due to the epistemological concerns from the *Metaphysical Foundations of Natural Science* mentioned above, this position is dismissed. This recasting of hylozoism as a form of weak panpsychism veils the shift in the argument. It is not inertia but the inability to produce and maintain a form (unity) that prevents matter from being considered alive, since aliveness involves the intentional acts of being irritable *and* reacting to stimuli accordingly to maintain its form. As Goy puts it: "Thus Kant argues that while organisms are material machines, they must be designed and animated by something immaterial—not because matter is ruled by inertia, but because it is never a true unity."[131]

It is the inability of matter to give itself a form or to self-organize that entails the antinomy of teleological judgement and the rejection of hylozoism. However, since judgements on the appearances of organized beings are reflective, they ought to be treated *as if* they conformed to our cognitive faculties. Even if we try to think otherwise, "our reason will still force us to subordinate such products ultimately [...] to the causality in terms of purposes."[132] Such a "force" of reason has to be presupposed, if we are confronted with the antinomy of teleological reason, while at the same time the teleological antinomy only appears under the assumption of such a "force." The foundation of a "force" of reason that unifies all particulars under universals can, however, not be critiqued itself, since it is not subject to a genesis in the sensible. Rather, it must be postulated, as Mensch suggests, as "the organic unity of reason."[133] It is itself, however, grounded, as is teleology, in morality, as we will see.

---

130  Ibid.
131  Paul Guyer, "Organisms and the Unity of Science," in *Kant and the Sciences*, ed. Eric Watkins (Oxford: Oxford University Press, 2001), p. 277.
132  Kant, *Critique of Judgement*, p. 415.
133  Jennifer Mensch, *Kant's Organicism: Epigenesis and the Development of Critical Philosophy* (Chicago: The University of Chicago Press, 2013), p. 133.

# THE ORGANIC IMAGE OF THOUGHT

## ORGANIC HISTORIES AND ENDS OF THOUGHT

Genealogy played a crucial role in Kant's deduction, posing the question of birthright in relation to the origin of the forms of sensation. And he repeats this genealogical movement in relation to reason's rightful place in the ancestral line.

The very end of the *Critique of Pure Reason* reveals a key point about the organic function of reason. The "History of Reason" can at first glance be seen as a process of maturation, with dogmatism being its infancy, skepticism its youth and criticism its maturity. The latter is the only suitable place for metaphysics to find a safe haven from the "marauding nomads,"[134] though it can only occupy this place after having failed and grown as a response to the failure. While Kant in the "Doctrine of Elements" had conceived of intuition, concepts and ideas from a material standpoint, he considers them in the "Doctrine of Method" from a systematic perspective in relation to reason (or the system of reason). The architectonic model of these elements, based on material considerations, now "matures" into a more organic model of growth. By conceiving of the whole of the system of reason (as well as its history) as an "organized unity (articulation)" rather than an "aggregate (coacervation)," Kant makes it function "like an animal body."[135] Growth in such an organic body works neither by the addition of parts nor by the alteration of proportion, but by rendering every member of the whole "stronger and more effective for its purposes."[136] Conversely then, this whole, which determines the relation, proportion and end of each member is already contained in the germ. Similarly, the unity and hence the completion of the task of reason—the end of history as reason's self-completion

---

[134] Kant, *Critique of Pure Reason*, A761/B789.
[135] Ibid., A833/B862.
[136] Ibid.

in a unified whole—had been implicated in the self-conception of reason from the beginning as an "original germ."[137] Subsequently, the unfolding of the history of reason is the "sheer self-development of reason"[138] towards its unification according to its disposition.

Ultimately, "the teleological course taken during the natural history of reason took on the cast of destiny."[139] The conception of such a destiny is, however, not only dependent on the assumption of an "original" germ, but on a "self-development" that in its development discovers its own purposiveness. Through genealogical research it puts its ancestry in order. But such a genealogy is only possible by the assumption of the very order it is supposed to ground. Hence, thinking must first determine itself to find the birthrights that justify such a conception. For Deleuze, it is exactly this unavoidable self-problematization of thought that challenges the possibility of an overarching narrative in the history of thought. Rather than uncovering universals through a continuous debate or discussion on the same problems, the self-construction of thought layers, through its auto-critique and subsequent auto-positing, different "images" of what thinking thinks that it is, one over the other, creating plateaus or sedimentary layers.[140] A history of thought according to such a "geology" of images is called "noology" by Deleuze. Such a history is not concerned with the continuity of ancestry, but with the "untimely" element of such a development. It is a cartography, mapping the coordinates with which we orientate ourselves within the dynamic system that is thinking. It is a history made by uncovering the images at the foundation of thinking.

---

[137] Ibid., A835/B863.
[138] Ibid.
[139] Mensch, *Kant's Organicism*, p. 128.
[140] Wittgenstein, in his later works, develops a similar approach with the "pictures" that thought is based in. See Ludwig Wittgenstein, *Philosophical Investigations* (Malden: Blackwell, 2009), p. 53.

## NOOLOGY

What an "*image* of thought" is can be expressed in the meaning of the Greek idea (εἶδος), which is itself an image (εἴδωλον).[141] If thinking is reflected back onto itself, it needs an image of what thinking means to have an object of this thought. Hence, one must identify thinking from amongst all the possible and actual subjective activities to account for its specificity if one wants to hold that thinking is different from, say, remembering, seeing or dreaming.

The example of Descartes's critique of Aristotle provided by Deleuze in *Difference and Repetition* is instructive here. It revolves around the dialogue between Epistemon and Eudoxus from Descartes's *The Search for Truth by Means of the Natural Light*, in which they discuss the proper way of conducting philosophical inquiry. Epistemon holds that philosophical inquiry entails (at least to some degree) an encounter with and an investigation of the external world. Knowledge can therefore only be justified by empirical evidence. As in Aristotle this implies that the investigation, as well as its results, might not be necessarily or inherently systematic, as would be the case in an approach that is purely internal to reason. This method of empirical investigation has two weaknesses, as Eudoxus is happy to point out by contrasting his method against Epistemon's. Conducted by pure reason, the mind has "at its disposal all the truths it comes across" and therefore "does not dream there are others to discover."[142] Therefore, given that it is executed in its proper form, all inferences made by thought through pure reason are true and certain, a quality that Epistemon's approach lacks. More importantly though, all the terms used in order to think are derived from reason alone and are thus transparent to it; they do not need to be investigated any further.[143] In a way, by not think-

---

141  Gregg Lambert, *In Search of a New Image of Thought: Gilles Deleuze and Philosophical Expressionism* (Minneapolis: University of Minnesota Press, 2012), p. 1.
142  Henry Somers-Hall, "Feuerbach and the Image of Thought," in *At the Edges of Thought: Deleuze and Post-Kantian Philosophy*, ed. Craig Lundy and Daniela Voss (Edinburgh: Edinburgh University Press, 2015), p. 255.
143  See ibid., p. 256.

ing properly, Epistemon is guilty of not really thinking at all. Because his terms are *necessarily* obscure, he does not really think what he thinks: the object of his thoughts is indeterminable and therefore empty. Thought therefore legitimately distinguishes truth and falsity by conducting its investigation purely internal to reason, in the "natural light" of (or attributed to) reason, not letting itself be confused by the possibly erroneous impressions of the other faculties. At the end, however, Eudoxus turns to Polyander (the everyman) to demonstrate that if the latter employed the former's method of radical doubt, he would arrive at the conclusion that the only thing he can't doubt is his own existence. The way the famous *cogito*-argument is set up seems to prove Deleuze's assertion that Descartes claims that "good sense is of all things in the world the most evenly distributed."[144] This even distribution of good sense establishes "good will on the part of the thinker" and an "upright nature on the part of thought."[145] We can therefore see that beyond thought's *passive* and reflexive use of its own image, the image also has an *active* and prescriptive function, insofar as it describes how to engender thinking proper. Thus, it doesn't simply prompt the question of how one begins to think, but of how one ought to begin to think properly in order to think at all. It's not that the philosopher models thinking thereby *de facto* after an image, but that the image determines *de jure* what counts as thinking. Consequently, an image of thought excludes (or ignores) certain activities as not legitimate for systematic reasons. Once it has determined what legitimate thought is, it has already defined the objects of thought that these specific activities encompass. It is however worth noting that Descartes (and also Kant, for that matter) do not actually believe that thought works like this *in fact*,[146] but rather that it does so in (and by) principle. It thereby at once legitimates and limits what can be thought. Philosophy thus abstracts from

---

[144] Ibid., p. 257.
[145] Deleuze, *Difference and Repetition*, p. 131.
[146] "It cannot be regarded as a fact that thinking is the natural exercise of a faculty, and that this faculty is possessed of a good nature and a good will. 'Everybody' knows very well that in fact men think rarely, and more often under the impulse of a shock than in the excitement of a taste for thinking." Deleuze, *Difference and Repetition*, p. 132.

the particular thought and thinker to the acts universal to all thought, moving to a generality of the form "Everybody knows, no one can deny."[147]

This assumption has two aspects. Firstly, what Descartes attempts here is nothing short of an account of, as Hegel would call it, "thinking as such,"[148] because it is at once aware of its presuppositions and wants to part with them. Although it is Descartes who makes it possible to criticize the images of thought by bringing the impossibility of philosophy grounding itself in itself to light, in establishing this "good will" he falls prey to another illegitimate presupposition. In his *Meditations* we can see this double structure again, insofar as Descartes seeks to justify our knowledge of the world through God, while the knowledge of God is already based on our ability to conceive of him in a clear and distinct manner. The natural light leads the way and cuts through the mist soaring up from the dizzying depths of the sensible, straight to the bottom. Thinking, we are told, is a benevolent activity for good people. Secondly, this assumption takes the form of a discourse of representation enabled by common sense, because it negates the line between thinking and its self-presentation. As Feuerbach already notes in his critique of Hegel, this move subjects thinking to the rules of communication and communicability, not to thought itself.[149] As we have seen in Descartes's use of Polyander in the *cogito* argument, thought for him ought to be presented in a comprehensible manner. In turn this also means that one strips away all that which is considered accidental and only presents what is essential in thought, while the distinction between these categories can only be drawn by assuming what it is that makes a thought recognizable to another person. Thought is thereby determined by a common sense that trumps all other "unrecognizable" senses. This critique is one that Deleuze echoes in his definition of philosophy as above all *not* communication, i.e. neither dissolved into vari-

---

147 Ibid., p. 130.
148 Georg Wilhelm Friedrich Hegel, *Lectures on the History of Philosophy: The Lectures of 1825–1826*, trans. Robert F. Brown, J. M. Stewart, and H. S. Harris (Berkeley: University of California Press, 1990), p. 137.
149 Ludwig Feuerbach, *Towards a Critique of Hegel's Philosophy* (New York: Prism Key Press, 2013), p. 32.

ous forms of opinion nor subjected to a transcendental structure common to all thinking.[150] Common sense justifies thereby the model of recognition as the only legitimate pre-philosophical model for thought. In the establishment of common sense and good will, we can more clearly see that the active nature of the image of thought is a moral obligation at the heart of philosophy. The natural light is something thinking is supposed to imitate.

Rightly criticized by Hume, who conceives of reason as just a higher form of habit and thereby unfit to ground philosophy, Kant, for whom reason left only to its own devices easily falls prey to illusions created by its speculative interests, and Hegel, who objects that one might begin with consciousness alone, as Descartes did, but still would not be able to account for its "abstract unity,"[151] reason loses its natural *right*. But the natural *light* never fades out.[152] It lingers in the assumption that proper thinking is achieved as soon as philosophy has purified itself by expunging all presuppositions from its ground. In an a-hierarchical attempt to 'thinking', Hegel, for example, brings natural consciousness into position against a form of thinking that is the imitation of the philosophical theory proposed by Descartes, thereby championing a view of consciousness compatible with everyday experience. Rather than assuming the transparency of thought to itself, he posits a model of immanent dialectic, in which he lets the problems of consciousness play out in contradictions without presupposing one mode of thinking over another. While this developmental model of thinking takes philosophy's quest for eliminating its presuppositions further than any other, it does so only within the presupposition of

---

[150] See Deleuze and Guattari, *What is Philosophy?*, p. 28.
[151] Georg Wilhelm Friedrich Hegel, *Encyclopedia of the Philosophical Sciences in Basic Outline, Part 1: Science of Logic*, trans. Klaus Brinkmann and Daniel O. Dahlstrom (Cambridge: Cambridge University Press, 2010), § 213.
[152] Heidegger, by being the arché and point of departure of the German-French discourses on being and difference, seems at first glance inseparable from Deleuze's ontological project. But, beyond the Hegelian approach to the history of thought, it is Heidegger who in a twofold way reinstates for philosophy common sense as well as the good will of thinking and thinker. By rooting phenomenology in the primacy of hermeneutics, the existential analysis of Heidegger always opens up a relation of ontological superiority of one mode (also a mode of thought) over another, in giving the practical a grounding function in relation to the theoretical, assuming it holds less presuppositions.

common sense that informs the "pre-philosophical or natural Image"[153] of thought that is left when all other presuppositions are stripped away.

## ORGANIC REPRESENTATION

The problem of establishing natural law, as shown above, derives from the difference in kind between the sensible and the intelligible, or between intuitions and concepts. The transcendental deduction of the *Critique of Pure Reason* could be considered a solution to the problem of establishing a common sense between the faculties that ensures knowledge despite their difference in kind. The three syntheses laid out in the deduction proceed by the faculty of intuition, which runs through the manifold. For these connections established in the first synthesis to appear connected, the imagination must take them up, insofar as in experience past moments are not only reproduced, but also recognized as such. Therefore, in the third synthesis, the conceptual determination ensures that all presentations form the experience of a successive disclosure of the same object.[154] Insofar as thinking is related to a manifold of intuition, the good nature of thought will provide a common sense between the faculties. We must however not confuse this common sense with the "I think." For Kant, though "it must be possible for the 'I think' to accompany all our representations,"[155] this does not mean that it does so all the time in fact. In claiming that it did, we would be confusing Kant with Descartes, who provides the common sense through the cogito. In Kant, conversely, the "I think" is established by the transcendental unity of apperception, which in turn furnishes the common sense. In this "logical common sense,"[156] unlike in Descartes's, the notions of object and common sense presuppose or posit each other. The synthetic activity of the

---

153 Deleuze, *Difference and Repetition*, p. 131.
154 See Martin Heidegger, *Kant and the Problem of Metaphysics* (Bloomington: Indiana University Press, 1997), p. 89.
155 Kant, *Critique of Pure Reason*, B131–132.
156 Deleuze, *Difference and Repetition*, p. 137.

subject enables the notion of an object, which serves subsequently as a point of reference for representations of the object, enabling the subject to differentiate between itself and its representations. This transparency of the mind is the cornerstone of Kant's transcendental deduction. The good will of the thinker and the good nature of thought presuppose one another, and this in turn conditions the model of recognition.

This mutual conditioning ensures what Deleuze calls "organic representation," which is characterized by "identity in the concept, opposition in the predicate, analogy in judgement and resemblance in perception."[157] This tames difference by making any form of non-conceptual difference unthinkable: "every difference which is not rooted in this way is an unbounded, uncoordinated and *inorganic* difference: too large or too small, not only to be thought but to exist."[158] These limits to difference are expressed in Kant's model of the syntheses. The synthesis of recognition organizes the different representations around the *identity* of the object. But only if there is an analogous relationship between knowledge and the object (via the *analogy* of the rules that govern them) can this be done at all. To relate two representations and make them conform to a unity, they must have an affinity with each other that is established by a property of the object, a property which is the same now as it was in the past. The present object can only be judged as an instance of a type if the notion of *opposition* is already given (it is either an instance of a type or it is not). But still the two presentations of the object with their now determined properties must be compared to see if they have the same properties, to see, that is, if they *resemble* each other. While the concept functions as the *focus imaginarius* of unification, all other operations traverse the faculties or work between them. Between the intuition and imagination, as we have seen, resemblance is constituted. Insofar as a unified experience of objects obtains, the whole apparatus of representation is necessarily working properly.

Deleuze's objection to this is not that there is no representation or that this is not how representations are produced, but rather that this model is

---

[157] Ibid., p. 262.
[158] Ibid., my emphasis.

"organic." It totalizes everything in a self-sustaining form that ignores everything—that is, ignores everything that is beyond the limits or beneath the threshold of sensibility—and rejects everything that threatens its organic consistency. It is organic not only because the elements of experience are organized, but because they are being organized by principles that invariantly recreate themselves in this organization. The good will of the thinker acts as a principle of natural growth, a teleological development, which ends in the establishment of the organization from within, without the need for external forces. Common sense provides a principle that runs through all the faculties, organizing all the parts into a whole by establishing communication between them, a whole which is only for the parts, but irreducible to them. Through recognition the genetic conditions of its formation are obscured, just as organisms are when they are weakened by dependence on a specific environment and growing autarky. At the same time as thinking is subjected to "organic representation"[159] as a structure of thought, it also becomes thought for the organisms. One thinks as an organism or not at all. Or rather, one ought to think as an organism or not at all. This organic model of thought is not a fact as it is not a general law. If it were, one could not infringe upon it. But one can think things that do not abide by these organic limits; one can ingest the infinite (which is not the organism as a whole) or feel the intensities of the infinitely small (which are not yet parts of the whole), but one ought not to, because it is a threat to organic consistency. The representation, aided and instated by good will, common sense and recognition, acts as an upper and lower limit to experience, while at the same time enabling representational thought as such. Everything that does not abide by the limits of the large and the small—everything, then, that is under or above the limits of tolerance for the organism—is cut out. Representation acts as a tendency, a homeostatic principle that *naturally* tames difference to ensure survival; "good" organic growth against "bad" chaotic disorganization.

---

[159] Ibid., p. 29.

## TRACING THE TRANSCENDENTAL

What can be found to be the common denominator in all eight postulates Deleuze identifies as characteristics of the dogmatic (or, as I have called it in relation to Kant's specific formulation of it, the "organic") image of thought is a critique of Kant's method of tracing the transcendental from the empirical.[160] As we have seen, common and good sense work in tandem to restrict the field of thinking to recognition, making it the model (or image) of thought as such. If, however, what it means to know is predicated upon the identity of the object, guaranteed by the reciprocal relation of the form of the object and the transcendental unity of apperception, then only what can be recognized can be known or experienced. This *essentializes* the empirical. By accepting only recognition as the model of thinking, Kant acknowledges only the determinate qualities of an object as salient and not the indeterminate, because not recognizable, process of the production of these properties. Kant assumes (consequently) that the conditions of the empirical must resemble the empirical. This, again, implies a hylomorphic relationship between conditions and conditioned; the forms as conditions mold the matter of the empirical, while the empirical remains the passive receiver of the form. This, however, leads to a "vicious circle" at the level of grounding:

> The error of all efforts to determine the transcendental as consciousness is that they think the transcendental in the image of, and in resemblance to, that which it is supposed to ground. In this case, either we give ourselves ready-made, in the "originary" sense presumed to belong to the constitutive consciousness, whatever we were trying to generate through a transcendental method, or, in agreement with Kant, we give up genesis and constitution and we limit ourselves to a simple transcendental

---

160 Compare Joe Hughes, *Deleuze's Difference and Repetition: A Reader's Guide* (London; New York: Continuum Books, 2009), p. 71.

conditioning. But we do not, for all this, escape the vicious circle which makes the condition refer to the conditioned as it reproduces its image.[161]

The empirical is supposed to be grounded by the transcendental, a grounding which is in fact its *only* function. At the same time, the empirical here resembles the transcendental, since the latter is traced precisely from the empirical. The empirical is thus grounded in its double. When, in rare cases, Kant considers the process of the production of properties, it is retroactively made to conform to recognition. Take, for example, the blossom of a flower, which emerged by a free and non-conceptual interplay of forces. Once the process has produced the blossom as its product, it is retroactively designated as the end of the process and the forces subsumed as conditions *of* the blossom. The conditions become exclusively bound to the product, incorporated into a teleological movement that is external to the conditions themselves. Hence, the actual existence of the conditioned is a mere actualization of a possibility and therefore does not affect the conditions. At the same time the conditions remains indifferent to what they condition, making them invariant and a-temporal, in the sense that, whenever the empirical is produced, its conditions are reproduced in the exact same way in every instance. This indifference has a twofold function: on the one hand to restrict what can be known or experienced to what is possible, and on the other hand to prevent this possibility from being subject to change, allowing for the localization of the transcendental in the unity of apperception.[162] As Deleuze argues, Kant therefore never bridges the gap between conditioning and generation of experience or knowledge, and hence the transcendental, due to its resemblance to the empirical, is unable to "found" what it is supposed to ground.

Due to the difference in kind between intuitions and concepts, this problem returns at the level of the schematism. Concepts of the under-

---

161 Deleuze, *Logic of Sense*, p. 105.
162 See Diane Beddoes, "Kant, Deleuze and Indifference," in *Deleuze and Philosophy: The Difference Engineer*, ed. Keith Ansell-Pearson (London: Routledge, 1997), p. 25.

standing, characterized by spontaneity, and of sensible intuitions, characterized by receptivity, are entirely heterogeneous, but since they only together yield cognition, a third thing must be assumed to serve as mediator.[163] But "[t]his mediating representation must be pure (without anything empirical) and yet *intellectual* on the one hand and *sensible* on the other."[164] Kant's introduction of a third element, however, only defers the question, since "the schematism only reinforces the paradox introduced into the doctrine of the faculties by the notion of pure external harmony,"[165] since it again falls into a vicious circle. What the schematism is supposed to explain is the application of concepts to intuitions. To do so, a schema must be assumed because concepts are applied to intuitions by a schema. The schema, rather than founding the harmony of the faculties and therefore enabling cognition, is already predicated on said harmony. Again, the empirical harmony is projected into the transcendental. The rejection of a continuity between the sensible and the intelligible, which, as we have seen, is the basis of the rejection of hylozoism, has to propose an external harmony between them, while such a harmony cannot be justified from within its own restrictions. Hylozoism, however, does not face such predicaments. It is only when intuition is not able to give itself a form, as Kant argues especially and repeatedly in the B-text of the deduction, that the problem of an impossible mediation arises.[166]

If, therefore, "[t]ranscendental philosophy discovers conditions which remain external to the conditioned," then these "principles are principles of conditioning and not internal genesis."[167] Even if they only obtain insofar as they are applied, in their application they are always the same: eternal and invariant. The critical project, however, should be, as Kant conceptualizes it, an *immanent* critique. The foundational values such a critique is constructed upon can, however, not be critiqued within the representational model, since such a critique (uncritically) reproduces them as their

---

163  See Kant, *Critique of Pure Reason*, A137/B176.
164  Ibid., A138/B177.
165  Deleuze, *Difference and Repetition*, p. 173.
166  Kant, *Critique of Pure Reason*, B129.
167  Deleuze, *Nietzsche and Philosophy*, p. 85.

conditions. The critique extends to "all claims to knowledge and truth," but not to "knowledge and truth themselves," and equally to "all claims of morality and not [to] morality itself."[168] Leaning on Nietzsche's genealogy, Deleuze remarks repeatedly that every image of thought is predicated upon a moral image as its foundation. But "while Kant denounces the *transcendent,* these values and categories are nonetheless transcendent to the manifold of intuition they condition insofar as they themselves are not the result of a genesis."[169] Omitting the genetic conditions of the values and categories which provide the guiding principles for critical philosophy results in either obscuring the question of life or situating it within a field of binary oppositions external to it: either unity or chaos, either representation or no experience at all, either being or non-being, either mechanical causation or teleological spontaneity, either conservative limited economy of the bounded organism or destructive unlimited economy of the outside, either true or not true, either moral or immoral. A transcendental philosophy of life is a critique external to its object and subsequently leads us to the wrong questions when it comes to the matter of life. If the moral grounds for reducing the transcendental to the unity of apperception are themselves not a possible subject of critique, then Kant's critique necessarily remains only partial or regional. Instead, "[w]e require a genesis of reason itself, and also a genesis of the understanding and its categories."[170]

---

168 Ibid., p. 83f.
169 Levi R. Bryant, "Deleuze's Transcendental Empiricism: Notes Towards a Transcendental Materialism," in *Thinking between Deleuze and Kant: A Strange Encounter,* ed. Edward Willatt and Matt Lee (London; New York: Continuum, 2009), p. 32.
170 Deleuze, *Nietzsche and Philosophy,* p. 85.

# THE DESIRE FOR ORGANIC UNITY

### THE POSSIBILITY OF THE DISCORD OF THE FACULTIES

To achieve an account that is able to subvert the organic image of thought, it is, first of all, necessary to demonstrate the genesis of the *sensus communis* which has made any such account impossible and has hence created aporias. The *Critique of Judgement* presents the possibility for such an opening through the idea of the discord of the faculties. Deleuze notes that, in Kant, faculties (*Vermögen*) have two distinct roles. The "higher form" is "autonomous," since "it finds *in itself* the law of its own exercise,"[171] whether as the conformity of a subject's representation to an object (faculty of knowledge), as the causality between a subject's representation and the object it realizes (faculty of desire), or as the strengthening or weakening of the subject's "feeling of life"[172] (*Lebensgefühl*). These faculties govern appearance in accordance with the speculative and practical interests of reason. The other role is played by the lower faculties, which can be said to realize the purposes of reason that the higher faculties have determined. The understanding, sensibility and reason hence produce intuitions, concepts, and ideas to fulfill the task (as interest) given by the higher faculties. Counterintuitively, this gives the lower faculties a greater degree of freedom, since they are only beholden to their own judgement. As we have already seen, to produce representation, the lower faculties must relate to each other according to a *sensus communis*. To establish such a harmonious relation, the first two *Critiques* see a dominant lower faculty working as a reference point for the others, while abiding by the interest of the corresponding higher faculty. In the *Critique of Pure Reason* the dominant lower faculty is the understanding, which produces objects in line with the speculative interest

---

[171] Gilles Deleuze, *Kant's Critical Philosophy: The Doctrine of the Faculties*, trans. Hugh Tomlinson and Barbara Habberjam (Minneapolis: University of Minnesota Press, 2007), p. 4.
[172] Kant, *Critique of Judgement*, p. 277.

of reason and is hence beholden to the faculty of knowledge, while in the *Critique of Practical Reason* it is practical reason that, while acting in the practical interest of reason, produces moral legislation.

The *Critique of Judgement* breaks this pattern in the idea of aesthetic judgement. Neither morality nor cognition can determine the results of the encounter of the understanding and the imagination that occurs when we "like" something; the experience is "devoid of all interest."[173] In the first two *Critiques*, the dominant faculty directs the others so as to enable a certain kind of truth, be it (scientific) knowledge or (moral) action. While the discord of faculties was always possible, it was avoided by demanding accord under one dominant lower faculty. This guaranteed the possibility of truth. Now it is not truth but the forms of accord between non-hierarchical faculties that is of interest. As such, an object that (purposefully) causes harmony between the faculties produces pleasure and, conversely, an object produces displeasure if it causes them to be in discord. In the "free play" of the faculties, the understanding and the imagination, for example, enter into a relationship *as if* they were to produce knowledge, but instead their free accord arouses pleasure. Deleuze, therefore, detects a romantic element in the heart of the late work of Kant: elective affinities, capable of harmony and accord without jurisdiction, a philosophy "beyond the state."[174] No action of any higher faculty would be possible unless it rested on a prior "free spontaneous accord, without legislation, with neither interest nor predominance"[175] in the lower faculties.

Granting power to "pathos beyond all logic,"[176] however, only gives us the *possibility* of a *sensus communis* born from the "free play" of faculties, but not its genesis. Although the third *Critique* can make the *sensus communis* itself the object of critique for the first time, it still presupposes it rather than explaining it. There are, however, genetic (or quasi-genetic)

---

173 Ibid., p. 211.
174 Georg Wilhelm Friedrich Hegel, Friedrich Wilhelm Joseph Schelling, and Johann Gottlieb Fichte, "The 'Oldest System-Programme of German Idealism'," *European Journal of Philosophy* 3, no. 2 (1995), p. 200.
175 Gilles Deleuze, "The Idea of Genesis in Kant's Aesthetics," *Angelaki: Journal for Theoretical Humanities* 5, no. 3 (December 2000), p. 60.
176 Deleuze, *Kant's Critical Philosophy*, p. xii.

accounts of the striving for reason's unity, or organicity, in the *Critique of Pure Reason*, the *Critique of Judgement* and other writings, which legitimize themselves through life, liveliness or animation. These amount to three kinds of "striving": conative, natural and cultural.[177]

### THE CONATIVE STRIVING TOWARDS ORGANIC UNITY, OR LIFE AND LUST

The conative striving towards unity can be found in the animation of the mind (*Gemüt*) in the reflective judgement in aesthetics. To understand the role played in Kant by the "feeling of life" (*Lebensgefühl*), which is a feeling of "the powers of the mind reciprocally promoting each other,"[178] we first have to consider the role of feelings of pleasure and displeasure in the systematic approach of the third *Critique*. Reflective judgement must be understood as performing a function or action by "means of which it strives to rise from intuitions to concepts in general."[179] It operates, since it lacks the directions commonly provided in determinative judgements by the understanding, by obtaining or creating its directions based on the dynamic interplay of the faculties. Since the unity of the systematic whole of nature and freedom must present itself as a finality, the realm of the faculty of reflective judgement is that of ends, while for reason it is freedom and for the understanding the cognition of the object. The "modes of the mind"[180] that Kant designates as corresponding to these registers are cognition (understood in a strict sense), which relates to the understanding; desire, which relates to reason; and the "feeling of pleasure and displeasure,"[181] which relates to reflective judgement. The di-

---

177 This list and the following remarks may be incomplete and might be supplemented by an aesthetic striving or moral one. However, the three desires towards organic unity discussed here are particularly interesting, because they all employ a certain, distinctively Kantian, notion of life and liveliness for their justification.
178 Kant, *Critique of Judgement*, p. 230.
179 Ibid., p. 249.
180 Ibid., p. 207.
181 Ibid., p. 206.

rections that reflective judgement obtains are based on these "feelings," which, as we will see, are initiated by the (dynamic) interplay of the faculties. Strictly speaking, this "feeling" is not a third power (*Vermögen*), since firstly it "neither is nor provides any cognition at all"[182] and secondly it is a way of combining representations that is simultaneously non-legislative and non-cognitive. It is, as Kant says, "heautonomous": since it has no domain it only has legislative power over itself.[183] Therefore, while in the representations of the first two powers an object is related to a subject, in feeling representations are "referred only to the subject."[184] If, however, these representations are only valid as mine and do not refer to an object, and since the subject itself is not such an object, then these representations "are themselves the basis only for preserving their own existence."[185] Hence, "[t]he feeling of pleasure is the maintenance of the representation for itself."[186] The question of whether desire or knowledge trigger pleasure or displeasure is contingent; hence Kant is hesitant to infer, from the empirical connection of the powers and feeling, the possibility of finding an a priori principle that would yield a system of the faculties.[187] In §12 of the *Critique of Judgement* we find already the reinforcing point that a representation causing a feeling "can never be cognized otherwise than *a posteriori*."[188] However, the introduction of reflective judgement would not yield any benefit if Kant had not introduced exceptions to establish "feeling" as a means of connection between the faculties. Such an exception can be found in the categorical imperative. When operating under the principle of the will, freedom is the object of cognition, and this gives rise to a "feeling of pleasure."[189] However, this seems not to give Kant a principle for the unity of experience, for three reasons. Firstly, the feeling of pleasure only follows from the will or is identical

---

[182] Ibid.
[183] Deleuze, *Kant's Critical Philosophy*, p. 48.
[184] Kant, *Critique of Judgement*, p. 206.
[185] Ibid.
[186] Jean-Luc Nancy, "Kant's System of Pleasure," *Pli: Warwick Journal of Philosophy* 8 (1999), p. 151.
[187] Kant, *Critique of Judgement*, p. 207.
[188] Ibid.
[189] Ibid.

with the sensation of self-determination; it has no determinative power itself and hence does not provide an a priori principle of unity. Secondly, the implied connection to the first power only functions partially, since the knowledge it yields is with the perception of comprehension. It is only a *blind* cognition. Thirdly, as the *Critique of Practical Reason* shows, the feeling following from the self-determination of the will is "respect" and, unlike in the *Critique of Judgement*, the category of respect here emphatically rejects any connection to pleasure or displeasure either as its content or its cause.[190] As the incentive of practical reason, it is directly the representation of the law and not one of its objects. The reason why Kant establishes this connection in the aesthetic judgement is, however, apparent. Like pleasure, respect can only be described as the basis of the maintenance of a representation that refers only to itself and not to any object. Pleasure and respect resemble each other in structure and there is indeed an a priori connection, albeit one of repulsion, between feeling and the power of will, since pleasure is a priori expelled from the respect that follows from the moral law. Nonetheless, this does not give us "feeling" as a higher form; instead, "feeling" is an "intellectual analogue"[191] in relation to the faculty of desire.

Considered only as "the union of perceptions with laws in accordance with the universal concepts of nature (the categories),"[192] knowledge also does not contain any pleasure. In the application of the reflective judgement however, e.g. in the unification of two (heterogenous) laws of nature in one principle, we might feel "a quite noticeable pleasure, often [...] admiration."[193] Not unlike religious or moral feeling, feeling seems to provide at least something akin to or "analogue" to these sentiments. This analogy between knowledge and freedom in the feeling of admiration might be an incentive to the exercise of the understanding, as if a hint were given to cognition as to a commonality in the ends of both faculties. What is given to cognition as a hint can, however, not be freedom, since

---

190 Immanuel Kant, *Critique of Practical Reason* (New York: Palgrave Macmillan, 1993), p. 76.
191 Deleuze, *Kant's Critical Philosophy*, p. 46.
192 Kant, *Critique of Judgement*, p. 187.
193 Ibid., p. 211.

it is unrecognizable, but a sense of directedness, "and would therefore be knowledge of freedom as knowledge enjoying itself."[194] Such an enjoyment is not only possible in cognition, but necessary. Kant suggests that, while today in the encounter with the "incomprehensibility of nature" we do not find pleasure anymore, "this pleasure certainly did exist once, and it is only because even the most everyday experience would be impossible without it, that it has little by little merged with simple cognition and is no longer particularly noticeable."[195] Such cognition doesn't operate according to universal law but instead moves from particular laws and empirical concepts towards the universal.

Insofar as the unity of nature and its laws is the minimal condition for the unity of experience, the feeling of pleasure provides an a priori distinct from the schematism (the forms of intuition or categories), which accounts for the activity of cognition as such. It functions as the incentive for the combination of the sensible manifold and the unification in the concept as an enjoyment of a representation for itself and in itself of unity in general. One might explain Kant's exclusion of pleasure from the workings of the understanding when they proceed according to universal law with the special mode of forgetting, insofar as the feeling of pleasure is not a faculty itself but is active *as* or *within* theoretical or practical reason.

Such an animating principle is able to give credence to Kant's introduction of the idea of "spirit" as the mind's animating principle in §49. If one only understood the function of reflective judgement in its schematic role (manufacturing accord in determinative knowledge), neither its motivation nor the introduction of spirit would be plausible. Rather, reason has the inner drive to attain a "maximum,"[196] which means unity or the unconditioned. In the reflective judgement then, imagination strives to emulate or mimic the "precedent of reason in attaining to a maximum."[197] The striving towards organic unity in reflective judgement must be understood as an (almost Spinozist) conatus, an effort to obtain more being by

---

194 Nancy, "Kant's System of Pleasure," p. 157.
195 Kant, *Critique of Judgement*, p. 221.
196 Ibid., p. 312.
197 Ibid., p. 314.

striving, gesturing or grasping towards the unconditioned. Neither such a striving nor the operations of the imagination could be understood without the function of pleasure as elaborated above. The pre-logical function of reflective judgement acts therefore as a "metabolic filter of the psychic system,"[198] converting everything heterogenous into digestible elements, whilst at the same time affirming and recreating the homeostasis of cognition.

Still, the legitimacy of the use of such a power (or quasi-power), which is the end of all critique, is still only presumed and not proven yet. Our approach to pleasure in Kant has revealed a striving towards unity, which is animated by a pleasure that in turn is only plausible if such unity is already presupposed as an (even only analogical or symbolic) commonality in the ends of the faculties: a natural end. Trying to ground the genesis of common sense in conative striving affirms it on another level—even at the level of pre-philosophical or "everyday experience"—but does not give us a *real* genesis.

## THE NATURAL STRIVING TOWARDS ORGANIC UNITY, OR THE BIOLOGICAL ROOTS OF THE CATEGORIES

*Transcendental Affinity and the Reef of Transcendental Realism*
The "deduction," as a method of critical philosophy derived from jurisprudence, depends on the notion of a birthright. Jurists separate "the question of right [*quid juris*] from the question of fact [*quid facti*]."[199] Before approaching the question of fact, the question of right has to be established, firstly by searching for a certificate of birth to legitimate the claimant, and secondly by comparing the substantiated claimants, building on the results of the first step. It is especially Locke who in Kant's

---

[198] Louis Schreel, "Idea and Animation. A Study of the Immanent Sublime in Deleuze's Metaphysics," (Ph.D. diss., University of Antwerp, 2018), p. 404.
[199] Kant, *Critique of Pure Reason*, A84/B117.

view fails these requirements for a proper deduction, since he is only concerned with the physical derivation of knowledge. The question of origin the empiricist poses in this derivation needs, according to Kant, to be replaced by a proof of descent other than from experience. As the question of fact might give an "explanation of possession of pure knowledge,"[200] it cannot, by itself, form a deduction lacking any account of the question of right. While the primacy of genealogical investigation, i.e. the question of right, can operate with relative independence from the question of fact in disputes over inheritance in everyday disputes, Kant's transcendental deduction seems not to subscribe to this logic. If we consider again the case against Locke, we can see that the question of birthright is not lost on him, and formally Kant's approach to demonstrating and therefore proving the descent of the categories from reason, rather than from experience, seems to be tied to the same argumentative structure we find in Locke and other empiricists. Moreover, "Kant's real argument against the empiricists' claim did not rest on a demonstration of the *quid juris*, on a proof of the rightful claim to the objective necessity of the categories for experience at all."[201] If we return to the setup of the division of labor of the deduction mentioned before, the problem Mensch is referring to is not obvious yet. While the metaphysical deduction is concerned with the origins of the categories, the transcendental deduction attempts to show the necessity of their application to experience. But the latter then seems to rest on the results of the former, although it is supposedly independent from it. The final proof of the deduction is given by a genealogical investigation *de facti* not *de juris*, in what Kant calls "transcendental affinity,"[202] understood as the principle of reason's organic unity.

Since the different parts of cognition yield cognition, they must, as we have seen above, stand in a harmonious relation to each other, or, in other words, they must have an *affinity* for each other. For Kant, since Hume did not distinguish between empirical concepts in a posteriori judgements

---

[200] Ibid., A87/B119.
[201] Mensch, *Kant's Organicism*, p. 2.
[202] Kant, *Critique of Pure Reason*, A101.

and pure concepts in a priori synthetic judgements, he was unable to see the latter's origin in the understanding, and so, subsequently, defaulted to experience for their birthplace. Kant therefore holds that Hume is exclusively concerned with *natural* affinity and did not properly consider the condition that grounded it: *transcendental* affinity. This affinity, dubbed "organic affinity"[203] by Mensch, ensures the unity of apperception, which provides the transcendental condition of unified experience, and hence also the natural affinity of appearances that Hume described with the laws of association. Only in this manner could it be explained that "all appearances stand in thoroughgoing connection according to necessary laws."[204] Hume had leaped from the *fact* of "the contingency of our determination *according to the law*" to the "contingency of the *law* itself."[205] The principle of affinity is only found "in the principle of the unity of apperception."[206] Affinity served as the right concept to ground "all association of appearances,"[207] since it established a connection to his transcendental theory of truth. He had prepared this connection earlier, since "[t]he same functions which give unity to the various representations *in a judgement* also give unity to the mere synthesis of various representations *in the intuition*; and this unity, in its most general expression, we entitle the pure concept of the understanding."[208] Transcendental affinity subsequently not only supplies the relation of every part of the experience to a unified whole, but the grounds of the logical connection as well, since he uses the idea to establish "that the means for making a logical connection between subjects and predicates" are "the same for connecting concepts and objects."[209]

Affinity in its transcendental function, however, might present certain problems for transcendental idealism, as Kenneth R. Westphal shows in his reconstruction of Kant's possible but never realized transcenden-

---

203 Ibid., p. 133.
204 Ibid., A114.
205 Ibid., A766/B794.
206 Ibid., A122.
207 Ibid.
208 Ibid., A79/B104.
209 Mensch, *Kant's Organicism*, p. 135.

tal proof of realism. Against Kant (and Henry E. Allison's interpretation of him) he argues "that there is a necessary, formal, yet non-subjective condition for the possibility of self-conscious experience."[210] Such a condition is concerned with the relations of the characteristics of experienced objects, while being neither conceptual nor intuitive, hence formal. It is, however, also material—as even Allison recognized—insofar as it is either derived from or at least dependent on the matter of sensation, since we have a manifold of sensation. The existence of this condition (the *affinity of the sensory manifold*) poses a problem for transcendental idealism since, as the B-Deduction repeatedly stresses, connections among sensations can only be produced by the understanding and cannot arise from sensation itself. Or, in other words, *combination* as the prerequisite for self-conscious representation and reference is the product of an intellectual synthesis. Hence, Kant argues that "combination is a representation of the synthetic unity of the manifold. Thus, the representation of this unity cannot arise from the combination."[211] While it is clear that objects of experience must be reconstructed with some properties derived from sensations and others from active synthesis of the mind, sensation alone does not suffice to account for the possibility of representation. However, even if we grant that active mental synthesis produces a combination of sensory or conceptual elements, the specific elements thus combined must be selected nonrandomly. Hence, "combinability must be a function of the elements thus combined."[212] For sensations to play any role in empirical judgements, the understanding must possess some information as to which sensations can be combined or not. Giving up the idea that this primitive information is carried by sensations and locating it within the understanding would be a reversion to subjective idealism, insofar as the reconstruction, as well as the construction, of representations would be entirely located within the mind and, hence, the order of nature would be constructed *tout court* in this manner. Sensations would then not matter

---

210 Kenneth R. Westphal, *Kant's Transcendental Proof of Realism* (Cambridge: Cambridge University Press, 2004), p. 87.
211 Kant, *Critique of Pure Reason*, B130.
212 Westphal, *Kant's Transcendental Proof of Realism*, p. 89.

in empirical judgements to the extent Kant grants them, a problem Sellars picked up on.[213] The converse, however, would be the endorsement of a transcendental realism which undermines or regionalizes transcendental idealism. If we concede that combinability is indeed dependent on a characteristic of sensation, i.e. if sensation possesses a structure able to provide guidance for empirical judgement, then we would have to conclude that intellectual synthesis is able to reconstruct the order of nature but is not able to construct it. This would immediately, however, clash with idealism's basic principle, i.e. that the formal structure of experience, from conceptual structures (the categories) down to intuitive structures (space and time), is given by the understanding. This inconsistency is apparent in the *Critique of Pure Reason*'s core doctrine. While in the doctrine put forth in the appendix to the "Dialectics" he argues that affinity is not concerned with categorial or intuitive form, but rather content, the perhaps most essential doctrine proposes that the matter of sensation is given *ab extra* to us, while the form of sensation is contributed by the mind alone. Or, while in the A-Deduction Kant asserts that the principle of affinity lies in the object, he also inconsistently holds that all grounds for transcendental conditions are subjective. This inconsistent triad "presses Kant's transcendental idealism in either of two directions,[214] both of which Kant sought to avoid. One is subjective (or 'empirical') idealism, the other transcendental realism."[215]

---

[213] Sellars observed that Kant says very little, and most certainly too little, about the role and functioning of sensation in empirical judgement. See Wilfried Sellars, *Science and Metaphysics. Variations on Kantian Themes* (London: Routledge, 1968), p. 1–30.

[214] Husserl follows this Kantian hint on the synthesis of the manifold (especially by pointing to the difference of the A-Deduction and B-Deduction), by positing a passive synthesis as the ground of the active ones, while both operate within the bounds and structures of consciousness. Deleuze will pick up the possibility of a transcendental proof of realism more explicitly, subverting the theory of passive synthesis within consciousness by pointing out that with passive synthesis something constitutive within consciousness happens, which is not amenable to judgement nor a mere precursor to it; rather, consciousness and its structures are constituted by something prior to the activity of consciousness: a logic of sensation, as we will see in the next section.

[215] Westphal, *Kant's Transcendental Proof of Realism*, p. 110.

## From Affinity to Germs

Staving off a relapse into absolute idealism on the one hand or naïve realism on the other, Kant defends the unstable middle ground of transcendental idealism. The opposition to absolute idealism is rather dogmatically brushed aside, as in the addition to the *Critique of Pure Reason* after the *Göttingen Review* (*Göttinger Gelehrte Anzeigen*). The transcendental realism that affinity seems to suggest is, however, rejected upon a different set of assumptions, presuppositions Kant frames in decidedly biological terminology. In Kant's later added conclusion "Outcome of This Deduction of the Concepts of the Understanding," apparently borrowing terms from his 1772 "Letter to Herz," he renders the possibilities for grounding the necessary agreement of experience and concepts in their objects as the exclusive disjunction that "either experience makes the concepts possible, or the concepts make experience possible."[216] Following the presupposition that passive sense data alone could not account for the emergence of transcendental grounds, the first option would amount to a "sort of *generatio aquivoca*."[217] Thus, he holds firm to the idea that Humean natural affinity must be grounded by transcendental affinity, but rejects transcendental realism on account of the passivity of sensation. This decision on the birthplace of transcendental grounds leads Kant to debate the kind of disposition that would be necessary for this kind of birth. To structure the debate, he introduces Leibnizian innatism as a halfway point between Humean empiricism and his own position. This "kind of preformation-system of pure reason" rejects, as Kant does, the reliance on experience to ground the concepts. However, it does not acknowledge that the concepts are "self-thought first principles a priori of our knowledge,"[218] instead claiming that they are given from the first moment of existence.

Although Kant had in the past held preformist positions to account for the conditions of experience, he now dismisses the possibility of divine

---

216 Kant, *Critique of Pure Reason*, B167.
217 Ibid.
218 Ibid.

implantation of the subjective dispositions, which would be set up by the Creator to work in harmonious accordance with nature to produce experience.[219] To balance the scale on the empiricist side, he argues that this account degrades the knowledge that is the result of the functioning of the categories, since it would simply propose the accordance of the categories and experience in their objects, making any transcendental proof of their accordance superfluous. But without such a transcendental proof of their coherence, their functioning depends exclusively on the divine fiat, which could disappear at any point; what is supplied are therefore only contingent grounds for the possibility of experience, not necessary ones.[220] Navigating and avoiding both the preformism of innatism (the *genertio aequivoca* of the transcendental realism that affinity seemed to suggest) and the danger of subjective idealism, Kant discovers the "epigenesis of reason" as the only proper ground for the possibility of experience, retracing "the pure concepts to their first germs [*Keimen*] and dispositions [*Anlagen*] in the human understanding, in which they lie prepared, till at last, on the occasion of experience they are developed."[221] The epigenetic approach can also be found in the very structure of the *Critique of Pure Reason*, mirroring reason's growth. While at first glance the progression from sensible intuition to intellectual concepts and finally to rational ideas, terminating in the possibility of experience, suggests a linear "bottom up" approach, the work is actually constructed non-linearly. The "Doctrine of Method" forces the reader to reread the book from the beginning from the vantage point of the now achieved unity. To see that the teleological development of the progression was already structured by an underlying unity provided by the understanding, one had to follow the expression of the dispositions to their maturity; the *Bauplan* was tied, "in other words, to the idea that arguments too could be organically presented."[222]

---

[219] See Günter Zöller, "From Innate to A Priori: Kant's Radical Transformation of a Cartesian-Leibnizian Legacy," *The Monist* 72, no. 2 (1989), p. 222–235.
[220] See Kant, *Critique of Pure Reason*, B168.
[221] Ibid., A66/B91.
[222] Mensch, *Kant's Organicism*, p. 141.

Although the explicit reference to germs and dispositions situates Kant firmly within the eighteenth century discussion on organic generation, this facet of critical philosophy has mostly either been debated ahistorically, mainly in the context of innatism, or simply ignored as a pre-critical remnant stemming from the *Inaugural Dissertation,* and only recognized by a few.[223]

*Eighteenth Century Organic Generation Theory*
The discussions on organic generation among Kant's contemporaries are not without consequence for the development of his own theory, and evidence suggests that Kant was not only familiar with many contemporary theories on epigenetics but also inserted himself actively in the debate.[224] It stands to reason that the paradigm shift towards epigenetic theories steered Kant towards the renegotiation of the "birthplace" of transcendental structures that became core to critical philosophy. "Epigenesis," however, was a heavily contested and ambiguous term in eighteenth century debates in natural history and science.

---

223 See Lorne Falkenstein, "Was Kant a Nativist?," *Journal of the History of Ideas* 51, no. 4 (1990); Graciela de Pierris, "Kant and Innatism," *Pacific Philosophical Quarterly* 68, no. 3 (1987), p. 285–305; Norman Kemp Smith, *A Commentary to Kant's "Critique of Pure Reason"* (Basingstoke: Palgrave Macmillan, 2003), p. 175; Phillip R. Sloan, "Performing the Categories: Eighteenth-Century Generation Theory and the Biological Roots of Kant's A Priori," *Journal of the History of Philosophy* 40, no. 2 (2002), p. 229–253; Anthony C. Genova, "Kant's Epigenesis of Pure Reason," *Kant-Studien* 65, no. 1 (1974), and Thomas Haffner, "Die Epigenesisanalogie in Kants Kritik Der Reinen Vernunft: Eine Untersuchung Über Herkunft Und Bedeutung Der Begriffe Epigenesis Und Präformation in Kants Transzendentaler Deduktion" (Ph.D. diss., Saarland University, 1997).

224 Although an exhaustive list of all Kant's mentions of and comments on theories of organic generation is beyond the scope of this book, the textual evidence highlights that Kant was simultaneously grappling with and being inspired by these theories. While Buffon's work is already mentioned in *Lectures on Physical Geography* from 1756, the 1763 *Only Possible Proof of the Existence of God* contains these theories in a more explicitly philosophical context, see Immanuel Kant, *Der Einzig Mögliche Beweisgrund Zu Einer Demonstration Des Daseins Gottes* (Berlin: Preußische Akademie der Wissenschaften, 1900), p. 68. The "Letter to Herz" of 1772 makes frequent use of the epigeneticist terminology of the time, see Immanuel Kant, *Briefwechsel 1747–1788,* Akademieausgabe, vol. 10 (Berlin: Preußische Akademie der Wissenschaften, 1900), p. 125. Buffon's distinction between race and variety appears in his "Lecture on Race" from 1775, see Immanuel Kant, *Von den Verschiedenen Racen der Menschen zur Ankündigung der Vorlesung der Physischen Geographie im Sommerhalbjahre 1775* (Berlin: Preußische Akademie der Wissenschaften, 1900), p. 429.

The first line of epigenetic reasoning to look at relied on the mechanistic outline proposed by Descartes and attempted to deduce the possibility of organic generation and individuation from the three laws of nature, vortices as well as contact forces, grounded in a particular conception of matter that is without any reference to a vital power or *entelechia*. Such a deduction was, however, even if combined with theories of weak preformation, rejected by the scientific community by the late seventeenth century, especially by embryologists. Due to the failure of Cartesian epigenesis, strong preformism offered a way to hold true to the minimal mechanistic metaphysics, disputing the existence of any obscure, non-mechanical vital force, while still accounting for generation. Although it is more accurate to speak of it as a pre-existence theory of preformed germs, Augustine's theory of the *rationales seminales* provided a basis for later preformist theories (as is evident in the work of Perrault, for example). Long standing as the authoritative work on generation, Augustine's *Literal Interpretation of Genesis* proposes that all germs must have been created by God and then distributed. After they have been consumed by an organism with its food and activated through fertilization, the preformed germ would, under proper nourishment, unfold within the host.[225] Opposed to epigenesis, such theories proposed first and foremost a temporal reorganization of the genetic process. Here it is not historical time that provides the conditions for genesis, i.e. it is not that organic existence is shaped by chains of ancestors. Instead, true formation of the individual is due to essential properties already created with the creation of the world. The general paradigm of preformist theories at least until the 1730s was the encasement theory, formulated by Malebranche and later Leeuvenhoeck and Boerhaave. This was widely accepted in medical textbooks and curricula of the time. While the former situated the preformed germs in the ovaries, for the latter the spermatozoa was the locus of the pre-existing structure, waiting since the beginning of the world to be unfolded.[226]

---

[225] Augustine, *The Literal Meaning of Genesis* (New York: Newman Press, 1982), no. 40f.
[226] The seminal work, representing the expert consensus until at least the 1760s, was Boerhaave, see Hermann Boerhaave, *Institutiones Medicinae* (Paris: Leyden, 1708).

In stark opposition to these theories, which emerged from the ruin of mechanical epigenesis, is the Aristotelian line of conceptions, which assume a non-mechanical vital power that guides the process of structuration from unorganized matter to organized being. Such a neo-Aristotelian approach can be found in William Harvey's *Observations on Animal Generation* from 1651, supplemented by the possibility of a serial addition of parts, putting it firmly against strong preformist claims.[227] Supporting these attempts with his microscopic studies, Wolff's dissertation identified the *vis essentialis* (essential force or "wesentliche Kraft") as governing the genetic process from unstructured matter to embryo.

From these fault lines, the epigenetic theories of Buffon and Maupertius emerge and will assert a strong influence on Kant. The former's *Histoire Naturelle Générale et Particuliére* conceived of the organism as comprised of *molécule organiques* and organized by a micro-force called the *moule intérieure*, analogous to the micro-forces in Newtonian physics that accounted for the formation of crystals.[228] Supplying the causal grounds for the organization, nutrition, growth and reproduction of the organism, the interaction of the *molécule* and the *moule* seemed to satisfy the metaphysical parsimony of the mechanical approaches while also providing a more consistent theory of the development of the embryo. With the microscopic experiments Buffon performed together with Needham in 1748, which led to the discovery of conglomerates of organic molecules, the predictions of this theory seemed confirmed. The *Histoire Naturelle*'s publication in German translation in 1751 stirred up widespread philosophical and theological controversies, due in no small part to the pointed introduction by Albrecht von Haller. In the *Vorrede*, he outlined the basic issues and consequences of the theory, putting emphasis on matter's internal, self-organizing powers and forces, which account for organic generation without the need for pre-existent germs. Debating the broader philosophical and theological question of divine

---

227 See William Harvey, *Exercitationes de Generatione Animalium* (London: typis Du-Gardianis; impensis Octaviani Pulleyn in Coemeterio Paulino, 1651).
228 See Conte de Buffon, *Histoire Naturelle Générale et Particuliére, Vol. 4* (Paris: L'Imprimerie Royal, 1777), p. 339.

cause and intervention in organic generation, Haller held that the organization of matter into organized being could be explained by Buffon's theory, given the assumption that a teleological directionality is internal to natural forces.

However, after the insights from the microscopic studies of his friend Bonnet, as well as his own, Haller rejects this form of radical epigenesis for a new reformed preformism, the concrete form of which sets the course for a paradigm shift that would also affect Kant's critical philosophy. Unlike strong preformistic theories, Haller and Bonnet did not propose individual preformation, i.e. that the embryo would lay fully formed in miniature in the germ, but only a preformation of primordia which unfold in time. In other words, the germ doesn't resemble the embryo or the grown organism; "the forms, proportions and situations"[229] of the parts in the germ differ from the mature specimen. This crucial difference necessitated the assumption of an ordering force, which would be neither identical with the germs nor a pure supplement like the Aristotelean vital power. In his studies on chicken embryos in 1758 Haller explains this new relation of dissimilarity:

> the essential parts of the fetus [...] are arranged in such a fashion that certain prepared causes, hastening the growth of some of these parts, impeding that of others, changing positions, rendering visible organs which were formerly diaphanous, giving consistency to the fluidity and to the mucosity, form in the end an animal which is very different from the embryo, and yet in which there is no part that did not exist essentially in the embryo.[230]

As Bonnet puts it even more bluntly, but also with a more explicit preformist bent: "The germ carries the original imprint of the species, not individuality."[231] Variation within the species could be accounted for

---

229 Charles Bonnet, *Considérations Sur Les Corps Organisés* (Neuchâtel: Faulche, 1779), p. 461.
230 Albrecht von Haller, *Sur La Formation de Coeut Dans La Poulet* (Lasanne: Bousquet, 1758), p. 186.
231 Bonnet, *Considérations Sur Les Corps Organisés*, p. 338.

without relying on strong preformation to guarantee the proliferation of species boundaries and forms.[232]

While this use of the term "germ" became widespread after Haller and Bonnet's theories found a public audience, the other part of Kant's "epigenesis of reason," the dispositions (*Anlagen*), which also came out of the same theories, was rather technical in nature and not as widespread. This not only points to Kant's in-depth understanding of epigenesis, but also reveals a crucial turning point in his own theory of the organic genesis of reason. In Kant's *Only Possible Proof of the Existence of God*, he had already taken up, but also criticized, Buffon and Maupertius's approach. While acknowledging the limitation of biology to natural causes—and therefore the rejection of divine preformation—as necessary, he regarded the mechanistic approach as a threat to a proper teleological understanding of nature, without which organized being would become incomprehensible. Already he hints at a possible third option by introducing the notion of "dispositions."[233]

### Kant's Relative Epigenesis of the Transcendental

The tension in Kant's work between the reformed mechanistic epigenesis and the new moderate preformism finally came to a head in Kant's lecture in the summer of 1775. Grappling with the problem of explaining the differences of the races, as well as their proper typology, and the failure of a Linnaean approach to provide a sufficient explanandum, Kant adopted Buffon's distinction between race and variety to advance to a genetic explanation. While Linnaeus only considered the external characteristics of similarity and difference to justify the taxonomic grouping, Buffon proposed that organisms with immense differences in external characteristics could still be classified as members of one biological

---

232 Bonnet explains this in the following way: "The germ carries the original imprint of the species, not individuality. [...] Those of the same species are not perfectly similar. I see nothing identical in Nature, and without recourse to the principle of indiscernibles, it is very clear that all the germs of a single species are not developed in the same womb, at the same time, in the same place, in the same climate; in short, in the same circumstances. Thus are the causes of varieties." Ibid.
233 Kant, *Only Possible Proof of the Existence of God*, p. 126.

species due to a shared *moule intérieure*.[234] To that Kant added his own conjecture: that such a development of external varieties with internal similarity could only be explained by proposing not only germs, but dispositions in intimate relation to them. The germ would still be activated by an external cause and in its unfolding provide the basis for the expression of certain physical traits. Since the individual was not already present as a miniature in the germ, what was preformed in the germ was a range of possible outcomes for specific parts when activated. The relation to external conditions, however, as well as the relations between the parts, is determined by the dispositions.[235] These dispositions assumed the ordering function of the teleological force that Haller had speculated on but could not properly account for.

Against this theoretical backdrop, we can reinterpret passage A66 from the *Critique of Pure Reason*. The language of germs and dispositions—which are said to lie prepared in the understanding "until developed on the occasion of experience and through one and the same understanding, freed from the attending empirical conditions, are displayed in their purity"[236]—is the same as in the lecture in 1775. The preformed germs seem to supply an a priori structure to thought, which is only manifest in relation to external circumstances, but is nevertheless biologically pre-existent within us. Hence, they are objectively and subjectively necessary. As we have already seen, Kant rejected a strong preformist theory like Leibniz's, since it would downgrade the necessary coherence of intuitions and concepts in the objects of experience to a contingent one. In line with the theory of germs and dispositions, Kant therefore rejects preformistic subjectivism, i.e. that the foundations for the categories are individually specific biological characteristics given by divine implantation, while

---

234  See Carl Linnaeus, *Systema Naturae* (Stockholm: Salvius, 1758).
235  In the same lecture, however, this theory is applied to morality, making human character thought in terms of moral properties (as well as physiognomy) contingent on the existence of specific germs and dispositions. While these germs are present in every human being, Kant makes a decidedly racist addition: that, although the uncivilized peoples (he mentions for instance the "savage Indian and Greenlander") possess the same germs responsible for the possibility of morality, these are not developed. Kant, *Briefwechsel 1747–1788*, p. 694.
236  Kant, *Critique of Pure Reason*, A66.

still holding that they are biological properties. With this Kant could ensure that the categories would still be limited in number and immutable, much as several specimens could vary in external characteristics but still be immutably confined to one biological species by the non-individual but shared *moule intérieure*. This gives us an epigenetic theory but, I would suggest, only a relative or weak one.

To assess the full consequences of this middle course, we must measure it against a more radical interpretation of epigenesis, which Kant vehemently rejects: the approach by his student Herder. As we saw above, Herder's vital, genetic force in the *Ideen* served, for Kant, as a cautionary tale about the excesses of unrestrained speculative nature philosophy operating with naïve epistemological assumptions about the attainability of knowledge of real natural history. "When discussing it from the point of view of the theory of germs and dispositions, however, Kant's critique of Herder's pan-vitalist approach is more dogmatic. The piece in the *Allgemeine Literaturzeitung* containing Kant's review of Herder's *Ideen*, while often paraphrasing Herder unfavorably, also concedes some ground, insofar as it reinterprets Herder's generative "vital force"[237] as constrained by germs and dispositions, so as to give it a ground for structuration. Nevertheless, he rejects Herder's attempt to render the idea of germs redundant by transferring its formative power to the vital force itself, precisely on account of the consequence that such a principle, knowing no bounds and fixed forms for its self-structuration process, would not guarantee the preservation of species boundaries, nor account for their unbroken lineage. The review of Herder's work falls exactly between the first and second edition of the *Critique of Pure Reason* and the references are apparent.[238] For the *Bauplan* of the first *Critique*, accepting Herder's radical epigenetic account would have meant reworking the whole non-linear structure, al-

---

237 Immanuel Kant, "Erinnerungen des Recensenten der Herder'schen Ideen zur Philosophie der Geschichte der Menschheit' (1785)," in *Abhandlungen Nach 1781* (Berlin: Preußische Akademie der Wissenschaften, 1923) p. 43–66.

238 John Zammito provides an in-depth discussion of Kant's refutation of Herder, while also acknowledging the influence. See John H. Zammito, *The Gestation of German Biology: Philosophy and Physiology from Stahl to Schelling* (Chicago; London: The University of Chicago Press, 2018), p. 172f.

lowing not only for changes in the number of categories, which would have discredited their deduction, but also, even worse, for their mutability over time. Grounding the categories in germs and dispositions ensures that their number is limited and that they remain immutable over time (the germs being themselves unchangeable). To highlight this point, let's consider Kant's essay in *Teutsche Merkur* in 1788. Written when Kant had just started conceiving of the third *Critique*, this essay reiterates the importance of teleological principles for philosophy and, interestingly, also discusses the work of the German naturalist Georg Forster. While sailing the world with Thomas Cook, Forster had formed a theory about the taxonomy of the human races, differing significantly from contemporary consensus, in that he claimed that, although differentiated—in composition, organization and in relation to the drives—through climatic conditions, they were essentially the same. In the end he settled on the theory that there must have been two primordial human stocks. Kant, to the contrary, claimed in his 1775 lecture and again in the *Teutsche Merkur* essay that there had been four separately created human lineages, establishing four races, with their differing characteristics being rooted in different "implanted purposive primordial *Anlagen* [dispositions]."[239] He saw this as necessary, since the possibility of historically developed races called into question the taxonomic model, and also subjected race as a category to contingency, ultimately plunging the human into a genetic abyss: evolution. In the same way that, for Kant, germs and dispositions prevent the transformation of a species, they secure the unchanging nature of the categories, and hence only provide a relative epigenesis, contingent on preformation and a preformist natural striving towards unity.[240]

---

239 Immanuel Kant, "Über Den Gebrauch Teleologischer Principien in Der Philosophie," in *Abhandlungen Nach 1781* (Berlin: Preußische Akademie der Wissenschaften, 1923), p. 169.
240 Even in a favorable discussion of Blumenbach's *nisus formativus*, itself designed to replace the assumption of germs and dispositions, Kant holds firm to his former position, whilst also adapting it. Still rejecting the Herder-Wolff idea of epigenesis, he dynamizes germs and dispositions, making them no longer static relations of parts, but rather inner purposive relations.

## THE CULTURAL STRIVING TOWARDS ORGANIC UNITY, OR THE WHOLE LIFE

In his *Lectures on Metaphysics*, Kant presents a different, but closely related, model of the relation of life and pleasure to the one we saw above:

> Life is threefold:
> 1. *animal*,
> 2. *human*, and
> 3. *spiritual* life.
> There is thus a threefold pleasure. *Animal pleasure* consists in the feeling of the private senses. *Human pleasure* is feeling according to universal sense, by means of the sensible power of judgement; it is a middle thing and it is cognized from sensibility through an idea. *Spiritual pleasure* is ideal, and is cognized from pure concepts of the understanding.[241]

Kant couples this typology with ascending degrees of freedom: "the feeling of the promotion of life is pleasure, and the feeling of the hinderance of life is displeasure."[242] Thus, freedom is the highest degree of activity, as well as the highest degree of pleasure. The animal is animated only by the desire for an object that follows from the feelings of pleasure in a representation of it. It doesn't possess an inner principle, or, in other words, as the "False Subtlety of the Four Syllogistic Forms" has it, the "the faculty of making one's own representations the objects of one's thought."[243] The pleasure of spiritual life can be only understood as moral life, that is, as the "harmony of freedom with itself," which does not yield gratification "but instead approval [*Beifall*],"[244] since it is only reflective. In the highest degrees of freedom, we therefore also find the

---

[241] Kant, *Lectures on Metaphysics*, p. 247.
[242] Ibid.
[243] Kant, "Erinnerungen des Recensenten der Herder'schen Ideen zur Philosophie der Geschichte der Menschheit' (1785)," p. 104.
[244] In the German original, Kant uses *Beifall*, which is more accurately translated as "applause." Kant, *Lectures on Metaphysics*, p. 250.

highest degrees of pleasure, and hence life, since *"Whatever harmonizes with freedom, agrees with the whole of life. Whatever agrees with the whole of life, pleases."*[245] The human life, however, is not distinct from the animal one because of a biological difference in species, but by education. In the *Notes and Fragments*, Kant establishes that human life does not begin with birth, which is merely the beginning of animal life. Rather, the "complete spiritual life" of the human can only be attained by the "death of the animal,"[246] whose death is nothing other than the death of sensibility. This introduces a twofold paradox between life and its ground in existing organized beings. Since this account, as Jan Völker correctly notes, makes human life begin with death and, as Hans Werner Ingensiep adds, establishes a hierarchy between organized beings in terms of their liveliness, it is breaking with the possibility of a unified notion of life.[247] It does, however, still confirm what we have called the *organic image of thought*. In the tripartite division of life in the *Lectures on Metaphysics*, the death of the animal in the human is achieved by a movement away from private towards universal sense. One can feel pleasure through universal sense only after one has had to "consider the object according to private sense"[248] via the communal sense arising from the intercourse among people in a society. Hence, "[t]he beautiful and the ugly can be distinguished by human beings only so far as they are in a community"[249] and being able to abide by this universal sense in such a community means having taste. Common sense is hence also justified culturally, as Derrida observes.[250] This results in a common recognition of beauty and reason as cultural values, as Feuerbach recognizes critically:

---

245 Ibid., original italics.
246 Jan Völker, *Ästhetik Der Lebendigkeit: Kants Dritte Kritik* (Paderborn: Wilhelm Fink, 2011), p. 88, my translation.
247 Hans Werner Ingensiep, "Tierseele Und Tierethische Argumentationen in Der Deutschen Literarur Des 18.Jahrhunderts," *Internationale Zeitschrift Für Geschichte Und Ethik Der Naturwissenschaften, Technik Und Medizin* 4, no. 2 (1996), p. 21.
248 Kant, *Lectures on Metaphysics*, p. 248.
249 Ibid.
250 See Derrida, *The Truth in Painting*, p. 35.

the artist presupposes a sense of beauty—he cannot bestow it upon a person for in order that we take his words to be beautiful, in order that we accept and countenance them at all, he must presuppose in us a sense of art [...] [Similarly] in order that we recognize [the philosopher's] thoughts as true, in order that we understand them at all, he presupposes reason, as a common principle and measure in us as well as himself.[251]

The link between cultural teleology and aesthetic common sense again reaffirms the harmony of the faculties as a condition of possibility for a communicability which bridges the gap between the private and the social, since the outer commonality becomes predicated on the inner. Hannah Arendt has, in her *Lectures on Kant's Political Philosophy*, transformed this common sense into a principle for a "cosmopolitan existence"[252] built and maintained by a discordant accord. In his *Idea for a Universal History with a Cosmopolitan Aim*, Kant had translated the accord that follows from the free play of the faculties into a political vision. Humanity, due to their rational predisposition and through their discord, would achieve a common purposive progress without the necessity of a universal governing body, "and hence transform a *pathologically* compelled agreement to form a society finally into a moral whole."[253] Crucial for this movement is the desire (in accordance with our free will) to "obtain a rank among fellows, who [we] cannot *stand*, but cannot *leave alone*,"[254] which Kant calls "unsocial sociability."[255] Hence, discord is at the dialectical heart of culture, since "the human being wills accord; but nature knows better what is good for his species: it wills discord,"[256] and, as Arendt notes, "without it, no progress can be imagined."[257]

For Deleuze, the free play of the faculties unifies and grounds the three

---

251 Feuerbach, *Towards a Critique of Hegel's Philosophy*, p. 103.
252 Hannah Arendt, *Lectures on Kant's Political Philosophy*, trans. Ronald Beiner (Chicago: University of Chicago Press, 1990), p. 75.
253 Kant, *Anthropology, History, and Education*, p. 21.
254 Ibid., p. 21.
255 Ibid., p. 20.
256 Ibid., p. 21.
257 Arendt, *Lectures on Kant's Political Philosophy*, p. 52.

*Critiques*, insofar as aesthetic common sense validates moral and empirical common sense, and taste provides the grounds for the determinate relations of the faculties in cognition and morality. Due to the fundamental role given to the aesthetic, Kant's idea, then, that common sense must be presupposed *as* a condition of communication, as well as a condition for the possibility of taste, is rather begging the question.[258] Further comments from Arendt on the lack and even impossibility of a genetic explanation for common sense refer the striving towards commonality back to the human drive for community, suggesting that ultimately human beings long for community with the unconditioned, the cosmos itself. This refusal of a genetic account of common sense seems to be affirmed in the second half of the *Critique of Judgement*.

Such optimism about our commonality with the cosmos is, however, as unfounded as the assumption of such a drive itself. To legitimize aesthetic common sense through culture, as in Kant's and Arendt's account, means to accept the imposition of a teleological approach on humanity's history and development. Moreover, such an explanation must assume a universal harmony between nature and humanity. Although "disinterested," and hence not governed by the speculative or practical interest of reason, beauty in nature or culture is still of interest for reason. In it the guiding assumption of reason—that nature is in accord with its interests, hence also with those of knowledge and freedom—is at least hinted at. Deleuze attempts to explain such a community by considering Kant's "Analytic of the Sublime."

---

[258] Recently, Scarry took up this line of argumentation, contesting our forgetfulness of beauty in institutional and everyday life. She argues that the encounter with beauty demonstrates the abstract concept of fairness within the realm of perception, thereby liberating us, however momentarily, from our self-preoccupation. Such a line of defense in relation to the beautiful reduces political discord and the ethical implied in it to a transcendental common sense by presupposing the unquestionable value of fairness. See Elaine Scarry, *On Beauty and Being Just* (Princeton: Princeton University Press, 2010).

## THE MONSTROUS SUBLIME

In a section considered by Kant as "a mere appendix to our aesthetic judging of the purposiveness of nature,"[259] another possible relationship to the *sensus communis* that is the *sensus communis* is given in the form of the sublime. The sublime both prepares the teleological *sensus communis* and takes the aesthetic *sensus communis* to its *inner* limits. He characterizes it as follows:

> Nature is thus sublime in the appearances, whose intuition brings with them the idea of their infinity. Now the latter cannot happen, otherwise than through the inadequacy of the greatest effort of our imagination in the estimation of an object's magnitude.[260]

While it is factually the case, for example in encountering a shapeless mountain mass, that the object presented in intuition is not infinitely large—since it could, through use of the understanding, be measured—the object does still cause an internal feeling of sublimity because it cannot be unified in a single intuition. The object can invoke the idea of the "absolutely large" in the failure of the imagination to apprehend it. It becomes a series either of parts whose number is too big to retain or of moments which stretch towards infinity.[261] Such a failure of the imagination to create unity would not yield anything if it were not for another faculty, which demands that something be produced.

In the discussion of the mathematical and dynamical sublime in paragraphs 26 to 29 of the third *Critique*, Kant attempts to tame the sublime by splitting each mode into on the one hand a moral and central side, and on the other an illicit and fringe side. The sublime inspires religious sentiments, which supersede superstition, which invoke fear through feelings of reverence. The abolishment of the mind's freedom must be rejected in

---

259 Kant, *Critique of Judgement*, p. 246.
260 Ibid., p. 112.
261 See ibid., p. 103.

favor of passion and enthusiasm, the animation of imagination; the mind must avoid slipping into fanaticism, the becoming anomalous of imagination. In Kant's discussion of the negative aspects of the sublime and his subsequent dismissal of these as abnormalities, their difference is always one of degree. However, it is the border between the colossal, that is, "[t]he mere presentation of a concept [...] which is almost too great for all presentation,"[262] and the monstrous, which "by its magnitude annihilates the end which its concept constitutes,"[263] that appears most fragile. Since "crude nature" cannot present the monstrous itself—nature does not contain anything "horrid" —the concept's function is merely negative and serves to render the edges of the colossal clearer. Alas, this "frame doesn't fit," as Derrida remarks, because the demarcation used in order "to stop the category of the almost-too-much,"[264] i.e. the colossal, from degenerating into the excessive magnitude of the too-much already relies on the determination of the monstrous. The colossal seems to appear on the edges of the monstrous, as an experience of a limit, a threshold not yet crossed, constituted by the outside of representation. This aporia—that the monstrous is unrepresentable but must be determined to negatively constitute the colossal—is instructive for our view of the whole third *Critique*. In this mere appendix, not only is the very possibility of the sublime at stake, but also the systematic unity of Kant's project as such. For Kant the ultimate symbol of the good is the beautiful, and the sublime complicates the connection between vision and truth, or vision in regard to its ability to give a reliable index of the true. He writes: "The beautiful in nature concerns the form of the object, which consists in limitation; the sublime, by contrast, is to be found in a formless object insofar as limitlessness is represented in it, or at its instance, and yet it is also thought as a totality."[265] For the limitless to be represented, the multiplicity of it must be bound; this is necessary in order to think and experience an object at all. Hence, the sublime is never fully formless, which allows for judgement to take

---

262   Ibid., p. 253.
263   Ibid.
264   Jacques Derrida, "The Parergon," *October* 9 (1979), p. 30.
265   Kant, *Critique of Judgement*, p. 244.

hold. However, if the size of the object were to increase just a little more, if the magnitude were just the smallest quantum bigger, such unified experience would disintegrate. A purely quantitative difference between the almost-too-much and the too-much would therefore lead to varying results: an object could be legitimately judged as sublime one moment, but "appear" as monstrous the next; it would fall in and out of representation. Kant thus adds a qualitative distinction. The "negative pleasure"[266] that the sublime proper invokes is a "vibration [...], a rapidly alternating repulsion from and attraction to one and the same object,"[267] while the monstrous is the cessation of this movement.

In the sublime, reason "demands absolute totality as a real idea,"[268] but imagination cannot abide this demand; the power of reason is therefore felt or makes itself felt in its superiority to nature. The resulting discord, while producing displeasure, is however "purposive for the whole vocation of the mind."[269] It grounds the harmony of faculties, according to Deleuze: within this discord, he argues, both find "the principle of their genesis, one in the proximity of its limits, the other beyond the sensible."[270] Unlike in the intuition of the beautiful, in the sublime it is not the object that is represented as purposive, but the aesthetic judgement itself. While the imagination is brought to the limits of its power by reason, the feeling of the sublime is nevertheless produced by a "discordant accord"[271] at the "point of concentration."[272] Rather than from harmony, the sublime is engendered by a "differential"—as Deleuze says, alluding to Maimon. Here, common sense is not just assumed, but *generated*, as "the suprasensible unity of all faculties"[273] in the discordant accord of reason and imagination. The free accord of the understanding and the imagination that we found to be the "beautiful" is made possible by the (intellectual) interest

---

266   Ibid., p. 245.
267   Ibid., p. 258.
268   Ibid., p. 250.
269   Ibid., p. 259.
270   Deleuze, "The Idea of Genesis in Kant's Aesthetics," p. 63.
271   Deleuze, *Kant's Critical Philosophy*, p. xiii.
272   Deleuze, "The Idea of Genesis in Kant's Aesthetics," p. 63.
273   Ibid.

of reason in it. In the breakdown of schematizing, the matter of the beautiful object is connected, by what Deleuze calls symbolization, to reason's Ideas according to its interest. This reaffirms the external harmony of our capacity to judge and nature. Freely associating, for example, the concepts of moral qualities with intuitions of colors, reason breaks free from the constraints of cognition. In such an activity, the imagination is freed from these constraints as well, because reason expands the concepts of the understanding, making it undetermined.

Rather than seeing the genesis of common sense in Kant's third *Critique* as part of a teleological account of human sociability and communication, Deleuze sees it as a gift of reason, engendering in its own interest the harmony between humankind and nature. It can do so, however, only if it has encountered and passed through its own "state of nature": the sublime, as the genetic model internal to itself. Having passed through this, reason frees the other faculties, as we have seen in the case of the understanding and the imagination in the beautiful, and "animates" them in indeterminate accords. Unlike Heidegger, who sees schematization and synthesis as functions of the productive imagination, for Deleuze the *Critique of Judgement* reveals that it is reason that provides the possibility of such operations. This is why Deleuze, echoing Whitehead, states that the third *Critique* should have been the first one, since it grounds the other two.

Against Lyotard, who sees a contradiction between sensibility and reason in the sublime, we should, however, emphasize the difference between its mathematical and its dynamic form.[274] The latter is concerned with discordant accord from the standpoint of the faculty of desire "as the pivot point of nature and freedom and as such as the turning point of the entire CPJ [Critique of the Power of Judgement]."[275] In the sublime, the intelligible comes into view without it being reducible to nature, while

---

[274] Jean-François Lyotard, *Lessons on the Analytic of the Sublime: Kant's Critique of Judgment* (Stanford: Stanford University Press, 1994), p. 162.
[275] Donald Loose, "The Dynamic Sublime as the Pivoting Point between Nature and Freedom in Kant," in *The Sublime and Its Teleology*, ed. Donald Loose (Leiden: Brill, 2011), p. 53.

nature at the same time rises to the suprasensible. The harmony is strictly external and, unlike in Hegel, this difference cannot be sublated by a dialectical transition from the imagination to reason. Provocatively, Deleuze claims that the contra-purposiveness of the sublime, which reveals a higher finality in the faculties, already foreshadows "the advent of the moral law."[276] The faculties' suprasensible destination gives us the whole of nature not simply as purposive in itself, but as acting according to ends from the perspective of freedom. Nature becomes an unexpected ally in the tasks of human freedom, while not being thereby elevated to a suprasensible unity; this prevents the theory falling back on physico-theology. While in the sublime reason is represented in its superiority to nature, the latter is nonetheless at least sympathetic to its ends; this shows that freedom is possible in nature. Freedom, as revealed in the sublime, appears as the realization of a predisposition of humans and while culture cultivates taste to prepare for the moral law, the former is the condition of the latter. The whole cosmos becomes transformed into an animal, an ally to freedom.

This reading of the sublime gives us an idealist account of the possibility of the free accord of the faculties, insofar as Deleuze stages the drama between humans and nature as internal to the mind and its powers. By positing the sublime as the genetic model for the beautiful, he uses Kant's specification that the sublime "is not contained in anything in nature, but only in our mind"[277] to prevent any other extra-mental grounding. While Kant explicitly refuses any genetic explanation of the mind's functioning, Deleuze's romantic leanings lead him to invent them from the material of the Kantian system by reading him through Maimon's intuitive intellect. If Deleuze, in his abandonment of the social and cosmic teleology of the *sensus communis*, might appear the crudest kind of respondent to Kant's critical system, three aspects of his strategy here should be considered to soften such a critique. Firstly, by demanding a genetic explanation rather

---

[276] Deleuze, *Kant's Critical Philosophy*, p. 52; see also Joshua Rayman, *Kant on Sublimity and Morality* (Cardiff: University Of Wales Press, 2012), p. 94.
[277] Kant, *Critique of Judgement*, p. 264.

than presuming it, and then restricting this genesis to the mind, Deleuze is able to avoid Kant's "naturalization" of common sense. Secondly, this allows him to prepare his own Schellingian move towards a philosophy of nature (*Naturphilosophie*) through transcendental philosophy. Thirdly, this genetic account is still only preparatory to his reading of the difference between aesthetic and teleological common sense.

### FROM AESTHETIC TO TELEOLOGICAL JUDGEMENT

The connection between aesthetics and teleology has not always been seen as secure: Schopenhauer, for example, called it a "baroque union" and saw it as the consequence of Kant's disposition as an "architectonic psychopath."[278] Deleuze, however, is devoted to maintaining the consistency of the *Critique of Judgement* in itself and with the other critiques. The structural plan prepared in Kant's analysis of aesthetic judgement is the starting point for the examination of teleological judgement, which investigates living nature from the point of view of the subjective maxim of reflection. The speculative interest, forming Ideas which have a regulative function without themselves having an object (according to the faculty of knowledge), produces a maximum of systematic unity in the concepts of the understanding. It can, however, only do so if it also endows phenomena with a similar unity, which can be understood as the final unity of things, or the greatest possible variety endowed with a maximum of unity. Such a finality cannot be conceived other than as a natural end, which is the assumed reconcilability of particular empirical and individual laws with the unity. This is necessary insofar as the understanding does not a priori determine the content of an intuition, and hence its particular laws. To conceive of an understanding capable of

---

[278] Peter McLaughlin, *Kants Kritik Der Teleologischen Urteilskraft* (Bonn: Bouvier, 1989), p. 145. McLaughlin cites Erich Adickes's *Kants Systematik als systembildender Faktor* as the root of the idea that the notion of systematicity structured not only the works but the decisions Kant makes, without being able to justify such choices. See Erich Adickes, *Kants Systematik als Systembildender Faktor* (Berlin: Mayer und Müller, 1887), p. 171.

conferring a priori a unity on phenomena according to the particularity of empirical laws is to conceive of an inhuman understanding, an "archetypal intuitive understanding."[279] This would thus serve as a substratum, insofar as the whole would be caused by a representation of it. For Kant, rather than serving as a proof of divine existence, the very inexistence of such a supreme understanding transforms the notion into an indication of the point at which our understanding encounters its limit. Without any reference to a supreme cause or an intentional finality, our understanding is unable to conceive of the final unity of phenomena. Because causality in nature can only be thought through reason, natural ends are a product of reason's Ideas. Unlike an Idea of reason, however, the idea of natural purpose has a given object, and unlike a concept of the understanding it is not legislative for that object. The idea of natural purposes can only be thought in its generality if the objects of experience present this purposiveness themselves or, in other words, if the effect that indicated a certain causality is already given in the object. This difference to the aesthetic judgement is enacted on the one hand when the understanding attempts to determine an object but the concept of natural ends interjects in the imagination, which prompts reflection, so that in accordance with the Idea of reason the understanding can acquire concepts of these ends. On the other hand, the presentation of finality in the objects of experience themselves allows for an analogous determination of the object of the rational Idea, although by itself it would have no object. This reciprocal determination is the basis for Kant's attempt to solve the aforementioned antinomy of teleological judgement. As McLaughlin has shown, establishing what has come to be regarded as the "reigning wisdom,"[280] the solution presented in the *Critique of Judgement* relies on a qualitative limit unique to our understanding, which means that we are not able to determine the relation of the parts to the whole without relat-

---

279  Deleuze, *Kant's Critical Philosophy*, p. 62.
280  John Zammito, "Teleology Then and Now: The Question of Kant's Relevance for Contemporary Controversies Over Function in Biology," *Studies in History and Philosophy of Science Part C: Studies in History and Philosophy of Biological and Biomedical Sciences* 37, no. 4 (2006), p. 756.

ing such unity to an intuitive understanding of God as intentional cause. By introducing the "non-constitutive particularity of our understanding, which we cannot, however, overcome,"[281] the antinomy resolves itself, insofar as only mechanical causality can be conceived by our discursive mind. And hence, we cannot understand the unity of mechanical and teleological causality from our finite perspective but can still judge organized beings according to such a unity by referring them to an intuitive understanding.

Here, the most important difference between the two kinds of reflective judgement is revealed. The aesthetic judgement does not imply ends in nature, rather "nature only gives us the *external* opportunity"[282] to reflect upon the *internal* finality in the relation of the faculties. Hence, *we* judge nature favorably, not it us. Conversely, in the teleological judgement nature does us a favor. Reflection does not mean here, as it did in aesthetic judgement, "the formal reflection of the object without a concept," but rather "the concept of reflection through which the content of the object is reflected on."[283] While in the aesthetic judgement the harmony of nature and the faculties is external to the *sensus communis*, this harmony is internal to the *sensus communis* in the teleological judgement. The transition from aesthetic to teleological judgement therefore excludes the problem of the genesis of the *sensus communis*, insofar as the reflection without a concept of beauty prepares for the introduction of the idea of natural purposes, which is itself fully constituted only in the application of reflection upon nature. This point of application, in which the understanding forfeits its claim to legislation, is still not outside of the faculty of knowledge but at the heart of the speculative interest to establish a maximum of unity.

It is the relation of these two common senses (aesthetic and teleological) that is at issue in the turning point of Deleuze's analysis of Kant's *Critique of Judgement*. While reflective judgement provides the possibility

---

281 McLaughlin, *Kants Kritik Der Teleologischen Urteilskraft*, p. 169.
282 Deleuze, *Kant's Critical Philosophy*, p. 65.
283 Ibid.

of a "transition from the faculty of knowledge to the faculty of desire," it "prepares the subordination of the former to the latter."[284] The appeal to teleology to supply morality is, however, empty; i.e. it does give rise to wisdom if we do not introduce the moral idea of man as the final purpose of nature.[285] If such an assumption is made, however, the thought of an (omniscient, omnipotent and wise) intelligence directing nature to produce rational beings becomes necessary.[286] While physico-theological proofs of God cannot be admitted, teleology still prompts the question of a final purpose and hence "drives us to seek a theology"[287] and demands of us that we are moral. According to Paul Guyer, the novelty of the argument in the *Critique of Judgement* consists in the break from the systematicity of the whole through the introduction of the purposive organization of organized beings, which prompts the need for a final end to reestablish systematic unity. While the theoretical understanding cannot provide a candidate for such an end, practical reason can: "our own existence as moral agents."[288] This again establishes the analogy between the purposiveness of the organism and our own, since we are prompted by the moral law to assume an additional principle to the mechanisms of matter and when we judge organisms as purposive, we endow them with the same immaterial principle we had to assume for our purposive actions. The organism becomes the locus of the realization of the natural disposition towards freedom, which is revealed to be the purpose of nature as a whole itself. Organic nature therefore points to the possibility of an ultimate reconciliation of man and nature, while the rest of nature is literally "dead weight."

---

[284] Ibid.
[285] See ibid., p. 411.
[286] See ibid., p. 444.
[287] Ibid., p. 440.
[288] Paul Guyer, *Kant's System of Nature and Freedom* (Oxford: Oxford University Press, 2005), p. 267.

# LIFE AND TWO WORLDS PHYSICS

### TRANSCENDENTAL PHILOSOPHY'S NATURE: ORGANIC ANTI-PHYSICS

Very few have gone as far as Deleuze in trying to make Kant's *Critique of Judgement* consistent in itself and establishing a systematic unity of the three critiques from the perspective of the third. Howard Caygill has gone even further in this attempt to unify the seemingly disparate elements by tying the two parts of the *Critique of Judgement* together under the notion of life:

> The two aspects of reflective judgement, the differential activity pleasure/displeasure of the "Critique of Aesthetic Judgement" and the dispositional activity of finality in the "Critique of Teleological Judgement" are united in a notion of formative activity or "life". This comprises the negation of the active and passive aspects of human being in the world which appear in the ordering and disposition of nature, self and others.[289]

His characterization of the connective tissue that runs through readings of life and nature in post-Kantian philosophy implies a metaphysical consequence: a two-world physics. Here, the two meanings of "organicity" we have used equivocally so far—describing on the one hand the *organic* image of thought, and on the other existing *organized* beings—converge and reveal the extent to which the critical project is not merely limited by its organicity but remains incomplete because of it.

In the conclusion of this chapter, we will see that, while the Kantian organic image of thought gives us a phenomenalism and somatism which introduces the gulf between the organic and the inorganic as a lack of formative power in the latter (a *relative* anti-physics), the subordination of the speculative to the practical interests of reason at once grounds the organic image and extends its consequences. The world is split into two

---

[289] Howard Caygill, *Art of Judgement* (Oxford: Blackwell, 1989), p. 302.

realms and their relation becomes not only unbridgeable but also asymmetrical, with the potential for activity in the organism becoming the locus of freedom not merely in but against (inorganic) nature (an *absolute* anti-physics).

The modern misconception introduced by Nietzsche that it is Plato or Platonism which first introduces a "two worlds" philosophy has often overshadowed the real root of contemporary world dualism. It is not Plato's decidedly one-world "physics of the All,"[290] but rather the critical philosophy of Kant, introducing a "physics of all *things*,"[291] that produces two incommensurable realms. On the characterization and genealogical power of this project for contemporary philosophy, Grant argues:

> it consists solely in the determination of nature by intellect, so that nature is reduced to a nature of the phenomenalizing conscious subject's own manufacture in accordance with essentially ethico-practical ends. This principle, inherited from the ontological quietism attendant upon the Kant-Blumenbach restriction of organic causation to subjective judgement alone, informs the vast majority of postkantian [sic!] developments in the philosophy of nature.[292]

We should, therefore, not only be concerned with the driving force of this project—the reduction of nature to what is given to consciousness—but also the perpetuation of its structure and premises even in critiques of it. For example, both Bergson's critique of the alleged subordination of biology to mechanics, a critique of pure formalism in favor of the organic duration, as well as its inversion in Badiou's formalist critique of the organic are premised on the exclusion of inorganic externality.[293] The co-

---

[290] Plato, *Timaeus. Critias. Cleitophon. Menexenus. Epistles*, trans. Robert Gregg Bury, vol. 9 (Cambridge, Mass.: Harvard University Press, 2005), 25a5.
[291] Iain Hamilton Grant, *Philosophies of Nature after Schelling* (London: Continuum, 2008), p. 33.
[292] Ibid., p. 16.
[293] Keith Ansell-Pearson, "Bergson's Encounter with Biology," *Angelaki: Jounal for Theoretical Humanities* 10, no. 2 (2005), p. 59–72; see also Sergei Prozorov, "Badiou's Biopolitics: The Human Animal and the Body of Truth," *Environment and Planning D. Society and Space* 32, no. 6 (2014), p. 951–967.

ordinates supplied in the tension between the understanding and reflective judgement in the *Critique of Judgement* still inform such disputes, while inorganic matter *as such* cannot be found on either side. The external (aesthetic) and internal (teleological) harmony between nature and freedom in their mutual exteriority is repeated, to uphold the distinction between physics and ethics in favor of the latter. This enables autonomy to be grounded exclusively in the ethico-practical substrate and hence introduces a lower limit to activity: the organism as the avatar of indeterminacy (freedom) against mechanical determinacy (nature). These discussions have never left the gravitational pull of the "Antinomy of Teleological Judgement."

Schelling already argued that Kant "locates the standpoint from which to examine the world itself not within the world but outside of it."[294] Despite this, philosophy, especially in its Fichtean continuation, becomes trapped in a two-worlds *meta*physics. The organism as a principle of transcendental philosophy supplies the irreversibility of the move to a two worlds *physics*.

## RELATIVE ANTI-PHYSICS: KANTIAN PHENOMENALISM AND SOMATISM

Critical philosophy's approach to nature and in particular its expulsion of inorganic externality deserves to be called a *relative* anti-physics, since its movement needs to first dispose of substantial nature, only to reintroduce it again later as subjectively determined within the limits of the "primacy of pure practical reason."[295] Or, as Badiou remarks bluntly, Kant's "logic of appearance depose[s] ontology."[296]

We have already seen from the organic image of thought that Kant limits philosophy to only dealing with that which is recognizable and can be

---

[294] Friedrich Wilhelm Schelling, *Sämmtliche Werke*. Vol. 1 (Stuttgart: Cotta'scher Verlag, 1856), p. 400.
[295] Kant, *Critique of Practical Reason*, p. 119.
[296] Alain Badiou, *Theoretical Writings*, trans. Ray Brassier and Alberto Toscano (London; New York: Continuum, 2004), p. 171.

the object of a representation, excluding all non-representational difference. This image in turn was grounded in values it had to propose to make it work and could therefore not itself criticize. In his account of nature, following the organic image of thought, nature is defined as "the sum total of all things," an approach which we will call *somatism*, but only "insofar as they can be objects of our senses,"[297] which marks Kant's simultaneous *phenomenalism*. These guiding principles of Kant's philosophy of nature —the corporality of nature without remainder (somatism) and the reduction of nature to the sensible (phenomenalism)—are not only intertwined but determine and entail each other. Both converge in Kant's formulation of nature as "the whole of all appearances."[298] The *Metaphysical Foundations of Natural Science* elaborates on this understanding, insofar as it gives the doctrine for a metaphysics of nature as the foundation of natural science proper. Since natural science is understood to be empirical science— hence representational, according to the image of thought —"such a doctrine is an actual metaphysics of corporeal nature."[299] To ground such a doctrine transcendentally, meaning not in the things themselves but in the governing laws of the possibility of things, Kant turns to the concept of matter. Following the somatic axiom, he defines matter as "divisible to infinity, and indeed into parts each of which is again matter" and therefore concludes that no concept of matter could ground nature as "the sum total of all things."[300] If matter were understood as substantial, it could not be part of nature in the sense of the "whole of appearances," since in division of it we would only discover more appearances but no matter. This is why Kant follows Aristotle's somatic doctrine of empirical heuristics, in which matter, if it is part of material nature, can only be so if it is given to intuition. Physics collapses into phenomenology. If matter is given to intuition, it is a body. By eliminating the possibility of conceiving of matter as the non-phenomenal or conceiving of the non-phenomenal within matter, Kant renders it a priori sensible. It is also necessarily corporeal insofar as its phe-

---

297   Grant, *Philosophies of Nature after Schelling*, p. 7.
298   Kant, *Metaphysical Foundations of Natural Science*, p. 467.
299   Ibid., p. 471.
300   Ibid., p. 503.

nomenality implies formation through the understanding. This prompts Kant to radically transform the concept of transcendental dynamics. While at the beginning of the book Kant still concedes that the concept of matter is "reduced to nothing but moving forces,"[301] nothing can give us the a priori possibility of such forces, since they do not appear themselves and are not deducible as *necessary* for the experience of material nature. Kant must consequently conclude that these original forces (*Grundkräfte*) are not part of material nature. Accordingly, to ground material nature, Kant supplies a non-phenomenal, hence non-material, condition. The grounds of nature, its "[m]etaphysical foundations of dynamics"[302] introduce a split between bodies and forces, which itself is the result of the tracing of the transcendental from the empirical. Schelling, noticing this, calls it therefore an "empirical idealism," in which empiricism denotes the restriction of nature to finite consciousnesses, which phenomenalize it and hence reduce nature to mechanism. Nature, therefore, does not extend further than the body, corporality, or organized beings as such, and hence is incapable of material dynamics and self-organization. Whatever is dynamic in nature must be outside of nature. Thus, the idea of a genesis of things in forces is expelled from the outset since these forces could never be an object of possible experience and hence are not material. Due to this, Kant has to solve the same problem as Aristotle in his somatism: the question of how to find a "hypokeimenon," that is, a substrate "common to all things in nature."[303] But, since there is a formal divide between the phenomena of nature that we understand as *merely* mechanical and such appearances in nature that we cannot conceive of as other than self-organizing, the resulting antinomy of teleological judgement prompts the search for such a substrate that would unite all the concepts of nature and freedom.[304] And this stratum is the deepest or highest point of inquiry, making a "Newton of a blade of grass"[305] impossible and making the researcher of the "archeology

---

301  Ibid., p. 524.
302  Ibid., p. 507.
303  Aristotle, *Physics* (London: Kessinger Publishing, 2004), 192a.
304  See Kant, *Critique of Judgement*, p. 176.
305  Ibid., p. 400.

of nature"[306] come up empty handed. As Schelling rightly noted, Kant provides a "merely logical concept of ground"[307] unable to provide a concept of matter that is itself synthetic. Hence, the investigation of organic nature cannot be part of general natural science, which limits nature to the visible. In short, an insurmountable gulf between the organic and the inorganic results from Kant's comparison of just "two kinds of body"[308] and not the forces that generate them but can only be attributed to them, which is necessarily so, since dynamics are not considered part of nature because they are non-phenomenal. Somatism and phenomenalism create the gulf, and both are based on the organic image of thought.

The dominance of transcendental philosophy's dogmatism over nature is, however, relative, as shown not only by Schelling's radicalizing transformation of the transcendental philosophy into a nature philosophy (*Naturphilosophie*), but also by Kant's own late attempts, in the *Transition from Metaphysics to Physics*, to give nature a material and substantial ground again. By moving away from the static concepts of forces as they appear in the *Metaphysical Foundations of Natural Science*, the *Transition* attempts to see the materiality of experience itself as "agitating forces of matter"[309]—not matter as it is felt, but forces as "they make themselves felt,"[310] as Deleuze will later say. As the proofs of aether had already attempted to show, based on the assumption that an empty space could not be conceived, the generative power that produces bodies must precede them and is therefore proto-somatic and proto-phenomenal.[311] This moves away from the idea of a substrate of insubstantial dynamics underlying bodies, toward their production, and parts with the question of matter's phenomenalization. Ultimately, it seems to open a possibility of overcoming the gulf between the two worlds. Making experience dependent upon forces that the *Metaphysical Foundations of Natural Science* had

---

306 Ibid., p. 286.
307 Friedrich Wilhelm Joseph Schelling, *Einleitung in Die Philosophie* (Stuttgart: Frommann-Holzboog, 1989), p. 5, my translation.
308 Kant, *Metaphysical Foundations of Natural Science*, p. 507.
309 Immanuel Kant, *Opus Posthum* (Berlin: de Greuyter, 1936), p. 577.
310 Deleuze, *Difference and Repetition*, p. 230.
311 Kant, *Opus Posthum*, p. 476.

labeled "real," but then removed from the domain of the metaphysics of natural science proper, removes the constraints of phenomenalism and somatism, at least partly. The *Transition* asks, "how does matter produce a body?," instead of "what underlies all bodies?." But even this attempt remains partial because forces are still only considered phenomenally, and hence not in themselves but only insofar as they make themselves felt, revealing themselves in a product. As Kant says: "[H]owever diverse the objects of physics may be, they are, nonetheless, merely phenomena."[312] Similarly, forces are only considered insofar as they produce bodies. Again, the transcendental is traced from the empirical, giving us a matter that is "grounded *logically* [...] not *physically*."[313] This approach, however, allows for the question of what the nature of the nature is that it cuts out, since the gulf is an effect of Kant's assumption. However, Fichte's alleged completion of the Kantian system consolidates the gulf between the organic and the inorganic world by ontologizing the radicalizing of the practical, making the split unquestionable.

### ABSOLUTE ANTI-PHYSICS: FICHTE'S RADICALIZATION OF THE PRIMACY OF THE PRACTICAL

Johann Friedrich Blumenbach earned Kant's admiration by supplying an immaterial principle from outside of philosophy to justify his metaphysical conclusions on the teleology of organized beings: the formative drive (*Bildungstrieb*). In turn, Blumenbach seems to develop his approach on Kantian grounds. It might, however, turn out that this mutual recognition was a historical misunderstanding. As Blumenbach describes it:

> [I]n all living creatures, from man to maggot and down, from the cedar to the mold, there lies a specific, inborn, effective drive that acts throughout life to take on from the beginning its determinate form, then to maintain

---

312  Ibid., p. 477.
313  Ibid., p. 586.

it, and if it be destroyed, where possible to repair it; a drive (or tendency or striving, by whatever term one calls it) that is as wholly distinct both from the general properties of the body in general, as from the other forces of the organized body in particular; the one seems to be the first cause of all generation, nutrition and reproduction, and which, to fend off all misinterpretation and to distinguish it from the other forces of nature, I here give the name of the Bildungs-Trieb (*nisus formativus*).[314]

Despite the Aristotelian ductus, this concept is almost indistinguishable from Stahl's vital force (*Lebenskraft*), which in a similar way both counters the chemical or mechanical reducibility of organisms *and* accounts for the purposive organization of the body. While in the discussion on the mechanical reducibility of organized bodies between Stahl and Boerhaave, Kant had adopted a position closer to the former, he still dismissed its metaphysical foundations, namely the vital force as a type of soul. What Stahl and Blumenbach share is an ontological understanding "of the immense gulf that nature has appointed between animate and inanimate Creation, and between organized and non-organized creatures."[315] For Kant, however, this divide is between two powers, the understanding and judgement, which are in conflict, leading to the antinomy of teleological judgement.

Fichte's attempt, then, to solve this apparent problem of being able neither to posit metaphysical principles in nature as Blumenbach does, nor to resolve the antinomy of teleological judgement within the Kantian system (i.e. solved as a territorial dispute), leads him to reject Kantian somatism and phenomenalism in favor of a radicalized formalism (itself non-phenomenal and non-somatic).

Holding, as Kant also did in the *Metaphysical Foundations of Natural Science*, that "[a]ll change is contrary to the concept of nature,"[316] since

---

[314] Johann Friedrich Blumenbach, *Über Den Bildungstrieb Und Das Zeugungsgeschäfte* (Leipzig: Johann Christian Friedrich, 1781), p. 12, my translation.

[315] Ibid., p. 71, my translation.

[316] Johann Gottlieb Fichte, *Foundations of Natural Right* (Cambridge: Cambridge University Press, 2000), p. 105.

there is no indeterminacy in matter because "mechanism cannot apprehend itself"[317] and hence cannot act, Fichte concludes that freedom is not possible in or through nature. Or, in other words, the forces manifested in things are always already exhausted in their determination. But as the whole of the Kantian system breaks down without the primacy of practical reason, which supplies the concept of cause proper, Fichte radicalizes it in the direction of formalism, by first situating nature and freedom in two different worlds and then subordinating the former to the latter by positing that the not-I derives from the I. Since only the practical interest of reason supplies the concept of cause proper, "mechanical causality becomes an abstraction from the reciprocal affinity of organic matter for itself."[318] Fichte's "speculative egoism"[319] therefore subordinates being to action to solve the antinomy of teleological judgement, understood as a conflict of territorial demands between nature and freedom, by simply eradicating the former. He completes the radicalization of the primacy of the practical by making nature *only* conceivable insofar as it is determinable by freedom. Which, in turn, overhauls the concept of matter. As he states: "'Raw matter':–really only an (empty) abstraction from the efficacy of the drive; just as the drive *in general* (as not determined through and through) is only an abstraction."[320] Hence, organization cannot be a property of matter, but must be one of action. Organization can therefore only be understood in its actualization, not in the abstract. The same is true, as Kant had already remarked, for the productivity of the categories. Applying the synthetic dynamism of the categories allows Fichte to solve the dialectical illusion of the mathematical and dynamic application of the law of continuity, since categories can only be understood in terms of actualized empirical determination, which was relocated into the I, hence making the latter the substrate for "the most intimate unity of this

---

317  Johann Gottlieb Fichte, *The Science of Knowledge* (Cambridge: Cambridge University Press, 1982), p. 79.
318  Grant, *Philosophies of Nature after Schelling*, p. 99.
319  Friedrich Heinrich Jacobi, "Idealism and Realism," in *The Empiricist Critique of the Theoretical Philosophy* (Cambridge: Cambridge University Press, 2000), p. 175.
320  Johann Gottlieb Fichte, *Fichtes Werke, Vol. 9* (Berlin: De Gruyter, 1971), p. 364.

all (One force, one soul, one mind)."³²¹ Either something is actualized, meaning it is part of the I's organic form or incorporated in its organism, or it is not actual, and hence not part of the whole of the cosmos. Everything that is acts, since if it does not, it is a mere abstraction. Additionally, since it is only the "I" that acts, every force and thing is either part of the "I" or not actually existent. Hence, Fichte exorcises the specter of inorganic externality, by making it either organic as part of the whole or not existent. Everything in Fichte is organic or it is not at all. Therefore, this anti-physics, which reduces physicality to action, deserves to be called absolute, since it allows neither for the question of a physics that is not subject to metaphysics, nor for a concept of the inorganic that is independent from the judgement of the organic. In Fichte, instead of a "Geology of Morals," we get the "Morality of Geology."

## LESS THAN NOTHING

Fichte's approach is not only non-hylozoistic but anti-hylozoistic in its formalism. While hylozoism and speculative egoism establish continuity, the latter shifts the formative force to action entirely, excluding passive matter as an abstraction or even something non-existent, while the former would imply the determination of the "I" by the "non-I." Fichte begins his *Science of Knowledge* with a rebuttal of the Platonic physics of the "All" in favor of the infinite "One" expressed in the formula "A=A."³²² Positing the existence of inorganic particulars would limit the absolute One constituted by the I, insofar as it would introduce exhausted forces into thought, and therefore discontinuity in the continuity of action. The "I" would lose a part of its "infinite quantum"³²³ to the abstract All and, without boundaries to prevent this slippage, the One could dissolve in the inorganic All of exhausted forces. Hylozoism appears for the

---

321 Ibid., p. 366.
322 Ibid., p. 165.
323 Ibid.

Fichtean ontology of action as a death-drive or anti-drive: the unethical descent into non-actuality. Hylozoism, then, is a matter of ethics (or an affront to it), insofar as it introduces a continuity between the sensible and the intelligible or the material and the formal, threatening the autonomy of the latter. Fichte's solution also relies on the separation of nature and freedom to establish continuity from the standpoint of the latter, but the establishment of the substrate remains fragile and needs to be defended in an ethical effort. Inorganic externality always threatens to creep in because the incorporation of nature always remains partial.

While the expulsion of the inorganic in Fichte is ethico-practical, in Kant it is also scientific and speculative. Without the difference in kind between the sensible and the intelligible, already introduced in the *Inaugural Dissertation*, the possibility of synthetic knowledge a priori is unsustainable. Since it is the same functions that bring unity to the synthesis of representations in intuition which are also operative in bringing unity to representations in a judgement, the unifying function of recognition according to the organic image of thought is necessary for the possibility of truth. The antinomy of teleological judgement in the third *Critique* follows from organic representation, which is dominant in the first *Critique*, insofar as it provides the conditions for truth. This conflict between powers enables Kant, in the end, to establish external and internal harmony between nature and freedom, ensuring their mutual exclusivity. Hylozoism is hence for Kant a threat to truth, insofar as it establishes the continuity between the sensible and the intelligible, and hence also to freedom, insofar as it threatens to contaminate the purity of the moral law with sensibility. It might dissolve the is/ought distinction and imply a life guided by the sensible (pleasure, happiness), which is worth "less than zero,"[324] instead of by duty. Even if one tried to balance the scale in the direction of happiness, one would not be happy and one can't be happy; however, one can always be good and free, at least in principle. Therefore, living and judging according to freedom, understood as life's purpose, always has positive value, while making happiness the criterion for judgement makes

[324] Kant, *Critique of Judgement*, p. 434.

this value most likely negative and positive only by accident. It could be said that, for Kant, accepting hylozoism would also put an end to progress in society as such, since it would propose a continuity between freedom and nature, while progress, for Kant, relies on their dialectic; no new accord could come without this discord. This accord would be unnecessary anyway, since no communication would be possible in a hylozoistic world, where no common sense could be established.

Kant's system is a finely tuned framework of boundaries—sensible/intelligible, material/formal, freedom/nature, bodies/forces, being/thinking, etc.—which must be maintained to realize the values of the truths of knowledge and freedom. Hylozoism is the anti-thesis to such truths and is kept out by the Orphic guardian of the organism, which prevents our descent into the depths of inorganic externality. The maintenance of these boundaries puts "dead matter at the summit of a conventional hierarchy,"[325] as Georges Bataille notes, which gives us an idealist notion of matter. As Schelling writes in response to Kant:

> From the inception of philosophy up to the present day, in very different forms, admittedly, but always recognizably enough, matter, in by far the majority of so-called systems, has been assumed as a mere given, or postulated as a manifold, which has to be subordinated to the supreme unity, as an existing stuff, in order to comprehend the formed universe in terms of the action of the one upon the other.[326]

This twofold critique, implicitly commenting on Kant's somatism and phenomenalism, attacks not only the basic hylomorphic tenet of Kant's system, which makes it impossible to achieve any "real knowledge of the supersensuous,"[327] but also Kant's reintroduction of supreme unities in

---

[325] Georges Bataille, *Premiers écrits: 1922–1940; Histoire de l'œil. L'anus solaire. Sacrifices. Articles*, Œuvres complètes, Georges Bataille, Vol. 1 (Paris: Gallimard, 2004), p. 179, my translation.

[326] Friedrich Wilhelm Joseph von Schelling, *Ideas for a Philosophy of Nature as Introduction to the Study of This Science* (Cambridge: Cambridge University Press, 2001), p. 179.

[327] Friedrich Wilhelm Joseph Schelling, *On the History of Modern Philosophy* (Cambridge: Cambridge University Press, 1994), p. 103.

the form of the Ideas of God, the subject and the world. The reinscription of transcendence was already a consequence of the organic image of thought: as we saw in the problem of the transcendental double, the transcendental fails to ground the *sensus communis*, since its genesis cannot be given, but rather remains in an invariant, transcendent realm. The boundaries Kant maintains are, however, not assumptions following from transcendence, as was the case in Kant's predecessors; rather, transcendence emerges from the field of immanence and occupies it retroactively. The idea of the organism as the sole locus of the formative is in turn a consequence of such a transcendence.

## THE UNLIVABLE

This cat's cradle of life; this reality volatile yet determined;
This intense vibration in the stones
That makes them seem immobile to us.[1]

---

[1] MacDiarmid, "On a Raised Beach," p. 149.

# THE TRANSCENDENTAL EMPIRICISM THAT HAS NEVER BEEN

## THE JUDGEMENT OF GOD

The relation of God and His judgement changes in Kant's turn to the categorical in the *Critiques,* as Beaufret notes.[2] Rather than the Law from the Good, in Kant the Good follows from the Law as "a pure form that has no object, whether sensible or intelligible. It does not tell us what we must do, but what subjective rules we must obey no matter what our action."[3] As such, the final verdict is infinitely deferred and replaced with preliminary judgements only referring to ends; or, equally, since there is no final verdict, every day is judgement day: the Law is applied infinitely. This inverts the idea of divine immortality, since "it distills a 'slow death', and continuously *defers the judgement of the Law.*"[4] As in Kafka, one is always before the Law. Nietzsche had, in his doctrine of judgement in the *Antichrist,* already described a genealogy of judgement, beginning with the creditor/debtor relation, which operates without the use of judgement and is expressed in the (painful) extraction of debt in tribal rites.[5]

Debt, however, shifts to the gods understood as creators and rulers, so that "the gods give lots to men, and [...] men, depending on their lots, are fit for some particular form, for some particular organic *end.*"[6] In a last twist, Christianity again dispenses with prefigured lots for men but retains judgement itself, and hence transfigures the individual into a self-judge, which in turn, as Foucault has shown, becomes the principle for the

---

2   Jean Beaufret, "Hölderlin et Sophocle," in *Friedrich Hölderlin: Remarques Sur Oedipe/ Remarques Sur Antigone* (Paris: Christian Bourgois, 1965), p. 17.
3   Deleuze, *Essays Critical and Clinical,* p. 32.
4   Ibid., p. 33.
5   Bogue gives a concise description of the relation between tribal rites and judgement, see Ronald Bogue, "The Betrayal of God," in *Deleuze and Religion,* ed. Mary Bryden (London: Routledge, 2001), p. 20.
6   Deleuze, *Essays Critical and Clinical,* p. 128.

individuation of the sinful subject.[7] Such infinite deference is the form of the judgement in Kant.

As we have seen in the previous chapter, the operation of judgement relies on good sense and common sense while simultaneously grounding them. It provides not only the principles to make the singular into the regular by relating it to the identity of a subject or the form of the object, but also the categories. Hence, organic representation serves the form of the judgement of God. As was demonstrated earlier, for the *Critique of Judgement*, in aesthetic and teleological common sense the harmony of man and nature was given externally and internally respectively. It proposes that we can only understand the purposiveness of organized beings by analogy to our purposes, which ultimately relates these beings as well as the ends to the whole of nature, whose teleological organization implies a divine creator, although a merely hypothetical one. This is true for speculative interest, insofar as the solution to the antinomy of the teleological judgement relies on the assumption of an intuitive understanding, and also true for practical reason, since the ends of nature can only be understood as the self-realization of freedom in nature.[8] This uniting function is translated by Deleuze into Kant's judgement of God, now understood as the operations of a disjunctive syllogism:

> God is defined by the sum total of all possibilities, insofar as this sum constitutes an "originary" material or the whole of reality. The reality of each thing "is derived" from it; it rests in effect on the limitation of this totality, "inasmuch as part of it (reality) is ascribed to the thing, and the rest is excluded—a procedure which is in agreement with the 'either-or' of the disjunctive major premise and with the determination of the object, in the minor premise, through one of the members of the division." In short, the sum total of the possible is an originary material from which the exclusive and complete determination of the concept of each thing is derived

---

7   See Michel Foucault, *History of Sexuality, Vol. 1* (New York: Vintage Books, 1978), p. 58.
8   John Protevi, "The Organism as the Judgement of God: Aristotle, Kant and Deleuze on Nature (That Is, on Biology, Theology and Politics)," in *Deleuze and Religion*, ed. Mary Bryden (London: Routledge, 2001), p. 35.

through disjunction. God has no other sense than that of founding this treatment of the disjunctive syllogism.⁹

The reality of a thing is produced by the limitation of possibilities and hence negation of all others. The disjunctive syllogism—"either-or"— works exclusively, determining everything as what it is and excluding from it what it is not, thus subjecting everything to identity in the concept. God restricts disjunction to only a *"negative and limitative use,"*[10] which in turn relies on the integrity and self-identity of the body as an internally organized being, realizing and reproducing only what it is. Sartre describes this tension as a dual desire: to not want to be nothing but also to not want to be (a bound and limited) something, a situation which is the sole privilege of God, who is both singular and infinite. As he puts it: "The being of human reality is suffering because it rises in being as perpetually haunted by a totality which it is without being able to be it because it could not attain the in-itself without losing itself as for-itself."[11] The unhappy consciousness thus arises from the bounded life that rejects its own conditions, making such unhappiness unsurpassable.

It is, however, not the idea of God as the sum total of all possibilities that makes the restricted use of the disjunctive syllogism necessary, but the form of the judgement, which instates God as a modal totality. Deleuze shows in *Bergsonism* that the concept of reality as deriving from the realization of a pre-given set of possibilities is predicated on a misuse of negation, which creates a false problem through a "retrograde movement of the true,"[12] as Bergson puts it. The illusion of the ontological primacy of possibilities arises from an abstraction "in which being, order, and the existent project themselves back into a possibility, a disorder, a non-being that are supposed to be primordial."[13] Whenever we encounter an unexpected or

---

9   Deleuze, *Logic of Sense*, p. 295f.
10  Ibid.
11  Jean-Paul Sartre, *Being and Nothingness: An Essay on Phenomenological Ontology* (London: Routledge, 1989), p. 90.
12  Henri Bergson, *The Creative Mind: An Introduction to Metaphysics* (New York: Philosophical Library, 1946), p. 6.
13  Gilles Deleuze, *Bergsonism* (New York: Zone Books, 1988), p. 18.

not understandable order, contrary to the regular order of experience, we negate that order and call it *disorder*. Similarly, in an unexpected experience we negate the being in the experience and experience it as *lack*. If we retrospectively consider what has been given in experience as something that could have been otherwise or as something we wish would have been different, we negate the real and turn it into the *possible*. The concept of possibilities existing prior to the real is hence a confusion about the temporal order caused by retrospection (*Nachträglichkeit*). From the negation of the real we can derive the necessity of limitation again, since only one possibility can be realized. The other possibilities must be cancelled out, introducing not only the negation of the real, but creating that, which is not as Plato has it. If the real, then, is falsely conceptualized as a realization of possibilities, these possibilities have to resemble the real, since possibilities *only* differ from the real by existence, which, as Kant has demonstrated, is not a real attribute.[14] As we have seen in the tracing of the transcendental from the empirical, this relation of resemblance turns out to be a projection, since the only way to determine the possible is the real, which retrospectively is characterized as a realization of that which it itself determined.[15] To avoid this circular logic, Deleuze moves from the conditions of *possible* experience to *real* experience. Due to the identity of thinking and being, this is achieved, as we will see, by moving towards real existence, introducing the couple "virtual-actual" to supplant the possible-real opposition to move towards a positive philosophy. The actual and the virtual are the two halves of the real and while the latter is ideal, it is nonetheless real, as we will see.

## THE INORGANIC LIFE OF PASSIVE SYNTHESIS

*The Extension of Synthesis*
Although we have discussed the dogmatic image of thought in relation to Kant, Deleuze's claim that each of the eight postulates he outlines for

---

14  See Kant, *Critique of Pure Reason*, B627.
15  See Deleuze, *Logic of Sense*, p. 105.

this image "presupposes a certain distribution of the empirical and the transcendental"[16] is less specifically tied to one philosopher, but rather describes a tendency or tendencies in philosophy to model thinking according to certain presuppositions. As in Merleau-Ponty's characterization of intellectualism and empiricism[17] as ways to dogmatically think about thought which never fully coincide with one philosopher, Deleuze's claim is directed to philosophy understood as a whole composed of superposed images, each philosopher being a layer.[18] This provides *The Phenomenology of Perception* with the freedom to place its own position between the two tendencies, without having to resort to a synthesis of the two.

These presuppositions are pre-philosophical, insofar as they are not the result of a philosophical thinking without presuppositions. But philosophy does not overcome them by its thinking, rather they determine philosophical thinking in advance and hence make themselves necessary. As in the case of Bergson's claim that the philosophical tradition has modelled its thinking about time after space based on our pre-philosophical knowledge, or Nietzsche's accusation that philosophy is possessed by a moral image, which masks historically contingent values as universals and conditions of thought as such, either the empirical has been declared a transcendental principle or the transcendental traced from the outlines of the empirical. While both Bergson and Nietzsche propose new methods to remedy the specific predetermination of thought, it is Husserl who introduces a method for systematically dismantling such presuppositions: the bracketing of the natural attitude in the phenomenological reduction. Although *Difference and Repetition* is expressly Kantian in tone, it is Husserl's lack of specificity in relation to the pre-philosophical determination of thinking that drives most of the book. Neither space nor history are specifically problematized in Husserl's work, but rather the fact that

---

16 Deleuze, *Difference and Repetition*, p. 133.
17 "Empiricism cannot see that we need to know what we are looking for, otherwise we would not be looking for it, and intellectualism (rationalism) fails to see that we need to be ignorant of what we are looking for, or equally again we should not be searching." Maurice Merleau-Ponty, *Phenomenology of Perception*, trans. Donald A. Landes (Abingdon; New York: Routledge, 2012), p. 28.
18 Deleuze, *Difference and Repetition*, p. 132.

our familiarity with a world constituted by consciousness covers up the very act of constitution. To give an account of the constituting life of consciousness, i.e. to move from an already constituted world of objects and meaning to "the problem of the constitution of the world,"[19] first requires a method for avoiding the reversion to the empirical as a template for the transcendental and instead turning inward towards world constituting consciousness, i.e. the transcendental itself without reference to the empirical.[20] In employing the phenomenological reduction, at its most basic a "bracketing" of the "natural attitude," neither the objects nor their already constituted meaning remain the object of study, but instead their constitution in various layers of consciousness. The unity of the object, for example, that is given in the natural attitude, dissolves as soon as one traces its constitution in the lower levels of consciousness, and hence one cannot "remain with a piece of wax," as Lyotard quips with an allusion to Descartes, and "describe only what is given without presuppositions."[21] When relating to the transcendental, then, the phenomenological position is strictly empiricist in nature, insofar as the *noema* is the result of a reduction to immanent experience, which indicates the process of becoming a phenomenon. This method intrigued Deleuze, although he was not without reservations.[22] As Lawlor suggests, Husserlian phenomenology

---

19  Merleau-Ponty, *Phenomenology of Perception*, p. 69.
20  Take, for example, Deleuze on the "noematic sense," which is a phenomenon prior to being an object of consciousness: "When Husserl reflects on the 'perceptual noema', or 'the sense of perception', he at once distinguishes it from the physical object, from the psychological or 'lived', from mental representations and from logical concepts." Deleuze, *Logic of Sense*, p. 20; see also Eugen Fink, "The Phenomenological Philosophy of Edmund Husserl and Contemporary Criticism," in *The Phenomenology of Husserl* (Chicago: Quadrangle Books, 1970).
21  Jean-François Lyotard, *Phenomenology* (Albany: State University of New York Press, 1991), p. 33.
22  See Richard Murphy, *Hume and Husserl. Towards Radical Subjectivism* (Dordrecht: Springer Netherlands, 1980), p. 10. Hence, the noematic sense of the *Ideas I* is characterized by Deleuze as a phenomenon that to the consciousness that it precedes is neither the represented external object nor a pure psychic object, but rather pure presentation or pure event. The relocation of the sense-event into the transcendental was intriguing to Deleuze, although he points out "Husserl's definite tendency to understand the noematic nucleus as the formal identity pole of the object-in-general," which realigns Husserl's radical philosophical departure with Kant's apperception, insofar as it "sets in advance a transcendental object that, as isolated opposite, unifies the subject's power of comprehension." Marc Rölli, *Gilles Deleuze's Transcendental Empiricism: From Tradition to Difference*

and Deleuze's philosophy intersect in at least three ambitions.[23] Firstly, both attempt to reverse Platonism: Husserlian phenomenology through the phenomenological reduction, which situates every transcendence *within* experience, and Deleuze by means of an "intensive reduction." Secondly, both realize this project by searching for the transcendental rather than the transcendent ground of phenomena, which amounts to a reduction to immanence. Thirdly, this grounding, the transcendental, must escape the vicious circle which the reduction to immanence might entail. While the ground must remain within what is grounded, it cannot resemble what it grounds, or in other words, "[i]t must be the case that what is being grounded is not presupposed in the ground."[24]

In its transcendental function however, consciousness is not given as a homogenous field or process, but rather as stratified or layered, each layer providing the basis for the next higher function. Husserl's *Ideas I* provides an accurate picture of the genealogy of this method, taking its point of departure from Kant's first *Critique*. Although Husserl claims that phenomenology has been "the secret nostalgia of all modern philosophy,"[25] the germ of what would become the method of phenomenology is to be found more specifically in Kant's transcendental deduction. While Kant was already "operating inside the realm of phenomenology,"[26] he mistook this for psychology and, fearing his whole critical project might collapse into it, consequently dismissed it. This is evident in the significant structural changes in the three syntheses that are evident when one compares the A-Deduction in the 1781 edition of the *Critique of Pure Reason* to the B-Deduction in the reworked edition.

The A-Deduction presents specific syntheses belonging to particular faculties, i.e. "the synthesis of apprehension in the intuition" (sense), "the synthesis of reproduction in the imagination" (imagination) and the

---

(Edinburgh: Edinburgh University Press, 2016), p. 97.

23  Leonard Lawlor, "Phenomenology and Metaphysics, and Chaos: On the Fragility of the Event in Deleuze," in *The Cambridge Companion to Deleuze*, ed. Daniel W. Smith and Henry Somers-Hall (Cambridge: Cambridge University Press, 2012), p. 103.

24  Ibid., p. 103.

25  Edmund Husserl, *Ideas I* (Dordrecht: Kluwer Academic Publishers, 1998), p. 142.

26  Ibid.

"synthesis of recognition in the concept"[27] (apperception), which in turn have their respective aspects: intuitive synopsis, imaginative synthesis and conceptual unity.[28] Though the three stages are interdependent and enable representation only by functioning interrelatedly, the A-Deduction frames this as an accord without domination. The "first and synthetic principle of our thinking in general,"[29] apperception, which provides for the subject not only numerical unity but the very possibility of the free and spontaneous acts of the transcendental I, is regionalized into one stage of the triple synthesis. Sense and imagination, meanwhile, only participate in this activity by becoming subject to volition but are never its grounds. Hence, they operate "blind," insofar as "we are seldom ever conscious"[30] of them, and passively, insofar as they are not spontaneous like the acts of the transcendental "I." Despite their blindness and passivity, they are nonetheless syntheses, combining sensibilia below the level of apperception and without its jurisdiction. They are productive without being each a self-conscious "self-activity"; they are unconscious syntheses, which are "not carried out by the mind" but do occur "*in* the mind."[31] The B-Deduction revises this by eliminating the possibility of this kind of unconscious production. Combination is recast as exclusive to the understanding, because "the combination (conjunction) of a manifold in general can never come to us through the senses, and therefore cannot already be contained in the pure form of sensible intuition."[32] Such a process, for the B-Deduction, can only be one of spontaneity; since sense and imagination are passive, they do not combine by themselves but only through and under the jurisdiction of apperception. They are thus activi-

---

[27] Kant, *Critique of Pure Reason*, A94.
[28] The passage reads: "There are, however, three original sources (capacities or faculties of the soul), which contain the conditions of the possibility of all experience and cannot themselves be derived from any other faculty of the mind, namely sense, imagination, and apperception. On these are grounded 1) the synopsis of the manifold a priori through sense; 2) the synthesis of the manifold through the imagination; finally 3) the unity of this synthesis through original apperception." Ibid., A94.
[29] Ibid., A117.
[30] Ibid., A78/B103; see also ibid., A124.
[31] Ibid., B130.
[32] Ibid., B129.

ties of the understanding. While the (subjective) A-Deduction presents cognition as the mutual coordination of intuition, imagination and understanding, and therefore presents a temporal account of the nature of consciousness, the B-Deduction diminishes the role of sensibility in cognition and reduces combination to an affair of the understanding alone (two aspects that will return in the "Analytic of the Sublime" with a vengeance). Despite the revisions of the B-Deduction, Kant did discover in the A-Deduction something new. Husserl, therefore, can conclude as follows: "Luckily, Kant's theory is better than Kant himself knows. [...] Just one example: Kant comes across the intentionality that builds up in steps in consciousness."[33]

In his later works, Husserl takes up the idea of combination below the level of self-activity. The study of these passive syntheses, rather than revealing a homogenous field of experience, unearths heterogenous strata or layers of experience.[34] *Experience and Judgement* does not constitute Husserl's most decisive description of these layers in the passive temporal and bodily syntheses of sensory data that bring about the formation of the object (his "transcendental aesthetics") but does contain an application of the passive synthesis to provide a foundation for logic. His "genealogy of logic" marks a shift away from his earlier "logistic phenomenology"[35] towards a genetic phenomenology, which seeks to retrace logic's foundation and subsequently follow its emergence. Paramount in the investigation into these foundations is the question of the presuppositions of predicative judgement. Insofar as judgement requires a substrate, it refers to an individual object, which is necessarily first given in a "prepredicative experience."[36] Husserl locates the individuation of such an object which is amenable to judgement however in temporal, kinesthetic and passive

---

33  Edmund Husserl, *Erste Philosophie. Erster Teil: Kritische Ideengeschichte*, Husserliana, Vol. 7 (The Hague: Nijhoff, 1956), p. 404.
34  See Edmund Husserl, *Analyses Concerning Passive and Active Synthesis: Lectures on Transcendental Logic* (Dordrecht: Kluwer, 2001), p. 401.
35  Donn Welton, *Origins of Meaning: A Critical Study of the Thresholds of Husserlian Phenomenology* (Dordrecht: Springer Netherlands, 1983), p. 121.
36  Edmund Husserl, *Experience and Judgment: Investigations in a Genealogy of Logic* (Evanston: Northwestern University Press, 1973), p. 26.

synthesis. As the "Introduction" of *Experience and Judgement* already lays out, the constituting consciousness is stratified, with an internal flow of time at the deepest level of the ego, on top of which flows unorganized data, which on a third level is progressively organized by (passive) synthesis. These combinations produce a "life world" populated by affections and intensities, which in turn become the ground for judging and determinate thought, that is, active synthesis. The act of constitution, which Husserl earlier only understood as the interplay of "the voluntarist and 'judging' actions of the transcendental ego (the active side of genesis) and the simple reception of the 'ready-made' found object (the passive side of genesis),"[37] is now radicalized beyond the activity of the subject: for an object to be "ready-made" before the intervention of the subject, a passive synthesis must not only have taken place, but must be considered as the primary or fundamental synthesis. This would amount to a productivity under the level of the structure of judgement, in short, a non-organic synthesis or an inorganic life.

### The Outer Edges of Genetic Phenomenology

Merleau-Ponty is, however, quick to point out the contradiction here: "A passive synthesis is a contradiction in terms, if the synthesis is a process of composition, and if the passivity consists in being the recipient of multiplicity."[38] Husserl tackles this problem already in depth in his *Analyses Concerning Passive and Active Synthesis*, where he expressly uses the term "passive production" to denote an "in-between,"[39] something that is not fully an act but also not the pure reception by consciousness of pregiven content or static relations.[40] If, therefore, on the one side passivity is not to be misconstrued as an activity, on the other side it ought also not to be confused with receptivity. This new domain, neither act

---

37  Alain Beaulieu, "Edmund Husserl," in *Deleuze's Philosophical Lineage*, ed. Graham Jones (Edinburgh: Edinburgh University Press, 2009), p. 275.
38  Merleau-Ponty, *Phenomenology of Perception*, p. 496.
39  Husserl, *Analyses Concerning Passive and Active Synthesis*, p. 276.
40  See also Elmar Holenstein, *Phänomenologie Der Assoziation: Zur Struktur Und Funktion Eines Grundprinzips Der Passiven Genesis Bei E. Husserl* (The Hague: Nijhoff, 1972), p. 216.

nor reception, circumscribes the field of genetic phenomenology. Relying on the productive character of the "passive constitution" he had discovered in Kant's *Critique of Pure Reason*, Husserl Husserl had to redefine the basic coordinates of the problem of justification at the root of transcendental philosophy, the problem of a logic *immanent* to sensation.[41] Kant's transcendental analytics are already an attempt to solve this problem, which is one of reconciliation: every proof of such a logic will rely "on empirical findings as well as intellectual self-production of experience,"[42] which must be reconciled somehow. By taking recourse to apperception, which is a necessary presupposition to ensure the success of the deduction, he was able to suspend claims of cognitive processes below the level of apperception or simply relegate these processes to transcendental psychology and hence, in the end, made it possible for experience to catch up with itself. To justify the idea that "activity necessarily presupposes, as the lowest level, a passivity that gives something beforehand,"[43] would therefore mean to reject the Kantian solution, which renders the pre-subjective inaccessible. One would need instead to conceptualize it on new grounds, namely the experience of experience, without presupposing the (categorial) unity of experience, and while still rendering the constituent syntheses as well as the laws governing them accessible (intuitively). Because of this, Husserl is not so much concerned with apperception, which is the uppermost unity of experience, but rather with the workings of the lower levels of the constitution of experience, i.e. apprehending perception and reproduction. This becomes apparent in Husserl's emphasis on the figural synthesis "capable of composing a manifold of given space-time representations in view of their objective unity," instead of the intellectual one. Since the life-world experience is constituted and structured, Husserl must assume the "functioning understanding's"[44] synthesizing performance to

---

41  Compare Iso Kern, *Husserl Und Kant: Eine Untersuchung Über Husserls Verhältnis Zu Kant Und Zum Neukantianismus* (The Hague: Nijhoff, 1964), p. 256.
42  Rölli, *Gilles Deleuze's Transcendental Empiricism*, p. 102.
43  Edmund Husserl, *Cartesian Meditations* (Dordrecht: Kluwer, 1999), p. 78.
44  Rölli, *Gilles Deleuze's Transcendental Empiricism*, p. 106.

be at work, even if unnoticed. This introduces, however, an ambiguity into the functioning understanding, since a difference appears (even if only formal and not numerical) according to the justification problem mentioned earlier, that is

> on the one hand, understanding interpreting itself, in explicit self-reflection, as normative laws, and, on the other hand, understanding ruling in concealment, i.e. ruling as constitutive of the "intuitively given surrounding world" as always already developed and always further developing sense-configuration.[45]

Due to the "concealed" rule of the understanding, which points to the pre-representational domain and therein the proto-logical structures that guide passive synthesis, which cannot be conceptualized as "a result of [Kant's] regressive method," Husserl introduces a "double functioning understanding,"[46] in order to demonstrate that the same categorial functions are at work in categorial thinking as in pre-predicative constitution, hence ensuring the unity of experience without presupposing it. This allows him to circumvent Kant's harsh rejection of empiricism, which systematically expels any possibility of passive synthesis, insofar as the spontaneous understanding is seen as the sole source of justification for the necessary (and general) conformity to natural laws, while the passive syntheses cannot be considered as intelligible evidence for them. Hence, Husserl takes up the empiricist domains of habit and affection to address the ontological precondition of active cognition, effectively subverting the distinction between the active understanding and passive sensibility. Moreover, as he remarks on the transcendental aesthetic, the very notion of pure receptivity is a fictional limit, disguising the synthetic nature of both temporality and affectivity,[47] the two

---

45 Edmund Husserl, *The Crisis of European Sciences and Transcendental Phenomenology* (Evanston: Northwestern University Press, 1970), p. 103.
46 Ibid.
47 Therefore, the syntheses of the analytic must also be redefined and grounded by the (passive) syntheses described by the transcendental aesthetic.

aspects that will provide a foothold for Deleuze's appropriation of Husserl's passive synthesis.[48]

From this vantage point, the two reductions, the transcendental (or phenomenological) and the eidetic—the first reducing phenomena to constituting consciousness, the latter evoking the lawfulness of experience by moving from the concrete to the trans-empirical—must be reconsidered. While, in a note on his translation of *Ideas I*, Ricœur repeats Husserl's sentiment that "the possibility is excluded of a phenomenological reduction without eidetic reduction," he nonetheless points to the consequence of omitting the eidetic reduction; a "transcendental empirical phenomenology."[49] Genetic phenomenology's tracing of the object to its original constitution, moreover, makes the eidetic reduction either impossible or superfluous. The practical irrelevance of the eidetic reduction and Husserl's refraining from it in many of his later works gives us a central philosophical insight into the nature of the passive syntheses: that they are not only blind but essentially transgressive, i.e. they are not rule governed but rather productive (including the production of the rules governing production). This is why Ricœur concludes in his essay on Husserl's *Cartesian Meditations*: "If this entailment [the transcendental reduction] is not followed up [by the eidetic reduction], phenomenology, in effect, becomes only a transcendental empiricism."[50]

Since the passive syntheses operate on the level of pure perception and enable the higher, active faculties, and since they are not rule-governed, what the passive syntheses supply is the constitution of the transcendental, without tracing it from the empirical. Deleuze remarks on the consequences of this not-realized possibility in phenomenology that the passive synthesis "is not carried out by the mind, but occurs *in* the mind."[51] Ricœur's essay on *Existential Phenomenology* goes even further:

---

[48] Compare Deleuze, *Difference and Repetition*, p. 57, 68, 98.
[49] Paul Ricœur, *Key to Edmund Husserl's Ideas* (Milwaukee: Marquette University Press, 1996), p. 116.
[50] Paul Ricœur, *Husserl: An Analysis of His Phenomenology* (Evanston: Northwestern University Press, 1967), p. 91.
[51] Deleuze, *Difference and Repetition*, p. 71.

Thereafter it is clear that the progression toward an ever more originary original destroys every claim of constituting the world "in" consciousness or "beginning from" consciousness. The idealistic tendency of transcendental phenomenology is thus compensated for by the progressive discovery that one does not constitute the originary but only all that one can derive from it.[52]

Phenomenology as transcendental empiricism therefore holds the potential for a twofold approach towards grasping the possibility of an outside of consciousness which is nonetheless constitutive of it. Firstly, transcendental empiricism begins with an experience constituting consciousness. But, secondly, since there is nothing within consciousness that does not begin with such an experience, it points to an outside of consciousness constituting it. The latter is already what is alluded to in Sartre's "impersonal transcendental field"[53] or Bergson's "impersonal perception."[54] As Deleuze reflects, "Empiricism truly becomes transcendental [...] only when we apprehend directly in the sensible that which can only be sensed."[55]

Considering that phenomenology, already in Husserl's late work, held the possibility of becoming a transcendental empiricism, the pressing question is not only where it falls short of such aspirations, but more importantly why it had to. More precisely, to clarify and illuminate the insufficiently considered question of how Deleuze picks up Husserl's concept of the passive syntheses for his transcendental empiricism, although he himself "is not a phenomenologist" (not just a post-phenomenologist), the question has to be posed in a typical Deleuzian manner.[56] To help il-

---

52 Paul Ricœur, "Existential Phenomenology," in *Husserl: An Analysis of His Phenomenology* (Evanston: Northwestern University Press, 1967), p. 205.
53 Jean-Paul Sartre, *The Transcendence of the Ego: An Existentialist Theory of Consciousness* (New York: Routledge, 2004), p. 33.
54 Bergson, *Matter and Memory*, p. 25.
55 Deleuze, *Difference and Repetition*, p. 56f.
56 Since "there is not much consensus in the current critical literature when it comes to the question of Deleuze's relationship to phenomenology" (Joe Hughes, *Deleuze and the Genesis of Representation* [London; New York: Continuum Books, 2008], p. 3), the critical sentiment is sometimes even more hyperbolic on the question, making Deleuze an

lustrate what *problem* it is that forms the basis of Deleuze's own project, the question is not only where Husserlian genetic phenomenology falls short of being a transcendental empiricism, but why Husserl stops right before the edge.[57] The primary contention will be that Husserl's reservations in regard to transcendental empiricism are, in fact, designed to safeguard phenomenology from becoming mere psychology. Deleuze's use of the passive syntheses will have to deal with the same impasse Husserl faced, namely the problem of the origins of normativity and unity. Far from simply adopting Husserl's passive syntheses, Deleuze rejects the wholeness of experience both as presupposition and termination. The resulting problem of the normativity of the syntheses will lead Deleuze to radically *reinvent* the passive syntheses and find new means to justify their rule-basedness, as well as ways to ground the individuation of experience beyond any claim to necessary unity. But, he does so within the coordinates of two fundamental problems Husserl had outlined: reduction and constitution.[58] This invention, grounding the reinvention of the concept of passive syntheses, is the Idea, i.e. the power of the inorganic life.

What, we might ask now, is Husserl afraid of?

"anti-phenomenologist." See for example, Michel Foucault, "Theatrum Philosophicum," in *Language, Counter-Memory, Practice: Selected Essays and Interviews*, ed. D. Bouchard (Ithaca: Cornell University Press, 1977), p. 165; Leonard Lawlor, "The End of Phenomenology: Expressionism in Deleuze and Merleau-Ponty," *Continental Philosophy Review* 31, no. 1 (1998), p. 15–34; Dorothea Olkowski, *Gilles Deleuze and the Ruin of Representation* (Berkeley: University of California Press, 1999), and Pierre Montebello, "Deleuze, Une Anti-Phénoménologie ?," *Chiasmi International* 13 (2011), p. 315–325.

57  While, in the same manner, it is not actually important whether Deleuze is or is not a proper phenomenologist, it is certain that "[i]t is not enough to say, that Deleuze is anti-phenomenological because there is no absolute consciousness at the base of the genesis or because there is no theory of intentionality." Hughes, *Deleuze and the Genesis of Representation*, p. 19. Perhaps it is even in the nature of phenomenology to be unfaithful to itself. As Beistegui notes, "there is no 'letter' of phenomenology: no primordial word, no consecrated text, no originary truth that one could betray: only an endless series of heresies, which is, at least in philosophy, the only possible form of fidelity, that is, the fidelity in and through genuine questioning." Miguel de Beistegui, "Toward a Phenomenology of Difference?," *Research in Phenomenology* 30, no. 1 (2000), p. 68.

58  Fink defends Husserl against his Neo-Kantian critics by pointing out that phenomenology is misunderstood if framed in Kantian terms, which would miss that "the theory of reduction and the theory of constitution make up the systematic ideas for phenomenological philosophy as such." Eugen Fink, "The Phenomenological Philosophy of Edmund Husserl and Contemporary Criticism," p. 102.

## Being Awoken

Since Kant, the question of life and living has been inextricably tied up with the problem of law-making generally or autonomy specifically: the question of the justification of rules, and secondarily also their origin.[59] The transgressive nature of the passive syntheses helps reformulate the question of a presupposed rule for their functioning, opening the realm of a possible inorganic life, not justified by law, but rather justifying it by presenting itself as the law's very condition. Adorno, in his *Lectures on Negative Dialectics*, attempting to radicalize Husserl's credo of philosophy by moving towards "the things themselves," sets out to salvage empiricism's commitment to the idea "that cognition always proceeds in principle from below to above," albeit by transforming the idea into the dialectically convoluted concept of "intellectual experience."[60] The move towards this kind of dialectical model—prefigured in Hegel's and Fichte's criticisms of Kant—is seen here as necessary to counter the current tendency of empiricism (as a theory of cognition) to exclude any Otherness or radical novelty. If we, however, take seriously the way the German idealists "announced" the identity of the concept of experience and the content of such an experience, we can discern two paths for the empiricist model.[61] The concept of experience can be contrasted with deduction, however "the contents of such experience provide no models for categories, but they become relevant because they enable the *new* to show itself."[62] Such a subversion of deduction, in turn, comes with the high cost of either declaring this novelty a (non-normative) outside, only determinable negatively and hence demanding an ethics of distance and non-violent observation, or making the new the condition for rule-based experience at all. Despite the differences in consequence, both point to the fundamental problem posed if one forgoes representation as the sole

---

[59] See James Murray, *Deleuze & Guattari: Emergent Law* (Abingdon: Routledge, 2013), p. 133.
[60] Theodor W. Adorno, *Lectures on Negative Dialectics: Fragments of a Lecture Course 1965/1966* (Malden: Polity Press, 2008), p. 82.
[61] Although this identity was only ever announced, and not seriously followed up on, as Adorno mentions. See ibid.
[62] Ibid.

model for the reconstruction of experience, and the inexplicable origin of normativity thereby threatens its unconditional legitimacy. A structurally similar complication presents itself for the unity of experience as well.

This question is echoed in Husserl's account of genetic phenomenology, insofar as it is still relatively tied—or at least more than intended—to the model of recognition and therefore to negation. As Marc Rölli correctly suggests, Husserl seems to follow two conflicting heuristic maxims at once: firstly, that constitutive parts of concrete experience are to be examined abstractly; secondly, that his reconstruction is supposed to "satisfy in detail the phenomenological *criteria of evidence* as well."[63] Hence, we end up with the foundational ambiguity in the functioning understanding between intuition and reconstruction mentioned above, which Kant had bypassed by relying on the necessity of the unity of experience to guide the deduction. This conflict in Husserl plays out first of all in an approach to experience which makes visible all the parts of it not accessible to the natural perspective, highlighting and enlarging certain aspects of experience, which therefore gain intuitive independence. In a second movement, however, such independence is forfeit, insofar as these aspects are delegated to subareas of the whole of experience in its reconstruction. In this twofold movement even the passive syntheses are subordinate to the object's identity as preconditions for its regulation in consciousness— "the activity's mere precondition (the past for Husserl)."[64] The consequence of this conflicting heuristics comes to bear on the concrete practice of genetic phenomenology. Since Husserl attempts a philosophical description of pre-predicative experience, he must reconcile the difference between that which is pre-linguistically given (even given before the *form* of judgement) and the reflexive comprehension of it. However, it is not clear in Husserl how such a difference can even be conceived of. On the one hand, it could be that "any and every 'reflexion' has the character of a modification of consciousness, which in principle can be experienced

---

[63] Rölli, *Gilles Deleuze's Transcendental Empiricism*, p. 107, my emphasis.
[64] Beaulieu, "Edmund Husserl," p. 276.

by every consciousness."[65] Hence, *de jure*, consciousness encompasses all possible (pieces) of experience, asserting its homogeneity by integration, thereby making passive syntheses pre-forms as well as pre-conditions of the wholeness of experience. If, on the other hand, one forfeits the foundational coherence of the logical circularity of reflection, then any pre-reflexive experience becomes inconceivable. We can see from this that Husserl can only approach the passive synthesis in the idealist manner by describing it in terms of consciousness.[66]

This points to the foundational problem of the description of a life that is not active or organic and thereby does not satisfy the criteria of evidence. Deleuze will insist on conceiving of the passive syntheses as conditions of real experience; therefore, they must be thought as a "fore-field," which cannot be dissolved into active syntheses or relegated to a pre-condition of the wholeness of experience. Thinking them *as such*, however, means not grounding them in the circular self-founding which for Husserl guaranteed the reconciliation between intuition and reconstruction. Instead, Deleuze will ground them in their transcendental "ungrounding" or abyssality. Deleuze, however is not blind to the inherent dangers in such a forfeiting of safe grounds. While such a position seems to pit Schellingian nature philosophy against Hegel's dialectics, the former's "romantic turn" sacrifices free differences for an indifferent "unground." Deleuze extends this critique to *Lebensphilosophien* more broadly: "We see this with Schelling, with Schopenhauer, and even with the first Dionysus, that of the *Birth of Tragedy*: their groundlessness cannot sustain difference."[67]

What is philosophically at stake here is best demonstrated not only by Husserl's claim of a continuity between the lived experience of Euclid and himself (or anybody else for that matter), which Derrida so eloquently ex-

---

65  Edmund Husserl, *Ideas: General Introduction to Pure Phenomenology* (London: Routledge, 2012), p. 219.
66  For an account that uses this ambiguity to move from an eidetic to a structural reduction, see Bernhard Waldenfels, *Phänomenologie in Frankreich* (Frankfurt am Main: Suhrkamp, 1983), p. 177.
67  Deleuze, *Difference and Repetition*, p. 276. Compare this with the more affirmative mention of the Dionysian fluid world as the place of individuation, which Deleuze explicitly pits against Schopenhauer's indifferent ground, ibid., p. 258.

posed as the conclusion to philosophy's tendency towards logocentrism, but also by his insistence on the immortality of the transcendental ego.⁶⁸ As McDonald paraphrases Husserl, "the mundane man will have to die, the transcendental ego cannot perish," because, as Husserl himself states in the *Analyses Concerning Passive and Active Synthesis*, "even if the presently 'enduring' unitary object or event can cease, the process of the 'enduring' itself cannot come to a halt. The 'enduring' is immortal [...]. This implies that the process of living on, and the [pure] ego that lives on, are immortal."⁶⁹ While Husserl approaches the outside, he nonetheless integrates it into consciousness for *methodological* reasons; he remains a phenomenologist, even when phenomenology has been pushed to its outermost limit, where it starts to break down. As a proper transcendental idealist, life and consciousness are necessarily correlated (if not mutually constituted). But the pre-history of consciousness cannot be construed as a construction of consciousness, and hence must be impossible, since the transcendental ego cannot be considered as dead or non-existent. So, Husserl resorts to the assertion of an absolute consciousness, developed from a set of sleeping monads in an evolutionary process, to maintain idealistic consistency, so that "every physical thing is a body of consciousness, even if it be only a dull consciousness"⁷⁰ and "the being of nature leads back to the being of sheer consciousness, eternal consciousness."⁷¹ Hence, there was a time, according to Husserl, when all monads were asleep, but with an essential potential to wake up. This establishes a continuum between the bare Earth of a time before conscious beings and the teeming Earth on which present consciousness resides. The evolution of life is thus tied to the development of the monads, with inorganic nature's "dull monads" (or "sleeping monads") as ancestry and pre-condition. Such an insistence on integrating the inhuman (or inorganic fore-field) is not only motivated

---

68 Compare Jacques Derrida, *Voice and Phenomenon: Introduction to the Problem of the Sign in Husserl's Phenomenology* (Evanston: Northwestern University Press, 2011).
69 Husserl, *Analyses Concerning Passive and Active Synthesis*, p. 467.
70 Husserl, *Cartesian Meditations*, p. 72.
71 Dermot Moran, *Edmund Husserl: Founder of Phenomenology* (Malden: Polity Press, 2005), p. 230.

by the requirements of the reduction to pure consciousness (phenomenological reduction), which cannot investigate its genesis in something other than itself, since it would have to presume itself as not-yet-given, but is also, more importantly, built on the subsequent impossibility of an eidetic reduction, which amounts to an impossibility of accounting for the normativity of experience.[72] It is, however, in relation to the "monads" that Husserl confronts what is at stake metaphysically when moving from the inorganic to the organic. The time before time is described as "unconsciousness, sedimented foundation of consciousness, sleep without a dream, a form of Birth of subjectivity, the probable Being before being born, death, after death."[73] Considering the "universal teleology"[74] Husserl wants to maintain in the development of absolute consciousness, we can see that the question of the awakening of the monads arises in a twofold way. Firstly, Husserl argues that no monad can stay asleep forever, since in this case they would be unknowable, and nothing is unknowable in principle. But there seems no logical nor material necessity for the monads to awake arising from the existence of "sheer" consciousness as such.[75] Secondly, beyond the modal problem, the universal teleology, rather than solving it, highlights the problem of the process of "being awoken" or the emergence of consciousness.[76] Typically, the involuted monad starts being affected by *hylé* and subsequently begins its life as a conscious, world-constituting and self-objectifying being.[77] If conscious life depends on an

---

[72] Smith therefore rightly poses the question in relation to the concept of sleeping monads: "The real problem is, rather, in understanding what changes could take place in sleeping monads that might be rule-governed." A. D. Smith, *Routledge Philosophy Guidebook to Husserl and the Cartesian Meditations* (London; New York: Routledge, 2003), p. 205.

[73] Edmund Husserl, *Zur Phänomenologie Der Intersubjektivität: Texte Aus Dem Nachlaß, Dritter Teil: 1929– 1935* (Dordrecht: Kluwer, 1973), p. 608.

[74] Husserl describes this "universal Teleology" as a history in which "the temporal world process is, considered transcendentally, the life-process of monads who communicate with each other." Ibid., p. 609. In a distinctly anti-Leibnizian turn, monads have windows and they communicate.

[75] See ibid., p. 157.

[76] Compare James G. Hart, *Who One Is. Meontology of the I: A Transcendental Phenomenology* (Dordrecht: Springer, 2009), p. 391.

[77] See Edmund Husserl, "1917. Transzendentale Phänomenologie Als Wissenschaft von Der Transzendentalen Subjektivität Und Der Konstitution Aller Objektivität" (unpublished manuscript, 1917), B II/1, 16.

outside, the *hylé*, in order to come into being, the possibility opens up of a genesis of the monads in time. Husserl, however, dismisses this possibility, since he has characterized consciousness already as an immortal "streaming-present,"[78] which takes place within the constitution of time but is itself not a mode of time. Therefore, he notes:

> A time before all consciousness can only mean a time in which no animal was alive. That has a sense. But a time and no absolute consciousness: that has no sense. Absolute consciousness is "before" objective time, and is the non-temporal ground for the constitution of infinite time and of a world infinitely stretching out in time.[79]

There was no constitution or emergence of consciousness; it was, rather, awoken. Eugen Fink, Husserl's student, clearly saw the paradox Husserl was facing, which became the foundational problem of temporalization in phenomenology: how to explain the emergence of the temporal from the non-temporal? Husserl "tries to grasp time in its emergence from the timeless-eternal [...] and subjects in the self-articulation [*Selbstung*] of absolute being."[80] Not straying from the path set out by the criterion of evidence, Husserl, especially in his later works, set out to locate this origin within lived experience, forgoing any chance of developing a transcendental empiricism.[81] He "announces," however, a way to leave the constraints of "lived" experience —not by thinking the subject as primordially dead, as Hegelians like Lacan or Derrida had suggested in the "wake" of Husserl, but by thinking it as being in a constant discontinuous process of being born from or being awoken by something unlivable, or incommensurable by any organic metric.

---

78   Husserl, *Zur Phänomenologie Der Intersubjektivität*, p. 668.
79   Ibid., p. 16.
80   Eugen Fink, *Nähe Und Distanz: Studien zur Phänomenologie* (Freiburg im Breisgau: Alber, 2008), p. 233, my translation.
81   "In the manuscripts of the last years of his life, Husserl came to the remarkable thought that the most primordial depth of the life of consciousness might not be found by drawing the distinction between essence and existence, that, rather, this depth would be the original ground [*Ur-Grund*], and on this ground the separation of fact and essence, reality and possibility, examples and species, one and many, first appear." Ibid., p. 224, my translation.

While Husserl insists on the temporal self-affection of absolute consciousness, Lyotard, radicalizing phenomenological premises, rejects such self-affection, since it is only ever plausible in a transcendental philosophy that already presupposes the givenness of consciousness a priori. Without this self-grounding, consciousness is no longer given, but is being given or awoken from the outside. Lyotard writes:

> The soul does not affect itself, but is only affected by the other, from the "outside." Here existing is not the fact of a conscience aiming at its noematic correlative nor that of a permanent substance. Existing is to be awoken from the nothingness of disaffection by something sensible over there. An affective cloud lifts at this moment and deploys its nuance for a moment. Sensation makes a break in an inert nonexistence. It alerts, it should be said, it *exists* it. What we call life proceeds from a violence exerted from the outside on lethargy. The anima exists only as forced.[82]

This very violence, the inorganic affection, engenders, as we saw in the previous chapter, the birth of the soul in the discordant accord of the sublime. Existence is necessarily servile—it relies on the *aistehon*—and at the same time excited and propelled from nonexistence. If the organic separation of the sensible and the intelligible left us with a nihilism due to the splitting of existence and meaning, the sublime, by invoking the same split, overcomes nihilism by mending the gulf between the intelligible and the sensible.[83] It is not necessary to assume sleeping monads, since something is awoken, a soul, that was not already there, but brought into existence. Breaking with Husserl's continuity of absolute consciousness on the ground of genesis, however, leaves us with the problem that the phenomenologist tried to avoid by using this continuity as a guideline to reconstruct phenomena while still being able to satisfy the criterion of evidence. If we want to hold that phenomenology could become a

---

[82] Jean-François Lyotard, "Anima Minima," in *Postmodern Fables* (Minneapolis: University of Minnesota Press, 1997), p. 243.

[83] Ashley Woodward, "Nihilism and the Sublime in Lyotard," *Angelaki: Journal for Theoretical Humanities* 16, no. 2 (2011), p. 51–71.

transcendental empiricism, we are obliged to provide a consistent reconfiguration of the basic structural ideas of phenomenology: reduction and constitution, the two poles of Deleuze's own approach.

### SUSPENDING THE LIVED BODY

The concrete process of such an "awakening" is described or at least hinted at by Husserl. Since the affection by *hylé* requires kinesthesis—so that a world of objects can be constituted for the subject—it presupposes a body: "the constitution of nature [...] is from the start indissolubly interwoven with the constitution of a body."[84] This sentiment, echoed throughout phenomenology as a tradition, prompted a phenomenology of embodiment that sought to challenge Husserlian idealism. It is, however, this positing of the body as the new pole of identity, a substitute for consciousness, that reintroduces the logic of the negative, as is apparent in Merleau-Ponty's philosophy. The account given in *The Structure of Behavior* can be viewed as an attempt at a transcendental empiricism that radicalizes Husserl's insight into the constitutive function of embodiment, while at the same time avoiding the classical dichotomy between the idea that the transcendental ego grounds experience and behavior, and the idea that pseudo-physical and physical processes can ground them entirely. This dichotomy was reiterated by Husserlian phenomenology, which strengthened the former by refuting the latter. Faced with the danger that without such grounding structures embodied beings might appear to "exist on a sea of processes of which we know and experience nothing"[85] (i.e. the danger of forgoing the criterion of evidence), he attempts to describe the processes for the organization of embodied beings and their structures. The analysis cannot reduce behavior to organic or mechanical processes, since such "impersonal" life can only

---

84 Edmund Husserl, "Weltzeitigung Und Weltmodalitäten" (Unpublished Manuscript, 1930), 45b.
85 Maurice Merleau-Ponty, *The Visible and the Invisible: Followed by Working Notes*, trans. Alphonso Lingis (Evanston: Northwestern University Press, 1968), p. 232.

function when it is permeated or motivated by personal, symbolic, and meaningful life. Instead of reducing experience to physical processes, one must make sense of the physical in terms of experience. The only phenomenology of perception that would be possible is hence one that not only values the physical body and consciousness equally, but that posits that in every human activity both are indistinguishable in terms of process. The question of the genesis of the subject and the question of the genesis of the world, neither of which Husserl had satisfactorily answered, are thus inextricably linked.[86] To experience this integration, kinesthesis is necessary to allow for the multiplication of representations and the active engagement towards the world of the body. For our purposes, we will focus on Merleau-Ponty's account of kinesthesis and perception from the *Phenomenology of Perception*, which Deleuze takes up in *Difference and Repetition*, since it contains a description of the genesis of the illusion of identity.

Due to the perspectivism of embodied experience, objects are never perceived fully, an aspect of perception Husserl described with the word *Abschattung*. If I change my perspective on the object by moving around, and then by repeating my original perspective while remembering the others, I experience the implication of an infinite number of possible perspectives on the object, totalized in the object's identity, a "memory of the world".[87] With such an understanding, the current perspectival experience of the object becomes logically posterior to the object and hence inessential. If the object can no longer be considered as constituted by perception, both object and perception must be grounded in relation to each other. Such a relation is determined by mutual limitation, presupposing negation, so that, "obsessed with being, and forgetful of the perspectivism of my experience, I henceforth treat it as an object, and deduce it from a relationship between objects."[88] This "well founded" illusion of identity is reconstructed in *Difference and Repetition* as the idea of infinite representation in the con-

---

[86] Jack Reynolds and Jon Roffe, "Deleuze and Merleau-Ponty: Immanence, Univocity and Phenomenology," *Journal of the British Society for Phenomenology* 37, no. 3 (2006), p. 236.
[87] Merleau-Ponty, *Phenomenology of Perception*, p. 70.
[88] Ibid.

vergence of points of view in one point (the *same* object, the *same* world, the *same* Self), "which gathers and represents all the others."[89] As we have seen in the process of Kant's deduction in the last chapter, the in-itself of representation and the for-itself of the representant constitute each other through limit and hence negation. All points of view are centered around a single perspective and the subsequent "peripheral" ones are degraded to mere oppositions without any independent existence in relation to the center. Counter to this, in retrieving Merleau-Ponty's perspectivism, Deleuze suggests multiplying points of view by decentering representation, so that "each composing representation must be distorted, diverted and torn from its center. Each point of view must itself be the object, or the object must belong to the point of view."[90] This implies, however, a more radical shift away from a perspectivism grounded in the lived body. Insofar as the body in the perspectivism Merleau-Ponty proposes is the condition for perspectival perception, it becomes a point of convergence yet again. Rather than giving a fully genetic account of perspectivism, the body operates as an identity pole gathering and centralizing all possible points of view. Perspectivism is itself in need of explanation. While the lived body serves as a basis for the proper description of phenomena, these phenomena neither reveal in analysis nor present in themselves their genetic process.

Deleuze first examines the consequences of such a conception of the body in *The Logic of Sense*'s critique of phenomenology's *Urdoxa*, which then becomes radicalized in *Francis Bacon*. Both he and Merleau-Ponty criticize Husserl's notion of *Urdoxa*, "the primordial belief, predominant in memory and perception, that posits the world as real and certain."[91] Merleau-Ponty, however, by framing the affective and embodied encounter with the world as primordial experience in order to question this belief, establishes an *Urdoxa* of his own.[92] The spatialized conception of

---

89 Deleuze, *Difference and Repetition*, p. 56.
90 Ibid.
91 Sara Heinämaa, "Merleau-Ponty's Modification of Phenomenology: Cognition, Passion and Philosophy," *Synthese* 118, no. 1 (1999), p. 53.
92 See Judith Wambacq, *Thinking Between Deleuze and Merleau-Ponty* (Athens: Ohio University Press, 2017), p. 122.

perception Merleau-Ponty puts forth entails a pregiven harmony between the body and the world, which is itself not subject to genesis: the body is "intimate" with the world as if the world was made for it and the body for the world.[93] Hence, the possibility of unified embodied experience is not explained through difference but presupposed, making the body-world relation of Merleau-Ponty functionally akin to Kant's *sensus communis* or Husserl's *Urdoxa*. This kind of "good" union of existence is a consequence of tracing the transcendental from the empirical, since the relation between body and world is not established by a relation of difference and discord, but of harmony without genesis. It is not a coincidence that Merleau-Ponty's bodies are constantly moving, expressing their athletic capacity in almost frantic gestures. The lived body here prevents "difference" from becoming "the element, the ultimate unity."[94] The relation of the body to the world in Merleau-Ponty is not properly differential—in a way, the body bites off from the world only what it can chew, and the world obliges.[95]

Analogically, as we have noted, just as the impersonal life is for Merleau-Ponty always already permeated by personal, meaningful life, the structure of the *Urdoxa* is also operative on the level of meaning, generated by the affective encounter of the body with the world. *The Phenomenology of Perception*'s attempt to ground intellectual knowledge in a more primordial, non-cognized, embodied relation with the world already presupposes the inherent meaningfulness of (or as given in) experience. His notion of perceptual faith (for example in permanent figures) is based on the idea that "our experience is organized as if we had a perceptual guarantee to support this faith."[96] Even if the relation to the world is differen-

---

93  See Bernard Flynn, "The Question of Ontology: Sartre and Merleau-Ponty," in *The Horizons of the Flesh: Critical Perspectives on the Thought of Merleau-Ponty*, ed. Gillian Garth (Urbana: Southern Illinois University Press, 1973).
94  Deleuze, *Difference and Repetition*, p. 56.
95  Lash makes a point of acknowledging that for Deleuze it is not simply the case that our bodies are not defined by their biological unity, but also that we *should not* perceive our bodies as so unified and unifying. Compare Scott Lash, "Genealogy and the Body: Foucault/Deleuze/Nietzsche," *Theory, Culture & Society* 2, no. 2 (June 1984), p. 9.
96  The whole quote reads: "The presumption that these permanent figures will never prove to be illusory is based merely upon a perceptual faith—we would be astonished upon dis-

tial in nature, the organization of experience (in the relation of the body and the world) is geared towards meaning as if nature itself wanted us to know it. This is an iteration of the presupposed good sense of thinking, which, left to its own devices, will produce meaning by itself. Again, for Deleuze, this traces the transcendental from the meaningful experience of the empirical, making the transcendental solely the precondition for the personal. Again, phenomenology is trapped in a vicious circle: it presupposes as ground what it is supposed to ground. With that phenomenology falls short of its own ambitions and "the whole of Phenomenology is an epiphenomenology."[97]

These trajectories, which are pushed in Merleau-Ponty's later work *The Visible and the Invisible* even further as "natal bond, natal secret, perceptual bond, pre-logical bond, or natal pact,"[98] return in contemporary discussions on the embodied mind at the intersection of neuro-science and phenomenology, which constitute what is known as the affective turn or, somewhat misleadingly, the vital turn.[99] Such investigations are interested, on the one hand, in the brain's self-organizing dynamics and how such processes of emergence could function as models for a life without any prior plan. On the other hand, they seek to remove the brain from its central position in the constitution of the mind and to integrate cerebral functions into the larger network of corporeal activity. This follows Merleau-Pontyian lines by rejecting the thought of a brute material world to which meaning would have to be added, and replacing it with primordial meaningful experience for a living system, which is understood as an open, responsive, embodied and dynamic system. Consider the anti-Cartesian sentiment in such a venture, for example in Maturana and Verela: "the process of cognition is the actual (inductive) acting or behaving in this domain [*milieu*].

---

illusionment—but our experience is organized as if we had a perceptual guarantee to support this faith. At this point we are said to know particular natural objects." Merleau-Ponty, *Phenomenology of Perception*, p. 343.
97  Deleuze, *Difference and Repetition*, p. 52.
98  Reynolds and Roffe, "Deleuze and Merleau-Ponty," p. 245.
99  Compare Patricia Clough and Jean Halley, *The Affective Turn: Theorizing the Social* (Durham, N.C.: Duke University Press, 2007); see also Nigel Thrift, *Non-Representational Theories: Space, Politics, Affect* (London: Routledge, 2008).

Living systems are cognitive systems and living as a process is a process of cognition. This statement is valid for all organisms, with and without a nervous system."[100] The problem of binding affections is the problem of the organism as such and tying meaning to such physical acts, making them inherently meaningful acts, transforms the outside implicated in any affectivity into an outside *for* the living system.[101] Insofar as the outside can be processed, it is an outside with meaning *for* the organism and beyond these conditions of possibility of meaning, the outside does not "appear." The proposed correction of "Descartes's error: the abyssal separation between mind and body"[102] closes itself in its organic embodiment, unable to think the conditions for real experience, instead remaining within the bounds of meaningful experience, regionalizing affectivity to organisms and meaning to the ability to process information or cognize.

Interpreting Klossowski's characterization of the relation between divinity and the body, Deleuze gives us this relation as the concept of a *theological* body:

> The order of divine creation depends on bodies, is suspended from them. In the order of God, in the order of existence, bodies give to minds (or rather impose on them) two properties: identity and immortality, personality and resurrectibility, incommunicability and integrity. [...] God must depend upon the body.[103]

God depends on the bodies He creates and has dominion over. For that reason, Rilke asks so fearfully, "What will you do God, when I die?."[104]

---

[100] Humberto R. Maturana and Francisco J. Verela, *Autopoiesis and Cognition: The Realization of the Living* (Boston: D. Reidel Pub. Co., 1980), p. 13.

[101] This ascription of the world to a body is very prominent in Varela's work with the philosopher Thompson. See Francisco J. Verela, Evan Thompson, and Eleanor Rosch, *The Embodied Mind: Cognitive Science and Human Experience* (Cambridge, Mass.: The MIT Press, 2016).

[102] Antonio R. Damasio, *The Feeling of What Happens: Body, Emotion and the Making of Consciousness* (London: Vintage, 2000), p. 249.

[103] Deleuze, *Logic of Sense*, p. 292.

[104] Rainer Maria Rilke, "What Will You Do God, When I Die?," in *Selected Poems* (Oxford: Oxford University Press, 2011), p. 13.

But, inversely, the integrity of the body depends on God, who is the objective guarantee of self-identity, insofar as its unique internal organization prevents the essence of an individual self being attributed to somebody else, just as the endowment of a soul prevents thoughts from being somebody else's (e.g. the Cartesian horror contained in the argument on the continuity of the mind during sleep). And the jurisdiction of this order is stretched into infinity through the immortality of the soul. This body, understood as something organized internally and self-identical, i.e. an organism, hence provides the material condition of the incarnation of the image of God, as well as oppositional models for this: good growth against bad decay, good activity against bad passivity, good organization against bad chaos. Hence, as Colebrook remarks, situating life exclusively in the activity of the body "is at once a normative privileging of the bounded organism over other forms of life and movement, at the same time as it is eminently theological."[105] That is why Deleuze rejects both the "lived body" (*Leib*) of phenomenology and the linguistic co-optation of matter. In *Anti-Oedipus* he shows that the "body image" of phenomenology is "the final avatar of the soul, a vague conjoining of the requirements of spiritualism and positivism,"[106] which subjects the body to both unity and givenness. As the other pole of divine organization, "the identity of language as the power of *denoting* everything else"[107] subjects the materiality of the body to a normative order (of language). This denotative tendency still proliferates in performative theories of the body. Butler's account of the body as only "mattering" insofar as it is recognized, renders it inconceivable as an extra-discursive object and hence subjects it to the normativity of language and Hegelian dialectics—as if matter had only ever existed for culture and speech.[108]

---

[105] Colebrook, *Deleuze and the Meaning of Life*, p. 108.
[106] Gilles Deleuze and Félix Guattari, *Anti-Oedipus: Capitalism and Schizophrenia I* (New York: Penguin Books, 2009), p. 239.
[107] Deleuze, *Logic of Sense*, p. 292.
[108] Even referring to the material body as something not yet fully subjected to discourse or "to refer naively or directly to such an extra-discursive object will always require the prior delimitation of the extra-discursive." Judith Butler, *Bodies That Matter: On the Discursive Limits of "Sex"* (New York: Routledge, 1993), p. 10. Since such delineation is also discursive, for Butler, "matter" is only ever discursive. Elisabeth Grosz's *Volatile Bodies* presents,

## ON NOT BEING AT HOME

Heidegger's lectures on *The Fundamental Concepts of Metaphysics* contain the most consequential and at the same time most absurd expression of this approach. In it, he does not only conclude that the "animal is poor in world," this poverty resulting from it lacking the ability to *form* a world, but also that "the stone is worldless, it is without world, it has no world."[109] It does not *ex*-ist. Even though it touches the earth beneath it, this "touch" is not really touching, since touching for Heidegger is an experience that makes a difference in meaning. For the stone, there is no difference in meaning in whether it lies on a path or is crushed on a construction site. Since there is no meaning for the stone and experience is always meaningful, the stone is therefore not experiencing anything. It is thus not even affected. There is no meaningless world for Heidegger, since the world is always *for* a living being; hence, the stone cannot have a world. This expresses the *Urdoxa* that the world is *essentially* for us and we are *essentially* of this world, that there exists a harmonious relation of body and world in living beings. Such a prioritization of living organic systems which are capable of autopoiesis and response to stimuli presupposes the inherent meaningfulness of experience and excludes the possibility of a genesis of meaning beyond the level of the organic. Such a Heideggerian position incorporates the human in the world, in that they are a priori, before all knowledge and theory, interwoven. Even the material resistance of the world is made out to be nothing other than playful interaction with the lived body held together via perceptual intentionality. As Bachelard claims: "Life begins well, it begins enclosed, protected, all warm in the bosom of the house."[110] Even Heidegger's *Angst*, a basic concept in his analysis of mood, only deepens this relation to the world. Even

in contrast, a performative philosophy of the body that is far less tied to and restricted by the limits of speech. See Elizabeth Grosz, *Volatile Bodies: Toward a Corporeal Feminism*, Theories of Representation and Difference (Bloomington: Indiana University Press, 1994).

109  Martin Heidegger, *The Fundamental Concepts of Metaphysics: World, Finitude, Solitude* (Bloomington: Indiana University Press, 2012), p. 192.
110  Gaston Bachelard, *The Poetics of Space* (Boston: Beacon Press, 1994), p. 7.

in *Angst* the world remains a house we live in, which essentially belongs to us intact.[111] By universalizing hermeneutics as the structure of experience, both Heidegger and Merleau-Ponty decree that "mood and body are two ways in which subjectivity is inextricably and pre-thematically tied to the world."[112]

This can be seen in Heidegger's famous tool analysis. Heidegger holds that the hammer is primarily given in an always already understood way as ready-to-hand (*Zuhandenheit*). Only if it breaks, is misplaced or annoys us do we notice the heavy, iron head mounted on a wooden shaft, i.e. the hammer in its presence-at-hand (*Vorhandenheit*). While the first mode is "natural," the second one is derivative of the first. Deleuze and Guattari, on the other hand, reject such categorization and rather describe the interaction with the hammer in terms of territories, with meaning being part of one process.[113] Heidegger's pathos of *authenticity* and *inauthenticity*, which builds on the aforementioned distinctions, is decidedly not an attack on the univocity of being, but is founded in the fact that being is always mine (*jemeinig*).[114] It is exactly this phenomenological commitment to present a unified horizon that leads Heidegger into the trap of common sense. By stripping away the presuppositions of philosophy, he establishes the natural "image of thought" as an existential hermeneutics and claims that it is irreducible. Through the idea of "conscience as the call of care"[115] Heidegger solidifies common sense in the form of being-for-

---

[111] The pre-thematic bond of world and human subject—even if the latter is disavowed—can be found in the linguistic idealisms of Derrida and Lacan.
[112] Dylan Trigg, "'The Horror of Darkness': Toward an Unhuman Phenomenology," *Speculations* (2013), p. 114.
[113] The process of working with tools, for example, might be described as follows: the hand seizing the hammer deterritorializes it from what Heidegger would call its presence-at-hand (*Vorhandenheit*). At the same time, the hammer is reterritorialized on the hand (as Heidegger would say, it now is ready-to-hand [*zuhanden*]), while the hand deterritorializes itself from the body in order to enter into a symbiosis with the tool. That is to say, the hand, too, reterritorializes itself on the tool. Rather than separating the modes of being of presence-at-hand (*Vorhandenheit*) and readiness-to-hand (*Zuhandensein*), as Heidegger would do, Deleuze and Guattari consider both to be the two sides of one and the same process. See Stephan Günzel, "Deleuze and Phenomenology," *Metodo. International Studies in Phenomenology and Philosophy* 2, no. 2 (2014), p. 37.
[114] See Martin Heidegger, *Being and Time*, trans. Joan Stambaugh and Dennis J. Schmidt (Albany: State University of New York Press, 2010), p. 68.
[115] Ibid., p. 264.

others, which becomes the authentic mode of living in a moralist manner. The rejection of such an Image of thought, although rarely explicit, can be implicitly seen in Deleuze and Guattari on the many occasions that they deliberately favor the inauthentic over the supposedly authentic modes: the pronoun "one" (*man*) against mineness (*Jemeinigkeit*), indirect speech against the authentic conversation.[116] Even in his later work, by proposing the goal of philosophy to be the investigation of being as such and not *Dasein*, Heidegger is still searching for the being that is common to all beings, while Deleuze dissolves the common being in a Bergsonian manner with the formula "monism=pluralism."[117] The Heideggerian *common being* then serves as the basis for Heidegger's history of philosophy as the forgetting of being (*Seinsvergessenheit*), which again binds all primary images of thought into one narrative and makes them comprehensible for each other under the banner of metaphysical decadence. Even this history of absence is illuminated by a kind of natural light.

Deleuze does not have much love for such grand histories. Sometimes he and Guattari laugh about it, Heidegger's return to the Greeks, his *destruction* of the history of metaphysics; they smile: "We don't need the Greeks." Although he is firmly occupied with the problem of finding a new image of thought—and "its genesis in thought itself"[118]—Deleuze does not believe that there is an underlying continuous history of thought; there are only breaks, cracks and emergences. There is no history, but there is "*a* Life" of thought.

A bind such as that demonstrated by Heidegger not only comes with the epistemological drawback of encountering an anthropomorphist cosmos instead of the things themselves, but also provokes the phantasm of the great Outdoors as the opposite to this subjective relation. However, as Levinas demonstrates in his early work *Existence and Existents*, this kind of idealism is not necessarily the fate of phenomenology. While Heidegger will first tie temporality to finitude and later to Being, Levinas

---

[116] See ibid., p. 68.
[117] Deleuze and Guattari, *Thousand Plateaus*, p. 20.
[118] Lambert, *In Search of a New Image of Thought*, p. 2.

is interested in the alterity of duration in this period. Though the bond between beings and Being is also established and preserved in Levinas, the "adherence of beings in Being" is not "given in an instant [but] rather accomplished by the very stance of an instant."[119] The event of the emergence of beings carries with it its origins, insofar as it emerges from a pre-existence. They are born into *something*. The concept of "birth," however, only frees us from idealist-phenomenological constraints if we consider this *something* as non-historically or non-culturally determined Being, not yet tied down by manifest specificity. For Levinas, the Heideggerian hermeneutic circle, always bound on returning home, has to be broken: one must refuse to confer a "personal form"[120] upon it, thus thinking it through its anonymity. As such, however, "Existence is not synonymous with the relationship with a world; it is antecedent to the world,"[121] because it logically precedes the personal establishment of a world and is hence not dependent on there being a world in the first place. And indeed, the world can be lost and existence endures, or, as in the case of sleeplessness, one endures existence, even though the meaningful world has fallen away. This anonymous state of Being undercuts Heidegger's fundamental finitude, death, making it a derivate mode, since "in the situation of an end of the world the primary relationship which binds us to Being becomes palpable."[122] Therefore, however, the relation to this Being without existents can only be described in analogy,[123] avoiding the localization of Being, because Being is "not a person or a thing, or the sum total of persons and things; it is the fact that one is, the fact that there is (*il y a*)."[124] Folding back on itself in the experience of the contingency of the world or of being a subject, the anonymity of Being endures in beings while at the same time resisting them, so that "Being is essentially alien and strikes

---

[119] Emmanuel Levinas, *Existence and Existents* (Pittsburgh: Duquesne University Press, 2001), p. 2.
[120] Ibid., p. 3.
[121] Ibid., p. 8.
[122] Ibid.
[123] While Deleuze also invokes the "faceless existence," he additionally provides a metaphysical principle for thinking Being not through analogy, but as univocal.
[124] Ibid.

against us. We undergo its suffocating embrace like the night, but it does not respond to us."[125] How far one ventures towards the loss of the world might be to a certain degree a matter of choice, but even if the world is lost, one cannot not exist; one is awoken, not into a home, but into alien Being. One is not at home here. One is not in an organic and meaningful relationship with the world. And this meaningless being can emerge everywhere. As Deleuze puts it, "something of the ground rises to the surface, without assuming any form but, rather, insinuating itself between the forms; a formless base, an autonomous and faceless existence."[126] Günther Anders, a student of Heidegger, already invoked in his critique of his teacher Kant's fundamental insight that we are always come belated to the world; that the basic experience of living is not being immersed in a meaningful world; that existing is essentially not being at home in the world (*Weltfremdheit*); that the world must always be established, since all knowledge is a posteriori.[127] Rejecting the organic and immersive image of the world, both as an a priori and pre-thematic home and as the lived body, is therefore a prerequisite to conceptualizing inorganic life.

For a proper transcendental empiricism, the outside that awakens the soul must be traced beyond the organism and the lived body, because relying on the phenomenological hypothesis of the lived body only serves to reveal that "the lived body is still a paltry thing in comparison with a more profound and almost unlivable Power [*Puissance*]."[128] Simply substituting consciousness with the body as the identity pole does not give us a life free from the (organic) form of judgement, but means that we remain trapped within a logic of negativity. As such, the body functions as a substitute for the theological concept of the soul,[129] simultaneously presupposing and guaranteeing unity and identity (through negativity). The concept of the

---

125 Ibid.
126 Deleuze, *Difference and Repetition*, p. 275.
127 See Günther Anders, *Die Weltfremdheit Des Menschen. Schriften Zur Philosophischen Anthropologie* (Munich: C.H. Beck, 2018).
128 Gilles Deleuze, *Francis Bacon: The Logic of Sensation* (Minneapolis: University of Minnesota Press, 2005), p. 44.
129 As Deleuze and Guattari note in *Anti-Oedipus*: "The 'body-image'—the final avatar of the soul, a vague conjunction of the requirements of spiritualism and positivism." Deleuze and Guattari, *Anti-Oedipus*, p. 23.

body is the last bastion of God.[130] The lived body functions as an Orphic Guardian, keeping us from descending into "the intense world of differences, in which we find the reason behind the qualities and the being of the sensible, [which] is precisely the object of a superior empiricism."[131] We must suspend the lived body—meaning the belief in its primordial naturalness and self-evidence—to find the inorganic element, the being of the sensible: the unlivable.

[130] There is ample evidence that Deleuze might underestimate Merleau-Ponty's position on the flesh at times, or even that Merleau-Ponty might have a concept close to Deleuze's "body without organs." See, for example, Dylan Trigg's reading of Merleau-Ponty, where he is read as an non-phenomenologist, whose work provides a non-unified image of the body (Dylan Trigg, "The Role of the Earth in Merleau-Ponty's Archaeological Phenomenology," *Chiasmi International* 16 [2014], p. 255–273). Accounts of how Deleuze might underestimate Merleau-Ponty's late developments, especially the "flesh," can be found here: compare Jeffrey Bell, "The World Is an Egg: Realism, Mathematics, and the Thresholds of Difference," *Speculations* (2013); Henry Somers-Hall, "Deleuze and Merleau-Ponty: An Aesthetics of Difference," *Symposium, the Canadian Journal of Continental Philosophy* 10, no. 1 (2006), p. 213–222; Judith Wambacq, "Depth and Time in Merleau-Ponty and Deleuze," *Chiasmi International*, no. 13 (2011), p. 327–348; Judith Wambacq, "Maurice Merleau-Ponty and Gilles Deleuze as Interpreters of Henri Bergson," in *Transcendentalism Overturned*, ed. Anna-Teresa Tymieniecka (Dordrecht: Springer Netherlands, 2011), p. 269–284, and Judith Wambacq, "Maurice Merleau-Ponty's Criticism on Bergson's Theory of Time Seen Through The Work of Gilles Deleuze," *Studia Phaenomenologica* 11 (January 1, 2011).
[131] Deleuze, *Difference and Repetition*, p. 57.

# THE MONSTROUS EPIGENESIS
# OF THE TRANSCENDENTAL

### THE UNLIVABLE, OR THE TRANSCENDENTAL ENCOUNTER

In a letter written on July 7, 1688, William Molyneux poses the following question to his friend John Locke: would a blind person, who has learned to distinguish between a cube and a globe by touch, be able to recognize the shapes through his vision only, were he to suddenly gain sight?[132] This thought experiment, today known as Molyneux's problem, captured the seventeenth century imagination and beyond, and has prompted answers from many of the most important scholars debating the relation of perception and understanding.[133] The appeal of this question could be rooted in the interest in illuminating the processes of understanding by defining the outlines of both visual and tangible perception, especially with respect to their differences, which in turn must be considered in the broader context of the Enlightenment, and would later culminate in what is now known as cognitive science and psychophysics.[134] Another, more speculative, reason for this appeal might be that the author of the *Dioptrica Nova*[135] touches on the exact same themes of mediation and/in aesthetics which underlie the beginnings of Western philosophy. The idea of the blind man starting to see mirrors the scene in the cave described in Plato's *Republic*: Ἀλήθεια, moving from ἡΛήθη to λόγος.[136] As Galloway notes on this parallel: "Just as Plato's pupils must

---

132  John Locke, *An Essay Concerning Human Understanding* (Oxford: Oxford University Press, 1979), p. 146.
133  Notably, of course, Berkeley, Leibniz, Diderot, Voltaire, La Mettrie, Helmholtz, William James, and many more.
134  See Nicholas Pastore, *Selective History of Theories of Visual Perception, 1650–1950* (Oxford: Oxford University Press, 1971); Jessica Riskin, *Science in the Age of Sensibility: The Sentimental Empiricists of the French Enlightenment* (Chicago: University of Chicago Press, 2002), and Alessandra Jacomuzzi, Pietro Kobau, and Nicolo Bruno, "Molyneux' Question Redux," *Phenomenology and the Cognitive Sciences* 2, no. 4 (2003), p. 255–280.
135  Molyneux, himself a physician, must be credited with helping to establish the field of optics as a science, in particular the understanding of visuality as translucence.
136  That it is primarily a problem of mediation also explains the recurrence of this thought

wrestle with the murkiness of false knowledge and the hope of higher cognition unified by the light, Molyneux's blind man must determine if and how his newfound sensory ability will aid the communicative interplay between self and world."[137] In a certain sense, the communicative faculties are transformed in this encounter with the world, however rationalist or empiricist the description of this transformation might be. With the first successful cataract operations of Cheselden and Grant in the early eighteenth century providing actual examples of the problem, Locke's empiricist answer came to seem like the most plausible. While detractors like Condilliac or Diderot were quick to dismiss the results of the operations due to alleged disturbances of the eyes' proper functioning after the operations, subsequent repetitions of the procedure rendered this discussion a moot point.[138] The records of Marius von Senden give a clear account of the experiences of congenitally blind persons being able to see again after cataract removal operations. They give testament to the turbulent and often frightening chaos of colors and forms within which neither shape nor space as such seem to emerge initially. To be able to distinguish by sight between objects which were previously only known by touch, it is first necessary to establish ordered, pre-reflexive sense experience by developing the schemata common to ordinary experience. Such a process proved to be one of hard work and often painful learning.[139] The encounter between human and world is not a pleasant dialogue; being is rather a constant clamor, as are we.

experiment when discussing sensory substitution systems. See Mazviita Chrimuuta and Mark Paterson, "A Methodological Molyneux Question," in *Perception and Its Modalities*, ed. Dustin Stokes, Mohan Matthen, and Stephen Biggs (Oxford: Oxford University Press, 2014).

[137] Alexander R. Galloway, "Love of the Middle," in *Excommunication: Three Inquiries in Media and Mediation*, by Alexander R. Galloway, Eugene Thacker, and McKenzie Wark (Chicago: Chicago University Press, 2013), p. 26.

[138] Compare Daniel Smith, "Space and Sight," *Mind* 109, no. 435 (2000), p. 496. However, a possible way to dismiss the results of Cheselden and Grant's operations might be to argue that *in principle* or *de jure* the blind man, on being able to see again, could distinguish both objects by sight, but is hindered from doing so by the purely *de facto* physical weakness of the eyes. While this argument helps to shift the weight of the burden of proof back to the other side, it only succeeds in doing that.

[139] Compare Marius von Senden, *Space and Sight: The Perception of Space and Shape in the Congenitally Blind before and after Operation* (London: Free Press, 1960).

Given the implications of these results, especially the implication that space is neither unified nor a priori, it is all the more puzzling that Kant, even though aware of the findings,[140] did not deal with them when constructing his critical philosophy. Some have even claimed that "had Kant considered Molyneux's question and the evidence provided by the Cheselden operation, then he would not have written the Transcendental Analytic."[141] If space is an a priori form of intuition, as the first argument of the Exposition demonstrates, and space is "one," which is the claim of the third argument, then the newly sighted person should not have any difficulty identifying objects by sight. Since there are substantial difficulties in doing so, one or even both premises must be wrong—a point that the early empiricist critics and reviewers Feder and Pistorius made.[142] Even though one could argue that their Lockean, empiricist critique misconstrues Kant as nativist with respect to the "common scheme of space and its division in all sorts of figures, distances and outlines,"[143] as Feder had it, this does not delegitimize the problem they raised. As an example, let us consider the following as a Kantian defense: one might dispute the relevance of such empirical evidence for an investigation into the transcendental conditions of perception. Even though the difference in visual and tangible perception *might* indicate a transcendental heterogeneity and thereby call into question the essential oneness of space, this is not a *necessary* conclusion. While the difference of the functioning of the senses is an empirical matter, it is not necessarily a transcendental one. It is very well possible to grant that, empirically speaking, space is perceived differently by the different senses, but say that this experience is grounded in a homogeneous transcendental space that is actualized only empirically as heterogeneous. This solution, however, sidesteps the actual problem, since it intentionally

---

140   Sutara lists all the occasions Kant mentions them in his lectures; see Vladimir Satura, *Kants Erkenntnispsychologie in Den Nachschriften Seiner Vorlesungen Über Empirische Psychologie* (Bonn: Bouvier, 1971), p. 83f.
141   Brigitte Sassen, "Kant on Molyneux's Problem," *British Journal for the History of Philosophy* 12, no. 3 (2004), p. 471.
142   For a detailed account of this early criticism, see Brigitte Sassen, ed., *Kant's Early Critics: The Empiricist Critique of the Theoretical Philosophy* (Cambridge; New York: Cambridge University Press, 2000), p. 16f., 26f.
143   Sassen, "Kant on Molyneux's Problem," p. 122.

obfuscates the connection between the a priori form of intuition and actual visual and tangible perception by simply circumventing the criterion of evidence. This would suggest the opposite conclusion, namely that the difference in perceptions of space does not hint at a homogeneous spatiality across the senses, but an essential multiplicity of space. While such issues are almost unavoidable for psychological-temporal readings of the Transcendental Aesthetic, the epistemic reading might offer an ad hoc solution—but only through the triple sacrifice of weakening the scope of it, endorsing a position Kant himself probably would not have held[144] and finally abandoning the question of origins when it comes to the grounds of spatial representation. This last drawback was already anticipated by Kant's early critics, who conceded that space is the *de jure* condition of all figuratively determined representations of objects of outer sense, while simultaneously noting that this shrouds the *de facto* origins of this condition in mystery even more—an impasse that the Molyneux problem would highlight. Epistemic readings with a nativist twist, e.g. Sassen's deflationary solution, again presuppose a good will of thought, insofar as experience strives towards unity *naturally*. Even if the faculties fail in establishing such unity, these cases are to be regarded as failures of an otherwise primary drive towards representation, which is justified by falling back on nativism. Hence, a solution for the Molyneux problem cannot be found without giving credence to the empiricist solution of the problem.

In terms of acquiring proficiency in synthesizing sensations and hence simultaneously in forming and applying a schema as the transcendental ground for representational experience, the newly sighted person is confronted with similar obstacles to an infant learning to see. Studies in developmental psychology indicate that the world of the infant is initially populated by pure intensities—floating colors, sleepiness, hunger, disconnected sounds etc.—which are organized over time.[145] Though the infant does not distinguish itself from the world at this early point, it is not

---

[144] There is significantly more textual evidence in favor of the psychological-temporal reading of the Transcendental Aesthetic than the epistemic.

[145] Compare Daniel N. Stern, *Interpersonal World of the Infant: A View from Psychoanalysis and Development* (New York: Basic Books, 1985).

because of a primordial (all-encompassing and personal) bond between world and organism but because of the free interplay of intensities, which have not yet formed the conditions necessary for even pre-thematic meaning. Following Husserl's criteria for both evidence and reconstruction, Straus inserts a radical genetic perspective into phenomenology, firstly by distinguishing between perception and sensation, the former being a rational organization of the latter.[146] This allows him, secondly, to investigate the pre-rational domain of sensation as coextensive with perception but temporally prior. This is best illustrated by the difference and relation between geography—the perceptual, conceptual and non-perspectival representation of the world as recorded on maps—and the actual landscape as sensory, perspectival and pre-thematic; or Merleau-Ponty's differentiation of touching and pointing.[147] However, such distinctions, while providing a limited genetic account, still rely on the unifying workings of a ground of synthesis, most predominantly the lived body, which provide the (external) logic of sensation. Deleuze, however, will attempt to think the logic of sensation from the being of the sensible. In a similar way, the landscapes of Cézanne do not represent the interactive surroundings of a lived body; rather, they aim to capture the "world before humanity."[148] The painter is instructed by Cézanne to paint always at close range, to lose themselves in the landscape until the "stubborn geometries"[149] of the world, that is, forms and even matter, collapse and only forces remain.

It is this catastrophe which Kant's sublime foreshadows and Deleuze universalizes, insofar as he recognizes the fundamental fragility of the relationship between synthesis and its ground. There is always the pos-

---

146 See Erwin Straus, *The Primary World of the Senses* (New York: Free Press, 1963).
147 Merleau-Ponty describes cases in which patients were able to scratch their nose without hesitation when a mosquito bit them, but were unable to point to their nose with their fingers, if asked to do so. While the former is an intentional corporeal act, which relies on the space of the body created by sensation, the latter requires more conceptual coordination within the external space of perception. Ordinary experience relies on the transition from one to the other, which in some pathological cases is interrupted; see Merleau-Ponty, *Phenomenology of Perception*, p. 102–106.
148 Joachim Gasquet, *Joachim Gasquet's Cézanne: A Memoir with Conversations* (London: Thames and Hudson, 1991), p. 160.
149 Ibid.

sibility of something formless emerging from beneath the ground, something groundless, and for this to interrupt the synthesis. This unlivable emerging element, the inorganic life of nature or chaos, which disrupts the "proper" or usual workings of the synthesis, is, however, precisely and paradoxically the germ of rhythm and order itself. This makes the breaking point of normal perception not an exception but the revelation of an ungroundedness, the genetic foundation of synthesis. What Cézanne does, then, is not render the visible, but render visible the forces that are the conditions of sensibility but are themselves not sensible. He stages an encounter. Similarly, "the Literary Machine," itself concerned with the production of signs, is, as Proust once suggested about his own work, a "kind of magnifying glass"[150] able to produce a literary effect, much like we would speak of an electromagnetic or optical effect. It enacts creation from an "unground" by producing signs of different orders to function effectively, shifting the task of literature from meaning to problems of use. Most significantly, Deleuze discovers this shift in the work of Artaud, who introduces a difference in kind between the image of thought and thinking into his work, in that he "opposes genitality to innateness in thinking."[151] The opposition to the notion of reason as the true medium of the encounter which we have already seen in Feuerbach reoccurs in Artaud's theatre of cruelty, which is essentially a theatre of the nervous system. Shocking sounds and music, disturbing lighting and frenetic speeches disclose the "cruelty at the foundation of every spectacle," so that "in the state of degeneracy in which we live, it is through the skin that metaphysics will be made to re-enter our minds."[152] Instead of rejecting language as the beginning of philosophizing, as Feuerbach does, favoring intuition in its place, Artaud subverts the traditional poetic use of language, concerned either with meaning or harmonious form, by introducing the forces back into it which form the genetic conditions of it. The flow of air that makes speech possible becomes perceptible through

---

[150] Gilles Deleuze, *Proust and Signs* (Minneapolis: University of Minnesota Press, 2000), p. 145.
[151] Deleuze, *Difference and Repetition*, p. 147.
[152] Antonin Artaud, "The Theatre of Cruelty: First Manifesto (1932)," in *Antonin Artaud. Selected Writings* (New York: Farrar, Straus and Giroux, 1976), p. 251.

a stutter or by using breath as an effect itself. The schizophrenic connections of words and sounds, which reject any pre-existing categorial framework, are paradigmatic encounters with the forces which give the sensible, without being sensible within the framework of representation. The deformation or *deterritorialization* of language, as Deleuze would say, provides a model for the proper transcendental use of a faculty, i.e. the use of language becomes properly transcendental when it operates at the very limits of its sustainability, opening up to its conditions, which are themselves not representable within language, in the same way that structures of thought rely on conditions (for their genesis) that cannot be represented properly in thought. Thus, as Deleuze notes in the *Essays Critical and Clinical,* "Literature is a passage of life that traverses outside the lived and the livable";[153] it can move from the personal to the impersonal, which, while not being lived, is still very fundamentally our life, as Proust notes.

There is always something that cannot be lived, which traverses presence and at the same time operates outside it. Derrida, in his critique of Husserl's characterization of historical genesis as grounded in the presupposition of subjective genesis (i.e. the present subject can intuit something true for any subject ahistorically), already indicates this irretrievably lost element as the core of the structuration of the present: death. If the Husserlian conception of truth as the eternal within the finite is refused, life then becomes the bearer of a constitutive forgetting of the non-living as a genetic element of the lived, which affects even the auto-affection of a lived body and prompts the constitutive link between auto-affection, hetero-affection and auto-immunity. While, for Derrida, any return to the genesis is (always already) impossible because of the operation of the structuring effects brought about by the genesis, Deleuze solves this impasse metaphysically by eradicating the opposition between genesis and structure. In his later work, this unlivable element is the event, which

---

[153] Deleuze, *Essays Critical and Clinical,* p.1.

is not the state of affairs. It is actualized in a state of affairs, in a body, in a lived, but it has a shadowy and secret part that is continually subtracted from or added to its actualization: in contrast with the state of affairs, it neither begins nor ends but has gained or kept the infinite movement to which it gives consistency [...] The event is immaterial, incorporeal, unlivable: pure reserve.[154]

It is this unlivable event, which resists communicability, that is, the condition of intentional reference and identity. This highlights the paradoxical tasks of inorganic vitality. It must simultaneously produce (or abstract) singularities and establish conjunctions between them, forming a whole that affects these singularities without closing in on them.[155]

In order to fulfill this radicalization of the epigenesis of the transcendental, which will not trace it from the outlines of the empirical, Deleuze follows the scent of violence, already present as a "chaos germ"[156] in Kant's third *Critique*, the "sublime image" that "makes the sun explode."[157] As we will see, proper transcendental philosophy must traverse the livable only to engage with the unlivable and move from the primacy of ontology to the process of ontogenesis. As we have seen, Deleuze identifies the ground of the common sense of the faculties of the first two *Critiques* in the genetic model of the sublime, which in the third *Critique* enables the faculties' "free agreement, indeterminate and unconditional."[158] Here, in the attempt to apprehend the "absolutely great," the imagination is pushed beyond its limits by reason demanding the unity of phenomena, and in the breakdown of aesthetic synthesis turns to Ideas to think its potential infinity. Hence, it reveals or makes comprehensible the Idea of Nature, which as super-sensible unity grounds our faculty of reason

---

154 Deleuze and Guattari, *What is Philosophy?*, p. 156.
155 Due to Deleuze's empiricist credo that all relations are external, the connections of the singularities must be established in and as addition.
156 Deleuze, *Essays Critical and Clinical*, p. 83.
157 Deleuze, *Difference and Repetition*, p. 89.
158 Deleuze, "The Idea of Genesis in Kant's Aesthetics," p. 61.

as well as Nature. It is the "negative pleasure"[159] of this "vibration"[160] or "conflict,"[161] the "harmony in pain,"[162] that Deleuze is interested in. For him, it is within the "pain of childbirth," as Nietzsche had it, that thinking inclines towards a "superior empiricism,"[163] shedding the conditions of possibility of the human. It is violence, which is also a new mode of communication, that informs the transition from Kant's conditioned to Deleuze's absolute epigenesis: "each faculty communicates to the other only the violence which confronts it with its own difference and its divergence from the other."[164] This discordant accord, revealing the determination of sensation by a super-sensible Idea, "manifests and liberates a depth which remained hidden."[165] That depth determines sensation without the determination being conceptual: this is what becomes the model for internal genesis.

### EXTERNAL AND INTERNAL DETERMINATION

As we have remarked before, the separation of thinking and being in Kant is due to his rejection of any possibility of the internal determination of the sensible/material, which necessitates an extrinsic application of the concept through the schema. The genesis of this mediator could not be explained, and hence the material from an internal perspective must "remain undetermined."[166] Hence, Kant has recourse to empirical differences to determine things "negatively" in relation to each other, whilst not being able to give an account of the positive constitution enabling such negation. Having no account of an internal genesis that would determine things prior to negation, empirical differences must ground the

---

159 Kant, *Critique of Judgement*, p. 213.
160 Ibid., p. 258.
161 Ibid.
162 Deleuze, *Kant's Critical Philosophy*, p. 62.
163 Deleuze, *Difference and Repetition*, p. 69.
164 Ibid., p. 146.
165 Deleuze, *Kant's Critical Philosophy*, p. 60.
166 Kant, *Critique of Pure Reason*, B134.

relation between things by establishing a resemblance on a level of generality that is external to each individual thing. In Kant, things (in general) resemble each other in their objectivity and hence differ only in degrees of various kinds (temporal duration, causal efficiency, spatial extent and so on), as per the relation of phenomenalism and somatism we saw in the last chapter.

Instead of resting content with the extrinsic application of concepts to sensation, Deleuze attempts to find the internal relation between the undetermined, determinability and the determined. A Leibnizian rationalist's solution would insist on the complete a priori determination of a (determinable) object by the concept. The idealism of Hegel would posit the necessary sublation of both elements into a new (indeterminable) unity.[167] What both methods have in common is that they fill the gap between the determinable and determination, leaving no space for an internal genesis of the thing, which would avoid the incongruence of determination and determinant by making the determination no broader than the thing itself. To describe such internal genesis, Deleuze must recover the unconditioned, or that which is not yet subject to the conditioning of transcendental apperception, but is at the same time able to determine both the condition and the conditioned. As we saw in the previous chapter, Kant had already tried to provide such a ground by applying the form of the syllogism, under the direction of the categories, to the synthetic unity of intuition, producing pure concepts of reason or transcendental Ideas. For Deleuze, the Kantian conception of Idea is promising for an account of internal genesis because it seems to contain all three moments of determination. The Idea is undetermined insofar as it cannot be the determinate object of any intuition. Even if only applied to the manifold of sensation, the Idea remains both immanent and transcendent to experience, insofar as it can fulfill its regulative role only if none of the objects in experience ever exhaust it, or in other words, the Idea "remains a problem to

---

[167] See Beth Lord, "Deleuze and Kant," in *The Cambridge Companion to Deleuze*, ed. Daniel Smith and Henry Somers-Hall (Cambridge: Cambridge University Press, 2012), p. 86.

which there is no solution."[168] Hence, it differs in kind from the actual and is therefore not subject to categories or concepts, something which prevents the resemblance of the transcendental and the actual. But, insofar as the Idea regulates the use of the understanding, it is to a certain extent determined "in respect of the employment of our reason in respect to the world"[169] and is hence determinable. Furthermore, insofar as we assume an object to be completely determinable, the Idea provides the totality of all possible properties an object could possess as contradictory pairs and allows for the determination of the one that actually obtains in the object. The Idea is thus present in the determined object as a totality. Although undetermined, insofar as it cannot be an object of experience, the Idea is determinable in the process of predication through analogy and determined in the actual object as the totality of all sustainable predicates; thus it seems to provide the ground for internal genesis.

Making the Idea amenable to judgement only serves, however, to orient the use of the understanding towards the unity of moral or natural law, which then affirms the organic image of thought. The use of the Idea is strictly regulative and not productive, systematizing the knowledge of already constituted empirical differences and excluding the problem of their genesis. This limited use of the Ideas in Kant enables our thinking to encompass the sum total of all possible relations between representations in three forms: "the absolute (unconditioned) unity of the thinking subject," or the Idea of the subject, "the absolute unity of the series of conditions of appearance," or the Idea of the world, and "the absolute unity of the conditions of all objects of thought in general."[170] While these Ideas cannot be an object of experience, they are nonetheless thinkable and must be thought in their regulative function, to attain the highest degree of systematicity in knowledge. Although not being beyond experience, they still have structures amenable to judgement and hence incorporate into organic representation everything that would potentially fall outside it by being

---

[168] Kant, *Critique of Pure Reason*, A328/B384.
[169] Ibid., A698/B726.
[170] Ibid., A334/B391.

imperceptible. Through the progressive use of the Idea in relation to the empirically given and hence conditioned, the Idea serves only "to further and strengthen in infinitum (indeterminately) the empirical employment of reason"[171] and hence is restricted to the regulative role of systematizing our knowledge of the world and not the constitution of the world itself.

While the Idea might give an account of the process of movement from the ideal problem to its empirical solution, Kant refers the problem back to its solution, hence establishing a resemblance between the two. As such the determinability and the determination of the Idea remain external characteristics, referring not to the Idea itself, but to actual empirical things. According to Deleuze, Kant thus organizes the three aspects (the determination, the determinable and the undetermined) as belonging to different Ideas: God as the sum total of all possibilities is the ideal for determination, the determinable world and the undetermined subject. Kant proceeds like a biologist ordering every living thing, according to their similarities and differences, into kingdom, phylum, class, order, family, genus, and species, *assuming* the existence of a systematic unity in nature. A taxonomic account such as this cannot give us any idea of onto- or phylogenesis. Instead, taking this systematization to be the goal of reason, it excludes them. An account of internal genesis must therefore establish the connection between the ideal real and the empirical real internally, hence giving an account of the problem which gives rise to a solution that does not depend on the latter as a condition.

### THE IDEA AS NON-ORGANIC LIFE

Forfeiting the possibility of investigating the internal relations of the concept and the Idea to being, Kant restricts the sensible to what can be given in experience, excluding any consideration of its being in itself. Sensation within the critical project is always already anticipated, restrained by representation. Deleuze, in contrast, recovers the ontologi-

---

[171] Ibid., A680/B708.

cal dimension of what Kant called "empirically real," what, in Kant, was the "element which cannot be anticipated."[172] He shifts towards the transcendental principles of genesis in the passive intuition of sensation prior to the synthesis performed by the transcendental unity of apperception. The violence of thought in the discordant accord of the sublime already provides us with the model for the non-conceptual determination of sensation. As we have seen, the faculties must pass through the model of the sublime in order to free themselves from common and good sense by each transcending its limits in their discordant exercise. This confrontation of the faculties was engendered by the encounter with a paradoxical element. Hence, rather than our spontaneity in the act of thought being its own ground, something else engenders thought, but what "forces us to think [...] is not a sensible being, but the being of the sensible. It is not the given but that by which the given is given. It is therefore in a certain sense the imperceptible."[173] This "certain sense" refers to organic representation, for which only what conforms to good and common sense can *be*. The being of the sensible, however, is the inorganic, imperceptible and disruptive, or what is for representation the unlivable at the heart of the lived.[174]

To characterize this accordance in discord, Deleuze relies on Maimon's readings of Kant's transcendental philosophy (particularly his notion of "differentials"), which prefigure transcendental empiricism in certain respects, though Deleuze will, of course, turn these readings on their head. In his *Essay on Transcendental Philosophy* Maimon had already identified the separation of the understanding and sensibility as the reason for the failure both to explain experience *de facti* and to solve the question of the application of concepts *de jure*. Within the investigation of possible experience, "this problem is insoluble"[175] due to the difference in kind of the two sources of cognition; an account of real experience, however, sidesteps

---

172 Ibid., A167/B209.
173 Deleuze, *Difference and Repetition*, p. 140.
174 Compare Jeffrey Bell, *Deleuze and Guattari's What Is Philosophy?* (Edinburgh: Edinburgh University Press, 2016), p. 201.
175 Gideon Freudenthal, ed., *Salomon Maimon: Rational Dogmatist, Empirical Skeptic; Critical Assessments* (Dordrecht: Kluwer, 2003), p. 118.

this problem by examining qualitative sensation in its genesis. Maimon circumvents the problem of the difference between being and thinking by referring the finite understanding to the infinite intellect, as Spinoza or Leibniz had similarly done, which operates by producing its objects while and through intuiting them. In the understanding, "differentials" give the rules for the generation of intensive qualities, the ideas of the understanding. While Deleuze equally attempts to explain the ideal genesis of the real, for him it is sensation that must be considered primary, which helps avoid the rationalist or even absolute idealism of Maimon. Insofar as thought always comes to us through intensity, which can only be felt, thinking can only be thought of as something conditioned by a "transcendental sensibility."[176] Refining the identity of being and thought, "the intensive or difference in intensity is at once both the object of the encounter and the object to which the encounter raises sensibility."[177] This gives rise to a violently forced movement from the sensibility to the imagination, from the imagination to memory and from memory to thought, each faculty through its difference pushing itself and the other faculties to the limit.

This depth of Ideas, therefore, cannot pre-exist the experience but rather must be expressed in it. However, since Ideas do not resemble the surface of the sensible, because they are not traced from its outline, they remain conditions irreducible to real experience. Hence the super-sensible realm of Ideas cannot be actual, but it is still real or, as Deleuze characterizes the virtual, which is the ideal part of the real, "real but not actual, ideal but not abstract."[178] They are real and not abstract because they follow from an encounter with the being of the sensible.

This movement towards the being of the sensible informs the structure of *Difference and Repetition*, which could be viewed as a rereading of the first *Critique* through the third, and the critique of the possible in *Bergsonism*. Integrating many earlier works, the book takes the capacity to mediate between the faculties from the Transcendental Analytic and trans-

---

176  Deleuze, *Difference and Repetition*, p. 144.
177  Ibid., p. 145.
178  Ibid., p. 94.

poses it into the realm of the Transcendental Aesthetic, presenting the synthesis of reason and sensibility as non-conceptual through a process of spatio-temporal individuation. In the absence of the conceptual subsumption of the aesthetic manifold, unity is explained through the incarnation of the dialectical Idea, which in turn is the (super-sensible) depth of sensation and hence not preceding it. Or, in other words, because individuation determines the actualization of a virtual multiplicity, the transcendental is not bigger than the empirical, the condition is coextensive with the conditioned. At the same time, the transcendental is not derived from the empirical, since the Idea is not a possible object of experience. We will proceed by elaborating on the concepts of the Idea, intensive difference and individuation, as well as their intricate relation, but it is worth pausing first to recapitulate the ambitious aims of Deleuze's approach. His move towards real experience and hence "intrinsic genesis, not an extrinsic conditioning,"[179] must conceptualize conditions that are determined simultaneously with the conditioned, or in other words conditions that are singular rather than universal. However, something must determine the conditions as well as the conditioned to account for internal genesis, something itself unconditioned. Hegel had already provided such an account in his notion of "totality," which is necessary for the possibility of individuation through negation, since determination for Hegel is only possible by determining what the determinate differs from.[180] If such a negation is applied to something for which all relations to other objects are not exhaustively known, no determination is possible, due to the fact of it not being a totality. But Deleuze, who opposes negation as determination, must give a positive or affirmative account of individuation. He will do so through the "differential." It is his opposition to Hegel that informs his further move away from a developmental model of genesis (e.g. through historical determination) to a genesis from the virtual to the actual, or, from the virtual multiplicity of Ideas to actual entities. We will proceed by calling the Ideas which make up the virtual *structures*, as does Deleuze: "Structure is the reality of

---

[179] Ibid., p. 154.
[180] Dean Moyar, *Hegel's Conscience* (Oxford: Oxford University Press, 2011), p. 29.

the virtual."[181] Hence, the concepts of structure and Idea will be used interchangeably in the following. By situating the Ideas within the sensible, breaking with the identification of the Ideas with Reason, Deleuze resituates them within experience. The noumenal is immanent. Yet, the intensities and Ideas that condition experience are not exhausted in actual experience, i.e. they remain supra-sensible. Even though they operate below and above the human's threshold of the conditions of lived experience, they draw on the human, dragging her into nonhuman becomings. This power of Ideas to engender becomings, presenting itself as the deformed or unformed in Nature, is the force of inorganic life:

> The non-organic life of things, a frightful life, which is obvious to the wisdom and limits of the organism [...] It is vital as potent pre-organic germinality, common to the animate and the inanimate, to a matter which raises itself to the point of life, and to a life which spreads itself through all matter.[182]

In essence, therefore, the overcoming of hylomorphism, and thus the suspension of the organic image of thought, is predicated on solving the problem that these models of external determination were a solution to. This means providing an account of determination that does not rely on external but instead on internal determination, or which relies on internal genesis instead of extrinsic conditioning—in short, a positive and affirmative account of the absolute epigenesis of the transcendental.

As we will see in the next section, the passage through transcendental idealism for Deleuze is opened by a reconceptualization of non-chronological time, which through the analysis of the temporal fracture of the "I" reveals an account of internal determination proper.

---

[181] Deleuze, *Difference and Repetition*, p. 270. As Protevi jokingly remarks, one could substitute the title *Difference and Repetition* with "Structure and Genesis." See John Protevi, "Preparing to Learn from *Difference and Repetition*," *Journal of Philosophy. A Cross-Disciplinary Inquiry* 11, no. 5 (2010), p. 35–45.

[182] Gilles Deleuze, *Cinema 1. The Movement-Image* (Minneapolis: University of Minnesota Press, 1986), p. 50, 55.

# THE INORGANIC LIFE OF THE IDEAS

### TEMPORALITY AND NORMATIVITY

*The Three Syntheses of Time: I. Habit*
If one substituted the notion of "structure" for "time," Schaub asks, in Deleuze's "How Do We Recognize Structuralism?," what would happen?[183] Although she leaves the answer open to debate, the question indicates already the strong correlation of time (the paradoxical element of structure) with normativity, i.e. of the genesis and application of rules. As mentioned above, structures give rules for determination (or individuation), while having an internal relationship to what is determined (the actual). The model for such a determination will be provided by time, as we will see. There are two things to consider here. On the one hand, the question of life is, as we have seen, inextricably linked to normativity. Traditionally, the property of autonomy characterizes the organism's specificity. Therefore, the conceptualization of the conditions of structuration (i.e. the conditions of the formation of rules and their application in the processes of production and action) forms a crucial element for the understanding of "life." On the other hand, the connection of time and structuration in Deleuze's ontology is expressed in various (sometimes inconsistent) ways: as radicalization of transcendental philosophy after Kant, as process ontology after Whitehead, as structuralist serialization after Lacan, as system theoretical functions after Bateson, etc. We will clarify below which approach we are going to follow, in order to render the *Bauplan* more transparent.

Much like Schelling's *Weltalter*-project, Deleuze's philosophy of time attempts to ground all modal temporality in becoming, which is understood as qualitative change without external cause, engendered by an im-

---

[183] See Mirjam Schaub, *Gilles Deleuze Im Wunderland: Zeit- Als Ereignisphilosophie* (Munich: Fink, 2003), p. 45.

manent equitemporality of all temporal modes.[184] It is the coexistence of all temporal modalities that is able to supply a proper concept of becoming but is the most incomprehensible or paradoxical aspect of Deleuze's philosophy at first glance. The second chapter of *Difference and Repetition* demonstrates the consistency of such an equitemporality by laying out three distinct syntheses—the grounding, ground and ungrounding of time—which correspond to the three temporal modalities. The employment of the third synthesis (thought) provides, paradoxically by failing, a model of time as radical openness, novelty and event, i.e. becoming. The architecture of the chapter betrays both his proximity and his distance to Kant. The employment of the three syntheses mirrors to some degree the structure of the synthesis in the transcendental in the *Critique of Pure Reason*. Also, Deleuze utilizes a very similar retrospective technique to the one Kant utilized in the "Doctrine of Method." But while Kant consolidated the *Bauplan* non-linearly, Deleuze's rereading of the first synthesis from the vantage point of the third establishes radical linearity. In the first and the second synthesis, Deleuze proceeds from an active to a passive synthesis, which conditions the former, meaning a synthesis that while occurring in the mind is not a result of this mind's activity. The third synthesis in its failure, then, reveals the first two as being conditioned by pure difference (meaning radical disunity) or the pure and empty form of time.[185]

The first synthesis contracts repeated independent instances to form the living present, grounding time. The temporal modalities of the past and the future are created and appear as ecstasies of the present, which Husserl described in terms of retention and protention.[186] By thus

---

[184] Compare Friedrich Wilhelm Joseph Schelling, *Weltalter-Fragmente* (Stuttgart: Frommann-Holzboog, 2002).

[185] The following depiction of the three syntheses of time is reduced to an absolute structural minimum, since only the third synthesis is of interest for the present work. For in-depth analysis and commentary on Deleuze's philosophy of time, see James Williams, *Gilles Deleuze's Philosophy of Time: A Critical Introduction and Guide* (Edinburgh: Edinburgh University Press, 2011), and also Keith W. Faulkner, *Deleuze and the Three Syntheses of Time* (New York: Peter Lang, 2006), for a well-structured account of Deleuze's three syntheses of time.

[186] See Edmund Husserl, *On the Phenomenology of the Consciousness of Internal Time (1893–1917)* (Dordrecht: Kluwer Academic Publishers, 1991).

schematizing successions, it creates a horizon of anticipations, which the field of past instances can be related to. Drawing on Hume, Deleuze describes this contraction of instances as a novelty that breaks mechanical repetition by introducing a difference, namely the formation of a habit, thus creating a generality. The pre-reflective grounding of time in the passive synthesis of habit moves therefore from the past to the future and from the particular to the general. This generality, created by the imagination, differs from the conceptual generalities that the understanding produces. While the latter stores sequences of events quantitatively, the former's formation is qualitative, like a "sensitive plate"[187] capturing the relation of the instances, not their sequence. It is hence not mathematical time but a system of anticipations that is grounded in the synthesis of habit. Moreover, the possibility of the active synthesis of the higher faculties that Kant described is thus conditioned by the prior passive synthesis that grounds time, enabling the relation of remembered, present and anticipated sensations and establishing the reference point for transcendental apperception, the subject. Once these conditions are furnished by the passive synthesis, the "past is then no longer the immediate past of retention, but the reflexive past of representation, of reflexive and reproduced particularity."[188] The subject in this empiricist conception is conceived of as the organization of impressions, which is itself not the agent of synthesis but constituted as a system of anticipation. Building on the consequences of the basic empiricist assumption of the externality of relations to their objects, that is, the assumption is that contraction does not change anything in the repeated instances themselves but rather in the contemplating mind, Deleuze reverses the Kantian idea of constitution. Insofar as the subject or transcendental apperception is itself produced by and as habit, a pre-subjective imagination must be supposed as the agent of the formation of habits without the condition of the subtle cognitive apparatus Kant describes. While Hume is willing to extend this ability to contract instances to animals and small children, expanding the psycho-

---

[187] Deleuze, *Difference and Repetition*, p. 70.
[188] Ibid., p. 71.

logical realm, Deleuze attempts to further ground this mental synthesis in a material realm.[189] Unlike in the Kantian model, whenever we encounter rhythmic behaviors in nature, e.g. the heartbeat, there is a self, i.e. the subjective organization of time by a formation of a habit. Various habits coexist next to or are nested within each other. This has been followed up with a transdisciplinary attempt to better explain temporalities in biology, that is, in the science of organized beings,[190] but the consequences of Deleuze's conception that "everything is contemplation"[191] are far wider reaching. These will be examined in the next chapter ("Absolute Xenogenesis") of this book.

*The Three Syntheses of Time: II. Memory*

The grounding of time in the first synthesis is insufficient for explaining time as a whole, including the past. Exposing the gap in the lived experience in the present and guiding the subsequent analysis of the pure past beyond the present are three paradoxes, which arise from the attempt to conceive of the past in terms of the present, and which Deleuze seeks to resolve. The first paradox relates to the problem of how the present becomes the past. Insofar as past experiences are only relevant in the first synthesis as procedural memory, they are only retained as long as they are involved in the formation of the living present. The past appears for the living present only as instances for the formation of anticipations. This is crucial because the living present is not coextensive with time itself, since the present passes. Such a passing would however not be possible within the present itself. This dilemma becomes apparent when we try and remember a past moment. We represent not only the past but

---

[189] See David Hume, *A Treatise on Human Nature* (Oxford: Oxford University Press, 2000), 1.3.16.
[190] Protevi discusses this "organic time" in multiple places: see John Protevi, "Larval Subjects, Autonomous Systems, and E. Coli Chemotaxis," in *Deleuze and the Body*, ed. Laura Guillaume and Joe Hughes (Edinburgh: Edinburgh University Press, 2011), p. 35, and John Protevi, *Life, War, Earth: Deleuze and the Sciences* (Minneapolis: University of Minnesota Press, 2013), p. 155f. A more in-depth analysis of habit and biological time can be found in Tano Posteraro, "Habits, Nothing But Habits: Biological Time in Deleuze," *The Comparatist* 40, no. 1 (2016), p. 94–110.
[191] Deleuze, *Difference and Repetition*, p. 75.

the present at the same time, bracketed as the present within which we remember. Because we can remember the past, something in the present must already be past while present, otherwise the constitution of the past would be inexplicable. The present could not pass on account of there being nothing it could pass into. To resolve this paradox, a second synthesis is needed, which accounts for the possibility of the present passing: a ground upon which a grounding of time can take place that is coexistent with the present. The second paradox relates to how the past coexists with the present. If the past is understood as isomorphic to the present as in Hume's account of memories as faded sensations, the past does not differ in kind from the present. Rather, it is conceived as an extended present, insofar as its coexistence with the present would consist in particular past instances relating to other particular present instances without any characteristic that distinguishes between the two types of instances.[192] If the passing of the present therefore entails a coexistence of the present and the past, with the latter not being derived from the former, they must be different in kind and not only in degree. Accordingly, because the lived experience is composed of atomic and self-sufficient presents, the past must be non-atomic. The past is hence not coexistent with the present as instances but as a whole. It is therefore more accurate to say that the past does not *exist* so much as *insist*. The third paradox arises when the past is thought of as a consequence of the present and the instances of the lived subsequently cannot pass. Deleuze insists that contrary to this the past must exist (or insist) prior to the grounding of the living present as its condition.

The account of Hume is here not contrasted but complemented by a modification of Bergson's critique of associationism from *Matter and Memory*. In the synthesis of reproduction, according to Kant, a past experience is related to a present one by the establishment of an affinity between both. The principles of such an affinity must be resemblance or contiguity. Building reproduction on resemblance causes problems, however, when the concrete application of the principle is considered: there are no

---

[192] Hume, *A Treatise on Human Nature*, p. 275.

two ideas or experiences that do not resemble each other in one aspect or another. Similarly, "why should an image which is, by hypothesis, self-sufficient, seek to accrue itself to others either similar or given in contiguity with it?"[193] This repeats the critique Kant had leveled against Hume's principles of association. Yet, opposing transcendental idealism, Bergson offers a different solution for the problem of reproduction. Prior to the constitution of individual parts, which are subject to active synthesis, resemblance is perceived or, in other words, the whole as an aggregate of continuous parts is perceived, before the individual parts emerge. Hence, the past conditions the affinity necessary for the grounding of time in the living present and therefore the past does not resemble the present.[194]

Bergson's reconceptualization of reproduction illuminates a key component in Deleuze's vitalism: the critique of the law. For any law to be applied, a certain territory must be presumed with discretely determined objects which it has legislative power over. This form of legislation, however, faces a twofold problem. Firstly, it is impossible to determine the conditions and processes of determination of the territory itself and the determined objects in it. Rather, such determinations (the demarcation of a territory and the designation of possible objects in it) must be presupposed as conditions without genesis. Secondly, since no such genesis of the territory and its objects can be given, the principles of their relation are either unthinkable or dogmatic. Since they must be presumed as already determined and since their relation cannot be internal, an external force must be employed that legitimizes such a presumption and imposes relations onto the objects: the activity of consciousness.[195] For any non-despotic employment of the rules, the inner genesis of the law and its objects must be accounted for by giving their real conditions, meaning also their conditions in the real.

---

[193] Bergson, *Matter and Memory*, p. 165.
[194] A more detailed analysis of the Bergsonian basis for Deleuze's philosophy of time can be found in Alia Al-Saji, "The Memory of Another Past: Bergson, Deleuze and a New Theory of Time," *Continental Philosophy Review* 37, no. 2 (June 2004), p. 203–239.
[195] The critique of the hypothetical law can be found in Deleuze, *Difference and Repetition*, p. 2.

*The Three Syntheses of Time: III. Thought, the Failing Synthesis*
The analysis of the "fractured I" in the third synthesis of time—the apex of the second chapter of *Difference and Repetition*—demonstrates the process of determining the solution from within the problem, although this is not yet characterized as an ideal process but instead as the "furtive and explosive moment which is not even continued by Kant"[196] from which the idea of transcendental empiricism springs. While the first two syntheses of time, the ground and grounding of time respectively, operate as passive syntheses underlying the active syntheses, the third "synthesis" of ungrounding is not subject to the active/passive dichotomy. The second chapter of *Difference and Repetition* mimics this involution from the active constitution of time in the activity of consciousness to passive synthesis by structuring it as a progressive deduction, in which the first synthesis is predicated on the functioning of the second to resolve the paradoxes of the present, while the *internal* workings of both habit (first synthesis) and memory (second synthesis) rest on the functioning of the pure and empty form of time (third synthesis). The three syntheses do not occur successively, but rather the ground and grounding of time are predicated on its ungrounding. The "fractured I" marks the point of Kant's introduction of time into thought.[197] Descartes's cogito proposed that from the determination "I think" one could infer the "I am" as undetermined existence, which, in thinking itself as a thinking thing determines itself. For Kant, the description of this inferential step lacks an account of how the determination of the undeterminable is possible and "therefore he adds a third logical value: the determinable, or rather the form in which the undeterminable is determinable (by the determination)."[198] As we have seen, for Kant, the production of determinate representation requires the spontaneous act of the understanding to combine and determine the manifold. The self is intuited in the inner

---

[196] Ibid., p. 58.
[197] A clear characterization of this aspect can be found in Daniel W. Smith, "Analytics. Concept, Time and Truth," in *Essays on Deleuze* (Edinburgh: Edinburgh University Press, 2012), p. 131.
[198] Ibid., p. 85.

sense, and remains therefore undetermined and hence unthinkable, if its manifold is not combined by the understanding. However, insofar as the understanding relates the manifold to the "I think," the indeterminate self is therefore necessarily the same self which determines it, while also differing from it. The thought of my own indeterminate existence is already implicated in the determination of intuitions by the "I think," but such implication does not yet determine it, since it is an activity that determines it. To determine the indeterminate existence of the self it must be intuited in time, since it must be given to passive receptivity as per any other object. But in determining its existence as given in time, it determines something differing from itself. Insofar as time is the condition of determinability of the indeterminate existence of the self, it is exactly the temporal hiatus or the irreversibility of the sequence that makes it impossible to adequately think the spontaneity itself. It can be represented only in the experience of passive receptivity, but not as itself. As Kant notes: "I cannot determine my existence as that of a self-active being; all that I can do is to represent to myself the spontaneity of my thought, that is, of the determination."[199] Hence, the self can neither be its own thinking activity nor enact it: it differs endlessly from itself. While Kant does not follow this paradox of inner sense, which resides in the difference between transcendental self and empirical ego, to its conclusion, but rather grounds one in the other in moral action and passive receptivity, the self-differentiation of the self can provide a model for non-conceptual differentiation. Time is therefore simply "the formal relation through which the mind affects itself."[200] Or, as Deleuze praises Kant's dynamic of the thinking self:

> It amounts to the discovery of Difference—no longer in the form of an empirical difference between two determinations, but in the form of a transcendental Difference between the Determination as such and what it determines; no longer in the form of an external difference which separates,

[199] Kant, *Critique of Pure Reason*, p. 158 footnote.
[200] Deleuze, *Essays Critical and Clinical*, p. 31.

but in the form of an internal Difference which establishes an a priori relation between thought and being.[201]

The determination of the "fractured I" demonstrates therefore the internal relation of the three moments of the problematic unity of the Idea necessary for an account of internal genesis. In the differentiation of undetermined being and determinant thinking, the "fractured I" is undetermined as the existence of the "I am," but determinable as self-affection under the formal condition of time and determinant as the "I think," while such determination never exhausts the undetermined existence of the "I am." The third *synthesis* of the pure and empty form of time is thus the formal condition of the determinability of the "I think" through its differential auto-affection. Or, in other words, "thinking determin[es] its own being *as* the unfolding of time. Time is the form of the determinability of being by thought."[202] Kant's answer to the paralogism of the substantial subject in the form of the transcendental subject rests, falsely as Deleuze claims, on the assumption that there would be no synthesis without the agency of a subject. Thought, the third synthesis, constitutes the most revolutionary element of Deleuze's recasting of Kant's system, because it is a synthesis without a subject, a synthesis that always fails but that, in its failure, produces the moment of internal genesis.[203]

### THE PROBLEMATIC AND THE LAW

Because the relations between the undetermined, the determinability and the determination are internal to each other in the production of the fractured I, which represents itself as an other through its narcissistic contemplation, Deleuze will go on to say that "Ideas are exactly the

---

201 Deleuze, *Difference and Repetition*, p. 86.
202 Lord, "Kant and Deleuze," p. 93.
203 Eleanor Kaufman points out the connection between the dialectics in Deleuze and Sartre, which are both engendered by a conception of "solid time," meaning time as irreversibility; see Kaufman, *Deleuze, the Dark Precursor*, p. 31.

thoughts of the Cogito."[204] This connection is, however, not at all plausible from the outset and needs further explanation. In the same way that Kant could not think himself as self-active being, and hence "receives the activity of [his] own thought as an other," the actual Idea is animated by the problematic other as the "being of the sensible."[205] The fact that Deleuze's transcendental empiricism is constructed by taking the structural framework Kant provides (i.e. the notion of the "problematic" or the Idea) and reframing it by using Maimon's rationalist interpretation of the genesis of the transcendental makes it potentially susceptible to an idealist interpretation. Merleau-Ponty and Bergson provide the instances of the "problematic" he uses to undercut such idealism. *The Structure of Behavior* already problematizes the relation between stimulus and reflex response: no strict causal connection can be assumed to exist between the two. This is due to the fact that the same stimulus can, in various contexts (which are non-specific to the stimulus), yield different reactions. This dialectical, instead of causal, approach is extended to perception in the *Phenomenology of Perception,* where the sensible datum at the limit of being felt poses a question, or a "muddled problem for my body to solve."[206] In turn, the body will find an attitude which enables the problematic instance to sustain predicates, in other words, to become determinate in the representation *as* something. The question posed to my body does not resemble the solution, while the former still expresses itself in the latter, or, as Merleau-Ponty says, "I must find the reply to a question which is obscurely expressed."[207] The question is obscure because its answer differs in kind from it, i.e. the clear empirical phenomenon does not resemble the "muddled" vague sensation posing the problem. This understanding is inherited from Bergson's characterization of excitation as a question, which "solicits my activity"[208] (my motor activity as well as memory) and informs actions based on past

---

[204] Deleuze, *Difference and Repetition*, p. 169.
[205] Deleuze, *Essays Critical and Clinical*, p. 30.
[206] Merleau-Ponty, *Phenomenology of Perception*, p. 248.
[207] Ibid., p. 249.
[208] Bergson, *Matter and Memory*, p. 46.

experiences. As Descombes notes, sensibility is a faculty for the apprehension of problems.[209]

Accordingly, the Idea for Deleuze, which has the *virtual* problem as its object, determines itself insofar as it integrates itself into *actual* solutions, the former remaining undetermined in regard to the latter. It must, therefore, become determined as an actual solution in the realm of the sensible, while at the same time not being exhausted by it, or it "must be represented without being able to be directly determined."[210] As already demonstrated in the "fractured I," the Idea/problem provides a model for internal determination because it is self-differing, producing qualitative experience and hence representing itself as another while staying fundamentally undetermined. Once again, the synthesis of thought always fails and in that failure produces empirical phenomena. This places Deleuze in stark contrast to Heidegger's interpretation of the faculties in Kant.[211] Although for both philosophers the third synthesis has a relation to the future, for Heidegger's idea of transcendental recognition such futurity results from the successful coordination of the first and second synthesis and is hence a regulatory future. The third synthesis must therefore function prior to the first two. For Deleuze, on the other hand, the future is the failure to regulate and harmonize the syntheses of imagination and memory, since there is no ground for such coordinated synthesis anymore; the "I" is fractured; common sense is lost in the passage through the sublime. The good will of thinking has lost its system of coordinates, the truths of nature and morality.

Hence, thinking starts with a shock or θαυμάζειν, insofar as the encounter with this intensity catalyzes the transcendent use of the faculties, so that, "From the *sentiendum* to the *cogitandum* there develops the vio-

---

209 "A behavior pattern is not the reaction to a stimulus, but rather the response elicited by a situation. The faculty of apprehending the situation as a question to which it will reply must thus be ascribed to the organism whose behavior is under consideration." Vincent Descombes, *Modern French Philosophy* (Cambridge: Cambridge University Press, 1979), p. 58.
210 Deleuze, *Difference and Repetition*, p. 169.
211 Daniela Voss stresses that Deleuze, unlike Heidegger and Hegel, reconsiders the third Kantian synthesis of recognition and gives it priority. See Daniela Voss, *Conditions of Thought: Deleuze and the Transcendental Ideas* (Edinburgh: Edinburgh University Press, 2013), p. 24.

lence of that which forces us to think [...] Instead of all the faculties converging and contributing to the common effort to recognize an object, we witness a divergent effort, each faculty being confronted with what is 'proper' to it in what essentially concerns it."[212] In opposition to the empirical and concordant exercise of the faculties, the discordant exercise opens the faculties to their problematic (and hence ontological) dimension: the *sentiendum*, as the imperceptible being of the sensible, indicates something immemorable in memory, the *memorandum*, which then compels thought to confront that which is un-thought, the *cogitandum*. It is hence the transcendent exercise of the faculties which brings thinking into being, while being is the object of the encounter in thinking. The first two faculties fail to determine the object properly while unfolding their problematic dimension; thought determines the problem and thus produces the object. But it is a thought that is always forced.[213]

In the encounter with the unlivable, life and thought enter into a new relationship, one not mediated by the useful, the true or the good. As Deleuze asserts:

> Life would be the active force of thought, but thought would be the affirmative power of life. Both would go in the same direction, carrying each other along, smashing restrictions, matching each other step for step, in a burst of unparalleled creativity. Thinking would then mean discovering, inventing, new possibilities of life.[214]

Seen from the vantage point of the perpetual crisis of recognition in the failure of the synthesis of thought, time becomes the difference internal to the Idea. Being and thinking are hence not opposed as concepts and objects, as if thinking determined being *in* time. It is rather that both time, understood as the difference internal to the Idea, and the "fractured I" establish an a priori relation between thinking and being, both traversed

---

[212] Deleuze, *Difference and Repetition*, p. 231.
[213] See Deleuze, *Proust and Signs*, p. 100.
[214] Deleuze, *Nietzsche and Philosophy*, p. 101.

by inorganic life. Experience is therefore not conditioned but generated and we, confronted with its unpredictability, are shocked into thinking, into constant creation with no presupposition of organic unity: inorganic cognition.

We now return to the consideration of Deleuze's Bergsonian vitalist reframing of the Law. Reconsidering lawfulness from the vantage point of time in its pure state (the real) locates its emergence in real conditions beyond the world as given to us (to a subject, to the human, as lived experience, to the body) and beyond chronological time. The task of thinking and in particular philosophy for Deleuze is to create a viewpoint that conceives of the real generation of lawfulness, instead of determining how it is possible conceptually.[215] Hence, one moves from the question of which languages, concepts or institutions the law requires to "the question of how concepts are created and what reality must be if something like societies of law and lawful relations have evolved."[216] Deleuze's commitment to the Idea as the virtual makes it possible to interrogate the real emergence of the Law without tracing the transcendental conditions from the empirical, while still being able, in contrast to Derrida,[217] to provide positive determinations of such conditions. One can in this mode of thinking examine the actual-historical conditions of an event *and* its non-actualized potentialities, which are not reducible to mere unrealized possibilities. Considering the function of thought as a failing synthesis, it is not concerned with the determination of ideal conditions or definitive statements about the actual, i.e. the most accurate material repetition of what

---

215 Raastrup Kristenses, "Thinking Normativity in Deleuze's Philosophy," in *Revisiting Normativity with Deleuze*, ed. Rosi Braidotti and Patricia Pisters (London: Bloomsbury Academic, 2014), p. 18.
216 Claire Colebrook, "Legal Theory after Deleuze," in *Deleuze and Law: Forensic Futures*, ed. Rosi Braidotti, Patrick Hanafin, and Claire Colebrook (London: Palgrave Macmillan, 2009), p. 12.
217 Smith stresses this point with reference to their respective relation to metaphysics, almost aligning Derrida with negative theology; see Daniel W. Smith, "Deleuze and Derrida, Immanence and Transcendence: Two Directions in Recent French Thought," in *Between Deleuze and Derrida*, ed. Paul Patton (London; New York: Continuum, 2003), p. 48f. Even more pronounced is this counter-positioning in Gordon C.F. Bearn, "Differentiating Derrida and Deleuze," *Continental Philosophy Review* 33, no. 4 (2000), p. 441–465.

is, but "to produce the problematic."²¹⁸

Life, for Kant, could only be determined by referring to external law, a supra-sensible unity of nature and thinking, because the conditions of the lawfulness of life could not otherwise be fitted to the frame of the understanding. In opposition to Kant's external conception of law, the immanent Idea provides an account of the internal generation and application of law, i.e. normativity in its properly transcendental form. Autonomy, traditionally the measure of life, is thus universalized and singularized at the same time. The Idea engenders an inorganic life and since there is nothing that is not individuated by the actualization of Ideas, everything is traversed by an inorganic life. The Idea seems to provide a means for breaking down the three objections against hylozoism that Kant had raised. It provides an account of the emergence of lawfulness without presupposing any agency or activity. It supplies an explanation of the production of unity, whilst neither presupposing nor totalizing it. And it eradicates the boundary between the phenomenal and the noumenal, which served to distinguish between organic and inorganic beings.

To properly account for hylozoism in terms of the immanent Idea, we will examine the constitution of the Idea as well as its individuation in actual entities.

### VITALISM AND MATHEMATICS

As Deleuze notes, what we encounter are not the recognizable and benevolent gods, but those who lurk under the surface, hidden, powerful and violent: the demons.²¹⁹ We should take this suggestion of the heretic po-

---

218  Bent Sørensen, "Immaculate Defecation: Gilles Deleuze and Félix Guattari in Organization Theory," *The Sociological Review* 53 (2005), p. 120–133, p. 121.
219  Deleuze, *Difference and Repetition*, p. 37. Ansell-Pearson picks up on this Deleuzian theme of the demonic, developing it from *Difference and Repetition* into the realm of psychoanalysis; see Keith Ansell-Pearson, "Spectropoiesis and Rhizomatics: Learning to Live with Death and Demons," in *Evil Spirits: Nihilism and the Fate of Modernity*, ed. Gary Banham and Charlie Blake (Manchester: Manchester University Press, 2000).

tential of the encounter seriously.[220] And as St. Augustine already knew, it is the mathematicians who are most often seen in the company of demons.[221] But it is exactly this demonization of mathematics that has obscured its vital potential. Traditionally, life and calculation are anathema, vitalism often enough being defined as the opposite of and essentially in opposition to systematicity. Heidegger's rejection of mathematics as embedded in the technical worldview represents a classical argument of *Lebensphilosophie*,[222] which in its conservative sentiment finds an extension in Spengler's warning about the "Faustian symbol of the *machine*."[223] On the other hand, James's critique of the deadening potential of the concept, which, while stemming from actual experience and action, can separate us from actual experience and action when we unthinkingly overuse structural thought, is a paradigmatic example of the pragmatist critique of mathematics for its own sake.[224] This is also apparent in Bergson's critique of the intellect's capacity to reduce difference through the formation of concepts in order to facilitate efficiency, which results in a

---

220   Elaine Pagels's study *The Origin of Satan* characterizes the demon not as a self-identical entity, but as a differentiator on various levels. Firstly, in the theological as well as political process of demonization, the demonic is related to the threat of the outside (pagans, infidels), the internal boundary between inside and outside (non-Christian Jews) and the threat from the inside (heresy). See Elaine H. Pagels, *The Origin of Satan* (New York: Vintage Books, 1996). Thacker adds to that the idea of the differentiation that the demonic engenders as the relation of the human to the inhuman; see Eugene Thacker, *In The Dust of This Planet: Horror of Philosophy, Vol. 1* (Winchester: Zero Books, 2011), p. 25.
221   "Quapropter bono christiano, sive mathematici, sive quilibet impie divinantium [...] cavendi sunt, ne consortio daemoniorum irretiant." Augustine, *De Genesi Ad Litteram* (Kassel: Schöningh, 1964), Liber 2, Caput XVII, Nr. 37. The English translations usually have "astrologers" instead of "mathematicians," which is a mistranslation.
222   Heidegger discusses mathematical physics, and in what sense it is mathematical in "What is a Thing?." He bases his analysis on the Greek difference between *mathemata* and *mathesis*. While the former is identified with a knowledge that presupposes and seeks to found an a priori knowledge, and hence deals with quantification and number, the latter is a learning that is predicated on the practical, on indefinite and general knowledge (or familiarity) with the world. And, of course, mathematical physics is identified with *mathemata*. See Martin Heidegger, *What Is a Thing?* (Chicago: H. Regnery Co, 1967), p. 73.
223   Oswald Spengler, *The Decline of the West* (Cambridge: Cambridge University Press, 1991), p. 340.
224   "No abstract concept can be a valid substitute for concrete reality except with reference to a particular interest in the conceiver. The interest of theoretic rationality, the relief of identification, is but one of a thousand purposes. When others rear their heads, it must pack up its little bundle and retire till its turn recurs." William James, *The Will to Believe and Other Essays in Popular Philosophy* (New York: Longmans, Green and Co, 1907), p. 70.

self-reification that hinders life in the process.²²⁵ Although far from being unfounded, these rejections nonetheless underestimate mathematics' potential to engender non-representational thought. Relying on these influences, Deleuze himself runs the risk of slipping into a biological vitalism, setting aside mathematics, as van Tuinen has noticed: "Instead of a mathematical formalism, Deleuze [...] follows Bergson in proposing an onto-biological materialism."²²⁶ This accusation rests on the assumption that mathematical and biological truths are mutually exclusive and that vitalism can only be grounded in the latter at the expense of the former.

In Spinoza, however, we find a different approach, which by "pulling vitalism away from biology and reconnecting it with pantheism"²²⁷ suspends life's determination by teleological principles and ends and characterizes it as constant creation of forms (animal, organic and beyond). Taking up the post-scholastic pantheism of Cusa, Deleuze asserts, "the traditional couple of *explicatio* and *complicatio* historically reflects a vitalism never far from pantheism."²²⁸ Deleuze's own interpretation of Spinoza's philosophy of expression is highly indebted to Maurice de Gandillac, who acted as a supervisor on *Difference and Repetition*, and his writings on Cusa. In his seminal study, he warns against reducing *complicatio* and *explicatio* to either the preformist model or the epigenesist model of a miniature individual in a germ, and instead defines them by an overabundance and superlative generosity, and hence a constant, excessive creation.²²⁹ Spinoza radicalizes this anti-biological approach by reflecting it methodologically, rejecting Cusa's spiritual mysticism in the tradition of Meister Eckhart for an axiomatic, mathematical approach.²³⁰ Ferdinand Alquié,

---

225   Although this critique is repeated at various points in his work, the most poignant depiction of the deadening tendency of the intellect is laid out in Henri Bergson, *Time and Free Will* (London: Allen and Unwin, 1931).
226   Sjoerd van Tuinen, "Difference and Speculation: Heidegger, Meillassoux and Deleuze on Sufficient Reason," in *Gilles Deleuze and Metaphysics*, ed. Alain Beaulieu (Lanham: Lexington Press, 2017).
227   Thacker, *After Life*, p. 209.
228   Gilles Deleuze, *Expressionism in Philosophy: Spinoza* (New York: Zone Books, 1990), p. 18.
229   See Maurice Gandillac, *Nicolas de Cues* (Paris: Ellipses, 2001), p. 27.
230   It should be noted, however, that neither Cusa nor, when viewed strictly, Spinoza are "pantheists." The term "pantheist" emerges first in the so-called *Pantheismusstreit* in the seventeenth century and neither Cusa, Meister Eckhart nor Spinoza advocate the complete

Deleuze's advisor on *Expressionism in Philosophy*, acknowledges this shift as the central contribution of Spinoza's work. Since Spinoza inherits the concept of the Divine as the coexistence of Nature with God from Renaissance thought, the contribution of Spinoza consists primarily in methodically recasting this legacy, freeing it from mysticism. As Alquié claims in his 1958–1959 lecture on Spinoza: "What will permit Spinoza to give to spiritual processes a rational and precise sense, what will permit him to think Nature apart from the shadow of finality, will be the mathematical method, and that alone."[231]

The Spinoza of Martial Guéroult, the long-time rival of Alquié and an influence on Deleuze's monism, sets the *more geometrico* of the *Ethics* apart from a system of formal logic of inferences. The use of definitions, propositions and demonstrations does not progress deductively from what is most self-evident to synthetic a priori knowledge, but instead axiomatically grounds the definition of God as a single substance with attributes, which are qualified substances, formally distinct from substance in reality but not distinct numerically. Hence, "God is motley but unfragmentable."[232] The attributes describe a genealogical line of elements that (constantly) constitute the substance synthetically. This depiction of perpetual creation parallels the method of construction in mathematics, especially geometry, which is essentially synthetic. In his article on Guéroult, Deleuze highlights this entanglement of construction or genesis with the synthetic method characteristic for Spinozism, before going on to credit his work with having shown the Spinozism of Fichte. Both Guéroult and Deleuze situate Fichte's genetic method in

---

immanence of God to the world, all three insisting on God's transcendence in relation to the world. However, Gandillac reinterprets Cusa, just as Deleuze reinterprets Spinoza, as a monist and pantheist. These reinterpretations are much more "associations" with their respective interlocutors or creations of concepts rather than historically and philologically accurate retellings. On the reinterpretation of Cusa, Bruno, and Meister Eckhart as pantheists, see Tomáš Nejeschleba, "Why Do We Speak about Pantheism in Renaissance Thought?," *Pro-Fil* 19, no. 1 (2018), p. 2.

231  Ferdinand Alquié, *Nature et Vérité Dans La Philosophie de Spinoza* (Paris: Le Table Ronde, 2003), p. 32, my translation.
232  Martial Guéroult, *Spinoza, Volume 1, Dieu (Ethique, 1)* (Paris: Éditions Montaigne, 1969), p. 234.

opposition to Kant's analytics. In his seminar given in 1956–1957, which was later published as *What is Grounding?*, Deleuze reiterates this point by stressing that Kant starts from the simple hypothesis that the objectivity of experience will supply sufficient grounds to justify the objective validity of the categories.[233] While Kant remains constrained by his analytics and has to fall back on an appeal to simple facticity, Fichte attempts a genetic approach to thinking the transcendental grounds of experience and knowledge.[234] Demanding access to the unknowable self as the unconditioned condition for experience as well as free action, Fichte's method of investigation, "intellectual intuition," is derived from geometrical construction. The forms of the mind should be determined in the same way as the construction of a geometrical figure in pure intuition, i.e. synthetically.[235] The degree to which this proximity of Deleuze to Fichte is advantageous or disadvantageous for the former's transcendental empiricism will be the subject of a later chapter ("Passivity"); for now, it is enough to acknowledge Deleuze's recognition of the distance between the geometrical method and Kant's analytics.

In the "Doctrine of Method" geometrical cognition is regionalized to mathematics alone, having no metaphysical ramifications. Since philosophy operates through the "discursive use of reason in accordance with concepts" and geometry by the "intuitive use [of reason] through the construction of concepts,"[236] the former only supplies a pure concept for the subsumption of possible empirical intuitions, while the latter constructs quanta, i.e. pure objects understood as spatio-temporal magnitudes. Kant claims that the application of geometry, which allows for the construction of synthetic concepts in pure intuition, would only result in "houses of cards"[237] when applied to philosophy, but the stark distinction is not fully

---

233   Gilles Deleuze, *What Is Grounding?* (New York: &&& Publishing, 2015), p. 116f.
234   In his 1956–1957 seminar, Deleuze stresses this point: "The simple hypothesis subsists in the Kantian attempt. Fichte says that Kant remains attached to simple facticity, and that he [Fichte] himself searches for genesis." Deleuze, *What Is Grounding?*, p. 151.
235   See David W. Wood, *Mathesis of the Mind: A Study of Fichte's Wissenschaftslehre and Geometry* (Amsterdam: Rodopi, 2012), p. 79.
236   Kant, *Critique of Pure Reason*, A719/B747.
237   Ibid., A723/B751.

convincing. Schelling, in his "Über die Construction in der Philosophie" subverts Kant's sharp distinction, arguing that the mathematician realizes, in his construction of a geometrical figure, the universal within the sensible. In the same way, the task of the philosopher is to realize the ideal within the real by demonstrating the features of the contingent particular as instantiations of the Absolute.[238] This is the Spinoza-Schellingian line which Deleuze derives his theory of genesis from, and which will lead to the conceptualization of the inorganic life of Ideas.

## CONSTRUCTION AND GENESIS

### From Analytics to Dialectics

In *On the Improvement of the Understanding*, Spinoza lays out a substantial critique of the possibility of nominal definitions, which will later become the basis for various critiques of Kant's critical philosophy. He begins his argument by giving a definition of a circle: "a figure, such that all straight lines drawn from the center to the circumference are equal."[239] Such a definition, however, only gives one of its properties, providing no means for the production of the figure, meaning for its actual reality. Maimon, in his *Essay on Transcendental Philosophy*, discusses this example of the definition of the circle, stating that, although the nominal definition supplies the conditions or the rule for it, it lacks "material completeness,"[240] which can only be provided by an explanation of its generation. Additionally, "Should it be incapable of fulfilment, then the concept here expressed in words would have no objective reality: its synthesis would be found only in words but not in the thing itself."[241] Deleuze will pick up on this definition of a circle in *Difference and Repetition*, when he attempts to appro-

---

[238] Friedrich Wilhelm Joseph Schelling, "Über Die Construction in Der Philosophie," in *Sämmtliche Werke. Vol. 7* (Stuttgart: Cotta'scher Verlag, 1859), p. 125.
[239] Baruch de Spinoza, "On the Improvement of the Understanding," in *Works, Vol. 2* (New York: Dover, 1955), p. 35.
[240] Saloman Maimon, *Essay on Transcendental Philosophy* (New York: Continuum Books, 2010), p. 50.
[241] Ibid.

priate the synthetic method from geometry for philosophy. Mirroring the Maimonian movement, Deleuze states: "Whereas Analytics gives us the means to solve a problem already given, or to respond to a question, Dialectics shows how to pose a question legitimately."[242] As mentioned above, rather than a model in which the solution (the empirical) determines the question (the transcendental), Deleuze is interested in a question-solution complex, which is not grounded in the resemblance of the two.

Picking up Leibniz's discussion of infinitesimal magnitudes, which he posed to allow for the determination of instantaneous velocities, Deleuze seeks to recover the "buried treasure in the old so-called barbaric or pre-scientific interpretation of differential calculus."[243] For his solution, Leibniz introduces the symbols dy/dx as representations of a differential and infinitesimal difference. This gives rise to an immediate contradiction, since dx must have a determinate value in order to form a ratio, but at the same time it cannot have a magnitude greater than 0, since it would otherwise capture the gradient across a length of the curve and not at a point. While modern readings of this problem operate, rather pragmatically, with the concept of limit to circumvent the issue, Deleuze uses this paradox to point out the flaw in the assumption that dx must have a sensible magnitude, hence, that it must be representable in order to account for the determination of a value.[244] He will attempt to show an alternative reading of the infinitesimal as the differential with reference to Bordas-Demoulin, Maimon and Höené-Wronski.[245]

---

242 Deleuze, *Difference and Repetition*, p. 160.
243 Ibid., p. 70.
244 Deleuze chooses this pre-scientific and distinctly pre-set-theoretical approach for metaphysical, not logical reasons, as Badiou, himself proposing a set-theoretical interpretation of ontology, notes. See Daniel W. Smith, "Badiou: Mathematics & Theory of Multiplicities," in *Essays on Deleuze* (Edinburgh: Edinburgh University Press, 2012).
245 These three thinkers are not just references in *Difference and Repetition*, but are aligned in a progression. Bordas-Demoulin supplies the tools to express the differential as non-representable and, through his Cartesianism, allows for the concept of the emergence of discrete entities from continuous matter. With Maimon this concept is transposed into the realm of experience and put in opposition to Kant. Lastly, in Höené-Wronski, Deleuze finds a defense of the barbaric interpretation of the differential and, combining the mathematician's counter-Lagrangean theory on singular and ordinary points with the Bordas-Demoulin-infused Maimonian concept of phenomenal generation, he arrives at a proper theory of the Idea and internal genesis.

## The Circumference in Itself

Jean Baptiste Bordas-Demoulin was, as a Cartesian, primarily interested in how discrete magnitudes can be thought if matter is continuous, as Descartes claims.[246] To try to think these, he first attempts the representation of mathematical universals as they are in themselves, without proposing the distinct magnitudes he wants to deduce from the continuum. The Cartesian algebraic equation for the circumference of a circle ($x2 + y2 - R2 = 0$) only provides, according to Bordas-Demoulin, particular circumferences, but not circumference in itself. Only if one assumes determinate values for x, y and R, does the equation *produce* a particular circumference, but, since there are infinite values that could be inserted, it never produces circumference itself. Much as in Kant's notion of a condition or Russell's theory of sense, by inserting particular values we only ever determine the structure of this or that conditioned or functional outcome, but never the experience or sense itself. Bordas-Demoulin insists that this can be solved by using the differentials $dy$ and $dx$, where x and y are understood as 0, and hence he can do away with the need to give them a determinate value to describe the circumference. However, by reversing the operation of differentiation, through integration, actual particular circumferences can be determined. Hence, $ydy + xdx = 0$ expresses the circumference in itself. Differentials, as Deleuze infers from this, are not representable as quantities, but can nevertheless provide a structure for the genesis of individuals without reference to the empirically given. The equation $dy/dx$ implies the cancellation of individual values and their variation; because the relation of dy to dx stays the same through the actual variation of the values, it is elevated to a universal. As Duffy puts it, even as they are vanishing they still subsist as a "pure relation."[247] This primacy of the *relation* over the *relata*, as

---

[246] Buchdahl underscores the consequence that Descartes is forced to accept the existence of only one continuous form of with uniform density; see Gerd Buchdahl, *Metaphysics and the Philosophy of Science: The Classical Origins, Descartes to Kant* (Lanham, MD: University Press of America, 1988), p. 95.

[247] Simon Duffy, *The Logic of Expression: Quality, Quantity, and Intensity in Spinoza, Hegel, and Deleuze* (Aldershot: Ashgate, 2006), p. 49.

Bordas-Demoulin expresses himself, implies a rigorous Spinozism: "According to this metaphysics, one might say, by way of comparison, that the God of Spinoza is the differential of the universe, and the universe, the integral of the God of Spinoza."[248] This Cartesian Spinozism avoids the issue Leibniz encountered, when he was seeking to represent the infinitely small to account for individuality. But at the same time, it makes the Hegelian infinite expansion of representation, which he utilized to account for infinity, redundant. This dual rejection of the orgiastic tendency of representation[249] renders superfluous the introduction of contradiction to account for the dialectic:

> Just as we oppose difference in itself to negativity, so we oppose dx to not-A, the symbol of difference [*Differenzphilosophie*] to that of contradiction. It is true that contradiction seeks its Idea on the side of the greatest difference, whereas the differential risks falling into the abyss of the infinitely small.[250]

Not only does the differential subvert Hegelian negation with a purely affirmative account of determination, it also at the same time supplants the Kantian God of the disjunctive syllogism with the immanent God of (Deleuze's) Spinoza.

### *The Construction of the Phenomenal World*

While Bordas-Demoulin reveals that the differential can provide the universal for a circumference (and particular mathematical figures in general), Maimon had already gone further insofar as he realized his critique of Kant's account of the a priori by taking the differential as the genetic element of the construction of the phenomenal world. Rejecting the Kantian investigation into the relation of the faculties, Maimon focuses on the actual genesis of phenomena. Hence, starting from a differ-

---

[248] Jean Baptiste Bordas-Demoulin, *Le Cartésianisme, Ou La Véritable Rénovation de Sciences*, Vol. 2 (Paris: J. Hetzel, 1843), p. 172.
[249] See Deleuze, *Difference and Repetition*, p. 262.
[250] Ibid., p. 170.

ent point, the *Philosophisches Wörterbuch* takes the given not as a passive matter of the faculty of intuition, but as resistance to the understanding's drive for infinite expansion. If the faculty of thought was not limited, nothing would be given and everything would be thought.[251] Whereas Leibniz perceived the difference between infinite and finite being in their capacity for thinking as a difference in degree, Maimon establishes a difference in kind between them. As seen above, the differential function can produce sensible interpretations, but the infinitesimal itself cannot be represented. Like the Kantian noumenal, the differential cannot therefore be present in intuition but can be thought. Transposing this into the transcendental realm, Maimon takes the differential to be the grounds for the construction of phenomena:

> These differentials of objects are the so-called noumena; but the objects themselves arising from them are the phenomena. With respect to intuition = 0, the differential of any such object is $dx = 0$, $dy = 0$ etc.; however, their relations are not 0, but can rather be given determinately in the intuitions arising from them.[252]

If the understanding were infinite, it would be able to think the object in its totality, i.e. to conceive of differential relations without intuition. Alas, since the faculty of thinking is finite it cannot hold all the relations of differentials at once, which is what gives rise to sensible intuition. The synthesis of the object in intuition is not engendered by the extrinsic relation of the faculties, and nor is it ever complete; rather, the limitations of the faculty of thought produce intuition, rendering the synthesis of the object always incomplete, ongoing or procedural. Accordingly, Kant's approach to examining the a priori conditions of phenomena falls prey to the transcendental illusion that the inability to think the object as a totality which produces representations would imply that the original object

---

[251] Saloman Maimon, *Philosophisches Wörterbuch, Oder Beleuchtung Der Wichtigen Gegenstände Der Philosophie* (Berlin: Johann Friedrich Unger, 1791), p. 169.
[252] Ibid., p. 32.

was a representation too.²⁵³ Rather than being an account of conditioning, Maimon's conception of the differential as the noumenal provides an account of internal genesis as continuous "reciprocal determination."²⁵⁴

### The Singular and the Ordinary

Drawing on a discussion between Höené-Wronski and Lagrange, Deleuze solidifies the consequences of the above two approaches to the differential. In Maimon and Bourdas-Demoulin, Deleuze had found a way to establish the claim that the differential is logically and ontologically prior to the primitive function by demonstrating that the latter is a solution produced by the successive determination of the former.²⁵⁵

Attempting to render the "barbaric" interpretation of the differential obsolete, Lagrange had proposed in the *Theorie des Fonctions Analytiques* that calculus could be reduced to algebra by representing it as an infinite series of terms. Implicitly, however, this would equate the normal quantity to the differential. Höené-Wronski sought to show that these quantities "belong to two entirely different classes of knowledge: the finite quantities relate to the objects of our cognition, and the infinitesimal quantities relate to the generation of this same cognition."²⁵⁶ Lagrange, believing that he has supplanted the infinitesimal with the algebraic indefinite, still relies, according to Höené-Wronski, on the former to understand the latter, since the indefinite is the infinitesimal brought into an intuition. Lagrange's theory for Höené-Wronski is like Kant's focus on conditioning for Maimon: the result of a transcendental illusion. However, applying Lagrange's method does produce a series of differentials and enables the distinction between singular and ordinary points on a line. In ordinary points, the nature of the curve (or other figure) stays the same, while at singular points, for example inflexion points, turning

---

253 See Martial Guéroult, *La Philosophie Transcendental de Salomon Maimon* (Paris: Libre Félix Alcan, 1929), p. 66.
254 Deleuze, *Difference and Repetition*, p. 171.
255 See Aden Evens, "Math Anxiety," *Angelaki: Jounal for Theoretical Humanities* 5, no. 3 (2000), p. 111.
256 Józef Maria Höené-Wronski, *Philosophie de l'Infini* (Paris: P. Diderot L'Aíné, 1814), p. 35.

points, points of discontinuity or local minima and maxima, the behavior of the curve changes. Even more significantly, the behavior of the curve as such becomes apparent in the distribution and number of singular points, and this is then used to determine the species of the primitive function.[257] Hence, the ordinary points of the curve are determined by the singular point in a power series expansion and thus "to the extent that all of the regular points are continuous across all of the different branches generated by the power series of the singular points, the entire complex curve or the whole analytic function is generated."[258]

An assemblage of singular points surrounded by ordinary points is called a multiplicity by Deleuze, which is a system that changes its physical (or psychic) nature either at singularities, i.e. when something happens (a kettle boiling, a man breaking down in tears, a glass reaching its breaking point and cracking) or when one multiplicity "touches" another, changing its state (one billiard ball hitting another propelling it forwards, being unsettled by the change in another person's expression, burning the skin of the hand when reaching for a hot cup of coffee).

Thus, to conclude, dx and dy signify the elements of the structure (or Idea) which, while remaining undetermined with respect to the field of solutions, are nevertheless determinable through reciprocal determination and in a series of derivations disclose the singular points, which allow for the generation of the whole analytic function (solution). The work of Abel

---

[257] Deleuze's own interpretation of integration does not rely as much on Lagrange as on Weierstrass's analytic understanding of the function. Bowden mentions this in his interpretation of Deleuzian calculus; see Sean Bowden, *The Priority of Events: Deleuze's Logic of Sense*, Plateaus–New Directions in Deleuze Studies (Edinburgh: Edinburgh University Press, 2011), p. 106.

[258] Duffy explains this process with reference to Poincaré and Weierstrass: "A power series operates at each singular point by successively determining the specific qualitative nature of the function at that point, i.e. the shape and behavior of the graph of the function or curve. The power series determines the nature of the neighbourhood of that singular point, such that the specific qualitative nature of a function of the neighbourhood of a singular point insists in that one point. By examining the relation between the differently distributed singular points, determined by the differential relation, the regular points that are continuous between the singular points can be determined, which in geometrical terms are the branches of the curve. In general, the power series converges with a function by generating the continuous branch of a curve in the neighborhood of a singular point." Simon B. Duffy, *Deleuze and the History of Mathematics: In Defence of the "New"* (London; New York: Bloomsbury, 2013), p. 21.

is significant for Deleuze for this reason, insofar as his work is concerned with developing a method to determine whether a problem has a solution or not, rather than resolving the problem in the solution. Or, transposed into the register of transcendental philosophy, the field of differentials (the undetermined Idea) engenders both the concept (the determinable equation) and the intuition (determined value) subsumed by the concept.[259]

## DESIRE, TRUTH AND INORGANIC LIFE

Multiplicity therefore supplants the traditional category of substance as the definition of a thing, or, rather, definition and construction merge into one. The essence of a thing is replaced by the event as the expression of internal dynamics in the synthesis of forces. This transformation implies a methodological shift, most apparent in what is thought of as Deleuze's own second critique and first collaboration with Guattari. Despite Deleuze's open animosity towards Kant's second *Critique*, it has in common with *Anti-Oedipus* that it develops a theory of desire by examining the proper transcendental operations, that is to say, the higher form each faculty is capable of. It might even be justified to claim that *"Anti-Oedipus* remains an incomprehensible book as long as one does not see its overall structure as an attempt, on Deleuze's part, to rewrite the *Critique of Practical Reason* from the viewpoint of a strictly immanent theory of Ideas."[260]

---

[259] The process of the determination of Ideas is described in its specifics by Deleuze, referring to Poincaré and, more crucially, Lautman's interpretation of Poincaré's qualitative theory of differential calculus. See Deleuze, *Difference and Repetition*, p. 177. For a more detailed description of Deleuze's interpretation of these mathematicians' works, see Simon Duffy "The Mathematics of Deleuze's Differential Logic and Metaphysics," in *Virtual Mathematics: The Logic of Difference* (Manchester: Clinamen Press, 2006), as well as Miguel de Beistegui, *Truth and Genesis: Philosophy as Differential Ontology* (Bloomington: Indiana University Press, 2004), p. 268f. For a reinterpretation of Deleuze's work on Poincaré as a theory of phase spaces and an analysis more geared towards a scientific understanding, see DeLanda, *Intensive Science and Virtual Philosophy*, and Manuel DeLanda, "Deleuze in Phase Space," in *Virtual Mathematics: The Logic of Difference*, ed. Simon Duffy (Manchester: Climanen Press, 2006).

[260] Daniel W. Smith, "Deleuze, Kant, and the Theory of Immanent Ideas," in *Deleuze and Philosophy*, ed. Constantin V. Boundas (Edinburgh: Edinburgh University Press, 2005), p. 55.

As extensively outlined in the last chapter, Kant's conception of desire is as something productive, insofar as it is the faculty able to produce the object in a representation that corresponds to it. Hence, desire in Kant is concerned with the capacity to make objects real rather than knowing them; this is a result of critical philosophy's Copernican Revolution, which is still echoed in Deleuze and Guattari when they claim: "If desire produces, its product is real. If desire is productive, it can be productive only in the real world and can produce only reality."[261] The proper transcendental exercise in such a realization for Kant depends on elevating desire to its higher form, the will, i.e. the determination of desire by the representation of the pure form of universal legislation, the moral law. The possibility of free action according to the categorical imperative (the moral law) prompts the postulation of three transcendent Ideas —the cosmological Idea of a supra-sensible world, the theological Idea of God as the author of the "moral cause of the world" and the psychological Idea of the immortality of the soul which bridges the abyss between the first two in its infinite progress.[262] *Anti-Oedipus*, among various other things, is concerned with supplying an immanent theory of desire and, building on Kant, giving an immanent account of the Ideas that refuses the determination of desire by transcendence (the will). This conforms to the schema we saw above, whereby Deleuze refuses the external determination of desire and seeks instead to explore the immanent synthesis of it according to immanent Ideas. The immanent transformation of the Kantian Ideas conditioning the will, now finds expression as syntheses— World (connection), Self (conjunction), God (disjunction)—but without their transcendent status they do not engender unity anymore and are in a constant process of breaking down.[263] Kant had given the tran-

---

261 Deleuze and Guattari, *Anti-Oedipus*, p. 26.
262 Kant, *Critique of Judgement*, p. 340. While Kant denounces all three transcendent Ideas in the first *Critique*, the second *Critique* gives them practical determinations and introduces them back into the critical project one after the other.
263 *The Logic of Sense* circumscribes this movement: "The divergence of the affirmed series forms a 'chaosmos' and no longer a world; the aleatory point which traverses them forms a counter-self, and no longer a self; disjunction posed as a synthesis exchanges its theological principle of diabolic principle [...] The Grand Canyon of the world, the 'crack' of the self, and the dismembering of God." Deleuze, *Logic of Sense*, p. 176.

scendent Ideas of the first *Critique* practical determination in the second; Deleuze does the same with immanent ideas moving from *Difference and Repetition* to *Anti-Oedipus*. This is the reason why, in *Anti-Oedipus*, the vitality, the productivity that traverses through humans, animals, plants, rocks, the stars and so on is given expression in all its "machinic" glory.

The practical nature of the Ideas in the productivity of desire which Deleuze and Guattari invented in *Anti-Oedipus* highlights a methodological shift already implied in *Difference and Repetition* and prefigured in Deleuze's earlier works. The question of identity and essence is deposed by that of the multiplicity and the event, the logic of representation supplanted by a logic of production. Whitehead already formulates the basic point of inflexion for a method proper to processes:

> We can never get away from the questions: — How much, — In what proportions? — and in what pattern of arrangement with other things? [...] Arsenic deals out either health or death, according to its proportions amid a pattern of circumstances.[264]

The substance of a thing, understood as multiplicity, is not grasped by the Socratic question "What is …?." Rather, conceiving of a thing (or event) through its singular and ordinary points implies a variety of questions: "How much?," "Where?," "From which viewpoint?," "How?," "In conjunction with what?," "How fast?" and so on and so forth. As Deleuze remarks in *The Fold*, one might say with the same justification "Everything is ordinary!" as well as "Everything is unique!"[265] shifting the task of the philosopher away from determining invariable facts. The philosopher should rather treat whatever presents itself as fact as if it were a possible symptom of deeper differential relations (a multiplicity of intensities); in the same way Nietzsche characterized the philosopher as a physician.

---

[264] Alfred North Whitehead, *Process and Reality* (New York: Free Press, 1967), p. 173.
[265] Gilles Deleuze, *The Fold: Leibniz and the Baroque* (Minneapolis: University of Minnesota Press, 1993), p. 91.

Since truth is only concerned with the answers to questions, it does not distinguish between the ordinary and the singular; it always fails to conceive of the multiplicity of a thing. Philosophy, however, as Deleuze notes in his early book on Hume, is therefore not concerned with truth:

> a philosophical theory is an elaborately developed question, and nothing else; by itself and in itself, it is not the resolution to a problem, but the elaboration, to the very end, of the necessary implications of a formulated question. [...] In philosophy, the question and the critique of the question are one; or, if you wish, there is no critique of solutions, there are only critiques of problems.[266]

It is not what is true, since that is always only on the level of solutions, but the problems themselves that are of interest to the philosopher: not whether something is correct but whether something is remarkable, important and relevant. As Deleuze notes, teachers know very well that a common problem of homework assignments is not that the pupils produce falsehoods or mistakes, but rather that their descriptions are disinterested, their analyses lack a relevant problematic horizon and worst of all, they are filled with banalities mistaken for profundities."[267] The tautological mode of thinking, which Kant still presented as supplying the conditions of possibility of truth and morality, is exposed as a derivate mode dependent on the production of a non-tautological one. Rather than operating within a framework of an epistemology oriented around claims to truth, inorganic cognition is an account of transcendental learning.[268] While knowing already presumes the pre-existence of the object of knowledge and splits object and subject in the passive representation, leaving the object itself unaffected, the activity of learning transforms the subject, its relation to the world, as well as the ob-

---

[266] Gilles Deleuze, *Empiricism and Subjectivity: An Essay on Hume's Theory of Human Nature*, trans. Constantin V. Boundas (New York: Columbia University Press, 1991), p. 106.
[267] Deleuze, *Difference and Repetition*, p. 153.
[268] Levi R. Bryant, *Difference and Givenness: Deleuze's Transcendental Empiricism and the Ontology of Immanence* (Evanston: Northwestern University Press, 2008), p. 149.

ject itself.[269] Hence, although an ethical imperative guides thinking for both Kant and Deleuze, "the distinction between them lies in whether this ethical imperative is one of confirming the identity of a just accord or of being able to affirm the difference in itself without measure."[270] As Lyotard rephrases the task of the philosopher, who is no longer interested in wisdom and knowledge, but in that which cannot be traded at the market (the problem, learning or desire): "To philosophize is not to desire wisdom, it is to desire desire."[271]

An argument pertaining to the initial question of the organic and the inorganic image of thought can now be attempted. As laid out in the last chapter, Kant's rejection of hylozoism is grounded in the separation of the sensible and intelligible, which in turn was necessary to supply the conditions of possibility for truth and morality. The organic image allows for this grounding of truth and morality and makes them unquestionable as indispensable values by instating a *sensus communis* and a good will of the thinker and thought, which is supposed to give thought its proper (organic) ends. By radicalizing transcendental philosophy, Deleuze demonstrates the derivate status of truth and morality and proposes an immanent and internal theory of determination through the reciprocal determination of Ideas.

### THE INORGANIC LIFE OF THE TRANSCENDENTAL FIELD

*Immanence and Transcendence in Transcendental Empiricism*
In his spirited defense of the swindler, who he positions as providing an alternative to the destructive impulses of the idealist and the fanatic, Cioran provides us with the ethical core of maybe his entire work: "all of

---

269 Jeffrey Bell, "Postulates of Linguistics," in *A Thousand Plateaus and Philosophy*, ed. Jeffrey Bell, Henry Somers-Hall, and James Williams (Edinburgh: Edinburgh University Press, 2018), p. 73.
270 Patricia Farell, "The Philosopher-Monkey," in *Thinking Between Deleuze and Kant: A Strange Encounter*, ed. Edward Willatt and Matt Lee (London; New York: Continuum, 2009), p. 19.
271 Jean-François Lyotard, *Why Philosophize?* (Malden: Polity Press, 2013), p. 38.

life's evils come from a conception of life."[272] It is the vital paradox of Nietzsche's later work that, through a dark alchemy, life produces images of itself that possess the power to impoverish it. The basic ethical question, then, is how to live without a "conception" of life, or how prevent life from being amenable to judgement. If the organism is the instrument of judgement—ordering, assigning lots—it is with Deleuze's "inorganic life" that a metaphysical alternative can be attempted: a Life without properties.

As a preliminary summary, we could say that the distance between traditional empiricism and Deleuze's transcendental variety can be described in terms of their differences in the sources of knowledge. Deleuze goes beyond what is given, proposing that knowledge is derived from empirical ideas and not experience or the senses. This avoids subjectivism, in that determination in transcendental empiricism is an expression of being and not purely subjective. Heeding Bergson's call for philosophy "to go beyond the human state,"[273] Deleuze shifts from an epistemology of individuals to an ontology of individuation, since the human subject is no longer the locus to which the given is given. Hence, it is not human subjects that think, but being that thinks itself, occasionally involving human individuals in the process of a "Being identical to difference which, as such, thinks itself and reflects itself in man."[274] Difference is internal to being in Deleuzian ontology instead of external, i.e. being and thought are no longer asynchronic as in Kant, but identical in a Parmenidean manner.[275] Upon the grounds of this ontological basis, as demonstrated in the previous sections, knowledge is distinguished and distinguishes itself into the knowledge being has of itself (absolute knowledge) and the reflection of

---

272  Cioran, *Short History of Decay*, p, 5.
273  Henri Bergson, "Philosophical Intuition," in *Bergson: Key Writings*, ed. Keith Ansell-Pearson (New York: Continuum, 2002), p. 277.
274  Gilles Deleuze, "Review of Jean Hyppolite, Logique et Existence," in *Logique et Existence* (Minneapolis: University of Minnesota Press, 1997), p. 195.
275  Badiou explicitly aligns Deleuze with Parmenides on the identity of thought and being; see Alain Badiou, *Deleuze: The Clamor of Being* (Minneapolis: University of Minnesota Press, 2000), p. 30. The validity of this manner of equation, which Badiou achieves by reading Parmenides exclusively through Heidegger, is, however, questionable; see Clayton Crockett, *Deleuze beyond Badiou: Ontology, Multiplicity, and Event* (New York: Columbia University Press, 2013), p. 12.

and in man by being (empirical knowledge). Rather than the transcendental conditions of thought in fully constituted individuals, Deleuze examines the problems (Ideas) that the individual itself is constituted by and through. Thought's limits are therefore determined neither by the human nor by organic form, but in its problematic form becomes inorganic.

In a radicalization of Kant's introduction of the form of time to thinking, Deleuze's "fractured I," swarming with Ideas at its edges, supplies the real conditions of experience as an "impersonal and pre-individual transcendental field."[276] As Bryant puts it: "The notion of a transcendental field is thus the idea of time independent of subjects and objects and out of which subjects and objects are generated."[277] Sartre had already criticized Husserl's positing of the ego as the a priori guarantee for the unity of consciousness. He sought to demonstrate that the ego itself is only the product of a retrospective movement, and hence that in Husserl the transcendental ego is traced from the empirical unity of consciousness. This Husserlian retrospection becomes possible if the focus is shifted from the instantaneity of consciousness and thought's spontaneity to a supposedly underlying agent, the ego. But if such an a priori ego really existed, "it would violently separate consciousness from itself, it would divide it, slicing through each consciousness like an opaque blade."[278] Rather, the condition for the ego to appear for consciousness (a posteriori) is a background unity of consciousness to appear on, a unity which necessarily cannot be created by the ego but only by consciousness itself. The ego, therefore, transcends consciousness much like on the side of the noema the actual object transcended consciousness as well.[279] Experience, conditioned by the transcendental field, must therefore involve an impersonal, ego-less and non-intentional consciousness without the ego underlying it. This anonymous "stream of consciousness"—the self-actualization of

---

[276] Deleuze, *Logic of Sense*, p. 102.
[277] Bryant, *Difference and Givenness*, p. 181.
[278] Sartre, *The Transcendence of the Ego*, p. 4.
[279] See Sanja Dejanovic, "The Sense of the Transcendental Field: Deleuze, Sartre, and Husserl," *The Journal of Speculative Philosophy* 28, no. 2 (2014), p. 202.

experience without recourse to a pre-existent instance—is what Deleuze calls the "transcendental field." However, Deleuze stresses that for Sartre consciousness becomes "factum": the subject and the object in their double genesis transcend the transcendental field. For Deleuze, this transcendence within immanence is characteristic for (post-)phenomenological thought, reoccurring not only in Husserl and Levinas, but in Derrida as well in the structure of the Other.[280]

*The Idea of the Organism at the End of the World*
Understood from the immanent perspective, the transcendental field excludes not only the Kantian Idea of the Self, which is replaced by an egoless stream of consciousness, but also the world, which disappears as a unifying and ordering authority, as well as God's avatar, the body. The "world" as unifying Idea in Kant was legitimized by its practical application: to give the highest systematicity to the understanding. The world is posited "as if" it were a unified whole, designed to find the "lots" of things and enable determination. As Markus Gabriel has argued, such propositions, or at least such propositions' homologous function, persist in phenomenology's horizon and most notably in Heidegger's notion of the world.[281] The "world" is not defined as the sum total of either things, phenomena or facts, but is rather, as Heidegger puts it, "the domain of all domains,"[282] or the (conceptually) unifying domain of all others domains.[283] With the notion of the Idea as internal determination that Deleuze champions, such a totalizing and unifying ground becomes epistemologically superfluous and ontologically impossible; the world shatters. The thinking that destroys the world, however, reveals a profound cosmological sensibility.[284] Leibniz rejected incompossible worlds

---

280  Deleuze and Guattari, *What is Philosophy?*, p. 46.
281  Compare Markus Gabriel, *Why the World Does Not Exist* (Malden: Polity Press, 2015), p. 45.
282  Martin Heidegger, "Aletheia (Heraclitus Fragment B 16)," in *Early Greek Thinking* (New York: Harper & Row, 1975), p. 115.
283  Similar passages can be found in *Being and Time*, predominantly in §14, where Heidegger describes mathematics, science and even nature itself as something in the "world," since they can only be encountered there. See Heidegger, *Being and Time*, p. 63.
284  Anelli laments that the cosmological thought of Deleuze is often overlooked, considering how often Nietzsche-inspired geophilosophy overshadows Deleuze's Whiteheadian

with reference to a harmonious (rational) unity. Without such totalizing grounds (i.e. without a pre-established harmony) the coexistence of different worlds contradicting each other in their rational and organizational rules becomes possible. "Each actual world"[285] thus has the power to contradict the others and thus contradict the very notion of a natural order able to harmonize them. The universe is not a Leibnizian organic whole, but an inorganic Joycean "chaosmos."[286]

Most importantly for our purposes, however, the transcendental field rejects the claims to authority of the organic body. As stated at the beginning of the chapter, the organic body serves as the (last) avatar of the soul. After the logical identity of the subject and the metaphysical unity of the world have dissolved, universal becoming manifests itself in the dis-integration of the organic body. This disintegration results in the "body without organs," which, despite its name, does not actually describe an organ-less body, but a body wherein each organ is not defined by its functional relation to the wholes. The analysis of the Idea of the organism in *Difference and Repetition* takes up the work of Georges Cuvier, who thought that the anatomical determination of a part of an organism must follow from its independent function as well as the reciprocal functional relation with other parts. A difference in function thus, in this view, results in a difference in terms, as for example in the teleological difference between the fin of a fish and the arm of a man. With the advent of evolutionary theory, however, such a synchronic approach proved difficult, since it could not account for the diachronic changes of functions of the same parts over time, as for example the change in function of the hands facilitated by the adoption of upright posture during hominization

---

cosmology in contemporary debates; see Alberto Anelli, "Leaving Metaphysics? Deleuze on the Event," in *Gilles Deleuze and Metaphysics*, ed. Alain Beaulieu (Lanham: Lexington Press, 2017), p. 19.

285 Whitehead, *Process and Reality*, p. 230. Whitehead uses this notion in his philosophy of the organism to denote a universe within which all possible worlds are realized, even though they contain contradictions in regard to each other.

286 Joyce's neologism marks a subversion of the traditional opposition of chaos and order, in which both not only condition but also intersect each other. In Deleuze, as demonstrated above, virtual chaos (the non-representable inorganic life of Ideas) forces processes of differenciation and differentiation, creating order not out of but through chaos.

or the endosymbiotic evolution of mitochondria.[287] Cuvier's contemporary Geoffroy St. Hilaire, on the other hand, conceived of organisms as defined by the relations of parts, rather than functions, and was hence able to account for their functional change over time. His "transcendental anatomy" traces the homologies between organisms not through the direct comparison of organisms, but by describing them as instantiations of the transcendental structure of an ideal organism. For Deleuze, this search for the ideal connection beyond representable functional differences and visible resemblances constitutes Geoffroy's attempt to determine an organism through a field of differential relations. Opposed to Cuvier's comparative anatomy, Geoffroy established homologies not through actual terms, "but [the empirical terms] are understood as the actualisation of an essence, in accordance with reason and at speeds determined by the environment, with accelerations and interruptions."[288] However, the transcendental correlates of bones "still enjoy an actual, or too actual, existence,"[289] which is why Deleuze prefers the DNA model of modern genetics as an advancement over this relational account of determining organisms. The idea in *Difference and Repetition* of a body whose organs are determined by their relations (and their parts as fields of differential relations) and not by function and functionality will later become the body without organs.[290] Since the identity of the body confines life to a personal relationship with the world, as demonstrated in Merleau-Ponty, and enables the constraining judgement of God, as seen in Sartre, the body without organs sets life free: "not all of life is confined to the organic strata: rather, the organism is that which life sets against itself in order to limit itself, and there is a life all the more intense, all the more powerful for being anorganic."[291] The life unshackled by the organic form,

---

287  See Martin Ambley and William Martin, "Eukaryotic Evolution, Changes and Challenges," *Nature* 440 (2006), p. 623–630.
288  Deleuze, *Difference and Repetition*, p. 184.
289  Ibid., p. 185.
290  While the term is not mentioned in *Difference and Repetition*, it is prefigured in this conception of the organism. In *The Logic of Sense* and the two volumes of *Capitalism and Schizophrenia*, this term is developed in very different forms and across different territories.
291  Deleuze and Guattari, *Anti-Oedipus*, p. 503.

however, does not exist independently of organisms, but rather *insists* in their fixed dynamics as the force of the outside pulling them towards a becoming without negativity. This "vital topology that folds the outside into the inside" opens organisms up, freeing them from entropic containment, while at the same time constituting the regulating dynamics of the organism as emergent properties of a field of pre-individual singularities and intensities.[292]

*The Impropriety of Life*

Deleuze's last text, "Immanence: A Life," describes this dual movement in a manner differing from traditional vitalism, in that it does not propose the continuous immediacy of experience and the indifference of the ground, but that actualization of life is always involved within a framework of subjectivation within time:

> The indefinite aspects in a life lose all indetermination to the degree that they fill out a plane of immanence or, what amounts to the same thing, to the degree that they constitute the elements of a transcendental field (individual life, on the other hand, remains inseparable from empirical determinations). The indefinite as such is the mark not of an empirical indetermination but of a determination by immanence or a transcendental determinability. The indefinite article is the indetermination of the person only because it is determination of the singular. The One is not the transcendent that might contain immanence but the immanent contained within a transcendental field. One is always the index of a multiplicity: an event, a singularity, a life ...[293]

Constituting a correspondence between quantitability, qualitability and potentiality, the multiplicity integrates the three principles of sufficient ground in its expression in a singularity or a life. As we have mentioned

---

[292] Keith Ansell-Pearson, *Germinal Life: The Difference and Repetition of Deleuze* (London: Routledge, 1999), p. 85.
[293] Gilles Deleuze, "Immanence: A Life ...," in *Pure Immanence: Essays on a Life* (New York: Zone Books, 2002), p. 30.

at the beginning of this book, life can therefore only be grasped through the "middle," i.e. in the process of its expression, not earlier, not later, only in the continuous metamorphosis of its essential qualities. Precisely this is the reason why being deserves the name Deleuze gives it: Life.[294] When life is only ever accessible through the middle, there is no outside of life from which it could be evaluated. The rejection of the transcendent function of judgement renders life "neutral and literally in-valuable,"[295] since there is, as Nietzsche already knew, no life of life. There is only continuous becoming, the constant transition of life itself. Similarly, univocity is in Deleuze this indiscernible, impersonal movement of being, meaning that there is no being of being. Being is in the most profound sense beyond good and evil, therefore neutral. This "beyond" however implies neither transcendence nor negation, but signifies the constant production, dissolution and morphing into each other of good and evil, i.e. being creates value without itself being evaluated in the process. It thereby rejects the logic of "neither-nor" in favor of an affirmative "and and." The primacy of the relation over the *relata* which is expressed in the disjunctive synthesis disables the functions of identification in any categorial or conceptual sense. Instead, being is understood as power, the "powerful non-organic life that grips the world."[296] This, then, becomes the foundational principle of the Deleuzian identity of life and being. Conceiving of being means tracing its metamorphosis in the actualization of the virtual and the virtualization of the actual. Therefore, insofar as life and being are metamorphosis, they are also morphogenesis, i.e. they are both individuating and specifying as well as dissolving and unbinding. The logic of "and and" hence implies the inclusion of "and" "nor" and "or" into a superposition of "and-or-nor," the expression of a formula working against the logic of judgement, which is based on limitation, negation and identity.

---

294  Of course, we encounter a mereological paradox here, since "Life=Being" and "Being= immanence," but at same the time "immanence: A Life ... ." These two formulas—mathematically speaking—are not equivalent and might even contradict each other. We will return to this problem in the section "Passivity."

295  Alain Badiou, "Of Life as a Name of Being, or, Deleuze's Vitalist Ontology," *Pli: Warwick Journal of Philosophy*, no. 10 (2000), p. 195.

296  Gilles Deleuze, *Cinema 2. The Time-Image* (New York: Bloomsbury, 2013), p. 81.

Supplanting the form of judgement with the "and-or-nor," being is no longer exhausted by the properties assigned to it. Being, understood as this "in-between," is not determined by any properties but is rather the breaking down of properties in their virtualization. Life or being are strictly improper. To see what this might mean in Deleuze, one must gage his proximity and his distance to Plato. The latter, who gives being the name of "the Good" instead of life, already champions the necessary impropriety of being, since the Good cannot be identified with any actual property and does not designate any, but is instead what gives properties their power of division in the first place. According to Deleuze, this Platonist impropriety of being is, however, still ascribed as a transcendent property to the Good, which reintroduces judgement. Subsequently, to properly think the impropriety of being we cannot conceive it as a property itself and, while Deleuze will react to this problem with a call for immanence, it is not at all self-evident how this solves it. What the philosophy of immanence, conceiving of being as inorganic life, must therefore establish is a middle position between the false exclusive choice provided by transcendental philosophy, in which the transcendental grounds of being are understood as: "*either* an undifferentiated ground, a groundless, formless non-being, or an abyss without difference and without properties, *or* a supremely individuated being and an intensely personalized form."[297]

*Immanence Within and Beyond Consciousness*

What Deleuze's idea of "immanence" might entail as an answer to the problem of the impropriety of being is even more obscured by the fact that he in his middle works and then, surprisingly, in his last work, holds fast to transcendental philosophy. The problem at stake here is that Deleuze on the one hand seems "to have done with the transcendental,"[298] as Adkins notes, because he has taken the logic of conditioning *ad absurdum*. On the other hand, Deleuze never seems to make the transition into

---

[297] Deleuze, *Logic of Sense*, p. 121.
[298] Brent Adkins, "To Have Done with the Transcendental: Deleuze, Immanence, Intensity," *The Journal of Speculative Philosophy* 32 (2018), p. 533.

transcendental philosophy's opposite, *Naturphilosophie*.²⁹⁹ Even if one rejects the original leap of the subject, transcending itself to reach an outside, that underlies so much of transcendental philosophy and endorses the immanence of subject and object, one is still left with consciousness as the only secure starting point for transcendental philosophy. In this vein Rölli writes, "Immanence is defined by Deleuze as the transcendental field of an ego-less and non-intentional stream of consciousness," to which he then adds, "A Life consists entirely of virtuals that actualize themselves—in a consciousness to which they attribute themselves."³⁰⁰ Picking up such an interpretation of transcendental empiricism, Zourabichvili even draws the conclusion that Deleuze does not have an ontology at all.³⁰¹ Defenders of Deleuze's ontological project, he argues, pointing to the "univocity of being," misunderstand the problem this concept is an answer to, namely, how we can conceive of the conditions of experience without them being general and external to experience.³⁰² As such, Deleuze would not be concerned with being, but only experience or being qua experience, understood as affect, which "implies that a being can only be defined by the singular declination of its affects. This topples ontology into the problematic of experience."³⁰³ However, as was already apparent in the last section, such an understanding of being qua expe-

---

299  Schelling, for example, opposes transcendental philosophy and nature philosophy as incompatible, opting for the latter. His refutation of transcendental philosophy overlaps with Deleuze's critique of Kant's critical philosophy at most of the important points. However, while Schelling adopts a "speculative physics" *against* transcendental philosophy, Deleuze seems to attempt to reconcile them. However, it might be argued (and has been argued) that his reconciliation is rather uneasy or ultimately fails. See Grant, *Philosophies of Nature after Schelling*, p. 187.
300  Rölli, *Gilles Deleuze's Transcendental Empiricism*, p. 20.
301  See François Zourabichvili, "New Introduction (2004)," in *Deleuze: A Philosophy of the Event. Together with the Vocabulary of Deleuze*, ed. Kieran Aarons (Edinburgh: Edinburgh University Press, 2012), p. 37.
302  In a lecture course in 1974 on *Anti-Oedipus*, Deleuze even says this much when pressed on the difference between univocity and equivocity: "I'm not even interested in knowing if it's an ontological problem; it's just as much a problem of statements [énoncés]." Gilles Deleuze, "Sur L'Anti-Œdipe III," 1973–1974, 2nd session, 14th of January 1974, my translation.
303  Kieran Aarons, "The Involuntarist Image of Thought," in François Zourabichvili, *Deleuze: A Philosophy of the Event. Together with the Vocabulary of Deleuze*, ed. Kieran Aarons (Edinburgh: Edinburgh University Press, 2012), p. 4.

rience results in idealism, since the disjunctive synthesis is interpreted only according to the empiricist doctrine of the faculties, i.e. as being for consciousness (even if it is a consciousness without a subject).

In such a reading, Deleuze is all too easily conflated with Bergson and Spinoza (at least the Spinoza of Deleuze's own reading of the *Ethics*). Deleuze, however, is neither a pure Bergsonian nor a Spinozist, but first and foremost a Kantian. Although it is true that the transcendental field is only ever encountered (or registered) under the condition of consciousness, it is not identical with it. Consciousness is strictly coextensive with the transcendental field, as we saw already in Deleuze's critique of Sartre, since it does not transcend it. The converse however is not true:

> The transcendent is not the transcendental. Without consciousness the transcendental field would be defined as a pure plane of immanence since it escapes every transcendence of the subject as well as of the object. Absolute immanence is in itself: it is not something, not to something: it does not depend on an object and does not belong to a subject.[304]

Within the affective reading of Spinoza and Bergson, this is, however, impossible. The Kantian twist reveals the precarious Deleuzian solution: "The relation of the transcendental field to consciousness is only *de jure*."[305] To speak, in a Spinozist manner, of being without reference to the conditions of experience would be a relapse into pre-critical dogmatism. To claim on the other hand the identity of consciousness and the transcendental field would make it subject *to* something. Therefore, Deleuze takes up the *de jure* relation of the transcendental field and consciousness, while being very much aware of the weight of this decision, since "it is precisely at this point that Deleuze comes closest to falling into a speculative or dogmatic metaphysics."[306] *Difference and Repetition* establishes this problem by invoking Maimon's critique of Kant's false

---

[304] Deleuze, "Immanence: a Life …," p. 3.
[305] Ibid.
[306] Bryant, *Difference and Givenness*, p. 214.

choice between infinite and finite knowledge. If knowledge is finite, then we cannot not make any claims about the differential that constitutes experience and being. Conversely, however, such an appeal to differentials (infinite knowledge) would imply an infinite intuition, or the absolute understanding of God.

Since it is only ever the effects of the transcendental field that are registered, the existence of the transcendental field must be inferred—not, however, from axioms or principles but from experience. The "fractured I" mentioned above, which results from the introduction of time into thought, had already suggested to us the impossibility of deciding between finite and infinite knowledge, although without having a name for the third option, where the two are only differences in degree, not in kind. However, such a solution still relied on the discord of the faculties and hence presupposed the existence of an organism with sufficient cognitive capacities to attempt to determine itself (and to fail in this endeavor).

The speculative advance beyond consciousness is already foreshadowed in *Difference and Repetition,* not simply in the fact that the subject is split because it is given to itself in time, but also because it is only ever given on the condition of a time independent of the subject. Time exists as a whole in memory and as the radical crack of the eternal return, as a manifold and as pure and empty form (i.e. radical linearity), which depends epistemologically on consciousness,[307] but is ontologically only immanent to itself.

To go beyond consciousness therefore means to follow the speculative route of the transcendental field understood as time, well aware of the hazardous epistemological position of speaking "as if" one were not a subject but already in contact with the transcendental field *both* ontologically and epistemologically.

---

[307] Of course, this is only true if one understands "epistemology" in the traditional sense as the study about the nature of, justification of and our access to knowledge.

## ABSOLUTE XENOGENESIS

All is lithogenesis—or lochia.[1]

---

[1] MacDiarmid, "On a Raised Beach," p. 146.

# SPECULATIVE HYLOZOISM

## THE UNFATHOMABLE DEPTH OF TIME

*Forget the Earth! (Philosophy and Geology)*
In the aptly-named "When the World Screamed" from Sir Arthur Conan Doyle's *Professor Challenger Series*, the titular scholar endeavors to embark on his greatest research project yet. It rests on the idea, as he explains it to Mr. Jones, "that the world upon which we live is itself a living organism, endowed, as I believe, with a circulation, a respiration, and a nervous system of its own."[2] The vast swamp of metaphors conjured by Professor Challenger to prove that the earth indeed resembles an animal only serves to show that, "clearly, the man was a lunatic."[3] The exophobic expulsion of inorganic externality (i.e. the rejection of the earth itself as the Outside) in favor of organic internality (i.e. the proposition of the earth as a teleological whole) present in the scientist's words is mirrored today by a manifold of approaches, such as the Gaia hypothesis or deep ecologies. These alchemical philosophies, attempting to produce flesh from stone, while pretending to give the earth back its depth, in reality restrain it to purely terrestrial territory and hence strip it of any cosmic outside.

The intimate connection of philosophy and the earth is of course evident in their historical co-development: from the geographical and geological studies of Kant, to Nietzsche's fidelity to the earth, to Husserl's ark-ization of the earth, to Heidegger's re-romanticization of ground (*Boden*), all the way to current eco-philosophy. However, these images of the earth portray it as a "dead body and mute cradle,"[4] which is at the same time *sine qua non* for thought and in need of thought to properly be.

---

2   Sir Arthur Conan Doyle, *When the World Screamed (Professor Challenger Series)* (London: John Murray Publishers, 1968), p. 71.
3   Ibid.
4   Ben Woodard, *On an Ungrounded Earth: Towards a New Geophilosophy* (New York: Punctum Books, 2013), p. 6.

Within this tradition of philosophy that stays true to the earth is an insular discourse, imagining the earth and thought as islands, surrounded and constantly affected by the sea, storms and harsh winds—in short, a location confined and threatened by death trying to overtake the land of the living. Speculative visions such as the Atlantis myth as related by both Plato and Bacon, Ibn Tufayl's Islands in the *Philosophus Autodidactus* and Kant's island of truth understand the ground as traversed by alien forces trying to ablate it. Traditionally philosophy has pushed back against this limitropic porosity by denaturalizing the earth, turning it into a given or stable ground for thought itself. Philosophy has always been the rejection of the ungrounded earth by a thousand subterfuges, which stop the infinite speed of thought that introduces the infinite into the ground itself and thereby threatens the organicity of the earth.[5] One scouts the *terra cognita*, defines its borders, since the *terra incognita* outside has nothing to offer but desolation and insanity.

The most vehement rejection of this porosity of the earth comes from Hegel. As Hutton established geology as a proper science, introducing the immense timescales needed to understand the features of the earth's crust, and Lyell's uniformitarianism, building on this work, introduced deep time as a counter model to Cuvier's catastrophism, Hegel sensed the possible consequences and was appalled. Aware of the danger of extending the explanatory scope of observable natural causes to the earth's features, Hegel denounces the significance of geology for philosophy to prevent its implications from corrupting thought itself. Hutton's *Theory of the Earth*, however, is *prima facie* not philosophically threatening in itself. Although he proposes a naturalistic explanation of the earth's fea-

---

[5] Giordano Bruno, for example, takes up Teofilio's dual meaning of matter either as potency or substratum; see Werner Beierwaltes, *Identität und Differenz* (Frankfurt am Main: Klostermann, 2011), p. 188. Trying to reconcile both, Bruno's radical materialism attempts to formulate an ontology by proposing that being is only made up of forces (or potencies). Confronted with the consequences of reducing one to the other—if potency is canceled out there is no differentiation or formation; if the substratum is eliminated the unity of the One is impossible—Bruno halts his philosophical mining into the grounds of the earth, returning, in the last instance, to Aristotelian substance. See Giordano Bruno, *Cause, Principle, and Unity*, trans. Robert de Lucca (Cambridge; New York: Cambridge University Press, 1998), p. 66–77.

tures, he still maintains that regarding the formation of the earth, "we find no vestige of a beginning—no prospect of an end."[6] It is only at the furthest point of the investigation into the history of the earth that Hegel and Hutton, both agreeing on the eternity of the earth, diverge. The oldest rocks are, the geologists propose, "the last of an antecedent series,"[7] an antecedence which is not recoverable in real time. Since, therefore, this antecedence is a non-recoverable exteriority, Hegel must eliminate it to accomplish the total recovery in and of the Notion. The *Encyclopedia* addresses these concerns about the earth's relation to the Notion: "The earth is a whole, as a system of life, but, as crystal, it is like a skeleton, which can be regarded as dead because its members seem still to subsist formally on their own, while its process falls outside it."[8] The integration of the earth into the organic system of Life (as *one* Life) expressed by the movement of the Notion therefore hinges on the expulsion of antecedent exteriority. In a recapitulation of the formal-vitalist principle, "the organism makes itself into its own presupposition," because "the inwardisation of the Idea of Nature within itself to subjective vitality [...] is the judgement or partition of the Idea into itself and into this processless immediacy."[9] All non-recoverable exteriority, like the antecedent series of the rocks, must therefore be expelled to ensure that all members of life caught be integrated into a unity, furthering subjective vitality. Hence, "all externality is inorganic"[10] and always carries with it the threat of annexing the movement of the Absolute, of subjecting Life to the inertia of the "outwardly actual" turning the earth into a wasteland. With the (real) natural forces of geology, however, Hutton had introduced a non-recoverable externality and, although he himself denounced all cosmogonic ambitions, Hegel realized the implications of the idea and set in motion philosophy's immune response. Geology was not only to be ignored by philosophy but rejected,

---

6    Charles Lyell, *Principles of Geology* (Harmondsworth: Penguin, 1997), p. 16.
7    Ibid.
8    Georg Wilhelm Friedrich Hegel, *Encyclopedia of the Philosophical Sciences in Basic Outline, Part 1: Science of Logic*, trans. Klaus Brinkmann and Daniel O. Dahlstrom (Cambridge: Cambridge University Press, 2010), §338, addition.
9    Ibid.
10   Ibid.

since the oldest rocks necessarily implied an antecedent to the planetary object (the ground) itself, refuting the eternity of the earth and hence the possibility of the total recovery of the Notion. Hegel must, therefore, stop the process of mining, halt progress at the earth's crust, making it eternal through the function of judgement.

Attempting to restore the earth's philosophical relevance and wrest it away from its subjugation to the movement of the Notion, Husserl ends up immobilizing it completely in his 1934 manuscript text "Grundlegende Untersuchungen zum phänomenologischen Ursprung der Räumlichkeit der Natur." As a "doctor of civilization," he finds Europe in a crisis caused by science's "delirious" objectification and reification of the Cosmos. Misunderstanding the teleology of science, which finds its realization of the λόγος in the proximity to the *Lebenswelt*, Husserl here attacks modern science, but Copernicus and Galileo in particular, for reducing the Cosmos to pure abstraction. As the root of θεωρεῖν implies, the remedy to this loss of teleological experience is a reconnection of science with phenomenology, with the former grounded in the latter. Rooting knowledge in a *Lebenswelt* which can be grasped neither by the intellect nor the senses but can only be intuited, phenomenology's cosmology is concerned with the constitution of the world (or cosmos), rather than with its empirical description. Whether helio- or geocentric, Husserl criticizes modern (empirical) science for conceiving of the earth only as a celestial body, misconstruing its "archaic"[11] function. Conceived as a phenomenological entity, not a celestial body, the earth as "ground"[12] (*Boden*) does not appear to move, but rather by being immobile provides us with a stable ground that enables all navigation and distinction; even the distinction between movement and non-movement is only teleologically possible relative to an immobile ground. The relative determinations necessary for

---

[11] The manifold meanings of *arché* —as special vessel (as in Noah's ark) and as the Greek "fundamental principle," which derives its legislative power from its temporal status as the "primordial" and has genetic power as the "ancestral"—are encompassed in this Husserlian notion.

[12] Edmund Husserl, "Grundlegende Untersuchungen Zum Phänomenologischen Ursprung Der Räumlichkeit Der Natur," in *Philosophical Essays in Memory of Edmund Husserl* (Cambridge, Mass.: Harvard University Press, 1940), p. 414.

establishing any metric—ones as simple as up, down, left, right—occur primordially on the immobile earth. Similar to the Greek *telos*, the earth provides a universal and common ground wherever we go; it is an unmoving home. Such a "geostatism" follows from Husserl's epoché. In line with the tradition of transcendental philosophy he reduces the earth to what can be experienced while simultaneously establishing a common sense— the universalized, nourishing *Boden*—that is invariable, unmoving and eternal. The world's constitution remains at the level of the earth's crust, where the feet touch the ground. Just as Kant refused the idea of a genetic dimension to the *sensus communis*, so Husserl prohibits any investigation into the origins of the immobile earth; it is the *Ur-Arché*, subjecting everything to the judgement of Mother Earth (or God).

This subsumption of the earth under the judgement of God, i.e. under the form of the organism, is never total. As Land notices, a "dark fluidity at the roots of our nature rebels against the security of *terra firma*, provoking a wave of anxiety in which we are submerged."[13] The faint remnants of cosmic horror in Deleuze's cosmology—the Invisible, the Unground, the Unknown—reveal Husserl's to be a "pseudo-cosmology." Asking for the genetic dimension of the immobile ground renders the earth porous and dynamic—animated and maintained by non-sensible forces, which cannot be made to resemble their empirical products. Consequently, the earth, rotating around its axis, revolving around the sun, traversed by cosmic rays and constantly (de-)formed by tectonic forces and geological processes, does not provide a stable ground or metric, but is implicated in a cosmic unground in non-metric space. Husserl cannot imagine any shift in the common universal ground and therefore any possibility of radically different experiences outside the limit of the current transcendental framework. The same earth was under Euclid's feet when he assembled the basic axioms of his geometry, as the one that provides an immobile reference point for non-Western philosophers, as the one we stand on today. As long as the earth is an ark, everything is conditioned by and hence subjected to its unchanging nature. Deleuze, however, invoking the *terra*

---

[13] Land, *The Thirst for Annihilation*, p. 107.

*incognita,* reveals the production of the earth itself by real forces that are neither recoverable by the notion of lived experience nor present in lived experience. This unknown earth in turn implies the possibility of experiences not yet predetermined by an unchanging earth. The infinite speed of thought mines deeper than living experience, shattering the earth that was conceived as a dead celestial body for science or as immobile ground for experience, transforming it into a territory constantly woven in a process of deterritorialization and reterritorialization. We forget the earth to stay true to it, we must plunge it into the ἄπειρον.

## Time and Ground

By inquiring into the anteriority implied in Hutton's earliest rocks, Deleuze reveals the unrecoverable exteriority of cosmic forces within deep time, which are not integrable into organic unity. This temporal shift illuminates the problem that occurs when leaving the organic image of thought, namely the relation of time and ground, or more precisely, the problem that no ground can be provided that either allows for the conditioning and constitution of time or the deduction of temporality. Rather, any supposedly stable ground seems to be grounded in time, or must be deduced from it, and, in fact, the ground is constantly ungrounded by time.

As the previous section demonstrated, Deleuze reframes the relation of time and ground through three (non-consecutive) temporal syntheses. The first two are habit and memory, which provide the grounding and ground of time respectively. These are conditioned by the third, an unground, which enables the first two by introducing intensive difference. The relation between time and ground that emerges here is, however, not sufficiently explained by Deleuze and permits readings ranging from realist positions to transcendental idealist attempts at reconstruction. As Grant correctly notes in relation to Alliez's distinctly idealist reading of Deleuze, this ambiguity in Deleuze's statements about "the universal ungrounding" have even reopened the possibility of bringing him in close proximity to Fichte, conflating the former's ethology with the latter's primacy of the practical. This amounts to nothing less than the eradication of the earth (and nature) in favor of an ethical view of the world.[14] In answering the question of the relation of time and ground, what is at stake is the fundamental problem of the scope and limitations of transcendental philosophy's inquiry into the *real* conditions of cognition, rather than only its conditions of possibility.[15]

While it seems uncontroversial to claim that Deleuze's philosophy of time can be easily applied to organic life, the question remains whether these processes can be extended to all spatio-temporal dynamics, or conversely whether, contrary to Deleuze's protestations, the syntheses of time have conditions that are only satisfied within the realm of organic life. In his study on life and time, Keith Ansell-Pearson, for example, is willing to extend the first synthesis of time in *Difference and Repetition* beyond the human, but only up to the limit of the organic sphere: "The presentation of time he is developing is by no means restricted to human time—the contraction of habits through an originary contemplation is a feature of organic life in general."[16] The implicit restriction in this well-meaning extension is noted by James Williams in his study of Deleuze's philosophy of time, even if only in the endnotes.[17] Ascribing the formation of habits exclusively to organisms not only recapitulates the vitalist's rejection of the morphogenetic power of matter, but at the same iterates transcendental philosophy's regionalizing of time, making it conditioned on a pre-given form. Manuel DeLanda's *A Thousand Years of Non-Linear History* is, on the other hand, at the other end of the extreme, constructing a materialist history by conflating all processes of structuration, whether physical, linguistic, economic, biological, anthropological, etc., situating them all on the same ontological plane, thereby creating a "flat" ontology.[18] This history, however, simply accepts the results of Deleuze's

14   Compare Grant, *Philosophies of Nature after Schelling*, p. xi.
15   Iain Hamilton Grant, "Movements of the World. The Sources of Transcendental Philosophy," *Analecta Hermeneutica* 3 (2011), p. 1.
16   Keith Ansell-Pearson, *Philosophy and the Adventure of the Virtual: Bergson and the Time of Life* (London: Routledge, 2002), p. 186.
17   Compare Williams, *Gilles Deleuze's Philosophy of Time*, p. 166.
18   See Manuel DeLanda, *A Thousand Years of Nonlinear History* (New York: Zone Books, 1997). In particular, he attempts to reduce economy, linguistics and biology to interplays of matter and energy to provide a history that is not determined by human intentions.

philosophy of time, without tracing or explaining how they are even applicable to processes beyond consciousness. He achieves this by bypassing all epistemological concerns expressed in transcendental philosophy and adopting the standpoint of modern science's realism, thus implicitly accepting all its positivist and idealist metaphysical premises, which means his project eventually falls behind Deleuze's ambitions.[19]

In the vitalist understanding predominant in contemporary Deleuzian thought, the transition from phenomenological to metaphysical registers, as well as the shift from regional ontologies to metaphysics appears to be unproblematic and is consequently not well examined. As Ray Brassier notes, this might be due to the forgoing of reliable epistemological tools, and while Deleuze denounces the subjugation of ontology to epistemology, such a refusal does not solve the problems transcendental philosophy had sought to remedy.[20]

This problem and its consequences can be seen in Nathan Widder's book on Deleuze's philosophy of time and politics. Drawing on Deleuze's interpretation of Hamlet and giving the fractured Self a distinctly psychoanalytic slant, Widder enquires into the impersonal conditions of the living present. In this approach "time" names the structure, not the measure, of change: "It is a kind of *being out of sync* with oneself, which is the condition for anything to change or move."[21] This detaches time from any metric but also any norms, moralities and images of thought derived from it. In its failed self-constitution the fractured Self implies the possibility of a becoming-other, a constant difference from any equilibrium that might be misconstrued as an identity. Relying on the fractured Self to explain the workings of the third synthesis, however, can lead to a certain form of

---

Unlike the predominant anti-humanist tendencies in contemporary thought, which render history an interplay of discourses or power structures, his history is devoutly materialist and realist.

[19] See James Williams, "Science and Dialectics in the Philosophies of Deleuze, Bachelard and DeLanda," *Paragraph* 29, no. 2 (2006), p. 98–114.

[20] Ray Brassier, "Concrete Rules and Abstract Machines: Form and Function in A Thousand Plateaus," in *A Thousand Plateaus and Philosophy*, ed. Jeffrey Bell, Henry Somers-Hall, and James Williams (Edinburgh: Edinburgh University Press, 2018), p. 277.

[21] Nathan Widder, *Reflections on Time and Politics* (Philadelphia: Pennsylvania State University Press, 2008), p. 6.

idealism, which Widder acknowledges: "an ontology of time is a human (although not a humanist) ontology."[22] Viewed within the larger framework of Deleuze's metaphysics, however, this problem is compounded, insofar as the third synthesis is the creation of novelty. It seems as if without the human mind there could be nothing new under the sun. Reynolds, responding to this predicament in Widder's books, suggests a phenomenological restriction, i.e. that Widder is only speaking about time insofar as it manifests itself in the mind. Through this epistemological regionalizing of time, however, which makes it dependent on the mind, its metaphysical dimension, again, is made inaccessible.

Confronted with the epistemological and ontological double bind that the relation of time and ground presents in Deleuze's philosophy, one cannot be agnostic about either the realist or the idealist tendencies implicit in it. Since idealist interpretations do not draw out the full potential of the inorganic image of thought and agnostic interpretations remain incapable of tackling this problem (or continue to ignore the uneasy passage from phenomenology to metaphysics), the following will provide an attempt at a speculative approach, which will resituate vitalism as anti-phenomenology, to then rephrase the relation of time and ground in terms of an idea of individuation beyond consciousness.

### THE BERGSONIAN PROBLEM

*Vitalism as Anti-Phenomenology*
Having already sketched Deleuze's critique of how Husserl deformed the life-world with his introduction of a transcendence within immanence (the transcendental subject traversing all levels of constitution), and having considered the difficulties transcendental empiricism has leaving phenomenology for good, we will now examine the Bergsonian line of flight. The twentieth century front against phenomenology mostly draws its resources from either Marxist, structuralist or rationalist (especially

---

22   Ibid., p. 4.

Spinozian) traditions.[23] Deleuze leans on the vitalist tradition, most notably on Bergson, in his critique and methodological alternative. But, yet again, the opposition Husserl/Bergson is more uneasy than it first seems.

At the conference of the Göttingen Circle in 1911, Husserl perplexed his listeners with the exclamation: "We are the true Bergsonians."[24] Reading this statement in the context of the beginning of the twentieth century, we can see that Husserl and Bergson are allies in their respective rejection of both rationalism and dialectics (i.e. Hegel) as the dominant modes of thought.[25] It is, however, in the method of how these oppositions are maintained and how the "return to the things themselves" is achieved that the two differ. As Deleuze notes, Husserl's bracketing of consciousness restricts his philosophy to the traditional constellation of the problem of immediacy and mediation, insofar as he begins with sensible things (sensible immediacy) to arrive at the mind (constructed mediation), while Bergson attempted to reverse this relation.[26] According to Deleuze's "Bergson, 1859–1941," the eponymous thinker offers the change in perspective that

> we are separated from things; the immediate given is therefore not immediately given. But we cannot be separated by a simple accident, by a mediation that would come from us, that would concern only us. The movement that changes the nature of things must be founded in things themselves; things must begin by losing themselves in order for us to end up losing them.[27]

---

23  Of course, these traditions also traverse each other in their critique of phenomenology, compare Knox Peden, *Spinoza Contra Phenomenology: French Rationalism from Cavaillès to Deleuze* (Stanford: Stanford University Press, 2014).

24  Herbert Spiegelberg, *The Phenomenological Movement: A Historical Introduction, Vol. 5* (Berlin: Springer Science & Business Media, 2012), p. 399.

25  An account of the interesting connections and similarities between Husserl's and Bergson's conception of the relation of time and consciousness can be found in: Rafael Winkler, "Husserl and Bergson on Time and Consciousness," in *Logos of Phenomenology and Phenomenology of the Logos*, ed. Anna-Teresa Tymieniecka. (Heidelberg: Springer Verlag, 2006). p. 93–115.

26  Kathrin Thiele, *The Thought of Becoming: Gilles Deleuze's Poetics of Life* (Zurich: Diaphanes, 2008), p. 83.

27  Gilles Deleuze, "Bergson, 1859–1941," in *Desert Islands and Other Texts, 1953–1974* (Los Angeles; New York: Semiotext(e), 2004), p. 23.

Sartre's discovery of a non-thetic and non-positional consciousness behind the self had provided a novel way of thinking the transcendental according to this paradoxical scheme. The claim of the transcendence of the ego, however, affirmed for Deleuze that the fate of phenomenology is to sink deeper into the subjective realm of consciousness, untethered from the world. As we have already shown, in the end even the Bergsonism of Merleau-Ponty is restricted by the demands of phenomenology. And we have gestured towards Deleuze's move: to break the organic unity of phenomenology, Deleuze will instead investigate the genesis of concrete beings, i.e. the physical, biological, psychic individuation conditioned by a pre-personal and pre-individual reality of intensive difference. Such a reality is no longer exclusively constituted by the subject, but instead designates the subject's genetic condition as such. We have also, however, noted the methodological and subsequent epistemological difficulty of safely transitioning from the phenomenological to a more speculative (and realist) position, which cancels out the need for an impersonal spontaneity of consciousness by introducing a genetic power outside the subject. As we have stated at the outset of the work, such a position would be the hylozoism necessary to replace the organic image of thought established by Kant. The figure who provides the resources for the speculative passage in Deleuze is, as we will see, Bergson, who enables a reconceptualization of the relation of time and genesis.

Deleuze's reconstruction of Bergson's *élan vital*, in the former's 1956 as well as the 1966 text, introduces a non-phenomenological and non-dialectical notion of difference as internal difference. Demonstrating how Bergson characterizes the notion of abstract time as an amalgam of space and duration and space as a mixture of matter and duration, Deleuze wants to highlight that these couplings involve the tendencies towards relaxation (matter) and contraction (duration). The difference in their nature is not located between the two tendencies, but rather within one of them: the internal difference of duration. In a similar way to Kant, Bergson detaches time from the metric of space, with, however, different consequences. Unbound by the condition of metric space—the notion that some-*thing* must be presupposed to conceive of movement—duration allows us to think movement as continuous self-differentiation without an object. That notions of difference which rely on alterity, negation and contradiction (external difference) are replaced by a notion of internal difference sets this approach apart from dialectics (Platonic as well as Hegelian), but also renders Bergsonian vitalism an anti-phenomenology.[28] Overcoming the need for an external difference between two tendencies, internal difference is hence "*in an unmediated way*, the unity of substance and subject."[29] Sartre's protestations that Bergsonian duration is incapable of accounting for the existence of consciousness *through* duration only serve to highlight again the conceptual limitations of phenomenology. In describing the process of perceptual temporalization in Bergson, which would account for subjectivity, Sartre is reluctant to concede that it is a process that temporalizes itself, since he is not willing to think of movement and hence difference in any other terms than negation (via consciousness).[30]

*Vital Difference, Time and Genesis*

To understand this process, Deleuze draws attention to Bergson's reading of biology as a process of differentiation (as the expression of vital difference). He suggests that the *élan vital* is better understood not in terms of individual ontogenesis but rather in the context of (and in opposition to) Darwinian evolution. While Darwin's model relied on determination of species by negation implicit in his mechanistic interpretation of the development of the species, Bergson insists on the unpredictability of all living things. This indeterminacy, however, should not be misconstrued as just random chance, since it subjects evolution still to the logic of preconceived beginnings, causes and ends. Rather, change must be conceived of as due to an internal drive (*élan*), propelling the continuous differentiation of species forward by an explosive force rather than a series

---

28   See Pierre Montebello, "Deleuze, Une Anti-Phénoménologie ?," *Chiasmi International* 13 (2011), p. 315–325.
29   Gilles Deleuze, "Bergson's Conception of Difference," in *Desert Islands and Other Texts, 1953–1974* (Los Angeles; New York: Semiotext(e), 2004), p. 38.
30   See Sartre, *Being and Nothingness*, p. 113.

of reactions based on external differences of material causes and ends. This process of self-differentiation, or of a problem that determines its own solution, was already described in the previous chapter as the Idea in the Deleuzian sense. Hence, transposed into a transcendental empiricist register, such a model of evolution can be described as follows:

> Virtuality exists in such a way that it actualizes itself as it dissociates itself; it must dissociate itself to actualize itself. Differentiation is the movement of a virtuality actualizing itself. Life differs from itself, so we are confronted by divergent lines of evolution and, on each line, original processes. Still, it is only with itself that life differs; consequently, also on each line, we are confronted by particular apparatuses, particular organ structures that are identical though obtained by different means.[31]

Within his text on Bergson, Deleuze prefigures the decisive idea of *Difference and Repetition*: that the virtual produces the actual beyond the rule of limitation and resemblance, and thus operates outside of the realization of the possible.

Duration is hence the virtual that "defines an absolutely positive mode of existence"[32] reconfiguring the relation of genesis and time. Duration describes a time that is neither psychological nor chronological but rather the genetic condition of the difference between subjective interiority and objective exteriority, which makes both possible as specific degrees of duration. Deleuze's reading of *Matter and Memory* develops this de-psychological time further by separating the psychological present from the ontological past. The virtual here is transposed into a Bergsonian pure past, equivalent to that we saw in the last section: a whole which contains all degrees of contraction and at the same time exceeds its actualization in the present. Although this proposition is already implicit in *Matter and Memory* as described by Deleuze, the later *Creative Evolution* explores the entailed cosmological consequence of it by demonstrating its applicability

---

31  Deleuze, "Bergson's Conception of Difference," p. 40.
32  Ibid., p. 44.

to the whole universe: "Everything happens as if the universe were a tremendous Memory."[33] Human consciousness hence appears as a specific instance of nature, i.e. a degree of duration, but not as its ground or principle. While Husserl had still tried to reconstruct the ark as the immobile earth by subjecting it to the metric of the structure of intentionality of the lived present, precluding deep or cosmic time, Bergson's duration reveals the condition of such a metric to be the non-metric and non-linear self-differentiation of vital difference: "A flowing-matter in which no point of anchorage nor center of reference would be assignable";[34] a universal ungrounding underlies the livable world.

*Beyond the Human Condition*

What makes phenomenology uneasy in Bergson is, as Moore notes,[35] his ambition to go beyond the human condition, forgoing intentional consciousness as the inevitable condition of the world. Rather than the formula that "all consciousness is consciousness *of* something," the genetic dimension of duration implies that "all consciousness *is* something." As such, Bergson's is not a transcendental philosophy but a philosophy of nature in the Schellingian sense: the question: "How is nature possible for a mind?" becomes "How is the mind possible for (or within) nature?."[36]

Such a decentering of the human does not, however, mean abandoning it but rather, as Braidotti puts it, developing a "sensibility that aims at overcoming anthropocentrism,"[37] not humanity. Philosophy in particular is characterized by Bergson as the discipline that is capable of achieving this aim of surpassing the human condition. As such, however, it must formulate theories building on an internal relation of knowledge and life, not an

---

33  Deleuze, *Bergsonism*, p. 77.
34  Deleuze, *Cinema 1*, p. 57.
35  For an in-depth investigation into the connections and differences of conceiving between conceptions of this "beyond" of the human condition in phenomenology (especially Sartre and Merleau-Ponty) and Bergson, see F. C. T. Moore, *Bergson: Thinking Backwards* (Cambridge: Cambridge University Press, 1996).
36  For a recent study of Bergson's significance in and for contemporary discourse on the posthuman, see Keith Ansell-Pearson, *Bergson: Thinking beyond the Human Condition* (New York: Bloomsbury Academic, 2018).
37  Rosi Braidotti, *The Posthuman* (Malden: Polity Press, 2013), p. 56.

external or even antagonistic one. If human consciousness is considered as a product of evolution, philosophy is not able to start by deducing the possibility of experience and the limits of knowledge from the current framework presented by the intellect, but must consider its genetic condition, and therefore leave the framework. The question of the evolution of the intellect as well as the question of how it surpasses its own limits are therefore methodologically linked and opposed to Kantian analysis. While the latter attempts to reduce the object to the elements already familiar to the mind, (re-)constructing it as the mind's spontaneous action, which accounts for its structural similarity with other objects, Bergson proposes a method of intuition.

Although Schelling had already attempted to circumvent the analytic method with intuition, Bergson notes, this post-Kantian approach appealed to a non-temporal intuition, inspired by Spinozism's ambition to deduce concrete existence from the One or complete being. Such a reduction of intuition is characteristic for transcendental philosophy and its successors, which propose a concept of intuition as form devoid of sensibility. Bergson argues that such a tendency is not accidental, but typical for modern philosophy's reduction to the intellect. As described in *Creative Evolution*, intellect, viewed from the perspective of evolution, has an inherent tendency to spatialize, since it models itself after the geometrical properties of the matter it is used to manipulating. This "habit" of the intellect manifests itself in representational thought, most notably in the spatialization of temporality and the reduction of life to its visible elements. Through such a reduction of life to just one local manifestation—the intellect's pragmatic impetus to mechanize the universe—the "very inwardness of life" is reduced to the mere notion of "Life" as such, so that its plurality is collapsed into a single image. Philosophy's task, then, is a paradoxical one: to find a way to broaden the horizon of our perceptions beyond the habits of the intellect but to do so *through the intellect itself*. Returning to the evolutionary perspective again, Bergson's radical proposal in *Creative Evolution* is that nature produced human consciousness as one instance among others and that communication or encounter with these forms of plant or animal consciousness is possible without proposing a transcendental ground of similarities. This confrontation between consciousnesses produces affects and possibly even knowledge without first having to leave the realm of the sensible to establish a common schema or language. However, this implies two reworkings of philosophy. Firstly, the Platonic idea, still present in Kant, that the goal of philosophy is generality and the rules of subsumption of objects under it, must be revised. But "the idea, that for a new object we might have to create a new concept, perhaps a new method of thinking, is deeply repugnant to us,"[38] since it clashes with the intellect's tendency to spatialize and thereby subject every object to the same homogeneous structure. As Bergson admits, the inherent paradox becomes an aporia if this tendency can only be overcome by the intellect itself, since even the indeterminate encounter would be then determined by and retrospectively made to conform to the spatializing tendency of the intellect. Kant had demonstrated that there is no dialectical method that could ever produce reliable knowledge beyond the conditions of possibility of experience. He concluded that any metaphysics would therefore be an intuitive one, only to then claim that such a metaphysics would be impossible due to the lack of an intuition of this kind. And, as Bergson admits, "it would in fact be so if there were no other time or change than those which Kant perceived."[39] New perceptions of time and change are required. The task of finding an appropriate intuition thus forces philosophy outside of the domain of the sensible.

In contrast to Kant, Bergson wishes to demonstrate that intuition should not be reduced to the geometries of the intellect; instead, considering the genetic dimension of the intellect itself, one must make clear and distinct the power that produced the intellect in the first place. Rather than intuiting an object as something constructed by the mind, Bergson invites us to "enter" the object via the instinct or sympathy "by which somebody is transported into the interior of an object."[40] Intuition is both means and method; it is self-reflective and disinterested instinct,

---

[38] Bergson, *Creative Evolution*, p. 48.
[39] Henri Bergson, *The Creative Mind: An Introduction to Metaphysics* (New York: Philosophical Library, 1946), p. 136.
[40] Ibid., p. 135.

"capable of reflecting upon its object and enlarging it indefinitely."[41] As Deleuze explains, this idea of intuition does not refer to vague experiences or incommunicable feelings, but is a method peculiar to Bergsonism and aiming at precision. Through this method, mental life is revealed to be temporal, a time internal to itself and constituted by the dynamics of interpenetrating states, with duration as the immediate awareness of this flow of experience. However, mental life does not appear as one unified flow as such, but as different states of mind that occur simultaneously while at the same time merging into one consciousness. This form of constitution of elements, which are different in kind since there is no unifying metric and which form a whole through their difference and their relationships and not in spite of them, upsets the intellect's tendency for spatialization. The intellect strives to quantify duration into separable units, creating the problem, so salient for phenomenology, of how to incorporate these into a seamless whole through the synthesis of consciousness. Intuition exposes this as a false problem born from a misconception of duration. Intuition, then, is not identical with duration, "but rather the movement by which thought emerges from its own duration and gains insight into the difference of other durations within and outside itself."[42]

The reflection of mental life upon itself does not, however, yield what Bergson suggests, namely insight into the material or even cosmic dimension of life. As Lapoujade explains, Bergson's methodological approach to metaphysics would be incomplete without the movement of sympathy. Irreducible to intuition proper, this denotes an act of reasoning by analogy, not by external resemblance but by an internal communication between movements, images or tendencies.[43] The intuitive exploration of ourselves as degrees of duration depicts our mental life as being constituted materially and vitally by the same processes which make up the

---

[41] Bergson, *Creative Evolution*, p. 176.
[42] Keith Ansell-Pearson, "Beyond the Human Condition: Bergson and Deleuze," in *Deleuze and the Non/Human*, ed. Jon Roffe and Hannah Stark (London: Palgrave Macmillan, 2015), p. 91.
[43] See David Lapoujade, "Intuition and Sympathy in Bergson," *Pli: Warwick Journal of Philosophy* 10 (2015), p. 8.

universe, so that "the deeper the point we touch, the stronger will be the thrust which sends us back to the surface."[44] While we investigate ourselves, we may find inhuman states of consciousness and cosmic movements as a source to go beyond the human condition.

## Bergson's Residual Humanism

In Adorno's *Negative Dialectics,* Husserl and Bergson, who appear *prima facie* as enemies, are surprisingly lumped together as avatars of the same historical movement, insofar as "Both men stay within range of immanent subjectivity."[45] One might very well argue that many of the accusations he levels against Bergson in particular are misconceptions on Adorno's part: the argument that the constitution of the *temps espace* cannot be accounted for from the underlying *temps durée,* for example, or that "all dialectical salt was washed away in an undifferentiated tide of life."[46] These critiques result from Adorno's unwillingness to recognize the internal difference of duration. However, his alignment of Husserl and Bergson reveals the more decisive critique: that both rely on an immediate givenness to consciousness, which is supposed to circumvent abstraction, but, according to Adorno, leads both to remain in the positivism they sought to avoid. To assess the validity of this claim of positivism and finally idealism, one must distinguish it from the other "residual humanism"[47] Bergson harbors.

In his later work, Deleuze will accuse Bergson of recapitulating common human mnemotechnics and transposing them onto the universe. Such anthropomorphism is, however, methodologically inevitable, since sympathy remains a reasoning that works by analogy. Similarly, the organism is still the primary locus of life and is hence the object that vitalism is concerned with in Bergson. While Deleuze and Guattari hold the organism to be the negative limit of life, for Bergson it is precisely the positive condition of creative evolution, since the organization of life is

---

44  Bergson, *Creative Evolution,* p. 299.
45  Theodor W. Adorno, *Negative Dialectics* (New York: Continuum, 1983), p. 9.
46  Ibid., p. 334.
47  Ansell-Pearson, *Germinal Life,* p. 73.

necessary for any "free act" that engenders novelty. As we will see, there is a metaphysical reason why Bergson makes novelty conditioned on the organic form. In a way, this anthropomorphism deepens the essential paradox that human consciousness (dominated by the intellect) is for Bergson the "end" of evolution, engendering free will while simultaneously disabling it.

The problems these accusations touch on, however, are rooted in the metaphysical consequences of the epistemological reliance on immediate givenness. Following two interrelated methodological problems of intuition and sympathy might help to approach the question. While Deleuze draws from Bergson's attempt to explore the inhuman and superhuman durations we are composed of, it is the aforementioned step beyond the subject's consciousness entailed in this that is methodologically problematic or at least too optimistic in both thinkers. When Deleuze describes, in his very generous interpretation in *Bergsonism*, for example, the encounter between the rhythms of time in a bird's flight and his own durations, he writes:

> The flight of the bird and my own duration are only simultaneous insofar as my own duration divides in two and is reflected in another that contains it at the same time as it contains the flight of the bird: There is therefore a fundamental triplicity of fluxes. It is in this sense that my duration essentially has the power to disclose other durations, to encompass others, and to encompass itself ad infinitum.[48]

This triplicity of durations, according to Deleuze, is what discloses immanence, insofar as his duration, which encompasses the duration of the bird's flight, is in turn encompassed by a third duration not belonging to his consciousness. For an obvious reason, Deleuze will drop this method of Bergsonian intuition later: it is prone to tracing the transcendental (duration) from the empirical. This is because, firstly, for Bergson, the third duration is not immanence, but consciousness still, and secondly, even

---

[48] Deleuze, *Bergsonism*, p. 80.

if we grant that intuition might gesture towards or imply immanence, this comes at the price of making the empirical in its specific givenness necessary for the transcendental, reducing the latter to the rules of the former. As Bryant remarks, this does not challenge the traditional subject-object split, but merely provides another method for reducing the world to consciousness.[49] This becomes apparent in Bergson's notes on the application of intuition as method. Insofar as intuition is already a relation of mind to mind, a reflexive mediation, the immediacy of experience necessary for intuition seems to be always deferred. This problem of the distance between the lived experience and the analyzed experience is evident in Bergson's distinction between an authentic subject and an artificial subject in *Time and Free Will*. He espouses that the difference between intuition as practice and intuition as method is merely external, but he cannot give an adequate description of their internal relation without already relying on intuition in its dual function. It is exactly in the immediate self-relation in intuition, then, that a paradox arises: the immediacy is produced by the seemingly autonomous subject, which reflects upon itself, *willingly* suspending its intellectual habits. Such a free act is not just a methodological problem because it proposes a fully constituted self-sovereign subject, but also because there is no epistemological tool to distinguish reliably between the self-positioning of durations (and their distinctions) by the subject and "genuine" durations. Rather, Bergson seems to propose good will on the part of the thinker, which ensures that thinking, once it is properly engendered by intuition, leads "naturally" to the truth.

Adorno's note might thus be understood as indicating a methodological problem with the immediacy of intuition as put forward by Bergson: "Intuition, then, signifies first of all consciousness, but immediate consciousness, a vision which is scarcely distinguishable from the object seen, a knowledge which is contact and even coincidence."[50] Bergson's trust in the mind's natural affinity to the truth as soon as the distorting

---

49 Bryant, *Difference and Givenness*, p. 78.
50 Bergson, *The Creative Mind*, p. 30.

effects of the intellect are removed entails a rejection of all mediating dialectics that would disturb authentic lived experience. As such, Adorno is right, and Deleuze would agree, that Husserl and Bergson both rely on and limit themselves to lived experience. For the transcendental empiricist, they appear unable to think the unlivable, impersonal, genetic dimension of consciousness. While *Difference and Repetition* could still be read in "post-phenomenological" terms and has been criticized for its championing of intuition as a method, Deleuze's later writings will progressively abandon the idea of human consciousness and subjectivity as methodologically and metaphysically primary.[51] "Non-organic life," which human consciousness can participate in but is in no way already implicated in, is, however, not thinkable for Bergson. The method of intuition at the same time presupposes and terminates in metaphysical assumptions about the nature of matter and mind, or space and duration respectively. The tendency towards entropy is, according to Bergson, inherent to matter and would accomplish its end—the complete dissolution of all organized form—were it not for an inverse process traversing it: mind. Conversely, pure mind is pure creativity without object, never yielding actual inventions since there is no obstacle to overcome. We find here the answer to the aforementioned question of why the organism has such a prominent place in Bergson's metaphysics: it is the point where the constant tension between consciousness and matter, contraction and extension results in an invention, which can in turn prolong the impetus of life in a free act.

Already in *Difference and Repetition,* Deleuze announces his break with Bergson in his critique of intensive magnitude. If he formerly attempted to describe "difference" as the difference between the order of the difference in kind and the difference in degree, he now uncovers difference as intensity, informing and constituting both orders. Intensity, for Deleuze, is neither extensive nor qualitative, since both presuppose identity and resemblance. Rather than the qualitative differences

---

[51] See Matija Jelača, "Sellars Contra Deleuze on Intuitive Knowledge," *Speculations. Journal of Speculative Realism* 5 (2014), p. 92–126.

of durations that would rely on lived experience, Deleuze is interested rather in the "graduated scale" of intensity, the being of the sensible, which will later become the plane of immanence. As a clarification of this difference, Deleuze's response to the entropic tendency of the universe proposed by thermodynamics is hence not, as Bergson described it, the traversal of matter by the mind, but rather the idea of intensity as the transcendental itself. The entropic illusion of science, for Deleuze, results from a misunderstanding about the difference between extensity and quality, in that progressive extension makes the universe uniform and thereby annihilates qualitative difference according to a mechanical understanding of the universe. This understanding falls prey to the transcendental illusion that excludes the genetic dimension of both extension and quality, proposing them as "given." By putting forward two orders of implication as well as degradation, Deleuze attempts to reveal this genetic dimension, so that intensities are always enveloped in the explication of extensities and qualities, while in the other order intensity remains implicated, both enveloped and enveloping, in itself. The illusion of entropy rests, then, in subjecting the order of implication to the order of extensity, reducing it to the empirically given, localized and extended forms of energy. Bergson similarly assumes that extensity is already constituted, with its corresponding differences in degree and qualities ready-made as differences in kind. He then sides with the latter, while also reducing them to lived experience, the immediately given.[52] Deleuze thus champions the primacy of quantitative difference before qualitative difference and, therefore, against Bergson's protestations, the mathematizability of time. Intensity now denotes the transcendental condition for their genesis, difference itself, which announces what Bergson could not accept: the unlivable being of the sensible. Moving away from Bergson, he now states:

> In short, there would no more be qualitative differences or differences in kind than there would be quantitative differences or differences of de-

---

[52] See Deleuze, *Difference and Repetition*, p. 225.

gree, if intensity were not capable of constituting the former in qualities and the latter in extensity, even at the risk of appearing to extinguish itself in both.[53]

The Deleuzian philosophy of time, which provides a methodologically sound way to think time beyond human consciousness, must consider intensity in its impersonal nature. The closely related concept of the affect and its anonymity will provide a basis for the inquiry into the concept of intensity. To make this inquiry, we must first consider what the personal or impersonal nature of affectivity might signify.

### THE ANONYMITY OF AFFECTS

Levinas's *Totality and Infinity* gives a decisive argument against the existence of the unconscious that not only illuminates the methodological constraints but also the ethical or moral core of phenomenology. Sartre's rejection of the unconscious and subsequent replacement of it with the concept of bad faith[54] was still very much in line with Husserl's denial of the existence of a psychic realm outside of the immanence of consciousness, on the basis that consciousness is consciousness in all its phases.[55] Levinas's more specific considerations on the matter start with a critique of Heidegger's narrow view of life, which forces it into the structure of "care" (*Sorge*) to meet his ontological demands. Against this, Levinas proposes the affirmative vision that "Life is love of life, a relation with contents that are not my being but more dear than my being: thinking, eating, sleeping, reading, working, warming oneself in the

---

53 Ibid., p. 239.
54 For an in-depth reconstruction of Sartre's argument and a concise Freudian answer, see Richard Askay, *Apprehending the Inaccessible: Freudian Psychoanalysis and Existential Phenomenology* (Evanston: Northwestern University Press, 2006).
55 For a balanced assessment of the problem that the Freudian unconscious poses to phenomenology, see Talia Welsh, "The Retentional and the Repressed: Does Freud's Concept of the Unconscious Threaten Husserlian Phenomenology?," *Human Studies* 25, no. 2 (2002), p. 165–183.

sun."⁵⁶ Since being is risked for happiness, life is not subject to care primordially and can never be reduced to "naked existence," but is always already affectivity and enjoyment of life. The possibility of despair and *Angst*, ontologized by Heidegger, is for Levinas conditioned by a more essential contentment. But as such, Levinas continues, life is essentially always in reference to me: "And because life is happiness it is personal. The personality of the person, the ipseity of the 'I', which is more than the particularity of the atom and of the individual, is the particularity of the happiness of enjoyment."⁵⁷ No constitutive power of the subject can account for the personality of the "I," only the formal bond between I-ness and affectivity provided by the happiness of life roots the "I" in its affective and passive ground. The sensible enjoyment of life thus leaves the ontological horizon set by Heidegger and with it Levinas abandons his earlier considerations of anonymous being in *Existence and Existents*.

The passive and affective grounds of the I-ness, however, entail a threatening verso: the impersonal nature of the affect. If we see a marble head in deep anguish, or a marble head jubilant to the point of excess, the expressions on the statues' faces seem to detach from any personal emotion or depth and present themselves as impersonal affections. And the deeper we sink into the passive constitution of the "I" by enjoyment, the more we might feel the anonymous drive to life and the tug towards more enjoyment, a desire not foreign to *Totality and Infinity*. While Levinas will argue for the primacy of alterity in the passive constitution of the I, he does not mean the impersonal exteriority that affectivity seems to entail. There appear to be no phenomenological means available to remedy this problem, although theological ones are summoned.⁵⁸ While one might argue that Levinas's primary concern was to put the constitution back on its feet and that the personal nature of affectivity is merely a by-product of this attempt, with Michel Henry's defense of the personal nature of af-

---

56  Emmanuel Levinas, *Totality and Infinity: An Essay on Exteriority* (Pittsburgh: Duquesne University Press, 2011), p. 112.
57  Ibid., p. 115.
58  A (possible) theological solution is sketched out in Hans-Dieter Gondek and László Tengelyi, *Neue Phänomenologie in Frankreich* (Berlin: Suhrkamp, 2011), p. 133.

fect, which describes affectivity as essentially self-affection, this problem becomes an intrinsic feature of phenomenology. Although Henry praises Schopenhauer in *Incarnation* for having reintroduced the question of life back into European philosophy, he decisively rejects the idea of a blind, impersonal will or drive of life.[59] Tracing the Freudian unconscious back to this tradition, *The Genealogy of Psychoanalysis* depicts this blind will-to-life as the paradigmatic model for the modern understanding of life. Beyond sophisticated arguments against the theory of repression, the main arguments against the impersonality of the drive are specifically phenomenological. All wanting or desiring that can be analyzed phenomenologically because it presents itself in givenness can be reconstructed as an operation of self-affection. Schopenhauer and subsequently Freud, according to Henry, create a speculative double of this will by interpreting the occurrence of desire as a sign or allusion to a beyond: the impersonal, blind and destructive will-to-life.[60] In this speculative vitalism, the phenomenology of desire appears as a mere (superficial) translation of an underlying play of forces. Collapsing back into pre-Kantian metaphysics, the speculations of these philosophies of Life (*Lebensphilosophien*), do not hold up to epistemological scrutiny, being neither evident in nor reconstructable from experience.

Phenomenology (and post-phenomenology) is hesitant to accept the anonymity entailed in the passive constitution of I-ness, not only because of epistemological constraints, but also for moral reasons. As in Kant, it is not truth that is at stake, but a certain morality tied to the concept of life itself. In both Levinas and Henry, happiness is co-constitutive with I-ness, as either personal enjoyment or self-affection. The reverse, the Schopenhauerian will-to-power, on the other hand, suggests a concept of life that on the level of the impersonal appears as destructive and on the level of the personal presents itself in and as suffering. Both (theological) phenomenologists, Levinas and Henry, construct their philosophy to avoid a

---

[59] See Michel Henry, *Incarnation: A Philosophy of Flesh* (Evanston: Northwestern University Press, 2015), p. 36.
[60] See Michel Henry, *The Genealogy of Psychoanalysis* (Stanford: Stanford University Press, 1998), p. 164.

speculative turn that would problematize their phenomenological morality or even prove to be its impossibility.

Positioned equally against the destructive will-to-life of Schopenhauer and the philosophies that seek to reduce life to the given, (Deleuze's) Nietzsche might provide a passage to the impersonality of the affect without the metaphysical or moral presuppositions. Nietzsche diagnoses, on the one hand, Schopenhauer's life-denying affectations as a remnant of the Kantian will-to-truth, in which the thing-in-itself is transposed into a singular metaphysical entity, a misconstrual of life's plural nature. On the other hand, philosophies that reduce life to the given are, for Nietzsche, content with a universe of things and visibility, warranting "truth" while ignoring the reality of the play of forces that describes the genealogical line (or genetic condition) of things and visibility, their origin in discontinuity and struggle, i.e. becoming.

As Graham Parkes notes, the idea that affectivity is of a personal nature is dubious for Nietzsche since, looking inward, the soul does not appear as a single unified self that encompasses all affections, but rather as a polyphony of personae expressing the affection. Even the soul is a multitude of forces struggling for domination, meaning expression.[61] This psychological polycentricity hence calls for a genealogy of I-ness to discover its real genesis from forces. In his early study on Nietzsche, Deleuze constructs his first version of transcendental empiricism from this vantage point by reformulating the will to power:

> Now, difference in quantity, understood in this way, necessarily reflects a differential element of related forces—which is also the genetic element of the qualities of these forces. This is what the will to power is; the genealogical element of force, both differential and genetic. The will to power is the element from which derive both the quantitative difference of related forces and the quality that devolves into each force in this relation.[62]

---

61   See Parkes, *Composing the Soul*, p. 249.
62   Deleuze, *Nietzsche and Philosophy*, p. 50.

Deleuze's critique of Bergson, in which he demonstrates the primacy of quantitative difference over qualitative difference, finds its origin in Nietzsche's theory of forces. The will to power, as both "differential" and "genetic" principle, denotes a never-ending process of organization, whereby changing constellations of force, resisting, overcoming or affecting each other, become variable units. These physical relations of forces (i.e. intensities) precede consciousness or receptivity and the latter become inexplicable (save as acts *sui generis*) without the activity of these forces. Affection for Deleuze's Nietzsche is therefore the corresponding quality to a quantity-difference in a configuration or relation of quanta of forces. As such, Deleuze understands affection in the Spinozist manner, as a *capacity* to affect and be affected, whose power should not be understood as passive receptivity or suffering (*pathos*), but as sensibility.[63] The field of differences of force-relations is necessarily impersonal and a-subjective since it is anterior to the constitution of consciousness. In *Difference and Repetition* then, Deleuze claims that intensity is the sufficient reason for phenomena and the condition for phenomenality.[64] However, insofar as affection is quality corresponding to intensity (quantity-differences), it describes the knowable product of a genesis that, while producing the given, is itself not given.

Even though affect and intensity are not identical, their close conceptual bond can be seen in Deleuze's claim that even inorganic "things" have a lived experience. This idea appears for the first time in *Difference and Repetition* in his discussion of Humean habit, where Deleuze invokes Plotinus's *Enneads* to detach contemplation and the formation of habits from the human framework. Since everything is contemplation—i.e. everything is affecting and affected—everything must possess a lived experience. In *What is Philosophy?*, Deleuze and Guattari reiterate this point: "Even when they are nonliving, or rather inorganic, things have a lived experience because they are perceptions and affections."[65] Alain Beaulieu

---

[63] See ibid., p. 62.
[64] See Deleuze, *Difference and Repetition*, p. 222.
[65] Deleuze and Guattari, *What is Philosophy?*, p. 154.

argues for a reading of this passage that suggests even in the animal, plant or mineral kingdom there is a minimal consciousness produced by the passive synthesis in the first synthesis of time. Such an interpretation, however, seems to call for a panpsychism modelled after human consciousness.[66] Although there is textual evidence that Deleuze in *Difference and Repetition* proposes that "everything is consciousness,"[67] since repetition is everywhere engendering spatio-temporal dynamics that correspond to a (rudimentary) consciousness, in the later works this idealism will give way to a transcendental empiricism proper to the field of immanence. A possible counter-interpretation might be found in *Bergsonism*, where Deleuze insists that quality emerges from a difference in quantity and, since everything is a constellation of force quanta, these processes yield a "lived experience."

Far more instructive, however, might be his notes on Plotinus and contemplation in the lecture "On Spinoza" from 1980, where Deleuze characterizes Plotinus's reversal of Platonism as the detachment of optics (pure light) from touch, which reveals the primacy of spatialization before space. The idea that light is not in space but creates space was utterly foreign to the classical Greeks and finds its way into Plotinus from the Orient.[68] Even if spatio-temporal dynamics *might* yield consciousness,

---

66  Beaulieu, "Edmund Husserl," p. 269.
67  The whole passage reads: "Every spatio-temporal dynamism is accompanied by the emergence of an elementary consciousness which itself traces directions, doubles movements and migrations, and is born on the threshold of the condensed singularities of the body or object whose consciousness it is. It is not enough to say that consciousness is consciousness of something: it is the double of this something, and everything is consciousness because it possesses a double, even if it is far off and very foreign." Deleuze, *Difference and Repetition*, p. 220.
68  As Deleuze describes in his lecture: "he had a premonition of the kind of reversal [*retournement*] of Platonism that he is in the process of making. It's with Plotinus that a pure optical world begins in philosophy. Idealities will no longer be only optical. They will be luminous, without any tactile reference. Henceforth the limit is of a completely different nature. Light scours the shadows. Does shadow form part of light? Yes, it forms a part of light and you will have a light-shadow gradation that will develop space. They are in the process of finding that deeper than space there is spatialization. [...] Space is the result of an expansion, that is an idea that, for a classical Greek, would be incomprehensible. It's an idea that comes from the Orient. That light could be spatializing: it's not light that is in space, it's light that constitutes space." Gilles Deleuze, "On Spinoza" (Paris, St. Denis, 1980), http://deleuzelectures.blogspot.com/2007/02/on-spinoza.html (last accessed April 2, 2024).

they do not do so necessarily, not logically at least. Rather, the ubiquity of contemplation points to life as intensive process instead of lived experience in the phenomenological sense, spatialization instead of a world.

### DELEUZIAN PLATONISM

*Ideality and Abstraction*

At this juncture, to reiterate in other terms the problem we are facing in this section, we must touch on a structural proximity between Hegel and Deleuze on the question of synthesis. Kant, characteristically for his organic thought, localizes the synthesizing function in the capacities of the subject and uses pure apperception as the guideline of the transcendental deduction. The relational synthesis, constitutive of objectivity for Kant, is then transposed by Hegel outside of its localization in the subject into the relation of subject and object itself. Construing this synthesis as self-relating negativity, Hegel's objective idealism recodes synthesis as the self-synthesis or self-construction of reality that produces objective structure. But this echoes the problem we encountered in Deleuze's uses and critique of Husserl's passive synthesis: insofar as we grant that synthesis is essentially transgressive and not an activity of the transcendental subject, how does the continuous flow of non-discrete elements (the continuum of intensities, i.e. force-relations) ever yield discontinuity and discrete things, that is, objective structure?

While Hegel's solution is founded in the self-movement of negation and hence contradiction, Deleuze invokes the *élan vital* (Bergson) or Will to Power (Nietzsche), which relies on the primacy of the intensive before the extensive and hence affirmative self-differentiation without negation. As we have chosen an anti-phenomenological stance to properly pursue Deleuze's notion of inorganic life beyond human consciousness, it is necessary to pose the question of how intelligibility is encoded, or connected to physical reality, differently. To solve the problem of Deleuze's ideality, we must move him closer to Plato, construing Ideas as forms, rejecting the empiricist understanding of ideas as mental entities, and investigating

Deleuze's claim that thinking can occur beyond and without a mind, or non-cognitively.

If the previous chapter reconstructed the Idea/structure in Deleuze from the Kantian regulative Idea, this depiction remained within the epistemological framework instituted by critical philosophy. In contrast to Kant as well as the empiricists, Plato and Deleuze stress a conception of the Idea as an *ontological* category, which precedes actual (empirically given) entities and is never exhausted by them. While Deleuze's use of the Idea in *Difference and Repetition* hints at the mind-independent genesis of structure as well as its actualization in concrete entities, the later transformation of it into the notion of multiplicity in *A Thousand Plateaus* enables it to account properly for phenomena, geneses and becoming beyond consciousness. This conception of the Idea is, as Deleuze admits, distinctly Platonist: "If we think of the Plato from the later dialectic [e.g. *Philebus*], where the Ideas are something like multiplicities that must be traversed by questions such as *how? how much? in which case?*, then yes, everything I've said has something Platonic about it."[69] As we have seen, with the Idea, Deleuze attempts to demonstrate the constitution of the universal in the realm of the sensible, or the emergence of the intelligible from infinitesimal differences in the sensible. As such, like the Platonic Idea, the structure cannot be conflated with the empirical, but serves as the condition of possibility for particular events to occur (i.e. to be expressions of that structure), while at the same time the totality of the structure is constituted by the conjugation of these incorporeal transformations with their singularities.

Alfred Sohn-Rethel's depiction of the reality of abstraction might help to illustrate this expression of a "problematic" field (the Idea/structure) unconditioned by human consciousness. *Intellectual and Manual Labour* attempts to view the circulation of commodities not from the actual (social) exchanges of goods and services, but from the perspective of their exchangeability. Real abstraction occurs in the exchange of com-

---

[69] Gilles Deleuze, "The Method of Dramatization," in *Desert Islands and Other Texts, 1953–1974* (Los Angeles; New York: Semiotext(e), 2004), p. 116.

modities, since the commodities themselves, as well as the abstract exchange equivalence they are grounded in, are not present in the minds of the commodity owners. The physical exchange of commodities within a larger material network of exchanges of money and labor force, policies, international relations etc., produces as it occurs the conditions (e.g. exchange equivalence) of its possibility. Furthermore, "the conversion of the real abstraction of exchange into the ideal abstraction of conceptual thought"[70] takes place without any intentional structure on the part of the humans involved. Far from being a model for the emergence of political ideology, real abstractions furthering abstraction serves to iterate the sociological point that a society built on exchange equality, and hence quantifiability and measurability, will produce a science founded on the same values, which then serves to reinforce these values in the economic sphere.[71] While summing up the material reality of "real abstraction," he writes:

> Whether we are dealing with money or with religion, the crucial error is to treat real abstractions as mere "arbitrary products" of human reflection. This was the kind of explanation favored by the eighteenth century: in this way the Enlightenment endeavored [...] to remove the appearance of strangeness from the mysterious shapes assumed by human relations whose origins they were unable to decipher.[72]

Just as per the Deleuzian Idea, the mind-independent production of objective structure that is figured in this characterization of real abstraction does not yield a structure with an existence independent from its instantiations. This is because, as Sohn-Rethel puts it, "real abstraction arises in exchange from the reciprocal relationship between two com-

---

70   Alfred Sohn-Rethel, *Intellectual and Manual Labour: A Critique of Epistemology* (London: Palgrave Macmillan, 1978), p. 68.
71   See Alberto Toscano, *Fanaticism: On the Uses of an Idea* (London: Verso, 2010), p. 180.
72   Ibid., p. 184. Against the accusation of a too abstract model of human interaction, Adorno offers a spirited defense that can be read as a retrospective clarification of Toscano's points. See Theodor W. Adorno, *Introduction to Sociology* (Stanford: Stanford University Press, 2002), p. 160.

modity owners and it applies only to this interrelationship."[73] The structure of exchange equality can only be said to be *real* when it is producing actual exchanges of commodities. The structure is thus not bigger than its empirical instantiations, while also not being exhausted by them.

In a sense, then, Deleuze can be viewed as a structural realist, viewing structures not as *ante rem*, but *in rem*, insofar as they only have reality if they are expressed in concrete systems. However, since Deleuze is not a modal structural realist, like Hellman, since he would reject Aristotelian realism and affirm the reality of abstract objects, it would be safer to say that Deleuze is a realist in respect to the genesis of structure. Considering the metaphysical scope of Deleuze's proposal, which is implicit in the notion of the Idea as operating in nature and accounting for the structure of thought, it might be more appropriate to characterize him, as Bryant does, as a "hyper-rationalist."[74] Recoding transcendental empiricism as a rationalism removes the danger of regarding sensibility as passive or mere receptivity and hence tracing the genetic processes of the sensible from its qualitative empirical products. The consequences of this detachment from empiricism are, however, momentous, since one can no longer frame the genetic problem in phenomenological terms, i.e. in terms of the idea that the structure (and hence its genesis) is real insofar as it yields experience for consciousness. Instead, one must grant that structure (the virtual) is real (as produced) insofar as it yields empirical products that *might* manifest as experience in consciousness, but don't have to *necessarily*.

From this vantage point, we can fully consider the new function of time. The third synthesis of time in *Difference and Repetition* was primarily considered as thought. It was introduced through the idea of the split "I" as a failed synthesis, which left an ambiguity as to the applicability of the third synthesis of time to the non-cognizing or inorganic realm. Now, having left behind human experience as a condition for the reality of the virtual, we can see the ramifications of Deleuze's assertion that

---

[73] Sohn-Rethel, *Intellectual and Manual Labour*, p. 69.
[74] Bryant, *Difference and Givenness*, p. x.

"the only subjectivity is time, non-chronological time grasped in its foundation, and it is we who are internal to time, not the other way round":[75] time is the true agent. This presents another possibility of bifurcation, insofar as Deleuze characterizes the third synthesis of time as thought. We might read this characterization in phenomenological terms, as the idea that time is the condition that forces us to think and which *presents* itself within experience as a rupture or failed synthesis. In this case, the third synthesis of time would only operate as long as it manifests itself in human experience. However, taking into account that Deleuze's radicalization moves from the being of the sentendium to the memorandum to the cogitandum, we might be justified in the claim, unfairly referred to as Deleuzian "panpsychism" by Brassier, that "everything thinks."[76] By this we mean that the third synthesis of time, a failed synthesis, is the creation of novelty through repetition, which in human consciousness appears as "forced thought." Since time, however, is not interior to consciousness, but the inverse, everything is subject to the failed synthesis of time, which is to say, to thought, and is hence thinking.[77]

*The Trouble with Intensity in the Virtual/Actual Couplet*
The Platonic lesson meanwhile continues. Deleuze's Plato of the *Philebus* employs a method of "mixture," since "the people of old, superior to us and living in closer proximity to the gods, have bequeathed us this tale, that whatever is said to be consists of one and many, having in its nature limit and unlimitedness"[78] and everyone rushes to assert the dominance of either the One (Being) or the Infinite (Becoming) over the other. The virtual Ideas, which we have shown as the rules governing synthesis, are not the infinite from which the actual would emanate. Although Ideas have an intrinsic relation to their solutions, which they

---

75  Deleuze, *Cinema 2*, p. 80.
76  Brassier, *Nihil Unbound*, p. 198, see also the section "The Inorganic Life of the Ideas" in this book.
77  We will explore the specific claims and consequences of this approach in the "Post-Vitalism" chapter.
78  Plato, "Philebus," in *Complete Works* (Cambridge, Mass.: Hackett Publishing, 1997), 16c–d.

do not resemble, their application is an operation issuing from the Ideas itself. As we have seen, qualities are determined by relations of quantities, while quantities are determined by singularities. The example from differential calculus has provided the template of how singularities determine the form, i.e. the extensity and parts, of an object. The form of an object then, it seems, is nothing more than the organization of its qualities, which means that quality and extensity are coextensive. If, therefore, quality is an ordered constellation of intensive quantities and extensity an organization of quality, it follows that the Idea alone cannot account for the genesis of a determined actual object, or in other words, genesis is not an immediate relation between thought and representation. The exact process of how this works is not at all clear or precisely described by Deleuze. As Dale Clisby correctly notes, there seems to be a great deal of confusion around the exact role and placement of intensity within the virtual/actual couplet in Deleuze and Deleuze scholarship.[79]

Strictly speaking, we have two kinds of relations, one intensive and one ideal, two different processes belonging to two different "faculties." Deleuze thus faces the same problem as Kant of how the schematism actually operates in order to produce the empirical, or how the spatio-temporal dynamics (Deleuze's schematism) mediate between the Idea and the intensive field to produce a product. Or, framed in the language of Deleuze, how are the differen*t*iated structures actualized into differen*c*iated entities? This is even a more troubling problem for Deleuze than for Kant, since the two orders (intensive and ideal) belong to two different dimensions of time. While intensity denotes the immediate relation of force-quanta, i.e. affection, in the present, Ideas, on the other hand, belong to the future. The question then becomes, how is the future brought into the present? The answer to this problem, as well as to our initial question of how to construct a Deleuzian hylozoism that can supplant Kantian hylomorphism and is able to circumvent the opposition between teleology

---

[79] Dale Clisby, "Deleuze's Secret Dualism? Competing Accounts of the Relationship between the Virtual and the Actual," *Parrhesia* 24 (2015), p. 127–149.

and mechanism, lies in the fourfold structure of "differentiation-individuation-dramatization-differenciation."[80]

## THE PROCESS OF INDIVIDUATION

*The World is an Egg*

It is a mistake to claim, as some do, that Deleuze would only use the egg as a "metaphor" for the process of individuation.[81] When Deleuze exclaims that "The entire world is an egg,"[82] he summons the essential ethological similarity between the two terms—the world *does as the egg does*. There are, of course, many kinds of eggs and the Deleuzean Dogon egg differs significantly from Kant's teleological and epigenetic conception of the egg.

While Kant understood the ontogenesis of the fertilized egg in terms of germs, in line with eighteenth century organic generation theory, Deleuze conceives of the individuation of the organism as the encounter of DNA with an intensive field. We have already discussed the differing accounts of the determination of the organism by Cuvier and Geoffroy Saint-Hilaire. Deleuze portrays the sequence of deoxyribonucleic acid as the modern interpretation of the Idea of the organism.[83] Such an interpretation harbors a potential for three misunderstandings. Firstly, the structure (DNA) is a field of elements that does not resemble the characteristics of the actual organism. However, especially with the advent of the concept of genetic *information*, such a resemblance is often implic-

---

80  Deleuze, *Difference and Repetition*, p. 251.
81  Zdebik interprets this relationship between the world and the egg as a mere metaphor; see Jakub Zdebik, *Deleuze and the Diagram: Aesthetic Threads in Visual Organization* (London: Continuum, 2012), p. 171. Bryant calls it a "comparison"; see Levi R. Bryant, "The Ethics of the Event: Deleuze and Ethics without Αρχή," in *Deleuze and Ethics*, ed. Nathan Jun and Daniel W. Smith, Deleuze Connections (Edinburgh: Edinburgh University Press, 2011), p. 38. Hughes, especially, seems not to take the ontological claim seriously, calling the relationship a metaphor and stressing its relation and applicability only to experience; see Hughes, *Deleuze's Difference and Repetition*, p. 170.
82  Deleuze, *Difference and Repetition*, p. 216.
83  Deleuze's notes on embryology are scattered throughout the fourth and fifth chapter of *Difference and Repetition*, see ibid., p. 214–215, 248–249.

itly proposed in modern biology.[84] Since what the genes are and what "in-forms" the organism (i.e. that which shapes it) are the same thing, a resemblance is assumed that enables the tracing of the conditions (the DNA) from the product (actual organism) to subsequently deduce the latter from the former. This transcendental illusion, akin to Kant's tracing of the transcendental from the empirical, leads to the second misunderstanding: that the empirical result (the actual organism) could exhaust its generative structure (DNA). On the contrary, since the DNA is neither a model nor a miniature of the organism, there are always potentials within the structure that are unexpressed in the organized being. Thirdly, encompassing the former two, there is the misunderstanding of genetic determinism, which proposes that the DNA is solely responsible for the formation of the organism and sufficient for the unfolding of its form. As an alluring bridge between the seemingly inert matter of the egg and the intricate design of the organism, the proposed hylomorphism in which a material object housed in the egg (DNA) would organize the uncoordinated chemicals into an organized being, again, rests on the notion of genetic information. Modern biology's understanding of DNA vastly overestimates its productive power, seeing it as literally informing, shaping, and therefore producing the organism. This amounts to a reversion to the Aristotelian opposition of matter and form, with the dominance of the latter over the former. Such a determinism would turn the virtual (DNA) into the possible again, falling behind the ambitions of a philosophy of difference, since it would mean the presence of differenciation within differentiation. The Idea holds the rules for the production of actual entities, but not the actual entity itself, i.e. it does not contain the process of production of actual entities, for which it provides rules, in itself. If it did, the process of individuation would not yield novelty, i.e. would not give rise to differenciation, but would already pre-

---

84  Somers-Hall, in his study on Deleuze, cites the biologist Susan Oyama on this: "though we know that there are no hooves or noses in the genes, the accepted formulation is that the genes that are literally passed on make hooves and noses in ontogenesis." Susan Oyama, *The Ontogeny of Information: Developmental Systems and Evolution* (Durham, N.C.: Duke University Press, 2000), p. 43.

suppose it.[85] Instead, the individuation of the organism can only be understood as the encounter between a field of intensity and an Idea. Deleuze's critique of the determinist position prefigures the development of "developmental systems theory" in contemporary biology, in which the development of the embryo is considered as an interplay and network of various genetic and epigenetic factors, instead of a process governed by a transcendent and invariable genetic program.

In *Difference and Repetition*, the process that brings the field of intensities and the Ideas together is the process of individuation: "Individuation is the act by which intensity determines differential relations to become actualized, along the lines of differenciation and within the qualities and extensities it creates."[86] The egg not only contains the genetic material in the nucleus, but also cytoplasm. Despite its homogeneous appearance, the latter contains chemical gradients determining differences between zones and points in the egg. Such a field of undeveloped and undifferentiated intensities Deleuze calls a "field of individuation," i.e. "the individual in intensity."[87] The interaction of the pre-individual singularities (Ideas) and the field of individuation (intensities) results in what Deleuze describes as a movement of "dramatization." The distribution of intensities in the egg determines the speed of development of the different parts of the organism. Hence, the field of individuation determines the form of the organism in extensity, which is to say, it selects the Ideas that are actualized according to its intensive environment. For example, the visual perception of color is produced by the linkage of rates of change in electromagnetic vibrations (the Idea), which are then actualized according to the field of individuation (the intensities) of the eye.[88] On the other hand, these spatio-temporal dynamisms that "dramatize" the Idea are a movement according to the rules of the Idea:

---

85    Deleuze, *Difference and Repetition*, p. 248.
86    Ibid., p. 246.
87    Ibid., p. 250.
88    More precisely, the Idea is selected and expressed by the intensive field of the eye. The subsequent impulses (Ideas) moving along the optic nerve are then actualized as perceptual qualities according to the field of individuation of the brain, expressing some of the initial relations.

On the one hand, they create or trace a space corresponding to the differential relations and to the singularities to be actualized. [...] On the other hand, the dynamisms are no less temporal than spatial. They constitute a time of actualization or differenciation no less than they outline spaces of actualization. Not only do these spaces begin to incarnate differential relations between elements of the reciprocally and completely determined structure, but the times of differenciation incarnate the time of the structure, the time of progressive determination. Such times may be called differential rhythms in view of their role in the actualization of the Idea.[89]

In a striking similarity to Kant's *Critique of Pure Reason,* these spatio-temporal dynamics function as a schematism. They are the agents of actualization, although they act adhering to the role written by the Idea. The mathematician Ian Stewart provides a fitting example when talking about the development of frogs, which Cohen summarizes:

> Development seems to involve dynamics as well as chemical computation. When the developing frog embryo turns itself inside out during gastrulation, it looks just like a viscous fluid, flowing in an entirely natural manner. Some of the information required to make this process work may be specified by the laws of fluids, not by DNA.[90]

The spatio-temporal dynamics governing the behavior of the frog embryo, i.e. the laws of fluids, are not encoded in the DNA but are provided by physics, which makes the process more economical. The morphogenetic process of the frog embryo is hence not entirely guided by the DNA but is a field of intensity selecting the Ideas it expresses through spatio-temporal dynamisms.[91]

---

89  Deleuze, *Difference and Repetition*, p. 216–217.
90  Jack S. Cohen and Ian Stewart, *Collapse of Chaos: Discovering Simplicity in a Complex World* (London: Penguin, 2000), p. 294.
91  See Jeffrey Bell, "The World Is an Egg: Realism, Mathematics, and the Thresholds of Difference," in *Speculations IV: Speculative Realism*, ed. Michael Austin et al. (Brooklyn: Punctum Books, 2013), p. 67.

While intensity is the determinant in individuation, the Idea is expressed by it. Or, put differently, the Idea organizes an intensive field, while the nature of the field of individuation determines which particular Idea is actualized (i.e. the intensities express Ideas). Ideas are hence actualized according to an intensive field, which in turn gets differenciated, giving rise to extensity and quality. In this movement, alternately called "individuation," "explication" and "cancellation," intensity creates a qualified extensive system by getting drawn out of itself, cancelling itself out. Although intensities and Ideas end up covered over in the production of extensity, Deleuze establishes the former two as the genetic conditions of the latter. Without this priority, the actual process of embryogenesis becomes incomprehensible, since it depends on topological movements of the embryo, i.e. non-metric movements. The metric field of extensities is not able to perform such movements: "Embryology already displays the truth that there are systematic vital movements, torsions and drifts, that only the embryo can sustain: an adult would be torn apart by them."[92] As Ansell-Pearson notes, the classical opposition between preformism and epigenesis becomes redundant once it is understood that there is no resemblance between the differenciated organism and its genetic grounds.[93] Similarly, Deleuze dismisses the notion that species and genus have any constitutive power or meaning. As we have seen, there is a relation of non-resemblance between the DNA and the adult organism. We might still be tempted to view the individuation of the organism as if it were guided by the "encoded" information of the general species, with embryogenesis involving the application of the differentiating (universal) properties of species on the particular differenciated organic being. Such an understanding still relies on the hylomorphism implied in genetic determinism and must be dispelled once we recognize that individuation proceeds as the interplay of both intensities and Ideas that operate without general or universal concepts. Or, as Deleuze summarizes in a formula he attributes to Lucretius: "no two eggs

---

92   Deleuze, *Difference and Repetition*, p. 118.
93   See Ansell-Pearson, *Germinal Life*, p. 94.

or grains of wheat are identical."[94] Creative novelty precedes conceptual categorization, the latter being an inductive generalization of the former.

## The Egg is a Theatre

Reconsidering from this vantage point Deleuze's claim that the world is an egg, two non-exclusive interpretations of this are possible. Firstly, although we have described embryogenesis from the interplay of the field of intensity and the Ideas inside an egg, it is clear that more force-relations are important for the constitution of a field of individuation. Since the complete (worldwide) field of intensity (i.e. the *spatium*) does not have discrete parts, the boundary of the egg's shell is arbitrary or merely representational, while the milieu of embryogenesis extends over the whole of the field. The entire *spatium* is implicated in the egg. It is worldwide or even cosmic. Most differences, however, will be negligible for the development of the embryo, while other differences outside the shell, like temperature, atmospheric pressure and radiation, as well as their interplay,[95] might be more salient, i.e. the whole of the *spatium* is expressed confusedly, but some relations are expressed clearly. The life of the organism is not itself organic, rather it is *between* the organism's differenciated parts, and anterior to its organicity, interpenetrated and sustained not only by inorganic intensities, but also other (non-/trans-/meta-organic) forms of individuation:

> The indivisibility of the individual pertains solely to the property of intensive quantities not to divide without changing nature. We are made of all these depths and distances, of these intensive souls which develop and are re-enveloped. We call individuating factors the ensemble of these enveloping and enveloped intensities, of these individuating and individual differences which ceaselessly interpenetrate one another throughout the fields

---

[94] Deleuze, *Difference and Repetition*, p. 252.
[95] Temperature itself, of course, is an intensive difference, meaning a relation, and therefore connected to other relations *ad infinitum*.

of individuation. Individuality is not a characteristic of the Self but, on the contrary, forms and sustains the system of the dissolved Self.[96]

An individual is thus not defined by an identity, but a consistency that is determined by the field of intensities in the continual process of individuation, which never approaches full individuality without introducing a difference into the field from the outside.

Secondly, it is not only the case that everything is in the egg, but also that the egg is everywhere. The egg, as a biological mode of individuation, exemplifies the general model of individuation as morphogenesis. The beginning of *Difference and Repetition* already provides the example of the physical individuation of lightning: "Lightning [...] distinguishes itself from the black sky but must also trail it behind, as though it were distinguishing itself from that which does not distinguish itself from it. It is as if the ground rose to the surface, without ceasing to be ground."[97] A difference in the electrical potential between cloud and ground (individuation/field of intensities) triggers an equalization of charge (differentiation/Idea), which follows the path of least resistance (dramatization/spatio-temporal dynamics), finally producing the empirical phenomenon of lightning. Both lightning and embryogenesis yield an actual entity by introducing Ideas into a field of intensities that selects and expresses them, and hence actualizes the Ideas in actual objects, entities, events or phenomena. Here, Deleuze switches register from biology or atmospheric physics to ontology, in order to propose something philosophical. Changing the metaphor, he universalizes the process: "The world is an egg, but the egg itself is a theatre: a staged theatre in which the roles dominate the actors, the spaces dominate the roles and the Ideas dominate the spaces."[98] The world is no longer understood as comprising representable extensity, but as a process of the continual production of the extensive through the encounter of intensities and Ideas. We can now make

---

[96] Deleuze, *Difference and Repetition*, p. 254.
[97] Ibid., p. 28.
[98] Ibid., p. 216.

sense of Deleuze's more materialist use of Plotinus's idea of contemplation. John Protevi, when talking about the process of dramatization in Deleuze, takes up this understanding of "lived experience": "Deleuzian critique also commands the non-resemblance of both virtual multiplicity and actual adult individual to the intensive processes of morphogenesis or to what Deleuze calls the lived experience of the embryo."[99] The processes of differentiation (dynamic genesis) and the expression of these differentiated structures in fields of intensities (static genesis), i.e. the activities which make up the embryo's development, are *lived* by it.

## The Theatre is a Plane

Of course, as Deleuze notes with reference to Simondon, there are differences between different "forms'" of individuation. Physical (non-organic) individuation, for example, occurs all at once, involving only monocausal relations, at a boundary that is created or advanced, "whereas a biological system receives successive waves of singularities and involves its whole internal milieu in the operations which take place at the outer limits."[100] Social/collective or psychic individuation seem also to involve a set of behaviors peculiar to them. It is tempting, especially considering Deleuze's treatment of him, to read the different forms of individuation proposed by Simondon as merely heuristic, helping to further the general understanding of individuation. However, as Filippo Del Lucchesse notes, Simondon employs these differences as a critique of Bergson, since "the preindividual reality that every individual carries within itself belongs [...] to the vital rather than the prevital."[101] This attack on Bergson is a result of Simondon's interest in determining points of actual transformation—discontinuities or breaks within Being—and thereby discrediting the continuity between the vital and the pre-vital implicit in the notion of the *élan vital*. As such, Simondon, in an attempt to stave off

---

99   John Protevi, "Life," in *The Cambridge Companion to Deleuze*, ed. Daniel W Smith and Henry Somers-Hall (Cambridge: Cambridge University Press, 2012), p. 245.
100  Deleuze, *Difference and Repetition*, p. 255.
101  Filippo Del Lucchese, "Monstrous Individuations: Deleuze, Simondon, and Relational Ontology," *Differences* 20, no. 2 (2009), p. 184.

the accusation of vitalism, reintroduces an epistemological gap between the organic and the inorganic and ontologizes it into a gulf within Being. Even if Deleuze ultimately rejects Bergsonian vitalism for relying on a notion of negation, his use of Simondon's critique risks reinserting transcendence back into immanence, recapitulating the logic of genus and species in relation to the forms of individuation. Toscano perceptively notices the implicit danger in such a discontinuity between the pre-individual and the individual, not only for immanence, but for individuation itself, insofar as it grinds down differences into singular individuations, subsuming them under conceptual determinates that precede individuation's creative novelty. Or, in other words, it would mean that the pre-individual anticipates the possible forms the individual can assume and the possible paths it can take to achieve them. The Simondonian discontinuity between the pre-individual and the individual enables him to conceive of the former as a reservoir for creation, which implies the Anaximandrian cosmogonic narrative of an undifferentiated ἄπειρον, in need of transcendent principles to account for individuality. As Toscano suggests, speaking of the pre-individual "as such" already reduces the multiplicity and complexity of individuation and its forms.[102] Instead, one might speak of a multitude of fields engendering individual processes of individuation within *this* field, rather than asserting the existence of the field of *the* pre-individual or of Being as such. The untotalizable plane encompassing these fields might be called immanence, populated by events of modulation of energetic and material differences. Since every field is the real condition of a phenomenon, it cannot be detached from the actual product it produces, but at the same time is not exhausted by it. The "forms" of individuation are therefore as numerous as the processes of individuation that occur, i.e. *de facto* infinite, while the *de jure* rift between them reveals itself to be an arbitrary conceptual cut of the plane.

Hence, it is not the case that there is no difference between the forms of organic and inorganic individuation. Rather, since every process of individuation is different in kind (i.e. it only occurs as the individuation of *this*

---

[102] See Toscano, *The Theatre of Production*, p. 156.

field), establishing a difference in kind between organic and inorganic individuations to facilitate their opposition negates the differences in kind between particular individuations within the category of either inorganic or organic individuation, and can therefore ultimately only be achieved by the arbitrary insertion of opposition.

What Deleuze calls inorganic life, therefore, refers not only to physical, and hence non-biological, individuation (as DeLanda suggests), but also to the events of individuation of the multiple fields populating the plane of immanence. Such a life precedes any categorial classification, precluding any ascription of properties or limits, and hence cannot be subjected to the organic form of judgement. This is the meaning of life in Deleuze: that life does not simply belong to immanence, but immanence is always expressed as a generic individual: "What is immanence? A life ..."[103]

## Organicity and Totality

We are now in a position to reevaluate the essentially mereological question posed by Kant, which led to the gulf between inorganic and organic beings: insofar as the former are not able to produce and maintain unity, he proposes a hylomorphic model of the genesis of organisms. Always caught up in the characteristic tensions resulting from the incompossibility of materialism, empiricism and vitalism that characterizes his work, Deleuze might formulate an answer in various ways.

With the example of the individuation of the embryo, Deleuze has already provided a description of the formative process which results in an organism, without relying only on either mechanist mono-causality or teleology. Instead, he has shown that the necessity of assuming either of these explanations of the grounds of ontogenesis arose from a transcendental illusion, which misinterprets the intensive conditions for genesis as resembling their extensive products, and hence uses the unified individual as *explanans*: "The former [mechanism] assumes that everything is calculable in terms of a state, the latter [teleology], that everything is

---

[103] Deleuze, "Immanence: a Life," p. 28.

determinable in terms of a program."[104] Both kinds of explanation are hylomorphic, in that they conceive of matter as inert and homogeneous, and thus bind life to the structure of the organism. More explicitly than in *Difference and Repetition,* Deleuze will return to this critique of hylomorphism in *Anti-Oedipus.* The main theme of this latter work, translated into the terms of our problem, is the *intrinsic* relation of the relational production of individuation (machines) and a formative force (desire). Deleuze and Guattari might be seen as portraying the *extrinsic* relation of the two in one of two ways: either desire determines the functioning of the machine from which it at the same time miraculously emerges (primacy of vital force), or a machine produces desire as an epiphenomenon or even illusion (primacy of mechanism). In order to solve this aporia or misunderstanding regarding the relation between functioning and formation in Deleuze and Guattari, we need first of all to mount a critique of the problematic presupposition inherent to both vitalism and mechanism. Deleuze and Guattari name this presupposition "indexical vitalism," i.e. the idea that the essence of the living is in its unity of organization (something often insisted upon for moral reasons). Common to vitalism and mechanism is a mereological understanding of the organism as constituted by a totalizing principle, either by the abstract unified structure of the machine or by a unitary formative force. The determination of parts of the organism and the function of these parts within the organism as a whole is conceived as proof of the totalizing principle. The organism in turn, expressing this totalizing tendency, is construed as a homeostatic unit, entailing the question of finality. Crediting Samuel Butler as their inspiration, Deleuze and Guattari now attempt to discredit the grounds both the "vitalist thesis" and the "mechanist argument" share, by "calling into question the structural unity of the machine."[105] In order to conceptualize this critique, they define two regimes, the molar and the molecular. While the former is described as segmentary, often constituted or defined in relation to transcendent principles or plans of organization, and

---

[104] Deleuze, *Bergsonism,* p. 105.
[105] Deleuze and Guattari, *Anti-Oedipus,* p. 338.

is therefore classifiable in representational terms, the latter functions as a transcendental field, comprised of sub-representational intensive differences: while molar regimes are concerned with organization, molecular ones effect composition. To the degree that the molar regimes depend on the genetic activity of the molecular while also concealing it, the molecular can be seen as functionally similar to the intensities and Ideas in *Difference and Repetition*. As we have already seen, the multiplicities that comprise the virtual are not subject or subjectable to totalization without being conflated or confused with their actual products. The opposition between mechanism and vitalism only plays out, therefore, at the level of the molar, where life is conceived under the principle of (personal) unity. This totalization of the unity of the organism, then, as Nietzsche had already argued against Kant, entails the false notion of finality as (transcendent) program. Deleuze and Guattari do not actually solve this problem, but rather circumvent it by, in a Bergsonian manner, exposing it as a badly-posed question grounded in a transcendental illusion: the adoption of the fully individuated organism as the *explanans* of ontogenesis, which disregards the non-resemblance of the actual entity and its genetic conditions. In a materialist gesture, Deleuze and Guattari modify the process of individuation of *Difference and Repetition*, urging us to think it in terms of "haecceities," i.e. individuals consisting entirely of relations of speed and slowness, non-formed molecules (or particles), that are able to be affected and affect. The "this-ness" hence retains the anonymity of the intensive relations and processes it is constituted by. Recoding this in the terms of the initial problem of the relation between "formation and functioning," they argue that at the level of the molecular the two operations become indiscernible. Since vitalism and mechanism operate on the level of the molar and are thus not able to account for the genesis of either the functional structure or the unifying program, they have to appeal to *postulates* in order to determine tasks or inject life. While it could be argued that the homeostatic tendency, (self-)reproductive constitution and self-referential behavior of the organism supply sufficient grounds for the indissociability of formation and function, both these characteristics and their unity must be postulated, and no account can be provided of their genesis. In turn, they create the false question of abiogenesis.[106]

From this basis, Deleuze and Guattari undertake their critique of the "organism." On the level of the body, the production and the product become one without being identical; the organism as conceived by indexical vitalism is a product that transcends its production, gaining functional autonomy and personal unity. The Kantian *Ding an Sich*, non-relational and withdrawn from examination, is one result of this excess of product over production. The complete organizational closure of its functional autonomy entails its eidetic heteronomy, meaning its presentation as exterior totalization. By thus totalizing the potentialities of this organically conceived external entity, Kant suggests that it exhausts all its forces in every actual moment. Therefore, the transformative or morphogenetic potential of the organism must be isolated from the object and actualized into a separate entity. And, in the case of the organism, such an entity must be reintroduced into the actual organized being (as formative force or functional structure), which prompts the problem of their connection. This exclusion of the formative potential of the molecular means that the simultaneity of the organism's unity and variation on the molar level can only be achieved by centralizing and binding forces and potentialities into a representable force. The differences in intensities which result in qualitative change within the organism and external qualitative changes acting on it must therefore be limited to a certain threshold, which cannot be fallen below or exceeded. The potentialities of real metamorphosis entailed in the real conditions of possibility, i.e. the potentialities for anomalous individuation, are thus expelled for the sake of organic unity, which results from the totalizing principle both vitalism and mechanism are based on. The organism of "indexical vitalism," through this limita-

---

[106] The fundamental question of the chemical evolution that enabled the emergence of organic life from inorganic matter is an entirely scientific problem, insofar as the exact development of bacteria from less complex chemical compounds in the first eon (the Hadean) of the Precambrian era has yet to be reconstructed. There is, however, no metaphysical or philosophical problem of abiogenesis since the orders of the inorganic and the organic are only strictly segmented within the regime of the molar.

tion, constructs the transcendental in resemblance to the empirical, conceptualizing it as condition of possibility.

The reasons involved in individuation are neither logical nor possibilities, but rather "machinic." The "life-assemblage" might be *logically* possible with all kinds of molecules, e.g. silicon, but is not so "machinically," since "it does not distribute the zones of proximity that construct the plane of consistency."[107] Individuation, operating on the level of the molecular, in which formation and function become indiscernible, precludes the totalization of the vitalist/mechanist organism. Deleuze and Guattari's materialism, intensive and expressive instead of extensive and reductive, is thus a hylozoism able to supersede the dichotomy between mechanism and teleology by discrediting the foundations of both of them. Both rely on a conception of space as succession or as a continuum of extensive magnitudes that can be represented, because this enables the externality necessary for the operations of totalization. Space for Deleuze and Guattari, as they reiterate in *A Thousand Plateaus*, is rather understood as a *process* of spatialization, the production of extensity from intensive fields, within which the intensities cancel themselves out without losing their intensive quality. From the perspective of intensity, such a "smooth" space cannot be divided without changing its nature. Hence, within such a space no permanent coordinates can be established, since this space is constant variation. Hence, the stationary point of reference (e.g. the outside observer) becomes the result of a transcendental illusion that views space as segmented and comprised of discrete parts, i.e. as "striated."[108] There is hence only a view from *within* space, which precludes the totalization that theories of mechanism and teleology rely on.[109] Equally, the functional determinations of the parts of the organism—the lots God assigned—are cuts in the intensive space of the body, which segment it according to the totalizing principle of survival. Deleuze is interested in the embryo not only because it is a model of individuation, but because

---

107 Deleuze and Guattari, *A Thousand Plateaus*, p. 286.
108 See ibid., p. 474.
109 Bennett, *Vibrant Matter*, p. 62.

it presents ontogenesis as a process of production giving rise to an organism and its organs that involves constant variation and transformation of both the form and function of the organs and the organism. The indissociability of functioning and formation in the intensive process of embryogenesis thus presents a body with indeterminable organs, instead of the determinable organs of the organism in the "indexically" vitalist sense. It is a body without organs, which is an egg, which is the world, which is everywhere, and which has everywhere in it.

# ORGANS WITHOUT BODIES

## INDIVIDUATING MONSTERS

*The Disintegrating Body*

The judgement of God first appeared as a failure, as a false judgement about the lot assigned to the human being, which plunges her into delirium or madness, only to rescue her by imposing the rightful lot. The idea of the integrity of the body as a self-reproducing unity in form(ation) and function(ing) relied on the integrity of God and his judgement. With the destitution of his judgement, the dangers of false judgement return, universalizing the possibility of insanity.[110] Within immanence as portrayed by Deleuze and Guattari, false judgement does not denote a moral or factual failure measured by or in need of a correct one, but rather, on the one hand, the transcendental impossibility of a transcendent judgement, and, on the other, the productive and creative capacity of falsity. This power of the false does not account for the totalized form of the body and does not assign any lots to its organs, but transforms it into a process of successive as well as simultaneous variations, without pre-established coordinates, animated by an inorganic vitality. From the suspension of the judgement of God follows the disintegration of the body as an organism. Deleuze "considers madness an intensive experience that enables nonorganic life to be captured."[111]

In Bacon's figural distortions, Deleuze sees this non-organic life, i.e. forces and collections of forces that operate below the organizational unities of the human and the organism. While the latter serve to preserve the former in habitual forms and mechanisms, they nevertheless also hinder, limit and dampen them by reducing their potential for differential expression. The organism creates the minimal conditions for life, only to

---

[110] For a detailed discussion of madness in modernity, especially in Hume and Deleuze, see Jeffrey A. Bell, "Are We Mad? Intensity and the Problems of Modern Philosophy," *Deleuze Studies* 11, no. 2 (May 2017), p. 195–215.

[111] Anne Sauvagnargues, *Deleuze and Art* (London: Continuum Books, 2018), p. 61.

be deformed and decomposed by the forces that it cannot fully capture because they are its genetic condition. It is this more fundamental level of the body portrayed by Bacon, which operates prior to (and underneath) the phenomenological lived body, and is neither regulated by nor reducible to the organism, that Deleuze calls "body without organs" (BwO). Such a body, traversed by intensive forces, is not opposed to its organs but to the transcendent organization of the organism, which assigns the organs their lots, determining them and hence imprisoning life.[112] More explicitly than in *Difference and Repetition*, *Francis Bacon* ties this analysis to an idea of sensation that is not representational but bodily, i.e. is produced by forces flowing over the body on the non-organic level and encountering an external force. Not registered by the organism, these encounters still produce provisional "organs," which can change if the external force changes or another force is encountered. This determination of organs, according to Deleuze, is not related to the organs that empirical science might determine within functional, unified and unifying structures, but related to arrangements or constellations of forces that can "feel" even without being registered by the organism. The "powerful inorganic life"[113] Deleuze observes in the BwO is thus an intensive body as an abundance of forces, which constantly change and in their encounters produce sensation. From this vantage point we can say that, for Deleuze, inorganic life is this flow of forces, which, with the sensations it gives rise to and their concomitant provisional organs, presents a capacity for material synthesis beyond the organic conception. Sensation here thus does not conform to the conditions of possibility of experience beholden to a subject, with the former being the genetic condition for the latter. The BwO is therefore non-organized, non-stratified and non-formed but not chaotic or unordered. It is the continual variation of determinations of organs, their production, metamorphosis and disintegration. The orders of the forces are manifold, ranging from pressure, weight, gravitation, attraction and germination to desire or perception.

---

112  See Deleuze and Guattari, *A Thousand Plateaus*, p. 158.
113  Deleuze, *Francis Bacon*, p. 46.

In the theory of the germplasm conceived by the German biologist August Weisman, Deleuze finds an exemplification of the relation of the BwO and the organism. The embryo developing from the zygote, according to Weismann, sets aside the germplasm necessary for the transmission of features to the next generation, as well as the cell forming the body of the organism. The soma, the body of the organism, is produced to protect and nourish the germplasm as well as to combine it with the germplasm of the other sex. If we take up again the example of the egg, we could say that Weismann would hold that the developed organism (the chicken) is merely a device or mechanism for the creation of the next generation by laying an egg, i.e. the chicken is a "function" of the egg. If there were another way to convey the germplasm in a secure way or produce eggs, chickens would cease to exist; the developed organism is a detour. Deleuze highlights in this example that the BwO is contemporary with the organism but does not *necessarily* belong to the organism.

By progressive determination of the organs through the establishment of habits, which regulate the encounters between the differential forces of the BwO and external forces, the organs become fixed according to the needs and organizational structures of the organism. Such a regulation is at the same time a reduction of the multiplicity, realizing only particular arrangements of forces, limiting the expression of life. The BwO howls: "They've made me an organism! They've wrongfully folded me! They've stolen my body!"[114] Deleuze, when using this term, is not only speaking about biology; rather, various BwOs can be encoded and made to function according to different transcendent organizations, e.g. "strata, the State, organisms, the family,"[115] proper use of language, etc., regulating intensive flows. The world is a BwO that becomes stratified by geological processes as much as geographic ascriptions and industrial production on and destruction of its surface. The earth screams, not because it has a nervous system, but precisely because it doesn't.

---

[114] Deleuze and Guattari, *A Thousand Plateaus*, p. 159.
[115] Ibid., p. 157.

## Contagious Vitalism

The genetic dimension of the BwO meanwhile does not cancel itself out in the bodies it gets folded into, like the abovementioned intensities that, while cancelling themselves out in extensity, do not lose their intensive nature. It constitutes an alternative way of experiencing, right at the threshold of the organism, which invokes multiple forms of becoming beyond "control." William Burroughs's essay *The Electronic Revolution*, from which Deleuze borrows the new paradigm "societies of control," names Aristotelian logic as the foundational evil of Western civilization. Surprisingly, Burroughs refers to Korzibsky's *General Semantics* and Hubert's concept of the reactive mind as something like lines of flight to escape this framework, although these same ideas were used as tools for programming in Scientology. Korzibsky attempted to create a language that circumvents the use of the definite article and therefore avoids the need for an either/or logic. Hubbard's invention of a pseudo-church tied its promise of salvation to monetary obligations and solidified this coupling with mind-control techniques, eroding soteriology from within. The BwO as danger and hope appears in the form of a viral logic:

> I have frequently spoken of word and image as viruses or as acting as viruses, and this is not an allegorical comparison. It will be seen that the falsifications of syllabic western languages are in point of fact actual virus mechanisms. The IS of identity the purpose of a virus is to SURVIVE. To survive at any expense to the host invaded. To be an animal, to be a body. To be an animal body that the virus can invade. To be animals, to be bodies. To be more animal bodies, so that the virus can move from one body to another. To stay present as an animal body, to stay absent as antibody or resistance to the body invasion.
>
> The categorical THE is also a virus mechanism, locking you in THE virus universe. EITHER/OR is another virus formula. It is always you OR the virus. EITHER/OR.[116]

---

[116] William S. Burroughs, *The Electric Revolution* (Göttingen: Expanded Media Editions, 1970), p. 35.

The virus is a BwO, operating through continuous variation; it becomes-animal, becomes-human. The identity of the organism that is invaded by the virus is not independent from it; the organism is only a conduit to the virus's survival. The idea of a self-identical being is a function of the invasion of the virus pushing the logic of opposition on the body, creating its own conditions for survival. The BwO, as the virus demonstrates, is able to engender becomings by affecting and being affected by other intensities or bodies. On the level of DNA there can be a combination of animal and human genes. Barking along with a dog or jumping like a cat is a process of becoming-animal. The visual field might be expanded by being combined with various tactile sensations or even new senses altogether. But at the same time, it is the virus in Burroughs that invents the logic of the exclusive disjunction, creating the paranoia of contradiction and opposition. The virus introduces constant mutation and has no more specificity than the transformations it engenders. It is alive in a way that is too much to be an individuated specific living being, since it rejects all limits and boundaries. That is to say, from an ethological standpoint it is contagion, the creation and proliferation of difference; "it is nothing more than an event that occurs to *the* living."[117]

It seems that there is an inherent danger to the BwO. From the perspective of the organic model, Bacon's works will "appear only as trauma, damage, and expression of pessimism and nihilism: life disfigured."[118] It is a horror that is inherent to life, which occurs as pure becoming, as Deleuze notes in reference to Cézanne. And, while he claims that "[p]ainting transmutes this cerebral pessimism into nervous optimism,"[119] the persistence of the former in and against the latter is worth investigating, in order to help measure the power of inorganic life.

---

117 Colebrook, *Deleuze and the Meaning of Life*, p. 39.
118 Ashley Woodward, "Nonhuman Life," in *Deleuze and the Non/Human*, ed. Jon Roffe and Hannah Stark (London: Palgrave Macmillan, 2015), p. 36.
119 Deleuze, *Francis Bacon*, p. 52.

## Teratology as an Epistemological Problem

Canguilhem observes, with reference to Bichat, that biological nature allows for aberration and malformation, while classical machines do not: "there is no machine monster."[120] Anomalous individuation becomes here the mark of biological life as such. This is the contagious insanity of the body without organs. Hylozoism threatens to infect nature, since without Him (God) there is no transcendent immunology, no safeguard from virulently spreading immanence. Nature becomes mad, teratology is universalized. As Lucretius writes fearfully:

> It must not be supposed that atoms of every sort can be linked in every variety of combination. If that were so, you would see monsters coming into being everywhere. Hybrid growths of man and beast would arise. Lofty branches would spread here and there from a living body. Limbs of land-beast and sea-beast would often be conjoined. Chimeras breathing flame from hideous jaws would be reared by nature throughout the all-generating earth.[121]

Lucretius's 'body-horror,' extended to nature, does not entail the *apeiron* but rather the ubiquity of singular individuations, or provisional teleologies, which do not form whole organisms but nonetheless express themselves in organs, combining and splicing human, plant and animal traits. Teratology is as much a historical, a metaphysical and a moral area of study as it is a biological one. The chief surgeon of Charles IX, Ambroise Paré, catalogues side by side in his *On Monsters and Marvels* (1573) the birth of twins and triplets, monsters created by the wrath of God, hermaphrodites and creatures produced through corruption. Paré views these not merely as biological aberrations but, referring the order within nature back to the order of Creation, as moral failures as well. As Paré holds: "monsters are things outside the course of nature (and are usually

---

[120] Georges Canguilhem, "Monstrosity and the Monstrous," in *Knowledge of Life* (New York: Fordham University Press, 2008), p. 90.
[121] Lucretius, *On the Nature of Things* (Harmondsworth: Penguin, 1982), p. 80.

signs of some forthcoming misfortune)."[122] The concept of Creation, and hence of a perfect order of nature, calls for or entails a concept of moral failure *within* nature to account for the existence of monsters. They introduce the idea of an impersonal or natural evil. However, Paré's description of these aberrations is distinct from other scholastic works on necromancy, demonology or possession which might pose a challenge to or impose a limit on philosophy, since such boundaries are ontological.

From this tension between the flawless order of nature and the possibility of a failure of morality (of accidents falling outside the course of nature) or an immoral counterforce (an evil that opposes nature), however, there follows an epistemological problem: "The existence of monsters calls into question the capacity of life to teach us order."[123] Aristotle, insisting on the immutability of species, tarries with this problem even in the human:

> Still it is not easy, by stating a single mode of cause, to explain the causes of everything,——(1) why male and female are formed, (2) why female offspring often resembles the father and male offspring the mother, and again (3) the resemblance borne to ancestors, and further (4) what is the cause why sometimes the offspring is a human being yet bears no resemblance to any ancestor, sometimes it has reached such a point that in the end it no longer has the appearance of a human being at all, but that of an animal only—it belongs to the class of monstrosities [τέρατα], as they are called.[124]

As Upton argues, a monster is not unformed but actually manifests the traits peculiar to a genus or species; what is monstrous is that she doesn't resemble the father. This, for Aristotle, indicates a difference in the movements of the specific father and the universal genus/species in the sperm. In regular cases, these interact at certain stages of develop-

---

122  Ambroise Paré, *On Monsters and Marvels* (Chicago: University of Chicago Press, 1989), p. 3.
123  Canguilhem, "Monstrosity and the Monstrous," p. 134.
124  Aristotle, *Generation of Animals* (London: William Heinemann Ltd., 1953), IV, 3, 769b 4–10.

ment to produce a being that both resembles the specific and manifests the universal.[125] In the monstrous case, the father's movements in the sperm lacked in purposive effort or were impeded by material causes, and, hence, the "formal nature" was not able to control the "material nature" properly, forming a monster.[126] As Connell shows, Aristotle considers the phenomena rare and infrequent, or incidental, and one cannot know about incidental matters; thus, monsters do not yield knowledge about nature.[127] And, since they are caused by chance and are not per se causes, i.e. they are accidental, they are not explanatory and hence not scientifically explicable.[128]

Kant, as we saw above, equally insists on the immutability of species to ensure the invariable nature of the categories, i.e. to prevent them from being subject to epigenetic development and inherent contingency. The idea of "monstrosity" as deformation remains an unsolved, but potentially not unsolvable problem for Kant, even in the *Opus Posthumum*. Paragraphs 26 to 29 of the *Critique of Judgement* approach monstrosity in an aesthetic and moral manner, shifting its meaning. Examining the mathematical and dynamical sublime, Kant attempts rather tentatively to discern the moral and central side of the sublime from the illegitimate and fringe aspects. The animation of the mind by passion and enthusiasm engendered by the sublime risks slipping into fanaticism, which is seen as a form of abnormal imagination. Rooting out these abnormalities is always a matter of determining a difference in degree between the moral and illegitimate aspects of the sublime. Most fragile in this analysis, however, is the difference between the colossal, i.e. "[t]he mere presentation of a concept [...] which is almost too great for all presentation" and the monstrous, which "by its magnitude [...] annihilates the end which its con-

---

[125] See Thomas Upton, "Aristotle on Monsters and Generation of Kinds," *American Catholic Philosophical Quarterly* 77, no. 1 (2003), p. 27.

[126] That the formal nature is not able to establish control is one explanation for the cause of monsters in *The Generation of Animals*. See Aristotle, *Generation of Animals*, 770b, 16–17.

[127] Aristotle, *Generation of Animals*, 2.5; 197a 19–20; Aristotle, *Aristotle's Metaphysics* (Bloomington: Indiana University Press, 1966), 6.2, 1027a 19–23.

[128] Sophia Connell, "Aristotle's Explanations of Monstrous Births and Deformities in *Generation of Animals*," in *Aristotle's* Generation of Animals: *A Critical Guide*, ed. Andrea Falcon and David Lefebvre (Cambridge: Cambridge University Press, 2017), p. 207.

cept constitutes."[129] The function of the "monstrous" is merely negative here, since "crude nature" cannot present the monstrous itself; because it does not contain anything "horrid," it only serves to determine the outer edges of the colossal more clearly. Alas, as Derrida notes, the demarcation operating to stop the "almost-too-much" from tipping over into the "too-much" already relies on the determination of this monstrous outside of representation. The aporia of the colossal aspect of the sublime thus consists in it being constituted as a representation through the determination of the unrepresentable; "the frame does not fit,"[130] as Derrida remarks. The monstrous lurks transcendentally in the shadow of the colossal, determining it. With Deleuze's reconfiguration of transcendental philosophy through the prism of the Kantian sublime, the transcendental becomes monstrous, and every act of experience carries with it the anomalous excess of the unrepresentable as a virtual shadow.

### Teratology as an Ontological Problem

The wandering line moving from Aristotle through Kant to romanticist vitalism understands monstrosity as deformation or excess, aberrations in relation to either the teleology guiding the formative force in nature or the homeostatic economy presupposed or implied in genesis, with, of course, variations and combinations of these two conceptions sometimes occurring. With Deleuze and Guattari, however, we can find a positive account of monstrosity. Referencing *Difference and Repetition*'s discussion of natural history's efforts to determine the parts of the organism accurately, Deleuze and Guattari go further, asserting that "Geoffroy called forth Monsters, [while] Cuvier laid out all the fossils in order."[131] Prior to Geoffroy Saint-Hilaire, monstrosity could only be regarded as privation, i.e. as accidental and incidental, lacking proper cause and teleology, or unrepresentable and inconceivable, lacking measure and organization. But since deformed creatures do not lack organization *per se*, as Aristotle is ready to

---

129 Kant, *Critique of Judgement*, p. 253.
130 Derrida, "The Parergon," p. 30.
131 Deleuze and Guattari, *A Thousand Plateaus*, p. 46.

admit, they still follow the principles of the unity of composition. Geoffroy argues, following from this, that it is not that deformities imply a lack of organization or an excess, but rather, due to the different development of a part of the organism, that the whole of the organism (conceived from the point of view of composition not function) is actualized differently. This implies a non-teleological understanding of organs, leaving open the possibility for the mutability of an organ's functions or even the creation of new organs, i.e. deformities that take on new functions within a novel composition of parts. Cuvier, like Hegel, rejected all possibility for transformation and functional novelty, i.e. the evolutionary process, since it contradicted the teleological account of the determination and organization of the organism. Geoffroy's depiction of evolution, on the other hand, while still scientifically wrong in the end, introduced the non-teleological understanding of the organism necessary to account for evolution, as Darwin acknowledges: "Geoffroy Saint-Hilaire has strongly insisted on the high importance of the relative position or connection in homologous parts; [...] Nothing can be more hopeless than to attempt to explain this similarity of pattern in members of the same class, by utility or by the doctrine of final causes."[132] Evolution necessarily involves the existence of suboptimal organisms, whose organs do not adhere to their "proper" function, and whose structure can thus not be determined by it.[133] Rather than life being contained within the structure of the functional whole of the organism, the organism is in this view constantly pulled away from teleological stability by an inorganic life engendering universal becoming.

## From Body to Cosmic Horror

This universal becoming, incorporated in the concept of the BwO, thus calls forth different monsters, as Powell suggests:[134] creatures that adhere

---

[132] Charles Darwin, *The Origin of Species* (London: Dent, 1972), p. 414.
[133] An analysis of this difference between Cuvier and Geoffroy, as well as the connection to Darwin's theory of evolution, can be found in Henry Somers-Hall, *Hegel, Deleuze, and the Critique of Representation: Dialectics of Negation and Difference* (New York: State University Of New York Press, 2013), p. 229.
[134] For an analysis of the BwO in horror films, see Anna Powell, *Deleuze and Horror Film* (Edinburgh: Edinburgh University Press, 2011), p. 62–64.

to the formula "ENTITY=EVENT,"[135] characterized by "zones of indiscernibility or undecidability"[136] that envelop the subject and the body in a becoming below and above the limits of its identity. The fusion of human and fly DNA in Cronenberg's *The Fly* reveals Brundle's body to be at base a field of intensive flows (a BwO), which is combinable and indeed combined with the body of the fly on the molecular level, leading to the transformation of its appearance on the molar strata. This is distinct from the body horror of Kristeva, which is rooted in the abjection of the inside of the body rising to the surface, breaking the skin and destroying the body's integrity.[137] Rather, the surface of the body is revealed as depth itself, constantly subject to intensive fluxes of power that constitute and transform it, blurring the difference between the inside and the outside. The body as a productive product precludes conceptual determination, which is visible in the cognitively transgressive nature of monsters. As Noël Carroll notes, for this reason "[m]onsters are not only physically threatening; they are cognitively threatening,"[138] since they are either non-conceptual or, worse, imply specific concepts that are only applicable to them. Although there is a cosmos of biological creatures and species (factual and fictional) that is traditionally excluded from philosophical thought, as Ben Woodard shows, it is the tension between theology and biology that presents us with a hagiography of life that is losing determinability at its fringes.[139] The undead (being dead while alive), the living dead (being alive while dead), the demon (corporeal life and desire without a soul) or the phantasm (spiritual life without a body) are all contradictions in terms, which defy the judgement of God and only exist as aberrations. The horror of monsters, as is maybe true of horror in general, consists less in the threat of death than in the "creep" inherent to life.

135 Gilles Deleuze and Claire Parnet, *Dialogues* (New York: Columbia University Press, 1977), p. 66.
136 Deleuze, *Francis Bacon*, p. 19.
137 See Julia Kristeva, *Powers of Horror: An Essay on Abjection* (New York: Columbia University Press, 1982), p. 53.
138 Noël Carroll, *The Philosophy of Horror or Paradoxes of the Heart* (New York: Routledge, 1990), p. 34.
139 See Ben Woodard, *Slime Dynamics: Generation, Mutation, and the Creep of Life* (Winchester: Zero Books, 2012).

Monsters are not just essentially transgressive but transgressive against the very notion of essence. The epistemological problem they pose turns into an ontological one: "Transgressing the conceptual category of 'natural' that any given culture might champion, monstrous creatures not only pose a threat to an existing scheme, but also to the action of naturalizing any schematization."[140]

Deleuze and Guattari's invocation of Lovecraft in *A Thousand Plateaus* provides them with a description but also an experience of "becoming-intense"[141] in reference to his description of mixtures of human and inhuman, sentient and non-sentient life and creatures, which could only be characterized as mixtures of biological matter and nothingness. With vitalist fervor they insist on relative deterritorializations based on intensities below the threshold of the organism, sidelining Lovecraft's higher deterritorialization of life in intensities exceeding the limits of human consciousness. It is incorrect to characterize Lovecraft's work as supernatural horror. Rather, the basis for his horror as well as for his disdain for vitalism is hypernatural and materialist. As Houellebecq writes: "What is Great Cthulhu? An arrangement of electrons, like ourselves. The terror of Lovecraft is rigorously materialist."[142] There is, strictly speaking, no noumenal space left in Lovecraft; it has collapsed into the phenomenal, infusing the latter with an eeriness that can never be "placed." It is not only that our body is gripped by forces that transform it, but, as *The Music of Erich Zann* or *The Color Out of Space* make felt, there are forces implicated in the body that are nonetheless indifferent to it. As much as the body without organs is its own cosmos, the cosmos is itself a body without organs.

---

[140] Eckardt Lindner, "Absolute Xenogenesis: Speculations on an Unnatural History of Life," in *Diseases of the Head: Essays on the Horrors of Speculative Philosophy*, ed. Matt Rosen (New York: Punctum Books, 2020), p. 268.
[141] Deleuze and Guattari, *A Thousand Plateaus*, p. 240.
[142] Michel Houellebecq, *H.P. Lovecraft: Against the World, Against Life* (San Francisco: McSweeney's Publishing, 2005), p. 32.

## HYLOZOISM AS IDEALISM

*The Despotism of the BwO*

Despite the excess, the Dionysian rage, that seems to be implied in the BwO, and the richness of vitality in inorganic life, Badiou claims that Deleuze's philosophy is characterized by a distinct stoicism and asceticism, a demand for sobriety. Taking up Nietzsche's notion of the strong as the one who affirms the equality of being, i.e. the joyous struggle of forces, Badiou notes that the reality of forces is not self-evident and encountering them consciously not an easy matter. The removal of the transcendental illusion that adopts the actual as the *explanans* of genesis requires practice and renunciation. Judged from the standpoint of life it therefore appears as a normative duty towards life itself:

> Ascesis, because we are constituted and judged by life "according to a hierarchy that considers beings and things from the point of view of power." To be worthy of inorganic life is not to concern oneself unduly with the satisfaction of one's organs.[143]

To this extent, the notion of inorganic life entails an ethical demand. Being worthy of inorganic life means to become equal to the violence that being is and to perform that violence against what resists dissolution in oneself. It asks one to leave oneself as a subject, as a person, behind. Overcoming the limits of what one is to engender the breakthrough to that which one can be at one's most extreme point entails thinking of oneself as a disjunctive synthesis open to the impersonal outside (inorganic life) at the point of one's dissolution. This ethical imperative of becoming-no-one or becoming worthy of inorganic life, the character of the strong, is therefore in a certain sense absolute, if nonetheless only formal. Žižek's *Organs without Bodies* attempts to outline the consequences of this ethical demand from the point of view of inorganic life in a critique of the totalizing operations of the BwO, which arrives at the conclusion that

---

143 Badiou, "Of Life as a Name of Being, or, Deleuze's Vitalist Ontology," p. 196.

Deleuze's vitalism converges with Idealism. Although it remains questionable whether the book (as a whole) is based on a rigorous reading of Deleuze,[144] part of it is worth focusing on in relation to our problematization of inorganic life. Rather than looking at the Lacanian defense of *The Logic of Sense* against *Anti-Oedipus* which the text is most concerned with, we will take a closer look at Žižek's accusations that the concept of the BwO is hierarchical and beholden to a classical understanding of hylozoism which infuses matter with life qua self-organization. Although Deleuze has been properly defended by numerous commentators against the ontological and psychoanalytic challenges posed by Žižek,[145] it is the issue of idealism implicit in the aforementioned accusations against the BwO that highlights, I claim, a genuine problem in the Deleuzian understanding of inorganic life.

After recounting, fairly accurately, Deleuze's account of the BwO, Žižek questions the necessity of such a conception within a univocal ontology. He asks: "Why not Body as the space in which autonomous organs freely float?"[146] Deleuze's choice, framed as "strategic" by Žižek, in favor of a chaotic multitude (BwO) and against the "organs without bodies" (OwB) entails, for Žižek, an acceptance of the hierarchy of monads proposed by Leibniz. The latter argues that every monad, while expressing the whole of the world, can be characterized by its specific quantitative adequacy and intensity. Aligning Deleuze and Leibniz, in Žižek's account

---

[144] Chiming into a choir of rather unfavorable reviews and discussions, Lambert calls it "an extremely bad book on Deleuze." See Gregg Lambert, *Who's Afraid of Deleuze and Guattari?*, Continuum Studies in Continental Philosophy (London; New York: Continuum, 2006), p. 88. Smith, after having recapitulated the fair to middling account of the relation of Deleuze and Lacan, declares "*Organs without Bodies* a bit of a disappointment." See Daniel W. Smith, "The Inverse Side of Structure: Žižek on Deleuze on Lacan," in *Essays on Deleuze* (Edinburgh: Edinburgh University Press, 2012), p. 313.
[145] Beyond the overwhelmingly dismissive responses to the concept of the "organs without bodies" mentioned above, Bankston provides a more nuanced defense of Deleuze. See Samantha Bankston, *Deleuze and Becoming*, Bloomsbury Studies in Continental Philosophy (London; New York: Bloomsbury Academic, 2017), p. 56f. McQueen makes the concept productive against Deleuze by connecting it to Baudrillard's account of the mirroring of political and libidinal economy. See Sean McQueen, *Deleuze and Baudrillard: From Cyberpunk to Biopunk* (Edinburgh: Edinburgh University Press, 2016), p. 158–160.
[146] Slavoj Žižek, *Organs without Bodies: On Deleuze and Consequences* (New York: Routledge, 2012), p. xii.

of the monadology, what refuses the full expression of God in a monad is its creatural delusion, i.e. the attachment to its material identity. Žižek finds this sentiment mirrored in Deleuze's Bergsonism, which conceives of philosophy as the means to elevate the human beyond its condition. From a Hegelian perspective, Deleuze still fails to see that such an overcoming cannot be achieved by rejecting the creatural delusion but is attained by a stubborn insistence on the Self in its autonomy, which frees it from the necessities of life (generation and corruption), making its connection to eternity possible. Evil thus opens up the field for the good to exist.

Surreptitiously, Žižek foists the good will of life on Deleuze here, insofar as Deleuze's strategic creation of the BwO instead of the OwB suggests, for Žižek, that opening the human up to the "inhuman" is not only possible but occurs "naturally" when abandoning the autonomy of the organs, i.e. when giving up the creatural delusion. Hence, the BwO contains a normative or even despotic aspect. It demands the dismissal of the autonomous agency of the organs as a formal condition for its construction. Although this depiction of Deleuze is an intentional over-simplification, which ignores all the dangers associated with the creation of the BwO in *A Thousand Plateaus*, Žižek's deliberations echo a methodological problem mentioned above in relation to the inorganic life of the transcendental field. Deleuze, at times, speaks as if we had unmediated access to the plane of immanence, while at other times the field only presents itself as rupture and distortion from the perspective of constituted consciousness, indicating no *necessary* passage from ontology to ethics or vice versa. Hence, the inherent ethical demand of the BwO, from a Žižekian perspective, can therefore appear as idealist.

### *The Suspicion of Vitalism as Idealism*

This line of reasoning permeates Žižek's discussion of autopoiesis as well. Characterizing Deleuze's basic philosophical question as that of the emergence of the new, he adds that the condition for such an emergence would have to be given without appealing to any transcendence. Here, Žižek attempts to propose a parallel between Hegel and Deleuze, insofar as for both the possibility for freedom consists in the excess over its causes in every causal link. This "fundamental assertion of Deleuze's materialism," according to *Organs without Bodies*, describes not just an excess over the (totalized) material reality of causes, but one immanent "to the level of the bodies themselves."[147] Through this excess, an autopoiesis, understood as a construction by self-differentiation, is possible. Having located the problem of emergence in the body, Žižek has pushed Deleuze into a compromised position and is ready to begin his critique of hylozoism:

> Within the history of biology, this topic of autopoiesis is part of the "idealist" tendency of hylozoism: everything that exists, the whole of nature, is alive—it suffers and enjoys. There is no death in this universe; what happens in the case of "death" is just that a particular coordination of living elements disintegrates, whereas Life goes on, both the Life of the Whole and the life of the elementary constituents of reality.[148]

Following this characterization, Žižek proceeds by erroneously lumping Deleuze's univocal immanence in with ideas such as Diderot's claim that even trees feel pain, Schelling's World-Soul and contemporary theories of Gaia. After that, he maneuvers Deleuze's BwO so that it is close to Heidegger, Merleau-Ponty or Varela, insofar as all of these seek the unity of the body with the subject. Although all these alleged proximities and similarities are factually wrong and inapplicable to Deleuze, and are clearly provocative in nature, they hint at a more valid point. Within the discussion of the autopoietic process, Žižek is not so much concerned with the emergence of teleological structures from inert mechanical matter, but rather with the point where the autopoietic entity (e.g. an organism) breaks with the closure of its continuous self-reproduction to achieve an ecstatic openness, i.e. a reflexive self-relation, that is to say, (self-)consciousness, which is always also a relation to the Other.

---

[147] Ibid., p. 101.
[148] Ibid., p. 108.

Deferring the operations of biological life, self-consciousness introduces a Death-in-Life. Hylozoism for Žižek would result in an affective cosmos, since without it one could not account for the excess of effects over causes. However, this affective cosmos would still lack the difference self-consciousness entails, that is, death. Without death, or the rupture of consciousness, the subject would be the subject of its body and life would denote the point of their unity.

The problem here is not, as Leslie Dema suggests, that Žižek claims that Deleuze proposes an empty concept of emergence.[149] The alignment of Deleuze with the tradition of autopoiesis stemming from Varela and Margulis is, as we saw above, less problematic than perplexing, and simply incorrect due to the impersonal nature of individuation. The issue with Deleuze's notion of the BwO and inorganic life that Žižek reiterates in the book, the accusation of idealism, results from a (perceived) failed Hegelianism in Deleuze's philosophy of life. As Bruce Baugh suggests: "For all his criticisms of Hegel, there remains an element in Deleuze that is profoundly Hegelian: a notion of 'alienation' that stems from Deleuze's 'vitalism'."[150] Every organ, as a solution to a problem, says Baugh, alienates life from itself, insofar as the productive and constitutive intensities cancel (or alienate) themselves out in extensity. While the virtual only knows (intensive) difference, the actual introduces (the transcendental illusion of) negation and the dialectic of contraries. It seems "as if actual life were a degradation of virtual life; as if virtual life were a value higher than actual life and through which actual life is denounced."[151] The Life of the virtual, or the body without organs understood as unorganized vital matter flow, appear to be imprisoned or muffled in their differenciation, actualization or stratification. Life's journey or duty to itself, accomplished by the de-

---

[149] See Leslie Dema, "'Inorganic, Yet Alive': How Can Deleuze and Guattari Deal With the Accusation of Vitalism?," *Rhizomes. Cultural Studies in Emerging Knowledge* 15 (2007). Even if that were the problem, the proper solution would not be to suggest that not all theories of emergence are empty, as she does.

[150] Bruce Baugh, "Actualization: Enrichment and Loss," in *Hegel and Deleuze: Together Again for the First Time*, ed. Karen Houle and Jim Vernon (Evanston: Northwestern University Press, 2013), p. 143.

[151] Ibid., p. 144.

tour of philosophy, then, is the return to the ground that all its manifest organizations sprang from. Like Hegel's Absolute, such a ground would be difference before all unity. While it remains true that the teleology of this circle is different, with Hegel ultimately seeking the identity of "difference and identity" and Deleuze the differentiation of difference, both do nonetheless tarry with the alienation of life from itself, seeking a return to that which is not alienated.

Even though this depiction of Deleuze might prove to be based on a misunderstanding, it still poses a problem worth pursuing.[152] The problem is not whether Hegel or Deleuze are right with regard to a gain or loss in actualization or the teleology of the circular movement of philosophy, but rather what their difference is with respect to life's internal and external connections to idealism. The purported idealism of inorganic life raises a problem concerning the subject (or subjectivity) and its epistemological, ontological and normative relation to life, which poses a challenge to Deleuze's metaphysics (as metaphysics). We will explore this problem by subjecting it to Laruelle's razor, revealing that there is an idealist dilemma within transcendental empiricism's "inorganic life" that calls for a reconfiguration of the basic coordinates of Deleuze's vitalism.

---

[152] The chapter "Post-Vitalism" will recapitulate exactly this problem and reframe it as the contrast between the active vitalism in Deleuze and the passive vitalism his metaphysics can also enable.

# NON-LIFE

Than these stones, and inerrable as they are.
Their sole concern is that what can be shaken
Shall be shaken and disappear
And only the unshakeable be left.[1]

---

[1] MacDiarmid, "On a Raised Beach," p. 150.

# TO HAVE DONE WITH THE TRANSCENDENTAL

## GETTING CAUGHT UP IN LIFE

In a curious passage of *What is Philosophy?* Deleuze and Guattari, rather than contrasting the artist and the philosopher as they have done in the rest of the book, invoke something that is a constitutional force common to both of them: the encounter with the "plastic spectre."[2] The thinker as well as "the novelist or the painter returns breathless and with bloodshot eyes"[3] from her encounter with forces, which do not *belong* to her but she cannot stay indifferent to. This recurring encounter with the relational forces that make up the "Life in the Living" is suggestively described as a form of athleticism, although one which relies neither on muscular stratification nor organic unification, but on inorganic affectivity. Both artist and philosopher are confronted with an "experience" always too rich to sustain and too forceful to endure; it becomes too much to integrate it into one's finite organism, but one can train oneself to stay away from the shore without drowning. As Deleuze reminds us: what else is an elegy, this source of all poetry, if not a complaint? What is expressed in this complaint, however, is quite distinct from sadness and mourning: it is a misunderstood type of *eloge* or prayer, an expression of astonishment over the forces that take hold of oneself that cannot be incorporated, an amazed sigh in being confronted with, as we have called it, the immanent sublime of inorganic life. But the unsustainability of the intensive forces within the extensive organism, or the impossibility of (actually) living a (virtual) life, has physical consequences for the philosopher: "What little health they possess is often too fragile, not because of their illnesses or neuroses but because they have seen something in life that is too much for anyone, too much for themselves, and that has put on them the quiet mark of death."[4]

---

2    Deleuze and Guattari, *What is Philosophy?*, p. 172.
3    Ibid.
4    Ibid.

Here, a strange change of perspective seems to be necessary, typical for Spinozist monism, to maintain an affirmative image of philosophy. From the finitist perspective of the subject or the organism, Life appears in this encounter as something not primarily lived, or, if it is lived, without that being necessary. As Platonov's character Komyagin calmly explains in *Happy Moscow*: "After all, I'm not living—life's just something I got caught up in. I've got entangled in all this, but I wish I hadn't."[5] Looking out from the prisoner's cell or moving around as a body brittle from old age, the thought may dawn on you that life is a disease, something that takes hold of you, consumes you until nothing is left. Remember Castorp's "studies" on Life in *The Magic Mountain*, where it appears as a "sickening of matter."[6] Apparently then, once Life is separated from the volatility of the subject, the first question is not, how we can still affirm life, but if we still should. Gazing with "bloodshot eyes," experiencing the tears and cracks in the muscular texture of the body, feeling the proximity to madness—who would want to encounter Life? The weight of this question is what drives Freud to the strange note: "To tolerate life remains, after all, the first duty of all living beings."[7] Therefore, according to this injunction, there is nothing natural about the affirmation of life; rather, it is a function of the super-ego.

If we, however, change the perspective to the infinitist view of the inorganic forces themselves, which are not yet bound by organic forms, but generate, constitute as well as transform them, the affirmation of life is the result of a naturalist ethics;[8] injunctions following from nature in which—from this perspective—only relational forces exist. The very question of "whether one *should* affirm life or not" is in this view already born from a "sick" mind as a symptom of depression or lethargy, a weakening of life, and should be abandoned. This devotion to naturalism does not, however, mean that affirmation comes naturally, or is something

---

5   Andrei Platonovich Platonov, *Happy Moscow* (New York: New York Review Books, 2012), p. 66.
6   Thomas Mann, *The Magic Mountain* (London: Vintage Random House, 1967), p. 197.
7   Sigmund Freud, "Thoughts for the Times on War and Death," in *The Standard Edition of the Complete Psychological Works of Sigmund Freud, Vol. 14* (London: Hogarth Press, 1957), p. 299.
8   A discussion of the infinitist perspective of Spinoza and the finitist one already appears in the introduction to Freud's *Civilization and its Discontents*.

that did come naturally but that we have become alienated from over the course of time; we rather need philosophers and artists to incite the change in perspective. Since life's identification with itself is impossible because it too is necessarily in difference with itself, a higher form of reflection of life upon itself is needed to deliver us from organic stupidity: the difference of life to itself needs to be invoked or instigated to make us worthy of the becoming that nature is. If one *sees* inorganic intensity as productive, rather than destructive, the promise it carries on its sleeve becomes *visible*: joy instead of mere pleasure, the affirmation of the self-referential play of the drives, or, in short, *beatitudo*.

But it is exactly this *seeing* that is problematic. Since we have an organic perspective as default, to change the perspective, especially if it is to the detriment of the body, still needs to be motivated. The force that drives the reflection, moving us to change perspective and *see* the promise of *beatitude*, relies on it being *felt*. This is why, for Deleuze, the question of philosophical style always involves the affects and events a work can produce; a philosophical work should strive to invoke simmering intensities, which "make themselves felt, announcing the universal 'ungrounding'."[9]

Even if one holds that the argument that *beatitudo* has a motivational force introduces teleological thinking again, this rebuttal is only valid if the position in question and its implied values are already assumed to be right. And again, if this assumption is shown to be an affective one and not reducible to an argumentative rationale, this then begs the question. This type of circular logic implies the practical philosophical problem of which facts we assume to be transcendental and how to select them. Consider, for example, that someone, although accepting all the metaphysical assumptions about Deleuzian inorganic life, does not then accept the (meta-)ethical claim that an ethical injunction to affirm Life follows from them. Since she does not see everything as bursting with life but considers, perhaps, inorganicity as transforming the world into a wasteland, or as total "vacuity,"[10] as Hegel puts it, Life is as threatening to her as the

---

9     Deleuze, *Difference and Repetition*, p. 230.
10    Georg Wilhelm Friedrich Hegel, *Phenomenology of Spirit*, trans. A. V. Miller and John N.

confrontation with the noumena is to Kant. This might be exactly the position we find ourselves in when we place Deleuze and Lacan in confrontation with each other. As Aaron Schuster remarks:

> To put it bluntly: if for a Lacanian what appears to be alive is in fact already dead—Eros, the drives, the speaking being—for a Deleuzian what we usually think of as dead is actually bursting with vibrancy and life, but another kind of life, released from the familiar human coordinates, a machinic life or an inorganic life or a cosmic life, or—to quote the title of Deleuze's last essay—"immanence, a life."[11]

To mediate these *views*, to compare them on common grounds or even to try to solve the question of which one is the more radical, would be—as Schuster also notes—rather pointless, since both philosophers attempt to subvert the notions and distinctions that would make them comparable in this way. Rather, this confrontation leaves us with a philosophical question concerning the relation of life and philosophy: the question of how we decide what we take the realm of the transcendental to be if it does not resemble the empirical, and how this decision actually *works* or is *done* in practice.

## THE TRANSCENDENTAL SPLIT IN DELEUZE

### Questioning Standard Philosophy

It is François Laruelle who engages in most depth with this exact problem of philosophical decision, and simultaneously offers us a lucid critique of Deleuze's vitalism on this basis. His critical engagement with

---

Findlay (Oxford: Oxford University Press, 1977), p. 9; see also Slavoj Žižek, *In Defense of Lost Causes* (New York: Routledge, 2017), p. 112.

11  Aaron Schuster, *The Trouble with Pleasure: Deleuze and Psychoanalysis* (Cambridge, Mass.: The MIT Press, 2016), p. 45. Schuster misquotes the title of Deleuze's late essay here; actually, it's "Immanence: A life …." The difference, as Agamben notes, is vital; see Giorgio Agamben, "Absolute Immanence," in *Potentialities: Collected Essays in Philosophy* (Stanford: Stanford University Press, 1999), p. 220.

Deleuze will therefore be the focus of this section. In his analyses in *Philosophies of Difference*, he places Nietzsche's and Deleuze's vitalism with idealism, insofar as all actual existence is judged according to an immaterial principle—life or becoming—which means, therefore, that ideality and reality become identical. Nietzsche reaches this point, for Laruelle, by ontologizing the affirmation of relational forces against reactive forces in the Will to Power and then instating the Eternal Return as the transcendental. The epistemological justification of the reality of forces as self-determining and non-objective qualities through Nietzsche's generalized semiotics is thereby supported by the claim of a transcendental necessity for non-identical repetition. This, however, as we will see, can only be guaranteed if being is reflected back onto itself in the act of "the choice." Nietzsche, and subsequently Deleuze, thus introduce the divide between the empirical and the a priori structure of life into the transcendental in favor of the latter. The result of the transcendental deduction from the metaphysical premise of Nietzsche thereby presupposes itself and subordinates discrete being to continuous becoming.

This section will therefore attempt, firstly, to explain the problematic ground upon which the concept of philosophical decision can be posed. To do this we will examine the immanent split in Deleuze's understanding of the transcendental and then present the critiques of transcendental reasoning made prominently by Austin, Stroud and Körner. From the vantage point of this problematic, we can then, secondly, elucidate Laruelle's critique of (standard) philosophy in its attempt to solve such problems with an authoritarian gesture, a characterization of philosophical hubris in which he includes vitalism. After this elucidation, we can, thirdly, pose the question of what is left standing of Deleuze's inorganic vitalism and what elements Laruelle's rigorous "science of philosophy"[12] allows us to question. From there, we can move to a more robust account of inorganic philosophy as descriptive naturalism.

---

12   François Laruelle, *Principles of Non-Philosophy*, trans. Nicola Rubczak and Anthony Paul Smith (London: Bloomsbury, 2017), p. xviii.

## Philosophy "after" Life

The thought of a life beyond the human (or even organic form) understood in terms of transcendental philosophy seems to be anathema at this stage. If transcendental philosophy wants to describe the universal and general conditions for cognition and experience, it seems to clash with the singular reality of phenomena and instantiations that can only be retrospectively said to conform to these conditions. Especially considering that transcendental arguments run the risk of "degenerat[ing] into observations about how we do think, not arguments about how we must think,"[13] if they are unable to pinpoint the particular factors that *have to be present* (as conditions) and are thereby shared by *all* and *every* experience. Otherwise, the distinction between descriptive psychology and transcendental philosophy, or observations and normativity, breaks down. Following from Kant's architectonic, such a devolution of transcendental philosophy into psychology is exactly what needs to be avoided in order to not regionalize the transcendental.

But, if we follow Deleuze's vitalist critique, his radical temporalization of the transcendental and dissolution of the resemblance of the transcendental and the empirical, which makes the transcendental no bigger or more extensive than the empirical, the claim that certain transcendental factors obtain ahistorically and moreover atemporally in every experience becomes implausible, given that we accept Deleuze's arguments. His insistence on replacing the question of *possible* experience with the study of *real* experience by supplanting the possible with the virtual not only shifts philosophical focus away from an invariable transcendental, but also calls into question the validity of transcendental arguments in terms of Kant's architectonic project as such. But then, if there is something like "transcendental empiricism"—and if it is *one* method at all—the question of whether empiricism and/or transcendental philosophy are even capable of a purely materialist vitalism as proposed becomes a pressing

---

[13] Ralph C. S. Walker, "Kant and Transcendental Arguments," in *The Cambridge Companion to Kant and Modern Philosophy*, ed. Paul Guyer (Cambridge: Cambridge University Press, 2006), p. 254.

concern. Deleuze's notion of the transcendental needs to be evaluated.

There exists a Deleuze that expresses this perceived contradiction with unmistakable overtones of eighteenth and nineteenth century romantic historicism. As anti-Platonic transformation, "Life" became a new *prima philosophia*, deposing the invariant transcendental in favor of the creativity and productivity of becoming. In its encounter with biology and especially evolutionary theory, this dynamic ontology exchanges on first glance the universality and generality of dogmatic transcendental thought for contingent and singular experiences. This romantic line in Deleuze's œuvre encompasses Leibniz's intensive materialism, the vegetal mobility of the rhizome, the rejection of Oedipus in the name of desire and the experimental practices of art before theory. On the other hand, Deleuze's philosophy presents itself as the zenith of classicism: the stoic physics of incorporeal surfaces, the attention to universal history, the pure and empty form of time and the emphasis on the creation of concepts. There seems to be a split between structure and the resistance internal to structure, much like the one Deleuze locates in Kant.[14] Is this split not, as John Mullarkey suggests, the very after-life of Deleuze himself? It seems to be his legacy in the philosophy of immanence: that one either pursues the purely quantitative line of the abstract and the Idea, as Badiou's "mathesis" does, or takes Henry's route, tracing everything to its genesis in a purely qualitative affectivity, the "pathos" that is life. Is Deleuze not the genetic factor that posthumously splits the world into matheme or patheme without remainder?

Though every one of his readers—even his critics—seem to agree that Deleuze's transcendental empiricism is expressing something crucial about post-Kantian philosophy, it is not so easy to make out *exactly* what this is.[15] One certain aspect, already depicted here, is that Deleuze's construction or genesis of the transcendental makes it no more extensive than the empirical. By rejecting the category of the possible and replacing it with

---

[14]  Deleuze, *Kant's Critical Philosophy*, p. 57.
[15]  Alistair Welchman, "Schopenhauer and Deleuze," in *At the Edges of Thought: Deleuze and Post-Kantian Philosophy*, ed. Craig Lundy and Daniela Voss (Edinburgh: Edinburgh University Press, 2015), p. 246.

the virtual, the condition does not precede the conditioned but is created in the act of determination. *This* Deleuze is concerned with structural genesis as well as the genesis of structure. On the other hand, there is a Deleuze that insists on the importance of phenomena, things or imperceptible affections that resist any structure, especially that of representation. Paradoxically, this Deleuze is far closer to phenomenology, since this resistance appears as a break, a crack, a resisting element within structure. While one Deleuze is concerned with the genesis of representation, the other one is interested in what is left once representation is subtracted. Of course, one could, as Claire Colebrook actually does, make the argument that a vitalist theory must accept or even embrace such inner tensions as expressions of a vibrant thinking.[16] But the split within matters of vitalism and/or life cannot simply be mended by disjunctive synthesis. Rather, we will suggest a third Deleuze, neither one who is only interested in static genesis, i.e. the constitution of the actual by the virtual, nor one whose focus is the invariable ethical injunction to counter-actualize, but a Deleuze in the movement between the two in the pure and empty form of time.

This quasi-dialectical trait is already apparent in Nietzsche and in Deleuze's reading of him. Nietzsche's vacillations in relation to his conception of life are visible in a philological sense in some works that take a very clear materialist and even biologistic standpoint,[17] from which life ought to be seen as reducible to chemistry and physics. Other works, however, clearly reject this reductionist view in favor of a metaphysical and distinctly anti-reductive view of life.[18] There seems to be on the one hand a corpus of finitist works rooted in empirical biological ideas of physical life (which almost run the risk of becoming a vulgar materialism), including, for example, what Deleuze calls "the cosmological and

---

[16] See Colebrook, *Deleuze and the Meaning of Life*, p. 5.
[17] An account of the scientific basis of Nietzsche's theory of biology can be found in Gregory Moore, *Nietzsche, Biology, and Metaphor* (Cambridge; New York: Cambridge University Press, 2002).
[18] For example, Nietzsche's critique of Darwin's too reductive view of evolution, which does not consider the artistic and creative potential of organic life. See Friedrich Nietzsche, "Anti-Darwin," in *Twilight of the Idols* (Oxford: Oxford University Press, 1998), p. 50.

physical doctrine"[19] of the Eternal Return and Will to Power. On the other hand, there are the infinitist writings of the philosophy of unlimited immanent becoming(s), which transform the Will to Power into an a priori and include a version of the eternal return as an "ethical and selective thought."[20] This opens up a deeper philosophical problem, since it complicates the reading of Nietzsche's approach of the self-differentiation of the Will to Power into reactive and active forces, thereby allowing for or even inviting more "extreme" interpretations and approaches. This tendency is encapsulated by Bataille's identification of sovereignty with nothingness; here we can find a unique vision of the will to power as destruction, which operates through the eternal return, and entails a rejection of all gregarious and herd-like tendencies. The problem with the absolute anti-humanism of this "base materialism"[21] was best grasped by Klossowski, who refers back to the aforementioned dialectic:

> The very anthropomorphism he was fighting against, and which he criticized even in the most "objective" theories of science, was now reintroduced by Nietzsche himself—he became an accomplice, certainly not in order to safeguard human feeling, but rather to "overcome" it, as he said; in fact, to dehumanize thought.[22]

All the reactive tendencies of the Last Men cannot simply be eradicated totally and instantaneously without similarly destroying the basis upon which the Overman can arise. The necessity of subscribing at least in part to the leveling tendencies of reactive forces cannot be eliminated, since the expression of any conception of the Will to Power, which is necessary to become active, cannot be separated from the objects or concepts it represents. Hence, the notion of the Will to Power undergoes

---

[19] Deleuze, *Nietzsche and Philosophy*, p. 47.
[20] Ibid., p. 68.
[21] Benjamin Noys constructs an anti-vitalist materialism on this basis; see Benjamin Noys, "Georges Bataille's Base Materialism," *Cultural Values* 2, no. 4 (October 1998), p. 499–517.
[22] Pierre Klossowski, *Nietzsche and the Vicious Circle* (Chicago: University of Chicago Press, 1997), p. 113.

an internal split or bifurcation since it is always "at once *representations of* (the expression of Will to Power) and (representations of) *the expression of* Will to Power."[23] Although, as we will see, this dialectic does not work through negation and is distinctly anti-representational, it does not break completely with the structure of Hegelian dialectics. Negotiating the actual function of the dialectic in Nietzsche's vitalism will not only determine the extent and meaning of his (anti-)humanism and (anti-)organicism, but the role of thought and philosophy in his vitalism. To understand this dialectic as well as its overcoming by Nietzsche-Deleuzian vitalism, we first have to linger with the problem of transcendental reasoning, of which both philosophers represent the most radical form: a transcendental philosophy turned against itself.

### WHAT DO TRANSCENDENTAL ARGUMENTS DO?

While the general discussion on the validity of transcendental arguments has been very different in Anglo-Saxon and continental philosophy, these differences (as well as differences within the two traditional lines) hinge on distinct ways of dealing with the Kantian heritage, and don't constitute evidence for some kind of politico-philosophical geography á la Hegel.[24] One can sketch these diverging paths in numerous ways, for example as two conflicting "narratives" constituting the history of philosophy that evolve from encounters with Kant's work; one line stretching from Hegel to Derrida, while another encompasses everyone from Bolzano to Putnam. This Rortyan approach, which sees philosophy as merely a history of people reading certain books by other people, and subsequently not reading others, could be supplemented by the idea that, even though everybody is reading Kant, not everybody is reading the same Kant. Not only does Kant appear, albeit unwillingly,

---

23  Rocco Gangle, *François Laruelle's Philosophies of Difference: A Critical Introduction and Guide* (Edinburgh: Edinburgh University Press, 2013), p. 73.
24  See Georg Wilhelm Friedrich Hegel, *Philosophy of Nature*, trans. Arnold V. Miller (New York: Clarendon Press, 2004), p. 285.

as the philosopher of splits (between the transcendental and the empirical subject; between transcendental aesthetics and logic; between the human being fitting into nature and the human being being eternally separate from it; between man inhabiting the noumenal and the phenomenal world), but his work is perceived and used as such. There are multiple Kants,[25] sometimes within one work. It is not the case (even if it proves to be empirically true) that analytical philosophers only read the *Critique of Pure Reason*, while continental philosophers would consider the *Critique of Pure Reason* only as necessary groundwork for the *Critique of Judgement*. Rather, within the *Critique of Pure Reason*, a metaphilosophical approach might focus on the relationship between experience and our capacity to reflect on it, while the transcendental aesthetic might give a starting point for a radical critique of the ahistorical nature of the categories of the Deduction and lead the way to their temporalization via a genetic or deconstructive account. Similarly, because "[i]n the *Critique of Judgement* mature classicism and nascent romanticism are in a complex equilibrium,"[26] one can either follow the possibility of a free play and conflict of faculties in the sublime or marvel at the serenity and the reaffirmation of common sense in beauty. This question turns on the value and meaning of "critique" itself. While in continental traditions, philosophy cannot, as of yet, be completely separated from transcendental reasoning due to its adherence to the necessity of an auto-critique of philosophy (understood as questioning of the conditions of thinking), the analytical tradition has transformed this reflexive quality of philosophy into forms of meta-philosophy, effectively circumventing the transcendental by positing the primacy of language and logic to provide rigor for philosophical analysis.[27] While, therefore, in analytical traditions the search for "necessities" could be construed as pre-critical or as "necessity-mongering"[28] by continental philosophers, the continental reinvention

---

25  I fully acknowledge that such a claim is already more typically made by continental philosophers.
26  Deleuze, *Kant's Critical Philosophy*, p. 57.
27  Which, of course, could be construed as a minimally transcendental philosophy too.
28  Jack Reynolds and James Chase, "The Fate of Transcendental Reasoning in Contempo-

of the transcendental in its genealogical, deconstructive, phenomenological or constructivist forms, might appear to a Frege scholar as obscure at best.

Whether in Strawson's defense of transcendental arguments or the skeptical objections of Stroud and Körner, the analytic tradition has judged the validity of transcendental reasoning mainly by its form, detaching it thereby from the Kantian heritage and impetus. While occasional voices like Stapleford try to urge us to consider Kant's project as the attempt to close the gap between reality as cognized by us and external reality by giving priority to the relation of the a priori and the synthetic, he remains an oddity.[29] Moreover, the employment of transcendental arguments, as for example by McDowell or Davidson, is still confronted with an implicit accusation of non-analyticity.[30]

The twentieth century development of transcendental reasoning in the continental tradition, even though often written as a singular story, can also be read as a reaction to and interaction with emerging analytical, and more specifically scientifically-inclined, thought. Chase and Reynolds remark, albeit pointedly, that the survival and thriving of transcendental philosophy in continental circles—despite the critique it has received and the transformations it has undergone—takes up, at least in part, the form of Pascal's Wager: "believing in the efficacy of transcendental arguments, if they work, may result in tremendous results (a Copernican revolution); if they do not, some important concepts will have nonetheless been created. Better that, on this view, than disbelieving and

---

rary Philosophy," in *Postanalytic and Metacontinental: Crossing Philosophical Divides*, ed. Jack Reynolds and James Chase (London; New York: Continuum, 2010), p. 28.

[29] See Scott Stapleford, "Kant's Transcendental Arguments as Conceptual Proofs," *Philosophical Papers* 35, no. 1 (2006), p. 119–136.

[30] This persistent practice of drawing methodological lines in the sand might not be surprising at all. As with the early analytic empiricists like the logical positivists, for whom the synthetic a priori was close to non-sense or, even worse, poetry, transcendental philosophy has been a consistent counterpoint to help shape and sharpen the empiricist project. While it would also have been possible to go the route of the implicit synthetic a prioris in Carnap or Wittgenstein, the widespread adoption instead of Quine's radical empiricism shows the disengagement with traditional transcendental methodology. The rejection of non-positivist and non-empiricist approaches in the strict sense is at least implicated in the birth narrative of early analytic thought.

being the under-laborer of science."[31] Although this caricature is not unrecognizable, it remains true that phenomenology has in recent years engaged very productively with naturalism and post-structuralist concepts, especially ideas by Deleuze, which have inspired sciences as diverse as sociology and quantum physics. Rather than invoking the Wager, therefore, it would be better to reconstruct the continental attitude towards the transcendental, as we have already remarked, as a stance towards the necessity of "critique" in the Kantian sense that encompasses the conditions of critique itself. Even if we consider the transcendental in its most basic form as a system of relations between propositional contents, they will necessarily—if we want to hold that they obtain in experience and/or cognition—not be self-evident. This means that if we construct arguments in a transcendental manner, trying to present them as valid propositional inferences, these arguments will not be truth-apt until experience (actual or possible) is considered to satisfy the a priori factor in question. As we have already seen in the "image of thought," thinking cannot be abstracted from the act of thinking; there is no thinking about thought that does not involve the thinker itself. One can think of this thinker as always already existing in a world as *Dasein*, and transcendental reasoning turns into existential hermeneutics. But the same thinker can then be reconsidered as a corporeal subject and the body becomes the center of thought, as in Merleau-Ponty's phenomenology. One then discovers that the body is already the incarnation of (historical) discourses and the a priori becomes "historical." This pertains up to the point where the possibility of any category (historical or otherwise) is revealed to cover up how specific things are actualized and individuated in their particularity and the transcendental becomes "empirical," "sensible" and fully "temporalized." If in

---

[31] See Reynolds and Chase, "The Fate of Transcendental Reasoning in Contemporary Philosophy," p. 37. This claim certainly rings true for Husserl's relationship to Carnap, which went from extreme proximity, in terms of phenomenological and phenomenalistic approaches in their works and in terms of personal respect, to completely diverging paths, due in no small part to their stances on science. Likewise, it might apply to Heidegger's conservative defense of thinking against science, still present in deconstructive thought, which sees science as the prolongation of an instrumentality caused by a technological attitude towards the world.

the end no conversation seems to be possible any more, someone tries to rediscover the transcendental as the condition for a communicative society and for rationality.[32] What is common to the methodological approaches of the continental tradition in transcendental thought consists, therefore, in the question of anteriority, i.e. the question of how to actually execute the shift from the transcendental to the empirical.[33]

While Kant marks the point of departure for both traditions' attitude towards the transcendental, traditionally analytic philosophy was more concerned with the form and validity of transcendental arguments, while continental thinkers were more engaged in situating and reinventing the transcendental in light of the question of anteriority.[34] Most recent developments, however, have softened this division, with post-analytic philosophers embracing the possibilities of transcendental thought, while some continental philosophers, chief among them the Speculative Realists, have started to question Kant's critical project and transcendental philosophy as such.

It is, however, worth noting that Kant himself does not speak of transcendental arguments in the aforementioned sense. It is not the so-called "transcendental arguments" (*transzendentalen Argumente*) of the *Critique of Pure Reason* (mentioned at A627/B655) which are the object of the discussion, but rather the abstract form of the practice of transcendental exposition and transcendental deduction. But, as we have already seen, the transition from one to the other is no less controversial than the possibility of abstracting a consistent methodological form from them.

---

32   For all these positions, see respectively Heidegger, *Being and Time*; Merleau-Ponty, *Phenomenology of Perception*; Michel Foucault, *Archaeology of Knowledge*, Routledge Classics (London; New York: Routledge, 2002); Deleuze, *Difference and Repetition*; Agnes Bosanquet, "Luce Irigaray's 'Sensible Transcendental': Becoming Divine in the Body," *Transformations: Online Journal of Region, Culture and Society* 11 (2005); Dario Antiseri, *The Weak Thought and Its Strength* (Aldershot; Brookfield: Avebury, 1996); Karl-Otto Apel, *Karl-Otto Apel: Selected Essays*, ed. Eduardo Mendieta (New Jersey: Humanities Press, 1994).

33   Alan Murray, "Philosophy and the 'Anteriority Complex'," *Phenomenology and the Cognitive Sciences* 1, no. 1 (2002), p. 27–47.

34   Mark Sacks, "The Nature of Transcendental Arguments," *International Journal of Philosophical Studies* 13, no. 4 (December 2005), p. 444.

## THE TRANSCENDENTAL ARGUMENT AND ITS DISCONTENTS

But if, as we have seen, the problem of organicism follows from Kant's architectonic project, then we should view this detachment of transcendental arguments from the critical project as a positive opportunity, rather than a negative estrangement. If it would be possible to detach transcendental reasoning from the architectonic without collapsing into absolute Idealism, which could well be the consequence of such an undertaking,[35] we would have the chance to construct a transcendental philosophy capable of a materialist vitalism. This move is overtly counter-intuitive in terms of the above traditions, since it is continental philosophy, the safeguarder of the transcendental tradition, which seems also to shelter contemporary vitalist thought, while the Anglo-Saxon landscape does not attempt something of this kind. Still, as a methodological consideration, it makes sense to ascertain whether one really must go through the transcendental to overcome its boundaries, or if one can escape its constraints by removing the engine (transcendental arguments) from the architectonic project and using it elsewhere.

The first deterritorialization, to phrase it in Deleuzian terms, of the transcendental form of reasoning, which detaches it from Kantian heritage, occurs in Austin's "Are There A Priori Concepts?" With quite some rhetorical cunning he first transforms the discussion into one about "universals," which might seem to be in agreement with Kant's approach, insofar as we understand universals to be the factors which obtain in every experience. Given this shift in focus, he presents the form of transcendental arguments as follows: "This is a transcendental argument: if there were not in existence something other than sensa, we should not be able to do what we are able to do (viz. name things)."[36] This form of argument, obviously tailor

---

35 Just consider the fact that the antagonistic stance of Moore as well as Russell towards transcendental reasoning stems from their shared opposition to British Idealism, which inevitably leads them to adopt radical empiricist positions. A comprehensive look at this history can be found in Tom Rockmore, *On Foundationalism: A Strategy for Metaphysical Realism* (Lanham: Rowman & Littlefield, 2004), p. 73–75.

36 John Longshaw Austin, "Are There A Priori Concepts?," in *Philosophical Papers* (Oxford: Oxford University Press, 1961), p. 34.

made for a critique by ordinary language theory, offers us a very stripped down version of Kant's method, removed from the context of his critical project. Although the argument appears to simplify the problem of the ground of said capacity, we should acknowledge that this reduction allows Austin to pick out the form of the argument. Setting himself apart from traditional metaphysics, Austin does not simply start from scratch, but retrospectively levels the playing field by breaking the dominance of the transcendental method to create the conditions for philosophizing without the necessity of transcendental considerations. The transcendental argument therefore enjoys the benefit of being treated as a form of argument, or, in ordinary language theory terms, a standard argument form, equal in standing to, for example, *reductio ad absurdum*. Therefore, it is subject to the same critical scrutiny as any universally applicable argument. He by no means does away with transcendental arguments lightly, because, even though he wants to free himself from having to use them, they might still prove to be useful tools. Alas, it turns out they are not. This actually marks a point of connection with Deleuze's method of "pick up,"[37] where he constantly plucks concepts and arguments from their environments and original contexts in order to test their effects in other "machines" or constructions. Instead of performing an exegesis or a hermeneutics deconstructing Kantian ambiguities, Austin and Deleuze are both more interested in salvaging the useful parts of the philosophical tradition.

Problems arise, according to Austin, when we use transcendental arguments repeatedly, creating different arguments about universals, while we do not know how these universals are alike. In this light, it seems "odd to suppose that *any two* distinct transcendental arguments could possibly be known each to prove the existence of the *same* kind of thing."[38] Hence, if every transcendental argument proves the existence of something, which for a lack of any criterion for evaluation or identification is different in kind from any other thing proven by another transcendental argument, every use of a transcendental argument is a glass cannon.

---

[37] De Bolle, "Preface: Desire and Schizophrenia," p. 9.
[38] Austin, "Are There A Priori Concepts?," p. 36.

Against such harsh treatment Strawson has tried to rehabilitate transcendental arguments by endorsing a "descriptive metaphysics."[39] Such a method derives its necessity from the problem that, although the "close examination of the actual use of words is the best, and indeed the only sure, way in philosophy,"[40] such inquiries do not reveal the structures that enable understanding. However detailed the explanation of the meaning (or use) of a word, we will not uncover the structure that "the metaphysician wants revealed,"[41] but we can at best approximate some of it in the course of our examination of it. We therefore need the kind of argument that is able to function as an explanation *and* a description at the same time; we need, in short, a transcendental argument. Returning to our problem of transcendental arguments describing general factors obtaining in every experience, Strawson holds that it is descriptive metaphysics, not psychology, that gives us the basic elements of the structure of understanding, cognition and experience, but he dramatically reduces their claim for generality. The arguments he talks about *only* refer to the conceptual commitments we hold and thereby are *only* applicable to the "subjective order of our perception,"[42] which is forever split from the natural world. Therefore, insofar as, and only insofar as, we *only* formulate claims about "the rule-governed connectedness of our representations"[43] can we circumvent the need for any truth claims about external reality and ascribe objectivity to the rules of this subjective order. The world we must start with is, hence, not the external world, but the world "for us," the world as cognized by us.[44]

---

[39] Peter Frederick Strawson, *Individuals: An Essay in Descriptive Metaphysics* (London: Routledge, 1959), p. 9. He describes his method as follows: "Descriptive metaphysics is content to describe the actual structure of our thought about the world, revisionary metaphysics is concerned to produce a better structure." Ibid.
[40] Ibid., p. 10.
[41] Ibid., p. 9.
[42] Peter Frederick Strawson, *The Bounds of Sense: An Essay on Kant's Critique of Pure Reason* (London: Methuen & Co, 1966), p. 91.
[43] Ibid.
[44] Strawson, by questioning the role of the noumena in Kant's account, in the end formulates the reading now known as the "two-worlds" theory, in which appearances, which are comprehensible for human minds, and the things-in-themselves, which are completely incomprehensible to the human mind, inhabit two distinct worlds. Resting on textual evidence,

From this vantage point, we can attempt to recapitulate Strawson's argument in *Individuals* about "reidentification" as a response to Austin's accusations. Insofar as we can have individuating thoughts about particulars, we have to suppose the conceptual scheme of a unified (and single) system of spatio-temporal relations as the framework of such thoughts. But only if we accept the persistence of (at least some) particulars—also through periods of absence from our consciousness or non-continuous perception—is such a conceptual scheme possible. Without the acceptance of some persistent particulars, a unified system of spatio-temporal relations for organizing our individuating thoughts would be impossible. The belief in such persistent particulars is therefore justified, since they not only condition, but also explain the possibility of actual individuating thoughts about particulars. Although not bridging the gap between external reality and internal cognitive processes, this argument is supposed to show the validity of transcendental arguments for making claims about anything at all, since Strawson seeks to rehabilitate them as a method for philosophical investigation. As we have already outlined above, this effectively closes transcendental arguments off from considering any experience or thinking other than human, but also from the split in thought internal to itself. It excludes the question of the genesis of cognition and therefore amplifies the tendencies of Kant's architectonic to encase transcendental thought in the organic image. As we will see, the apparent methodological limitations of this strategy are considered a strength by his advocates. By using the figure of a sceptic questioning the usefulness of transcendental arguments, Strawson is able to illustrate the strength of his argument by trapping the sceptic with his own argument:

> Strawson makes his case for a two-worlds interpretation against the remnants of Berkeleyian metaphysics. He holds, as Kant would, that human experience arises from a (complex and quasi-causal) relation of phenomena and noumena. This is, however, Strawson claims, incompatible with Kant's own account, firstly because we do not know how we could know the things-in-themselves on an epistemic level, since they are necessarily not comprehensible, and secondly because on an ontological level we cannot say how the relationship between phenomena and noumena should be constructed, if not in space and time and not as causal in the strict sense. Strawson, therefore, making Kant an "inconsistent Berkeley," rejects Kant's proposed transcendental idealism. See Henry E. Allison, *Kant's Transcendental Idealism* (New Haven: Yale University Press, 2004), p. 4.

He pretends to accept a conceptual scheme, but at the same time quietly rejects one of the conditions of its employment. Thus his doubts are unreal, not simply because they are logically irresoluble doubts, but because they amount to the rejection of the whole conceptual scheme within which alone such doubts make sense.[45]

To utter his concern, the sceptic has to accept the framework he rejects, since any kind of proposition about particular things presupposes the existence of a conceptual scheme that allows for individuating thoughts, a scheme which is then in turn conditioned by our commitment to accept the persistence of (at least some) particulars.[46]

Not convinced by Strawson's rebuttal of the sceptic, Barry Stroud has defended the claims of the sceptic. As he expresses it in his aptly-named paper "Transcendental Arguments," Strawson's arguments may tell us something about the way we think things are, but not how things are, which is also true for the conditions of the refutation of the sceptic's position.[47] To transition from one commitment, e.g. that there is a conceptual scheme, to another commitment, e.g. that there are persistent things, this has to be backed up by another commitment, which actually leads us to accept *all* the commitments involved by acting as connective tissue and a criterion for truth (at least about the necessity to accept a commitment). To bridge this gap between the things we think about things (apparent commitments) and the commitments that are fact *because of* the initial commitments, we need a strong metaphysical commitment, e.g. idealism or verificationism. And since idealism is rejected by Strawson, there are not a great many options.

---

45   Strawson, *Individuals*, p. 35.
46   This interpretation of transcendental arguments—which is far more modest than even the Kantian account—is, however, not able to defeat the sceptic, despite all the sacrifices in philosophical scope. Allison (among others) rejects the "two-worlds" account, by holding that Kant is not talking about two things (phenomena and noumena), but about one thing conceived in two different (although distinct) ways, effectively rejecting the metaphysical approach of Strawson and replacing it with an epistemological one. This account, however, does not help us with our consideration of vitalism.
47   See Barry Stroud, "Transcendental Arguments," in *Kant's Transcendental Arguments: Disciplining Pure Reason*, ed. Scott Stapleford (London; New York: Continuum, 2008).

But if we make such a commitment, why would we still need transcendental arguments at all, since the conclusions could equally be supported by the framework of the strong metaphysical commitment?[48] In defending the possibility of the utility and function of transcendental arguments they become superfluous. We can see this playing out in the "additional factual premiss [sic!]"[49] that Strawson proposes, which, according to Stroud, is a necessary condition for transcendental arguments of this variety to be convincing. It runs as follows: "If we know that the best criteria we have for the reidentification of particulars have been satisfied, then we know that objects continue to exist unperceived."[50] However, this means that we sometimes know that these particulars exist independently of our perception of them, because certain conditions have been satisfied. And indeed, if the commitment to the existence of a conceptual scheme of a single and unified system of spatio-temporal relations is dependent on the commitment that there are (at least some) persisting particulars, the commitment to the conceptual scheme depends on the strength of the justification that the *actual* satisfaction of the conditions of (at least two) particulars persisting is true for all *possible* experiences. If, therefore, only particular cases of particulars persisting without our perception can be verified, the strength of the justification that there is a conceptual scheme, which is necessary to bridge the gap to our commitment, is regionalized. The only way to investigate further philosophically would be to follow this trajectory and work with narrower and narrower conditions, but then transcendental arguments would not be distinguished in any way from verificationist or empiricist arguments. So, either it makes sense to us that objective particulars persist *factually*, but in no way *transcendentally*, or transcendental arguments are regionalized by specific cases. Both conclusions make transcendental arguments either null and void or reduce them to psychological observations.

---

[48] This actually seems to be the case with Strawson's interpretation of Kant as a two-worlds philosopher, in which the latter is not considered a proper transcendental idealist but merely an inconsistent absolute idealist in the vein of Berkeley.
[49] Stroud, "Transcendental Arguments", p. 122.
[50] Ibid.

This "factual premiss" is close to moves we have seen above and see time and time again in continental philosophy: even if we only make claims on the level of commitments, a shift has to occur from the transcendental to the empirical in order for transcendental reasoning to work. Consider in this line of thought the phenomenological solutions that feature an existential twist, such as Heidegger's or Merleau-Ponty's. They propose that philosophy has always favored a theoretical approach to things, but that this enunciation of the thinker is "already always" conditioned by her practical involvement in the world, or in other words, that things are first and foremost known as "ready-to-hand" and accessible to it as "present-at-hand." The question arising from Heidegger's complicated relation to transcendental philosophy is whether this is simply a critique of the traditional (theoretical) transcendental forms of reasoning, which works by pointing out that the possibility of such a transcendental inquiry is conditioned by a practical a priori, or if this in itself is a transcendental argument. Rather than rejecting the autonomous validity of scientific knowledge, as Heidegger does on more than one occasion,[51] Merleau-Ponty builds on it, while still holding that such knowledge is conditioned by corporeal engagement with and towards the world. This "primacy of perception" thesis proposes that our constantly developing "body-schema" (involving the acquisition of skills, habits and new corporeal equilibria), serves, through bodily motility and involved bodily intentionality, as the transcendental condition for sensible sensory experience.[52] Privileging know-how above know-that, these conditions ensure that experience is not just a dispersed collection of raw sense data but a meaningful field

---

[51] Heidegger's pre-modern attitude towards the "impotence of the sciences," as expressed in "Science and Reflection," in *The Question Concerning Technology and Other Essays* (New York: Harper & Row, 1977), p. 176 and its consequences are explored in Babette E. Babich, "Heidegger's Philosophy of Science: Calculation, Thought, and Gelassenheit," in *From Phenomenology to Thought, Errancy, and Desire*, ed. Babette E. Babich, vol. 133 (Dordrecht: Springer Netherlands, 1995), p. 589–599, and in William J. Richardson, "Heidegger's Critique of Science," *New Scholasticism* 42, no. 4 (1968), p. 511–536.

[52] Compare Maurice Merleau-Ponty, *The Primacy of Perception: And Other Essays on Phenomenological Psychology, the Philosophy of Art, History and Politics*, trans. James M. Edie (Evanston: Northwestern University Press, 1971); see also Merleau-Ponty, *Phenomenology of Perception*, p. 102.

of unified experience. *If* we say that these approaches constitute reinventions (or resituations) of the transcendental—while not being mutually exclusive, as Dreyfus shows—they seem to be made for bridging the gap that plagues transcendental arguments in Stroud's critique.[53] Reformulating Strawson's rebuttal to the sceptic, we could make the following argument: "If one wants to make a critique of an existentially or corporeally conceived transcendental, one already has to use the practical or corporeal scheme that one doubts." *If* we want to make this argument and feel that it can be made uncontentiously, then "what's wrong with charitably interpreting Heidegger or Merleau-Ponty in such a way, and so protecting them from Stroudian critique?"[54] The problem is, however, that the way to immunize Heidegger or Merleau-Ponty is also the way to make them superfluous, as we have seen with Strawson. Again, both operate with a "factual premiss" as Strawson does, effectively regionalizing the transcendental. We are again then faced with a dilemma: either we give in to a residual realism—especially present in Merleau-Ponty but in Heidegger as well—to bridge the gap, or we can dissolve it in tautology. The first option would need an additional commitment that none of them would accept. Or as a second option, we could simply say, whenever we are immersed practically or corporeally in an act, it is the case that the conditions of such investment obtain. If we consider the latter option, a retrieval of transcendental arguments in the style of Stern's, which builds on the consistency and equilibrium of our judgements and pre-judgements, would be possible.[55] But Heidegger's anti-scientism especially suggests that the latter regionalization of the transcendental as well as Stern's very modest solution are not acceptable as well.[56] This problem is particularly pressing, since

---

[53] See Hubert L. Dreyfus, *What Computers Can't Do: The Limits of Artificial Intelligence* (New York: Harper & Row, 1979).

[54] See Reynolds and Chase, "The Fate of Transcendental Reasoning in Contemporary Philosophy," p. 41.

[55] Robert Stern, "On Kant's Response to Hume: The Second Analogy as Transcendental Argument," in *Transcendental Arguments: Problems and Prospects*, ed. Robert Stern (Oxford: Oxford University Press, 1999), p. 47.

[56] Still, despite all this critique, the claim that there would still be something missing in the complete picture of reality if cognition (and its structures) were universalized should be taken up.

the pre-scientific being invoked by Merleau-Ponty, which is inspired by Bergson and the openly anti-scientific *Welt* of the *Dasein* in Heidegger, and which draws heavily from Dilthey, has served as a basis or proof for (classical) vitalism.[57]

We could, however, approach this problem from the critique Stroud formulated with Körner.[58] They point out that the defense against the sceptic rests on a proposed conceptual framework (spatio-temporal, corporeal etc.) which can only be employed with an additional premise. If we want to hold that the sceptic uses the conceptual framework in question while she doubts it, we also have to prove that she could not have done her doubting otherwise. We would need to prove that she *necessarily* has to commit to the conceptual framework, because she could not have done it within another one. The fact that currently the conceptual framework in question seems to appear to be the only one is not conclusive prove of the conceptual framework's *necessity*. It could be a proof of our lack of imagination as well, which should never be taken as a proof of necessity, as Dennett remarks.[59] Furthermore, even if we accept that a necessity established by a transcendental argument appears to be necessary within the current conceptual framework, the necessity of the validating conceptual framework is not proven yet at all. It might still be contingent itself, which makes the proven necessity within the conceptual framework relative at best. Since we do not even know, as Austin has shown, how the factors described by any two transcendental arguments are alike, we also cannot find criteria to make them commensurable. As we have seen, we cannot solve this problem with verification, since it makes transcendental arguments superfluous. The only solution to this dilemma—as Kant might well have seen already—is dogmatism. The possibility of finding

---

[57] Compare Eric S. Nelson, "Heidegger and Dilthey: Language, History and Hermeutics," in *Horizons of Authenticity in Phenomenology, Existentialism, and Moral Psychology: Essays in Honor of Charles Guignon*, ed. Hans Petersen (Dordrecht: Springer Netherlands, 2015).
[58] See Stephan Körner, "Transcendental Tendencies in Recent Philosophy," *The Journal of Philosophy* 63, no. 19 (October 13, 1966), p. 63.
[59] "Philosophers' Syndrome: mistaking a failure of imagination for an insight into necessity." Daniel C. Dennett, *Consciousness Explained*, trans. Paul Weiner (Boston: Back Bay Books, 1991), p. 401.

alternative conceptual frameworks is exactly what motivates the "anteriority complex" that has brought about many of the phenomenological, hermeneutic or post-structuralist reinventions of the transcendental. It leads us back to Austin's question about how two distinct transcendental arguments could be alike.

As we have seen, the detachment of transcendental arguments from Kantian architectonics reveals the inherent difficulties in performing the shift from the transcendental to the empirical and subsequent problems in verifying a transcendental conceptual framework. To effectively use transcendental arguments, it is necessary to build a hidden bridge in the form of a suppressed premise, say a commitment to a metaphysical position that secures the way in which the transcendental and the empirical are connected and structured, or else to leap over the gap. This decision would also involve the selection of the transcendental factors or the situation/location of the transcendental from the overabundance of possible transcendentals. This problem leads us precisely to Laruelle's critique of transcendental philosophy and subsequently to the allegation of vitalist Idealism against Nietzsche and Deleuze.

# (NON-)PHILOSOPHICAL IMMANENCE

### TWO FORMULAS

The bifurcation of Deleuze's philosophical heritage (into matheme and patheme) is not simply a question of first philosophy, but of radicalizing monism, even as—and in Badiou's case, only as—illusion. As John Mullarkey sharply notes:

> To crystallize the difference between Badiou and Henry we might even paraphrase Kant and say that affectivity without mathematics is blind, and mathematics without affectivity is empty. But Henry welcomes blindness and Badiou resolutely grounds his ontology on the empty set, that is, on the void.[60]

The One of immanence splits, when in a reductive gesture both forms are eliminated by a predicative procedure that attributes existence to only one side and non-existence to the other. The idea that there are things that are and things that are not (or only are as illusions) is not only incompatible with ontological univocity but would bar us from employing the disjunctive synthesis as weapon of last defense and making immanence a plural but consistent plane. The plane is split by antagonism, rather than agonism. As we saw in Austin's critique, what precludes us from synthesizing Badiou's and Henry's accounts is not only an incompatibility of assumptions or assertions, but a methodological problem. Although their arguments appear to be polar opposites, implying a similarity or common ground that facilitates such an opposition, we find ourselves unable to express clearly what this commonality is. Since this is the case, we cannot begin to solve this antinomy, because there is no higher or deeper ground to gain from which we could root out their shared false presuppo-

---

[60] John Mullarkey, *Post-Continental Philosophy: An Outline* (New York: Continuum, 2006), p. 125.

sition. The mere possibility of such a division between quality (Henry) and quantity (Badiou) refers back to the bifurcation in Deleuze's philosophy itself. Even worse, by setting in place looping systems of reflexivity, both dig deeper in their reductive stance—there is always a new layer of affectivity to be discovered *by* affectivity (the feeling of feeling), as well as there is always a new set to be revealed as a set of sets. However, it is exactly the claim of being all-encompassing that makes these philosophies paradoxically similar. As Bergson once noted, if something is everything, every other thing that also claims to be everything is at least "formally" identical; in the end, it becomes synonymous with existence itself. To state, however, that something is everything implies the impossibility of determining that "something" at all.[61]

This, however, should make us suspicious of the formula Deleuze offers in a letter entitled "Immanence=Life" in contrast to the later formula "Immanence: A Life ...." Besides the greater informational richness of the second formula, unfolded literally to the dot by Giorgio Agamben, the first formula seems to be almost empty. However, to explain the difference between identity ("=") and expression (":") or, better, the sort of difference invoked by the latter and denied by the former, an additional reflexive step is necessary—a folding back of life upon itself. To understand this folding and its validity, we must consider the operation formally. This is what Laruelle provides us with.

## DECISION AS TRANSCENDENTAL AUTO-DEDUCTION

Despite being hailed by Deleuze as a thinker "engaged in one of the most interesting undertakings of contemporary philosophy,"[62] Laruelle remains an overlooked figure in current academic discourse. It is not

---

61   Compare Bergson, *The Creative Mind*, p. 48–50.
62   "Francois Laruelle is engaged in one of the most interesting undertakings of contemporary philosophy. He invokes a One-All that he qualifies as 'nonphilosophical' and, oddly, as 'scientific,' on which the 'philosophical decision' takes root. This One-All seems to be close to Spinoza." Deleuze and Guattari, *What Is Philosophy?*, p. 220, note 5.

clear whether this is a result of his distinct and unique style, which to the uninitiated can look like an amalgam of "deconstructionist sterility with constructivist extravagance,"[63] or rather another consequence of the inertia and stunted desire inherent to academic philosophy. The first is indisputable from an outside perspective, the second already in fact a philosophical point made by Laruelle, since he is not only the philosopher of non-dominance but philosophizes in a non-dominant manner. This means that he does not subsume the whole of the real into or under a superior concept, such as the Will, the Unconscious, Being etc., as academic philosophy usually does, proposing that everything is *philosophizable*. On the contrary, his "non-philosophy" rather uses philosophy itself as a material or object of study in a rigorous but inexact "science," constantly trying to reveal philosophy's decisional operations and demonstrating their equality, as well as their equality to other modes of theory in a non-decisional gesture—and what would be more dangerous to the structures of academic philosophy than real radical democracy in thought?

The practice of non-philosophy therefore necessitates a suspension of the "principle of sufficient philosophy,"[64] the spontaneous and automatic belief in the legitimacy of the authority of philosophy (including its methods, questions, etc.) in its attempts to ground itself *within* thought *through* thought *as* thought. Consequently, the style of Laruelle's own theoretical work distances itself from the standard model of philosophy, which includes eschewing (similarly to Derrida, but for wholly different reasons) comprehensibility and therefore communicability as ideals for philosophical writing, an idea not far from Deleuze's critique of the image of thought.

As we have already mentioned, philosophies (after Kant) can be said to be at least minimally transcendental, insofar as they must consider their own conditions to avoid the accusation of being pre-critical. According to

---

63  Brassier, *Nihil Unbound*, p. 119.
64  François Laruelle, "Summary of Non-Philosophy," *Pli. The Warwick Journal of Philosophy* 9 (1999), p. 139.

Laruelle, however, this strategy has a flipside: philosophies turn this relation to their own conditions into conditions of thought *as such*. Although this critique is not limited to post-Kantian philosophy,[65] it becomes a more pressing matter in it. Kant already attempts to formulate the task of philosophy in terms of immanence and innumerable critics have attempted to overturn Kant on the basis that he was not radical enough in his dedication to immanence, confining it to representation. Laruelle's approach is potent because it is not simply a repetition of these critics' canonical dismissal of representation, but a suspension of the grounds upon which such a critique is made: a critique of the structure of "decision."[66] This structure not only provides philosophy with the means but also an invariant strategy to constitute itself as self-grounding, reflexive thought.

Philosophy, for Laruelle, is thus not only in the grips of a certain desire but is that desire itself: to identify and comprehend "the ultimate unity of empirical manifestations of phenomena."[67] Keeping in mind the critique of transcendental arguments we have already seen in Austin and Stroud, this philosophical desire seems doomed to failure from the start, insofar as we can neither decide between different contenders for a ground (the true condition of a given phenomenon) or for the absolute ground (the condition of conditions), nor guarantee the universality of a proposed universal without making it superfluous. This is the primary corruption of the philosophical project (as such): that it must start without a *determinable* secure starting point. This predicament, Laruelle argues, does not preclude philosophy from starting, but means that it does so, paradoxically, first and foremost by a scission and not a grounding, or rather does so by

---

[65] Laruelle's critique of what he calls "philosophy" is, however, far broader and more historically far reaching. His project is close to Heidegger's *Seinsgeschichte*, and Laruelle acknowledges Heidegger as the one who reopened the question that makes the investigation of non-philosophy possible. But while Heidegger sought to find an essence in the history of Being, which turned out to be a history of decadence, Laruelle dismisses the question of a relation between essence and philosophy outright, since it is still only an expression of the very same structure Heidegger set out to criticize.

[66] François Laruelle, "Toward a Science of Philosophical Decision," in *From Decision to Heresy: Experiments in Non-Standard Thought*, ed. Robin Mackay (Falmouth: Urbanomic, 2012), p. 75.UK\\uc0\\u8239{}: New York: Urbanomic\\uc0\\u8239{}; Sequence Press, 2012

[67] François Laruelle, *Philosophies of Difference: A Critical Introduction to Non-Philosophy* (London; New York: Continuum Books, 2010), p. 187.

means of a scission that is also a grounding. The necessity for the self-validation of philosophy splits "radical immanence" or the "Real" into two in order to grant immediate access to the Real qua reflection, an operation which would be rendered pointless in a unified Real (the One). An immanence thus split can then be shown to guarantee the validity of the postulate of an ultimate unity for the Real by deducing one side of the split from other, i.e. it "retroactively renders intelligible the multiplicity on which its postulation depends."[68] In other words, the One can only be thought insofar as it is manifest in the empirical and at the same time conditions it, that is, if it simultaneously unifies the multiplicity of the empirical, therefore necessarily surpassing it, and *is* this multiplicity. The One can philosophically only be thought as the unity of "two contraries or differends that it unites."[69] If philosophy—especially in its anti-dogmatic stance—wants to rest on epistemic validation, the splitting of immanence provides the means to not only ground philosophy in what is given or in what conditions the given, but also in the principle of unity or synthesis of the two, alongside a conceptual inventory that makes the mechanisms of the unification or synthesis intelligible. This process of self-validation is operative through a split in the Real, which philosophy itself creates to legitimize itself as the thought that is able to unify this split. It does so by pretending that, if its postulates are accepted, the Unity of the Real is given and hence it can provide knowledge of the One. Philosophy fails to think the undivided Real, but by dividing it enables the failure to masquerade as absolute success, with the philosopher covering her tracks through synthetic a priori factors. In other words, philosophy proceeds from the splitting of the One to the reflexive and self-validating reconstruction of the One in *its* terms and then to the presentation of this double as One (which is at the same time multiplicity), i.e. the most radical One. This strategy, called the "principle of sufficient philosophy" by Laruelle, "articulates the idealist pretension of philosophy as that which is at least able to co-determine

---

[68] Michael Olson, "Transcendental Arguments, Axiomatic Truth, and the Difficulty of Overcoming Idealism," in *Laruelle and Non-Philosophy*, eds. John Mullarkey and Anthony Paul Smith (Edinburgh: Edinburgh University Press, 2012), p. 176.
[69] Laruelle, *Philosophies of Difference*, p. 187.

that Real which is most radical."[70] One of the consequences of the strategy for the practice of philosophy is the constant supplanting of different and more radical immanences or transcendental conditions, each one more anterior than the preceding one, which is what we have referred to already in the above section as the "anteriority complex." By invoking "radical immanence," Laruelle instead begins with an undivided One or the One as "Indivision," a Unity unlike any ever thought by philosophy, "indifferent to the Unity of which all philosophers speak."[71] While the synthetic unity of standard philosophy gathers together elements which are supposed to "always already" secretly obtain as the genetic or transcendental ground of actual phenomena, the non-philosophical One is unity prior to unification, or the "given-without-givenness."[72] This immanence is "lived prior to all representation."[73] By postulating immanence as Unity prior to the philosophical modus operandi of first splitting and then unifying immanence (through a transcendent or superior operation), Laruelle's One escapes the deadlock of decision by avoiding the dyad of transcendence/immanence altogether. Therefore, what non-philosophy proposes is not another representation of or thought about the Real—since this would necessitate the splitting and unifying of immanence again—but thought "alongside" and therefore according to the real.

How, then, is this different to thinking according to the "univocity of being," as spoken of by Deleuze? Insofar as Deleuze's articulation of the "plane of immanence" already proposes immanence in its absolute (or even pure) form, ideality and materiality are but expressions of the same substance: *one* immanent existence without any transcendence. There would be no abstraction or concept that would not be uttered (so to speak) in the same ontological register as every material aspect.[74] A

---

70   Laruelle, "Summary of Non-Philosophy," p. 139.
71   Laruelle, *Philosophies of Difference*, p. 12.
72   Laruelle, "Summary of Non-Philosophy," p. 141.
73   François Laruelle, *En Tant Qu'un: La "Non-Philosophie" Expliquée Aux Philosophes* (Paris: Aubier, 1991), p. 19, my translation.
74   On the surface, the very distinctions between material and ideal, or sensible and intelligible (and so on) seem to be, if not errors, then a simple ontological confusion, if applied beyond a purely methodological and provisional use.

transcendent use of concepts or a transcendental use of categories already seems to indicate either a confusion on the ontological level or a lack of radicality on the epistemological level, which then only serves to affirm "given" ideological forms. Abandoning the structural and structuring role of the Other(-structure), Deleuze outperforms even Derrida in his commitment to immanence.[75] In essence, the dyad of transcendence and immanence in Deleuze seems not to indicate a *real* opposition between the two, since no such struggle would be possible within (all embracing) univocal being, but rather a technical split within immanence, which accounts for the possibility and reality of transcendental illusion. Hence, it is not the case that being is grounded in an abyss of non-sense, negation or even lack; thought can only be thought of as an expression of immanence (at the same time *physis* and *noesis* or their differencial identity) or, say, the Real as pure "positivity of content."[76] Inversely, there can never be a thought that determines the nature of thought as such, since this would imply a determination of the Real or immanence itself, effectively making this concept identical with immanence itself, which would mean that immanence was the immanence *of* this concept and not absolute. It seems like one would have to say that, if all thought is univocally an expression of immanence, "all thoughts are equal," not because there is something determinable that would make them equal, that is, the same in kind, but precisely because there is no such ground for the "alike-ness," meaning all thoughts are different in kind, with no common measure to select which is the more accurate representation of the real.[77] All of them must be said to be equal, which thus circumvents Austin's "problem" or, even more, turns this perceived dead end of transcendental argumentation into a new principle for a philosophy of immanence. Here, for Laruelle, the problem with Deleuze becomes manifest. Although there is no way to determine the

---

[75] See Daniel W. Smith, "Deleuze and Derrida, Immanence and Transcendence: Two Directions in Recent French Thought," in *Between Deleuze and Derrida*, ed. Paul Patton (London and New York: Continuum, 2003).
[76] Ian James, *The New French Philosophy* (Malden: Polity Press, 2012), p. 62.
[77] See John Mullarkey, *All Thoughts Are Equal: Laruelle and Nonhuman Philosophy* (Minneapolis: University of Minnesota Press, 2015), p. 208.

nature common to all thought without betraying immanence, meaning that all thoughts must be said to be equal—which seems to be the claim following from Deleuze's philosophy of immanence—this is not what Deleuze actually does. Laruelle claims implicitly (and Badiou more explicitly) that Deleuze turns away from a "democracy in thought" to an "aristocratic" style of thinking, by dogmatically recasting immanence in terms of vitalist idealism.[78] This (Nietzschean) brand of vitalism—so runs the argument, especially in *Philosophies of Difference*—holds Deleuze back from actually "thinking alongside the Real" and transforms his philosophy into merely yet another thought of the Real. Ironically, although "all thoughts are equal," some thoughts are more equal than others, it seems.

Closer examination of this claim is necessary but we can cast the problem in familiar terms, referring back to our treatment of the image of thought, which can serve as a guiding thread for the next sections. While both the transcendental empiricist and the non-philosopher are concerned with images of thought, and while both their approaches critique traditional or standard philosophy for tying and restricting thought to communication, the consequences they draw are radically different. Acknowledging the necessity of an image of thought for thinking at all—or, better, philosophizing at all—Deleuze proposes the need for a method that selects different images and creates new images, while non-philosophy insists on a thought without image or a thought that takes these images to be simply images, suspending any determination of thought by one of them, "visioning" them in their abstract generality. In a Kantian manner, Deleuze still delivers judgements on the images of thought, splitting the common doxa from the real philosophy, opinion from (real) thought, whereas Laruelle brackets all judgements to establish radical democracy in thought. Vitalism, as we will see, not only provides criteria for selection, but the idea that such selection is necessary at all. Although Deleuze does not favor a single image of thought, his vitalism prompts a selection of these images to save philosophy, to revitalize it, turning it into a vital process itself, as we will see.

---

78   Badiou, *Deleuze: The Clamor of Being*, p. 11.

For Laruelle, therefore, he must be rejected, for he is still Deleuze, "the" philosopher par excellence.

## IDEALISM AT THE HEART OF PHILOSOPHY

This rejection of philosophy as such is at the same time the refutation of the philosopher's "world," or as Laruelle puts it hyperbolically: "I postulate that philosophy is the form of the world."[79] The world of philosophy is a "thought-world" insofar as by decision it "colors its world with its own chosen ideas—be it the plane of immanence, the event, or auto-affection."[80] This does not imply that everything is thought per se, but that, for philosophy, the world remains indeterminate until concepts are applied to determine it, which effectively negates the already autonomously fully determinate One (or radical immanence). The hubris of the philosopher is therefore the belief that her concepts are indispensable for the complete constitution of the Real and that "merely" living the Real is not enough. As Socrates claims, "an unexamined life is not worth living." He sets philosophy not only apart from but above ordinary life; there are the lives of the ordinary men and there are the extraordinary biographies of the philosophers. There seems to be an "idealism at the heart itself of thought"[81] and philosophy, rather than being corrupted by it, is being enabled by it. This transcendence at the heart of immanence manifests for Laruelle as the coinciding movement of the Greek thought of being and the Jewish thought of alterity, of being and difference, which are still constitutive of both Heidegger's onto-theology and Derrida's deconstructivist aporias. If there is such an idealism at the heart of philosophy, this would be of great concern for our investigation into the concept of inorganic life, since we have established that there is a tendency (or widely practiced inference) from idealism to noocentrism to biocen-

---

[79] François Laruelle, "What Can Non-Philosophy Do?," *Angelaki: Journal for Theoretical Humanities* 8, no. 2 (2003), p. 183.
[80] Mullarkey, *Post-Continental Philosophy*, p. 137.
[81] Laruelle, "What Can Non-Philosophy Do?," p. 183.

trism, and finally to organocentrism. If being depends on thinking and thinking depends on minds and minds depend on living beings and living beings are organic, the world depends on organisms.

If we want to understand Laruelle's critique of Deleuze's inorganic life, which claims his philosophy to be an "idealist vitalism", we must follow this idealism in actu. How, then, does philosophy's idealism manifest for Laruelle? To elucidate the mechanisms of this idealism—even within outspoken realist and materialist philosophies—we will work from Kant's 1787 addition to the *Critique of Pure Reason*, the Refutation of Idealism.[82]

Because the *Göttingen Review* (*Göttinger Gelehrte Anzeigen*) claimed that Kant's is a materialist idealism, he reacted by clarifying his own position vis-á-vis the traditional debate by working out the only empirical realism he deemed possible. His critical or transcendental idealism does not—like the material idealism alleged of him—claim that it is the content of knowledge (or matter) that is ideal, but rather that its form is ideal. Subsequently he offers a rebuttal to two forms of idealism that he sees as guilty of this confusion of matter and form: dogmatic and problematic idealism. While the dogmatic variety, denying in a Berkeleyian manner the material existence of objects external to the mind, is swiftly left by the wayside due to the results of the "Transcendental Aesthetic," Cartesian problematic idealism presents itself as a more robust approach. By asserting that the material existence of objects can only be inferred, if somewhat dubiously, from the undisputable fact of one's own existence, problematic idealism proposes self-consciousness as the unconditioned ground for spatial intuitions. Kant sidesteps this straightforward inference by showing that spatial intuitions are (in principle) epistemically reliable, insofar as they must be presumed as the condition for the indisputable fact of the temporality of our self-consciousness. It is uncontentious to claim that

---

82  This section was added as a reaction to the critique of the *Göttingen Review*, which situated his *Critique of Pure Reason* within the tradition of material idealism. It is important to mention that the development of transcendental or critical thought had complicated the debate between materialist and idealist positions. While traditionally the sufficiency of either position was the focus of the debate, following transcendental philosophy the struggle of determining who and whose philosophy was either materialist or idealist became more pressing.

we are conscious of our existence in time. But such consciousness of our location in time is only possible insofar as there is something persistent in perception, so that a specific temporal location can be determined by serving as a reference point. Referring to the "First Analogy of Experience" he reminds us that we are "unable to perceive any determination of time, save through change in outer relations (motion) relative to the permanent in space."[83] In other words, the consciousness of our existence in time is only as epistemically reliable as the reality of external relations, or the inner sense only as certain as the outer. Here, the argument turns towards the external reality of these persistent objects:

> [T]his permanent cannot be an intuition in me. For all grounds of determination of my existence which are to be met with in me are representations; and as representations themselves require a permanent distinct from them, in relation to which their change, and so my existence in the time wherein they change, may be determined.[84]

Hence, a robust account of empirical self-consciousness is only possible on the premise of an (at least implicit) metaphysical realism. Although things cannot be known in themselves, the transcendental idealist is at least a realist on the metaphysical irreducibility of real objects to representation. Since this rejection of idealism is rather weak in terms of its scope—rejecting specific forms of idealism—it might be worth pausing to ask whether current philosophies of embodiment are in any way stronger than Kant in their commitment to materialism.[85] He weakens the problematic idealist's claim about the unconditioned givenness of self-consciousness by making it a datum conditioned by the existence of permanent objects external to itself as its a priori condition (as a fac-

---

83 Kant, *Critique of Pure Reason*, p. B277.
84 Ibid., B275.
85 If we take embodiment to mean the thesis that consciousness can never fully be distinct or separated from physical corporeal being, then this seems to be nothing more than a recasting of Kant's Refutation. If we take it to mean that consciousness is conditioned, at least in part, by a body external to it, then we have just recast Kant's argument in different words but have not improved it.

tum). This Real that is external to consciousness, however, can only be presupposed as given for consciousness as a condition of possibility for consciousness and not in itself. Such a Real is, therefore, secure in being epistemically valid and undogmatic, since this metaphysical realism is rooted in the relation of an ideal conditioned and real condition. But this can only be achieved by turning this external real against itself, insofar as the external real must be presumed as (and only as) the outside of representation, but only insofar as it is conceived through these representations and as their condition. Hence, "[t]he permanence of external reality is only external, in other words, to the extent that it is both presupposed and posited by that consciousness to which it is supposedly external."[86] Far from being, therefore, an external reality, the implicit metaphysical realism of the "Refutation of Idealism" limits the Real's autonomy from and anteriority to self-consciousness to the function of constituting self-consciousness. Therefore, the Real is constituted in turn by self-consciousness as consciousness's conditions of possibility or, in other words, the Real *is* insofar as, *and only insofar as*, it constitutes self-consciousness. Rather than refuting idealism, therefore, Kant, by making in a reflexive movement the Real into the co-constitution of the ideal and the real, solidifies an even deeper idealism, disguised as minimal realism. This is not an idealism because there is no reality outside the mind or because things cannot be thought in-themselves, but rather because *philosophically* the Real is constituted by self-consciousness as its necessary condition. Here, we find the inversion peculiar to transcendental thought: "There is thought, because there is being" turns into "There is being, because there is thought."[87]

To understand the structural isomorphy Laruelle sees manifest in *all* philosophy, we have to consider the structure of the "decision" in more detail. "The Transcendental Method" provides a systematic description of the invariant movement of philosophy as "a dyad of immanence

---

[86] Olson, "Transcendental Arguments, Axiomatic Truth, and the Difficulty of Overcoming Idealism," p. 177.

[87] Iain Hamilton Grant, "Foreword by Iain Hamilton Grant," in *Introduction to New Realism*, ed. Maurizio Ferraris (London; New York: Bloomsbury Academic, 2015), p. vi.

and transcendence, but one wherein immanence features twice, its internal structure subdivided between an empirical and a transcendental function."88 We have already seen these functions in action in the form of the empirical datum of self-consciousness, which gets coupled to the a priori factum of the existence of persistent objects external (or in other words, transcendent) to that self-consciousness. These objects are tied together by self-consciousness in its transcendental function to guarantee that the ideal and the real are always already united. Self-Consciousness features twice, once as conditioned by a factual condition and then as that which unites the two. This leads us to the three-step movement that is the "decision" for Laruelle. Firstly, the metaphysical distinction between the datum and the factum (or, in other words, conditioned and condition) has to be made, alongside the invention of an inventory that makes this distinction intelligible. Secondly, the local a prioris have to be gathered and united under a single transcendental a priori. This superior a priori (and only this a priori) therefore has to be able to make experience as such possible. It cannot be a result from another synthesis since it makes the form of synthesis possible in the first place. While, in other words, the categorial a priori factors are still in need of an a posteriori, the absolute condition (transcendental a priori) is no longer bound to regional experience (and necessarily not) but is a pre-synthetic condition unifying the regional categorial and metaphysical a prioris. The third movement seems to mirror Heidegger's idea of the "turn" (*Kehre*) as it pertains to the deduction, in that it turns "the superior pre-synthetic unity," which gathered the regional a priori, back towards the immanence of experience or, in other words, the empirical "in the form of a transcendental synthesis binding the a priori to the a posteriori, the logical syntax of the ideal to the contingent empirical congruencies of the real."89 The unity established in the second step now gets reformulated in and as the constitutive function for experience, using empirical immanence to legitimate both the first and second step of the deduction. Experience as such can be shown to be only

88   Brassier, *Nihil Unbound*, p. 123.
89   Ibid., p. 125.

possible assuming certain metaphysical and categorial a prioris, which in turn are conditioned by the transcendental a priori, which simultaneously binds the regional a prioris reliably to experience, hence legitimizing the auto-deduction.

Reconsidering the argumentative structure of Kant's *Critique of Pure Reason*, we can find this threefold movement several times. The division of condition and conditioned occurs, for example, in the metaphysical deduction of the a priori forms of judgement (categories) as well as in the metaphysical exposition of the a priori forms of intuition (space and time). Pure apperception, as the indivisible unity and condition of the synthetic a priori as such, gathers and unifies, in a version of the second step, the categorial and metaphysical a prioris, effectively transcending experience absolutely rather than relatively.90 The transcendental deduction of the categories, then, transcribes this gathering together in terms of the unity of possible experience to guarantee that the datum and the factum are reciprocally entanglement and immanence to each other. The transcendent (superior or pre-synthetic unity) is therefore unbound, since it encompasses the whole of the field of empirical sense into which all a prioris are folded, while on the other hand the empirical is confined to the conditions of possible experience.

While it could be argued that Laruelle's account of Kant is oriented on the neo-Kantian interpretation of Hermann Cohen, which identifies the core of the transcendental synthesis in the first *Critique* in the principles of pure understanding, the opposing—for example Heideggerian—emphasis on the schematism of the imagination does not solve the structural problem.91 As we will see, the problem lies not with the sort of concepts or entities proposed, but with synthetic a prioris and their condition as such.

---

90 Depending on the specific philosopher, Laruelle already points to a corruption in the claim of absoluteness, since it must refer to a metaphysical entity—the facultative apparatus and the "I think" in Kant or the Ego (pure phenomenological consciousness) in Husserl—which can only be presupposed.
91 Brassier, *Nihil Unbound*, p. 255, note 12.

# DELEUZE'S VITALIST IDEALISM

## THE DELEUZIAN DECISION

The importance of the discovery of the synthetic a priori cannot be understated, in no small part due to the fact that Kant finds with it the means to explain cognition in its actual or empirical reality, as well as, transcendentally, its a priori reality. For Laruelle, this discovery is at the heart of the "decision" and post-Kantian philosophy as such, as it allows for the synthesis of logos and physis in a "specifically philosophical sense which is that of the concrete synthetic unity of the empirically real and of an a priori or ideal possibility."[92] Since the synthesis is indivisible —because necessary to account for the possibility of experience—the superior a priori constitutes reality as this synthesis of real and ideal, thereby affirming its own transcendental status. The decision, hence, is exclusively operative neither in the empirical reality of a thing or proposed entity, nor in the ideal a priori in its metaphysically transcendent form, but rather in their synthesis. But, as Kant's successors—chief among them Schelling and Hegel—already argued, the synthetic a priori must be considered also beyond the tight bounds of the pure apperception in the sense that it must be de-objectified and de-subjectivized. If, then, the transcendental synthesis constitutes reality as the indivisible unity of real and ideal, thereby constituting the conditions for experience and thought, it necessarily operates on a pre-subjective and pre-objective (or even non-objective) level. What makes Laruelle's analysis interesting at this point is that this critique not only targets the obvious philosophers like Kant and Husserl, but also, because the transcendental a priori is also operative on the pre-subjective level, extends it to Deleuze as well.

Two questions, therefore, need to be posed, from the perspective of the aforementioned method of non-philosophy, and given answers, even

---

[92] François Laruelle, *Au-delà du principe de pouvoir* (Paris: Payot & Rivages, 1978), p. 697, my translation.

if these are interlocking, in the hope that it will be possible to clarify the accusation of vitalist idealism. Firstly, how and why is Deleuze's philosophy not only a vitalism, but also decisional (in terms of the structure laid out before)? Secondly, how could it *therefore* be said to be an idealism?

Laruelle is adamant to point out that non-philosophy follows a tradition (or secret line) through the Kantian approaches of Fichte, Hegel or Feuerbach. For Laruelle, these, despite their differences, have a common feature in the proposition of a pre-philosophical or "pre-speculative state"[93]—instances that are free from philosophy, with each such domain being the margin of non-philosophy that every philosophy tolerates. However, this domain is only to be tolerated by philosophy as "momentary ignorance," as something to be overcome by philosophy. The non-philosophical in turn becomes a function of the philosophical syntax, a function which rules this syntax retrospectively by giving (and satisfying at the same time) its conditions of possibility. It might seem unjustified to include Deleuze, despite certain affinities, in this line of transcendental thought, considering that the non-philosophical domain of absolute immanence is in Deleuze the "plane of immanence," of which philosophy is an expression, rather than its condition. But if we consider the decisional structure to be an indication of transcendence and idealism, we might be able to reevaluate the positing of the plane of immanence as event. The choice, which Deleuze proposes as fundamental, between identity ("Only what resembles differs") and difference ("Only what differs resembles") is not solved in favor of difference for an unquestionable reason, but through a decision.[94] This decision, however, is then folded back formally onto being itself, affirming philosophy's justification (or rather, affirming that there is no need for such justification) for the choice of difference over identity.

It still remains to be seen, however, how, according to Laruelle, the mechanism of this decision in Deleuze works in practice, as well as which readings of Deleuze and his predecessors the non-philosopher's judge-

---

[93] See Mullarkey, *Post-Continental Philosophy*, p. 136.
[94] See Deleuze, *Difference and Repetition*, p. 154.

ment is based on. A closer look at the reading of Nietzsche and Deleuze (and Deleuze's Nietzsche) in *Philosophies of Difference* might help us answer the two questions posed above and respond to the accusation of idealism. For the sake of comprehensibility—willingly giving into the temptation to philosophize—we will reconstruct Laruelle's metaphysical exposition of Nietzschean-Deleuzian vitalism in order to show how the movement towards the transcendental is seen to be instigated.

### THE EVENT AS THE NAME OF BEING

Let us first consider briefly the unique theory of the sense-event from *The Logic of Sense* as a starting point for our analysis.[95] Reconfiguring Stoic physics, Deleuze reinterprets the properties of an object as events or processes, e.g. the "redness" of an apple is transfigured into an active "becoming red." As a consequence of this prioritization of pure events, while there is still an empirical difference between "X eats Y" and "Y eats X," it is undercut by a differential (impersonal) event, i.e. "eating/being eaten."[96] The infinitive subverts the logic of the nominative form, which is conditioned by individuated representation and can thus be predicated upon. It becomes the primary series, which, by coordinating the communication of events, conditions the secondary (nominative) series in a metaphysical twist. Since predicates are therefore exclusively relational, they are not even properties anymore, but rather unbound processes. If the self-subsistence and identity of the object is refused because it only holds on an empirical, but not on a transcendental level, there is simply nothing that the properties could refer to. Or in other words, if everything is an impersonal event and the infinitive form takes precedence, either properties become non-referential, which is a contradiction in itself, or there are no properties that could be said to be referring to only one

---

[95] Since the interpretation of the sense-event is not very controversial within the research on Deleuze, I will restrain my explanations to the necessary minimum. Excellent presentations of the argument can be found in Bowden, *The Priority of Events*.

[96] A discussion of impersonal events can be found in Deleuze, *Logic of Sense*, p. 4f.

individuated thing. This priority of relations over things is what Laruelle identifies as the basic structure of Nietzsche-Deleuzian metaphysics, as he writes:

> What is a differential "relation of forces" for Nietzsche? It is the a priori structure of experience, the a priori or ideal constituent of the Will to Power that would be from its side its transcendental essence, its supreme principle of unification. Now such a relation is truly a "difference," but this difference is integrally relative and ideal as a relation, each of the differends exhausts itself in its relativity to the other.[97]

The critique that Laruelle is making here is straightforward. Nietzsche's Idealism consists in, firstly, giving priority to relation over individuated objects, therefore degrading "[r]eal beings" to "only a moment of the ideal field of presence, a field of presence that is never really present."[98] Becoming is here "relatively" prioritized over Being. This only becomes problematic, however, if, secondly, this ideal principle of becoming, the Will to Power, the event, becomes *absolute*, if, that is, "each of the differends exhaust itself in its relativity."[99] There are only and exclusively relational forces because Being itself can only be conceived as (pure) event, and Being can exclusively be conceived as event because there are only relational forces without remainder. The Idealism in question, then, is that there is *nothing besides* the immanent production of differences, hence identity, actual being and representations become mere empirical illusions without metaphysical reality. In other words, Nietzsche-Deleuze identify ideality (the Will to Power, becoming, the event) with reality, which is the basic movement of the "decision." This however does not yet give us a vitalism, nor does it explain how this identification is made and justified.

To highlight this turn (or *"Kehre"*), we can consider Deleuze's distinctly Nietzschean rereading of Leibniz's theory of compossibility as

---

[97] Laruelle, *Philosophies of Difference*, p. 82.
[98] Ibid.
[99] Ibid.

providing the binding element in the genesis of sense between the sense-events (of the surface) and the depths of bodies.[100] While incompossible predicates, according to Leibniz, are not contradictory in the strict sense of negation, they cannot be posited (at the same time) for one subject. If identity and contradiction are logical, Leibniz's conception is *onto*logical, since also non-contradictory predicates can be incompossible. All possible permutations of compossible predicates can be taken to form a class: possible worlds. But, since of all possible worlds, only one is actual, God has to be introduced to function as the selection mechanism that makes the rational (and therefore benevolent) choice of the "best of all possible worlds." Here, Deleuze introduces a Nietzschean razor to cut away the axiom of the *transcendent* principle of selection and supplant it with an *immanent* one. The removal of God establishes communication between possible worlds (and their differences) through this immanent principle of selection: the eternal return.

At this Leibniz-Nietzsche-Deleuze intersection, we can see why Laruelle points out that Nietzsche's reversibility of contraries is not the logical assertion that one predicate implies its opposite and thereby "it's all the same," but the ontological assertion that no such sameness can be said to actually exist, since the relations of forces are not "ideal" (spoken from a representational standpoint), but actual material forces. Moreover, to hold that "affirmation" and "negation" are the same would be a local, reactive expression of the Will to Power, culminating in nihilism, but still an expression of actual relational forces and *nothing besides*. Since everything is the local expression of the Will to Power without remainder, for Deleuze, the principle of selection (which grounds ethics) must be immanent to it too. This means, in Deleuze's reinterpretation of the Stoic ethics, "not to be unworthy of what happens to us,"[101] but rather to affirm it (*amor fati*) by "becoming-active." This affirmation of non-identical repetition as/and becoming is therefore the identification of the "Idea and

---

100 Again, this interpretation of the sense-event is not controversial and pretty straightforward in the literature, so I will refrain from repeating it here. To clarify I suggest the aforementioned interpretation.
101 Deleuze, *Logic of Sense*, p. 149.

the One, or ideal and real immanence" without remainder, because it "is simply itself infinitely, unlimitedly at stake; it is *integrally reversible.*"[102] If this were not so, the opposition to affirmation would become mere logical opposition with an actual reality of its own and Being could not be interpreted as pure event without remainder. In other words, if difference would not be at stake "absolutely," given that, because of the reasons given above, being is *nothing but* the expression of the Will to Power, then it is not only the case that it must be "integrally reversible," but also that the victory of active over reactive forces is "possible without remainder," since every such remainder would be more than the "objectivation-without-being" or the "reality-without-the-real"[103] that being as pure event allows for. Conversely, then, there can never be a force that is *purely* reactive, since this would be a complete withdrawal from relational forces. As the end of *On the Genealogy of Morals* assures us: "man would rather will *nothingness* than not *will.*"[104] The Will to Power, the metaphysical a priori of the Nietzschean-Deleuzian philosophy of difference (the Will to Power), proper for a philosophy of immanence, issues from an examination of experience. Empirically, the struggle for life, the Darwinian battle for the chance to reproduce, serves as a sign for an interaction of forces that determine each other relationally. In a section of the *Twilight of the Idols*, appropriately titled "Anti-Darwin," Nietzsche turns this problem of selection around. Since the Darwinian interpretation merely supplies us with signs, which can hinder or encourage thinking, it misses the underlying question: how is it possible that the instances of struggle between living beings (that is, differential phenomena) function as *signs* of this struggle

---

102 Laruelle, *Philosophies of Difference*, p. 82.
103 Ibid., p. 83.
104 The whole passage reads: "We can no longer conceal from ourselves what is expressed by all that willing which has taken its direction from the ascetic ideal: this hatred of the human, and even more of the animal, and more still of the material, this horror of the senses, of reason itself, this fear of happiness and beauty, this longing to get away from all appearance, change, becoming, death, wishing, from longing itself—all this means—let us dare to grasp it—a *will to nothingness*, an aversion to life, a rebellion against the most fundamental presuppositions of life; but it is and remains a *will*! ... And, to repeat in conclusion what I said at the beginning: man would rather will *nothingness* than not *will.*" Nietzsche, *On the Genealogy of Morals*, p. 162.

at all? And what ought we to do with them?

By introducing perspectivism as a meta-perspective, the Will to Power becomes a "generalized semiotics," through which differential phenomena can be interpreted or *read* as metaphysical a priori. But far from being external to these material struggles, the semiotics is necessarily itself involved in the struggle. In other words, the forces that constitute the struggle of living beings are not material coated with a semiotic exterior layer but are interpretive forces. While the empirical objects in the struggle might be driven by forces, the forces themselves are not objective and are therefore expressions of self-determining or self-relating difference. This quality will become the measure of how active a force is, of the degree of self-overcoming, of the identification with becoming that instigates a "becoming-other." The metaphysical a priori (Will to Power) frees the forces from their representational determination through objects towards a self-determination, or, in other words, it enables a dynamic conception of forces as such. This movement is not only the basis for Deleuze's interpretation of Nietzsche, but for Deleuze's own reinterpretation / renaming of this structural (metaphysical) a priori in *Difference and Repetition*: difference as such.

## THE ETERNAL RETURN AS TRANSCENDENTAL A PRIORI

As we have already suggested, this metaphysical a priori must still transition into the transcendental realm, since it would otherwise remain a rather weak form of existential hermeneutics. The Eternal Return, which functions as the transcendental determination, is for this purpose established as and through the non-identical repetition of relational forces. But, unlike the Will to Power, the metaphysical determination of difference, it cannot be read on the empirical level. Here, we encounter the core paradox of the Eternal Return: it is a sovereign choice or decision (*Wahl*), but at the very same moment the choice is made it annihilates all sovereign positions that would be able to make the choice, or, in other words, the choice can only be made from the position of a Self in its objectivized, representational and finite being, but any such position is denied *actual* existence by the Eternal Return. This is why Nietzsche formulates the Eternal Return not as a factual statement, but as a thought experiment or literary aphorism; it is not a fact like all the empirical facts, but a temptation—a desire for infinite, powerful, inorganic life. The thought of the return of everything we have lived so far *ad infinitum* challenges us, mocks us and maybe even terrorizes us: "If this thought were to gain possession of you, it would change you, as you are, or perhaps crush you."[105] To think about why this forces us to become adequate to the event, we should consider Deleuze's reformulation of the categorial imperative: "whatever you will, will it in such a way that you also will its eternal return."[106] What Deleuze shifts in Kant's formula is precisely the locus of repetition.[107] Rather than the recurrence of the action, which then can be judged categorically, what comes back in the Eternal Return is a situation or state of affairs, which is always singular. There is, then, no universal rational law to guide us, since an action must be chosen from the vantage point of a unique constellation of forces, incommensurable to the law. Hence the only thing we can become equal to is the event.

Here we must clarify the shift from the metaphysical (Will to Power) to the transcendental (Eternal Return) in order to understand better the logic of Laruelle's critique. Two misunderstandings must be avoided: the Will to Power and the Eternal Return do not coincide without remainder, but they are also not distinguished from each other by an "ontic-real" remainder. Rather, they are both difference, meaning their content is

---

105 The whole passage reads: "How, if some day or night a demon were to sneak after you into your loneliest loneliness and say to you, 'this life as you now live it and have lived it, you will have to live once more and innumerable times more; and there will be nothing new in it, but every pain and every joy and every thought and sigh and everything immeasurably small or great in your life must return to you—all in the same succession and sequence....' Would you not throw yourself down and gnash your teeth and curse the demon who spoke thus? Or did you once experience a tremendous moment when you would have answered him, 'You are a god, and never have I heard anything more godly.' If this thought were to gain possession of you, it would change you, as you are, or perhaps crush you." Friedrich Wilhelm Nietzsche, *The Gay Science: With a Prelude in Rhymes and an Appendix of Songs*, trans. Walter Arnold Kaufmann, 1st ed. (New York: Vintage Books, 1974), p. 273f.
106 Deleuze, *Nietzsche and Philosophy*, p. 77.
107 This spatial analysis can be found in Hughes, *Philosophy after Deleuze*, p. 72.

the same, but their functions are nonetheless formally distinct. Rather than dissolving individuated empirical beings, the Eternal Return rather *consumes* or *incorporates* the whole sphere of beings without remainder; hence, a notion like the Kantian "thing in itself" is not actually dissolved by relational forces, but rather "suspended in a preliminary manner."[108]

We can see this mechanism in its application in Deleuze's presentation of the problem in the context of European nihilism. "What happens," Deleuze asks us, "when the will to nothingness is related to the eternal return?"[109] Here, the Will would break with reactive forces in an "active negation"; i.e. the "strong spirits" are willing to destroy reactionary tendencies within themselves, even at the cost of their own demise under the weight of the Eternal Return. Nihilism thereby actually acts not only as a precursor but as a condition for its own overcoming through the pressure of the Eternal Return. This is its operational or practical determination as principle of selection after the death of God: the "active negation" as the singular practice of making reactive forces *active*. It is this application of the Eternal Return to the history of philosophy with which Nietzsche attacks the truth world/appearance distinction. Equally, the distinction gives coherence to his genealogical project, in which Nietzsche seeks to transform philosophy from an idealist exercise into a materialist (untimely) history and open-ended project. It is not the universalized sphere of nature, society, thought or things-in-themselves but the sphere of vital material struggles that provides the "real genesis of the concepts."[110]

In this turn, Nietzschean-Deleuzian "difference" establishes itself, not only as a metaphysical a priori, but as a transcendental, insofar as the ideality of difference is identified with the actual real existence of beings, insofar as the Eternal Return takes them up into the form of ideal difference. By deploying the Eternal Return, the merely empirical identity of things is overwritten or re-written by self-differentiation, by becoming active; ethics and ontology become reversible.

---

[108] Laruelle, *Philosophies of Difference*, p. 41.
[109] Deleuze, *Nietzsche and Philosophy*, p. 70.
[110] Nietzsche, *The Will to Power*, p. 579.

## THINKING THROUGH IDEAL DIFFERENCE

If we consider this conception of ideal difference, in which it is a metaphysical and transcendental a priori, Deleuze's interpretation of the Eternal Return can give us a hint towards the Laruelleian problem of the identity of thinking and being as indicative of Idealism. The Spinozian method of starting from infinity (the absolute), instead of approaching it from the finite, is adopted by Deleuze in the same way as he adopts the notion of immanence without outside, namely, by reconceptualizing it with Nietzsche; it is as if Spinoza had been subjected to the Eternal Return himself. Common to Spinoza and Nietzsche is the assertion that thought is the result and not the prerequisite of a relationship with actual material forces, the result of being grasped and changed by them. Hence, the very nature of thought is affective. The creation of concepts can therefore be seen as reconfigurations through these material forces (active affects), the same way power comes from the joyful affirmation of these forces. But rather than making knowledge the strongest affect (also against the affections of the body), which is even Spinoza's position, Deleuze sees rather a Nietzschean vital force operating behind all the intellectualist facade of logical rigidity.[111]

The ethical injunction of the Eternal Return combined with the reconceptualization of thought as affect, then, gives us the formula "to think is to create."[112] If we take the Will to Power to be the plastic principle that Deleuze makes it out to be, a thought equated with the Eternal Return is therefore not generated by the condition of possibility, but the "exigencies of real experience."[113] Thought, rather than being a possible action, becomes embedded in the state of affairs *within* which it is a singular action. Hence, when the Eternal Return "makes willing a creation," since it determines or rather creates its own conditions of possibility as a situated singular action, it then simultaneously produces the "possibility of

---

111 See Stuart Pethick, *Affectivity and Philosophy after Spinoza and Nietzsche: Making Knowledge the Most Powerful Affect* (London: Palgrave Macmillan, 2015), p. 16.
112 Deleuze, *Nietzsche and Philosophy*, p. 97.
113 Hughes, *Philosophy after Deleuze*, p. 72.

transmutation as a new way of feeling, thinking, and above all being."[114] Thought becomes, by virtue of being affect (relational force), a tool for life that can redirect, recombine and reconfigure forces by making itself adequate to them.

Thinking thereby becomes identical with the Real, insofar as Being and the philosophical syntax of difference are made reversible. By shifting from the metaphysical a priori to the transcendental, philosophy becomes not only co-constitutive of the Real, but, as creation through thinking, identical to it. This identity is expressed best in *What is Philosophy?* in a description of the plane of immanence:

> And how could truth itself not turn away from thought when thought turns away from it? However, this is not a fusion but a reversibility [...]. Infinite movement is double, and there is only a fold from one to the other. It is in this sense that thinking and being are said to be one and the same. Or rather, movement is not the image of thought without being also the substance of being. [...]. The plane of immanence has two facets as Thought and as Nature, as Nous and as Physis.[115]

This structure of the fold as reversibility is what constitutes the identification of philosophical syntax with the real, so that, as Laruelle puts it rather bluntly in "Résponse à Deleuze," this identification could be expressed in the formula "philosophia sive natura."[116] Despite how it

---

114  Deleuze, *Nietzsche and Philosophy*, p. 69.
115  The whole quote reads: "And how could truth itself not turn away from thought when thought turns away from it? However, this is not a fusion but a reversibility, an immediate, perpetual, instantaneous exchange—a lightning flash. Infinite movement is double, and there is only a fold from one to the other. It is in this sense that thinking and being are said to be one and the same. Or rather, movement is not the image of thought without being also the substance of being. When Thales's thought leaps out, it comes back as water. When Heraclitus's thought becomes polemos, it is fire that retorts. It is a single speed on both sides: 'The atom will traverse space with the speed of thought'. The plane of immanence has two facets as thought and as Nature, as Nous and as Physis." Deleuze and Guattari, *What is Philosophy?*, p. 38.
116  François Laruelle, "'I, the Philosopher, Am Lying': Reply to Deleuze," in *The Non-Philosophy Project: Essays by François Laruelle*, ed. Gabriel Alkon and Boris Gunjević (Candor: Telos Press Publishing, 2012), p. 41.

might appear, even from the manner in which we phrased things above, Laruelle does not actually accuse Deleuze himself of fusing being and thought, and nor does he claim that Deleuze would presuppose such an identity. Rather, it is the transcendental a priori that determines in Deleuze what thought is and ought to be. As Ramey puts it, writing about the secret hermeticism in Deleuze's demand that we always think from the perspective of immanence: "What this prescription assumes is that, at least under certain conditions, thought can adequately express being; that is to say, the conditions of philosophy, for Deleuze, are those under which there is no longer any difference between thought and being."[117] This recapitulation of the Greek ἓν πάντα considers the plane of immanence equally as the plane of matter/life/thought. Through the living/lived relation a unity in multiplicity is created always anew, rather than being given. Deleuze thereby doesn't accept the unities of God, the World or the Soul, but only "the strange unity that can only be said of the multiple."[118] This is the plane composed by vital differences of living individualities, which as incomplete actualizations of the virtual participate without pregiven unity or identity in a universal becoming. In Deleuze's depiction of the plane of immanence, we can therefore find the same dyadic structure as in the Will to Power and Eternal Return, which are the structural a priori of difference. Immanence is not immanence of something, e.g. God, the Ego, the body etc., but only immanent *to itself*. This reflexive self-relation is the philosophical syntax of difference, which—as we have already seen—implies an ethical vision of the world in the name of becoming active. It introduces hierarchies into immanence, which are at the same time legitimized and executed by the inner split in difference between the metaphysical and the transcendental. This self-referentiality gives Deleuzian immanence an axis of transcendence, establishing a hierarchy between beings and the pure event

---

[117] Joshua Alan Ramey, *The Hermetic Deleuze: Philosophy and Spiritual Ordeal* (Durham, N.C.: Duke University Press, 2012), p. 2.
[118] Marjorie Gracieuse, "Laruelle Facing Deleuze: Immanence, Resistance and Desire," in *Laruelle and Non-Philosophy*, ed. John Mullarkey and Anthony Paul Smith (Edinburgh: Edinburgh University Press, 2012), p. 46.

of being, the living and life, actual and virtual etc. always in favor of the latter term. Badiou also notes this, when he writes that: "Being is formulated univocally as: One, virtual, inorganic life, immanence, the nonsensical donation of sense, pure duration, relation, eternal return, and the affirmation of chance."[119] The lack of a term like "actual" in this list is a harsh critique of the dominance of the virtual in Deleuze. "[T]he world," del Bufalo writes, on Deleuze's philosophizing of the world, "is the actual of philosophy, philosophy is the virtual of the world."[120]

The genesis of the philosophical project is taken up in the project itself—this is the apex of philosophy as Idealism. For clarity's sake, we will risk pointing out a structural similarity between Heidegger's and Deleuze's ontological projects regarding their genesis. The fundamental ontology of *Being and Time* describes the journey of Dasein from its average everydayness towards a more proper and authentic meta-physical stance, which Dasein obtains in confronting herself with her "being-towards-death."[121] Since this (thanatological) finitude is already the "own-most potentiality" of Dasein according to this fundamental ontology, the project depends on the analysis of finitude. But at the same time, the analysis of finitude is grounded in Heidegger's fundamental ontology, which in turn is legitimized by results that turn out to be its condition of possibility.[122] Laruelle holds that the same problem is true for Deleuze. He outlines his project, especially in *Nietzsche and Philosophy,* as the description of the shift from reactive to active forces through the Eternal Return as well as the injunction to perform it. Since we are—and everything else too is—just Will to Power and nothing besides, we are constantly tempted by it to

---

119 Badiou, *Deleuze: The Clamor of Being*, p. 78.
120 Erik Del Bufalo, *Deleuze et Laruelle: De La Schizo-Analyse à La Non-Philosophie* (Paris: Editions Kimé, 2003), p. 37, my translation.
121 Heidegger, *Being and Time*, p. 233.
122 See Brassier, *Nihil Unbound*, p. 126. See also Marion's critique of Heidegger's conception of boredom as an existential phenomenon. Boredom does not provide a *necessary* way to confront oneself with one's mortality, unless we have already accepted Heidegger's analysis of being-unto-death. Hence, what should lead us to ask the questions which we ask because we are finite beings does not do so unless we have already asked the question. Instead, real boredom has no intention, no function—it is nothing. See Jean-Luc Marion, *God Without Being: Hors-Texte*, trans. Thomas A. Carlson and David Tracy (Chicago; London: The University of Chicago Press, 2012), p. 115.

affirm (which means to actively negate reactive forces). When we do so, we do philosophy the way Nietzsche-Deleuze prescribe it. Both Heidegger and Deleuze, Laruelle claims, construct self-sufficient philosophies, whose conditions of possibility are contained within them and do not lay outside, in what Laruelle would call non-philosophy. The paradox is apparent: Deleuze holds that it is true that "The nonphilosophical is perhaps closer to the heart of philosophy than philosophy itself, and this means that philosophy cannot be content to be understood only philosophically or conceptually, but is addressed essentially to nonphilosophers as well."[123] But at the same time, to actually become non-philosophical can only be achieved philosophically, namely by accepting all the hierarchies it puts in place. Or, in other words, philosophy's aim is non-philosophy, but it can only reach it by already conceptualizing the non-philosophical real it wants to approach philosophically and becoming equal to it. Rather than a simple levelling of the boundary between philosophy and non-philosophy, this is indicative rather of an infinite reflexive deferral of the syntax/reality boundary. As Gangle expresses this point in Laruelle: "Syntax/(syntax/(syntax/...) ... reality)=Syntax=Idealist Difference."[124]

**IMPERSONAL DISPERSION**

Thinking as a practice therefore involves an extraction of the virtual or incorporeal events of life. One must unbind the flow of matter/energy from the concrete (sometimes organic) bodily mixtures and make oneself adequate to it, to unearth the genetic power that brought the mixtures about: impersonal or inorganic life. By breaking with the everydayness of pre-given structures and structurings in a becoming-infinite of thought, one can pass into an intensive existence. As a consequence of this acceleration of thought, Deleuze proposes an infinite number of modes of existence, which, while not different in kind, but in degree, are

---

[123] Deleuze and Guattari, *What is Philosophy?*, p. 41.
[124] Gangle, *François Laruelle's Philosophies of Difference*, p. 85.

still hierarchical according to their degrees of intensification. This ethical prioritization of the one who becomes adequate to life by losing his identity is explicit in *Difference and Repetition*, where she is the only one who deserves to be called "the universal individual."[125] While Deleuze seeks to escape organic stupidity, but can only do so by "way of presupposing that humans need philosophy to live more intensively," Laruelle wants to avoid vitalist trappings altogether by instead detaching the Real/One from any philosophical conception of being or thought.[126]

The full scope of his critique of inorganic life comes to the forefront in "Rèsponse á Deleuze." The letter was drafted as a reaction to the (very favorable) mention of his non-philosophical project in *What is Philosophy?*, which we quoted above, and to which Laruelle took serious offense. In it, he not only reiterates the hierarchical implications of Nietzschean-Deleuzian vitalism, but also considers its consequences in the realm of the sensible. He writes:

> The consequences for "empirical data" are disastrous: not only are they deprived of reality, they are also above all conceived as deficient or degraded, as the reification or "actualization" of becoming. [...] This is the most general presupposition of every absolute idealism, and perhaps of all philosophy, an idealism that is here equally an absolute realism ("real without being actual, ideal without being abstract"): "experience" is generally construed from the outset as devoid of reality.[127]

Quite obvious here is the provocative mention of Deleuze's famous characterization of the virtual ("real without being actual, ideal without being abstract"[128]), which is taken by Laruelle to be a sign of the identification

---

125 Deleuze, *Difference and Repetition*, p. 254.
126 See Gracieuse, "Laruelle Facing Deleuze," p. 47. Since it does not offer any insight into the topic of inorganic life to pursue Laruelle's line of thought further—which instates the human, or the "Man-in-person" as the living identity at the center of non-philosophy—we will not stress it here. Most commentators, while still acknowledging the legitimacy of Laruelle's critique, have abandoned Laruelle's own positive approach or outright ignored it.
127 Laruelle, "I, the Philosopher, Am Lying," p. 70.
128 Deleuze, *Difference and Repetition*, p. 208.

of the ideal and the real. In Laruelle's interpretation of this credo, actualizations are degraded to mere actualizations of the virtual and *nothing besides*. Since the virtual has a necessary surplus over the actual and harbors the potentialities for creation, the actual is not only poorer, but also something to be overcome through its chiasm with the virtual. There seems to be a split between life and the living.

This position can aptly be called virtualism. For an example of the consequences of this position, we can turn to Graham Harman's critique of DeLanda's Deleuzian ontology. DeLanda conceives the virtual as a multiplicity of singularities and/or attractors that govern the genesis and behavior of actual beings. Since the attractors are virtual, they are themselves never actualized, although they have "a monopoly on the world's causal power."[129] The response to such a conception of Deleuzian virtualism must be that "DeLanda's *actual* world is made up of sterile nodules unable to affect one another or to relate in any way."[130] This illustrates the seemingly paradoxical position of virtualism, which conceives every actualization as a loss,[131] while at the same time wanting to adhere to the transcendental empiricist movement from the conditions of possibility of experience to real experience; the real therefore is on the side of the virtual. Peter Hallward has investigated this paradox on the political level. The ethical injunction to always intensify expresses itself as a "minor politics" at the political level. But every attempt to actually enact such a politics is thwarted by the constant call to negate the actual, and therefore also all "concrete" political and real conditions.[132] Hence, by rejecting the concrete real *on principle*, Deleuze's "otherworldliness" prevents his philosophy from ever being politically effective. We can find this sentiment

---

[129] Graham Harman, *Towards Speculative Realism: Essays and Lectures* (Winchester: Zero Books, 2010), p. 175.

[130] Ibid., p. 177.

[131] An account of Deleuze's "actualization" in confrontation with Hegel's, which characterizes Deleuze's movement from the virtual to the actual as loss, can be found in Bruce Baugh, "Actualization: Enrichment and Loss," in *Hegel and Deleuze: Together Again for the First Time*, eds. Karen Houle and Jim Vernon (Evanston: Northwestern University Press, 2013).

[132] See Peter Hallward, *Out Of This World: Deleuze And The Philosophy Of Creation* (New York: Verso, 2006), p. 186.

foreshadowed in Lyotard's critique of Deleuze and Guattari's political project in *Anti-Oedipus*. Lyotard prefers a critical analysis of the constellations and circulations of affects (as in *Libidinal Economy*), because the ethical juncture of intensification, he claims, has no real consequence, since in the concrete situation of capitalism, there is no discernible or justifiable starting point to fulfill this demand.[133]

---

[133] For a good account of Lyotard's passive politics in *Libidinal Economy*, see Ashley Woodward, *Nihilism in Postmodernity: Lyotard, Baudrillard, Vattimo* (Aurora, Col.: Davies Group Publishers, 2009), p. 199f.

# LIFE AFTER IDEALISM

### VISIONING THE REAL

From the outset, one cannot help but notice the massive scope of Laruelle's project; it is a gesture reminiscent of Heidegger's "destruction" of the whole history of occidental metaphysics. Ironically, Laruelle also reinscribes this Heideggerian movement into the larger history of "the philosophy" which should be overcome. But ironically, in a way, he seems to make the same inductive error as Heidegger: "Laruelle has conflated the critique of a certain kind of philosophizing with the critique of philosophy *tout court*."[134] As Brassier notes, this inference is aided by the French language, since "philosophie" is always accompanied by "la," the definite article.[135] No such thing is necessary in the English language, which can help us to see philosophy as an open-ended "doing," rather than a definite essence. Not surprisingly, then, since the definite article *die* is also commonly prefixed to *Philosophie* in German, idealists like Hegel or Heidegger have always identified the material and historical practice of philosophy as an unfolding, a coming to light or a corruption of its "true" essence. Even if Laruelle were able to accomplish the physically and theoretically impossible task of boiling down all actually existing philosophies to a single structure of self-sufficiency, it would still not prove philosophy's *essential* corruption. Far from being a vulgar epistemological point, this observation leaves us with the question of the relation between totalization and positioning. Since Laruelle's accusation is not that philosophy, by making everything philosophizable, is totalizing philosophy, but that philosophy is itself an act of totalizing, he also marks the entry point for non-philosophy:

> The "capital P" of "Philosophy" [*le "la" de "la philosophie"*] is understandable first as a self-auto-affecting Whole, and this is the affair of philosophy

---

[134] Brassier, *Nihil Unbound*, p. 121.
[135] Ibid., p. 133.

itself, philosophy understood a second time as the Whole('s)-identity, and this will be the affair of non-philosophy.[136]

But the characterization of philosophy as a totalizing activity is already a non-philosophical claim and is the condition for the identity of any one philosophy, an identity which in turn calls for a non-philosophical reconstruction. Non-philosophy as an activity becomes its own condition and is therefore not exempt from its own critique of auto-positional transcendence. This foundational problem of non-philosophy is evident when we consider that the "auto-affecting whole" philosophy creates is not given in any form of self-evidence, but has to be "interpreted" as such, which already requires non-philosophy to be called upon. Due to the impossibility of deducing, inducting or simply intuiting the object of his investigation (the essence of philosophy), it becomes impossible for Laruelle to prove his claim without bringing about a circularity. His approach, which falls into non-concrete generality instead of achieving concreteness without generality, is characteristic for Laruelle's engagement with philosophers, who only embody an invariant structure for him, up to and including Deleuze and inorganic philosophy. Although Mullarkey tries to construe this in a positive light, seeing Laruelle as a performative philosopher who repeats the whole of philosophy in one gesture, this gesture is too big to be sustained or even really possible. We have, therefore, two options. Either we say that Laruelle's philosophy cannot provide a satisfying answer to the question of how philosophy's identification with auto-positioning transcendence is related to the actual existing history of philosophy—the non-philosopher would find herself hard-pressed to explain how, for example, Hume[137] or Churchland would fit in, or how Quine, with his unsurpassed distrust of philosophy's independence from science, is a *standard* philosopher. Or we say that Laruelle's philosophy is

---

136 François Laruelle, *Struggle and Utopia at the End Times of Philosophy*, trans. Drew Burk and Anthony Paul Smith, 1st ed. (Minneapolis: Univocal, 2012), p. 193.
137 It might even be possible that Laruelle himself is a kind of Humean philosopher, or even "ultra-Humean," as Mullarkey seems to suggest. Mullarkey, *Post-Continental Philosophy*, p. 145.

unable to register conceptual nuances and therefore has to resort to tendentious and uncharitable readings to force philosophies to fit the mold. Subsequently, this leaves us with the question of this self-positioning, especially in relation to Deleuze and inorganic life, and how this act effects his readings.

In a discussion between Derrida and Laruelle, the former—already quite frustrated by his interlocuter's evasiveness—confronts him with the question of how he could come up with non-philosophy if not philosophically. In other words, what is non-philosophy if it is not born out of philosophy or even a philosophical position itself. To which Laruelle—with incredible consistency, but to Derrida's frustration—answers: "*I get it from the thing itself.* This is as rigorous an answer as I am able to give."[138] However infuriating, this is the only answer that does not betray non-philosophy's core value of not being (standard) philosophy. Any sufficient reason would transform thought according to this reason and make it something other than itself (be it consciousness, call, affect etc.). For consistency's sake, it is necessary to say, therefore, that it is not, as Laruelle notes, that philosophy as it presents itself gives rise to non-philosophy, but that the Real itself does, and hence the starting point has to be "discovered."[139] By this process, he means what he calls "vision-in-One," which is "*the being-given-without-givenness.*"[140] This quasi-phenomenological notion is one he best exemplifies in his non-photography.[141] However, it reiterates our epistemological concerns rather than resolving them. Furthermore, as Meillassoux notes: "Laruelle gets to his first position just by force, just by a *coup de force*. The Real is *posited* as indifferent and as non-related to thought."[142] The theory of axiomatics that engenders such a positing in

---

[138] François Laruelle and Jacques Derrida, "Controverse Sur La Possibilité d'une Science de La Philosophie," in *La Décision Philosophique* (Paris: Osiris, 1988), p. 71, my translation.
[139] Which, again, is a problem in relation to Laruelle's description of how non-philosophy actually works, namely through the resistance *of* philosophy to its outside. See Mullarkey, *Post-Continental Philosophy*, p. 140.
[140] Laruelle, "Summary of Non-Philosophy," p. 141, original italics.
[141] See François Laruelle, *Le Concept de Non-Photographie, The Concept of Non-Photography* (Falmouth: Urbanomic, 2011).
[142] Ray Brassier, Iain Hamilton Grant, Quentin Meillassoux, and Graham Harman, "Speculative Realism," in *Collapse III: Unknown Deleuze* (Falmoth: Urbanomic, 2007), p. 420.

Laruelle—building on Hilbert and Frege —already implies the grounding of the real in the relation of being and thought.

### IN DEFENSE OF DISPUTATIO

From this vantage point, we can formulate a rebuttal to Laruelle's critique of Deleuze. The self-sufficiency of the real, indifferent to all philosophical conception or intellection, has to be already proposed, to justify Laruelle's sometimes tendentious readings of the Nietzschean-Deleuzian concept of difference. Or, in other words, it is a critique coming from the outside in relation to Deleuze's philosophy and therefore only takes effect if we already accept all the assumptions—really, for him, axioms—that Laruelle proposes, even considering the ontological quagmire of "being-given-without-givenness." Or, again in different words, while Laruelle's readings of Deleuze seem like a critical analysis of difference, they are rather a self-positioning of non-philosophy vis-à-vis Nietzschean-Deleuzian ontology. In the confrontation between non-philosophy (according to Laruelle) and philosophy (according to Deleuze), "Not surprisingly [...] the stage is set for a complete mismatch."[143] Univocity is exclusively considered "in terms" of the Real.

Recalling the allegedly "disastrous" consequences of Deleuzian ontology for "empirical data," we might now be inclined to ask: what empirical data? Likewise, Hallward's critique of Deleuze's "otherworldliness" might now be subjected to the question: what actual, concrete "" is Deleuze supposed to be neither in nor of? Both questions can be answered with a unique concept of the actual, which again is distinct from Deleuze's account. Laruelle's and Hallward's critiques of Deleuze's rejection of actual empirical data or the actual world are not founded on his notion of the actual, but on theirs—thus, they are external to Deleuze. To say otherwise would be to assert that Deleuze's conception of the virtual/actual is simply self-contradictory, without proving this. What is actually at stake

---

[143] Mullarkey, *Post-Continental Philosophy*, p. 146.

here is not Deleuze's but Laruelle's and Hallward's "actuals." It is almost superfluous to also add that Harman's critique of Deleuze's virtualism is only viable insofar as we already accept that "actual things," firstly, have to and/or should exist as non-relational self-identical objects and, secondly, have to and/or should have causal power on their own—an assertion that is problematic even within his Object-Oriented-Ontology. The argument that could be made for both premises is again external to Deleuze, insofar as it does not touch his argument at all. Again, a complete argumentative mismatch.

However, all these critiques are not entirely unmotivated and do not randomly pick Deleuze as their focal point. While Harman pushes back against what he perceives as the "under- and overmining" of objects and Hallward grounds his anti-virtualism in a Badiouian politics of the actual, Laruelle's motivation can best be explained by his insight that "human kind needs to be protected against the authoritarian conceptions of man and of the world."[144] Since he conceives philosophy as essentially anti-democratic, taunting and threatening man with ever-changing regimes of determination foreign to him, humanity seems to be in the service of philosophy, not the other way around. To further the cause of democratic practices, he first wants to restore the democracy of and within thought by breaking the dominance of philosophical regimes, be they "Being, Text, Power, Desire, Politics, Ethics"[145]—or Life.

This impetus becomes apparent in his sometimes tendentious or reductive readings of Deleuze's inorganic vitalism. Foreshadowing his allegation of vitalist idealism again Nietzsche-Deleuze, the passage from *Nietzsche contre Heidegger*, which reads Nietzsche's vitalist politics as a kind of hermeneutics, to *Au-delà du principe de pouvoir* already indicates a shift from an infinitist position to a finitist position closer to Heidegger than to Nietzsche.[146] The problem, however, does not concern the choice for a position or whether either position can be defended, but rather the rela-

---

[144] Gracieuse, "Laruelle Facing Deleuze," p. 44.
[145] Laruelle, *Philosophies of Difference*, p. xxii.
[146] See François Laruelle, *Nietzsche contra Heidegger : thèses pour une politique Nietzschéenne* (Paris: Payot, 1977).

tion of the "content" of infinity and finitude, and the possibility of forming a relation between the two terms: a meta-difference. Because the idea of a difference without remainder would again point to an identity of syntax and reality, Laruelle instead opts for an (impoverished) finitude, which introduces a break with the reversibility of the real and the ideal.[147] The opposition of Heideggerian finitude to Nietzschean infinity then informs his subsequent readings. This becomes apparent in Laruelle's reduction of Deleuze's pluralistic philosophy to a one-note Nietzschean philosophy, which also in turn reduces the latter in the same way. In construing them both as *only* philosophers of difference, he unjustifiably condemns them tout court. But here we have to concede, alongside Gangle, that Laruelle's critique is justified insofar as we regionalize it (or restrict its scope). By reading Nietzsche and Deleuze together, or as one, Laruelle "extracts" a philosopheme not accessible without such a juxtaposition. Hence, "[i]nstead of adequacy to their respective textual corpuses, the relevant criterion becomes that of utility in clarifying a new philosophical 'object,' that of an Idealist Difference."[148] But if such an object *exists*, it seems to also *insist*, insofar as it demands a rereading of Deleuzian ontology in light of it. Although inadequate for a full-fledged critique, this idea of Idealist Difference might, then, be a useful conceptual tool to reexamine and reconfigure the idea of inorganic life so as to avoid any accusation of Idealism.

### SINGULAR AND GENERIC LIFE

After all this critique, one might read "Letter to a Harsh Critic" in a wholly new light. As Deleuze notes, it is possible to read him in a "malevolent" way, constantly trying to prove how he stays locked within philosophy, saying disparagingly that he "remains Greek."[149] Or it is possible to choose a more amorous or "benevolent" reading of his philosophy, which

---

[147] See François Laruelle, *Au-delà du principe de pouvoir*, p. 17.
[148] Gangle, *François Laruelle's Philosophies of Difference*, p. 82.
[149] Mullarkey, *Post-Continental Philosophy*, p. 146.

draws from the outside, is in connection with it, and has the non-philosophical at its heart. The second option does away with distinctions such as "observing" and "living" or "thinking" and "becoming." Deleuze's collaboration with Guattari —a non-philosopher—is an example of this, not only by virtue of being a cooperation, but also by being an encouragement to work from the perspective of the *problem*, which is neither philosophical, artistic, political etc. but marks the very genesis of thought.

To put it in already familiar terms: while Deleuze's account of the Image of Thought does not reject it outright, but instead advocates a certain creation and selection of these "images" with the express aim of unbinding thinking, for Laruelle, every image of thought, if taken seriously, infects immanence with philosophical transcendence. However, both philosophies therefore attempt radical pluralisms of thought. The *mathesis universalis* Laruelle describes reconfigures the transcendental not as conditions of possibility, but as real "force (of) thought";[150] a similar thing could be said to be true for Deleuze. The difference then, as Mullarkey correctly notes, lies in the difference between laterality and univocity, between space and voice. While non-philosophy does not lay claim to the content of radical immanence, and hence does not think *about* the Real, but thinks *alongside* it, for Deleuze all thinking is a univocal expression of immanence, and hence one cannot help but think the Real/immanence. Laruelle therefore avoids every accusation of being attached to a dogmatic image of thought by not determining thought at all, while Deleuze, in an effort to intensify expressions of immanence through thought, creates and selects images that enable new modes of thought.

Mullarkey thus contrasts Deleuze, the pluralist philosopher operating from and universalizing "his" concept of a highest thought, which "is one that does *not* do what it says," with Laruelle's more consistent position of "non-philosophy," which "*does do what it is saying.*"[151] Or at least "it *says that it does* (such consistent practice is easier said than done)."[152] It is

---

150 Ibid., p. 104.
151 Mullarkey, *All Thoughts Are Equal*, p. 162.
152 Ibid., p. 163.

worth putting special emphasis on the bracketed part of this quotation for reasons elaborated upon above.

But unlike Mullarkey, we would like to say that both are consistent in what they are saying and doing. The inconsistency described in Deleuze's philosophy is only a valid observation insofar as we accept as fact what Laruelle is telling us that Deleuze is saying and doing. But as we have seen, Laruelle's reading already passes through non-philosophical axioms, which ensure that Deleuze fits the standard philosophical mold. In the conversation with Derrida mentioned above, Laruelle responds thus to his discussion partner's opening statement on the relation of philosophy and terror:

> Do I practice terror? There are obviously two readings of my text. There is a philosophical reading, one in which I do practice terror. And there is a non-philosophical reading, which is obviously my reading. And from the latter point of view, I am reluctant to concede that I am practicing terror.[153]

Leaving Derrida's protestations aside and considering that we were able to propose a benevolent reading of Deleuze's philosophy, we should give the same benefit of the doubt to Laruelle: non-philosophy does not practice terror. But it is precisely the nature of "terror" that needs to be specified. If terror actually consists, as Laruelle would probably say, in the philosopher's gesture of splitting immanence into two and, on this basis, introducing a hierarchy between thoughts, or, in other words, in claiming that not all thoughts are equal, then Deleuze does practice terror. But Deleuze would call this gesture "agonism": a non-democratic feature at the heart of democracy, which only resembles terror if practiced without *philia*.[154] While for Deleuze, democracy as societal reality depends on non-democracy in thought, for Laruelle this democracy in thought is a prerequisite for its material manifestation among people. Both are

---

[153] Laruelle and Derrida, "Controverse Sur La Possibilité d'une Science de La Philosophie," p. 69.
[154] See Deleuze and Guattari, *What is Philosophy?*, p. 4.

consistent in their respective pluralisms—one, inorganic vitalist agonistic and one, radically axiomatic egalitarian. "No thoughts are equal" or "all thoughts are equal"—singular or generic.

### VITALISM AFTER IDEALISM, OR THE THINGS TO COME

The question of the differences between these two pluralisms is not yet resolved after this brief sketch. But the above considerations provide us with the key points we need to discuss to produce a critical theory of inorganic life.

The connection of pluralism and thought points to an important shift in Deleuze's own work, away from the focus on difference (in the 1960s and 1970s) towards a more radical theory of multiplicity (in the 1980s and 1990s). Later we will examine his radical changes to the idea of the "Body without Organs," which moves precisely from a conception based on difference in *Anti-Oedipus* and *The Logic of Sense* towards one based on multiplicity in *A Thousand Plateaus*. But here our focus is on the concept of the virtual, which undergoes dramatic changes in Deleuze too. Keeping this in mind, we should consider Hallward's questioning of this concept:

> You might expect, then, an explanation of how the causal depths determine these surface effects. Deleuze duly accepts that every event does indeed emerge from the "depth of corporeal causes." However, the general effort of the book is to complicate if not disrupt the mechanics of this production.[155]

If the verdict he passes here on *The Logic of Sense* is accurate still needs to be determined, but it is clear that this conception shapes the perception of Deleuze's work as a whole. It is therefore not surprising, considering the state of the reception of *Difference and Repetition*, that Hughes writes that "the current interpretations of the book [...] read it more or

---

[155] Hallward, *Out of This World*, p. 43.

less as a theory only of the static genesis. They emphasize only the virtual [...]."[156] Hallward, however, subsequently claims that no theory on the emergence of the virtual from the actual (consistently) exists in Deleuze, and that the virtual should be dropped from our philosophical vocabulary.[157] Although these claims, I suggest, are wrong, in order to rebuff them we need to show how Deleuze in fact has a theory that encompasses the constitution of the virtual from the actual as well as the constitution of the actual from the virtual, and how a theory that describes this two-way dynamic is superior to one that only considers either the virtual or the actual to be primary, or considers one of them to be non-existent. The position that considers everything only in and as its genesis in the virtual, and therefore imposes the universalized ethical injunction on the actual to always counter-actualize, we call "active vitalism."

Active vitalism, despite being a popular position among Deleuzians, is, I want to suggest, not able to harness the full potential of Deleuze's inorganic vitalism, since it, in the best case, is neither able to think the inorganic nor to think inorganically, and, in the worst case, not only makes thought but the world a (super-)organism. This becomes apparent in the focus on "becoming-animal" in scholarship on Deleuze, which currently serves to limit the forms of becoming that man is capable of instead of increasing them. Becoming-animal is the organic bastion of a thought of immanence that has become static. The position that focuses on it embodies the tendency of Deleuzian approaches to the inorganic and to inorganic thought to project the traditional properties of the organic, which are derived from the division of matter into living and non-living, onto the inorganic. Hence, this projection of organic properties onto the inorganic conceives of matter (albeit unwillingly) as endowed with capacities like agency, formative powers, consciousness and teleology. Consequently, despite the genuine effort to do the opposite, it renders all matter organic. In doing this it re-introduces normativity into matter, with all the anthropocentrism that accompanies such ethical perspectives on matter.

---

[156] Hughes, *Deleuze and the Genesis of Representation*, p. 103.
[157] Hallward, *Out of This World*, p. 80f.

We will discuss this "active" vitalism, as well as the implications of taking the animal to be the (unjustified) limit of Deleuze's vitalism, at length in the next chapter. And, to go a step further, we will see that such an active vitalism, carried to its logical conclusion, becomes a theory of virtual extinction. It is embodied best by Land's libidinal materialism, since from this perspective all actualizations have to be considered a loss in richness of potentiality and should therefore be overturned. Against this "mad black Deleuzianism," the apex of active vitalism, we will consider a passive vitalism, which is "a *hyper*-philosophy or *theory* (if we take theory to be an acceptance of the distance or relation that necessarily accompanies any perception or looking)."[158] Against the active variety, the passivity of this vitalism does not take every problem to be practical first but embraces the connection of philosophical thinking and life, thereby permitting it to present itself as a speculative philosophy, which is primarily descriptive instead of prescriptive.[159] If we understand immanent vitalism as a speculative naturalism instead of a prescriptive ethics, inorganic thought can emerge without being tied down by any anthropocentrism or organicism, and hence can meet the demands of radical immanence and univocity. As a critical tool for analysis, inorganic life, if applied to situations or states of affairs, *entails* an ethics, rather than presuming one. It allows us, for example, to reconsider the cultural problem of exhaustion in relation to active vitalism (including its injunction to always affirm and intensify). The ethical injunction to affirm—as a constant demand for production, intensification and maximization—which is already the driving force of capitalism, becomes underpinned with an ontology that presents these insistences as inescapable. Elizabeth Grosz's book *The Incorporeal* exemplifies this demand for self-exhaustion in a Deleuzian flood of words: "*live optimally, thrive, maximize, enhance, intensify, go to the limit, affirm, expansion, maximization, affirmation, enhancement, intensification, well-being, capacity for more, excess, extra 'charge',*" etc.[160]

---

[158] Colebrook, *Deleuze and the Meaning of Life*, p. 7.
[159] Mullarkey, *Post-Continental Philosophy*, p. 37.
[160] Elizabeth Grosz, *The Incorporeal: Ontology, Ethics, and the Limits of Materialism* (New York: Columbia University Press, 2017), p. 48, 86, 132, 134, 149, 153, 157, 174, my italics.

Even if such programs of intensification suggest an expansion of intensities beyond the level of the organism, it is only to facilitate growth in and of the organism to extract a surplus value that can be harnessed. *Intensification as an end in itself*, however, is at best reckless and at worst leaves us with a naïve politics of effective, well-oiled machines (as we will see in the next chapter). Inorganic life, understood from the vantage point of passive vitalism, can provide a counterweight to this kind an uncritical (and organic) vitalism and instead offer a necessary critique of life.

Refuting this type of vitalism, however, brings us back to the foundational problem we discussed when considering Austin's and Stroud's critiques of transcendental philosophy. This leads us to Laruelle, who showed how philosophy, by using a sleight of hand, solves this kind of problem, namely how to choose our transcendentals and thereby choose our philosophy (thereby choosing the very grounds upon which such a decision could be made.) What is true for Hume's association theory[161] or Wittgenstein's ladder[162] is equally true for Deleuze's inorganic vitalism. Insofar as we accept that the self-conscious choice for any idea is merely an illusion, how do we then choose that we must choose according to the eternal return philosophically? If it were only a *practical* problem, philosophy would not be needed—or only needed as a vehicle. If this is the case, then the value that informs our choice of this and not that philosophy cannot be provided within philosophy, and nor can it be proven by means external to philosophy. Every possible answer seems already based on circular reasoning. If we take the intensification of life as the value that provides criteria for the choice, we have just deflected the question, since this

---

161  If *all* ideas are just a coalescence of perceptions tied together by the (mechanically working) rules of association, then how is Hume's philosophy any more true (or even more truth-apt) than any other philosophy? But if this question cannot be answered, the grounds for the question disappear alongside Hume's philosophy.

162  The conclusion of the *Tractatus* rejects its foundations: "My propositions serve as elucidations in the following way: anyone who understands me eventually recognizes them as nonsensical, when he has used them—as steps—to climb beyond them. (He must, so to speak, throw away the ladder after he has climbed up it.) He must transcend these propositions, and then he will see the world aright." Ludwig Wittgenstein, *Tractatus Logico-Philosophicus*, trans. David Pears and Brian McGuinness (London; New York: Routledge, 2001), 6.54.

value is already based on the acceptance of Deleuze's core claims. Also, to repeat Mullarkey's problematization, if we assume "machinic values" based on the correlation of a type of input and maximization of output, we cannot back up or justify the value of this value except by insisting on its self-evidency or by putting forth a claim which follows from the assumption of the value of the value itself. If we, for example, assume that the body finds its highest level of joy in production and therefore we *should* bring it into certain affirmative relations (milieus), we have already accepted the core premise instead of proving it. Vincent Descombes characterizes this problem in Deleuze as a form of moralistic fallacy: "measuring *that which is* according to the standard of *that which is not, but which ought to be*."[163] This allegation of Fichteanism in Deleuze, even though it actually targets only one possible Deleuze, does not dismiss his onto-ethical or naturalistic ethics tout court. Rather, the problem is a matter of the *theory*—or rather epistemology and meta-ethics—which the early Deleuze embodies. Badiou notes, "Life makes the multiplicity of evaluations possible, but is itself impossible to evaluate."[164] So, if we want to accept the inherent value of life/the event/becoming, we have the problem of what measure would make it possible to determine and know such value?

But even if such epistemological difficulties could be avoided and an inherent value of life could be rendered knowable, the meta-ethical problem of why we should also live according to these values, folded into nature itself, persists. This problematic conjunction of naturalistic facts/values and epistemic norms can, however, be overcome with a vitalist theory that does not start from the ethical prescription but from a radical description, that entails an ethics rather than presupposing one. This makes it possible to fulfill Deleuze's promise of a philosophy of nature as a "description in thought of the life of the world, such that the life thus described might include, as one of its living gestures, the description."[165] We

---

[163] Descombes, *Modern French Philosophy*, p. 180.
[164] Badiou, *Deleuze: The Clamor of Being*, p. 97.
[165] Alain Badiou, "Review of Gilles Deleuze, The Fold: Leibniz and the Baroque," in *Deleuze and the Theatre of Philosophy*, ed. Dorothea Olkowski and Constantin V. Boundas (London; New York: Routledge, 1994), p. 63.

will therefore offer the portrait of an inorganic vitalism, which does not side with the ethical injunction "become what you are," but instead begins with the naturalist formula "you are what you become"[166]—in short, a passive vitalism.

---

[166] Alain Badiou, *Court traité d'ontologie transitoire* (Paris: Éditions du Seuil, 1998), p. 68, my translation.

# POST-VITALISM

So let us beware of death; the stones will have
Their revenge; we have lost all approach to them,
But soon we shall become as those we have betrayed,
And they will seal us fast in our graves
As our indifference and ignorance seals them;
But let us not be afraid to die.[1]

---

[1] MacDiarmid, "On a Raised Beach," p. 155.

# PASSIVITY

## VITALISM, ACTIVE AND PASSIVE

*A Force That Acts But Is Not*

One might trace the manifold fractures within contemporary vitalism by investigating their relation to the membrane of the organism and its permeability. One vitalism insists on the physical boundaries of the organism being conditions for *meaning,* and hence the living being's "personal" life. The limits of the organized being are continuously in contact with the *Umwelt,* the outside it is constituted by and lives directed "towards." Unsurprisingly, such theories, for example those of the extended mind, autopoietic systems and embodiment, find their resources in (existential) phenomenology. Life is, first and foremost for these theories, practical, and lived by being embedded in and projecting meaning. Another vitalism, however, conceives of the organism as constituted by *sense,* i.e. incorporeal, impersonal and inorganic events that occur above and below the organism's bounded capacities for perception and abstraction. The body of the organism, bound to the world and binding the world to it, is only possible because of these sub-representational and unbound events, the distribution of nomadic singularities that constitute the border between the inside and the outside, while constantly traversing and shifting it. This vitalism, a (possible) Deleuzian ontology of life, considers life as primarily theoretical, as an act of θεωρεῖν prior to and exceeding the practical meaningful life of the bounded organism.

In their late work *What is Philosophy?*, Deleuze and Guattari frame this opposition in historical terms:

> Vitalism has always had two possible interpretations: that of an Idea that acts, but is not—that acts therefore only from the point of view of an external cerebral knowledge (from Kant to Claude Bernard); or that of a force

that is but does not act—that is therefore a pure internal awareness (from Leibniz to Ruyer).[2]

The peculiar line of development from "Kant to Claude Bernard" suggests the assumption that Deleuze and Guattari retrospectively read the history of vitalism from the vantage point of Ruyer's *Néo-Finalisme*. Here, the specificity of "organicism" is construed as the rejection of both mechanist and vitalist interpretations of the organism: neither an attempt at a physio-chemical reduction of the constitution and functioning of the organism, nor an appeal to an intervening dynamic principle responsible for the occurrence or development of vital phenomena.[3] By conceptualizing the organism as an (organized) totality, such a whole is not reducible to the sum of its parts, hence is not in need of external principles of animation and precludes mechanical reduction. Despite appealing simultaneously to scientific positivistic experimentation and philosophical (and ethical) interpretation, Ruyer summarizes, "this advantageous doctrine has the weakness of only existing verbally. Organicism is an empty concept that designates nothing real; it is a 'square circle'."[4] The whole itself remains *necessarily* inexplicable. In Kant, Ruyer finds this "organism" founded and legitimized in its philosophical form in the antinomy of teleological judgement. Holding on to the universality of mechanical and deterministic causes in the physical world while acknowledging the empirical evidence for purposiveness in nature, the teleological judgement is deemed legitimate only as reflective judgement and not as the cause of phenomena. As we saw above, the conflict between the understanding, which conceives of the world as deterministic, and reason, which regards (living) nature as purposive, must be resolved by the faculty of judgement, which unites them in the supra-sensible principle, i.e. through the perspective of God's understanding, which can, once considered, be cancelled out again. This final cause, the point of unity, is then "not a

---

2 Deleuze and Guattari, *What is Philosophy?*, p. 213.
3 See Raymond Ruyer, *Néo-Finalisme* (Paris: Presses Universitaires de France, 2012), p. 225.
4 Ibid., p. 226.

force, but only a point of view, legitimate moreover and indispensable, not only for living beings but also for the entire world."[5] Similarly proposing that all biological phenomena are guided by an idea that is not part of or reducible to the physical world, Charles Bernard, in his *Lessons on the Phenomena of Life Common to Animals and Plants*, is also unable to provide an account of the interaction between the ideal and the physical that produces the biological, and therefore, mimicking Kant's turn to God, resorts to an "initial impulse," which is supposed to traverse both the cosmic and biological unfolding.[6] Despite guiding the formation of organized beings, the idea has no physical existence of its own, which is to say, it "acts, but is not."

### Philosophy as Active Vitalism

As Colebrook suggests, one might also map out this split within vitalism according to the tension between πρᾶξις and τέχνη, which not only characterizes the relation of man and machine, but also a relation within human capacity itself.[7] The lived body, in its practical performance, furthers its life in a meaningful engagement with the world. For its purposes, these corporeal movements engage with technical extensions that ought to enhance its capacity to act, but always carry with them the danger of imprisoning life by alienating it from its vital source and incorporating it in its monstrous inorganic exteriority. For Bergson, although the intellect can enhance effectivity by reducing difference in adopting the extended and quantifiable geometry of space as a model of thought, this might end up with it reifying itself and deadening all intuitive (vital) potentiality. Similar sentiments might be found in philosophers as diverse as Dilthey and James, the former claiming that the positivist attempt to extend its quantifying approach to feelings will eliminate the notion of an inner life, the latter going further in claiming that concepts that were once created to further life's reach might, when overused, end

---

5    Ibid., p. 228.
6    See Ronald Bogue, "The Force That Is but Does Not Act: Ruyer, Leibniz and Deleuze," *Deleuze Studies* 11, no. 4 (2017), p. 520.
7    See Colebrook, *Deleuze and the Meaning of Life*, p. 1.

up precluding man from feeling life's rich intensity.[8] These claims about the acceleration of praxis through technical means do not simply mourn or indict the body's or mind's descent into a quantifiable extensity that neutralizes all inwardness, but rather locate the life-denying tendency in the organism's preoccupation with self-preservation, which is achieved through technological means. Vitalism can hence pose the question of how, given life's self-affirmative nature, it is possible for it not to flourish.

An active vitalism, based on the ontological primacy of the practical or livable over the theoretical, considers technological extensions as enhancements of life's capacities, which are legitimate only insofar as they do not alienate life from its original abundance and complexity. Hence, it construes the technical as a means that is inherently parasitic to life's vibrancy. Even if the technical is considered as a capacity of life itself, it appears still as a difference within life or harmful transcendence within life. For active vitalism, life is imprisoned in systems of its own design, which have lost the connection to their vitalizing origins. Despite Nietzsche's protestations to the contrary, one might claim that this inherent vitalism is the mode of traditional philosophy as such. Even more, the very claim that metaphysics becomes life-denying can only ever be justified by proposing that life is something that is seduced by the promise of power at the core of philosophy, even if such a commitment to the *techne* that is metaphysical thought turns out to be a trap in the end.

Could one not read Nietzsche's rival Kant as cloven in exactly these terms? On the one hand, Kant seems to impose the empty formalism of judgement upon life, imprisoning experience within conditions of possibility. On the other hand, Kant rejects any transcendence imposed on life and experience, attempts to remain within immanence as far as possible and is chiefly concerned with health and vitality (understood as the feeling of animation of the mind). One could construe judgement as the limit of life and its self-forming potential, which at the same time guarantees vitality and the prevention of any transcendence that could not be justified

---

8   James, *The Will to Believe and Other Essays in Popular Philosophy*, p. 70.

within lived experience. Critical philosophy simultaneously limits and intensifies life, is both vitalist and anti-vitalist. Even Descartes's subjectivism, which results from his proposition of the existence of two substances, so often critiqued by later vitalists, sought to return thinking to a ground of truth and representation secure from any doxa or dogma that would halt it.

Philosophy, thus, constructs itself and operates from the standpoint of life, even if the means for construing and reaching its concept (if it is a concept) differ. This is the ethics of thought par excellence, upon which all others are built. The history of philosophy since Kant has been a constant flow of (often misconceived) accusations against precursory and contemporary philosophies for being systems unable to provide an accurate account of their genesis. What describes active vitalism philosophically is not just the assertion of a formative force presiding over the organization of matter in living beings, but precisely what we described above as the "a priori complex." The philosophical mode of thinking proper to this inherent vitalism rejects all doxa, ideas or systems which cannot provide their own conditions of genesis, i.e. an account of how what is claimed to be came into being, and how the claim about how something came into being is possible in the first place. In Laruelleian terms, such an auto-positioning of philosophy, which traces the transcendental from the empirical to then deduce the empirical from it, makes the world as such philosophical and organic, since it incorporates everything in its movement.

Philosophy, in this active vitalist mode, thus seeks to return *techne* back to the praxis it originated from, and which it potentially escapes from. The autonomous supplement must be reincorporated into or overwritten by the originary ground of creation. The reification of the intellect, which turns its quantification and spatialization onto itself, must, for Bergson, be liberated from this preoccupation with efficiency by an intuition of itself as spirit. For James, constituted language, which had become a limiting form of conceiving of thought, must be understood as a dynamic response to the powers of perception that ought to be reawakened. Along these vitalist lines, it is phenomenology that fulfills the philosophical promise. *Lebensphilosophie* for Husserl is still paltry, not vitalist enough, in that it merely restores generative power to (the praxis of) living beings, while pursuing the disclosure of a transcendental life (the lived) as the condition of possibility of specific lives.

### The Auto-Positioning of Deleuzian Vitalisms

At first glance, this ethics is perpetuated by Deleuze's Nietzschean ethics of active and reactive forces, as already demonstrated. Within the active vitalist reading of Deleuze, the problem of life is its imprisonment in systems or identities, which results in an alienation of the living being from its dynamic and generating powers. The inverse movement is then presented in concise, normative terms. Rosi Braidotti's normative ethics gives us precisely this "politics of life itself"[9] by invoking the "endless vitality of life as continuous becoming,"[10] which must be the object of a pure affirmation, which unbinds the pre-human and non-logocentric vitality of the manifold qualitative becomings of the human, chief among them the becoming-animal. This liberation of bio-power, which is supposed to engender a micropolitics of becoming, is not only framed in expressly vitalist-normative terms, but as a τέλος τελειότατον:

> Given that intensity is the body's fundamental capacity to express its joy, positivity and desire, [...] to put a stop to it marks the death of desire. In the ethics of sustainable nomadic subjects, "unhealthy" states are those which kill the affirmative powers of expression of positive passions (*potentia*). In other words, they are not sustainable and do not endure. [...] The transcendental empiricism of the non-unitary subject is such that becoming is a forward-looking activity. The joyful expression of becoming is a way of writing the prehistory of possible futures, that is, to take care of the unfolding of possible worlds.
> In other words, futurity or possible futures are built into the logic of sustainable affirmative interrelations. The point is to allow the embodied to express

---

9   She quotes this term from Rose but misinterprets it quite significantly. Rose uses this term in a purely descriptive sense to denote a politics characterized by the advancing ability of human beings (as living beings) to monitor, manipulate, govern and modulate vital processes—the opposite of what Braidotti means. See Nikolas S. Rose, *Politics of Life Itself: Biomedicine, Power, and Subjectivity in the Twenty-First Century* (Princeton: Princeton University Press, 2007), p. 3.

10  Rosi Braidotti, *Transpositions: On Nomadic Ethics* (Malden: Polity Press, 2006), p. 41.

its powers of affirmation, by increasing his or her capacity to be affected and to affect in the positive sense of sustaining enriching encounters.[11]

Among the manifold maneuvers executed here is the affirmation of a hygienic power of life, i.e. the idea that only the joyful expression of the body is sustainable, which betrays the active vitalist ethics. While claiming to accomplish the transition from an ethics to a politics, this "prehistory of possible futures" de-politicizes life, expelling all struggle, hierarchy and alienation within and inherent to life from it, oblivious to the circumstance that "nomadic subjects" can be not only an active resistance to but also the dynamic force of the body without organs that is capital.[12] This "reckless"[13] political strategy indicates a philosophical inversion of inorganic life into an organic good will on the part of life itself, insofar as life, when properly engendered, naturally results in joy and the morally good, i.e. life is presented as politically, ontologically and ethically unproblematic. In lieu of a morality, which is exposed as the operation of transcendent values and discredited in the name of life, becoming posits itself as the formal criterion (or norm) for an ethics, effectively making itself a principle of judgement. Life (or becoming) judges actuality, introducing transcendence precisely in the name of immanence, of a life of life. The ethical demand of this purified life can, as we have mentioned, only be met by a constant intensification of experience.

Nietzsche is aware of the danger of the practice of freeing life by merely intensifying feeling and experience. For him, "[t]he ascetic ideal is employed to produce orgies of feeling,"[14] which then must be paid with guilt.

---

11   Ibid., p. 209.
12   Commentators, such as Žižek, have claimed that "[t]here are, effectively, features that justify calling Deleuze the ideologist of late capitalism." Žižek, *Organs without Bodies*, p. 184. Even if this sentiment rests on a (Lacanian) misreading of *Anti-Oedipus*, Deleuze becomes more aware in his later works of the degree to which his concepts rather describe than resist capital, e.g. the rhizomatic nature of millennial capitalism. See Gilles Deleuze, "Postscript on the Societies of Control," *October*, no. 59 (1992), p. 3–7.
13   Saar, for example, portrays Braidotti as an emblematic figure for the contemporary tendency to construct from Spinoza (and Deleuze) a vitalist politics solely concerned with unbinding life from all structures, boundaries or constraints. See Martin Saar, *Die Immanenz Der Macht. Politische Theorie Nach Spinoza* (Berlin: Suhrkamp, 2013), p. 212.
14   Nietzsche, *On the Genealogy of Morals*, p. 139.

The priest encourages frenzied intensifications of feelings to avoid the melancholic withering away of the human soul, only to then demand penance for the exuberance. Life is always already caught up in systems and machinations of power and the liberation of "vitality" can and will be used against it. Braidotti's approach of framing "Life" as a force that is bound and that ethically demands to be free, that is without any restraints, thwarts any attempt to investigate the complex nature of life's entanglement with power, and elides the problematic aspect of inorganic life. Epistemologically, it demands an untangling of the social, the political and the vital in order to liberate vital forces against or in spite of social or political constraints, even while such entanglement, by Braidotti's own admission, cannot be broken. The ethical injunction of infinite affirmation of life becomes a purely formal criterion for an ethics.

*On the Genealogy of Morals* traces the genealogical line of the critique of vitality that occurs in the name of an ideal transcendent to it, and frames this process as actually life's auto-critique. The emergence of life-denying morality from life marks not only the genesis of all systems and relations in life, but life's strange self-mutilations in expression. In this anti-Spinozist turn in Nietzsche, there is a stupidity and malevolence *inherent* to life, which is not just based on a misunderstanding of the true nature of the relations between ideas and bodies. Rather, there is a cruelty and power of the false in life that cannot be mastered by thought. A passive vitalism must confront the impropriety of inorganic life.

### DELEUZE AGAINST FLAT ONTOLOGIES

*Grinding Down Difference*
Lecercle, in his "The Pedagogy of Philosophy," describes the curious scene of a tailored-suit-wearing yuppie reading a book expressly written against yuppies: Deleuze and Guattari's *What is Philosophy?* The incongruity might elicit a smile.[15] But what, as Žižek suggests, if we instead find

---

15  See Jean-Jacques Lecercle, "The Pedagogy of Philosophy," *Radical Philosophy* 76 (1996), p. 44.

the yuppie full of enthusiasm about the book, in respect to, for example, the way that the idea of impersonal affects seems to relate to his newest advertising campaign or the delimitation of subjectivity in man's combination with machine.[16] Even if this, again, is a misreading of Deleuze, on the part of the yuppie as well as Žižek, the unmistakable Jamesonean overtones of this accusation indicate a serious question about the status of the contemporary use of the concept of "immanence." Frédéric Neyrat's *Atopias* formulates this question using the idea of "saturated immanence," which is immanence without any transcendence, purified of all hierarchies in the name of an equality of all beings that is grounded in univocity. In the face of such a levelling of all ontological levels, he asks, "How has immanence, as a category necessary for contesting the spiritualities that negate life, come to mean the grim machine that destroys difference, a mill for grinding out a sort of ontological flour, an ontology spread flat?"[17] The "flat ontologies" alluded to here are a loose collection of philosophies, including approaches from New Materialism and Object-Oriented Ontology, which draw inspiration from Deleuze's impersonal, inorganic vitalism. The characterization of flat ontologies by Levi R. Bryant unites them through four negatively formulated theses held by all of them. Firstly, they reject any transcendence or presence that indicates that one kind of entity (e.g. consciousness) is the genetic ground of all others. Secondly, therefore, there is harmonious unity encompassing all entities (e.g. a Heideggerian world). Thirdly, the primacy of epistemological considerations, which follows from the privileging of the human-world relation and the resulting concern with the human's cognitive access to the world, is to be dispensed with by ontology. Fourthly, "flat ontology argues that all entities are on equal ontological footing and that no entity, whether artificial or natural, symbolic or physical, possesses greater ontological dignity than other objects [...]. Existence, or being, is a binary such that something either is or is not."[18] This last

---

16    Slavoj Žižek, "The Ongoing 'Soft Revolution'," *Critical Inquiry* 30, no. 2 (2004), p. 292.
17    Frédéric Neyrat, *Atopias: Manifesto for a Radical Existentialism* (New York: Fordham University Press, 2018), p. 6.
18    Levi R. Bryant, *The Democracy of Objects* (Ann Arbor: Open Humanities Press, 2011), p. 245f.

thesis collapses the distinction between reality and appearance in a Parmenidean gesture, disavowing both the being of non-being and the Platonist dialectic of the mixture of being and non-being. This univocity establishes a desired equal ontological footing for all entities at the cost of making being binary. The steep cost of the loss of degrees of and difference in being, however, is presented as a gain.

### The Epistemological Reef of Flat Ontologies

While the idea of a flat univocity presents interesting epistemological as well as ontological problems for object-oriented ontologies, the problems with the New Materialist flat ontology of DeLanda will be more instructive for our discussion, since this ontology provides an account of what it means to actually intuit inorganic life and this ontology's impasses.[19] The widely discussed *Intensive Science and Virtual Philosophy* takes off from the concept of individuation described above. The primary ontological commitment adhered to throughout is to the existence of concrete individuals nested at various stages of spatio-temporal individuation, which results in a sharp distinction between actual individuals on the one hand and virtual and intensive individuation on the other. Since every actual entity is the solution to a virtual structure, representation, operating only on the level of ready-made actual individuals, is therefore excluded as a means of grasping the real genesis of phenomena. Instead, the epistemology follows from the ontological premises, or is included in the ontology. The representational categories of truth or falsity are replaced by the concepts of the singular and the ordinary. This framework is translated into terms of systems theory, which conceives of linear knowledge as a special case of non-linear dynamics.[20]

---

[19] For a more epistemological approach to these problems, see Ray Brassier, "Deleveling: Against 'Flat Ontologies'," in *Under Influence–Philosophical Festival Drift (2014)*, ed. Eva van der Graf (Barcelona: Omnia, 2014), and for more on the ontological problems, see Iain Hamilton Grant, "Mining Conditions," in *The Speculative Turn: Continental Materialism and Realism*, ed. Levi R. Bryant, Nick Srnicek, and Graham Harman (Melbourne: Re.Press, 2011), p. 41–46.

[20] The details of DeLanda's impressive translation of Deleuze's ontology in terms of nonequilibrium thermodynamics and dynamic systems theory are immaterial here. For an accurate reconstruction and discussion of his approach, see Williams, "Science and Dia-

Along these lines, the constitution of such knowledge, in terms of science, is described thus:

> A true problem, such as the one which Newton posed in relatively obscure geometric terms and which Euler, Lagrange and Hamilton progressively clarified, would be isomorphic with a real virtual problem.
> Similarly, the practices of experimental physicists, which include among other things the skillful use of machines and instruments to individuate phenomena in the laboratory, would be isomorphic with the intensive processes of individuation which solve or explicate a virtual problem in reality.[21]

This objective "problem-solving" is then mapped onto theoretical as well as experimental physics via an isomorphism. Using textual evidence in Deleuze, DeLanda claims that, even though there is no analytical resemblance, the difference between the planes does not preclude isomorphism. The skillful use of machines individuates phenomena in a manner "isomorphic" to that of natural processes.

However, this isomorphism raises the question of how the macro-physical perceptual skills of individuated researchers (e.g. theoretical knowledge of science or competency in the manipulation of machines) is *like* the capacities of micro-physical pre-individual processes of individuation. Having discarded representation as a means of bridging the planes through resemblance, DeLanda must fall back on a Bergson-inspired method of intuition to achieve isomorphism with the virtual, quasi-causal operator underlying individuation. Having dismissed the mind, i.e. consciousness, as the locus of the performance of intuition, meaning it is not the mind that mirrors nature, DeLanda grafts the mirroring onto the corporeal performance of the scientist. Even though experimentation involves regulation, standardization and representation, "the physics laboratory may be viewed as a site where heterogeneous assemblages

---

lectics in the Philosophies of Deleuze, Bachelard and DeLanda," p. 98–114.
21  DeLanda, *Intensive Science and Virtual Philosophy*, p. 136.

form, assemblages which are isomorphic with real intensive individuation processes."[22] There is, however, no argument or convincing demonstration that such a relocation of the epistemological grounds is justified or that it yields any results. The attempt to justify the legitimacy of the isomorphism seems to be grounded in the assumption that the knowledge is rooted in corporeal practices caused by virtual problems. Causation, however, does not equal justification. Rather, the isomorphism of the corporeal performance of the scientist and the pre-individual process of individuation is premised on the presupposition of a flat ontology that levels the ontological distinction between thought, theories, skillful actions and micro-physical processes, instead of justifying it. The dismissal of epistemological clarification in favor of ontological assertions, e.g. the postulation of an isomorphism between a historically contingent scientific practice and the intensive flows of matter-energy that constitute individuation fails to solve the Kantian problem of representation. The "dogmatic" solution of flat ontology is also consequential for DeLanda's attempt to map intensive processes in terms of dynamic systems theory. Since he considers all representation to be linguistic, the epistemological burden of proof is shifted to the non-linguistic representation of mathematical modelling. Alas, the isomorphism between mathematical modelling and individuation is a consequence of the flat ontology it was supposed to ground.

Taking into account the difference between philosophy and science outlined in *What is Philosophy?*,[23] in DeLanda's approach this epistemological problem in mapping inorganic life reappears: "the philosopher must become isomorphic with the quasi-causal operator, extracting problems from law-expressing propositions."[24] By identifying with the virtual, the philosopher "extracts" what is irresolvable in actual solutions, i.e. the "reserve" of the virtual. Again, an appeal to the superior faculty of

---

22  Ibid., p. 165.
23  A discussion of the difference between the formulation of scientific functions and the creation of concepts can be found in Deleuze and Guattari, *What is Philosophy?*, p. 117–162.
24  DeLanda, *Intensive Science and Virtual Philosophy*, p. 136.

intuition does not resolve the problem of isomorphism but exacerbates the problem of the absence of epistemological clarification.[25]

The embedding of epistemology in ontology in the name of an impersonal and inorganic vitality can, and in the case of New Materialism also does, yield, paradoxically, an absolute organo-centrism in the form of an ontologized traditional hylozoism, i.e. matter is endowed with (organic) life.

### TRAPPING THE COSMIC ANIMAL

*The Number and the Animal*
At a central juncture, despite their philosophical animosity, Badiou's and Laruelle's philosophies align in their respective critiques of the totalizing tendency of Deleuze's vitalism and constructivism. Like Laruelle, who exposes the decision in Deleuze's ontology that entails an auto-positioning of philosophy, Badiou also emphasizes that a choice informs Deleuze's vitalism: "The animal or the number? This is the cross of metaphysics, and the greatness of Deleuze-Leibniz, metaphysician of the divergent world of modernity, is to *choose* without hesitation for the animal."[26] He depicts this choice as the one between Plato or Aristotle: a fundamental rift between the mathematical or the organicist schema. Seen from *within* this dichotomy, Deleuze-Leibniz seems to renounce mathematics as the scheme of individuation,[27] allowing Badiou to further his peculiar reading of *The Fold* as portraying a metaphysics of the large animal (the multiple), comprising smaller animals multiplied ad infinitum. This understanding of "the multiple as *living tissue*," which changes by expanding and contracting, entails "the capture of a life that

---

[25] A critical account of "intuition" in light of its epistemological problem regarding representation and knowledge can be found in Jelača, "Sellars Contra Deleuze on Intuitive Knowledge," p. 92–126.
[26] Badiou, "Review of Gilles Deleuze, *The Fold*," p. 55, my emphasis.
[27] "In mathematics, individuation is what constitutes a determination; now the same does not hold for physical things or organic bodies." Deleuze, *The Fold*, p. 65.

is both total and divergent."²⁸ He insinuates here that the dual commitment to both the claim that there is just one world and the infinite variety found in it prompts Deleuze's assertion that the plane of immanence is "a texturology that attests to a generalized organicism, or to a ubiquitous presence of organisms."²⁹ The world thus becomes an (intricately) folded but indivisible totality, within which all distinctions are always local, and only conceivable as folds. Thus, even the most radical heterogeneities are compossibilized in this opening, "capturing" everything.

The accuracy of this depiction of Deleuze-Leibniz turns on the notion of the singularity and more specifically on the "honeymoon of concept and singularity,"³⁰ or, to speak more clearly and distinctly, what it means to begin philosophy with the fait accompli of their marriage. The "event" is introduced as an answer to this by Deleuze, who proposes that "We begin with the world as if with a series of inflections or events: it is a *pure emission of singularities.*"³¹ This conceptualization of the singular-as-event, as Badiou points out, presents a seeming *contradictio in terminis*, insofar as there appears to be nothing truly singular if everything is. Hence, Deleuze asks: "What are the conditions that make an event possible [if everything is an event]?"³² As we have already seen, the event, when understood as the singular, is not a rupture, i.e. the introduction of discontinuity, negation or alterity, but rather designates a structural and creative genesis in which the transcendental is not bigger than the empirical. Or in other words, it is the instance in which the continuity is singularized *locally* in its folds, i.e. it is the genesis of a truth (a concept) of *this* singularity. Epistemologically speaking, therefore, the true is subordinated to the remarkable. In Badiou's reconstruction of Deleuze's organicism, every event is for this reason accompanied by the "shadow" of the *pre-existing*

---

28  Badiou, "Review of Gilles Deleuze, *The Fold*," p. 55.
29  Deleuze, *The Fold*, p. 115.
30  Ibid., p. 67.
31  Ibid., p. 60.
32  Ibid., p. 76. The English translation omits the most important part of the question from the French original, so I added it again. The French original reads: "Quelles sont les conditions d'un événement, pour que tout soit événement?" Gilles Deleuze, *Le pli: Leibniz et le baroque* (Paris: Éditions de Minuit, 1988), p. 103.

*All*; it occurs as if it was a spontaneous gesture against the background of "global animality," which envelops the event in turn. The creation of the concept of the singular, therefore, always demands the conjoining of the situation and the infinite.

This ontological commitment and its epistemological consequences lead Deleuze to his most radical and fundamental assertion, namely that "[e]verything has a concept," or, expressed logically, "Every predicate is in the subject,"[33] which is a formulation of the principle of sufficient reason. In this maneuver he subverts nominalism, for which the Multiple exists but the One is reduced to language, and universalism, for which the One exists at the expense of the multiple, by claiming that "the Multiple exists in the One."[34] Therefore, from *within* the Multiple, the one is extracted—this is precisely the function of the monad—and the one in turn provides a concept of the multiple. We can see now how Badiou's claim—that for Deleuze-Leibniz the world is an animal comprised of smaller animals—is justified by the nature of the monad as functor of truth.

At the same time, Deleuze holds on to the principle of indiscernibles, introducing a seeming contradiction: everything is bound to everything, since everything possesses a concept according to the principle of sufficient reason, while everything is unbound from everything else, since there is no thing that is identical to another according to the principle of indiscernibles. He solves this by refining his ontological commitment to the "organicist scheme," attributing the surface level contradiction to a more fundamental continuity, which means the cuts introduced in the continuity by the principle of indiscernibility are not gaps or interruptions, but rather distribute continuity in the "best way" to avoid discontinuities. The commitment to this universality is a commitment to the universality of continuity, which entails that everything has a concept, understood as a fold, i.e. determined through its inclusion in the continuity or in the cosmic animal.

---

33  Deleuze, *The Fold*, p. 41, 42.
34  Badiou, "Review of Gilles Deleuze, *The Fold*," p. 58.

## The Cosmic Animal

The uncharacteristic admiration for *The Fold* which informs Badiou's review, especially in comparison to *The Clamor of Being*, indicates that this is not so much a straightforward critique, but rather both an elucidation of the fundamental (and arbitrary) choice animating Deleuze's ontological commitments (to intensity, the differential, quality and continuity) and an auto-positioning of his own philosophy, which opts for the opposite choice (for extensity, the set, quantity and discontinuity). In order to examine the merit of this reconstruction of Deleuze-Leibniz as organicists, one must first avoid a confusion of terminology. Indeed, in the lower floor of the baroque house matter is presented as folded and continuous by way of its superabundance, i.e. there are always more caverns in the caverns in the folds ad infinitum, and the organic is therefore continuously folded into the inorganic and vice versa. The organicism described by Badiou, however, encompasses these organic/inorganic folds and even grounds them. Moreover, Badiou's characterization of Deleuze points to an issue with Deleuze's ontology and specifically with the philosophy of the event that extends beyond *The Fold*.

Firstly, to state that Badiou is simply misreading Deleuze's ontology is to make a moot point without getting at the *problematic* core of the accusation. One might have already spotted the misconception of Deleuze's ontology in the skewed genealogy Badiou draws. While, for Deleuze, Plato as well as Aristotle are on the side of infinite representation, obstructing any idea of difference beyond contradiction and opposition, here Deleuze-Leibniz is aligned with Aristotle against Plato. As Iain Hamilton Grant already observes, this creates a dichotomy between pure formalism and organicism, which repeats the post-Kantian movement of limiting nature to the animal (or the plant in the case of Fichte), making the inorganic inconsequential for thought.[35] Discussing nature only in terms of the organic or embodied is, of course, inadequate to Deleuze's inorganic "philosophy of nature," which undoes the exclusive disjunction offered by Badiou. However, even if we allow the extension of φύσις beyond animal-

---

35  See Grant, *Philosophies of Nature after Schelling*, p. 9.

ity *within* Badiou's dichotomy, his characterization of Deleuze-Leibniz as organicists would hold.

The description, found in Badiou's review, of Deleuze's philosophy as a "mannerism" at first glance appears adequate. One might, as Jon Roffe does, reformulate the two theses of univocity in mannerist terms: "beings are all expressed in the *same manner*, even though they differ from each other and, more fundamentally, are synthetic products of difference-in-itself."[36] As such, the background of "global animality" does not merely resemble being, understood as substantial or emanative, but *is* being-as-difference. At the very moment of its constitution Being dissolves into difference, which is why, to evoke this conception of being, Deleuze refers to Nietzsche's eternal return. Badiou's assertion that Deleuze is a philosopher of the One at the expense of the multiple, which makes him an organicist, is, again, on the face of it, *merely* a misreading.

The depiction of and the central role Badiou allots to the event in his review marks the real point of encounter between the two philosophers.[37] The later engagement with the event in *Logics of Worlds* reiterates the construction of Deleuze-Leibniz as organicists on another level and makes it retroactively clearer:

> The event is the ontological realization of the eternal truth of the One, of the infinite power of Life [...] The event is the synthesis of past and future. In truth, as the expression of the One within becomings, it is the eternal identity of the future as a dimension of the past. For Deleuze, just as for Bergson, the ontology of time does not accept any figure of separation.[38]

Encapsulating the grounds upon which Badiou will judge Deleuze, this characterization encompasses three distinct determinations. Firstly, the

---

36 Jon Roffe, *Badiou's Deleuze* (Durham: Acumen, 2012), p. 14.
37 It is telling that Badiou's review of *The Fold* holds up the event as the central concept in Deleuze's ontology and the *Logics of Worlds* devotes a whole section to "The Event According to Deleuze," while *The Clamor of Being* does not contain any sustained discussion of the event, but rather passing characterization and (false) equivalences with other Deleuzian concepts. See Badiou, *Logics of Worlds*, p. 381f.
38 Ibid., p. 382.

event is bound to the notion of the One, something Badiou supports by citing Deleuze's assertion that "a life is composed of one and the same Event, despite the variety of what might happen."[39] By aligning this Event (the *eventum tantum*) with the One it is made unary and enjoys ontological priority over actual states of affairs. Secondly, because they ontologically subsume the future to the past, events are in a way effects, establishing continuity between temporal dimensions, instead of being causal actors themselves. As such, the Event (*eventum tantum*) is Being and insofar as everything is singular and everything is evental, the all-encompassing (i.e. organic) nature of the One prevents any dissent or separation from it, which prevents any radical novelty from arising. More specifically, the harmonious relations of time, truth, the singular and the One in Deleuze's theory of the Event as constructed by Badiou precludes the separation that engenders the constitution of the subject. Beginning with the singular in the name of life (which is the name of Being) therefore prevents radical singularity; the universalization of novelty makes its emergence (as break) impossible. The cosmic animal incorporates everything.

### *The Stellar Void*

To reframe this opposition, we might turn to *The Clamor of Being*, where Badiou, in order to clarify his reservations about inorganic vitality, presents different interpretations of the event, or dice-throw, in Mallarmé.[40] He opposes the maxim of the subtractive ontology of Mallarmé: "the Infinite proceeds from Chance—that Chance you have negated" to affirmation (according to Deleuze): "Chance proceeds from the In-

---

39   Deleuze, *Logic of Sense*, p. 170.
40   It is indeed, as Badiou acknowledges, surprising that Deleuze refers to Mallarmé, since the subtractive ontology of the latter seems incompatible with the affirmative metaphysics of the former. If we take into consideration, however, the conceptualization of Mallarmé by Rancière, which was written against the Badiou-inspired one by Meillassoux, it becomes clear that Mallarmé might escape both subtraction and affirmation. See Jacques Rancière, *Mallarmé: The Politics of the Siren*, trans. Steven Corcoran (London; New York: Continuum, 2011), and Quentin Meillassoux, *The Number and the Siren: A Decipherment of Mallarmé's* Coup de Dés, trans. Robin Mackay (Falmouth: Urbanomic, 2012).

finite—that Infinite you have affirmed."[41] In line with his treatment of the event in *Logics of Worlds,* Badiou paints the Deleuzian dice-throw as unique, in that there is only one throw (Event) which is the One (Being) and therefore chance is affirmed in its productive totality (Eternal Return). Hence "[t]he numerical results are only superficial stampings or simulacra of the Great Cast,"[42] i.e. the former is ontologically subordinated to the latter. This Deleuze abnegates the possibility of decision in order to affirm the totality of chance as the unquantifiable One of consistency.[43] Contrary to this, the Badiouian dice-throw in its (Maoist) militancy is a subtraction from ontological consistency through a quantification of the infinite which is determinate but locally indiscernible. As such, given a specific state of affairs and the political, transcendent principles of ontological unity they are embedded in, the event cannot be recognized, but rather engenders the constitution of the subject in their fidelity to that which cannot be recognized, i.e. the truth. Thus, while Deleuze's One-All insists on the virtual unity of the dice-throw, making the event unique but ubiquitous, Badiou's subtractive void splinters this into a plurality of dice-throws, of singular and rare events. Since ontological choice, for vitalism, thus entails that the event is always prior to truth, it demands the destitution of the subject, while in subtractive ontology the choice would be the condition of the subject's emergence. To enable the militant "no," Badiou must therefore oppose the ascetic "yes." He must ward off the engulfing forces of the cosmic animal and wrest from them, from the ontological excess of the One, the void understood as subtraction from the ontological (organicist) consistency which

---

41    Badiou, *Deleuze: The Clamor of Being*, p. 71.
42    Ibid., p. 73.
43    This construction of Deleuze as a philosopher of the One has political resonances, as seen in Badiou's harsh review of Deleuze and Guattari's concept of the rhizome, published as "The Fascism of the Potato." Here Deleuze and Guattari are portrayed as the "cunning monkeys of multiplicity" and "the heads of the anti-Marxist troupe," who invoke the unity of the One in movement (meaning that "all is process") and thus prevent the "scission," i.e. refuse the Marxist dialectic, which conceives of all process as having "its internal being in scission." Alain Badiou, "The Fascism of the Potato," in *The Adventure of French Philosophy*, trans. Bruno Bosteels (London: Verso, 2014), p. 193. In this portrait it is as if Deleuze and Guattari were embedded in a constant becoming-counter-revolutionary.

generates the subject: "the quantification of the stellar void punctures the qualitative unity of the cosmic animal."[44]

Having elucidated the motivation for Badiou's characterization of Deleuze, we might easily dismiss it as idiosyncratic exegesis, pointing to the fact that for Deleuze, events are plural and not unified in the One, but are univocal. Badiou reads univocity in the same ill-conceived manner as the proponents of flat ontologies do, seeing it as putting all beings on the *same* ontological level, their similarity guaranteed by the One at the cost of the multiple. In stark contrast, in the mannerism of Deleuze, touched on above, being "is said in a single and same sense *of* all its individuating differences,"[45] i.e. the equality in univocal Being can only be said *of* that which is not equal, which means that difference is prioritized over Being. It follows from this that events do have a (quasi-)causal power and are not mere effects of a state of affairs or emanations of the One.[46] The event in Deleuze thus introduces novelty, while retaining an excess in regard to the actual state of affairs. Within these processes, the individuation of psychic phenomena and the constitution of a subject understood as continuous subjectivation are of the utmost importance for Deleuze in their ontological and political dimensions.[47]

All these defenses in favor of Deleuze, however, only serve to establish a "correct" reading of Deleuze (if there is such a thing),[48] but do not solve the problem we have stated in the previous chapter and that has re-

---

44  Ray Brassier, "Stellar Void or Cosmic Animal? Badiou and Deleuze on the Dice-Throw," *Pli: Warwick Journal of Philosophy* 10 (2000), p. 216.
45  Deleuze, *Difference and Repetition*, p. 36.
46  Denying the causal power of events, Žižek proposes two inconsistent definitions of the basic ontological operation in *Anti-Oedipus* and *Logic of Sense*: either the event is the effect of corporeal states of affairs or states of affairs are products of incorporeal events. See Žižek, *Organs without Bodies*, p. 18–19.
47  Especially in his reading of the late Foucault Deleuze turns to various modes of existence and forms of subjectivation, as well as their relation to the enunciations of power, which he was not as interested in in his earlier work.
48  Considerable work has been done to defend Deleuze by dismissing Badiou's reading of his alleged "organicism" as erroneous; see James Williams, "If Not Here, Then Where? On the Location and Individuation of Events in Badiou and Deleuze," *Deleuze Studies* 3, no. 1 (June 2009), p. 97–123, and Roffe, *Badiou's Deleuze*, p. 104–127, or by pointing out the fundamental decision of vitalism against subtractive ontology with heavy leanings for the former; see Clayton Crockett, *Deleuze Beyond Badiou: Ontology, Multiplicity, and Event* (New York: Columbia University Press, 2013), p. 137–139.

turned in this one; rather, they serve only to delay a creative solution. We are thrown back to the Laruelleian decisional structure, whether for the cosmic animal or the stellar void, at the heart of these *philosophies* of immanence. Instead of stopping with these defenses, we will assess whether, by sustaining the accusation and therefore acknowledging the problem it poses without dismissing it as mere misreading, we can create a line of flight within and from Deleuze's vitalism.

Taking Badiou's accusation seriously to the degree that it exposes the auto-positioning operations within both philosophies of immanence and recalling the epistemological problems with the method of intuition mentioned earlier, we are presented with two problems: firstly, the problem of the nature and extent of Deleuze's materialism in relation to the organic and inorganic; secondly, the question of whether there is an implicit panpsychism within inorganic vitalism.

## THE FICHTEAN ORGANICISM OF NEW MATERIALISM

### *Deleuze's Physicalism*

The inorganic openness Deleuze creates is foreshadowed in his early work on Hume, which already alludes to a (possible) radically naturalistic and physicalist position. He remarks early on that empiricism and especially Hume's philosophy is a kind of physicalism.[49] The self-contradiction of the term transcendental empiricism begs the question of how plausible a fulfilment of the promise implied in this classification is, namely, that matter and experience are connected, identical or dialectical in an immanent naturalism. The merger of these two terms in Deleuze plays out in heterogeneous lines: we find, on the one hand, in *The Fold* or *A Thousand Plateaus,* a methodological union of matter and experience in the language of geology, dermatology and textures, while, on the other hand, we find in *Difference and Repetition*'s assertoric approach

---

[49] See Deleuze, *Empiricism and Subjectivity,* p. 66, 103, 109, 119.

something like an identity of matter and mind.[50] As Iain Hamilton Grant points out, this indecision about the relationship between physics and experience is indicative of Deleuze's inability to leave behind transcendental philosophy for a proper nature philosophy like Schelling's. Because he is unable to provide an account of this merger of matter and experience, he leaves room for the false binary decisions (the number *or* the animal) that encompass philosophy in his wake.[51] While Schelling proposes a radical naturalism for which grounding is the explication of the phenomena, which is achieved by "tracing the original conditions of matter itself,"[52] Deleuze's universal ungrounding conditions, drives and undoes any grounding. The former therefore presents a one-world physics, while the latter proposes a one-world transcendentalism.[53] Since the world is swept up and gripped by the powerful ungrounding, which makes the differentiation of its empirical and transcendental dimension itself transcendental, Deleuze becomes unable to maintain his commitment to naturalism. Rather, he reiterates the Kantian question of what the unifying ground of nature and freedom could be, insofar as he takes both up into the universal ungrounding, only to maintain their antithesis. This recapitulates the problem of the impossible merger of matter and experience in transcendental empiricism, insofar as ethos and physis are in danger of limiting (or regionalizing) each other in the same way as matter and experience. Deleuze's hesitation to commit to a Schellingian immanent physics sustains the antithesis of ethos and physis as well as of experience and matter and leaves his philosophy open to being read in terms of the Fichtean ethical alternative, which elides the whole of nature. It is this reading—the Deleuze of the *Thathandlung*—which, I claim, dominates much of the contemporary discussion about his phi-

---

50  See Mullarkey, *Post-Continental Philosophy*, p. 14–15.
51  See Grant, *Philosophies of Nature after Schelling*, p. 9.
52  Schelling, "Über Die Construction in Der Philosophie," p. 76.
53  As Grant notes, if it is true what Deleuze says and the depth or volcanic *spatium* of *Difference and Repetition* "is like the famous geological line from NE to SW" (Deleuze, *Difference and Repetition*, p. 135), then it is necessary to ask the question of what the meaning of this likeness is, i.e. in which way or manner the transcendental *is* physical. See Grant, *Philosophies of Nature after Schelling*, p. 200.

losophy of matter and inorganic life, and which is especially associated with New Materialism.

## The Organicism of New Materialism

This neo-Fichtean turn can be found most prominently in Deleuze-inspired materialisms like DeLanda's morphogenesis or Bennett's vital materialism. It aligns with a broader tendency within contemporary metaphysics to attempt to retrieve (inorganic) matter's potential for activity and creativity. However well meaning, these ontologies suffer from an discrepancy between their intended goal and their philosophical consequences, i.e. while they intend a revaluation of inorganic matter (a "vitalization" of matter), they end up eliminating (inorganic) matter altogether.

Generally speaking, these philosophies start from the traditional distinction between *passive* matter and *active* organisms/human beings, only to then subvert this distinction. Within this traditional division between the realms of mechanism and teleology, they argue, matter is construed as inactive and uncreative in order to elevate the ontological position of the organism, or human beings, or the mind, whose activity is necessary to account for the creation of forms. This anthropocentrism "deprives" matter of its inherent creative capacities and hence these must be rediscovered, whether as agency, thing-power or capacity to self-organize.

However, by attributing activity to matter, one accepts the conceptual distinction between the organic and the inorganic (and its consequences), only to then project organic properties onto the inorganic. The notion of activity as capacity is based on the distinction between nature and freedom (and subsequently between the inorganic and the organic), and denotes the limitation (or regionalization) of nature with respect to freedom. If capacities for activity are ascribed to the inorganic, therefore, the antithesis is retained and the organic is extended to everything. This satisfies Fichte's demand that the physical be determined by the ethical, i.e. activity, only with the slight variation that activity is not restricted to the human. Subsequently, these neo-Fichtean materialisms insist on an ethics of activity, intensification and creation which extends to human-object relations as well as to the material world itself. This Fichteanism, however, betrays the most important insight of Deleuze's inorganic vitalism of the event, namely that at the heart of life is inactivity.

The Kantian trajectory of vital materialism becomes apparent in the readings of Deleuze's materialism by DeLanda which Bennett draws from. They present Deleuze's concept of life as a "capacity" for novelty and creative becoming, which extends to inorganic matter as well and manifests in the "self-organizing processes" which even "drive the geological cycle."[54] The recourse to self-organization, a concept that was crucial for Kant's biophilosophy, recapitulates the projection of organic properties onto inorganic matter. As we have seen already in our treatment of Maturana and Verela, autopoietic systems are networks of productive processes which create, reproduce and maintain their components and engender their own unity both topologically and functionally. This corresponds to and builds on Kant's operational notion of self-organization, "defining an organized being as one whose elements or component parts are its own products, whose causality is circular and whose production is self-referential."[55] The idea of an exception to the universal law of mechanics led Kant to the assertion of an activity peculiar to such systems. Again, ascribing the capacity for self-organization to inorganic matter in the manner of DeLanda incorporates everything into the organic model, which retroactively binds all of the free forces of inorganic life.[56]

Bennett's vital materialism, to take another instance, builds on Deleuzian materialists like Protevi or DeLanda to introduce the notion of "thing-power" to describe the capacity of material configurations to "produce effects," i.e. to "act" and "alter [...] the course of events."[57] With the centerpiece of *Vibrant Matter* being a reconceptualization of Latour's

---

54 Manuel DeLanda, "Non-Organic Life," in *Incorporations*, ed. Jonathan Crary and Sanford Kwinter (New York: Zone Books, 1992), p. 142.
55 Toscano, *The Theatre of Production*, p. 56.
56 For an account of the difference between the production and breaking of symmetries in Deleuze and DeLanda which alludes exactly to this problem, see ibid., p. 185.
57 Bennett, *Vibrant Matter*, p. viii.

concept of an "actant," an (irreducible) source of action within a network of interlinked relations, which can but do not have to involve the human, Bennett claims to "stretch" the notions of action and freedom to render the capacities of vital matter visible. This move, however, solidifies the anthropocentrism she attempts to vanquish, since the organic categories are not stretched and transformed but mapped, in a form much like Spinoza's organic model of the conatus, onto inorganic life. Although she cites Nancy Levene's position that "Spinoza continually stresses this continuity between human and other beings,"[58] this continuity can only be accounted for by the assertion of a peculiar vitality, in that "[e]ach thing [*res*], as far as it can by its own power, strives [*conatur*] to persevere in its own being."[59] On epistemologically rather insufficient grounds, Bennett extends this conatus to inorganic matter and material processes in general by calling on our ability to recognize "that human agency has some echoes in nonhuman nature."[60] This ability resembles Bergsonian intuition, and this justification through intuition of the extension of conatus into matter is exactly what Deleuze opposes. Not only does Deleuze transform the method of intuition, as we have already shown, but he breaks with the idea that the *élan vital* is active, no less than he breaks with the idea that the conatus is active. As demonstrated above, Deleuze's syntheses are strictly passive, meaning that they do not act. With respect to Bergson, Deleuze argues against the idea of an active selection by the living being, in favor of an unfree selection that the living being itself is a result of: the event. It is the temporal modality of the future that ungrounds every activity and suspends the "capacity" for creation. Instead,

---

[58] Nancy Levene, *Spinoza's Revelation: Religion, Democracy, and Reason* (Cambridge: Cambridge University Press, 2004), p. 3.

[59] Baruch de Spinoza, "The Ethics," in *A Spinoza Reader: The Ethics and Other Works*, ed. and trans. Edwin Curley (Princeton: Princeton University Press, 1994), IVp34s1.

[60] Bennett, *Vibrant Matter*, p. xvi. In subsequent chapters, this hypothesis is supported by incongruent analyses, like the phenomenological account of the "encounter" with material forces (p. 2), the Deleuzian account of the "activity" of the assemblage (p. 20) and the scientific account of the unpredictable behavior of inorganic materials like metal (p. 52). This method is then used to further a political ecology that introduces material "actors" into the democratic process. This seeming elevation of matter, which muddles the question of the demos, again reinforces the obfuscation of the actual potential of a thought of inorganic life: its inactivity.

the future is the indifferent production of novelty through the irreversible break between the past and the future.

### The Feminist Critique of Karen Barad's Agential Realism and the Revaluation of Passivity

A more deceptive form of this neo-Fichtean organo-centrism can be found in Karen Barad's agential realism and its ethical claims. In her (sympathetic) critique of Foucault's approach to the historicity of the body, Barad claims that in his genealogy of corporality the body only ever appears as the effect or product of the judicial system of power which then represents it.[61] Following Butler, Barad tries to show how in Foucault the materiality of the body itself is a discursive object, dependent on forms of knowledge which are subject to discourses within a given power structure. Matter for Foucault, according to Barad, is thus not conceptualized in terms of "performativity" but merely as the object of discursive activity.[62] If Foucault wants to hold simultaneously that "the deployments of power are directly connected to the body—to bodies, functions, physiological processes, sensations, and pleasures"[63] and that in such a formation the body is not effaced as such, then according to Barad, he would need a robust theory of *materialization*, i.e. a theory of how the physio-biological, physical and historical are interwoven. Hence, she claims that even though Foucault exposes the workings of disciplinary power, "he [...] fails to offer an account of the body's historicity in which its very materiality plays an active role in the workings of power,"[64] which means he cannot give an account of the relation between discursive and non-discursive practices. Against the objection that every account of non-discursive practices would itself be dis-

---

61  See Karen Barad, "Posthumanist Performativity: Toward an Understanding of How Matter Comes to Matter," *Signs* 28, no. 3 (2003), p. 804.
62  Even though it is fairly obvious that such an assumption about Foucault is factually wrong (i.e. Foucault spends much of his late works in the 1980s considering the body's resistance to dominant discursive formations), it might appear this way in Barad's interpretation of Foucault, which she quotes to substantiate her claim about Foucault's reduction of matter to power. The source for her interpretation of Foucault is most likely Judith Butler, *Gender Trouble: Feminism and the Subversion of Identity* (New York: Routledge, 1990), p. 2.
63  Foucault, *History of Sexuality, Vol. 1*, p. 151.
64  Barad, "Posthumanist Performativity," p. 809.

cursive, she claims that such a representationalism can be (and must be) overcome by a performative theory of matter (i.e. an account of the materialization of human and non-human bodies). Drawing on Niels Bohr's epistemology, she demonstrates her idea of this performative understanding of matter in relation to the production of phenomena emerging from scientific measurement. She proposes a reworking of the traditional concept of causality in the form of "intra-actions": in contrast to inter-action, which presupposes pre-existing *relata* antecedent to the relation, intra-action poses relations without *relata* as "ontologically primitive"[65] in the constitution of a phenomenon. The *"relata*-within-phenomena" emerge rather from an "agential cut" enacted by an intra-action, which involves a specific material configuration Barad calls the "apparatus of observation," i.e. "the agential cut enacts a *local* resolution *within* the phenomenon of the inherent ontological indeterminacy"[66] of being. As such, the agential cut constitutes a local or regional set of causal relations between the emerging components of the phenomenon. The measuring process thus isn't a purely human activity, and the relevant devices can't be understood as mere detectors of objectively existing entities—both measurement and device are elements in the material production of phenomena. In this way, Barad can claim that even the seemingly discursive domain of science is constituted by an intra-action between social/cultural and material practices as well as between human and non-human agents. From this, Barad expands this agential realism to include the whole of the universe, which constitutes itself in its spatio-temporal, procedural and historical intra-activity. Or, "in summary, the universe is agential intra-activity in its becoming."[67]

Agency is thus not aligned with human subjectivity or intentionality, but instead the aforementioned "dynamism [intra-activity] *is* agency. Agency is not an attribute but the ongoing reconfigurings [sic] of the world."[68] Hence, agency is performed by matter rather than being an

---

65  Ibid., p. 815.
66  Ibid., original italics.
67  Ibid., p. 818.
68  Ibid.

attribute of matter.[69] The dead and passive matter of traditional Western philosophies is thus, according to Barad, reanimated or rather given a "new sense of aliveness"[70] as intra-activity, which actively involves matter in the constitution of the universe. If this dynamism operates with a "primitive" materiality, the distinction between notions such as those of animate and inanimate matter, or active organic and passive inorganic processes of individuation, is suspended a priori. Everything is equally active, so that "this new sense of aliveness applies to the inanimate as well as to the animate, or rather, it is what makes possible the very distinction between the animate and the inanimate."[71] Her extension of activity to the inorganic real is therefore both the leveling of a distinction and the subversion of a dualism. Claiming, however, that there is no dualism between the animate and the inorganic does not necessary entail that the distinction between passive matter and active beings (humans, organisms) is also removed. Rather, the latter can only be achieved if the two sides are equalized in a third term, i.e. that of "activity." As we have already seen in DeLanda, this move creates significant epistemological problems. Barad must, at the same time as depicting the overthrow of the dualism (dead/alive), provide grounds for this overthrow.[72] From the descriptions in *Meeting the Universe Halfway*, it seems that the reason for her proposed idea of intra-active dynamism is that the dualistic approach is empirically inaccurate, insofar as it does not conform to the empirical findings of quantum physics. Such a claim, however, is wholly unsubstantiated since quantum physics does not propose to be or even entail a metaphysics. Furthermore, tracing in this way the transcendental dynamism of the universe from the empirical finding of just one branch of physics repeats Kant's error of tracing the indeterminate and the determination from what is determined.

---

69  Barad, *Meeting the Universe Halfway*, p. 178.
70  Ibid., p. 177.
71  Ibid., p. 437.
72  See Chris Calvert-Minor, "Epistemological Misgivings of Karen Barad's 'Posthumanism'," *Human Studies* 37 (2013), p. 135.

As Ahmed in her feminist critique of the so-called New Materialisms already mentions, such undertakings as Barad's should be understood not as ontologically or epistemologically motivated projects, but ethically and politically motivated metaphysics.[73] Barad's presentation of her project as "an epistemological-ontological-ethical framework that provides an understanding of the role of human *and* nonhuman [...] factors in scientific and other social-material practices"[74] corresponds *prima facie* to this categorization. This presents a specific double bind, which is never resolved by Barad: because everything (animate and inanimate) is *actively* engaged in the intra-active constitution of the universe, everything is accountable for the constitution of every phenomenon (and the *relata* within the phenomenon). Conversely, however, the metaphysical grounds of this accountability (the agential realism) can only be thought or conceived of if and only if one assumes the activity and thus the mutual accountability to be true. Or, only the ethical version of the world ("everything is accountable for the specific materializations it is a part of") can ground the construction of the intra-active metaphysics ("everything is active"), but in turn such an ethical vision is purported to follow from the metaphysics. This problem is especially significant when Barad attempts to further define what this "accountability," or the ethics entailed in the metaphysics, consists of. As well as not specifying the ethical injunctions following from the metaphysics, she doesn't specify why any ethics would

[73] Ahmed argues that the New Materialisms display a certain "biophobia," insofar as they make a proper engagement with biology and gender impossible. In an approach wherein matter subverts all boundaries and creates them itself, the societal mechanisms of exclusion and effective hierarchies in biology become imperceptible. See Sara Ahmed, "Imaginary Prohibitions: Some Preliminary Remarks on the Founding Gestures of the New Materialism," *European Journal of Women's Studies* 15 (2008), p. 25–39. Davis, in her response to Ahmed, has proposed that this critique of New Materialism is built on a rather specific and classical understanding of what it means to engage with biology from a feminist perspective. See Noela Davis, "New Materialism and Feminism's Anti-Biologism: A Response to Sara Ahmed," *European Journal of Women's Studies* 16 (2009), p. 67–80. However, Davis underestimates Ahmed's critique, since the latter does not claim that New Materialism's approach to biology is wrong but that it is superfluous at best and harmful at worst. The claim that the social and the natural are intertwined is a banality for Ahmed (i.e. nobody would disagree with that). To dissolve this distinction entirely in the name of an affective matter, however, renders the mechanisms of power acting between the realms imperceptible and epistemologically inaccessible.
[74] Barad, *Meeting the Universe Halfway*, p. 26.

follow from an agential realism. By collapsing the cultural and the natural domains into the notion of ubiquitous "agency," Barad forgoes all the options for critique present in Butler's account of materialization, i.e. the investigation of the production of bodies within and guided by a given power structure. Such a critique is only possible if the ethics animating it is supplied by a principle of vulnerability, which in turn entails the distinction between animate and inanimate beings. However, even though she proposes this distinction, Butler's critique is not rooted in an understanding of the active formation of the world by human subjectivity or intentionality but rather an account of the passive production of the subject (and the body), which involves natural *and* cultural factors. The overcoming of the dualism between inanimate and animate objects does not *necessarily* entail the erasure of every possible distinction between the living and the non-living. Ethics becomes impossible if all distinctions have been blurred, as is the case in Barad's ontology.

One should situate Barad's ethics in the Fichtean tradition sketched earlier. By ascribing "activity" to matter as such (or materialization), she first accepts the gulf between active organisms and passive matter, only to then subvert this distinction by extending the dynamic and creative "activity" of the organic side to the inorganic realm as such. Instead of grounding or ungrounding both realms in a dynamic process, Barad shows how the inorganic is *like* the organic, i.e. she traces the inorganic from the organic. As we have seen above, the devaluation of the "passivity" of matter in the name of the repressed or overlooked "activity" of matter cannot be grounded in the empirical findings of quantum physics. If one, however, regards this rejection of passivity as ethical in nature, then this would presuppose an "inherent" value of activity, which amounts to a Fichtean ethics. Furthermore, as Braunmühl notes in her feminist critique of Barad, the implication of the inherent value of activity and the subsequent "devaluation of passivity accords with hegemonic, male-supremacist discourse, which feminizes that attribute."[75] Barad's metaphys-

---

75  Caroline Braunmühl, "Beyond Hierarchical Oppositions. A Feminist Critique of Karen Barad's Agential Realism," *Feminist Theory* 19 (2018), p. 231.

ics reinforces and reproduces the privilege and primacy of activity in relation to passivity that is produced by masculinist discourses. To understand how to avoid such a projection of organic activity into the inorganic, which effectively eliminates the latter, we must further confront this ethical vision of the world.

*The Ethical Vision of Nature and its Discontents*
Recapitulating the Kantian problem of the "activity" of the synthesis and projecting organic properties onto inorganic matter not only prevents the possibility of an inorganic image of thought, but, paradoxically, undermines the alleged "materialism" of New Materialism. The progression we hypothesized as following from Laruelle's critique of Deleuze's vitalist unity of being and thinking now seems inverted in active vitalism: while the series still terminates in the same "image," it now runs from organo-centrism to biocentrism to noocentrism to idealism (entailing anthropocentrism).

The ontological movement, having transmuted everything into activity, feeds into the ethical movement, completing the Fichtean trajectory. The empirical difference in operation (teleology) from inanimate matter and the ontological dignity of the organism provide sufficient grounds to account for the exception of the organism from the universal mechanical laws. In a radicalization of Kant's grounding of pure in practical reason, Fichte's demand that the material be determined by the ethical sought to banish from philosophy everything which is not activity. New Materialism recapitulates this demand, following a line of reasoning present in Deleuze, by asserting that inorganic life is at the same time an ontological, descriptive assertion and a prescriptive injunction. The vitalization of assemblages or structures, and hence the call to transpose what is passive into activity, is in itself motivated by an ethical and political "value" *deduced* from the ontological premises. As we have already seen in Laruelle's critique of Deleuzian vitalism, the ethical demand implicit in the eternal return assures the transition from the metaphysical to the transcendental by forcing a decision. This moralizing vitalism is not yet done with judgement; rather, it *judges against* judgement to install an ethics of intensification. Inorganic life is thus used to judge against the organic and, in a dialectical turn, is made to mimic the properties of its opposition. With fervor, proponents of New Materialism attempt to disrupt anthropocentrism, only to leave a human-shaped hole in the world around which everything gravitates. The organic reveals itself to be the secret core of the vital materialist ethics of inorganic life.

Instead of being a thinker who ascribes activity to matter in the name of life (as is often claimed), Deleuze is interested in introducing passivity into life in the name of time.[76] The ontologies of New Materialism, then, do not go as far as Deleuze. Ultimately, then, New Materialism falls back behind critical philosophy, insofar as it inherits its problems, but offers only solutions that do not hold up to the epistemological rigor demanded by transcendental philosophy. One is reminded of Kant's discussion with and critique of Herder's bio-philosophy and its proposal of an organic force animating all natural processes. By linking the empirical phenomena of material behaviors (e.g. the unpredictable line of a fracture in metal) to a transcendental *capacity* of matter to produce such novelties, New Materialism introduces the problem of the agency of inorganic matter solely through the way the question is posed, without any reliable epistemology to justify its claims. By conflating ethology with praxis, the New Materialists mirror a movement in contemporary analytic philosophy of mind towards pan-intentionalism. This tendency identifies, in Karl Pfeifer's account, physical dispositional states with intentional mental states because of the similarity (or analogy) of their behaviors and capacities.[77] Such an account is, however, not able to explain consistently whose intentionality mental and physical states are identified with.[78]

---

[76] Although not fully fleshed out, this reversal can already be found in Joseph Barker, "Against 'Vital Materialism': The Passive Creation of Life in Deleuze," *Mosaic: An Interdisciplinary Critical Journal* 48, no. 4 (2015), p. 49–62.

[77] See Karl Pfeifer, "Pantheism as Panpsychism," in *Alternative Concepts of God*, ed. Andrei Buckareff and Yujin Nagasawa (Oxford: Oxford University Press, 2016), p. 47.

[78] Although Pfeifer's theory seems to suggest a materialist panpsychism, the answer to the question of whose intentionality he is talking about reveals it to be a pantheism first and foremost. But this leaves this account in a bind, since either God is perceived as a "mass noun" to accommodate monism, but then no consistent description of "intentional" mental states is possible, or He is conceived of as a numerically distinct subject, but this sug-

This impasse in the paralleling account points to a problem in the New Materialist framework, namely the proposed subjectivity of inorganic nature, i.e. the problem of panpsychism.

## THE POVERTY OF PANPSYCHISM

*Deleuze's Vitalist Hypostatization*

Reacting to Laruelle's exaggerated critique of "la philosophie," Brassier suggests instead a reconfiguration of non-philosophy as a critique of the transcendental synthesis and auto-positional transcendence that correlationism calls upon. This shift brings non-philosophy—at least with respect to its impetus—almost in line with Meillassoux's rejection of correlationism. In *After Finitude*, Meillassoux writes:

> By "correlation" we mean the idea according to which we only ever have access to the correlation between thinking and being, and never to either term considered apart from the other. We will henceforth call correlationism any current of thought which maintains the unsurpassable character of the correlation so defined.[79]

The Copernican revolution impedes any thought of the separation or identity of thought and being in favor of an asynchronous correlation. Translated into non-philosophical terms we could say that only the auto-positional transcendence invoking transcendental synthesis is thinkable. But neither can thinking and being be thought separate from each other nor can they be conceived as identical, because philosophical thought is (co-)constitutive of the real by thinking being. Thus, for Meillassoux, Deleuze's levelling of the noumenal/phenomenal distinction is an absolutization of the correlation, insofar as the notion of "life" not only cor-

---

gests ontological pluralism. For an exploration of this problem in Pfeifer's account, see Joanna Leidenhag, "Unity Between God and Mind? A Study on the Relationship Between Panpsychism and Pantheism," *Sophia* 58, no. 4 (December 1, 2019), p. 543–561.

[79] Meillassoux, *After Finitude*, p. 5.

relates being and thinking but proposes that there is nothing to think beyond this correlation. He accuses Deleuze of a "vitalist hypostatization"[80] of the correlation, i.e. Deleuze conceives everything (even "ancestral events") as a correlate of "a Life" and is hence a strong correlationist. One might understand this point as a repetition of Badiou's contention that Deleuze's vitalism is a quasi-ontotheological metaphysics, insofar as life/becoming becomes a new ground and principle, which betrays the basic tenets of Deleuze's own ontology.[81] This, however, does not clarify the nature of the correlation Deleuze is allegedly guilty of, since on the surface life does not appear in Deleuze as a metaphysical principle nor does it imply a similar structure to other strong correlationists (like Husserl, Heidegger or Wittgenstein). While *Subtraction and Contraction* and *Spectral Dilemma* both contain clues to better understand the relationship between Deleuze and Meillassoux and shed light on the critique, the heavy focus on the Bergsonian side of Deleuze in these texts blocks the real potential of the accusation.[82]

## Deleuzian Panpsychism

If we are, however, willing to take the detour through Ray Brassier's critique of the same (or at least similar) issue in Deleuze, we can see the correlation more clearly. Brassier reconstructs Deleuze through his theory of individuation with the explicit aim of demonstrating Deleuze's subjectivism. He argues that the Deleuzian "encounter,"[83] as the starting point of individuation, triggers the discordant exercise of the faculties, pushing every faculty to its limits, and it is "through this transcendent-discordant as opposed to the empirical-concordant exercise that each faculty accesses its own problematic-ontological dimension."[84] Every faculty is hence confronted with what is not experienced (*sentiendum*) in sen-

---

80  Ibid., p. 64.
81  Badiou, *Deleuze: The Clamor of Being*, p. 70–72.
82  See Quentin Meillassoux, "Subtraction and Contraction," *Collaps* 3 (2007), and Quentin Meillassoux, "Spectral Dilemma," *Collaps* 4 (2008).
83  Understood as the "confrontation with the paradoxical instance which defines the being of its proper object." Brassier, *Nihil Unbound*, p. 169.
84  Ibid.

sibility, is not remembered (*memorandum*) in memory and remains unthought (*cogitandum*) within thought. Through this transcendental deduction, Deleuze reveals that the sensible has a privileged position in the series, since it is the place of the encounter which enables the other two dimensions: "From the intensity to thought, it is always by means of an intensity that thought comes to us."[85] Hence, he concludes, the answer to the question of who it is that thinks is: an intensity. Brassier seeks to demonstrate this by insisting that Deleuze claims that actualization unfolds along three series: spatial, temporal, and psychic. As we have seen, thinking is engendered by an encounter with an intensity. This plays a crucial role in individuation, since it is the process of implementing virtual ideas into actual physical systems.[86] Such ideas in turn are the result of thinking, which breaks with the present and orients organization towards the future; hence, individuation is the creation of the new. However, since Ideas are irreducible to the sensible because they are not immediately encountered in the present, something is needed to perform the thinking necessary for creating the dimension of the future that individuation hinges on. This is why Deleuze, according to Brassier, must introduce "larval-subjects," which account for the spatio-temporal dynamism in individuation and guarantee intensity's independence from representational consciousness.[87] It is intensity that thinks, but only as a latent form of consciousness. Hence, in Deleuze's ontology, "ideality and sensibility ultimately converge in a double genesis of thinking and being,"[88] while thinking is still in need of subjectivity or proto-subjectivity. In short, a panpsychism is necessary to conflate being and thinking, but is itself only justified by said conflation, from which follows the circular structure of conditioning typical for strong correlationism.

---

85  Deleuze, *Difference and Repetition*, p. 144.
86  Deleuze takes this to be the main focus of his magnum opus *Difference and Repetition*, insofar as this gives an account of the diversity of being, without falling back into Kantian constraints.
87  The reading of Deleuze attempted by Brassier is, however, heavily contested; see for example Woodward, "Nonhuman Life", p. 27–30. On the "larval subjects," see Deleuze, *Difference and Repetition*, p. 78.
88  Brassier, *Nihil Unbound*, p. 171.

Ultimately, due to the univocity of being, there can in Deleuze be no being without thinking and vice versa. In a twisted way, Deleuze could be construed as a subjective idealist à la Hegel. This seems to invite the critique of the speculative realist, since for the speculative realist "There is contingent being independent of us, and this contingent being has no reason to be of a subjective nature."[89]

With the copula of being and thinking being a form of consciousness, Deleuze seems to inherit all the problems of panpsychist theories. He would be unable to describe the real genesis of mind from nature, since mind would always already be presupposed in it, in a way akin to Husserl's sleeping monads. Panpsychism, in contemporary discourse, is mostly made plausible via an abductive argument (e.g. in Strawson or Brüntrup).[90] The form of the question therefore only allows for two answers, which are both reflective of the reductive manner in which the problem is posed in the first place. Either consciousness is made a "factum" and is considered as a property (or as "mental properties"), or it is a ground or condition for higher cognitive functions.[91] Both answers quite obviously fall prey to the transcendental illusion described earlier (see section "The Transcendental Empiricism That Has Never Been"). From this vantage point, panpsychism is organic metaphysics par excellence, extending judgement to all regions of being.

Deleuze, in Brassier's reading, seems also to pose panpsychism as the result of an abductive argument, which is necessary to explain the iden-

---

[89] Meillassoux, *The Number and the Siren*, p. 63.
[90] Even Galen Strawson is ready to admit that he rejected the theory at first, until he realized that there is "no alternative." See Galen Strawson, "Realistic Monism: Why Physicalism Entails Panpsychism," in *Consciousness and Its Place in Nature: Does Physicalism Entail Panpsychism?*, ed. Galen Strawson and Anthony Freeman (Exeter: Imprint Academic, 2006), p. 25. For Brüntrup, the recursive nature of the argument not only leads to panpsychism, but to pantheism. See Godehard Brüntrup, "Introduction," in *Panentheism and Panpsychism: Philosophy of Religion Meets Philosophy of Mind*, ed. Godehard Brüntrup, Benedikt Paul Göcke, and Ludwig Jaskolla (Leiden; Boston: Brill, 2020).
[91] Take, for example, Skrbina's definition of panpsychism as "the view that all things have mind or a mind-like quality. [...] Mind is seen as fundamental to the nature of existence and being." David Skrbina, *Panpsychism in the West* (Cambridge, Mass.: MIT Press, 2005), p. 2. Or Nagel's position that panpsychism is "the view that the basic fundamental constituents of the universe have mental properties, whether or not they are parts of living organisms." Thomas Nagel, *Mortal Questions* (Cambridge: Cambridge University Press, 1991), p. 181.

tity of being and thinking according to the principle of the univocity of being. But then, Brassier claims, he shifts gears to assert this mechanism as not merely the explanatory grounds but the ontological grounds for the identity of being and thinking. Even though no longer tied to representational consciousness, Ideas are *expressed* in the realm of the sensible by the "thinking" of intensity.

The nature of this thinking is crucial for Brassier's argument. To clarify it, he makes an insertion into the quotation of the following passage from *Difference and Repetition*:

> The individual in intensity finds its image neither in the organization of the self nor in the specification of the I but, on the contrary, in the fractured I and the dissolved self [i.e. the larval subject], and in the correlation between the fractured I and the dissolved self.[92]

Brassier's addition in this quote as well as his conflation of various Deleuzian notions such as "agent," "the originary subjectivity of habit," "the passive self," "the fractured I," suggest the primary role of psychic systems in the process of individuation. In his reading of Deleuze, the transcendent exercise of the faculties, i.e. human thought, is a *conditio sine qua non* for individuation in general, since "only the psychic individual can become equal to the conditions of its own intensive individuation."[93] This interpretation does not imply a panpsychism akin to Whitehead's, which would ontologically prioritize sentience ("feeling") before cognition, thinking or even vitality;[94] nor does it imply any kind of pan-experientialism. Rather, this depiction of Deleuze rests on the notion of the universal individual, as described in *Difference and Repetition*:

---

[92] Deleuze, *Difference and Repetition*, p. 254, as cited in Brassier, *Nihil Unbound*, p. 181.
[93] Brassier, *Nihil Unbound*, p. 185.
[94] As Shaviro notes: "Sentience is a more basic category than life or vitality. Life is possible because there is already sentience, rather than the reverse. (A difference between Whitehead and Deleuze, as noted by Brassier.)" Steven Shaviro, "The Consequences of Panpsychism," in *The Nonhuman Turn*, ed. Richard A. Grusin (Minneapolis: University of Minnesota Press, 2015), p. 41.

Everybody, every thing, thinks and is a thought to the extent that, reduced to its intensive reasons, it expresses an Idea, the actualization of which it determines. However, the thinker himself makes his individual differences from all manner of things: it is in this sense that he is laden with stones and diamonds, plants "and even animals". The thinker, undoubtedly the thinker of the eternal return, is the individual, the universal individual.[95]

The thinker is thus both the condition for the expression of individuating factors and "universal." However, as Brassier notes, since "the principle of explication [...] is not an 'objective' aspect of bio-physical reality but rather an empirical dimension of experience,"[96] this universal individual belongs to psychic systems. As we have seen in Laruelle, the Nietzschean-Deleuzian metaphysics necessitates a sovereign decision, which annihilates this sovereignty to satisfy the eternal return as metaphysical principle and establish the Will to Power as empirical principle. The psychic system then marks the point at which the eternal return is "performed," in that the eternal return is the locus wherein pre-individual intensities surface and turn against the Self and the I. As such, only the human thinker can partake properly in the affirmative becoming of immanence. Insofar as this is true, it seems that Brassier's paradoxical claim—that for Deleuze every individuation involves the human thinker—is justified. Even if we loosened the strength of the argument by proposing that "thinking" in Deleuze is ascribed to non-human processes as well, this would solidify the accusation of panpsychism, since every material individuation would then involve the individuation of a psychic system as well, and subjectivity would thus become universal, which absolutizes the correlation between being and thinking.

Both Brassier's characterization of Deleuze's philosophy as an anthropocentric noocentrism or the weaker panpsychist version run, of course, counter to Deleuze's ontological ambitions. While it is possible to rebuff

---

95 Deleuze, *Difference and Repetition*, p. 254.
96 Brassier, *Nihil Unbound*, p. 191.

these accusations as resting on a misreading (and unjustified conflation) of Deleuzian concepts, I claim that they do in fact reveal a problematic aspect of Deleuze's theory of a Parmenidean identity of thinking and being.

## On the Micro-Souls

*Prima facie*, Brassier's accusation of the subjectivity implicated in (and explicating intensities in) individuation seems to be supported by textual evidence from *Difference and Repetition*, e.g. "Every spatio-temporal dynamism is accompanied by the emergence of an elementary consciousness."[97] This is compounded by this text's overemphasis on examples from biology rather than physics. However, as Roffe points out, Brassier surreptitiously conflates all the various manners of "thinking" that Deleuze mentions, in order to locate them in psychic systems and identify them as "subjective" qualities.[98] The "elementary consciousness," for example, is not a subjective phenomenon, but an objective one, as it describes only the auto-unifying form Ruyer called "overflight" (*survol*). It is "a *form in itself* that does not refer to any external point of view [...]. It is an absolute consistent form that surveys itself independently of any supplementary dimension."[99] It is therefore incompatible with the hylomorphic model of an indifferent (material) substratum formed by a static (ideal) structure. The notion of consciousness that is involved in individuation, for Ruyer and Deleuze, does not resemble any phenomenological or human consciousness belonging to the subjective order, but is instead a "dark vision and not a non-vision [...], it is primarily consciousness of its own form."[100] Of course, there is the subjective order of actual constituted consciousness, or the "I." But, contrary to what Brassier suggests, individuation does not rely on the dissolution of the self through the transcendent exercise of the faculties, since individuation and the self belong to different orders:

---

97  Deleuze, *Difference and Repetition*, p. 220.
98  Jon Roffe, "Objectal Human: On the Place of Psychic Systems in *Difference and Repetition*," in *Deleuze and the Non/Human*, ed. Jon Roffe and Hannah Stark (London: Palgrave Macmillan, 2015), p. 48.
99  Ruyer, *Néo-Finalisme*, p. 26, my translation.
100 Ibid., my translation.

the individual to intensity and the "I" to differenciation. But the "I" (the subjective order) does not detach from its sub-representational genesis, which makes the transcendental illusion of its representation possible in the first place, and in its encounter with intensity calls the identity attributed to the thinker into question (the fractured I). Brassier's attempt to prove the subjective nature of synthesis by references to Deleuze's notion of "larval subjects" falters in the face of this distinction. The Humean associationism, reconfigured by Neoplatonism, with which Deleuze describes the formation of habits (understood as passive contractions) involves egos that are precisely the auto-contemplations in the conjuncture of impressions and elements in passive synthesis as such. Since actualized psychic systems are constituted by these passive syntheses, one finds a multitude of these "micro-Souls" in them. But since they are a base feature of synthesis *as such,* they exist in nature, beyond the human mind, and can be constituted without it. By abandoning the spontaneity of the human mind as a *conditio sine qua non* for (passive) synthesis, Deleuze opens transcendental philosophy up to various speculative approaches, for example that found in the visions of Samuel Butler, which conceive of habit as the synthetic power of the complex material ensemble of reality:

> These component souls are of many and very different natures, living in territories which are to them vast continents, and rivers, and seas, but which are yet only the bodies of our other component souls; coral reefs and sponge-beds within us; the animal itself being a kind of mean proportional between its house and its soul, and none being able to say where house ends and animal begins, more than they can say where animal ends and soul begins.[101]

Even though the accusation of panpsychism as such is not wholly justified, it is also not without merit. The analysis of the third synthesis of time and the spatio-temporal dynamics of individuation especially are expressed in *Difference and Repetition* in distinctly transcendental philo-

---

[101] Samuel Butler, *Life and Habit* (London: A.C. Fitfield, 1910), p. 110.

sophical terms and retain a close methodological proximity to the phenomenological adherence to the maxims of reconstruction and evidence. This methodological "routing" on Deleuze's part results in a constant "zig-zag" between a quasi-phenomenological account of the rupture of the subjective order of the self, which leads to the genesis of consciousness as a psychic system from the sub-representational, and an anti-phenomenological account of the objective intensive processes that constitute the world (with or without the subjective order of actual consciousness) as ongoing self-referential becoming. This is what Brassier notices in Deleuze: "he is constantly equivocating between the claim that he is providing an account of the genesis of actual experience and the claim that he is giving an account of the genesis of actuality *tout court*."[102] Brassier's argument simply conflates the second genesis with the first, instead of conceiving of the genesis of experience as a "dimension" of the genesis of the world.

### *The Activity of Thought as Topological Operation*

The question of the subjective "ground" of individuation follows from Badiou's problematization of the Parmenidean identity of being and thinking in Deleuze. As we have seen, Badiou conceives of Deleuze's One/Being as life or production, which, due to its alignment with plenitude, affirmation and activity, rejects any subtractive logic. This productivity itself, or at least an aspect of it, is thought as a fold of being, the point of the identity of being and thought. However, to distinguish this folding from the production of (inert) simulacra, Badiou reintroduces the idea of the subject. The folding activity in and of thinking produces an "internal pocket,"[103] which doubles the coextensive outside. This "double" constituted qua thinking *is* the subject and hence the point of identity of being and thinking. Such a subjectivity, as Badiou acknowledges, is dissimilar to any Cartesian, Kantian or phenomenological account of subjectivity, since it is neither autonomous, constitutive nor spontaneous, and because

---

[102] Brassier, *Nihil Unbound*, p. 199.
[103] Badiou, *Deleuze: The Clamor of Being*, p. 89.

it is not separate from the outside, but is precisely exteriority folded in on itself. Viewed through the lens of the "paramount formal opposition of the active and the passive,"[104] which pervades much of Deleuze's work, this alignment of the fold, thinking and the subject falls in line with Badiou's aforementioned critique of the idea of inorganic life. In the same manner as he identifies the virtual with production (life), and thus demotes the actual to the order of passive products, he now ascribes activity to thinking, with the subject as the passive product of the topological operation of folding. Life—identified with Being, production, the virtual, the Fold, the Event and thinking—becomes pure creative activity. This despite Deleuze's constant protestations that at the heart of life is passivity.

Badiou and Brassier draw from Deleuze's Parmenidean identification of being and thinking two classical panpsychist impasses: either understanding psyche as a subjective aspect or as a property of everything. Parmenides's fragment 3 (Το γαρ αυτό νοείν εστίν τε και είναι) only states that, as Cornford has it, "[i]t is the same thing that can be thought and can be,"[105] but from this the panpsychist draws the conclusion: "whatever is, thinks." This leap already adds an unjustified qualification to being, namely that to be is to be a discrete object or thing. Both of Deleuze's detractors, however, accuse him of an even more absurd interpretation of the identity thesis, namely that "it is the same thing to think and to be." Yet, neither fragment 3, however outlandish the interpretation, nor fragment 8, which establishes the identity of thought and its object, say anything about the "thinker." Rather, fragment 3 seems to suggest that only being itself could be the thinker and therefore that being thinks itself. This translates only to the thinking of things if being is unjustly qualified as *exclusively* composed by them (e.g. according to Aristotle's physics of bodies), but the fragment makes no allusion to a subject or consciousness at all. The question of the subject only arises when not only being but also thinking is qualified retrospectively, by conceiving of thinking as a capa-

---

[104] Ibid., p. 52.
[105] Francis McDonald Cornford, *Plato and Parmenides* (London: Routledge, 1964), p. 43.

bility which implies a ground (the spontaneous subject) that this activity issues from, or even that something *is* by virtue of its thinking, which would allude to an auto-positional subject. Hence, Brassier proposes a subject (an actualized psychic system) as the agent of the eternal return to ground the capacity to think, i.e. to become equal to its intensive condition. Badiou, on the other hand, proposes that the subject is a necessary product of the *activity* of thinking as folding as an aspect of Being's productivity. In both cases, the assertion that a subject is *necessarily* implied in thinking is based on the assumption that thinking is an activity or capacity because Being is production.

### The Passivity of Thought

At first glance, Deleuze's universal individual seems to conform not to the identity thesis of Parmenides's fragments, but rather to the version Plato presents of Parmenides in the eponymous dialogue: "all things think."[106] As Grant notes, Parmenides's fragment 3 does not provide us with any clue as to whether the identity of being and thinking is said of the one or the many, either of the physics of the All or the physics of bodies/substances.[107] The Deleuzian identification of monism and pluralism further obfuscates the object and locus of the identity. While Deleuze rejects the subjectivist account of individualizing existents or objects, but ascribes to them the capacity to think, it is not clear how the identity of being and thinking is established in the One. One might construct the notion, according to the principle of Being as power, of a "being-thinking," with both terms united in an (epistemologically) indistinguishable One, or consider an aspect dualism like Spinoza's. Deleuze might be seen to either begin from the individuated individual, thus accepting the Platonist-Parmenidean idea of particulars that think, or from powers (κατά δύναμιν), in which case he could propose that being entails thinking. Both positions, however, contain an implicit asynchronicity and asym-

---

106  Plato, "Parmenides," in *Complete Works* (Indiana: Hackett Publishing, n.d.), 132c.
107  Iain Hamilton Grant, "All Things Think," in *Mind That Abides: Panpsychism in the New Millennium*, ed. David Skrbina (Amsterdam: John Benjamins Publishing, 2009), p. 284.

metry, in that, if there is thinking, then there is *necessarily* being, but not the reverse. In the first case, thinking can only be ascribed to everything once being has been qualified to consist only of beings. This, however, leaves the problem of the individuation of beings and what tools are left to account for the subject's individuation. In the second case, being would yield thinking, but due to the logical, causal or even temporal antecedence of being to thinking, they would not be the "same" all the time. Deleuze, however, does not espouse the panpsychist subjectivist account of thinking existents, nor the notion of a temporal or genetic difference between being and thinking; rather, he insists on the radical synchronicity of being and thinking by reconceptualizing thinking, not as production, activity or capacity, but as characterized by a specific passivity.

The monotony of Deleuze's work, what Badiou thinks of as his fidelity to the One, is expressed in the "subjective" nature of the Fold because it is the same as Memory, i.e. the virtual totality of the past, which is another name for Being. Even though the operation of memory is irreducible to the spontaneous act of the subject—in fact, the latter is a modality of the former —time, the subject/thought and the fold become identical at the moment of folding.[108] This, again, depicts memory, thought and folding (as aspects of the productivity of the One) as active against the backdrop of sensible time, which is passive. The active/passive dyad is used to collapse various operations into the activity of the One, e.g. in his characterization of the eternal return or the affirmation of chance in a single throw, "which returns as the active being of all casts."[109] Conversely, the products of the productivity of being are rendered inert or passive simulacra. While acknowledging a non-mechanical causality between events ("the communication of events") as well as their independence from efficient causality in relation to a state of affairs, Badiou ignores the often-repeated idea of an inverted causality in which states of affairs cause events in a non-active quasi-causality, i.e. serial interlacement. As *The Logic of Sense*

---

[108] See Badiou, *Deleuze: The Clamor of Being*, p. 90.
[109] Ibid., p. 113.

has it, there is an impassivity and sterility inherent to events.[110]

It seems, with respect to Deleuze's concept of inorganic life, that, to avoid the Kantian and Fichtean trappings of New Materialism, the panpsychism of Brassier's critique and the organicism alleged by Badiou, and to maneuver between the Charybdis of the epistemologically unsound metaphysics of self-organization and the Scylla of the epistemologically restrictive reinstitution of the subject, we will have to counter the shared assumption of all these claims: that Being/inorganic life is continuous active production and creativity. If Badiou is right that time and thought are inseparable for Deleuze, but he is wrong to claim that thought is just an aspect of the active production of the One or Life, then an understanding of time, thinking and their relation as passive will provide a deeper and even novel understanding of inorganic life. Everything hinges on a better understanding of the passivity at the heart of (inorganic) life, which, I claim, is provided by a radical reading of the third synthesis of time.

---

**110** Deleuze, *Logic of Sense*, p. 5–8, 20, 31, 63, 95–96, 100, 129.

# DEATH

### THIS EVENT, DEATH

*The (Im)possibility of Mourning*
In his eulogy for Deleuze, "I'm Going to Have to Wander All Alone," Derrida emphasizes how his old friend was a thinker not only of the Event but of *this* event: the singular event, but also the specific event of death. This characterization, at first glance, seems at odds with Deleuze's deeply held alliance with Spinoza, whose *Ethics* proclaims: "A free man thinks of nothing less than of death, and his wisdom is a meditation on life, not on death."[111] But Derrida mentions Deleuze's reference to Jos Bousquet, recounts Bousquet's substitution of his own "inclination to death" with a "longing for dying," and then quotes Deleuze's interpretation of this "apotheosis of the will":[112]

> [F]rom this inclination to this longing there is, in a certain respect, no change except a change of the will, a sort of leaping in place [*saut sur place*] of the whole body which exchanges its organic will for a spiritual will. It wills now not exactly what occurs, but something in that which occurs, something yet to come which would be consistent with what occurs, in accordance with the laws of an obscure, humorous conformity: the Event. It is in this sense that the *Amor fati* is one with the struggle of free men.[113]

This substitution of the organic with the spiritual will—paralleling the secret replacement of the Spinozist conatus, which remained beholden to a Greek notion of form, with the Nietzschean Will to Power—entails a (certain) Stoic ethics, which supersedes the conservative economy of the

---
111 Spinoza, "The Ethics," p. 235.
112 Bousquet as quoted in Deleuze, *Logic of Sense*, p. 149; see also Jacques Derrida, "I'm Going to Have to Wander All Alone," *Philosophy Today* 42, no. 1 (1998), p. 3.
113 Deleuze, *Logic of Sense*, p. 149.

organism and opens the individual up to (pre-personal) inorganic life: an ethics of the event.

One might begin to think this movement from the situation of the eulogy itself. The moment of death, as Benjamin has it, becomes the point where a life turns into a tale and is rendered communicable *as a whole*.[114] This endless source of stories that is someone's death opens the possibility of mourning as an event itself. Philosophy, when seen from this vantage point, has been in large part obsessed with finding the answer to the question of how one might mourn *one's own* death, while still being alive. Such untimely lamentations are expressed in two contrary approaches: Heidegger's, in which it is impossible to mourn, and Hegel's, in which it is impossible not to mourn.[115] Deleuze, as we will see, will resolve this antinomy.

Heidegger's recasting of the temporality of death in *Being and Time* means that Dasein is individuated within and through its existential situation of "being-towards-death" (*Sein zum Tode*).[116] Dasein is always already stretched ahead of itself into a future it projects, which consists in the possibilities ultimately totalized by its finitude, death. Even if Dasein is therefore characterized as care in general, i.e. the existential condition of being stretched ahead of itself, Dasein is individualized by the totality of possibilities that its "ownmost" death constitutes and to which Dasein is always in relation (even if it denies it). As such it is always "not-yet": there is always something incomplete in its constitution, which is not a lack, since this would presuppose a split or separation in the whole, impossible for Dasein. Rather, Dasein is always already oriented towards the end of all possibilities, wherein these possibilities are realized and completed and can finally be understood; where, in other words, Dasein

---

[114] See Walter Benjamin, "The Storyteller," in *Illuminations* (London: Fontana Press, 1992), p. 93.
[115] See Brent Adkins, *Death and Desire in Hegel, Heidegger and Deleuze*, 1st ed. (Edinburgh: Edinburgh University Press, 2008), p. 193. This categorization, of course, relies on Freud's typology in "Mourning and Melancholia"; see Sigmund Freud, "Mourning and Melancholia," in *The Standard Edition of the Complete Psychological Works of Sigmund Freud, Vol. 15* (London: Hogarth Press, 1962).
[116] Heidegger, *Being and Time*, p. 237.

is made "whole" and the "not-yet" dispelled—but at the same time the event of dying has not yet happened. It is therefore at its core assigned a task (care) that it cannot complete because its goal is the end of possibilities. Death, as Heidegger states, can therefore not be experienced, since it is what constitutes the individuality of Dasein by virtue of being always "not-yet." Hence, the totality of possibilities is the totality of experiences excluding the event that is finitude itself. Or, the impossibility of any experience of death is also the possibility of experience. This profound inability to experience death leads Heidegger to deny and defer mourning, making him melancholic.

As such, Dasein is a movement towards something a priori unobtainable, a movement in place, a κίνησις in place with nowhere to go. In this catatonic movement, however, Heidegger discovers a fundamental mood, which acts as an interruption, revealing every lived task as just one realized possibility among countless others and presenting the "nothing" as the foundation of Dasein's formation: anxiety.[117] Faced with the most radical, own-most and non-relational possibility of its death, Dasein's anxiety reveals—in Deleuzian terms—nothing but the zero degree of intensity around which all projects (constituting the possible) and hence experiences are oriented, but which is itself always absent, and so Dasein never advances to an experience of death. Heidegger discovers in his concept of anxiety the Deleuzian "model of death" which is also "the body without organs."[118] Dasein can either deny the implications of anxiety and seek refuge in the "they," or face them (i.e. its constitutive finitude) to properly individualize itself authentically.

Adorno, in his *Jargon of Authenticity*, captured the paradoxical situation of Dasein precisely: "Thus he [Heidegger] singles out his authentic death as something that is extremely real and at the same time beyond all facticity."[119] However, for Adorno, such a mode of authenticity sim-

---

[117] Martin Heidegger, "What Is Metaphysics?," in *Pathmarks* (Cambridge: Cambridge University Press, 1998), p. 91.
[118] Deleuze and Guattari, *Anti-Oedipus*, p. 329.
[119] Theodor W. Adorno, *The Jargon of Autheticity* (Evanston: Northwestern University Press, 1973), p. 148.

ply mirrors the capitalist constitution of the subject as atomized individual. It serves to refine and purify numerous social grievances by framing loneliness and solitude as a transcendental condition for Dasein's authentic mode of existence. Other social problems, like "homelessness," are removed from the sphere of politics and reinscribed in the language of "Eigentlichkeit" by Heidegger, which reinforces the urban anonymity he himself sought to escape.[120] The paradoxical individualization of Dasein, together with such mystifications of social ills, entail a language producing tautologies that must be preached not proven, since authenticity no longer serves as a subjective relation to morality nor as an empirical condition of it.[121] Upholding a religious allure and a sanctity in his manner of speaking, while having adjured all actual transcendence, Heidegger insists on the inescapability of the existential choice, at once solitary and heroic. Deleuze would agree with Adorno's estimation that Heidegger takes the privatized individual of capitalism as his model and extracts from it the conditions of possibility of experience. Both capitalism and Heidegger, according to Deleuze and Guattari, interiorize anti-production as the foundation of production. The existential-hermeneutic approach meanwhile, by focusing and limiting any account of constitution to the individual (Dasein), is unable to conceive of any forces that would produce the "nothing" and hence retrospectively establish anti-production as fundamental. Heidegger is, therefore, unable to conceive of the "desiring production" underlying or grounding "nothing."

If Heidegger has a model of death but permits no experience of it, Hegel, conversely, knows only an experience of death but no model of it. Rather than the melancholic refusal to mourn, Hegel is concerned with the constant and continuous replacement of the lost object with another, which is the basic topography of consciousness. Since every new form of

---

[120] See ibid., p. 58.
[121] Adorno writes: "Nevertheless, once authenticity can no longer be either the empirical condition of mortality or the subjective relating to it, then it turns into grace. It turns, as it were, into a racial quality of inwardness, which man either has or does not have—a quality about which nothing further can be stated than that, tautologically, there is mere participation in it." Ibid., p. 132.

consciousness emerges from the overcoming (or death) of the previous one, the *Phenomenology of Spirit* turns the natural negation into a spiritual one. The life of consciousness and its progression is not a life sheltered from devastation but is a life that *is* constantly contaminated with its own death in its conception: a dismembered life.[122] In terms of content this movement finds its completion in "Revealed Religion," while in form it is accomplished in "Absolute Knowing." During spirit's education, as Hegel insists on pointing out, each negation is only determinate negation and never absolute negation; hence, every previous stage is "aufgehoben" (sublated), i.e. negated, preserved and elevated.[123] The continuous death of stages of consciousness leaves traces, a ghostly presence, even though it replaces the objects of mourning. The work of mourning is also a production of ghosts. However, these specters never form a zero degree or body without organs, and nor are they the product of a substance. Rather, Hegel refuses a model of death by subjugating this movement to the subject (as the absolute). In a quite similar manner to Heidegger, one might argue, following Deleuze and Guattari, Hegel presents what is produced as the foundation. If we conceive, however, of the changes between states of consciousness as a series of intensive or affective states, even though Hegel would certainly dismiss that, then we discover through these changes the production of a subject that is no longer the absolute. The idea of the subject as the driving force of the transition between stages functions to smooth out these changes without relying on any outside to the system, i.e. a model of death. Consciousness progresses as the continuous experience of death without loss or outside, like capital that yields capital—an absolute system of production and consumption without exteriority. As antithesis to Heidegger, who represents the atomized individual of late capitalism, Hegel presents a consciousness modelled after the anonymous flows of capital, which beget more capital in a frictionless economy.

---

122 With unflinching clarity Hegel writes: "But the life of the spirit is not the life that shrinks from death and keeps itself untouched by devastation, but rather the life that endures it and maintain itself in it. It wins its truth only when in utter dismemberment, it finds itself." Hegel, *Phenomenology of Spirit*, p. 19.
123 See ibid., p. 28.

To repeat once more: while Hegel's continuous experience of death in the work of mourning denies any model of death, Heidegger's discovery of the model of death tied to Dasein's ownmost finitude disavows any experience of death. Deleuze, however, will attempt to think death in its twofold nature as both model and experience, anonymous and empirical.

*Becoming-Mortal*

The communicability of life as a whole is predicated on a power that drives the production or fabrication of such stories and prevents the dead from being forgotten. With one's death "the unforgettable emerges and imparts to everything that concerned him that authority which even the poorest wretch in dying possesses for the living around him."[124] An example from Deleuze is the odious Riderhood in Dickens's novel *Our Mutual Friend*, who on his death bed summons from the people around him "an eagerness, respect, even love, for the slightest sign of life."[125] But Deleuze urges us to consider the death of the animal as an equally potent source of thinking and writing. He writes in "Literature and Life":

> One becomes animal all the more when the animal dies; contrary to the spiritualist prejudice, it is the animal who knows how to die, who has a sense or premonition of death. Literature begins with a porcupine's death according to Lawrence or with the death of a mole in Kafka: "our poor little red feet outstretched for tender sympathy." Karl-Philipp Moritz (1756–1793) said, one writes for dying calves. Language must devote itself to reaching these feminine, animal detours, and every detour is a becoming-mortal.[126]

Against the existential hermeneutics of Heidegger, the suffering-based ethics of philosophers from Bentham to Singer, Kant's critical philosophy (with its spiritualist prejudice) as well as the ethics of alterity, Deleuze

---

[124] Benjamin, "The Storyteller," p. 93.
[125] Deleuze, "Immanence: a Life …," p. 28.
[126] Gilles Deleuze, "Literature and Life," *Critical Inquiry* 23 (1997), p. 226–227.

portrays the death of the animal not simply as a personal, empirical death but also as impersonal dying. While alive, the products of individuation can be easily mistaken for beings with personal identity by representational thought. But at the edges of life, when the process of individuation begins to fail, the anonymous process of production (inorganic life) comes to the fore and implicates me, even if I'm not the one who dies. The twenty-first paradox of *The Logic of Sense* captures this double structure of death with reference to Blanchot: "Death has an extreme and definite relation to me and my body and is grounded in me, but it also has no relation to me at all—it is incorporeal and infinite, impersonal, grounded only in itself."[127] There is an empirical individual (a person) that dies, but they do so by being gripped by an impersonal force. This death-event is the model for the event's double structure as such, at once embodied in an individual or person, i.e. a definite state of affairs in the present, and at the same time circumventing the present and only grounded in itself. The latter aspect of the event—neutral, impersonal and pre-individual—is the past and the future of the event only in and for itself: "neither general nor particular, *eventum tantum*."[128] The future has no presence beyond the continuous division between the past and future, it is rather an insistence than an existence. As such, death is not just one event among others, but every event is like death. It is the point at which the impersonal most clearly—with minimal phenomenality —"appears" as the counterpoint to every actualization. It denotes the point at which Chronos, as self-sufficient present, dies and one is therefore gripped by a becoming-mortal, the finite faced with the infinity of the *eventum tantum*. There is a constant experience of death in every event.

On the other hand, *Difference and Repetition* pushes this point in a different direction by making death the (speculative) center of psychic individuation.[129] Death presents us with the "ultimate problem" or Idea, with a concept without any possible intuition but nonetheless still insolubly

---

127 Deleuze, *Logic of Sense*, p. 151.
128 Ibid.
129 See Christian Kerslake, *Immanence and the Vertigo of Philosophy: From Kant to Deleuze* (Edinburgh: Edinburgh University Press, 2009), p. 90.

tied to the end(s) of the subject.[130] As such, the "the last form of the problematic" is also "the source of problems and questions,"[131] and therefore the condition for the self-reflection and auto-critique of philosophy itself. There is, hence, also a model of death in Deleuze that is not tied to the death of the individual but to the event as death. Inorganic life thus appears at this point as the impersonal aspect of the event as well as the last form of the problem conditioning the production of the individual.

### THE DOCTRINE OF DEATH

*The Transmutation of the Will*
At this point, Laruelle's objection to Deleuze's alleged equation of philosophy with the Real might serve as a transition between two incompatible readings of this interpretation of the *eventum tantum*. Laruelle proposes that Deleuze's Nietzschean philosophy employs the deductive maneuver typical of transcendental philosophy by first introducing a metaphysical principle which grounds the empirical (the Will to Power) and then, in a second step, producing the empirical from this principle via a transcendental principle (the Eternal Return). While the Will to Power and the Eternal Return appear indistinguishable, they differ functionally, the former being a metaphysical principle, the latter a transcendental principle. While the latter grounds the former, the former justifies the operations of the latter. The Eternal Return demands, as Laruelle shows, a choice or transformation of the will: the affirmation of the metaphysical one, the Will to Power, as transcendental principle. At the same time, this choice is not sovereign; it is a choiceless choice guided by an ethical injunction. We traced this idea in Deleuze above and were even able to extend the initial concern with the ethical injunction to the active vitalism Deleuze seems to espouse, which led us to consider the forms of panpsychism seemingly implied by Deleuze's notion of thought.

---

[130] See Deleuze, *Difference and Repetition*, p. 112.
[131] Ibid.

Let us return to the antithesis between the Gods and the anti-God in Deleuze's theory of action. Deleuze draws on the Stoic distinction between (physical) corporeal instances or states of affairs and incorporeal events, highlighting the possibility of their transposition onto the temporal distinction between Chronos and Aion. While all creatures are (empirical) finite creatures detached from the cosmic perspective and are therefore living in the time of Chronos, such instances of life are only thinkable if they are placed in relation to an ideal temporal mode (past and future), which is itself infinitely divisible; every moment *is* because it *becomes* in relation to every other moment. This unlimited dimension of time—the time of the event—is the empty form of time ungrounding the present; the third synthesis of time as presented in *Difference and Repetition*.[132] *The Logic of Sense* proposes that the problem underlying the distinction between Chronos and Aion is not metaphysical but primarily ethical in nature, and marks a shift from the Stoic metaphysics of Chrysippus to the ethical view of nature in Marcus Aurelius.[133] As John Sellars shows in his seminal study, Marcus Aurelius's problem consists in the fact that from the perspective of finite beings, the chain of all causal events might seem incomplete or contradictory: parasitic processes, meaningless deaths and so on might be perceived as faults of nature, either as the nature external or internal to ourselves.[134] Only from the cosmic perspective—only by seeing Nature as whole—can one perceive the harmonic, measured and wise composition of all causal interactions and therefore accept what happens as it happens: *amor fati*. The (metaphysical) distinction is therefore made to create the possibility of the ethical doctrine of *amor fati*. The One is divided into two. Deleuze therefore formulates his

---

132 Or, one might say, "Aiòn is an all-encompassing time structure, while Chronos on the other hand is merely its chronological and organized expression. Chronos actualises Aiòn and provides it with a livable form." Piotrek Świątkowski, *Deleuze and Desire: An Analysis of Logic of Sense* (Leuven: Leuven University Press, 2015), p. 169.
133 See Bowden, *The Priority of Events*, p. 22. Corry Shores stresses, with reference to Goldschmidt, that the Stoic conception of time in Chryssipus only has one notion of time. See Corry Shores, *The Logic of Gilles Deleuze: Basic Concepts* (London: Bloomsbury, 2021), p. 127f. With the ethical view of nature and the greater pragmatism of the later Stoics, especially Marcus Aurelius, the second notion of time emerges.
134 See John Sellars, *Stoicism* (Berkeley: University of California Press, 2006), p. 126–128.

philosophy of the event in terms of action. On the one hand, the Gods only know the eternal present (Chronos), fully actualized and immortal; they exhaust all potentialities at once, making past and future aspects of the present, i.e. they only exist in relation to it. On the other hand, the actor (meaning "agent" as well as "performer") has a present that is infinitesimally thin and punctual, an unlimited past-future. The empty present of the anti-God appears only as the point of segmentation, rupture or scission which divides past and future. Deleuze presents the actor as performing not a character but a role or "the components of the event [...] liberated from the limits of individuals and persons."[135] However, in the actualization of this event Deleuze ascribes an ontic distinctiveness to it that turns into an ontological difference:

> The actor thus actualizes the event, but in a way which is entirely different from the actualization of the event in the depth of things. Or rather, the actor redoubles this cosmic, or physical actualization, in his own way, which is singularly superficial—but because of it more distinct, trenchant and pure. Thus, the actor delimits the original, disengages from it an abstract line, and keeps from the event only its contour and its splendor, becoming thereby the actor of one's own events—a counter-actualization.[136]

The counter-actualization, here, understood as a break within the actual, seems to be engendered by the actor, even if he is acting a role not of his own design. The ethical injunction to move towards a cosmic perspective, later repeated as Spinoza's *sub specie aeternitatis*, therefore informs the metaphysical or ontological framework of Deleuze's philosophy and not the other way around.

---

[135] Deleuze, *Logic of Sense*, p. 150. The English translation of *The Logic of Sense* retains the double meaning of the original French "l'acteur" by translating it with "actor"; compare Gilles Deleuze, *Logique du Sens* (Paris: Les Éditions de Minuit, 1982), p. 179. Since this ambiguity is not translatable, the German version is more decisive and translates it as "Akteur," i.e. an agent as the subject of an action; Gilles Deleuze, *Logik Des Sinns* (Frankfurt am Main: Suhrkamp, 1993), p. 188.
[136] Deleuze, *Logic of Sense*, p. 150.

This opening towards Aion/the virtual in the physical Chronos is also an aperture towards the death drive in its speculative form. Here, the connection to *Difference and Repetition* is at its clearest. Deleuze states that: "If the eternal return has an essential relation to death, it is because it promotes and implies the death of everything that is one 'once and for all'."[137] Since time *only* produces difference/novelty, only difference returns and everything that *is* (as the Same, identity, the negative) and doesn't *become* will perish, never to return. From a Laruelleian perspective, we might extend our suspicion of the Stoic *amor fati* in *Logic of Sense* to the Nietzschean version in *Difference and Repetition*. The self-overcoming of nihilism is predicated on the Eternal Return it engenders. The ethical injunction and the transcendental principle are not asymmetrical *prima facie* but become so in the retrospective movement Deleuze makes according to the doctrine of the primacy of the practical, i.e. Deleuze discovers the Eternal Return while searching for a metaphysics to ground his ethics, but then makes this metaphysics conditioned on the ethics—the Fichtean movement.

This suspicion concerns the concept of "inorganic life" at its heart, since such a move makes it susceptible to all the forms of active vitalism we have highlighted above. Therefore, we must trace the consequences of this ethical injunction for "inorganic life" to then try to find an alternative route.

### The Death That Is, and Is Not

In *Specters of Marx*, Derrida proposes that "absolute evil" might be understood as "absolute life, fully present life, the one that does not know death and does not want to hear about it."[138] A life unscathed by death, which only considers finitude as an external rather internal event would end up framing the process of dying as contingent or meaningless when

---

137 Deleuze, *Difference and Repetition*, p. 115.
138 Jacques Derrida, *Specters of Marx: The State of the Debt, the Work of Mourning and the New International* (London: Routledge, 1994), p. 175; see also Bruce Baugh, "Death and Temporality in Deleuze and Derrida," *Angelaki: Journal for Theoretical Humanities* 5, no. 2 (2000).

considered from the perspective of the absolute. If we absent this specter of death from within life, "there would be no reason to care about life,"[139] since the very question of value is meaningless without finitude. *Prima facie*, Deleuze's account of the event as death, or rather inorganic life as the future, seems designed to escape such an account of fully present life. However, the issue is not with presence. The danger of Deleuze's ontology lies with infinity, which turns every form of finitude (especially dying) into a *function* of Life. This transmutation and devaluation of the death of the empirical subject is the actually the main point of the hyper-Nietzschean readings of Deleuze in Bennett and Braidotti.

Both versions of active vitalism start from a perspective of "energetic love for the world," because "you have to love life before you can care about anything."[140] Such a "profound love for Life as cosmic force" is expressed in the affirmation of a non-anthropocentric and even inorganic Life, i.e. the creative process (Being as difference-in-itself), which is only immanent to itself or simply "difference-at-work."[141] From this post-human perspective, human life might appear meaningless or absurd, but, as Bennett suggests, first we must overcome this "victimization" of the human by entering without resistance into the cosmic creative process.[142] This gradual dismantling of the human is a model for the attitude towards harm as such, which we—in an injunction very close to Nietzsche's Stoicism—should face with "amor fati," achieved through the "depersonalization of the event."[143] Finally, then, we might gain the insight that even death as the "ultimate subtraction is after all only another phase in a generative process."[144] In this onto-bio-political framework, the possibility of us being able to "take on the future affirmatively" with "deep and careless

---

139 Martin Hägglund, *Dying for Time: Proust, Woolf, Nabokov* (Cambridge, Mass.: Harvard University Press, 2012), p. 113.
140 Jane Bennett, *The Enchantment of Modern Life: Attachments, Crossings, and Ethics* (Princeton: Princeton University Press, 2001), p. 4.
141 Rosi Braidotti, "The Politics of 'Life Itself' and New Ways of Dying," in *New Materialisms: Ontology, Agency, Politics*, eds. Diana Coole and Samantha Frost (Durham, N.C.: Duke University Press, 2010), p. 210.
142 See Bennett, *The Enchantment of Modern Life*, p. 12.
143 Braidotti, "The Politics of 'Life Itself' and New Ways of Dying," p. 213.
144 Ibid., p. 212.

generosity" rests on the denial of death as a singular event and its integration into immanent life as the functor extracting the Event, i.e. death as the ultimate subtraction is the model for all subtraction *embedded* in the *eventum tantum*.

In this context, Derrida's warning about absolute life being absolute evil rings true, not because immanent Life is absolute presence, but because loss is expelled from it, in a fashion similar to what Derrida describes in *Cinder*. Every empirical loss, if viewed from the perspective of cosmic life, is transformed and sublimated in the *amor fati* gesture, and recoded as just another site of production. Deleuze's famous formula "it is organisms that die, not life"[145] is not a denial of the empirical death of the organism. Rather, in the transvaluation Bennett and Braidotti propose, this death ceases to be a loss; if viewed from the perspective of Life and the *necessity* of change, this perspective comes to us as an ethical injunction from Life itself. Life does not die and loss (empirical death) is continuously ejected by an ethical demand.

## Existence as a Test, or Stoicism

This ejection, however, is not congruent with the Spinozist claim that death is always caused by forces external to a body's essence.[146] Ontologies predicated on the rejection of death's redemptive or redeeming functions as transcendent limits to the immanent flourishing of life strive to overcome death through active joys (Spinoza), the eternal return (Nietzsche) or a becoming-active (Deleuze). Spinoza understands the body not through negation or limit, but as a finite mode of the infinite substance, i.e. as "a power of existing or acting"[147] or in Deleuzian terms a degree of power or intensity. Hence, it is defined less by what it is not than by its non-privative relation to the infinite. This is to say, a mode/body is singular in the sense explained in the chapter "Absolute Xenogenesis." Such a characterization thus considers both *this* degree of

---

**145** Deleuze, *Negotiations, 1972–1990*, p. 196.
**146** See Deleuze, *Spinoza, Practical Philosophy*, p. 12.
**147** Deleuze, *Expressionism in Philosophy*, p. 89, 183.

intensity (finite mode) and the composition (constitutive relations) as eternal.[148] If, then, each finite mode constitutes an "eternal truth"[149] independent from its actualization in existing bodies, since duration only applies to extensive bodies, how is there any room for death in this philosophy of life? The extensive parts of actual existing bodies come into existence through the laws of nature, i.e. laws external to the essence of a finite mode, which also determine the "encounter" of the various parts of the body. Hence, the extensive parts of the body are extensive to each other and externally determined. The essence then is *expressed* through and in these extensive parts but is not constituted by them. Each finite mode thus endures as long as the relations between the extensive parts it expresses remain, but if the extensive parts enter into a relation with external forces incompatible with this organization and the forces it has, the existing body, as the expression of this essence, ceases to exist.[150] Hence, death is not internal to life, but always an accident, a chance encounter of forces with a body which cannot endure them without losing the relations that express its essence.[151] But because, and not in spite of, this externality of death to life, "there is no death that is not *brutal, violent* and *fortuitous*."[152] According to Deleuze, the same externality of death to life that makes every death an irredeemable accident is also the antidote to this loss. In a Nietzschean move, he writes that "[e]xistence itself is" transformed into "a kind of test [...] a physical or chemical test, like that whereby workmen test the quality of some material."[153] Passing this test entails living life as fully as possible in accordance with one's singular essence, since then, having exhausted the internal potentialities of this finite mode, this person has nothing to lose in death but all external determinations—a true Stoicism.

Badiou surmises a philosophy of death is secretly lurking in this ascesis:

---

148   See ibid., p. 304.
149   Ibid., p. 312.
150   See ibid., p. 238; see also Deleuze, *Spinoza, Practical Philosophy*, p. 21.
151   See Deleuze, *Spinoza, Practical Philosophy*, p. 100.
152   Deleuze, *Expressionism in Philosophy*, p. 239.
153   Ibid., p. 317.

if the event of thought is the ascetic power of letting myself be chosen (the Deleuzian form of destiny) and being borne, qua purified automaton, wherever hubris carries me; if, therefore, thought exists as the fracturing of my actuality and the dissipation of my limit; but if, at the same time, this actuality and this limit are, in their being, of the same "stuff" as that which fractures and transcends them (given that there is, definitively, only the One-All); and if, therefore, powerful inorganic life is the ground both of what arrays me in my limit and of what incites me, insofar as I have conquered the power to do so, to transcend this limit: then it follows that the metaphor for the event of thought is dying, understood as an immanent moment of life.[154]

Badiou is very clear in pointing out the double function of inorganic life: on the one hand the constitutive capacity to determine finite empirical beings and on the other hand what "incites" them to transform the will from organic to spiritual, i.e. *amor fati*. He therefore frames this explicitly not as mere *posse esse* or potentiality, but as an ethical injunction or temptation towards "authentic being" that grasps and becomes equal to its impersonal aspect or internalizes its pre-personal exteriority, meaning death. Furthering this point, *Logics of Worlds* thus aligns phenomenology with vitalism again, insofar as for both, "[t]o exist [...] means to be in the constituent movement of originary over-existence. In other words, to exist is *to be constituted* (by consciousness or life)."[155] In this constitutional binding of the finite to the infinite, the former is thus revealed to be nothing but its own dissolution in the latter, and precisely this "death" of the finite is ultimate proof of the power of the infinite. The Stoic indifference to death, therefore, is not merely due to the insignificance of actual empirical beings when measured against the infinite (Life), but is precisely an asymmetrical difference constituted by judging empirical beings from their furthest point (death), i.e. their ability to incorporate

---

[154] Badiou, *Deleuze: The Clamor of Being*, p. 12.
[155] Badiou, *Logics of Worlds*, p. 267.

death. As Mullarkey notes, "[v]irtualism judges *against* judgement"[156] and thus ontologizes an ethical position that advocates that the death of the individual is to be read as a sign of the powerful sovereignty of Life. As we have already mentioned in the last chapter, such a judgement is justified by a form of *sight* rooted in the specific experience of *beautitudo*, which had to be experienced to be believed, while in turn this experience already presupposed the sight it sought to ground.

Here, we seem to have reached a paradoxical point. We have attempted to show that for Deleuze, although he is still beholden to a version of it, the Bergsonian form of intuition is methodologically inadequate to grasp the unlivable or inorganic life.[157] However, the ethical injunction of Life to intensify, i.e. the demand for a finite being to incorporate death by living according to the possibilities of its eternal essence, must be instated and needs a register. Intuition served the dual role of inciting becomings *and* giving them a measure, meaning that it limited them to what the organism could register and endure. So, if this insistent demand for intensification persists but cannot be registered, measured and contained by intuition, i.e. if the injunction to intensify is unbound from the finite being and its lived experience completely, then inorganic life becomes unbound destruction—as we find in the libidinal materialism of Nick Land.

### THE THANATROPIC REASON OF UNBOUND INORGANIC LIFE

*Nick Land's Libidinal Materialism*

From the inception of the question of the living in Aristotle, Life and the living encounter each other in a mereological disproportion. While the living are the empirical manifestation of Life, the latter is never exhausted by the sum total of the individuals within it, and nor does their death diminish its power. Rather, the death of the individual propagates Life, which is a creative and destructive process indifferent to its instanti-

---

[156] Mullarkey, *Post-Continental Philosophy*, p. 36.
[157] See section "Speculative Hylozoism" in this book.

ations.¹⁵⁸ Even though Deleuze rejects such Schopenhauerian pessimism on the grounds of its misconception of Life as numerically one and unitary (a misconception about Schopenhauer on Deleuze's part as well),¹⁵⁹ there is a point at which their philosophies converge, which we might call their libidinal-transcendental materialism.

Land's "machinic practicism" emerges from a radicalization of the movement of destratification described by Deleuze and Guattari, which he extends to Kant's critical philosophy to level the transcendental/empirical difference. In the same manner as for Deleuze, this rejection of the structural condition of critical philosophy results in a critique and ultimately in a disapproval of representational thought as an illegitimate use of syntheses. However, as Deleuze and Guattari do in *Anti-Oedipus*, Land holds on to the Kantian notion of the primacy of transcendental synthesis, reconceptualizing it as the synthesis of matter itself. Since synthesis is the conjoining of heterogeneous terms, the process is productive, spawning new differences and triggering new syntheses. Untethered from any empirical experience rooted in a constitutive subject, synthesis denotes here the primary process of the self-differentiation of matter and its continuous production of production without outside.¹⁶⁰ This autoproduction thus becomes the production of the real understood as a function of matter itself, i.e. the productive product of continuous machinic construction—a techno-cosmos. The desire expressed in this desiring production, as Deleuze and Guattari already had it, is thus not human anymore; the empirical human being (understood as a subject as well as

---

158 See Eugene Thacker, "Darklife: Negation, Nothingness and the Will-to-Life in Schopenhauer," *Parrhesia* 12 (2011), p. 28.
159 Deleuze's rejection of Schopenhauer is rooted in a mereological misunderstanding inherited from Nietzsche. Deleuze claims that Schopenhauer conceptualizes Life/Will as destructive because it is essentially numerically one and unitary (see Deleuze, *Nietzsche and Philosophy*, p. 79), but the latter's claim is far more nuanced. As Welchman notes, Schopenhauer might be ambiguous about the correct mereological status of the Will on first glance, but this follows from his peculiar position: that the Will is neither unified nor multiple, since every unity or multiplicity can only be understood as the contrary of the other. See Arthur Schopenhauer, *The World as Will and Representation* (Cambridge: Cambridge University Press, 2010), p. 137f. Hence, Will is neither identity nor difference, which makes him unappealing for Deleuze; see Welchman, "Schopenhauer and Deleuze," p. 244.
160 Land, "Machinic Desire," p. 320f.

organic being) is merely "*a* part" of the machine that is the transcendental unconscious of the primary process. The Kantian subject is only produced at the edge of an impersonal production and thus any alignment of thinking with an autonomous subjectivity is broken. Instead, "[t]hought is a function of the real, something that matter can do."[161] It follows, then, that all conceptual distinctions, as well as representational thought itself, must be produced as a function of matter as well.

It is exactly at this point that his critique of metaphysics turns into a metaphysics of critique. Representational thought, according to Land, might emerge from the primary process but only as a transcendental illusion, i.e. in the illegitimate use of a synthesis. If everything is produced by the machinic unconscious and nothing is given, thinking thus cannot be oriented towards the congruence between ideas and things (or concepts and objects), but must itself be a praxis of the schizophrenic process of matter itself. Investigating the conceptual structures of "given" reality or the intelligible conditions of transcendental consciousness would therefore be an illegitimate use of synthesis rooted in a misunderstanding about the nature of matter and thought.[162] On the contrary, as the rhizomatic or schizophrenic mappings of *A Thousand Plateaus* suggest, the process of thinking and the thoughts produced amplify each other if they trace the productive process of matter itself. Thinking is becoming equal to and enacting matter's creativity by following its tendencies and movements. This Deleuzian epistemology, which we have already described in the section "The Inorganic Life of the Ideas," is no longer aligned with the distinction between truth or falsity, but with the singular and the ordinary. The common or ordinary is aligned with stratified or molar organizations, while the singular is always only molecular and smooth but covered over by the former; inorganic flows of intensities are everywhere calcified into rigid organic structures. For Land, then, thinking is inseparable from a process of destratification and therefore intensification. He

---

[161] Ibid., p. 322.
[162] See Nick Land, "Circuitries," in *Fanged Noumena: Collected Writings 1987–2007* (Windsor Quarry: Urbanomic, 2014), p. 302.

transposes this claim into politics, as Deleuze and Guattari do as well, with a call for the intensification of machinic production to transform it into the deterritorializing and destratifying movement of the "schizo." Instead of succumbing to the retardation of the primary process which representational thought and stratification instill, Land proposes constant acceleration and intensification as imperatives for political action, i.e. the destruction of every obstacle to the free expression of matter's production. Philosophy thus becomes both the organon and location of the reversal of the rigidity of structure, unity and tranquility that has dominated occidental thought.[163]

### Absolute Delimitation and Machinic Death

In a ferocious radicalization of *Anti-Oedipus*'s materialism, Land thus urges us to deterritorialize and destratify on a cosmic scale to counter the always already existing surplus of stratification or neuroticization. This constant acceleration only has a seeming limit: the catatonic schizophrenic body of anti-production, or death. However, Land identifies this body without organs as the *focus imaginarius* of any critique as such, describing such a death as the death of identity itself, i.e. the death of the organism frees the smooth surface of transcendental difference from the former's colonizing grasp.[164] Deleuze and Guattari are still concerned with tracing how pre-capitalist societies kept this cosmic schizophrenia in check, while for Land it needs to not only be liberated but introjected. Following this thanatropic logic, exploring the inorganic life *within* the organism is insufficient, instead it needs to be freed from the organism wherever it is found to be bound by it. Again, the death of the individual organism is sublated into a more fundamental movement of Life (or the machinic unconscious), which rids this movement of its empirical basis.

If, however, everything is the production of production, below and

---

**163** Nick Land, "Delighted to Death," in *Fanged Noumena: Collected Writings 1987–2007* (Windsor Quarry: Urbanomic, 2014), p. 125.
**164** See Nick Land, "Making It with Death: Remarks on Thanatos and Desiring Production," in *Fanged Noumena: Collected Writings 1987–2007* (Windsor Quarry: Urbanomic, 2014), p. 274.

above the threshold of the organism and all empirical individualized subjects, then this radicalized libidinal materialism encounters a methodological problem. As we have already seen, Deleuze must take recourse to Bergsonian intuition to be able to trace the intensive differences enveloped in extensive differences. For Bergson, however, such qualitative differences had a phenomenological correlate which manifested as a (lived) experience that is registered by an organism. As we saw in the section "Speculative Hylozoism," such a methodology is not suited to tracing unlivable, intensive differences or the pre-personal transcendental because to do so it would have to rely on a paradoxical "immediate givenness." With Land, this problem returns insofar as he cannot take (spurious) recourse to the intensification of experience, since the primary process circumvents all stratified registers (such as the organism's). If there is no "givenness," since everything is the production of production and there is no representation, the machinic unconscious of production thus seems *essentially* foreclosed to humanity and organisms. Lyotard, reacting to Deleuze and Guattari's *Anti-Oedipus*, already drew the consequences from this peculiar darkness. If all intensive differences are differences in kind inaccessible to representational thought, and if organisms or subjects are no longer the law-giving grounds for judgements but products of a material process indifferent towards them, then no resistance to the ever-intensifying processes of capitalism would be possible; no fulcrum for a ground to do so could be established which is not immediately subject to destratification. In lieu of any justification for the distinction between "good" revolutionary desire and "bad" fascist desire and hence any moral orientation, one must fall back on a cynical affirmation of intensification without pre-given plan.[165]

This inability to access production is not a problem for Land, since he has long abandoned the idea of humanity as the actor and enactor of the primary process; humans are rather just another stratification to be

---

[165] Jean-François Lyotard, *Économie Libidinale* (Paris: Les Éditions de Minuit, 1974), p. 311. For an in-depth discussion of this impasse in Lyotard's politics of libidinal economy, see Peter Kenneth Drews, *Logics of Disintegration: Post-Structuralism and the Claims of Critical Theory* (London: Verso, 1987), p. 138.

overcome. Due to this epistemic foreclosure of matter-flows, epistemology must eventually collapse into an ethics of absolute praxis, i.e. in the absence of any possible orientation one can only abandon "what" one *is* and become equal to the primary process. Unbound from experience (in organic terms), the process of intensification becomes the acceleration of material processes without limits, and thus, the approximation of cosmic schizophrenia becomes the normative core of libidinal materialist vitalism. Here, the hidden teleology of the ethical injunction embedded in active vitalism is laid bare, unconcealed by any promise of *beatitudo* or feeling of power. Being is becoming/Life. One ought to become equal to becoming, because otherwise one would hinder becoming/Life. One becomes equal to Life by intensification. Therefore, one ought to intensify. Spinoza and Nietzsche had attempted to justify the dubious premise that one ought not to inhibit Life with experiences that they could not prove but that they enticingly declared. Without such promises, vitalism becomes a self-contained, self-justifying and empty ethical injunction.

Paradoxically, this radical anti-dialectic ultimately mimics a Hegelian movement; it is a Hegelianism without the subject as the absolute. By infinitely affirming the ethical injunction to reintegrate all secondary processes (strata, organisms, territories) into the primary process, i.e. introjecting "death," Land conjures a serpent of absolute production as the ultimate figure of the process (akin to Hegel's serpent of absolute knowledge). This expulsion of the living from the process of production, following a thanatropic logic, parallels what Marx called "high organic composition production." In production settings with a high ratio of constant capital to variable capital, the replacement of (fragile and slow) labor power by machinery accelerates production to the (relative) speed-limit of the most cutting-edge technology of the time.[166] Approximating the absolute acceleration of frictionless, instant production, high tech capitalism's *focus imaginarius* is a "zero-work paradox," i.e. a system that generates an average profit range without human laborers, relying on ma-

---

[166] Karl Marx, *Das Kapital. Kritik Der Politischen Ökonomie, Vol. 1*, vol. 23, Marx-Engels Werke (Berlin: Dietz, 1988), p. 640.

chinery alone. Such (potentially infinite) "high organic composition" production would create profit competitively only if it could expand over the whole of the planet, making laborers obsolete everywhere by cutting out their troublesome psychological complexity and error-prone bio-machinery. This expulsion of the human from the process of production in machinic capitalism is today repeated in the de-anthropomorphizing tendency in philosophy, which dissolves the human into ever larger networks or into the all-encompassing process of Life. In the name of Life every loss, frailty, madness and death is sublated into a spiritual will or *amor fati*.

Nothing is ever lost. Everyone is a winner.

*Becoming-Loser and the Virus of Sadness*

As George Caffentzis explains, Marx already foresaw that an apparently infinite extension of high organic composition production on a planetary or cosmic scale would not yield the profits one might expect. Rather, the law of value holds also in this case since products of high organic composition production usually exchange above their value and commodities from lower organic composition production below it. The rate of profit in high organic composition can thus only stabilize through the "existence of a much greater mass of labor-power exploited in spheres of production with extremely low organic composition."[167] The end of high organic composition production (i.e. taking over and transforming the whole sphere of production) is at the same time the destruction of its condition of possibility (labor-intensive production of lower organic composition spheres). The approximation of the state of absolute frictionless, machinic production without remainder (i.e. pure Life) is, as Nick Land acknowledged, a race towards death. The only way for Life (pure machinic production) to accelerate or intensify is to rely on the loss and the losers implicated in the winnings who constitute its *internal* limit. The staving off of human frailty (finitude) in the name of Life recapitulates

---

[167] George Caffentzis, "Why Machines Cannot Produce Value," in *Cutting Edge: Technology, Information Capitalism and Social Revolution*, ed. Jim Davis and Thomas Hirschl (London: Verso, 1997), p. 31.

the parallel movement wherein new ways of thinking become news of living, but to hygienic ends. As Baudrillard notes, this end of humanity was heralded by such hygienic efforts:

> It would not be too farfetched to say that the extermination of mankind begins with the extermination of germs. Man, with his humors, his passions, his laughter, his genitalia, his secretions, is really nothing more than a filthy little germ disturbing the universe of transparency. Once everything will have been cleansed, once an end will have been put to all viral processes and to all social and bacillary contamination, then only the virus of sadness will remain.[168]

Everything is haunted by loss. Everyone might be a loser.

The idea that it is the essence of a finite mode to open itself up to the intensive power of inorganic life makes a possibility into a demand: one must do this or fail the test of existence. Nietzsche's "last man" flunks the "test of life," unable to overcome his internalized dialectic of self-limitation. But, as Derrida would argue, the deck might have been stacked against him from the start. For an actual existence to measure up to the eternal essence it actualizes nothing less is demanded than the renunciation of its actual existence itself. Deleuze rejected the horizontal function of death, i.e. it neither structures temporality nor does it follow from temporality *necessarily*. It is always only an accident brought about by the fortuitous interaction of extrinsic parts of existing modes. Derrida vehemently objects to this line between internal life and external death, since it prevents the actual existing parts of a being from having any effect or being in any way involved in the affirmation of life.[169] If a mode's essence is eternal (i.e. independent from its temporal determination), then the actual existence and duration of a finite mode neither adds to nor subtracts from the essence's determination. Deleuze clarifies that duration qualifies the existence of modes, but only in the way that time is the measure

---

[168] Jean Baudrillard, *The Ecstasy of Communication* (Los Angeles: Semiotext(e), 2012), p. 37.
[169] Jacques Derrida, *Life Death* (Chicago: Chicago University Press, 2020), p. 25.

of an essence's power of acting, i.e. the affects within time increase or decrease the mode's power of acting, while "states of essences are always as perfect as they can be."[170] If the essence of the mode is therefore not determined by the existence of external parts actualizing it *in time*, is it then not always already "after life" or "beyond life," i.e. beyond the variations of duration?

Thus, Derrida's analysis of Deleuze's philosophy of life would arrive at a similar point to Badiou's. Even if the actual moment of death of an empirical finite mode is only ever an event extrinsic to the mode's essence, the event of dying is always an eternal event contemporaneous with a lived duration (or *my* duration).[171] So, from the perspective of *sub specie aeternitatis* death is always extrinsic and Life eternal, but from the point of view of an embodied empirical subject, it is exactly *this* Life that presents itself as the continuous event of dying. Dying thus presents itself as the eternal *necessity* for empirical beings. From a Derridean perspective, it seems that every coming into existence of a mode would entail the death of another, since the prior mode's external parts are now subsumed under the new one. However, by conceiving of the event as continuous dying, Deleuze is (or would be) able to entertain a concept of temporality which might counter this Derridean logic of finitude. If the extended parts of modes are continuously brought into existence at the same moment as the Idea (essence) is determined, then the beginning of the existence of a mode within duration could be necessary while its end is not.

### THE DEMAND OF INASSIMILABLE INORGANICITY

*The Anterior Posteriority of the Death Drive*

The death drive, understood as trauma without any binding function, as we have presented it above, appears to be an anti-image of the hedonic regulation of psychic life on an empirical level. Topologically speaking,

---

170 Deleuze, *Spinoza, Practical Philosophy*, p. 40.
171 See Deleuze, *Logic of Sense*, p. 51.

however, both are consistent if not congruent, because Freud's discovery of an investigation into the unconscious has never been anything other than a "spectral archaeology."[172] From the earliest works on, the unconscious does not exist independently but rather *haunts* conscious life in the form of glitches or slides in everyday life, which are nonetheless constitutive of the latter. It marks the point at which consciousness becomes inconsistent or divided and therefore *insists* rather than exists, unrecognizable and unrecognized. It is a reservoir of unexperienced or repressed experiences, which nevertheless emerge as impossible recollections, as the insistence of a past which expresses itself only in affective antithesis. As such, the "timeless" unconscious has, in its expression as mark, trace or haunting, a specific relation to time. Moreover, one might say that Freud's diagnoses of pathologies describe specific or peculiar temporalities or relations to time.[173] His spectral archaeology reveals a temporal typology.[174]

In *Beyond the Pleasure Principle* Freud finds himself unable to explain the progression of a World War I veteran's psychological traumata[175] — especially his nightmares — within the sexual aetiology of the pleasure principle, and thus supplements his theory with a speculative hypothesis: the death drive. This interrogation of the depths of bodily drives anticipates the hauntological approach, presenting the death drive not a force distinct from the pleasure principle, but as a denaturalization of the seemingly natural teleology of the drives; it disorients pleasure and pain. Em-

---

172  Justin Clemens, Jon Roffe, and Adam John Bartlett, *Lacan Deleuze Badiou* (Edinburgh: Edinburgh University Press, 2014), p. 50; see also Schuster, *The Trouble with Pleasure*, p. 33.
173  E.g. melancholia, the refusal or inability to mourn, not only actively refuses to accept the loss of an incorporated object (and therefore refuses to unbind libidinal forces from it), but refuses to accept loss as such. It purports a temporality without the experience of loss, which is nevertheless determined by loss.
174  Adrian Johnston's innovative study on the essential splitting of the drive underlines this insight: "Psychoanalysis is, fundamentally, a *philosophical* insight into the subject's relationship with temporality." Johnston, *Time Driven*, p. xxix.
175  To this, Freud adds further situations that are not explicable by the rule of the pleasure principle: the "fort-da game," the peculiar forms in which patients repeat the past and their resistance to the results of the analysis, and the strange case of fate (as the compulsive repetition of previous structures or failures).

pirically, such a compulsion appears as a break or hindrance of the vitalist "natural attitude" towards the effortless flow of life, which is, however, a resistance from within. The drive for thanatropic regression doesn't conform to the organism, but is rather presented to it as the demand of a repressed primordial past—the call of the inorganic. With an anti-Spinozist twist, Freud states:

> If we are to take it as a truth that knows no exception that everything living dies for internal reasons—becomes inorganic once again—then we shall be compelled to say that "the aim of life is death" and, looking backwards, that "inanimate things existed before living ones" [...] For a long time, perhaps, living substance was thus being constantly created afresh and easily dying, till decisive external influences altered in such a way as to oblige the still surviving substance to diverge ever more widely from its original course of life and to make ever more complicated detours before reaching its aim of death.[176]

Here, Freud tries to be both Newton and Kant, concerned with the (empirical) physics of pleasure and the (speculative) conditions of the pleasure principle.[177] Ultimately, the transcendental will not only ground but undermine the self-sufficiency of the empirical. Thanatos is described here as the compulsive recapitulation of phylogenetic origins in organic ontogenesis. In the pre-history of life, organic interiority emerges from its inorganic origins by binding exteriority (death) in a dynamic interplay, e.g. by separating the interior of the organism from stimuli it is not able to incorporate into its conservative economy, using an outer layer that is "dead," and also, therefore, exterior. The death drive is an instinct that strives to repeat this scission which it itself is a trace of. In other words, the organism strives to repeat its own traumatic origin in the inorganic, or death. However, "that trace is the marker of an exorbitant death, one

---

[176] Sigmund Freud, *Beyond the Pleasure Principle* (New York: W.W. Norton & Company, 1961), p. 32.
[177] See Gilles Deleuze, "Coldness and Cruelty," in *Masochism* (New York: Zone Books, 1991), p. 112.

that even in dying, the organism cannot successfully repeat."[178] This impotence to repeat it is grounded in the peculiar temporality of the drive, of which three aspects are key. Firstly, since the inorganic is older than the organic and hence predates any possible empirical instances of organic life, the compulsion demands an impossible repetition, the recapitulation of a time that has *empirically* never been. Secondly, unlike symptoms that have an explicit binding function, thanatropic regression refuses integration into the habits, rhythms, thresholds and organization of psychic life ruled by the pleasure principle. It appears, therefore, at once destructive and pointless from the perspective of the bound organism—as pure Schopenhauerian blind will. The drive is essentially a-rhythmic. And lastly, what the drive demands is not within time but the *end* of time as such, in the form of a return to before its *beginning*. Paradoxically then, the death drive finds its end (and satisfaction) only in the universal cosmic dispersion of its host, i.e. in its self-destruction.

The compulsion towards thanatropic regression is thus a demand for organic life to integrate the trauma of its inorganic origins into its conservative economy. Although the organism always bears the trace of this scission, and is haunted by it, the demand proves to be impossible to fulfill. This means that the objective truth of the death drive is instated for the organism *a posteriori* (as the demand of the inorganic), while it is nevertheless for organic subjectivity *a priori*. Structurally, it is similar to what Levinas, in regard to the Other, called an "anterior posterior."[179] Not determinable by resemblance or analogy, Freud's speculative death drive is transcendental precisely as an impossible condition, an inassimilable traumatic ground (or unground). Unlike the constant tendency towards economic assimilation in the pleasure principle or the pragmatic survivalism of the reality principle, the death drive does not make death an inflection of life, but the reverse. Death is thus no longer the teleological end of organic life, "but rather life is a temporary anomaly in the order of

---

[178] Brassier, *Nihil Unbound*, p. 238.
[179] Levinas, *Totality and Infinity*, p. 170.

dysteleological death."¹⁸⁰ Being the medium of dissipation, the actualization of thanatropic regression is guided by the conservative economy of the organism. The incompatibility of the exorbitant demand of inorganic exteriority (the logic of dissipation) and the demand of the organic (the logic of sustenance) cannot be resolved instantaneously but follows the law of affordability of the bound organism. The qualitative and quantitative dissolution of all tension, the regression towards death, is thus always individual, since it is bound to the specific organism's inherent exigencies. Even if it might appear empirically as if the organic tendency towards negentropic complexity counteracted such dissolution, these are mere postponements of absolute entropy, the specific way the organism can fulfill the transcendental demand within the individual economic constraints of the organism. Weismann had even shown that in highly dynamic systems such complexity might accelerate the speed of dissipation.[181] Thus, "death needs time for what it kills to grow in [it]."[182] In other words, to kill each organism in the way immanent to it, death must take an indirect route. This detour (*Umweg*) is called life.

### The Death Drive's Non-Dialectical Negativity

The radical 'anterior posteriori' temporality of the trace of "aboriginal" or pregenetic death not only preclude it from being accessed by or from conforming to transcendental subjectivity, but also prevents any dialectical sublation. It introduces a radical temporal linearity that subverts the Hegelian circle. The "circle" of the dialectic's final form or rather the circular movement the dialectic is oriented towards might always be individual (or unique), as is the Freudian detour towards death called life, but the Hegelian topology describes a circle as the end point of a cycle of spirit's expression of its differential power of negation until, in the end, having traversed all possible expressions of negativity, it incorporates negativity (i.e. absorbs and absolves it) in the ultimate closure of

---

[180] Lindner, "Absolute Xenogenesis: Speculations on an Unnatural History of Life," p. 262.
[181] Freud, *Beyond the Pleasure Principle*, p. 43.
[182] William S. Burroughs, "Ah Pook the Destroyer," in *Dead City Radio* (London: Island, CD, 1990).

the totality. The topology must become its own projection temporally. In other words, Deleuze insists against Kant that the concept must form itself within the tumult of temporal becoming; once the circle is attained no repetition of the circle of the "piste" leading up to it can be repeated. Every ground is already recovered and hence there is nothing to repeat. Whatever appeared contingent in the process is transformed into necessity as the necessary contingency of every prior sublated movement. The way in which the concept becomes itself thus relies on the temporal vicissitude Hegel inscribes in it in the form of the determinate negation.

As Bataille, Foucault and Derrida attest, the essential relation and mutual determination of circularity, negation and temporality in the Hegelian dialectic cannot be simply dissolved without either falling back behind Kant or being inadvertently ensnared by even stronger problems of dialectical thought.[183] Schopenhauer, Kierkegaard and Nietzsche already sought to de-naturalize or de-essentialize these relations by supplying thought with the armamentarium to conceive of something that Hegelian dialectics excludes, i.e. an operation, relation or (non-)being, which could not be recovered and absorbed by and in the concept, something that is repeated endlessly because it resists the closure of totality. However, as Derrida rightly interjects, how can such a thing be conceived of, if re-presenting it already makes it susceptible to being incorporated into the dialectic?

Freud's death drive presents an answer to this, since it is "a negativity that escapes the concept,"[184] a "non-dialectical negativity"[185] or a negativity without negation. Derrida was interested in this peculiar resistance as it appears in analysis: as the refusal of the analysand to accept the results of the analysis. In Freud's earlier works such a resistance could still be integrated into the hermeneutic framework of analysis itself, but in the later

---

[183] See Benjamin Noys, *The Persistence of the Negative: A Critique of Contemporary Continental Theory* (Edinburgh: Edinburgh University Press, 2010), p. 8–10.
[184] Clemens, Roffe, Bartlett, *Lacan Deleuze Badiou*, p. 53.
[185] Reza Negarestani, "Drafting the Inhuman: Conjectures on Capitalism and Organic Necrocracy," in *The Speculative Turn: Continental Materialism and Realism*, ed. Levi R. Bryant, Nick Srnicek, and Graham Harman (Melbourne: Re.Press, 2011), p. 197.

works this compulsion radically refuses interpretation. It is a drive to repeat, a resistance, without inherent meaning and refusing any ascription of meaning through analysis. What the spectral archaeology unearths is a compulsion which is "analytic" in a double sense. It returns to its origin (or aboriginal trauma), and it dismantles or takes apart every complex structure. Thus, in the heart of psychoanalysis resides a drive that resists analysis and is the impossible condition of meaningful psychic life. Psychoanalysis, thus, resists itself and with that rejects the possibility of an archive free from contamination.[186] The Hegelian circle is just such a collection of filing cabinets, but the death drive prevents the final piece from being put in its place. There is always already a fire in the archive. Things will have to be sorted anew, must be continued and expanded on. The circle is always out of alignment with itself.

There is "always already" something dead within the living. The machine, the apparatus, with its repetitions without internal end, *haunts* the organism as its inassimilable trauma.[187] There is no pure life, there is only a life/death rejecting all conceptual sublation.[188]

*Further Beyond the Pleasure Principle*

This "demonic" power repeats itself in Deleuze when he aligns Freud's notion of neurosis with Kierkegaard's concept of repetition and Kant's paradox of asymmetrical objects as examples of repetitions which pose a problem for representation, but which are integrated into or disavowed by the logic of representation, their productive power obscured.[189] With the death drive, Freud had provided an even clearer example of a repetition (constitutive for experience), which rejected its subsumption under the law-governed structures of representation.[190] However, as Deleuze

---

186  See Jacques Derrida, *Resistances of Psychoanalysis* (Stanford: Stanford University Press, 1997), p. 24.
187  See Jacques Derrida, *Writing and Difference* (London: Routledge, 2001), p. 285.
188  See Derrida, *Life Death*, p. 359.
189  Deleuze, *Difference and Repetition*, p. 23.
190  Henry Somers-Hall, "Deleuze, Freud and the Three Syntheses," *Deleuze and Guattari Studies* 11, no. 3 (2017), p. 298.

demonstrates, ultimately Freud betrays this radical distinction between repetition and representation, by tying the former to the latter.

In *Anti-Oedipus* Deleuze and Guattari proclaim that "the only modern myth is the myth of the zombie."[191] This is the tale of a creature's internalization of anti-production, which drives it to desire and embody the empirical form of death; capitalism does not let its subjects live properly, but nor does it let them die. Such a tendency towards death (as empirical principle) is also apparent in Freud's account of the death drive. But, as Deleuze declares in *Difference and Repetition*, the transcendental illusion in Freud is not the consequence of considering the death drive as fundamental, but of misconstruing its proper transcendental function. The reconceptualization of the life of the organism as a detour towards death still remained dependent on the conservative economic order of the organism, which imposed a partial natural order on the death drive, limiting its dysteleological tendency. Rather than conceiving of the death drive as a unilateral demand, Freud, by making its expression contingent on the exigencies of the organic, makes the death drive bilateral and hence concludes his speculative hypothesis with a metaphysical dualism of drives. In other words, the death drive in Freud is not transcendental.

Deleuze, at the end of Chapter 2 of *Difference and Repetition*, attempts to retrieve the monism of drives refused by Freud. He determines Thanatos within a dialectical model, juxtaposing it with and against Eros, and repeats this opposition as the oppositional relation between organic interiority and inorganic exteriority. The inorganic is hence only conceived empirically as the inanimate that gives rise to the aboriginal trauma within the organism, which the latter unsuccessfully tries to bind. This impossible return is for Freud synonymous with the re-emergence of a time before time and without life, meaning that death is only considered as an empirical fact and not yet as a transcendental principle. Death for Freud is always only ever individual and personal. When he writes that death is necessary for the organism, he traces the transcen-

---

[191] Deleuze and Guattari, *Anti-Oedipus*, p. 355.

dental from the empirical, iterating Kant's movement of precluding any investigation into the impersonal genesis of the personal.

Freud thus *represents* the death drive from the vantage point of the individual organism as a tendency to return to the lowest possible state of energy, i.e. dissipation. While this model seems diametrically opposed to Bergson's model, which conceives of life as the affirmative tendency to counter entropic regression, both still remain within the same representational framework. Both conceive of these tendencies as active forces, at once destructive and creative, which escape the organism's boundaries only insofar as they can be reintegrated into its conservative economy. This proposition of an active tendency *within* or *for* the organism entails a false choice of priority or primacy. Where to begin? With death or life? *Either* the organism repeats its aboriginal trauma as the exorbitant demand of death (inorganic exteriority) *or* the organism affirms the negentropic tendency as the principle of life.[192] This false choice proposes that the problem of the inorganic could be determined completely by an empirical solution. Deleuze neither starts with life or death, but inorganic vitality, which is always already life/death or neutral, passive genesis.

Recently, Keith Ansell-Pearson has proposed a defense of Bergson's position against Freud's account of the death drive by drawing on the works of the biologist August Weismann.[193] While this analysis discredits the biological grounding for Freud's speculative account, as Ansell-Pearson admits, it nevertheless does not yet escape the tendency to only determine the virtual through the actual and hence must be superseded by Deleuze's transcendental empiricist account.[194] Colebrook tangentially comments on this false choice of primacy between Freud and Bergson ("'thrust' or 'crust'"[195]) as a divide between tendencies internal to Deleuze himself:

---

[192] This false choice is again repeated in Schrödinger's seminal account of the living organism and its tendency towards "negentropy"; see Erwin Schrödinger, *What Is Life?* (Cambridge: Cambridge University Press, 2012).
[193] See Ansell-Pearson, *Germinal Life*, p. 104.
[194] Ibid., p. 129.
[195] See Colebrook, *Deleuze and the Meaning of Life*, p. 40.

on the one hand we have a Bergsonian line, which traces the emergence of structure and systems from the active engagement of living bodies with the world (active vitalism), and on the other a Freudian line concerned with the detachment of meaning, systems and events from the living and lived body (passive vitalism). It is Deleuze's radicalization of Freud in the latter line that will provide the account of passive and neutral genesis that we sought.

## UNBINDING THE DEATH DRIVE

### Narcissism and Free Energy

Capitalizing on the energetic model of the psyche that Freud provides, Deleuze attempts to unbind the death drive from the conservative economy of the organism and think the emergence of the personal from the impersonal. In this reconfiguration, Thanatos is neither merely the excessive intrusion of alterity (the exorbitant demand of inorganic exteriority) for an organism, nor merely a traumatic interruption of an empirically given (and retrospectively transcendentalized) natural order. Rather than the anterior posteriori interruption of the empirical by this natural order, it is the suspension of this natural order a priori. It is the transcendental denaturalization of the genesis of the empirical as such. More recent readings of the death drive by Land or Brassier have followed Freud in declaring Thanatos an objective truth a posteriori, emphasizing only its destructive aspect.[196] Deleuze's a priori account, the transcendental Thanatos, subverts the false choice of destruction and creation with a neutral genesis.

Deleuze applies his three synthesis of time to Freud's account of psychic life, each time proceeding from an active to a passive synthesis. It is the third synthesis, the pure and empty form of time, which deals with the death drive. Deleuze attempts to leave the Freudian dualism of drives, which only appears when both are considered empirically, by

---

[196] See Land, "Making it with Death," and Brassier, *Nihil Unbound*, p. 234.

conceiving of the death drive as "the transcendental principle"; in contrast, "the pleasure principle is only psychological."[197] In other words, he makes the death drive transcendental, in order to ground the empirical expressions of both Eros *and* Thanatos. Freud's text *The Ego and the Id* already provided an account of narcissism and melancholia, in which he seems to hint at the possibility of a single form of libido traversing both the life and the death drive. In the case of an individual who is forced to part with a "sexual" object, Freud observes a compensatory process, within which the ego is altered in the process of "erecting the object within the ego."[198] The loss of the id is thereby compensated for by the ego, which presents itself as the love-object, saying: "There, you see, you can love me too—I look just like the object."[199] To relate itself to the id, the ego effectively forgoes its relationship to the outside, i.e. the individual gives up its sexual goals and relates directly to itself. In thus desexualizing the libido this narcissistic compensation acts against the rule of Eros and hence implies the existence of a "neutral, displaceable energy, essentially capable of serving Thanatos,"[200] or a libido equally expressed in the id and the ego (and their respective structures). This "energy" is what Deleuze calls intensive difference: "the state of free differences when they are no longer subject to the form imposed upon them by an I or an ego."[201] This intensive difference is not beholden to the (empirical) Thanatos or the Eros Freud proposes, but rather constitutes both these drives, which envelop intensive differences in their operation. Instead of following any principle (whether entropic or negentropic), this transcendental death drive constitutes principles according to its manifestation. From the vantage point of the conservative economy of the organism, such intensive differences can only be registered as a tendency towards thanatropic regression or death.

---

[197] Deleuze, *Difference and Repetition*, p. 16.
[198] Sigmund Freud, "The Ego and the Id," in *Beyond the Pleasure Principle and Other Writings*, ed. John Reddick (London: Penguin Books, 2003), p. 120.
[199] Ibid.
[200] Deleuze, *Difference and Repetition*, p. 111.
[201] Ibid., p. 113.

Following up this indication of a neutral energy, Deleuze attempts to trace its nature by engaging with Freud's peculiar temporal model in *Beyond the Pleasure Principle*. In this work, as Derrida also noticed, Freud did not discover the death drive in the context of aggression or destruction (the reference points for the discussions of Thanatos in Freud's later works), but as a peculiar form of repetition. For Deleuze, the compulsion to repeat a trauma which cannot be properly bound within the conservative economy of the organism indicates an element which, while itself not *appearing* in the repetition, still manifests itself disguised within the Eros it constitutes and as the motor of disguising itself. Thus, "Eros and Thanatos are distinguished in that Eros must be repeated, can be lived only through repetition, whereas Thanatos (as transcendental principle) is that which gives repetition to Eros."[202] The pleasure principle is therefore not a principle complementary to the death drive, but a manifestation of the latter. To this, Deleuze justifiably adds the question: "How is it that the theme of death, which appears to draw together the most negative elements of psychological life, can be in itself the most positive element, transcendentally positive, to the point of affirming repetition?"[203] Keeping in mind Deleuze's interpretation of Nietzsche's Eternal Return as the repetition of difference, which conditions and (un-)grounds empirical repetition based on resemblance, identity and opposition, we can see how the repetition of the death drive is no lack and involves no negativity. The apparent "failure" or "impossibility" in relation to the exorbitant demand of inorganic exteriority (i.e. the demand to repeat the original trauma), only appear as such for the individual organism or for empirical representation, but not when considered transcendentally. Rather than a lack (or the failure to repeat) being the means by which the death drive generates repetition, as is the case for Lacan, it is repetition itself that is for Deleuze the "motivation" of movement, which means time, considered as repetition, is not moved by something in it but is itself an empty form.[204] It

---

202 Ibid., p. 18.
203 Ibid., p. 16.
204 See Jacques Lacan, *The Four Fundamental Concepts of Psycho-Analysis* (London: Penguin, 1979), p. 139, 146.

is then intensive difference that is repeated in the death drive, and which cannot be completely synthesized into a representation but nevertheless envelops itself in the given. Death, in its impersonal or pre-personal mode, traverses life not as a disturbance, but as its very condition, which still remains unrecoverable by the living. The death drive, as the affirmation of intensive difference, is hence not the repetition of an "original" trauma, but of a disguised difference. Similarly, it is also not the repetition of an end implicated in the origin, since such teleological principles entail a repetition of the same in the constitution of the lived. Deleuze's dysteleological temporality ungrounds every attempt at grounding the lived in conatus, the "drive" of a body to preserve its existence, or rather its form.

### Lacan and Deleuze on the Crack

Even if one rejects the entropic tendency of transcendental Thanatos, however, it still raises the question of how exactly this intensive death is concomitant or coextensive with life. As Henry Somers-Hall writes: "Since intensive death is a part of life (the destabilizing of identities), our 'death' is coextensive with life."[205] Alas, this formulation still invites the misunderstanding of the death drive as an anterior posteriori. In her treatment of the death drive in Deleuze, Alenka Zupančič notes that one ought not to misconstrue Deleuze's affirmative approach as a rejection of negativity out of hand.[206] She notes that Deleuze discusses the death instinct as difference in *Difference and Repetition*, but as "crack" (*fêlure*) in *The Logic of Sense*. This distinction, I would argue, reflects a fundamental problem about Deleuze's inorganic vitalism, which we have discussed several times in this book: the problem of the perspective on life that follows from Kant's critical philosophy. Deleuze describes Life both from the perspective of the subject's experience (as a force of de-subjectivation and an a-subjective field within it) and from the vantage point of

---

[205] Henry Somers-Hall, *Deleuze's Difference and Repetition: An Edinburgh Philosophical Guide* (Edinburgh: Edinburgh University Press, 2013), p. 96.

[206] Alenka Zupančič, "The Death Drive," in *Lacan and Deleuze: A Disjunctive Synthesis*, ed. Boštjan Nedoh and Andreja Zevnik (Edinburgh: Edinburgh University Press, 2016), p. 171.

pure immanence. The former is traversed to reach the latter, but the latter can only be discovered through the former. The logic of the "crack" nonetheless differs substantially from that of "difference." Drawing on Zola's *La bête humaine*, Deleuze describes the crack in the context of a family drama: the (morbid) ancestral line weighing on and puncturing the protagonist's very body as a "hereditary taint [*fêlure*]."[207] However, he adds, "heredity is not that which passes through the crack, it is the crack itself—the imperceptible rift of the hole."[208] For Zola, the temperaments (or instincts) form and organize around this crack. The instincts and their objects, in Deleuze's translation, are the empirical (i.e. corporeal) phenomena of the imperceptible crack:

> If it is true that the instincts are formed and find their object only at the edge of the crack, the crack conversely pursues its course, spreads out its web, changes direction and is actualized in each body in relation to the instincts which open a way for it, sometimes mending it a little, sometimes widening it.[209]

This topology emerging and oriented around the crack is fused by Deleuze with the death instinct. In other words, the crack designates an emptiness, which is death.[210] *Prima facie*, this concept resembles Lacan's conception of a lack which produces the One, of a primary "hole" or ontological deficit from which the One emerges. Instead of following from a failed repetition, or being the impossibility of successful repetition, it is the impossible itself, which repeats in every repetition, because it is the repetition. This "entry door designated from the lack, from the place where there is a hole"[211] which the One emerges from is the premise on which the death drive for Lacan is based. Given the productive nature

---

207 Deleuze, *Logic of Sense*, p. 331.
208 Ibid.
209 Ibid., p. 321.
210 See ibid., p. 326.
211 Jacques Lacan, *Le Séminaire de Jacques Lacan, Livre XIX; ... Ou Pire* (Paris: Seuil, 2011), p. 147.

of this lack (hole or crack), Zupančič connects this negativity with Deleuze's notion of repetition:

> repetition is negativity taken in its absolute sense: not negativity in relation to something, but original negativity, negativity that is itself productive of what is there and what can be differentiated, compared, said to fail, and so on. We could also say that he takes negativity as such to be the original positive force —as opposed to a secondary notion of negativity (and difference). And the whole question now becomes how to eventually separate this "bad" negativity from a "good" one.[212]

She thus recasts Deleuze's *fêlure* as a lack which is primordial and repeated in every repetition and which transforms the problematic of repetition into a pragmatic or ethical problem. This reconceptualization follows a peculiar strategy in as much as Deleuze, as she acknowledges, would emphatically reject lack as a motor for repetition or as repetition itself, since repetition (in the empty form of time) is only motivated by itself. As we have seen, what returns in a repetition is not the same, but only difference itself and, hence, difference is being in its univocity. This notion of pure difference, therefore, logically precedes what was traditionally conceptualized as being and appearance (as well as their difference) and dissolves them both by undermining their mutual determination in negation. From this vantage point, the crack does not appear as a rupture but as pure difference repeating itself as the constant movement of and univocal Being itself. While Lacan's model appears to be topological, implying a small crack as the point of emergence of the One, Deleuze's is dynamic, entailing a grand crack or the constant affirmation of the whole as cracked Being in every repetition. Unsurprisingly, this contrast mirrors the opposition between Badiou's subtractive and Deleuze's affirmative logic, as discussed above. While this opposition is obvious in the case of Badiou and Deleuze, Zupančič's juxtaposition of Deleuze and Lacan is not as self-evident. The problem in these two interpretations of the death

---

[212] Zupančič, "The Death Drive," p. 172.

drive, I would suggest, is not one of differing conceptual premises, but a practical one: the question of realizing repetition and difference *in* repetition. Or, in other words, given that being is difference, *how* is this being-as-difference *repeated* to "realize" difference and avoid its reification.

For Deleuze, being-as-difference already provides the means for this realization, since it is itself a "centrifugal force," which thwarts the dialectical conception of being and repetition. The difference between being and appearing is thus collapsed and the confusion of them is avoided by replacing both with pure difference. The problem of difference and its realization thus coincide in the movement of being itself (as pure difference). In contrast, Lacan, instead of dissolving the distinction between being and appearance in an *ontology* of difference, introduces a third term between them, denoting their non-coincidence: the Real. Only this third term realizes difference, insofar as it helps explain why being "needs" to appear. The Real provides a conceptual name for the rift, crack or lack within reality, i.e. the primary ontological inconsistency of being, which in turn makes thought in the most emphatic sense possible. Only because there is something inconsistent within reality is the encounter from which thought emerges possible. Unlike in Deleuze, then, in Lacan difference is not auto-realizing, because the Real is an inconsistency that is neither auto-realizing nor something to strive for. Rather, it is a possible weapon of intervention, which needs active commitment to realize difference. Hence, while thinking is not fully on the side of the subject for either Deleuze's or Lacan's materialism of thought, for Lacan it can only occur in and as the effect of subjectivation, whereas for Deleuze it implies de-subjectivation.

From a Deleuzian perspective, this Real is nothing but the self-actualizing movement of being (or pure difference). From a Lacanian point of view, Deleuze ontologizes the Real and identifies it with being, thus confusing two conjoined but separate orders. Lacan is reluctant to simply identify the Real with being, for several reasons. Firstly, this identification defers the problem of the realization of difference to a metaphysics which only ever justifies itself. Deleuze arrives at this ontological model qua the speculative movement of presupposing the (transcendental) pre-individual, which can only be extracted from the (empirically given) individual by the force of thought, and then he justifies it by demonstrating how the empirical can be produced from the transcendental. Deleuze's ontology thus falls back to the situation before Kantian critical philosophy and becomes metaphysics in the dogmatic sense. This critique is not so far from Laruelle's non-philosophical approach. Secondly, since Deleuze forgoes the possibility of understanding thought qua subjectivation, he also forgoes the possibility of determining criteria for the selection within the repetition. The Nietzschean Eternal Return (also called the death drive by Deleuze) is not only a physical but an ethical doctrine, as we have seen. It selects in the repetition only that which is novel and repeats it, letting everything that stays the same die. Since such a drive is always satisfied with its repetition and is not motivated by anything but itself, the affirmative movement does not yet guarantee freedom from repression or an increase in liveliness. Because there is no value to life itself, i.e. no life of life, there is no "right" decision the drive can make. For this reason, Deleuze must artificially attach it to a ("dead") signifier: the promise of *beatitudo*. Only if the selection of the death drive by itself is expressed in the individual as "bliss" can Deleuze claim that the "spiritual turn" of the Will in the ethical doctrine of the Eternal Return (*amor fati*) is in step or in line with Life itself, or an expression of life itself. In this fusion of ontology and ethics (and consequently politics), Deleuze has—from a Lacanian perspective—abnegated all other options in order to follow a politics of intensification, i.e. the realization of the differential movement of being itself.[213] Of course, these two critiques intersect and, since in Deleuze's metaphysics ontology, ethics and politics are mutually dependent, they actually entail each other.

All the problems we have discussed so far in relation to Deleuze's inorganic vitalism are in evidence in these critiques: the problem of the

---

213 This critique becomes more salient if one considers that for Lacan, what is "beyond" the pleasure principle is an excess of enjoyment, which is inseparable from (and experienced as) suffering. This enjoyment is not emancipatory as such, but always dependent on a dead signifier to realize it as an intervention in the given order. See Lacan, *Le séminaire de Jacques Lacan, livre XIX; ... ou pire*, p. 151.

realization of difference qua thought,[214] the problem of the ethical decision underpinning his ontology,[215] which would either lead to an active vitalism grounded in the actions of a body[216] or a cancelling out of actuality by virtuality via an ethical demand.[217]

The question now is how we can use the critique of Kant's transcendental idealism as grounded in an organic image of thought,[218] the resources of Deleuze's concept of inorganic life as the power of the Idea[219] and his philosophy of individuation,[220] as well as our discussion of the problems with Deleuze's vitalism, to find a version of Deleuze that approaches *a* life: a Deleuze of passive, neutral genesis.

All the pieces are already in place.

### The Coldness and Impassivity of the Death Drive

As Land notices, there is something peculiar in the way that Deleuze "succeeds in detaching himself from Parisian temporality"; "the time of Deleuze is a colder, more reptilian, more *German* time."[221] This is not the temporality of Hegel, but of the Germans rebelling against these German roots, of Schopenhauer and Nietzsche—"a time of indifferent nature," an inhuman time, as well as the time of the demand of the inorganic, the time of the death drive. From the outset then, there are significant affinities between the (Schopenhauerian) temporality of Freud's *Beyond the Pleasure Principle* and Deleuze's own account. It gives metaphysical credence to the pessimist's assertion that Life is always already (or a priori) detached from the living and from what can be lived, that Life is not grounded in the living nor in any substance or principle but *is*—as Schopenhauer knew—a blind and impersonal Will, numerically neither one nor many. The independence of Time from what happens in

---

214   See section "Passivity."
215   See section "(Non-)Philosophical Immanence."
216   See section "The Transcendental Empiricism that Has Never Been."
217   See sections "Organs without Bodies," "Deleuze's Vitalist Idealism" and "Passivity."
218   See section "The Organic Image of Thought."
219   See section "The Monstrous Epigenesis of the Transcendental" and "The Inorganic Life of the Ideas."
220   See section "Speculative Hylozoism."
221   Land, "Making it with Death," p. 261.

it, the empty form of time (or death drive) creates a distinct silence, as Deleuze notes:

> The crack designates, and this emptiness is, Death—the death instinct. The instincts may speak loudly, make noise, or swarm, but they are unable to cover up this more profound silence, or hide that from which they come forth and to which they return: the death instinct, not merely one instinct among others, but the crack itself around which all the instincts congregate.[222]

There is a coldness and indifference towards what happens in it in such a drive, a mathematical impassivity instead of a biological affectivity. This "specific freezing point"[223] is felt in the masochistic scenarios of Sacher-Masoch, which Deleuze analyses in *Coldness and Cruelty* in the context of Freud's conception of drives and the idea of a free or unbound energy. As we have already seen, Deleuze first approaches the death drive by examining the unbound energy that narcissism presupposes. The distinction between free and unbound energy in Freud is derived from Breuer's earlier attempts to apply to the psyche Hermann von Helmholz's thermodynamic model of the degradation of energy. In the latter context, when "bound" energy is degraded within a thermodynamic system it manifests as heat, while "unbound" energy corresponds to the absence of heat, being the energy which is not degraded and thus remains convertible and usable. Applying this model, Deleuze conjectures that what the masochist is searching for is not the "heat" of either sensuality or sadism, but the absence of heat, the zero point of the death drive. Thanatos (in the Deleuzian sense) is constantly "bound" into the pendulum swings of sadism (hot) or sensuality (hot), which cover up the deeper absence of movement, the impassivity or coldness of the death drive which the masochist intuits and desires. If it were up to her/him, he would use or

---

[222] Deleuze, *Logic of Sense*, p. 326.
[223] Tracy McNulty, "Unbound: The Speculative Mythology of the Death Drive," *Differences* 28, no. 2 (2017), p. 99.

convert as little energy as possible in order to retain (and protect) the unbound energy as pure potentiality.[224] The coldness of the death drive is not a lack of sensuality or a mirror opposite of sadism, but itself transcendental and independent from such mutual determination. This mathematical, purely formal understanding of the drive is not opposed to the drive's liveliness, but rather seeks to trace the primary nature of the drive itself to something unlivable that cannot be approximated otherwise. This "zero point" of the death drive, upon which all the buzzing of the instincts occurs and from which all values and interests emerge, is itself neutral and formal.

At this point of our investigation, the alleged monotony of Deleuze's philosophy which Badiou decries, appears here as the compulsive drive to repeat the same motif at different levels or in different masks. In his analysis of Deleuze's philosophy of time, James Williams already notes that Deleuze's concept of repetition seems to be extracted from various instances of anomalous repetition in biology and psychoanalysis. Such a procedure, however, might make the resulting model either dogmatic or dependent on the historically contingent scientific truth that such repetitions exist. Yet, with the introduction of the death drive, Deleuze inherits from Freud a *speculative* account of repetition, which does not depend on theories which presuppose anomalous repetitions, but rather serves as a critique of such theories for conceiving of anomalous temporalities as secondary or derivative. Deleuze's speculative turn breaks with the Kantian (and phenomenological) requirement that every claim is based on evidence in experience (according to the value of truth), to proceed through what can only be thought to the creation of new forms of experience. This speculative account, then, allows us to draw various accounts of inorganic life together, insofar as inorganic vitality is the force of Thought, the Idea, the Event and Death (or the death drive), which is to say inorganic life is the empty form of time.

---

[224] Deleuze, "Coldness and Cruelty," p. 111.

# INERTIA

## THE SPECULATIVE NEUTRAL GENESIS OF PASSIVE VITALISM

*Caesura and Dysteleology*

If we're characterizing the empty form of time in terms of dynamic ruptures, it might be better to view it as a caesura between two asymmetrical parts than a crack within time. Hölderlin's poetic remark that due to an unequal distribution, time would stop "rhyming," elucidates Deleuze's creative use of the word "césure."[225] The term denotes a poetic hexameter where a pause divides a line of verse into two parts of five and seven syllables. The same unequal distribution is introduced by the cut in the third synthesis of time between before and after. The traditional linear model depicts time as a line made up of points and traversed by a presence, a moving point of actual existence, that determines each point as past or future in relation to itself. Deleuze seeks to radicalize this linearity by thinking of the cut itself as an event which orders all other events into a before and after in unequal parts. Instead of a logical point on a line denoting a presence, commensurable and equal in relation to all other points, the event of the Eternal Return is singular, i.e. incommensurable and unequal in relation to all other events. The former model still only considers time within a representational framework wherein before and after are logically entailed, but without there being any formal difference between them. Without such a formal difference, however, the future can only be conceived as the realization of possibilities (the past as condition of the present) within an instance of the present that is not yet. In other words, without a formal difference between before and after, there is no novelty. In contrast, Deleuze attempts to think time *from* the event of the cut, understood not as a representable instance in the present but as the unrepresentable event of the division of before and after.

---

[225] See Friedrich Hölderlin, *Essays and Letters on Theory* (New York: SUNY Press, 1988), p. 103.

Somewhat obscured by the English translation of the French "ensemble" as "totality," this orientation around the cut implies the gathering and then splitting of time as a whole or totality.[226] Hence, rather than saying that the cut splits a line into two segments, it would be more appropriate to say that there are only cuts with depth to them (i.e. all other events ordered into a before and after). That is to say, the past and the present become conditional on the third synthesis and thereby are subject to the irreversible loss it introduces.

Nothing will remain as it is. Time is forgetting.

In his critique of Bergson, Hägglund notes that in Bergson's conception of continuous duration (without negation) there is strictly speaking no temporality because there is no before or after, i.e. no succession. Although every moment, for Bergson, passes away, it doesn't cease to be but is integrated in the absolute continuity of duration. By conceiving of time as the affirmative movement of duration in which nothing ever passes away, Bergson, for Hägglund, denies the very condition of time: loss. By denying that temporality involves loss, Bergson is thus unable to think novelty (the future) and remains restricted to a repetition of the same which only poses as novelty. To solve this problem of the temporal-modal coexistence of the past with the present, Hägglund appeals to the Derridean conception of the negativity of time itself, which undermines both the idea of time as a mere succession of discrete moments and time as absolute continuity.[227] In doing so, he equates the idea that something passes away and something new emerges in its place with the movement of negativity in the present— without further explanation. Deleuze criticizes Bergson in the same manner but attempts to solve the question of the conditions of temporality (the constitution of a before and after), without resorting to negativity, by reversing the order of conditioning. This means that Deleuze is not interested in how the future can emerge from sufficient conditions rooted in the past and the present, but instead reconfigures the future as the condition

---

226 See Deleuze, *Difference and Repetition*, p. 94, 96, 115.
227 See Martin Hägglund, "The Trace of Time: A Critique of Vitalism," *Derrida Today* 9 (2016), p. 43.

for the past and the present. Or, in other words, the first and the second syntheses of time provide a topology of temporality, but the third synthesis provides a movement which at once facilitates the emergence of these syntheses and provides a principle for their operations. Hence, despite the immanent equitemporality of the three temporal modalities, there is a relationship of antecedence between them, which is itself not temporal but logical. Deleuze describes this transfer of authority from the dimension of the past to that of the future as: "The repetition of the future is the royal one as it subordinates the other two and strips them of their autonomy."[228]

The dimensions of the past and the present are hence radically transformed, becoming only dimensions of the future. The present becomes an actor or agent who is "destined to be effaced"[229] and the past becomes the failing condition of the future. From the perspective of the first synthesis, the present selects a singular series by contracting a (singular) past and (singular) future. With the second synthesis, the present and the future are founded in and by the dynamic relational variations of the past. The active subject of the first synthesis was already traced back by Deleuze to its constitution in the passive synthesis of contraction, while the activity of remembering is grounded in the passivity of memory in the second synthesis. The third synthesis not only rejects this active/passive distinction, but also breaks the hold of the passive synthesis over its constituted series by taking them up and ordering them within the totality (*ensemble*) of time. The present as an agent is now placed within a new series, where it is detached from past contractions, since they are not repeated as the same. Rather than constituting the difference between the past and the future, the singular living present is only a function in the determination of the new by the new for the new. In other words, the present is only an agent insofar as it is the locus of its own impotence to act. The end or goal of time is thus no longer determined by the present but only the future, understood as essential openness or aimlessness. Similarly, the operations of the pure past which make every present pass are overwritten when the

---

[228] Deleuze, *Difference and Repetition*, p. 94.
[229] Ibid.

past is taken up in the totality of time. The future is not determined by the past because otherwise no novelty would be possible. Rather, the past becomes the condition of the future *after* pure difference has returned. The past operates as a condition for the future by "default," i.e. it is a condition of the future only insofar as it fails to condition it and surrenders to the involuntary selection of past events by the future.

Every habit, every contraction, exists only insofar as it is repeated. But as repetition it is subject to the third synthesis of time and thus only returns as new. Hence, the very condition for the formation of a habit or contraction is that it never returns as the same. Every contraction is already the irreversible loss of *this* contraction itself and at the same time conditioned by the impossibility of returning as the same. Thus, there is a condition for the operation of the passive synthesis of habit/contraction, which cannot be incorporated or recovered by it and remains the unsynthesizable (un-)ground. Even the passing of a gesture from the present into the past is only possible because of the *movement* provided by the empty form of time, which gives the past its principle without itself passing into memory. In the movement of the future, it is not only the past but also the present that is irretrievably lost and superseded by the new. Every event is radically new, and not merely *for* the past and the present: every event changes the totality of time, i.e. transforms the whole of the past and every series contracted in the present. But there is nothing besides events within the Event of Being; everything is a Kierkegaardian "moment,"[230] a non-extended instance within which novelty occurs, which is thus an eternity within the realm of the finite. Deleuze's temporality is hence a non-eschatological apocalypse or a dysteleological Will.

### Death, Impassivity, Thought

In detaching the end (or goal) of time from the actions of the present and the conditions of the past, what the "eternal return imposes on time is

---

[230] Søren Kierkegaard, *The Concept of Anxiety: A Simple Psychologically Orienting Deliberation on the Dogmatic Issue of Hereditary Sin* (Princeton: Princeton University Press, 1980), p. 88.

an impassive and inflexible NEXT."[231] This irreversibility of time, the perishing of the same in every event, *is* Death or the continuous dying that is the Event. Deleuze, however, does not derive this model from an experience of time, but from enquiring into the unlivable conditions (the genetic conditions) of the livable, which can only be thought. He adopts Freud's speculative temporality of the death drive (the demand of the inorganic) but unbinds this inorganicity from the conservative economy of the organism. The death drive is not an inassimilable injunction of inorganic trauma *for* the organism, but the organism (understood as an actual being) is only an in and of the temporality of the death drive. The force of the future (the empty form of time) replaces the organism as the "actor" or "agent" (and "grounding") of time in the present and as a condition (or ground) of time in the past. The conservative economy of the organism is not violently disrupted by an experience of alterity, but its tendency for binding excitations and reiterating its form and unity has always already failed. All of its syntheses are conditioned by a synthesis that always fails and makes all subsequent syntheses inconsistent. Which is to say, all machines only work because they are in the constant process of breaking down. Badiou is hence correct to speculate that Deleuze's ontology is a philosophy of death. However, it is a philosophy in the tradition of Nietzsche, Bataille and Baudrillard, which insists on the persistence of the uneconomic excess of death, even in hygienic economies that (in order to establish frictionless transactions) seek to abolish all figures of death: the gift, theft, loss, unemployment.[232]

Paradoxically, it is therefore Brassier's critical account of Deleuze's vitalism that captures his speculative force most accurately. The thought following from the death drive, understood as an "adequation without correspondence," is describing, according to Brassier, the organism's inability to bind the demand of the inorganic (and time) and the necessity

---

[231] Jon Roffe, "Time and Ground: A Critique of Meillassoux's Speculative Realism," *Angelaki: Journal for Theoretical Humanities* 17, no. 1 (2012), p. 95.

[232] See Georges Bataille, *The Accursed Share: An Essay on General Economy*, vol. 3 (New York: Zone Books, 1988), p. 32, and Jean Baudrillard, *Symbolic Exchange and Death* (London: Sage Publications, 1993), p. 60.

of thinking beyond the organism's (or the body's) actions and intentions. This "cosmic" death, as Brassier's speculative move suggests, is an inhuman event, whose occurrence is not conditioned by the human, an encounter with nothingness, which enables a form of "thinking" that could escape the correlationist circle. However, since he insists on perceiving death as an objective truth a posteriori, he can only think this crack as an asynchronicity of being and time. Deleuze, on the other hand, because he makes the death drive a transcendental a priori, can detach life from the organism (and the body) while retaining the identity of thinking and being. Both Deleuze and Brassier acknowledge the potential of Freud's speculative temporality but pursue different notions of the inorganic. As we have seen, this leads Brassier to accuse Deleuze of philosophical idealism in relation to the latter's privileging of the psychic individual. From the standpoint of the notion of inorganic life sketched in the chapter "The Unlivable," this accusation would be credible: it seemed necessary to refer to consciousness in order to reconstruct and provide evidence for the temporal genesis of experience. But having arrived at the speculative interpretation of inorganic life as the temporality of the death drive, we can see that Deleuze does not presuppose the psychic individual (the thinker) as the "actor" that engenders the third synthesis. Rather, the "fractured I" is only one instance of the pure and empty form of time, an instance that appears as thought within consciousness—in other words, the thought of the psychic individual is but one mask of the death drive. Brassier's reading conjoins two notions in Deleuze: "thinking" and "the thinker." Deleuze understands "thinking" as the temporal determination of the Self, which ultimately fails to exhaust the undetermined ground of the Self but can produce empirical representations of the Self that involve a psychic system. Not all "thinking" involves such a system, however. Brassier confuses an instance of the third synthesis, which Deleuze uses to *demonstrate* the model of the pure and empty form of time—the thinking process of the psychic individual—with the full scope of the third synthesis as such.[233] In doing so, Brassier reconfigures and radicalizes the third syn-

---

**233** See Roffe, "Objectal Human," p. 53.

thesis by making it conditioned on an act in the present (the thinking of a psychic individual). Deleuze, however, instead of proposing this reflexive movement, wants to efface the actor and detach time's movements from the organism and the actions of the body. Time is grounded in nothing but its movement, which is not an action and cannot be grounded in any action. Rather, it is a constant ungrounding, which also suspends any grounding a priori.

### *Existence, Structure, Production*

If one reads Deleuze based on only the first and second synthesis of time, then the critiques by Hallward and Harman, to the effect that Deleuze neglects the actual in the name of the virtual, would be correct. However, in the third synthesis, actual existence not only matters but also introduces another process of differentiation. Which is to say that in his speculative turn Deleuze moves firstly from the conditions of the possibility of experience to the conditions of real experience, and then to the conditions of real existence. Working against Kant's argument that existence is not a real predicate and thus cannot be part of the concept, Deleuze's Leibnizian marriage of the singular and the concept conceives of existence as part of the concept because this actual existence makes a difference. Since the undetermined grounds of a virtual Idea do not resemble its determined products, actualization introduces a difference, a novelty irreducible to the present of the past. In other words, individualization is a process of differentiation. Insofar as the irreversible movement of time, understood as the production of the new, is not determined nor conditioned by the past (which fails as a condition) and the present (which is effaced as an actor), the movement from the virtual to the actual is not conditioned by any action nor reducible to it. Rather, the impassivity of time *is* the form of determination of an empirical actual existent being from undetermined grounds. The non-resemblance of the virtual and the actual is thus due to the production of novelty, which gathers, cuts into and orders time as a whole.

It follows from the above that structure and becoming are not mutually exclusive anymore. Rather, the virtual structure (Idea/problem) is determined by becoming, or time, which produces an actual individual. Conversely, the virtual problem is only ever determined as a field in the process of actualization. Although the problem exceeds the solution, the former does not precede the latter. The pure and empty form of time involves novelty *and* structuration; the perishing of whatever is structured and wants to return as the same means that a new (virtual) structure takes its place. Time encompasses both the dynamic and static genesis. This resolves the problem of Land's structure/death drive dualism in his Deleuzian libidinal materialism. Because Land only conceives of the death drive as an objective truth a posteriori every structuration becomes a hindrance to the implicit teleology of Life, which means its tendency is to return to its pure form: undifferentiated intensity. If we understand time, or the death drive, as a priori, however, it cannot be detached from the "disguises" it wears, i.e. the structures and processes of structuration it is enveloped in. Land's dualism might be rooted in a traditional understanding of engineering. As Dennett notes, engineering has never been taken seriously by philosophy since it was always overshadowed by science.[234] Kant's philosophy begins, in a sense, as an engineering problem, insofar as his break with empiricism consists in not conceiving of the world as given, but precisely as engineered.[235] However, the unity of nature produced by and presupposed in this model of engineering (or production) requires that it is thought outside of nature. The engineering problem is thus not conceived in terms of the internal production of nature, but in terms of the modern understanding of how science applies to nature. The *Critique of Pure Reason* attempted to solve this question, namely the question of how synthetic a priori judgements are possible, to do two things: firstly, to enable the application of pure mathematics and a priori geometry, i.e. Newtonian dynamics, to the world, and secondly, to reduce matter to its compliance with these dynamics. The technical-mathematical subjugation of engineering to science presented Kant with considerable

---

[234] Daniel Dennett, *Darwin's Dangerous Idea: Evolution and the Meanings of Life* (New York: Touchstone, 1996), p. 188.
[235] Alistair Welchman, "Machinic Thinking," in *Deleuze and Philosophy: The Difference Engineer*, ed. Keith Ansell-Pearson (London: Routledge, 1997), p. 216.

obstacles, since, as the paradox of incongruent counterparts already demonstrated, there is always a remainder of the real that escapes conceptual determination and hence it was uncertain whether a transcendental logic of concepts was capable of exhausting nature in its application. As Deleuze notes, in Kant one encounters "an always rebellious matter,"[236] since there is "a stubbornness of the existent in intuition which resists specification by concepts no matter how far it is taken."[237] The antinomy of teleological judgement is not the cause but the consequence of this fundamental decision to limit the scope of engineering.

The traditional divide of mechanism and vitalism, with the former being able to explain the functioning and proliferation of systems but not their genesis, and the latter accounting for the creation of these systems but unable to do so without the hypothesis of an immaterial *qualitas obscura*, is circumvented by Deleuze and Guattari. Rejecting the givenness of the unity of such functional systems as the explanans of ontogenesis because this unity can only be postulated but never proven or accounted for in its genesis, Deleuze's intensive materialism entails a universal engineering: the BwO organizes or stratifies itself without any transcendence; everything is self-organizing matter flows expressing themselves in extensity. In the peculiar structuralism proposed in Deleuze's *Difference and Repetition*, "there is no more opposition between event and structure [...] than there is between structure and genesis."[238] As such, he holds in *The Logic of Sense* that structuralism is defensible if and only if it accounts for its auto-genesis, which is not possible without considering the temporal determination of "structure" itself.[239]

In the work of Gilbert Simondon, there is a discontinuity between the pre-individual and the individual, in which the former is conceived of as a realm or field. This reintroduced the specter of conceptual determinations binding and limiting the process of individuation. However, as we

---

236  Deleuze, *Difference and Repetition*, p. 264.
237  Ibid., p. 13.
238  Ibid., p. 191.
239  See Edward Thornton, "The Rise of the Machines: Deleuze's Flight from Structuralism," *The Southern Journal of Philosophy* 55, no. 4 (2017), p. 460.

have seen, virtual Ideas are selected according to the nature of an intensive environment and actualized in it, thereby structuring and ordering this environment, i.e. transforming it. There is hence never a shared field of individuation or a field of individuation in general, but only ever *this* field of individuation for *this* event. But since every event is unconditioned novelty, all the fields of individuation in relation to each other as well as in themselves are different in kind. There is hence no communication between the different fields of individuation and the various events within the process of individuation, since such communication would presuppose a resemblance, communality or common ground between them. There is only violence between fields and events.

Thus, the formal conditions of the organism (i.e. autopoiesis, equilibrium, conservative economy, unity, homeostasis), which sustain it by binding life, have, in a sense, no future. The integrity of the organism is predicated on the construction of the future by actions in the present and according to the conditions of the past. The temporality of the death drive does not forcefully interrupt this ordering from the present in the form of an objective truth a posteriori but has always already destabilized the seemingly successful syntheses because they were conditioned by a failing synthesis. The metabolic filter of Kant's organic image of thought was predicated on the operations and establishment of a *sensus communis* whose conditions could not be given. First, Deleuze had attempted to detach responsibility for the harmony among the faculties from the spontaneity of the understanding and instead root it in passive synthesis. But these syntheses are in turn conditioned by a (failing) synthesis, which is neither active nor passive but impassive. In the determination of life, Kant had to rely on a reference to external law (i.e. the supra-sensible unity of thinking nature) to guarantee the conformity of the lawfulness of life with the understanding. By providing an account of the genesis of this common sense, Deleuze thus reveals that organic activity is already conditioned by a deeper passivity which in turn is subject to inorganic life, i.e. the death drive. With the death drive, the ordinary temporality (the pure, empty form of time) has reached its speculative peak. Deleuze shows how the discord of the faculties is an effect of the third synthesis of time. And, while the analysis of this discord can provide a "model" for the operations of the temporality of the death drive, the faculties are not a necessary condition for the impassive movement of time. Hence, no organism sustains itself without becoming inorganic.

## THE THREE FUNDAMENTAL CONCEPTS OF LIFE: MADNESS, STUPIDITY AND MALEVOLENCE

*Madness, or Life as the Power of the False*

Not enough attention has been paid, as Agamben notes, to the philological circumstance that both Deleuze's and Foucault's last writings are concerned with a reconceptualization of the notion of "life."[240] Already in his introduction to Canguilhelm's *The Normal and the Pathological* Foucault identifies the notion of "error" as the heart of the book, which is concerned with providing a concept of life.[241] In his last text "Life: Experience and Science" he returns to this thought, detaching life from the categories of the practical or the true. Life, instead, is what possesses the ability to stray, to err and to form delusions.[242] In a decidedly anti-phenomenological twist, he then proposes that experience and its knowledge cannot be fully contained in the lived or in intentionality but are rooted in a life that is essentially the potential for errancy *by right*.[243] Organic representation according to Deleuze, on the other hand, always strives to become orgiastic, stretching itself from the smallest to the biggest, and to root out any such chaos. Despite the attempts of organic representation to contain it, the potential for error persists even within organic representation. The catastrophes of madness, stupidity and malevolence (the

---

240 See Agamben, "Absolute Immanence," p. 221.
241 See Michel Foucault, "Introduction by Michel Foucault," in *The Normal and the Pathological*, by Georges Canguilhem (New York: Zone Books, 1991), p. 22.
242 See Michel Foucault, "Life: Experience and Science," in *Aesthetics, Method, and Epistemology: Essential Works of Foucault 1954–1984. Vol. 2*, ed. James Faubion (New York: The New Press, 2003).
243 See Agamben, "Absolute Immanence," p. 221.

"terrible Trinity"[244]) haunt thought still. Within the organic image of thought, such errors are but "a possible misadventure of thought,"[245] indicating a common sense against which the failure to think properly can be measured. This approach is, however, not able to satisfactorily critique the errors or ward them off, since their conception as a false solution to a problem or a simple fact conceals the real problem: that these activities are possible, but undesirable. While it is true that thinking can produce factual falsities or errors, the "terrible Trinity" is subsumed under this category and hence "arbitrarily projected into the transcendental"[246] to ensure that the failure of thought proper is always brought on by external causes, e.g. the confusion of the imaginary and the real. Deleuze notes, however, that these activities are not various deviations from common sense and the good will of thought but are "structures of thought as such,"[247] internal to thinking as such. While in the organic image of thought the "terrible Trinity" are mere empirical failures of recognition, Deleuze considers them in their transcendental function.

Within the organic image of thought, the false is always already informed by truth or considered only within the form of truth, while the false itself is formless. This means that the false arises when a false proposition takes the form of a universal and necessary *judgement*. The content of the judgement can be false, i.e. an error, but the form of truth is not affected by the false. Deleuze, however, notices a difference in the understanding of error in Kant from that of Descartes or Hegel, a concept of it "radically different from the extrinsic mechanisms of error,"[248] which could be understood to be the foundation of Kant's critical advance. Since thinking relies on the interrelation of faculties, the failure of one faculty to work in reference to another could create an error that emerges from an internal potential of thinking. As the "Transcendental Dialectic" shows, if reason attempts to create a system of knowledge, both unified and com-

---

244 Deleuze, *Difference and Repetition*, p. 149.
245 Ibid., p. 148.
246 Ibid., p. 150.
247 Ibid., p. 151.
248 Ibid., p. 150.

plete, some of the conditions of the creation of such a system are beyond possible experience. Since reference to other faculties is only possible within experience, the operation of reason yields errors (we have already seen such errors in the *Dreams*). The critical project could therefore be characterized as an auto-critique of reason. Ultimately, however, Kant argues that if we want to establish a systematic account of the conditions that are given, we must assume that *all* conditions *could* be given. Reason therefore operates under a "transcendental illusion,"[249] which simultaneously enables reason to perform its tasks, while also producing error. Kant seemed ready and equipped to move away from, maybe even to overturn, the dogmatic image of thought. Deleuze maintains, however, that in the end Kant betrays this immanent critique by remaining within the representational image, unable to critique its own founding values.

Nietzsche was perhaps the first to point out the *value* implied in this relation of the form of truth to the formless false, insofar as the preference of the former over the latter cannot be justified without resorting to circular reasoning.[250] Deleuze not only carries over Nietzsche's "experimental" questioning of the value of truth but surpasses him by providing an image of thought able to conceive truth as secondary to the false. The pure and empty form of time (the death drive) is what will simultaneously liberate the false from the form of the true and explain the true as a "power" of the false-in-itself. The radical temporality of the Eternal Return does not mean that the form of truth is understood in terms of its contents, i.e. by saying something like "what happens (the event) is true now, but will not be so in the next moment, and hence everything is false." Such a conceptualization would still consider the false according to judgement, understanding it as universal and necessary. In Deleuze's approach, however, the empty *form* of time, i.e. the independence of time from its contents,

---

[249] Ibid., p. 151.
[250] Conversely, the concept of morality can be employed to rescue the form of truth. Leibniz, for example, in his attempt to solve the problem of contingent futures with the concept of possible worlds, found himself on the threshold of discovering the power of the false, only to retreat to the moral concept of "the best of all possible worlds" and save the form of truth. See Deleuze, *The Fold*, p. 61.

dissolves the form of truth, i.e. judgement. As we have seen in Kant, judgement requires representation, which in turn presupposes identity and common sense. However, as Deleuze has demonstrated, in the pure and empty form of time nothing returns but difference, making being (understood as the Event) not amenable to judgement, because it cannot be represented. There is no God anymore to make the world amenable to judgement. Insofar, then, as it relies on the form of truth, "the organism has no future."[251] The function of judgement rests on the exclusion of loss (or the unrecoverable) and creation (or the novel), but now time is nothing but loss and creation (which converge in the Event). It is precisely the failure of the third synthesis, the forgetting in the Eternal Return and the loss in the death drive that produce novelty, without needing to be conditioned or limited by judgement. Time (or inorganic life), understood as the formless false-in-itself, thus disengages from the form of truth and operates with its own power. The genesis of the form of truth (judgement) can only be explained on the condition that the conditions of its production do not resemble the product (the form). Thinking is then always situated beyond the form of truth, always involved in a process of becoming-mad.

*Malevolence, or Life as Becoming-Loser*
In his lecture at the Collège de France in 1970/1971, Foucault mentions *en passant* Spinoza's ethical and aesthetic version of the "will to know":

> It has to be said that philosophical discourse is of little help in this investigation. Undoubtedly, there is hardly a philosophy which has not invoked something like the will or desire to know (*connaître*), the love of truth, etcetera. But, in truth, very few philosophers—apart, perhaps, from Spinoza and Schopenhauer—have accorded it more than a marginal status; as if there was no need for philosophy to say first of all what the name that it bears actually refers to. As if placing at the head of its discourse this de-

---

[251] Claire Colebrook, "Time and Autopoesis. The Organism Has No Future," in *Deleuze and the Body*, ed. Joe Hughes and Laura Guillaume (Edinburgh: Edinburgh University Press, 2011), p. 8.

sire to know (*savoir*), which it repeats in its name, was enough to justify its own existence and show —at a stroke—that it is necessary and natural: All men by nature desire to know ... Who, then, is not a philosopher, and how could philosophy not be the most necessary thing in the world?[252]

Spinoza, for Foucault, represents simultaneously the zenith of the Western tradition of the will to know and the threshold to overcome it, even though Spinoza never did so. For Aristotle, the natural desire for knowledge, which seems to pre-exist even actual knowledge, is animated by the "truth" which connects sensation and pleasure (i.e. the formation of knowledge from sensation is pleasurable). The general desire to know that knowledge engenders in its own movement is animated and justified by truth, insofar as it is truth that makes knowledge a possible object of desire and provides the grounds for identifying the subject of knowledge and the subject of desire. This systematicity relating desire and knowledge to truth is then transformed and pushed to its limits by Spinoza's ethical and aesthetic system.[253] An example of this can be found in *On the Improvement of the Understanding*:

> I finally resolved to inquire whether there might be some real good having power to communicate itself, which would affect the mind singly, to the exclusion of all else: whether, in fact, there might be anything of which the discovery and attainment would enable me to enjoy continuous, supreme, and unending happiness.[254]

The desire to know is transposed into a desire for happiness, which only *during* the search for happiness is revealed to be tied to the true idea, which is its precondition and the means to achieve it. The Aristotelean

---

[252] Michel Foucault, *Lectures on the Will to Know: Lectures at the Collége de France 1970–1971 and Oedipal Knowledge*, trans. Graham Burchell (New York: Palgrave Macmillan, 2013), p. 4.
[253] Ibid., p. 24.
[254] Baruch de Spinoza, "On the Improvement of the Understanding," in *Works, Vol. 2*, by Baruch de Spinoza (New York: Dover, 1955), p. 3.

premises of the will to know are overturned radically. In Aristotle, in order for sensation and knowledge to be connected by and situated in the realm of truth, a minimal (or even just potential) contemplative happiness had to be inscribed within sensation itself. Spinoza, on the other hand, proposes an adequation between happiness and the true idea. As Nietzsche realized with delight, this reversal removes the connection of desire and knowledge at the level of origins and therefore opens up the possibility of freeing desire from the form of truth, which would mean that desire is at the root of knowledge, not the other way around, and thus that knowledge is lived first. There is, however, a distinct form of madness associated with this primacy of desire over truth (and the former detaching from the latter), which Kant's philosophy attempted to exorcise from philosophy. Critical philosophy's insistence on the boundaries of knowledge is a defense against knowledge created from desire (e.g. the speculative interest of Reason) without possible relation to truth and morality, i.e. without the possibility of assessing whether truth is given or denied to knowledge.[255] As Nietzsche demonstrated, a critique of critical philosophy would first necessitate a critique of the "value" of truth, i.e. an attempt to (consistently) think of knowledge as independent of truth —a possibility Spinoza's *Ethics* at least seemed to hint at.

It is, however, also Nietzsche who realizes that and how Spinoza falls short of the consequences of his momentous discovery and therefore makes the connection of truth and desire inescapable. This is why Foucault reframes Nietzsche's relation to Kant and Spinoza thus: "Kant is the danger, the tiny daily peril, the network of traps; Spinoza is the great other, the sole adversary. [...] Spinoza is for Nietzsche the philosopher par excellence because he is the one who links truth and knowledge in the most rigorous way."[256] This connection between desire and knowledge, while not naturally given, is still rooted in truth (the true idea), which informs their connection and hence the direction of both; the desire for

---

[255] See Foucault, *Lectures on the Will to Know*, p. 26.
[256] Ibid., p. 27.

(absolute) happiness is expressed in the desire for knowledge measured by its proximity to truth. Exactly because knowledge for Spinoza is first of all lived rather than rooted in contemplation, and because the adequation between desire and knowledge is only achieved in the true idea, the injunction of truth is inescapable: if one wants to be happy, one must strive for truth through true knowledge. The affiliation of desire with knowledge and truth is here not natural but ethical (or normative).

For Spinoza, then, there can be no malevolence *de jure*, neither in thought nor in action. Deleuze accepts this limitation to the notion of malevolence, and even re-establishes it as a form of reactive thought or degeneration. This becomes apparent in Deleuze's peculiar reading of Dickens's *Our Mutual Friend*:

> No one told better than Dickens what a life is, taking account of the indefinite article as an index of the transcendental. At the last minute, a scoundrel, a bad subject despised by all, is saved as he is dying, and at once all the people taking care of him show a kind of attention, respect, and love for the dying man's smallest signs of life. Everyone tries to save him, to the point that in the deepest moment of his coma, the villainous man feels that something sweet is reaching him. But the more he comes back to life, the more his saviors become cold, and he rediscovers his coarseness, his meanness. Between his life and his death there is a moment that is nothing other than that of a life playing with death. The life of the individual gives way to an impersonal yet singular life, a life that gives rise to a pure event, freed from the accidents of internal and external life, that is, of the subjectivity and objectivity of what happens. "Homo tantum," for *whom everyone feels* and who attains a kind of *beatitude*.[257]

While Deleuze often highlights the violence and shock in every becoming, e.g. by invoking the horror involved in "becoming-animal" in *A Thousand Plateaus*, the introduction of *beatitudo* serves a peculiar ethical function that encompasses and justifies all this violence. The impersonal

---

[257] Deleuze, "Immanence: a Life ...", p. 28f, my emphasis.

life that rises to the surface in the in-between of the death struggle is a life of pure potentiality, with life understood as pure self-constitution, indifferent to subjective or objective exigencies and determinations, i.e. "as absolute immanence."[258] It is the immanent cause that expresses itself in its own movement and thus rests in itself (as in "acquiescentia in se ipso") in an impersonal yet singular life. Deleuze, as Agamben highlights, connects this self-expression of the immanent cause with an accompanying state of being "immediately blessed."[259] Such an inference is rooted in the identification of conatus and life, and because "*in* conatus *desire and Being thus coincide without residue,*"[260] the self-expression of the immanent cause is the liberation of desire to desire itself.

The presupposed assertion that the self-expression of the immanent cause is beatitude, however, requires a supplementary element that guarantees and justifies this blessing. What Spinoza proposes is a good will towards the happiness of life (or desire) itself, i.e. the idea that if desire properly conceives of itself (or desires itself) then a beatitude will accompany this (lived) knowledge of the true idea. In other words, impersonal life folding back onto itself (desiring itself) in the singular life (desire desiring itself) is *beatitudo* and thus knowledge of the true idea becomes desirable. While Spinoza asserts that true knowledge adequate to the conatus of a body (the force by which a being preserves its own being and strives to increase its power) is accompanied by a feeling of "joy," *beatitudo* is necessary to ground and justify this assertion. The desire which informed knowledge without yet being connected to truth is now oriented towards truth which, by means of the promise of *beatitudo*, now appears as the ethical (even if not natural) end of desire; an eschatology of life. Spinoza thus reaffirms and grounds the active vitalist interest in the animation and increase of the synthesizing power of the organism, which, if it acts according to the true idea, lives in *beatitudo*. As in Kant, the moral idea of life in Spinoza is justified by an aesthetic correlate.

---

258 Agamben, "Absolute Immanence," p. 237.
259 Ibid.
260 Ibid., p. 236.

Impersonal and inorganic life is taken into account by Spinoza if and only if it vitalizes the (human) organism and *beatitudo* justifies this reduction. Even Land's libidinal materialism, forgoing intuition and the focus on the organism, retains Spinoza's eschatology of an equation with Being or pure difference.[261] Life is portrayed in this Spinozist materialist eschatology as active and self-furthering, as if life itself strove to increase itself in power, capacity and actuality, i.e. as if life had a good will. Since from this perspective every malevolence is only a *de facto* (self-) perversion of organic life and not a *de jure* self-expression of inorganic life, Spinoza (and a certain version of Deleuze) finds himself incapable of answering the question of the dark alchemy of life: "the human organism can either hide within and maintain its normative image of dynamic, self-furthering, interconnected and sympathetic life, or ask 'what is life such that it generates capacities for self-annihilation, malevolence, inertia and theoretical detachment?'"[262]

Against this concept of moral beauty or pleasure (*beatitudo*), against the idea that life ought to return to the vitalizing grounds of life in accordance with the good will of life, the desire of life itself, Deleuze *could have* put forth a transcendental malevolence. Then life, subverting the good will of life implied by Spinoza, would encompass the life denying tendencies (i.e. threatening the self-sufficiency of organic life), not as perversions but essential characteristics. The "test" that Deleuze claims life is is thus rigged from the start.

As we have already seen, the pure and empty form of time only produces novelty, which means that every event is a difference in kind without transcendental ground. Insofar as time, then, entails the rejection of the form of judgement, it also rejects the universal grounds of communication—sympathy and recognition between each event or being—

---

[261] Even though the organism is no longer the actor or recipient of the animation, the eschatology of desire desiring itself is transferred by Land into matter itself. The primary process of matter, which is retarded and hindered by structuration, needs to be liberated from progressive reification, so that matter can desire itself in its self-movement. Without the organism as the agent of this intensification, *beatitudo* becomes a more radical resting-in-itself: the absolute serenity of destruction.

[262] Colebrook, *Deleuze and the Meaning of Life*, p. 60.

except for communication understood as violence and failure of recognition (the encounter). If one allows for a transcendental malevolence which suspends the good will of life, the promise of *beatitudo* is removed from becoming(s). Rather than being interested only in the increase of the affective capacities of the body or the subjective capacities of synthesis, the passive (or impassive) vitalism we have sketched above would allow us to consider expressions of life that resist human recognition and do not animate the organism. This "resistance" is not directed *against* the synthesizing capacities of the subject or the good will of life expressed in *beatitudo*, since this opposition would still only consider the inorganic within the realm of the organic (*as* a resistance *to* the organic). Instead, the movement of time is considered in itself: it is the Real foreclosed to the organism, or an evental Being that one cannot equate oneself with or access with the intent to animate the lived. If we begin to think from the aspects that would constitute this malevolent vitalism—the separation of life from the lived, and potentials that refuse to be determined in definitive relations—if we conceive of life as refusing to cooperate with the promise of *beatitudo*, this would allow for a revaluation of phenomena previously excluded from vitalism, such as inertia, decay, exhaustion or enfeeblement. Or, as Colebrook states: "Deleuze's concepts of passive vitalism and malevolence allow us to think of waste and detritus more positively."[263]

Thinking without the ethical vision of life, bearing in mind the malevolence inherent to life, one cannot give oneself over to life. The optimist is always already organic, expecting and insisting on animation and vitalization from the sustaining ground; she is the one who wants to be a winner. The pessimist is always already inorganic, embedded in the inertia and impassivity of life, a witness to the universal becoming-loser and malevolence of life. It is here that the potential of an actual beginning to the search for "reasons to believe in this world"[264] might emerge.

---

263 Claire Colebrook, "Beauty as the Promise of Happiness: Waste and the Present," in *Deleuze, Guattari and the Production of the New*, ed. Simon O'Sullivan and Stephen Zepke (London: Continuum Books, 2008), p. 130.
264 Deleuze, *Cinema 2*, p. 172.

As Cioran remarks: "The pessimist has to invent new reasons to exist every day: he is a victim of the 'meaning' of life."[265] Only without the lure of *beatitudo* can reasons be invented.

*Transcendental Stupidity, or the Natural Stupor of Being Human*
Derrida, in "Transcendental Stupidity," his commentary on Deleuze's use of *bêtise* in *Difference and Repetition,* takes issue with one particular formulation: "Stupidity [*bêtise*] is not animality. The animal is protected by specific forms which prevent it from being 'stupid' [*bête*]."[266] Malevolence and the false (in their proper transcendental operations) seem to entail a concept of inorganic life. Thus, the reintroduction of a difference between human and animal seems perplexing. This confusion has resulted in rather literal readings of Deleuze, which locate stupidity within (or tie it to) the dogmatic image of thought and thereby prevent the possibility of a positive reading of transcendental stupidity beyond the organic image of thought. This positive notion of stupidity is worth pursuing to help us reach a concept of inorganic life, even if it requires us to read Deleuze *against* Deleuze to achieve it. We will thus move from a notion of transcendental stupidity as that which disables thought to the notion of a superior transcendental operation of stupidity which emerges at the limits of what cognition is capable of.

In Patton's translation of *Difference and Repetition,* as Derrida points out, *bêtise* is not translated with "dumbness" but "stupidity." *Prima facie,* this translation is more accurate, since it represents the actual usage of the French word more adequately, denoting "not a bad judgement, but rather the inability to judge."[267] Stupidity is thus detached from the form of truth (judgement), i.e. not understood as a false judgement, but rather a non-judgement. Deleuze, similarly, considers stupidity not as an object of judgement (error), but as a structure of thought itself by asking a

---

265 Cioran, *All Gall Is Divided,* p. 12.
266 Deleuze, *Difference and Repetition,* p. 150.
267 Jacques Derrida, "The Transcendental 'Stupidity' ('Bêtise') of Man and the Becoming-Animal According to Deleuze," in *Derrida, Deleuze, Psychoanalysis,* ed. Gabriele Schwab (New York: Columbia University Press, 2016), p. 46.

transcendental question about it: "how is stupidity (not error) possible?."[268] This inability to judge can thus neither be analyzed within an epistemological regime that asks for access to or the justification of knowledge, nor be determined by any objects corresponding to or constituted by it. However, as Derrida notes, the transcendental method itself is only possible within the epistemological "economy" of knowledge. Posing the question in this way either risks exposing "stupidity" as a transcendental amphiboly (and thus entails the need to dispel it) or threatens to discredit the closed economy of knowledge transcendental philosophy is predicated on. Ultimately then, stupidity, insofar as it is possible, is concerned with the heart of philosophy (i.e. the transcendental condition of thought itself).

There is a perversion of and in the functioning of judgement that is *bêtise* paradigmatically expressed by the Cartesian notion of the precipitation of the infinite will when faced with the finitude of the understanding. Understanding, according to Descartes, involves an intervention of the will, i.e. a voluntary choice to know, and thus the latter will always form an abyssal excess in relation to the former. Neither the will nor the understanding, then, are stupid, but stupidity emerges as a possible relation between them. As we have seen, the traditional image of thought relies on an idea of the "good sense" of thinking to enable the distinction of truth from falsity, in which case stupidity is relegated to individual psychology: "there are imbeciles *de facto* but not *de jure*."[269] Deleuze, detaching stupidity from the epistemological regime of knowledge and "good sense," frames stupidity as a relation between ground and individual:

> Stupidity is neither the ground nor the individual, but rather this relation in which individuation brings the ground to the surface without being able to give it form (this ground rises by means of the I, penetrating deeply into the possibility of thought and constituting the unrecognized in every recognition).[270]

---

[268] Deleuze, *Difference and Repetition*, p. 151.
[269] Deleuze, *What is Grounding?*, p. 51.
[270] Deleuze, *Difference and Repetition*, p. 152.

Individuation, understood as the genesis of all empirical determinations, cannot be separated from the ground which rises to the surface in the production of the individual. Rather, even if the individual distinguishes herself from the ground, the ground persists (or insists) in the individual. The indeterminate ground, however, does not *appear* on the surface (as an empirical object), but rather *is* only insofar as it produces empirical products without being exhausted by them. The ground rising up within individuation thus disables the operations of judgement, insofar as the individual cannot become an object of judgement without being separated from the ground, which in turn is not possible without negating the continual genesis of the individual from the ground and thus negating the individual's existence. Stupidity concerns this relation between individual and ground, which, as we have seen, is itself an un-ground. How, then, can Deleuze claim that "[a]nimals are in a sense forewarned against this ground, protected by their explicit forms"?[271] Because, so Derrida argues, such a relation is, for Deleuze, only proper to human beings.

Stupidity, the ground "staring at us, but without eyes,"[272] is only possible for Deleuze "by virtue of a link between thought and individuation."[273] The exclusivity of this link to man in Deleuze's transcendental notion of stupidity stems, according to Derrida, from a commitment to a certain Schellingian conception of freedom. In the *Philosophical Inquiries into the Essence of Human Freedom,* Schelling, in attempting to distinguish between Being as "Grund" (ground) and being as "Existenz" (existence), proposes that there must necessarily be a Being prior to the difference of the two: an "Ungrund" (unground), which itself cannot be determined as an identity but must be conceived as "absolute Indifferenz" (absolute indifference). Any determination of human beings, any determination of their form, occurs against the background of this "unground" or groundless ground. It is precisely this relation which constitutes the freedom proper to human beings. Even if they have made themselves an object of

---

271 Ibid., p. 151.
272 Ibid., p. 152.
273 Ibid., p. 151.

judgement and resigned themselves to the regime of truth, even if the determinations of their forms protect them from the "stare" of the ground, the relation to the groundless ground (their freedom) insists. The animal, then, is protected from stupidity because it is not free, i.e. it is not determined with relation to the ground. Derrida thus aligns Deleuze with Lacan, Heidegger and Levinas, who all in their own way reintroduce distinctions between sovereignty and non-sovereignty, response and reaction, and freedom and non-freedom to justify the distinction between human and beast.[274]

However, Deleuze's formulation that the animal is "forewarned against this ground"[275] suggests that the animal is *de facto* in contact with the ground, which begs the question of why this is not *de jure* the case. Stupidity, for Deleuze, is only possible due to a link between individuation and thought and is hence conditioned by the conditions of thought and individuation as well. In Deleuze's characterization of the "fractured I," thinking occurs as the result of the (productive) inability of the thinking "I" to determine itself as this thinking activity in the form of time. Thinking thus introduces a (formal) difference between an indeterminate existence (ground) and the determinate "I" (individual), both not resembling each other. In this depiction of thinking, the "ground rises by means of the 'I', penetrating deeply into the possibility of thought and constituting the unrecognized in every recognition," meaning it only rises on the condition of the I's activity (and failure). As Derrida summarizes: "This amounts to saying that stupidity is the 'I', is the thing of the I, of the ego. It avoids naming something, in the form of a psychic life, that we could call ground or not, that wouldn't have the figure of the I."[276]

Derrida's interpretation of Deleuze's notion of stupidity as beholden to a certain "egology" has not only influenced Deleuze's detractors, but also the interpretations of Deleuze's notion of "transcendental stupidity" from

---

274 Derrida, "The Transcendental 'Stupidity' ('Bêtise') of Man and the Becoming- Animal According to Deleuze," p. 58.
275 Deleuze, *Difference and Repetition*, p. 151.
276 Derrida, "The Transcendental 'Stupidity' ('Bêtise') of Man and the Becoming- Animal According to Deleuze", p. 58.

his advocates and defenders.[277] Being concerned with stupidity's relation to animality, Derrida neglects to consider the functioning or nature of stupidity further. In an attempt to fill in the gaps, more recent interpretations of Deleuze's notion of stupidity have traced it from its Schellingian origins but have been far less favorable towards it than Derrida's commentary.[278] In a chapter of *Schelling's Practice of the Wild* titled simply "Stupidity," Jason M. Wirth takes up the trail, pointed out by Derrida, which leads from Deleuze's *bêtise* to Schelling's *Freedom Essay*. Rather than animality, however, Wirth is concerned with the question: *"How does stupidity expose the violence and madness incipient but repressed within dogmatic thinking?"*[279] Looking at stupidity enables us to see the subterfuge of the dogmatic image of thought, i.e. the cruelty of the (moral) reasoning employed to justify or hide the fundamental values that inform this image, because there is a double genesis of stupidity and the image, one constituting the other. The shock and seduction of, or the pull of and abhorrence before, the sublime as Kant described it, reoccurs in Deleuze's description of the formless ground rising to the surface in individuation, though "it is difficult to describe this ground, or the terror and attraction it excites."[280] Thought's inability to determine the unground, to make it an object of judgement, both arouses the mind (in the transcendent exercise of the faculties) and repels it (because of the loss of the *sensus communis* and the good sense). The confrontation with the abyssal unground, from which

---

[277] Stiegler and Ferreya, for example, offer defenses of Deleuze's notion of "stupidity" against Derrida's accusations of egology and anthropocentrism, but only insofar as they demonstrate that Derrida's interpretations rest on misreadings. See Bernard Stiegler, *States of Shock: Stupidity and Knowledge in the 21st Century* (Malden: Polity Press, 2015), p. 31, and Julián Ferreya, "Deleuze's Bêtise: Dissolution and Genesis in the Properly Human Form of Bestiality," *Comparative & Continental Philosophy* 8, no. 1 (2016), p. 1–11. They do not progress beyond an accusation against Derrida of hermeneutic failure, and they thus accept the reduction of stupidity to an empirical phenomenon.

[278] See Tano Posterano, "Transcendental Stupidity: The Ground Become Autonomous in Schelling and Deleuze," *Canadian Journal of Continental Philosophy* 20, no. 2 (2016), p. 2–22, and Gregory Kalyniuk, "Crowned Anarchies, Substantial Attributes, and the Transcendental Problem of Stupidity," in *Gilles Deleuze and Metaphysics*, ed. Alain Beaulieu (Lanham: Lexington Press, 2017), p. 181.

[279] Jason Wirth, *Schelling's Practice of the Wild: Time, Art, Imagination* (Albany: State University of New York Press, 2015), p. 94, original italics.

[280] Deleuze, *Difference and Repetition*, p. 152.

the individual (human) might separate herself but which does not separate itself from her, produces "the fear of life itself [*Angst des Lebens*]," which "drives man out of the centrum into which he was created."[281] Such a fear is both *genitivus objectivus* and *subjectivus*: the fear of an individual confronted with a groundless ground, which only produces determinations to immediately consume them. It is this stupefying life (objective genitive) and the fear produced by life itself as it expresses itself in the human, because for the human being to survive as an individual they must move away from the pure will ("the consuming fire") to the periphery. The life of the human being is thus torn between two poles, *Ungrund* and *Dasein*. The creation of the image of thought is animated by this anxiety, by the will to turn the unground into a solid ground and, at the same time, the unground is "represented" by the dogmatic image of thought as a threat to thought itself, either as error or madness. As Deleuze argues towards the end of *Difference and Repetition*, defending Schelling against Hegel, there is a transcendental illusion internal to representation, which suggests that the groundless ground should be an "indifferent night in which all cows are black" and that it "should lack differences, when in fact it swarms with them."[282] Within the dogmatic image of thought, the unground thus appears as the pure opacity of death, or absolute immobility. Stupidity, Wirth argues, is animated by this fear of life which is misconstrued by representation as (empirical) death or disintegration. The individual thus attempts to flee its genetic grounds and to determine itself in relation to and within a discourse of truth. Since the unground insists in the individual regardless, thinking is constantly called upon to react to the threat of the outside, to continuously establish homeostatic stability by acting as a metabolic filter; "we can even say that the representational-stupidity complex is to the subjectal what the membrane is to biological life."[283]

---

281 Friedrich Wilhelm Joseph Schelling, *Philosophical Investigations into the Essence of Human Freedom* (Albany: State University of New York Press, 2006), p. 47, brackets are my addition.
282 Deleuze, *Difference and Repetition*, p. 277.
283 Roffe, "Objectal Human," p. 52.

Already in *Nietzsche and Philosophy* Deleuze had portrayed such a way of thinking as stupidity: "The state of mind dominated by reactive forces, *by right*, expresses *stupidity and, more profoundly, that which it is a symptom of: a base way of thinking.*"[284] It is not the reaffirmation of truths, but submission under the form of truth (i.e. judgement) that detaches all determinations from its problematic grounds and in turn determines the problems from the perspective of its empirical solutions, i.e. "*Bêtise* is the rule of the result."[285] The idea of the baseness of such a mode of thinking is repeated in *Difference and Repetition*: "All determinations become bad and cruel when they are grasped only by a thought which invents and contemplates them, flayed and separated from their living form, adrift upon this barren ground."[286] Determinations must be regarded as events, which have *their* truth according to the problematic field they emerged from and in whose (symbolic, physical, psychic) order they *make* sense. Can we not see here, maybe unrecognized or unacknowledged by Deleuze, a similarity to Hegel's argument against the classical conservative idea of murder as a matter of private pathological psychology?[287] Detaching the solutions from their fields does not result in errors, but in cruelty, violence and ultimately melancholia. To ensure its place within the discourse of truth, the individual must shift the locus of its own genesis and determination (as well as the animating force of its thinking) into itself, separat-

---

[284] Deleuze, *Nietzsche and Philosophy*, p. 105, original italics.
[285] Wirth, *Schelling's Practice of the Wild*, p. 107.
[286] Deleuze, *Difference and Repetition*, p. 152.
[287] Hegel defends the idea that phenomena can only be understood in relation to the historical, political and societal fields they emerge from with the example of a murderer: "A murderer is led to the place of execution. For the common populace he is nothing but a murderer. Ladies perhaps remark that he is a strong, handsome, interesting man. The populace finds this remark terrible: What? A murderer handsome? How can one think so wickedly and call a murderer handsome; no doubt, you yourselves are something not much better! This is the corruption of morals that is prevalent in the upper classes, a priest may add, knowing the bottom of things and human hearts.
One who knows men traces the development of the criminal's mind: he finds in his history, in his education, a bad family relationship between his father and mother, some tremendous harshness after this human being had done some minor wrong, so he became embittered against the social order—a first reaction to this that in effect expelled him and henceforth did not make it possible for him to preserve himself except through crime." Georg Wilhelm Friedrich Hegel, "Who Thinks Abstractly," in *Hegel: Texts and Commentary*, ed. Walter Arnold Kaufmann (Garden City, N.Y.: Anchor Books, 1966), p. 115.

ing itself from the unground and thus closing itself off from the threat of becoming(s) drawing on the identity of the Self. One sees the problem (the genetic grounds) but does not acknowledge it in order not to risk the form of truth (judgement) being lost. Maintaining the form of judgement requires and fosters violence and cruelty. Becoming-animal, as *A Thousand Plateaus* demonstrates, was well known to the psychoanalysts as a phenomenon in fetishism and masochism, but "even Jung, did not understand or did not want to understand."[288] As a result "they killed becoming-animal"[289] by reducing the animal to a representative (of drives or of the parents), ignoring it as a form of affect in itself, a becoming that represents nothing. Closing the individual off from the intensive fields of individuation that produced it, separates it from the various becomings (assemblages of affects) that could have increased its power to exist (*puissance*). This catatonic stupefaction of life results in melancholy, a surrender to the sad passions, without any means to overcome them being left at the individual's disposal.

*Superior Stupidity, or Inorganic Life as the Unthought in Thought*
The "conceptual persona" able to oppose this organic stupidity would not be the Platonic "friend" who affirms the common desire for the truth by dialogically answering the question "What is ...?" together with another. Rather, it might be the jealous lover, violently asking: "Where? When? With Whom? How many? Why?." While the former's question is guided by the empirical object, the latter's thinking is animated by a problem. In James Joyce's *Ulysses*, Bloom is almost overcome with anxiety and panic over Molly's affair with Boylan and it takes him an entire "odyssey" to come to terms with it—an unexpected journey without a destination. Kant and Deleuze both distinguish between knowledge (a journey with a certain destination, even if one might get lost) and thinking (a journey without predetermined destination or return). But not all thinking is thinking in the proper Deleuzian sense. Leibniz already criticized Des-

---

[288] Deleuze and Guattari, *A Thousand Plateaus*, p. 259.
[289] Ibid.

cartes, not for his false inference from the "thinking I" to the existence of the "I," but for deriving an "I" from thought in the first place.[290] We might say that thought has taken place or that it thought us, but there is, according to Leibniz, no indication of an activity of thought that would entail an agent (the "I"). Such thought, as Deleuze acknowledges, appears as a "thought flow," one usually always already structured and determined by stupidity; in other words, one thinks as they (*Man*) think—in an inauthentic mode, as Heidegger had it. The problem is hence not that we think false things (errors), but "that we are not yet thinking."[291] The task is to wrest thought from its natural stupor and *"engender thinking within thought."*[292] In this negative image, "stupidity (not error) constitutes the greatest weakness of thought," but at the same time, as Deleuze notes, it is "also the source of its highest power in that which forces it to think."[293] So far we have sketched the movement from the empirical phenomenon of stupidity to the transcendental question of how it is possible, but Deleuze seems to hint at another (transcendental) operation of stupidity.

Although Derrida's critique of the notion of transcendental stupidity seems to resemble *prima facie* Brassier's accusation of an anthropocentric condition in Deleuze's notion of thinking, such conclusions do not necessarily follow. It is Derrida's allusion to a link between Heidegger and Deleuze on the question of thinking and sovereignty that is crucial for our discussion. Deleuze rejects the Heideggerian solution that works against the impersonal mode of thought, countering the inanity of the inauthentic mode of being with an authentic (sovereign) personal choice, and embraces instead the impersonal intensities that constitute thinking. Thinking-events are, as we have already described, *all* both unique and ordinary, but never personal. Thinking is thus never engendered voluntarily but is always the result of the forces of the outside. Deleuze provides

---

290  See Gottfried Wilhelm Leibniz, "Clarification on the Difficulties Which Mr. Bayles Has Found in the New System of Soul and Body," in *Philosophical Papers and Letters* (Dordrecht: D. Reidel, 1969), p. 495.
291  Martin Heidegger, *What Is Called Thinking?*, trans. Fred Wieck and Glenn Gray (New York: Harper & Row, 1968), p. 64.
292  Deleuze, *Difference and Repetition*, p. 147, original italics.
293  Ibid., p. 275.

examples of how to expose oneself to these forces of the outside in order to avoid the dangers of cliché in Bacon's techniques for emptying the canvas. Leaving random marks, throwing paint from various angles, wiping or scrubbing the surface of the canvas disturbs clichéd visual organization, creates a catastrophe (an encounter with material outside forces) or a problem that must engender novelty (or fall back to cliché). It is in this "chaos" that we might find the superior form of stupidity.

Returning to Schelling's notion of the *Ungrund* in her book *Stupidity*, Avital Ronell writes:

> In the preface to the *Phenomenology*, Hegel chastised Schelling for placing stupidity at the origin of being. Hegel, for once, was unnerved. Clearly, the imputation of originary stupidity to human Dasein was an "issue" for Hegel, tripping him up, effecting a phenomenal misreading. Schelling posits a primitive, permanent chaos, an absence of intelligence that gives rise to intelligence. Presumptuous man has refused to admit the possibility of such abyssal origins and is seen defending himself with moral reason.[294]

Instead of a relation between the individual and the ground of individuation, it is the absence of intelligence in the abyssal unground that Ronell highlights, an absence which is nevertheless the ground for intelligence. It is Hegel, in her account, who would be stupid in the Deleuzian sense by using moral reason to deny the dark origins of intelligence (or judgement). Ronell and Deleuze both understand stupidity in the same way: as the inability to think, that is, as a transcendental failure to engender thinking. Insofar as the human being is involved in a continuous process of individuation (*Vereinzelung*) determining itself, she is at once *necessarily* in relation with the unground *and*, in order to be at all, distinct from it. Insofar as a human being exists as an actual finite being, such an existence makes a difference, alienating her from this condition, which remains indeterminable:

---

[294] Avital Ronell, *Stupidity* (Chicago: University of Illinois Press, 2002), p. 37.

Man never gains control over the condition, although in evil he strives to do so; it is only lent to him, and is independent from him; hence, his personality and selfhood can never rise to full actuality [*zum Aktus*]. This is the sadness that clings to all finite life [...]. Hence, the veil of dejection that is spread over all nature, the deep indestructible melancholy of all life.[295]

The sadness resulting from the closing off of becoming for the individual, in Deleuze's account of stupidity, is for Schelling a feature of nature as such, because existence makes a difference. The transcendental stupidity portrayed by Derrida and Wirth is characterized by a disavowal ("They knew but did not want to understand") or cruelty and violence (the baseness of reactive thought). Nonetheless, even such modes of reflection (or representation) must be considered as within the univocal concept of thought, even if they are a kind of thinking that is "defined as minimally expressive."[296] *Difference and Repetition*, in its transcendentalist orientation, aims to conceptualize difference or "to specify the concept of difference as such";[297] such an endeavor depends on a thinking *of* difference, understood as a thinking that is itself a power of intensity and intensification: a thinking that pushes concepts to the limit of what they can do. For this reason, Derrida notes, in his commentary on *bêtise*, that Deleuze asks the transcendental question of stupidity "ironically," since the possibility of stupidity does away with the thinking *of* possibility as such; that is to say, Deleuze only asks the transcendental question to leave transcendental philosophy. Asking the question in such a way means, "to have done with the transcendental."[298]

From this methodological vantage point, the question of stupidity shifts. If representation is (minimally intensive) thinking, the ground rising to and penetrating the surface (of representational cognition) is the process of intensity attempting to comprehend itself, a process which

---

[295] Schelling, *Philosophical Investigations into the Essence of Human Freedom*, p. 62f.
[296] Daniel Whistler, *Schelling's Theory of Symbolic Language* (Oxford: Oxford University Press, 2011), p. 110.
[297] Deleuze, *Difference and Repetition*, p. 27.
[298] Adkins, "To Have Done with the Transcendental," p. 533.

*necessarily fails*. Due to the form of time, any understanding or circumscription within definite limits of the Idea/problem, i.e. any attempt to exhaust the problem in a determinate solution, fails. The misrecognition of the ground by the individual is, in a certain sense, inevitable, as Deleuze writes: "stupidity [...] is the faculty for false problems; it is evidence of an inability to constitute, comprehend or determine a problem as such."[299] There is a transcendental impotence or inability to determine the ground on an empirical level *inherent* to thinking, a stupidity *de jure*. Here, in one of the rare occasions and in a surprisingly nihilistic fashion, Deleuze leaves transcendental philosophy to speak from the perspective of a philosophy of nature:

> the presentiment of a hideousness proper to the human face, a rise of *bêtise*, of a rising tide of stupidity, an evil deformity, or a thought governed by madness. For from the point of view of nature, madness rises up at the point at which the individual contemplates himself in this free ground,— and, as a result, *bêtise in bêtise*, cruelty in cruelty—to the point it can no longer stand itself.[300]

At this point of melancholia, where the individual is contemplating not only the ground she fails to determine but also her own failure, a transformation can take place:

> It is true that this most pitiful faculty also becomes the royal faculty when it animates philosophy as a philosophy of mind—in other words, when it leads all the other faculties to that transcendent exercise which renders possible a violent reconciliation between the individual, the ground and thought. At this point, the intensive factors of individuation take themselves as objects in such a manner as to constitute the highest element of a transcendent sensibility, the *sentiendum*; and from faculty to faculty, the ground is borne within thought—still as the unthought and unthinking,

---

[299] Deleuze, *Difference and Repetition*, p. 159.
[300] Ibid., p. 152.

but this unthought has become the necessary empirical form in which, in the fractured I (Bouvard *and* Pecuchet), thought at last thinks the *cogitandum*; in other words, the transcendent element which can only be thought ("the fact that we do not yet think" or "What is stupidity?").[301]

As we have already seen, in Kant's version of the dynamic sublime it is the impotence of the empirical being that pushes the faculty of Reason to the limits of what it can do, to grasp the very idea of humanity: its superiority over nature. Although the faculty of Ideas for Deleuze is no longer identified with Reason, it is the inability to think (the impotence of the empirical mode of cognition in the face of the unlivable) that "exhausts" representation and engenders the transcendent exercise of the faculties. As Martin therefore rightly claims: "one enters a form of exhaustion, a superior form of stupidity which is like a new vigilance."[302] In its stupor before the unthought, in its impotence and non-sovereignty over the inorganic life *within* thinking, thinking occurs in a subtractive mode; the unthought engenders thought in the same way that the unlived engenders the lived. As we have seen, thinking is not exclusive to or predicated on the "I." Instead, thinking is the result of the transcendental death drive because it is produced by a failed synthesis due to the pure form of time. As we have shown, the Eternal Return, as a speculative principle, lets only difference return, which means that Being is a process of continuous self-difference. The stupidity of thinking (understood as empirical cognition) is thus only possible because there is a stupidity in Being as such, or in other words, because Life is stupid; inorganic life is the absolute inability or impotence of Being to synthesize itself, which thus engenders the involuntary, non-sovereign or passive production of novelty. This superior stupidity reveals, insofar as it animates, that such an animation is only due to refusal of the unlived to be lived, or the refusal of the inorganic to be used by the organic.

---

[301] Ibid., p. 152–153.
[302] Jean-Clet Martin, "Deleuze et Derrida, Ce Ne Pas Le Même Mouvement," *Chimére* 81 (2013), p. 53, my translation.

# CONCLUSION:

# FAILURE

But the world cannot dispense with the stones.
They alone are not redundant. Nothing can replace them
Except a new creation of God.[1]

---

[1] MacDiarmid, "On a Raised Beach," p. 149.

# CONCLUSION

## PRELUDE

## DELEUZE *AFTER* VITALISM

We started our investigation with even less than a suspicion of something, rather with the curious sense of an absence, an in/existence, and with the promise of Caillois's petrified thought as a spiritual exercise. Deleuze, it seems, retains some semblance of hermetic wisdom about the identity of being and thinking in his inorganic vitalism; the spiritual practice of the plane of immanence that situates non-philosophy at the heart of philosophy. We have investigated the unfathomable genesis of the stones, but we have not found a God, only time, or the Event. By constructing a passive vitalism, Deleuze introduces all the notions that have been exorcised from life by active vitalism back into the heart of life: alienation, death, loss, malevolence, stupidity, madness.

The opening of the first chapter introduced the problem of life and thought in a confrontation between Kant's and Nietzsche's ideas about the animating and debilitating effect of thought on life and vice versa.[2] We can understand Kant's rejection of hylozoism from the point of view of his peculiar "vitalism," which insists on the boundary between the sensible and the intelligible. This allowed us to circumscribe the problematic horizon of the creation of his "image of thought."[3] The image which critical philosophy creates of its own activity of thinking can be called "organic" since it presupposes the good will of thought, which engenders a common sense between the faculties, whose genesis is not given and would be seen as superfluous, since the experience and the operations of recognition produced by it justify its own assumption of this *sensus communis*; i.e. Kant traces the transcendental from the empirical and subjects everything to the form of judgement, which in turn allows for the realization of the values of truth and morality.[4] He does, however, provide various versions of a "demonstration" that there is a striving towards organic unity, which we attempted to show in following the parallel movement of

---

2 See section "On the Uses and Abuse of Thinking for Life."
3 See section "Hylozoic Madness."
4 See section "The Organic Image of Thought."

the development of his system and the conception of epigenetic principles in the eighteenth century natural sciences. We attempted to show how the function of common sense differs between aesthetic and teleological judgement, insofar as for the former the harmony between nature and the faculties is external to the *sensus communis* while for the latter this relationship is internal to it; this allowed the full scope of Kant's organicism to come into view.[5] As Schelling had already noticed, transcendental philosophy presents a two-worlds physics that bridges the gulf between the organic and the inorganic only on the condition of the neglect of the latter. Because inorganic nature resists yielding to the ethical vison of the world constituted by the primacy of the practical, it must, for Fichte, thus be either transformed into activity or extinguished.[6]

We have shown that Husserl's discovery of passive synthesis, modelled after the combinations in the manifold of intuition prior to the operations of the understanding in Kant's A-Deduction, might have provided a route to a concept of inorganic experience or even inorganic life. But alas, for methodological reasons, he retreats from the possibility of "transcendental empiricism" implied in these temporal, passive and transgressive syntheses. The long shadow of the retraction of the outermost consequences of genetic phenomenology is still apparent in later phenomenological philosophies. Aligning Merleau-Ponty's concept of the body with contemporary theories of embodied cognition and self-organization (e.g. Maturana and Verela), we saw how all of these approaches still rely on a Kantian *sensus communis* that guarantees a "meaningful" interaction with the world. While these corporeal philosophies always assume a co-constitution of the practices and functions of an organic body and the meaning of an environment, thus rendering both personal, Deleuze asks for the genesis of their harmonic relation and co-constitution in the impersonal encounter of pre-personal singularities.[7] Picking up the problem of how the transgressive passive syntheses could produce rules for the production of expe-

---

5   See section "The Desire for Organic Unity."
6   See section "Life and Two Worlds Physics."
7   See section "The Transcendental Empiricism that Has Never Been."

rience, which Husserl and subsequently the phenomenological tradition had found itself unable to solve for methodological reasons, Deleuze's notion of an internal determination of the sensible provided a first glimpse of the "inorganic" life of the Idea that would be able to provide the conditions for real experience and not just the conditions of possibility of experience.[8] The three syntheses of time (habit, memory, thought) provided us with a model of this process of determination, wherein the relation of indetermined, determinability and determined is internal to the three terms and thus does not require external activity (e.g. organic spontaneity). It is a purely passive process without activity or agency. The rules of production are thus created at the same time as production occurs; i.e. the transcendental is not bigger than the empirical. We found a predecessor to Deleuze in Maimon, with his idea that the phenomenal world is constructed by differential relations of unrepresentable infinitesimals. This notion of determination thus escapes the organic image of thought since it does not presuppose a *sensus communis* and is not amenable to judgement. Opposing the organism's judgement of God, the inorganic life of the Idea is always "improper."[9]

The problem is that this analysis is still centered around the animation of and determinations performed by the mind. We wanted to attempt to think this form of determination beyond consciousness, and so proceeded to question Deleuze's conflicted position on the *de jure* relationship of consciousness and immanence. Following the speculative aspect of Deleuze's ontology, however, presented methodological obstacles. The Bergsonian intuition which Deleuze relies on in *Difference and Repetition* to provide an epistemological and methodological through-line for his overcoming of critical philosophy still contains a "residual humanism"[10] and thus is predicated on (and interested in the furthering of) the organism. Rereading Deleuze's appropriation of Simondon's notion of individuation and connecting it to the internal determination of the sensible that

---

[8]   See section "The Monstrous Epigenesis of the Transcendental."
[9]   See section "The Inorganic Life of the Ideas."
[10]  Ansell-Pearson, *Germinal Life*, p. 73.

we analyzed in the section "Hylozoic Madness," we were able to construct a model for a process of genesis that moves beyond the mechanism-vitalism distinction.[11] Žižek's accusation that there is an idealism at the heart of inorganic vitalism led us to consider whether Žižek might have missed the "realism" and "materialism" (as notions opposing "idealism") implied in this non-organic vitality.[12]

Taking this accusation seriously, we used the non-philosophy of Laruelle as material but also as a method to investigate further. While Laruelle himself champions a "radical immanence" of the One, with a unilateral relation of being and thought (instead of a Parmenidean identity like Deleuze), he accuses Deleuze of betraying immanence. In a critique of the transcendental methodology in Deleuze, Laruelle claims that his forebear must first split being (or the One of immanence) into two (resulting in Deleuze's dyads, e.g. the virtual/actual, becoming/being, empirical/transcendental) to then favor one of the sides and to deduce the other from it, establishing a seemingly univocal ontology. Deleuze thus takes up the divide between the empirical and the a priori structure of life into the transcendental in favor of the latter. The result of the transcendental deduction from the metaphysical premise thereby presupposes itself and subordinates discrete being to continuous becoming. This operation, Laruelle claims, breaks with immanence (the One) in order to establish an ethical vision of the world, i.e. a vision of self-furthering life understood as pure becoming.[13]

Even though Badiou is diametrically opposed to Laruelle, the fifth chapter attempted to show that his critique of Deleuze's inorganic vitalism comes to similar conclusions. Accusing Deleuze not only of espousing a (counter-revolutionary) moralism, but also an organo-centrism rooted, not in failing to adhere to the One, but in adhering to it too strictly, Badiou claims that Deleuze, taking being to be a "cosmic animal" or "organic texture," asserts the identity of concept and singularity in order to

---

11   See section "Speculative Hylozoism."
12   See section "Organs without Bodies."
13   See chapter "Non-Life."

extract the One from the many and retrospectively order every event according to the *eventum tantum* or One. Being thus appears as self-furthering, insofar as no singularity is subtracted from the One. Ultimately, Badiou concurs with Laruelle that Deleuze subordinates the material to an ideal notion of becoming. We tested this accusation in an analysis of the New Materialisms of DeLanda, Braidotti and Barad and found it justified, but only with regard to these post-Deleuzian thinkers. By taking up the organic properties of activity, agency and formative force, which themselves result from the organic-inorganic divide, and projecting them on the inorganic (or matter as a whole), these thinkers recapitulate Fichte's ethical injunction to transform being (including inorganic nature) into activity. From a more properly Deleuzian perspective, these New Materialisms fall prey to a false equation of becoming and activity and hence, since being is becoming, extend organic activity over the whole of being. This elucidates a distinction we made at the beginning of the chapter between active and passive vitalisms, the former being directed to the recovery of the vitalizing grounds of genesis that have been covered up by opposing or perverting forces, and the latter being interested in the productive process itself, including its perversion and self-alienation. Thus, the former is interested in the revitalizing potential of these grounds for the organism and thus for activity, the latter focuses on the passivity of the impersonal and inorganic genesis, which is what conditions organic activity in the first place. We saw here how New Materialisms represent active vitalism, but the question remained of how Deleuze might help to formulate passive vitalism.[14] Following the thread of one of Badiou's accusations—that Deleuze's vitalism is a philosophy of death—we reread the connection between death and the event (or the event of dying), showing that Badiou is correct, but that this is not a flaw but a possibility. By rereading Freud's death drive (via Derrida, Land, Lacan and Brassier) as the compulsion of an organism to repeat the inassimilable trauma of its genesis in the inorganic, we discovered the temporal structure of the "anterior posterior" injunction. For Deleuze, however, the death drive is not

---

[14] See section "Passivity."

an objective truth to be discovered a posteriori, but rather an a priori condition, denoting the impassivity of time as pure and empty form. Time is here understood as a movement indifferent to and not engendered by its contents or the intensive movement within it.[15] The inorganic life of the transcendental death drive is thus the movement of the third synthesis of time, meaning a production of novelty by a synthesis that always fails. Hence, every event is a caesura, insofar as it gathers time as a whole and introduces an irreversible cut between the past and the future. Every event is different in kind. This process of production without activity thus grounds and explains the structural genesis as depicted in the chapter "The Unlivable." Individuation provides, then, a model for overcoming the mechanism-vitalism dichotomy, not because there is a process of individuation common to all beings (a "flat ontology"), but because the differences between processes of individuation are multiplied infinitely, insofar as every individuation is different in kind, as well as every event comprising it. At the end of our investigation, following this analysis, we attempted to recover three notions essential to the concept of inorganic life: madness, stupidity and malevolence. Even though Deleuze, somewhat surprisingly, conceives of them quite negatively, we were able from our reading of him to think these three notions in their rightful transcendental exercise and their expression of a passive, or even impassive, sterile inorganic vitalism.[16]

The title of this book is *Inorganic Life: On Post-Vitalism*. We have spent most of the text investigating, extracting and creating a concept of inorganic life, constantly pitting Deleuze's vitalism against classical (active) vitalism and showing its distance and proximity to the latter (the "Post-"), we have not yet considered this "after" in title. We have followed after Deleuze's vitalims, we were "after" this tradition temporally (*après* Deleuze), but also in pursuit of it. The Deleuze-inspired vitalisms we investigated were events engendered by this history. We might then also be tempted, even if just by association, to ask: what comes "after" inorganic life? We

---

15 See section "Death."
16 See section "Inertia."

cannot retreat to the Fichtean ethics of New Materialism or the active vitalists' ethics of vitalization, but is there an ethics or politics of inorganic life? In what follows, we will reflect on this question.

# EXISTENCE AND DE-CREATION

## THE ETHICS OF NON-PRODUCTIVITY

*Uselessness, Alienation and Life Out of Line with Itself*
For the organism life is essentially and crucially work. It is a constant effort to construct and maintain unity, to reproduce and reconstruct its form and to regulate and filter forces according to the conservative economy that secures its persistence. It is Nietzsche in the *Genealogy of Morals* who revolts against this "administrative nihilism," which conceives of life merely as "adaptation [...], that is to say, an activity of the second rank, a mere reactivity," instead of in terms of active, "spontaneous, aggressive, expansive, form-giving forces,"[17] that is, the Will to Power. After all we have said so far, we should be aware of the false choice Nietzsche presents to us: either docile passive adaptation or aggressive active creation; either being dominated or dominating. And it is no accident that Nietzsche frames this discussion as a revaluation of the nature of the life of the organism, since from the perspective of organized beings, the excessive, the uneconomic, unruly aspect of life *appears* as a Will (for domination and intensification). Nietzsche remains all too Kantian, ruling out the possibility of a passive, non-dominating, i.e. non-organic creation.

Laruelle is correct in noting that Nietzsche's description of the Will to Power is a metaphysical exposition which is still in need of a transcendental principle (the Eternal Return) to engender and ground it. The non-philosopher, however, neglects to note the distance between Deleuze and Nietzsche, which manifests in the subtle way the former overturns the latter precisely in the matter of *how* the metaphysical exposition is connected to the transcendental principle (i.e. the Eternal Return as the pure and empty form of time). To see this, we can link the transcendental interpretation of the death drive to the definition of "Chaos" that Deleuze and Guattari provide in *What is Philosophy?*: "Chaos is characterized less

---

17   Nietzsche, *On the Genealogy of Morals*, p. 79.

by the absence of determinations than by the infinite speed with which they take shape and vanish."[18] Rather than by a lack of determination, Chaos is defined by an infinite variability. In other words, the constant failure of synthesis to establish a rhythm, reference or consistency between determinations *produces* further determinations, which do not resemble the grounds of production. Everything is, therefore, a productive product because of the pure and empty form of time. But even time only ever persists as a form and not as content. Time itself can be defined by its detachment from any content determining it, including any temporal determinations like rhythms, contractions, memories and predictions. Instead of distinguishing between an originary (authentic) and a derivative (inauthentic) time as in Heidegger, Deleuze does away with the distinction: all time is primarily derivative, but only insofar as it is produced as its own self-difference or pure difference. It is an ordinary time.[19]

Life, understood in terms of chaos or the transcendental death drive, detaches from the conditions of the organism. Our analysis of the transcendental death drive in Deleuze revealed that, instead of being an anterior posteriori truth interrupting the conservative economy of the organism, the death drive suspends such conservative economies a priori. But it was the organism, the judgement of God, that assigned lots and guaranteed the teleological consistency of life and the world. As we saw in our use of the transcendental death drive to critique Bergson's residual humanism, Deleuze detaches life from its ends or goals and denaturalizes every ground, thus following Nietzsche's assertion that there is no life of life. Life, for Deleuze, is transcendentally useless and alienated from itself. Here, Deleuze appears to be *both* radically vitalist *and* anti-vitalist. Active vitalism, as described above, attempts to investigate the genetic grounds of the structures and practices which are empirically given, in order to uncover and access the vitalizing activity underlying the seemingly mechanical world. In short, these active vitalisms want to reintroduce the unlived

---

18   Deleuze and Guattari, *What is Philosophy?*, p. 64.
19   Daniel W Smith, "The Pure Form of Time and the Power of the False," *Tijdschrift Voor Filosofie* 81 (2019), p. 37.

or unlivable back into the living to intensify the lived under the conditions of the living. But with the inorganic vitalism of Deleuze, there is only ever the loss of these grounds and the impossibility of integrating the unlivable into the living. Life is transcendentally out of line with itself, insofar as it is the form of change; all ethical injunctions issuing from life are thus suspended a priori: the unlivable is not normative and nor does any ethical demand follow from it. The alienation of life from itself is thus not an accidental factum, but the movement of life, considered properly as inorganic, itself. Hegel still sought to release spirit (or life) from alienation: he created a philosophical narrative whereby spirit comes to recognize itself as actualizing itself and differing from itself, meaning that it becomes a power unto itself (and hence doesn't require external manifestations and actualizations anymore). Deleuze, on the other hand, espouses a "Hegelianism without sublation"[20] by introducing the idea of life as potentiality, from which emerges novelties which cannot be recognized, integrated or made to be useful. But this omission of the synthesizing function of sublation reverses the dialectics as a whole. Instead of the frictionless and lossless economy of Hegel, animated by "the Notion," Deleuze's economy consists only of friction and loss, i.e. the constant shattering of the Notion by its exteriority. The power of this inorganic life, therefore, does not coincide with an extension of power, but with counter-power, the becoming-useless of life or its becoming-unemployed. It is precisely this affirmation of unemployed potentiality (the unlivable), the affirmation of the Whole of chance, which removes the organism as a condition for life and releases life from the constraints of the conservative economy of the organism—Deleuze's most vitalist point. In *Difference and Repetition*, as we have shown, the operation of the faculties at the limit of their dysfunction or impotence is called the proper transcendental use of the faculties. They only operate in the process of breaking down, or, only insofar as there is an element (intensive difference), which cannot be represented or experienced is thinking and experience engendered.

---

20   Colebrook, *Deleuze and the Meaning of Life*, p. 13.

## Inorganic Life as Unemployed Negativity

In his reflections on the end of history in Hegel's philosophy, the time in which the tedious process of labor and negation will have concluded, the historical moment of reconciliation and the rational realization of *Geist* as an underlying unity, Kojève asks what will become or shall become of the human and nature if everything is already done. Once the process (or development) which had determined the human as a productive being has reached its final stage, once the gap between want and need has been closed, once there is no more work, no more employment, what will the human being do?[21] Bataille, in a letter to Kojève, answers this question with a theory of "unemployed negativity."[22] With this notion, Bataille attempts to overcome the totalizing aspect of Hegelian dialectics from within Hegel's philosophy and to find a way for the human to survive the end of history. In Deleuzian terms, one might say that Bataille, in order to subvert Hegel's empirical use of sublation, repeats sublation in its transcendent function to find a properly transcendental notion in it; i.e. he attempts to sublate the Hegelian notion of sublation in order to revoke its unifying and synthesizing function. To do so, he distinguishes between two economies. One economy transverses differences in order to relate to itself through the distance between the differing elements and thus only allows for alterity insofar as it can be integrated into the self or identity. The other economy exposes itself to the Other (or differential) without reserve or restraint and gets lost in it; i.e. it sublates itself in the Other. For Hegel a determination is only negated in order to be sublated in another determination which reveals the former determination's truth. Being and thinking thus proceed from determination to determination, from infinite indetermination to infinite determination, constituting and continuing "sense." Negativity and sublation are thus confined within the circle of absolute knowledge, which can neither break the continuity nor break with sense. Against this relative or limited

---

21  See Alexandre Kojève, *Introduction to the Reading of Hegel: Lectures on the* Phenomenology of Spirit (Ithaca: Cornell University Press, 1980), p. 159.
22  Georges Bataille, *Œuvres Complètes* (Paris: Gallimard, 1973), p. 369, my translation.

use of sublation within a conservative economy, Bataille proposes a radical understanding of sublation, which sublates the economy itself and is thus not bound to the connection of time, the notion, truth or sense. He attempts to demonstrate the internal connection of sense with non-sense and the constitutive relation between meaning and the irretrievable loss of coherence and "nonproductive expenditure." This means, much as Deleuze will criticize Kant, Bataille criticizes Hegel for lacking any genetic account of the unifying tendency of sublation. Contrary to Hegel, Bataille proposes that every limited and conservative economy can only be explained by the logic of expenditure, whose traces the absolute system can never fully extinguish.

Negativity, understood in these terms, is thus unemployed and unemployable, since it can never be fully integrated into the unity of absolute knowledge. This becomes apparent in Bataille's recasting of the notion of negativity and action in the absence of the unifying function of sublation. Action for Bataille (whether human or non-human) is the nonproductive expenditure of forces, which vanish in the act of their expression, never to return, never to be recovered. The forces appear and disappear too fast to establish any relation between values, meaning and truth. While for Hegel the duration of the present was the differential space for the recovery of that which, in the process of becoming-other, related to itself, Bataille theorizes an existence within which expenditure and loss contract into a moment without duration (or, in Deleuzian terms, an event). Unable to relate to itself within time, this expenditure points to an existence of a zone inaccessible to knowledge and thus (in the traditional sense) non-philosophical.[23]

If the inorganic life of expenditure, i.e. a life considered beyond the boundaries and conservative economy of the organism, is approached in this way as "unemployed negativity," Bataille's speculative question remains: how can the synthetic function of the Hegelian sublation be ren-

---

23   See Tony Corn, "Unemployed Negativity (Derrida, Bataille, Hegel)," in *On Bataille: Critical Essays*, ed. Leslie Anne Boldt-Irons (Albany: State University of New York Press, 1995), p. 89.

dered ineffective or suspended? Or, as Land reframes the problem: "energy must ultimately be spent pointlessly and unreservedly, the only questions being where, when, and in whose name this useless discharge will occur."[24] Expenditure can be carried out in the "name" of the Notion; i.e. the discharge can be folded back onto itself and retroactively integrated into the unifying function of sublation. Alternatively, it can be used to stand for the unrepresentable fringes or outer edges (non-sense, loss, non-productivity) of the Hegelian sublation (sense, recovery, productivity) at which and through which it constitutes itself. For Bataille, energy can be expended in such a way that the difference created by it is not the space within which identity can return to itself, but a non-space of loss which suspends such a return. The scenes offered by Bataille as examples of this sublation of sublation (the forbidden, the holy, the sacrifice, the war), remain, however, within Hegelian coordinates of negation, insofar as the Hegelian sublation is suspended a posteriori and not a priori. As we have seen in Brassier and Land, the conception of the death drive/non-productive expenditure as an anterior posteriori creates the illusion of a traumatic rupture, or, as Bataille has it, this follows from "the fact that the ground we live on is little other than a field of multiple destructions."[25] The dualism between structure and life which Land proposes has its origins in this Batailleian reserved negation, which seeks to break the Hegelian dialectic by subscribing to an eschatology of intensification or intensive death. The active vitalism personified by Bataille, seeking to liberate and wrest life free by force from the structures it is imprisoned in, ultimately counters the Hegelian notion of productive work with the non-productive expenditure of war—the trajectory Laruelle already identified in Nietzsche. For Bataille, war occurs either as a catastrophic expenditure of energy or as an inner (mystical) experience, the latter relating to a form of sovereign thought which recapitulates the dualist problem. Inner experience, understood as an invocation of the "intimate order" within thought,

---

24   Land, *The Thirst for Annihilation*, p. 56.
25   Georges Bataille, *The Accursed Share: An Essay on General Economy. Vol. 1: Consumption.* (New York: Zone Books, 1988), p. 23, my translation.

is an attempt to reverse the capture and homogenization of forces which emerged with production (e.g. the use of tools, diachronic temporalities, subject-object relations) and establish an intimate relationship between life and non-representable being. But, insofar as the thinker wants to think, she must situate herself within production, making absolute intimacy "impossible":

> The intimate order cannot truly destroy the order of things (just as the order of things has never completely destroyed the intimate order). But this real world having reached the apex of its development can be destroyed, in the sense that it can be reduced to intimacy. Strictly speaking, consciousness cannot make intimacy reducible to it, but it can reclaim its own operations, recapitulating them in reverse, so that they ultimately cancel out and consciousness itself is strictly reduced to intimacy.[26]

This intimacy or this thinking according to non-productive expenditure appears as the "impossible, yet there it is,"[27] allowing the sovereign subject to erase the distinction between interiority and exteriority for and in it. In order to achieve the active vitalist aim of recovering a vitalizing ground (intimacy) which has been obscured (in production), Bataille introduces a form of sovereignty that enables heterogeneous non-productive negativity in opposition to the homogeneous positivity of social production. Deleuze, on the other hand, thinks of inactivity as always already implicated in every production (the death drive), which entails an a priori suspension of sublation. Therefore, "anti-production" for Deleuze is not the "impossible" engendered by sovereign choice, but an ontological category. For Bataille, non-productive expenditure is understood empirically as negativity and opposition to the unifying and synthetic function of Hegelian dialectics and thus needs to be engendered by a sovereign subject. The inorganic life of Bataille is still in need of a judgement

---

26   Ibid., p. 100, my translation.
27   Georges Bataille, *La Souveraineté*, *Œuvres Complètes*, Vol. 8 (Paris: Gallimard, 1976), p. 257, my translation.

against judgement, or a sovereign activity of the organism against itself, to engender the inorganic.

## Inorganic Life as Destituent Power

In a critical engagement with Bataille and with reference to Deleuze, Agamben has attempted to supersede the residual Hegelianism of the notion of unemployed negativity with the notion of a non-sovereign, non-productive life understood as pure potentiality. While Deleuze's idea of passive vitalism as the "force that is, but does not act"[28] would satisfy this description, Agamben notes that this pure potentiality can only be thought by suspending the implied Spinozism. With reference to "Immanence: A Life ...," Agamben highlights the inseparable connection in Deleuze's Spinozism between political and biological life. On the one hand, life is characterized as conatus (i.e. life striving to only contain itself as the immanent cause). On the other hand, this self-constitution of desire as desiring is tied to a *beatitudo* engendered by life's self-furthering, nourishing and persistence. As we have seen (and Agamben affirms), *beatitudo* acts as a lure for binding zōē and bios together and, in the highest climax of the power to act (*puissance*), collapsing both in the beatific Being. For Agamben, however, it is exactly this conjunction of bios and zōē that constitutes the juridical order of biopower, and thus the idea of conatus, as "the element that marks subjection to biopower in the paradigm of possible beatitude," is inadequate for resistance to the law, and rather reaffirms its violence.[29] In our terms, we might say that Agamben identifies the active vitalism in Deleuze's Spinozism that prolongs the organic juridical order (of judgement) and impedes the profound (inorganic) passive vitalism that is able to penetrate biopower.

Rather than the self-affecting love of Spinozism, subscribed to by the cult of productivity, which comprises such figures as Althusser and Negri, what Agamben distills from Deleuze is "a non-dialectical negativity of

---

28   Deleuze and Guattari, *What is Philosophy?*, p. 213.
29   Agamben, "Absolute Immanence," p. 238.

*désœuvrement* or a non-synthesizing dialectic of impotentiality."[30] The idea of this "impotentiality" is already prefigured in Agamben's readings of Aristotle's *De Anima* and *Metaphysics*, which are leveled against Spinoza. In "Potentiality," for example, he quotes from Book Theta of the *Metaphysics:* "Impotentiality [*adynamia*] is a privation contrary to potentiality. Thus, all potentiality is impotentiality of the same and with respect to the same."[31] According to Agamben, privation (στέρησις) or non-Being is not opposed (αντιφασις) nor contrary (εναντίον) to the *dynamis*, nor is the *adynamis* erased in the actualization of potentiality; rather, *dynamis* itself is constituted and maintained "in relation to its own privation."[32] It is the *relation* of incapability and capability which is the essence of potentiality itself and therefore constitutes the condition of the Beings that *"are capable of their own impotentiality."*[33] Thus, "in potentiality, sensation is in relation to anesthesia, knowledge to ignorance, vision to darkness."[34] To translate this into our terms, there is an unlived ground that rises up within the lived but is never exhausted by it. There is, according to Agamben, not only a capacity to do but also a capacity not to do, not merely as a derivative mode of action but as a condition for activity itself; in other words, *dynamis* and *adynamis* are not considered in their logical but rather in their existential relation. Hence, at the heart of activity is a more fundamental passivity.[35] Instead of following the active self-affecting movement of Being (joy), Agamben thus proposes an ontology of the passive taking place of Being understood as a "whatever" existence, or, translated into our terms, the impropriety of Being.[36]

[30] Katja Diefenbach, "Im/Potential Politics: Political Ontologies of Negri, Agamben and Deleuze," *EIPCP -European Institute for Progressive Cultural Policies* (blog), 2011, http://eipcp.net/transversal/0811/diefenbach/en, original italics (last accessed 11 April 2024).
[31] As quoted in Giorgio Agamben, "On Potentiality," in *Potentialities: Collected Essays in Philosophy*, trans. Daniel Heller-Roazen (Stanford: Stanford University Press, 1999), p. 181.
[32] Ibid., p. 182.
[33] Ibid.
[34] Ibid.
[35] See Giorgio Agamben, *Homo Sacer: Sovereign Power and Bare Life*, trans. Daniel Heller-Roazen (Stanford: Stanford University Press, 1998), p. 45.
[36] See Giorgio Agamben, *The Coming Community* (Minneapolis: University of Minnesota Press, 1993), p. 1.

Tracing the source of the power of sovereign action to a passivity (potentiality) which is not erased in any actuality and which persists in every actualization, Agamben discovers the messianic power of a *de-activated* politics. *The Time that Remains* characterizes this messianic moment as the suspension and deactivation of the factual, juridical order in a reversal of act and potentiality; i.e. the potency bound up and implicated in the actual is released and returned to itself. The proper ontological question of our time, as Agamben reiterates, is thus not the activity of Being (or work) but inoperativity or the suspension of activity. If that is so, then "everything depends on what is meant by 'inoperativeness' [...] The only coherent way to understand inoperativeness is [...] as a *generic mode of potentiality* that is not exhausted [...] in a *transitus de potential ad actum*."[37] In Deleuze, we have seen this power (which the actual cannot exhaust) in the form of the Idea/problem constituted by the pure, empty form of time. Time is inoperativity as such, not engendered or dependent on the empirical phenomena that occur within time and not employable by anything in time; rather, time suspends all usefulness and all work a priori. As we have seen, this temporal ontology does not entail a communality or community of events; rather, every event is radically different in kind and thus continuously ungrounds its communicative ground. It is exactly under this condition that the political, in the Deleuzian-Agambenian sense, working without prior transcendental ground, is possible. It takes place not in communication but in encounter:

> We call a potential destituent that is capable of always deposing ontological-political relations in order to cause a contact [...] to appear between their elements. Contact is not a point of tangency nor a quid or a substance in which two elements communicate: it is defined only by an absence of representation, only by a caesura. Where a relation is rendered destitute and interrupted, its elements are in this sense in contact, because the absence of every relation is exhibited between them.[38]

---

37   Ibid., p. 61f.
38   Giorgio Agamben, *The Use of Bodies* (Stanford: Stanford University Press, 2016), p. 272.

To engender contact (an encounter) in this manner, Agamben proposes a "destituent" power that would suspend the juridical order as such and neutralize power instead of overthrowing it. A constituent power (e.g. of revolution) usurps a factual power violently and thus facilitates not only the return of that power but also the reinstitution of violence as a means of governance. However, "only a power that is made inoperative and deposed is completely neutralized"[39]—a destituent violence that breaks with the constituent power. Referencing Sorel's theory of the division of classes, it is Benjamin that provides the theoretical (and messianic) means for this suspension (*Entsetzung*) of the (mythical) forms of law. He takes up Sorel's distinction between the political strike and the proletarian general strike and compares the two forms: "While the first form [political strike] of interruption of work is violent since it causes only an external modification of labor conditions, the second [proletarian general strike], as a pure means, is nonviolent."[40] For Benjamin, it is the indifference of the proletariat in general strike to the possible material gains of their victory, as they are striving to depose the power of the state as such, that constitutes the destituent power. The messianic core of the general strike consists in the refusal to resume work or to be seduced into action again by concessions made by the state or the bourgeoisie, but instead to remain inoperative until a different kind of labor work, not imposed by the state, is possible. We might call this refusal to work in the attempt to depose the law that demands work under its conditions a power of inorganic life (of the passivity of the unlived) directed against the organic activity of the lived. The death drive understood as the pure and empty form of time provided us with a model for the separation of law and life, insofar as life, in relation to the death drive, is not only removed from the form of truth but also from the lure of self-furthering life justified by the promise of *beatitudo*. There are clear proximities between the passive vitalism of the event we have traced and the ethics of

---

[39] Giorgio Agamben, "What Is Destituent Power?," *Environment and Planning D. Society and Space* 32, no. 1 (2014), p. 71.

[40] Walter Benjamin, "Critique of Violence," in *Reflections" Essays, Aphorisms and Autobiographical Writings* (New York: Harcourt Press, 1978), p. 291.

the transformation of existence into inactivity: the idea of the impassivity of time does not facilitate an ethics of action but a movement closer to Agamben's, in which Being moves "towards its own taking place."[41]

However, *The Kingdom and the Glory* recontextualizes and specifies this inoperativeness at the same time by forcefully introducing the conatus and *beatitudo* back into the dialectics of "désœuvrement."[42] Reworking the third kind of knowledge in Spinoza's philosophy, Agamben takes up the 36th proposition of the fifth book of the *Ethics* to highlight the surprising equation of the mind's love for God and the love of God for man, whereby the intellectual love of the mind is the manner in which God loves Himself. The "acquiescientia in se ipso," which Agamben had previously rejected in connection with the conatus (understood as desire's self-constitution), is now reconsidered *within* the dialectics of inoperativeness, since we:

> discover here the Sabbatical connection between glory and inoperativity (*menuchah, anapausis, katapausis*—here rendered with the term *acquiescentia*, which was unknown in classical Latin), understood here in a specific way. Inoperativity and glory are, here, the same thing.[43]

To arrive at this conclusion, Agamben refers to the 52nd proposition of the fourth book: "Self-contentment is the pleasure arising from man's contemplation of himself and his power of activity."[44] Man in contemplation,

---

41  Agamben, *The Coming Community*, p. 3.
42  *The Kingdom and the Glory* was published earlier than *The Use of Bodies*. It is, however, discussed later here, because the depiction of "inoperativeness" as contemplation in the former is clearer and it can retrospectively be seen to problematize the later attempt to formulate the theory of a "destituent" power in regard to an implied Spinozism.
43  Giorgio Agamben, *The Kingdom and the Glory* (Stanford: Stanford University Press, 2011), p. 250.
44  Baruch de Spinoza, "Ethics," in *Complete Works* (Indianapolis: Hackett Publishing, 2002), Def. of Emotions 25. It should be noted that the Curley translation in the Princeton University Press edition interprets the basic concepts quite differently: "Self-esteem is a joy born of the fact that man considers himself and his power of acting (by Def. A:ff. XXV). But man's true power of acting, or virtue, is reason itself (by IIIP3), which man considers clearly and distinctly (by IIP40 and P43). Therefore, self-esteem arises from II/249 reason." Spinoza, *The Ethics*, p. 247.

for Agamben's reading of Spinoza, is not inactive; all specific *energeia* are inoperative and thus such a life "lives only (its) livability"[45] without effort or suffering. This *sui generis* praxis corresponds to the potency described above, insofar as both are the inoperative in every operation, or the passive condition of activity, which contains a messianic core, i.e. the moment in which all the potency or all the inoperativity bound up in actuality and the operations of life is returned and retained in itself. In the contemplative life, then, in the inoperativity understood as the sabbatism proper to human existence, for Agamben "*bios* coincides with the *zōē* without remainder."[46] In the liberation from their social or biological determinations, in their anthropogenesis in inoperativity, human beings are blessed; life and glory collapse into one. Agamben utilizes the structure of the conatus as a striving for the immanent cause but relocates the scene of *beatitudo* away from the nourishing self-affection of life to the contemplative inoperativeness of human beings. Instead of a Batailleian unemployed negativity, he envisages an unemployable subtraction, which does not negate merely the factual juridical or economic orders that are in place now, but the juridical and economic order as such. If one remains in the inoperative mode, one subtracts the ends, the benefits and any claim to ownership associated with the operations of life, and yet performs these operations effortlessly; is as if life were but a gesture or a game.

### Bartleby: the Living Stone, the Open Road

From the vantage point of this messianic promise a fundamental problem within life seems to arise: how can we find a univocal expression of life that negotiates between the immobility of inoperativeness, a life in which the human being expresses and is expressed as beatific Being in the contemplation of her own potency, *and* the frantic mobility of nomadic singularities, the expressions of a self-differential eventual Being (or pure becoming)? The eponymous antihero of Melville's 1853 nar-

---

[45] Agamben, *The Kingdom and the Glory*, p. 251.
[46] Ibid.

rative *Bartleby, the Scrivener: A Story of Wall Street* seems to embody a disjunctive synthesis of the swarming of singularities and the inertia of refusal: a becoming-stone. While American literature, especially in its French reception from Tocqueville to Baudrillard, is equated with infinite mobility (the movement across the great landmass crossed by open roads), Bartleby seems to be an expression of pure inertia and closed interiority.[47] He slowly lays down work, both refusing *to* work and to produce *a* work (the legal text) and increasingly decreases his "territory" or *Lebenswelt* by repudiating all requests to vacate the premises of the office, every denial punctuated by the formula "I would prefer not to."[48] Surprisingly, Bartleby's *désœuvrement* is translated into a philosophical problem both by Deleuze in "Bartleby; or, The Formula" and by Agamben in his (Deleuze-inspired) essay "Bartleby, or On Contingency" as a linguistic issue first and foremost. In a rather uncharacteristic allusion to the power of linguistic indeterminacy, Deleuze claims that the agrammatical formula ("I would prefer not to") "hollows out a zone of indetermination that renders words indistinguishable, that creates a vacuum within language."[49] The formula expresses a preference with object (or reference) *and* a refusal which is uttered as a preference. By way of an explanation, Agamben recontextualizes this zone of "indistinction"[50] into a logic of potentiality. The formula introduces an indistinction between the preferable and the nonpreferable, between yes and no, which is also a zone of indeterminacy "between the potential to be (or do) and the potential not to be (or do)."[51] The or-operator in this argument redoubles the indeterminacy, because the indeterminacy of affirmation and negation reoccurs *within* potentiality in the "both/and" of act and being. Because it cannot be resolved in a dialectics of opposites and clear readabil-

---

47 Kaufman, *Deleuze, the Dark Precursor*, p. 138.
48 Herman Melville, "Bartleby, the Scrivener. A Tale of Wall Street," in *Melville's Short Novels* (New York: Norton, 2002), p. 11.
49 Deleuze, *Essays Critical and Clinical*, p. 73.
50 The English translation of "indeterminazione" from Agamben's "Bartleby: La formula della creazione" is "indistinction" instead of the more appropriate "indetermination." Giorgio Agamben, "Bartleby, or On Contingency," in *Potentialities: Collected Essays in Philosophy*, trans. Daniel Heller-Roazen (Stanford: Stanford University Press, 1999), p. 255.
51 Ibid.

ity, the potential omnidirectionality of this inoperativeness thus appears as the immobility proper to the European tradition of thought. Bartleby refuses not only the factual work, but the protestant work ethic as such, including all its mechanisms of responsibility, discipline, accomplishment, success and competition. This refusal puts him in conflict with his employer, who exercises all registers of philanthropic morality in order to persuade or "guilt" his sickly and pale employee back into productive action. Thus, Deleuze reads Melville's "Bartleby" not as symbolic or allegorical, but exemplary:

> Whenever the attorney invokes philanthropy, charity, or friendship, his protestations are shot through with an obscure guilt. In fact, it is the attorney who broke the arrangement he himself had organized, and from the debris Bartleby pulls a trait of expression, I PREFER NOT TO, which will proliferate around him and contaminate the others, sending the attorney fleeing. But it will also send language itself into flight, it will open up a zone of indetermination or indiscernibility in which neither words nor characters can be distinguished—the fleeing attorney and the immobile, petrified Bartleby.[52]

What is most important for both Agamben and Deleuze in the "proletarian politics" of Bartleby is its specific mode of subtraction (and singularization). Between the repetitions of the negation ("to prefer *not* to collate, but thereby also *not* to prefer copying") there grows a peculiar "negativism beyond all negation."[53] The living stone, the petrified Bartleby, introduces a break with the "paternal function" (represented by the attorney) without resorting to the paternal means of revolt, instead attempting to suspend the law as such. He becomes fully inorganic, unemployable by organic functionality and indeterminable in his refusal; i.e. the denial of work cannot be understood in terms of any social role or end (political strike), but aims at the end of external determination

---

52 Deleuze, *Essays Critical and Clinical*, p. 76.
53 Ibid., p. 71.

as such (general proletarian strike). In his becoming-stone, his refusal beyond revolt, Bartleby appears as the embodiment of Agamben's inoperativity, refusing to actualize his own potency, and thus remaining in it (and the contemplation of it). In this mode of radical *epoché*, Bartleby seems completely immobilized, and politics, in a left-Heideggerian twist, seems only possible based on a fundamental absence. The question of how this immobility is compatible with the mobility of nomadic thought and "America" thus comes more clearly into focus.

In his essay "Deleuze, Bartleby and the Literary Formula," Rancière is perplexed by Deleuze's interpretation, exclaiming that "He transforms Bartleby, the voluntary recluse, into a hero of the open road."[54] To describe this paradox, Rancière contrasts Deleuze with Flaubert in relation to the Aristotelian counter-poles of character and action. While Flaubert makes narrative, and thus action, the center of a story at the cost of becoming, Deleuze maintains becoming by focusing on character. Rancière thus sets up a split between the privileging of *haecceitas* over character (Flaubert) or the privileging of becoming over narrative (Deleuze). This division is then located *within* Deleuze's own philosophy by Kaufman in her text "Bartleby, the Immobile" a split between being and becoming: on the one hand Deleuze and Guattari repeatedly emphasize the eventness of being as "thisness," while on the other Deleuze builds a topology of becoming around the rejection of "haecceities" in the essay on Bartleby. However, even from the commentary Rancière provides on Deleuze's "Whitman," this apparent paradox can be resolved by inverting it. To resolve the tension between interiority (the recluse) and openness (the open road), or between immobility and mobility, Deleuze applies the logic of Whitman, which he had earlier characterized as "sampling" in *Essays Critical and Clinical*: The world consists of non-totalizable singularities (samples or specimens), which are extracted from ordinary points. Instead of being best envisaged in terms of nomadic mobility in

---

54  Jacques Rancière, "Deleuze, Bartleby, and the Literary Formula," in *The Flesh of Words: The Politics of Writing*, trans. Charlotte Mandell (Stanford: Stanford University Press, 2004), p. 161.

an open desert, the world is "a collection of heterogeneous parts: an infinite patchwork, or an endless wall of dry stones (a cemented wall, or the pieces of a puzzle, would reconstitute a totality)."[55] What Rancière sees within the logic of the late Deleuze is a turn away from or a limit for the theory of becoming as portrayed in *A Thousand Plateaus*, a turn to something that corrupts the innocent vegetable and animal becomings with a more immobile, petrified thought. However, we can see how the subversive thought of becoming-stone is actually already the logic of Deleuze's earlier work, in the appearance in the essay on Bartleby of Whitman's wall: "a wall of loose, uncemented stones, where every element has a value in itself but also in relation to others: isolated and floating relations, islands and straits, immobile points and sinuous line."[56] As we have seen, Deleuze does not conceive of events and structure as opposites; rather, he claims that because everything is eventual, everything is already structural, due to the paradoxical element of structure that is Time, i.e. the Event. Bartleby's immobility is a *sign* of the impassivity of the pure and empty form of time and structure. Thus, we might be able to answer Rancière's question: "Why does the whole in motion that must guide the explorers on the great road have to be the image of the wall?"[57] The mineral logic of the wall (Bartleby's becoming-stone) disentangles mobility from openness, because it detaches movement from becoming. Everything is eventual, not because everything is in motion, but because the impassivity of time, whose operations are independent from the intensive movements within it, only lets difference return. Hence, every motion is conditioned by a more fundamental inertia, every action rests on a radical passivity and precisely because the whole is motion (i.e. every event is a cut into the whole of events) singularities themselves appear as "immobile points" within a wall (structure). One should, however, keep in mind that Bartleby fails in the end to subvert the law and dies incarcerated and alone. It seems like every becoming-stone carries with it not only the pos-

---

55 Deleuze, *Essays Critical and Clinical*, p. 57.
56 Ibid., p. 86.
57 Rancière, "Deleuze, Bartleby, and the Literary Formula," p. 161f.

sibility but the condition of becoming-loser, of a fundamental failure. It is Deleuze's encounter with Beckett that will think through this politics of failure and exhaustion—a truly inorganic politics.

*The Politics of Immobility and Exhaustion*

In his book *Infinite Mobilization,* Peter Sloterdijk identifies the dream of a "kinetic utopia" of perpetual mobilization as the central project of modernity, underlying both fascism and industrial production. Within mobilization, the "self-intensification" of the world, immobility can only appear as a planned rest that engenders later movement, or else as a failure to move with no political significance in itself.[58] In Bartleby, contrary to this tendency, we find the first hero of immobility. While both Agamben and Deleuze are interested in the subtractive logic of "becoming-stone" that Bartleby introduces into politics, their interpretations diverge drastically at a certain juncture. Ultimately, while Agamben presents us with a messianic anarchism, within which the riddle of Being and Life must be solved in the political, Deleuze champions an anarchist metaphysics of constant apocalypse (without a messianic core). In his essay on Deleuze's political gesture, Jérémie Valentin suggests that there is a "decisive difference between 'ne faire rien' (doing nothing) and 'faire le rien' (making the nothing)"[59] and claims that the latter describes immanent politics more accurately. Surreptitiously, the first formula seems to be directed at Agamben, who remains in a kind of *ataraxia* (entailing *apraghia*), refusing to live, while Deleuze suggests that "one remains active, but for nothing."[60] Instead of remaining in the contemplation of one's own being and capacity to act, Deleuze seeks to pervert the capacities and faculties.[61] The encounter with Beckett, the experiment Deleuze dares to

---

[58] Compare Peter Sloterdijk, *Infinite Mobilization: Towards a Critique of Political Kinetics* (Malden: Polity Press, 2020), p. 5, 10.
[59] Jérémie Valentin, "Deleuze's Political Gesture," in *Deleuze and Philosophy*, ed. Constantin V. Boundas (Edinburgh: Edinburgh University Press, 2005), p. 194.
[60] Deleuze, *Essays Critical and Clinical*, p. 153.
[61] As Deleuze and Guattari fittingly characterize this strategy: "The pervert is the one who acts without regard for the result but only for the sake of the event or the process itself." Deleuze and Guattari, *A Thousand Plateaus*, p. 357.

attempt with the affect of exhaustion, demarcates the point where Agamben and Deleuze part ways, the latter going places the former cannot risk venturing out to. The conjunction of contemplation (as pure inoperativeness) and *beatitudo* reveals, for Agamben, the fullness of Being that only takes place in itself. Wanting to retain the promise of *beatitudo* to fuel the messianic core of *désœuvrement*, Agamben must also restrict inoperativeness to the "fulness" of Being in contemplation. Deleuze, on the other hand, risks failing at *beatitudo* and experiments with destitution. As Audrey Wasser notes, this challenges the commonplace notion "that Deleuze's philosophy is wholly affirmative of the plentitude of being. Instead Deleuze finds that Beckett's genius lies in showing us 'how it is' that possibilities are exhausted and activity depleted."[62] In the experiment of Deleuze's Beckett, I claim, we can find a distinct inorganic logic that even exceeds Bartleby's becoming-stone, and which demonstrates in space and time the encounter with the pure and empty form of time that is exhaustion. And, although Deleuze claims that his text "The Exhausted" is not political since it is dedicated to Beckett, an involuntarist politics seems permeate the text.

Deleuze begins his treatment of Beckett with the fundamental distinction between tiredness and exhaustion:

> Being exhausted is much more than being tired. [...] The tired person no longer has any (subjective) possibility at his disposal; he therefore cannot realize the slightest (objective) possibility. But the latter remains, because one can never realize the whole of the possible; in fact, one even creates the possible to the extent that one realizes it. The tired person has merely exhausted the realization, whereas the exhausted person exhausts the whole of the possible. The tired person can no longer realize, but the exhausted person can no longer possibilize.[63]

---

[62] Aubrey Wasser, "A Relentless Spinozism: Deleuze's Encounter with Beckett," *SubStance* #127 41, no. 1 (2012), p. 133.

[63] Deleuze, *Essays Critical and Clinical*, p. 152.

As we have seen, God (the sum total of all possibilities) creates the world by applying a progressive disjunctive syllogism. Under the judgement of God, man realized the possible through the progressive exclusion of options (the possible), always retaining the idea that the possible is greater than the real. The tired person might lose the ability to realize possibilities, but they still exist independently of this inability. Conversely, living "according to certain goals, plans, and preferences,"[64] i.e. according to pre-existent possibilities, is what makes one tired.[65] The inorganic logic of exhaustion on the other hand works through an inclusive disjunction that combines the set of variables in and of a situation, but only on the condition that any pre-given preferences or ends are renounced, i.e. only if the possible is subtracted. Without collapsing into an undifferentiated ground (which would presuppose a whole of the possible again), these combinatory logics produce sets containing seeming contradictions which do not form a unity but zones of indeterminacy. The exhausted thus exhausts the possible in this combination of all possibilities without realization: "As for his feet, sometimes he wore on each a sock, or on the one sock and on the other a stocking, or a boot, or a sock and slipper, or a stocking and boot [...]."[66] Such a combinatoric is not restricted to the assemblages of things, but exists in every variable of a situation. This is embodied, for example, in Watt's strange form of locomotion, which, exhausting all cardinal directions at once, operates in a peculiar form of gyration.

The inclusive disjunction of the exhaustive combinatorics corresponds to a change in the "image" of God: "everything divides, but into itself; and God, who is the sum total of the possible, merges with Nothing, of which each thing is a modification."[67] Paradoxically, it is this impossibility of possibility in the exhaustion of the possible without realization that Deleuze frames as a "relentless Spinozism."[68] While more explicit

---

64  Ibid.
65  See Audronė Žukauskaitė, "Potentiality as a Life: Deleuze, Agamben, Beckett," *Deleuze Studies* 6, no. 4 (2012), p. 634.
66  Samuel Beckett, *Watt* (New York: Grove Press, 1953), p. 200.
67  Deleuze, *Essays Critical and Clinical*, p. 153.
68  Ibid., p. 152.

in his critique of the possible in his work on Bergson, Deleuze comments, in a lecture on Spinoza from 1980, on the latter's naturalism: "everything possible is necessary, which means that all relations have been or will be carried out. [...] That is identity in Spinoza, the absolute identity of the possible and the necessary."[69] Due to this identity, everything that "is" at all is necessarily real, and, hence, there is no possibility. It should give us pause, however, that Deleuze adds the strange qualification of a "*relentless* Spinozism," suggesting that one can be more or less Spinozist or even a "relenting Spinozist."[70] This ambiguity should be read as a symptom of a proper "encounter," leaving neither Spinoza nor Beckett who they were, because their confrontation does violence to both. While possibility and necessity are "unrelentingly" identified in Spinoza's *Ethics*, the exhaustion of possibilities in Beckett's novels requires a "relentless" attempt to include every combination of the set of variables in a situation without realizing them. Spinoza and Beckett do not sit flush. Rather, Beckett takes the "sub specie aeternitatis" and relocates it on earth: "Use your head, can't you, use your head, you're on earth, there's no cure for that!"[71] By doing so, the *amor dei intellectualis* (and *beatitudo*) of Spinoza's pure "discourse of the concept"[72] is suspended and the *sub specie aeternitatis* reconfigured within the logic of exhaustion. And thus, without this promise of joy, the project of Beckett seems to propose the opposite results as the summation of life from the point of view of eternity, as it shows "how one makes an inventory, errors included, and how the self decomposes, stench and agony included."[73] The heavenly *beatitudo* that accompanied the rising of impersonal life in Dickens's *Our Mutual Friend* is subverted by the decomposition of the immobile Murphy.

A certain redoubling of exhaustion understood as "the exhaustive and the exhausted"[74] takes place here, which alludes to a reciprocity of the

---

69 Gilles Deleuze, "On Spinoza."
70 Wasser, "A Relentless Spinozism," p. 128.
71 Samuel Beckett, *Endgame* (New York: Grove Press, 1958), p. 53, 68.
72 Deleuze, *Essays Critical and Clinical*, p. 138.
73 Ibid., p. 155.
74 Ibid., p. 154.

logical and the physiological. These two aspects of the same notion reinscribe finitude into Deleuze's philosophy. If time is a pure and empty form, it denotes the unlivable that nonetheless constitutes the lived, and thus all possibilities are always already exhausted. From this perspective, the reduction of evental Being to the possible, as we have shown, is a transcendental illusion. However, this illusion is not merely an error which fails to grasp a fundamental ontological truth but rather a mode of producing being itself. It is an illusion that does not require correction so much as disenchantment. Exhaustion, both in the physiological and logical aspects of the encounter, thus denotes a liminal state that makes the movement of time (the Event) "felt," something which has the potential to do away with the illusion of the possible. Exhaustion, as both that which exhausts and as the exhausted body itself, announces the finitude of the organic body. Being exhausted is the affective threshold, the tipping point of a change of state in a system and thus the point at which the infinite penetrates the finite, not by addition but by subtraction.

There is a physiological and postural correlate of the liminal state in the logic of exhaustion, to be found especially in Beckett's plays; people are bent out of shape, crooked or hunchbacked, blind and chair bound, confined to trash cans with only stumps for legs; Molloy sucks stones. The successive exhaustion of the possible, a movement from the organic tiredness of the possible to the inorganic exhaustion of time, is evident in the progression of Beckett's œuvre itself. Throughout his work, Beckett progressively exhausts the possible that exists within space, the image and language itself, thereby discovering methods beyond the combinatoric logic. According to Deleuze, Beckett attempts this exhaustion of the possible with four methods:

- forming exhaustive series of things,
- drying up the flow of voices,
- extenuating the potentialities of space,
- dissipating the power of the image.[75]

75  Ibid., p. 161.

It is always a method of reduction, restraint and subtraction. Every space contains possibilities as potential events that might take place in it. But in relation to what can an exhaustion of these possibilities take place? In *Quad* the players (in varying numbers) repeatedly cross a rectangular surface in a diagonal, only to suddenly turn left when approaching the center, thus forming a "danger zone." No words are spoken, no music plays, just sounds. Deleuze highlights in this play the difference between realization (they "realize and tire at the four corners of the square, and along the sides and diagonals") and exhaustion (they "accomplish and exhaust at the center of the square."[76]) They realize the square by combining lines, but they neutralize the possible event of a collision at the center, thus exhausting the square. The potentiality of the event is thus twofold: the possibility of the event realizing itself and the possibility of a place realizing the event. In the later plays for television this exhaustion of space in its double articulation is superseded by Beckett's shift from space to the image. In a passage similar to the passages on the crisis of the action-image in *Cinema 2*, Deleuze claims that "the image is more profound [than space] because it frees itself from its object in order to become a process itself, that is, an event as a 'possible' that no longer even needs to be realized in a body or an object."[77] The image exists only in relation to its own abolition. It has come loose from the "any-space-whatever," the space of its realization, and has become a free-floating close-up of a smile. Expressing the double aspect of logical and physiological exhaustion, the image for Murphy is thus connected to immobility: "But motion in this world [of the mind] depended on rest in the world [of the body]."[78] Thus, to exhaust a space properly, all possible relations to the sensory-motor conditions of the determinate bodies in the space, as well as any perceptual prefiguration, must be eliminated.

Finally, in the works for television, but also in the late poetry, "Beckett became less and less tolerant of words"[79] and of the use of language as

---

[76] Ibid., p. 163.
[77] Ibid., p. 168.
[78] As quoted in Deleuze, *Essays Critical and Clinical*, p. 169.
[79] Ibid., p. 170.

such. Language forms an impenetrable surface of tiring possibilities and ties words to the logic of the general and the particular. Words are soaked in habits, personal memories and the inanities of calculation, so that they form a "sticky" whole. Of course, visual and sonorous images can transform or even disrupt language, as seen in the television pieces. But Beckett also dispenses with words (as in *Quad*) or immobilizes language, lets it go nowhere, for nothing, by using it to enumerate everything without preference (as in *Molloy* or *Watt*), by reducing it to the function of acoustic ornament (as in *Ghost Trio*), by extenuating it to a murmur (as in *Hey Joe*) or trapping it in repetitions. By transforming the moving and flexible organic tissue of language into an immobile and rigid wall, Beckett loosens the elements enough to turn them against themselves, to form "boring holes" in the surface to find "what lurks behind it."[80]

### THE AFTERMATH OF EXHAUSTION

In Beckett, then, Deleuze finds a notion of potentiality differing from Agamben's. Instead of the negative positivity of the human being in contemplation of her own capacity and being, Deleuze insists on a positive negativity (beyond negativity), which is not a refusal to act, but a "play with the possible without realizing it"[81] in order to pervert it. The vagrants of *Waiting for Godot*, Estragon and Vladimir, still play at 'life' while waiting for their real lives to begin, waiting for a possibility they can realize, and they tire themselves out until nothing is left and there is nowhere to go. But they keep on going. As the Unnamable proclaims: "everything will continue automatically, until the order arrives, to stop everything."[82] In *Endgame* the end has come. There is no more outside, no more possibilities left to realize and still they play through and with possibilities. From this point onwards, according to Deleuze, the question of subtraction in

---

80 Ibid., p. 172.
81 Ibid.
82 Samuel Beckett, *The Unnamable* (New York: Grove Press, 1958), p. 115.

Beckett turns less around the potential not to do and more around the potential not to be. The immobilization of Beckett's characters is thus not accompanied by *beatitudo* (as in Agamben), but expressed in an often painful becoming-imperceptible. The characters lose their names and become functions ("F1," "F2"), they lose their bodies (like "MOUTH" in *Not I*) or their physical presence (like the off-stage voices in *Footfalls*); even the works themselves lose their individuality (like the play simply titled *Play*) or become a function of Beckett's preference for reduction (as in *Lessness*). They exist not in the fullness of being, but always at the edge of disappearing, opening onto the realm of nothingness (without negation).

Beckett's politics, implicit in his work, is concerned with dealing with the catastrophe that has already occurred or the apocalypse always already here: the predicament that is living. Whereas potency is retained in the contemplation of the livability of life, the exhaustion of the possible results in the total depletion of all capacities, which "corresponds to the abolition of the world."[83] It is a "politics of the aftermath," which takes place after the possible and the judgement of God have ceased to stabilize the world, and thereby takes place after the World itself. The futuriority of the "after" is, however, only enacted at the limit state in which one is no longer able to reproduce it, i.e. in a state of exhaustion. The "after" implied by exhaustion is thus only conceivable at the edge of the dissolution of the organism, when all its forms, including the form of truth it championed, are erased. Fatigue, the tiredness that comes from realizing possibilities, is still part of the dialectics of work and thus productive itself as the prerequisite for continuing production. The realization of possibilities is directed to a field of possibilities to which every realization adds. As Zourabichvili writes in relation to Deleuze's politics of exhaustion, the problem is not that there are no possibilities, but that "everything" is possible.[84] The possible itself must be subtracted. And thus, at the moment of

---

[83] Peter Pal Pelbart, *Cartography of Exhaustion: Nihilism Inside Out* (Minneapolis: University of Minnesota Press, 2015), p. 122.

[84] François Zourabichvili, "Deleuze et Le Possible (De l'involontarisme En Politique)," in *Gilles Deleuze: Une Vie Philosophique*, ed. Éric Alliez (Paris: Les Empêcheurs de Penser en Rond, 1998), p. 365.

least power (*puissance*), the new is produced involuntarily. A sleepless philosophy: in insomnia—which is a matter of exhaustion, as Deleuze says—when nothing is possible anymore, when the organism is not able to possibilize anymore, inorganic novelty emerges.

A new Creation.

# INDEX

absolute, the 21, 54, 55, 192, 216, 243, 358, 432, 439, 448, 472
activity 16, 20, 26, 37, 40, 44, 66, 70, 78, 90, 102, 118, 125, 131–133, 154–157, 170, 175, 199, 203–207, 211, 267, 269, 286, 367, 368, 405–414, 423–426, 480, 494, 499, 507, 508–515, 521–526, 532
actual 30, 40, 44, 86, 94, 140, 150, 173, 191–197, 207, 210, 211, 216, 218, 219, 232, 234, 243, 253, 261, 270, 273–276, 279, 2897, 302, 306, 318, 320, 323, 327, 353, 364, 369, 370, 375, 392, 437, 459, 477, 510, 523
*actual-virtual* 150
actualization 94, 139, 189, 196, 211, 229, 233, 234, 253, 270, 278, 306, 307, 363, 364, 417, 420, 434, 437, 441, 455, 477, 522
*counter-actualization* 318, 375, 437
Adorno, Theodor Wiesengrund 162, 258, 261, 271, 430, 431
affect 27, 236, 263–267, 286, 258, 259, 264, 265, 485, 498, 532
affinity 91, 103–109, 139, 202, 260
*natural affinity* 105, 108, 260
*transcendental affinity* 103–105, 108
affirmation 312–313, 315, 353–354, 358, 361, 376, 388–390, 400, 423, 426, 435, 439, 447, 450, 463, 465, 516, 527
Agamben, Giorgio 22, 45, 314, 336, 481, 488, 521–528, 531, 532
alienation 306–307, 388–389, 507, 511, 514, 516
amor fati 353, 428, 436, 438–440, 442, 467, 534
animal 23, 26, 43, 61, 77, 81, 84, 112, 113, 118, 119, 126, 167, 176, 213, 241, 255, 268, 293, 298, 354, 375, 376, 388, 395, 397–404, 422, 433, 434, 487, 491, 494, 498, 510, 530
*cosmic animal* 397–404
anthropocentrism 14, 22, 254, 375, 376, 405, 407, 413, 414, 495fn

Aristotle 88, 135, 296–298, 395, 398, 443, 485, 486
Artaud, Antonin 187
assemblage 26, 27, 40, 393, 394, 413, 498 533
auto-positional transcendence 415
Badiou, Alain 44, 72, 133, 217, 228, 234, 302, 225, 226, 342, 361, 378, 379, 395–402, 416, 423, 427, 441, 442, 452, 465, 470, 475, 510
Barad, Karen 408–412, 511
Bataille, Georges 45, 68, 142, 456, 475, 517–521
beatitudo 313, 448, 467, 487, 488–491, 521, 524–529, 532, 534, 538
Beckett, Samuel 45, 531–538
becoming 17, 43, 44, 51, 123, 198, 199, 231, 233, 234, 248, 266, 270, 273, 293, 294, 299–301, 313, 315, 317, 318, 319, 352, 353, 355, 357, 360, 362, 363, 372, 375, 378, 388, 389, 406, 409, 416, 420, 423, 433, 434, 437, 440, 445, 448, 449, 456, 473, 477, 478, 484, 487, 490, 498, 501, 510, 511, 516, 526, 529–532, 538
*becoming-active* 51, 353, 357, 360, 440
*becoming-animal* 43, 294, 375, 380, 487, 498
*becoming-imperceptible* 538
*becoming-loser* 449, 484, 490
*becoming-mad* 484
*becoming-mortal* 433, 434
*becoming-stone* 248, 335, 518
*becoming-useless* 516
*becoming-unemployed* 516
Benjamin, Walter 319, 425, 429, 433, 524
Bergson, Henri 28, 52, 53, 149, 151, 181, 203, 207, 213, 237, 247, 250, 251–262, 267, 269, 282, 333, 385, 336, 385, 387, 393, 399, 407, 447, 459, 472, 534
biology 18, 41, 58, 114, 128fn, 132, 148, 201 213, 247fn, 252, 276, 277, 281, 292, 317, 318, 411fn, 421, 470
Blanchot, Maurice 23, 434

541

# INDEX

body 31, 32, 34, 36, 51, 59, 63, 67, 68, 70, 74, 84, 134–138, 149, 165, 169–177, 180, 181, 186, 188, 207, 210, 230–232, 241, 287–295, 299–305, 312, 313, 323, 324, 331, 345, 358, 360, 374, 378, 383, 385, 389, 408, 412, 420, 428, 430, 432, 434, 440, 441, 446, 464, 476, 477, 488, 490, 508, 535, 536
  *animal body* 293
  *catatonic body* 36
  *lived body* 171, 176, 180, 186, 188, 291, 385
  *organic body* 84, 231, 292, 383, 508, 535
  *theological body* 174
  *body without organs* 34, 36, 231, 232, 289, 295, 374, 389, 430, 432, 446
caesura 471, 512, 523
Caillois, Roger 13, 14, 507
capacity 15, 18, 27, 65, 125, 172, 195, 212, 220, 224, 267, 290, 291, 296, 321, 326, 376, 385, 386, 381, 405–407, 414, 425, 426, 442, 489, 522, 531, 537
causality 30, 81, 83, 97, 128, 129, 139, 284, 406, 409, 426
Cioran, Emil Mihai 14, 67, 68, 70, 227, 228, 491
cogito 87, 88, 90, 204, 207
Colebrook, Claire 16, 36, 175, 318, 385, 459, 490
common sense (sensus communis) 43, 44, 88–92, 97, 98, 103, 119–127, 129, 142, 143, 172, 177, 189, 194, 208, 227, 245, 321, 480, 482, 484, 485, 507–509
conatus 27, 102, 407, 428, 463, 488, 521, 525, 526
consciousness 89, 93, 107, 132, 149, 152, 153, 155, 156, 159–170, 174, 180, 203, 204, 229, 230, 235–238, 248–263, 267–273, 301, 304–306, 328, 344–348, 368, 375, 391, 393, 417–424, 431, 432, 442, 445, 452, 476, 509, 520
contemplation 14, 201, 247, 267–269, 282, 287, 525, 526, 529, 531, 532, 538
crack (félure) 30, 224, 230, 318, 453–466, 469, 471, 476
death 7, 13, 20, 24–25, 31, 44, 50, 52, 54, 60, 62–63, 73, 79, 119, 147, 166, 179, 188, 211, 225, 242, 300, 305–306, 311–312, 354, 357, 361, 388, 428–435, 438–443, 446, 448–465, 467–470, 474–476, 478, 480, 483–484, 487, 496, 503, 507, 511–512, 514–515, 519–520, 524
death drive (thanatos) 7, 44, 446, 451–465, 467–470, 475–476, 478, 480, 483–484, 503, 511–512, 514–515, 519–520, 524
decisional structure 337, 350, 403
DeLanda, Manuel 16, 26, 29, 223, 247–248, 284, 364, 392–394, 405–406, 410, 511
democracy in thought 337, 342, 373
Derrida, Jacques 16, 19, 24–25, 50, 119, 123, 164–165, 167, 177, 188, 210, 230, 298, 320, 337, 341, 343, 368, 373, 428, 438, 440, 450–451, 456–457, 462, 472, 491–495, 499, 501, 503, 511, 518
desire 5–6, 14, 17–18, 20, 27, 31, 42, 77–78, 97, 99–101, 118, 120, 125, 149, 223–225, 227, 264–265, 285, 291, 300, 317, 326, 331, 337–338, 356, 360, 370, 388, 429, 436, 444, 447, 458, 484–489, 498, 508, 521, 525
destituent power 521, 524
determination 6, 35, 53, 55, 59, 67, 90, 101, 105, 123, 128, 132, 139–140, 148, 151, 190–194, 196–198, 203–206, 208, 210, 213, 217, 219, 221–224, 227–228, 230–231, 233, 252, 275, 278, 285, 291–292, 298–300, 341–342, 345, 355, 357, 370, 395, 410, 450, 456, 465, 470, 473, 476–477, 479–480, 493, 497, 509, 515, 517, 528
dialectics 107, 162, 164, 175, 206, 216–217, 248, 250, 252, 258, 299, 320, 456, 516–517, 520, 525, 527, 538
dice-throw 400–402
difference 6, 11, 28, 40, 57, 60, 64, 72–73, 75, 86–87, 89–95, 107, 113–114, 119, 123–125, 127–129, 136, 141, 151–152, 159–161, 163–164, 170–173, 176, 180–181, 184–187, 189–190, 194–197, 199–201, 203–209, 211–213, 216–217, 219–221, 223, 225–229, 231–233, 235–238, 246–248, 251–254, 257–258, 260–262, 266–268, 270, 272, 275–283, 285–286,

291, 294, 296–300, 306–307, 313–315, 320, 324, 335–336, 338–340, 342–343, 350–352, 354–357, 359–360, 362–363, 369–372, 374, 385–386, 390–394, 398–399, 402–404, 406, 413, 417, 419–422, 426, 434–439, 442, 444, 446, 457–458, 461–466, 471–474, 477–479, 482, 484, 489, 491–497, 499–503, 509, 515–516, 519, 530–531, 536

**differenciation** 277–278

**differentiation** 27, 44, 73, 186, 205–206, 212, 218, 231, 242, 252–253, 269, 276, 281–282, 305, 307, 319, 357, 404, 444, 477

**discord** 5, 20, 97–98, 120–121, 124, 142, 172, 194, 238, 480

**dramatization** 41, 270, 277, 281

**duration** 13, 132, 251–254, 257–259, 261, 361, 441, 450–451, 472, 518

**dynamism** 139, 268, 409–410, 417, 421

**ecology** 27, 407

**egg** 181, 275–278, 280–281, 289, 292

**ego** 156, 160, 165, 169, 205, 229, 236, 251, 312, 348, 360, 461, 494

**empiricism** 29, 41, 43, 74–75, 96, 108, 135, 151–152, 157–163, 167, 169, 180–181, 190, 194, 204, 207, 215, 226–228, 236, 249, 266, 268, 272, 284, 307, 316–317, 322, 388, 403–404, 418, 468, 478, 508
  *transcendental empiricism* 29, 41, 43, 96, 152, 157, 159–161, 163, 167, 169, 180, 194, 204, 207, 215, 226–228, 236, 249, 266, 268, 272, 307, 316–317, 388, 403–404, 418, 468, 508

**empty form of time** 44, 199, 204, 206, 317–318, 436, 460, 465, 470–471, 474–476, 478, 480, 483–484, 489, 514–515, 523–524, 530, 532

**encounter** 6, 23, 29, 33, 38–39, 41, 43, 51, 86, 96, 98, 102, 121, 132, 149, 171–172, 183, 187, 194–195, 201, 208–209, 211, 227, 234, 255–256, 259, 275, 277, 281, 311–312, 317, 355, 399, 407, 416–417, 422, 441, 443, 466, 476, 500, 508, 523, 531–532, 534–535

**epigenesis** 6, 39, 41, 43, 83, 109–111, 113–114, 116–117, 189–190, 197, 279, 468, 509

**eternal return** 6, 238, 315, 319, 353, 355–358, 360–361, 377, 399, 401, 413, 420, 425–426, 435, 438, 440, 462, 467, 471, 474, 483–484, 503, 514

**ethical demand** 302, 304, 389, 413, 440, 468, 516

**event** 6–7, 56, 72, 152–153, 165, 179, 188–189, 199, 210, 223, 225, 228, 231, 233, 236, 275, 294, 343, 350–354, 356, 360, 374, 378, 396, 398–402, 406–407, 424, 428–430, 434–439, 442, 451, 470–471, 474–476, 479–480, 483–484, 487, 489, 507, 511–512, 518, 523–524, 530–531, 535–536

*eventum tantum* 400, 434–435, 440, 511

**exhaustion** 7, 376, 490, 503, 531–539

**existence** 5, 7, 15–16, 19, 21–23, 44, 56–57, 63, 66, 71, 74, 79, 81, 87, 94, 100, 106, 108, 110–111, 114–115, 120, 128, 130, 140, 150, 166–168, 171–172, 174, 178–180, 193, 204–206, 218, 226, 228, 232, 238, 252–253, 255, 263–264, 271, 283, 296, 299, 315, 325–326, 329–330, 335–336, 340, 344–345, 347, 356–357, 362, 385, 387, 391–392, 402, 418, 431, 434, 440–442, 449–451, 461, 463, 471, 477, 485, 493–494, 500–501, 518, 522, 526

**expression** 15, 17, 31–33, 44, 55, 58, 61, 105, 109, 115, 176, 213, 218, 222–225, 228, 233–234, 252, 266, 270, 282, 290, 292, 294, 311, 319–320, 336, 338, 341, 350, 353–354, 372, 388–390, 399, 420, 436, 441, 446, 452, 455, 458, 467, 488–489, 512, 518, 526–528

**faculty** 63, 65, 75, 87, 90, 97–99, 101–102, 118, 122, 125, 127, 129, 154, 188–190, 195, 208–209, 220, 223, 384, 394, 416, 482, 502–503

**Feuerbach, Ludwig** 86, 88, 119–120, 187, 350

**Fichte, Johann Gottlieb** 5, 20, 53–55, 98, 137–141, 162, 214–215, 246, 350, 398, 405, 413, 508, 511

**field** 6, 26, 37, 93, 96, 143, 153, 155, 160, 164–165, 182, 222–223, 227, 229–233, 236–238, 267–268, 270, 274–275, 277–281, 283, 294, 300, 304, 326, 331, 348, 352, 463, 479–480, 497, 519, 538

finitude 23, 52, 176, 178–179, 361, 371, 415, 429–430, 433, 438–439, 449, 451, 492, 535
flat ontology 391–392, 394, 512
fold 225, 359, 378, 395–399, 403, 423–424, 426, 483
Foucault, Michel 24, 147–148, 161, 172, 324, 402, 408, 456, 481, 484–486
fractured 204, 206, 208–209, 229, 238, 248, 419, 422, 476, 494
Freud, Sigmund 44, 263, 265, 312, 429, 452–462, 468–470, 475–476, 511
genesis 6–7, 13–14, 16, 21, 26, 37, 43–44, 78, 83, 93, 95–98, 103, 111, 114, 124–125, 129, 135, 143, 156, 160–161, 167–168, 170, 172, 176, 178, 188–198, 203, 206–207, 214–219, 221, 223, 230, 251–253, 262, 266–267, 270, 272, 274, 282, 284, 286, 298, 302, 317–318, 328, 357, 361, 364, 372, 375, 387, 390, 392, 396, 417–418, 423, 459–460, 468, 476, 478–480, 484, 493, 495, 497, 507–508, 511–512
geology 20, 85, 140, 242–243, 403
god 6, 14, 56, 79, 82, 88, 110–111, 114, 130, 147–149, 174–175, 193, 214, 219, 224, 230, 232, 238, 245, 288, 290, 295, 300, 353, 356–357, 360–361, 384–385, 414–415, 437, 484, 505, 507, 509, 515, 525, 533, 538
ground 13, 31, 44, 77–78, 82, 85, 89, 93–94, 103, 105, 107–109, 116, 119, 134–136, 143, 153, 156, 161, 164, 167–169, 172–173, 180, 185–186, 189–192, 194, 198–199, 202, 204, 208, 230, 233, 235, 241–242, 244–247, 249, 254, 264, 281, 315, 326, 335, 337–341, 344, 387, 391, 394, 404, 411, 416, 418, 423, 425, 438, 442–443, 447, 453–454, 456, 461, 474–476, 480, 488–490, 492–497, 500–502, 514–515, 519–520, 522–523, 533
*unground* 164, 187, 245–246, 454, 493, 495–496, 500
Guattari, Félix 25–27, 30, 34–36, 38–43, 50, 54, 70, 89, 162, 175, 177–178, 180, 189, 194, 211, 223–225, 230, 232, 258, 267, 285–288, 290–292, 298, 301, 303, 306, 311, 336, 359, 362, 372–373, 383–384, 390, 394, 401, 430–432, 444, 446–447, 457–458, 479, 490, 498, 514–515, 521, 529, 531
habit 14, 89, 158, 200–201, 204, 246, 255, 267, 419, 422, 474, 509
Hegel, Georg Wilhelm Friedrich 88–89, 98, 120, 162, 164, 191, 196, 208, 218, 242–244, 250, 269, 299, 304, 306–307, 313, 320, 349–350, 364, 366, 418, 429, 431–432, 448, 456, 468, 482, 496–497, 500, 516–518
Heidegger, Martin 20, 22, 52, 89–90, 125, 176–180, 208, 212–213, 228, 230, 241, 263–264, 305, 323–324, 331–333, 338, 343, 347, 361, 366, 370, 416, 429–433, 494, 499, 515
horror 175, 177, 212, 245, 294–295, 299–301, 354, 487
human 13–15, 17, 19, 22, 24–25, 27, 33, 38, 58, 61, 67–68, 71–72, 74–75, 80, 109, 115, 117–121, 125–126, 131–132, 149, 170, 174, 176–177, 182–183, 190, 197, 201–202, 210, 212, 226, 228–229, 247, 249, 254–255, 257–259, 261, 263, 267–273, 290, 294–296, 300–301, 304, 314, 319, 321, 327–328, 354, 363, 370, 385, 388, 391, 405, 407, 409–412, 414, 419–422, 439, 444, 448–449, 476, 489–491, 493–497, 500–502, 517–518, 526, 537
*inhuman* 22, 39, 165, 212, 258–259, 301, 304, 456, 468
*superhuman* 259
Hume, David 28, 42, 89, 104–105, 152, 200–203, 226, 290, 332, 367, 377, 403
Husserl, Edmund 43, 107, 151–153, 155–172, 186, 188, 199, 229–230, 241, 244–245, 249–250, 254, 258, 261, 263, 268–269, 323, 348–349, 387, 416, 418, 508
hylozoism 5–6, 43, 60–62, 73, 76–77, 79, 82–83, 95, 140–142, 211, 227, 251, 274, 288, 295, 303, 305, 395, 443, 447, 468, 507, 510
hylé 166, 169
idea 41, 44, 128, 161, 189, 190, 191, 193, 196, 197, 206–211, 217, 219, 222–224, 230, 231, 243, 253, 271, 272, 274–281, 317, 353, 383, 420, 434, 451, 470, 477, 478, 502, 509, 523
*regulative idea* 127, 191–193, 270

idealism 6, 44, 54, 56, 98, 105–109, 135, 139, 169, 178, 191, 195, 197, 203, 207, 258, 268–269, 303–304, 306–307, 315, 325, 328–329, 334, 339, 342–346, 350–352, 358, 361, 363, 370–371, 374, 413, 468, 476, 510
   *transcendental idealism* 105–108, 197, 203, 328, 344, 468
   *vitalist idealism* 6, 334, 342, 370, 468
image of thought 5, 40–43, 52–53, 55, 60, 86–87, 89, 93, 96, 119, 131, 133–134, 136, 141, 150, 177–178, 187, 192, 197, 227, 236, 246, 249, 251, 323, 337, 342, 359, 372, 413, 468, 480, 482–483, 491–492, 495–496, 507, 509
   *dogmatic image of thought* 150, 372, 483, 491, 495–496
   *noology* 5, 41, 85
immanence 6, 27, 31, 39, 42, 44, 54, 69–70, 143, 153, 170, 210, 214, 226–227, 230, 233–237, 249, 259, 262–263, 268, 283–284, 290, 295, 304–305, 314, 317, 335–336, 338–343, 346–348, 350, 354, 358–361, 372–373, 375–376, 386, 389, 391, 396, 403, 420, 433–434, 468, 481, 487–488, 507, 509–510, 521
   *radical immanence* 44, 340, 343, 372, 376, 510
   *plane of immanence* 27, 42, 70, 233, 237, 262, 284, 304, 340, 343, 350, 359–360, 396, 507
impassivity 427, 469, 477, 490, 512, 525, 530
incorporeal 189, 270, 317, 362, 376, 383, 402, 434, 436
individuation 6, 37, 44, 59, 111, 155, 161, 164, 196, 198, 211, 228, 249, 251, 275–277, 279–288, 295, 306, 392–395, 402, 410, 416–417, 419–423, 426, 434, 468, 479–480, 492–495, 498, 500, 502, 509, 512
infinity 64, 122, 134, 175, 189, 219, 263–264, 358, 371, 434, 439, 454
   *infinite speed* 70, 242, 246
inner sense 205, 345
intensification 27, 365, 376–377, 389, 405, 443, 445–448, 467, 489, 501, 514, 519, 531
intensity 26, 58, 195, 208, 218, 235, 261–263, 267, 273–274, 277–280, 288, 290, 303, 313, 388, 398, 417, 419, 422, 430, 440, 478, 501

judgement 5–6, 20, 43, 50, 65–66, 68–71, 77–78, 80–81, 83, 91, 97–103, 105, 107, 118, 121–133, 135, 138–141, 147–149, 155–156, 163, 180, 189, 192, 224, 228, 232, 234–235, 243–245, 284, 290, 297, 300, 321, 348, 384, 386, 389, 413, 418, 443, 479, 482–484, 489, 491–493, 495, 497–498, 500, 507–509, 515, 520–521, 538
   *aesthetic judgement* 98, 101, 124, 127–129, 131
   *form of judgement* 163, 180, 284, 489, 498, 507
   *teleological judgement* 5, 20, 43, 80–81, 83, 127–129, 131, 133, 135, 138–139, 141, 148, 384, 479, 508
Kant, Immanuel 5, 20, 23, 28, 40–41, 43, 49–52, 55–85, 87, 89–91, 93–110, 112–130, 132–139, 141–143, 147–148, 150, 152–155, 157–158, 162–163, 171–172, 180, 184–186, 189–194, 198–200, 202–208, 211, 215–221, 223–224, 226–230, 236–237, 241–242, 245, 251, 256, 265, 269–270, 274–276, 278, 284, 286–287, 297–298, 316–317, 320–322, 324–325, 327–330, 332–333, 335, 337–338, 344–346, 348–349, 356, 383–387, 406, 410, 413–414, 433–434, 444, 453, 456–457, 463, 468, 477–480, 482–483, 486, 488, 495, 498, 503, 507–508, 518
Lacan, Jacques 167, 177, 198, 303, 452, 456, 462–467, 494, 511
Land, Nick 27–28, 73, 242, 245, 376, 443–449, 460, 468, 478, 489, 511, 519
Laruelle, François 41, 44, 73, 307, 314–315, 320, 334, 336–344, 346–354, 356–357, 359–363, 366–373, 377, 395, 413, 415, 420, 435, 467, 510–511, 514, 519
lebensphilosophie 20, 212, 387
Leibniz, Gottfried Wilhelm 73, 75, 81, 115, 182, 195, 217, 219–220, 225, 230, 303, 317, 352–353, 378, 385, 395–399, 483, 498–499
Levinas, Emmanuel 178–179, 230, 263–265, 454, 494
libido 461

life 5–7, 13–20, 23–26, 28–34, 36–37, 39–44, 49–62, 65–68, 73, 76–79, 82, 96–97, 99, 118–119, 121, 131, 141, 149–150, 156–157, 161–162, 164–169, 172–173, 175–176, 178, 180, 187–188, 193, 197–198, 201, 209, 211–213, 216, 223, 227–228, 231–237, 243, 247, 249–250, 253–255, 257–258, 261, 263–266, 269, 273, 279–280, 282, 284–288, 290–292, 294–296, 299–307, 311–315, 317–318, 336, 343–344, 354, 356, 359–364, 368, 370–371, 374, 376–378, 383, 385–392, 394–395, 399–400, 406–407, 413–417, 419, 422–424, 427–429, 432–436, 438–446, 448–455, 457–463, 467–468, 470, 476, 478, 480–481, 484, 487–491, 494, 496, 498, 501, 503, 507–510, 512–516, 518–522, 524, 526, 531, 533–534, 537–538
  *generic life* 371
  *inorganic life* 5–7, 15, 18, 28–30, 32–34, 36, 39–44, 60, 150, 156, 161–162, 180, 187, 197, 211, 216, 223, 227–228, 231, 235, 269, 273, 284, 291, 294, 299, 302–304, 306–307, 311, 313–314, 343–344, 356, 361–363, 368, 371, 374, 376–377, 389–390, 392, 394, 406–407, 413–414, 424, 427, 434–435, 438–439, 442–443, 445–446, 450, 468, 470, 476, 480, 484, 489, 491, 498, 503, 508–509, 512, 516, 518, 520–521, 524
  *organic life* 6, 23, 25–26, 29, 31–32, 193, 197, 234, 247, 261, 287, 290, 318, 406, 454, 489
  *singular life* 487–488
Lovecraft, Howard Philipps 72, 301
Lyotard, Jean-François 22, 125, 152, 168, 227, 365, 447
machine 25, 35, 41, 187, 212, 285, 385, 391, 457
machinic phylum 27
madness 5, 7, 20, 37, 43, 45, 65, 67, 70, 72–73, 290, 312, 449, 481, 486, 495–496, 502, 507, 512
  *insanity* 63, 68, 70, 242, 290, 295
Maimon, Salomon 124, 126, 194–195, 207, 216–217, 219–221, 237, 509
malevolence 7, 37, 43, 45, 390, 481, 484, 487, 489–491, 507, 512

masochism 453, 498
materialism 7, 19, 23, 26–29, 54–55, 59, 61–62, 79, 96, 213, 242, 284, 288, 305, 317–319, 345, 376, 391–392, 395, 403, 405–406, 411, 413–414, 427, 443–444, 446, 456, 466, 478–479, 489, 510
  *new materialism* 7, 26, 28–29, 391, 395, 403, 405, 411, 413–414, 427
  *base materialism* 319
mathematics 6, 181, 211–215, 217, 222–223, 230, 278, 335, 395, 478
  *geometry* 13, 214–215, 245, 385, 478
  *calculus* 217, 221–223, 274
  *topology* 233, 455, 464, 529
memory 53, 160–161, 170–171, 195, 201–204, 207–209, 238, 244, 246, 253, 426, 473–474, 509
Merleau-Ponty, Maurice 151–152, 156, 161, 169–173, 177, 181, 186, 207, 251, 254, 305, 323–324, 331–332, 508
metal 29, 407, 414
monism 178, 214, 335, 414, 418, 425, 458
multiplicity 50–51, 123, 156, 185, 196, 222–223, 225–226, 228, 233, 270, 282–283, 292, 339, 360, 364, 374, 378, 401–402, 444
Nancy, Jean-Luc 17, 23, 100, 102, 407
naturalism 312, 315, 323, 376, 403–404
Nietzsche, Friedrich 16, 25, 28, 41, 43–44, 49–53, 55–57, 59, 68–69, 95–96, 132, 147, 151, 172, 190, 209, 225, 228, 230, 234, 241, 266–267, 269, 286, 302, 315, 318–320, 334, 352–359, 361, 370–371, 386, 389–390, 399, 439–440, 444, 448, 450, 456, 462, 468, 475, 483, 486, 497, 507, 514–515, 519
nihilism 73, 168, 211, 294, 353, 357, 365, 438, 514, 538
non-philosophy 15, 41, 73, 315, 337–340, 342–343, 349–350, 359–360, 362–363, 367–369, 372–373, 415, 507, 510
normativity 6, 43, 161, 166, 175, 198, 210–211, 316, 375
noumena 27, 73, 220, 327–329, 445–446
object-oriented-ontology 370

organicism 5, 7, 43, 83, 85, 104–105, 109, 320, 376, 384, 396, 398, 402–403, 405, 427, 508

organism 13, 15, 19, 23–24, 26–27, 29, 34, 36–37, 39, 41–42, 58–59, 92, 96, 111–113, 130, 133, 140, 142–143, 148, 174–175, 180, 197–198, 208, 228, 230–233, 238, 241, 243, 245, 258, 261, 275–277, 279–280, 284–294, 298–299, 301, 305, 311–312, 375, 377, 383–384, 386, 405, 413, 440, 443, 446–447, 453–455, 457–462, 475–477, 480–481, 484, 488–490, 509, 511, 514–516, 518, 538–539

organo-centrism 15–16, 395, 408, 413, 510

panpsychism 7, 83, 268, 273, 403, 414–420, 422, 425, 427, 435

pantheism 213–214, 414–415, 418

Parmenides 228, 424–425

passivity 7, 20, 27, 29, 39–40, 108, 154, 156–157, 175, 215, 234, 376, 408, 412, 414, 424–427, 468, 473, 480, 511, 522, 524, 530

phenomenology 22, 24, 89, 134, 151–153, 155–156, 158–161, 163–173, 175, 177–178, 181–182, 186, 199, 207, 230, 244, 249–252, 254, 257, 263, 265, 313, 318, 323–324, 331, 333, 383, 387, 432, 442, 500, 508, 517

*anti-phenomenology* 161, 249, 252

*genetic phenomenology* 155–156, 159, 161, 163, 508

*post-phenomenology* 22, 261, 265

physicalism 403, 418

physics 5, 20, 27, 55, 77, 80, 112, 131–137, 140, 212, 236, 278, 281, 317–318, 323, 351, 393, 404, 410, 412, 421, 424–425, 453, 508

*anti-physics* 5, 131–133, 137, 140

Plato 73, 132, 150, 182, 235, 242, 269–270, 273, 395, 398, 424–425

pleasure 68, 98–103, 118–119, 124, 131, 141, 189, 313–314, 452–455, 457, 461–462, 467–468, 485, 489, 525

possible, the 42, 86, 148, 150, 195, 242, 253, 276, 283, 316–317, 430, 524, 532–538

*impossible, the* 33, 404, 457, 464

post-human 22, 254, 439

praxis 386–387, 414, 445, 526

preformism 109, 111, 113–114, 279

problem (see idea)

production 24, 27, 34, 38, 40, 59, 81, 93–94, 136, 154, 156–157, 159, 187, 198, 204, 206, 211, 216, 225–226, 234, 271, 276, 279, 281, 283, 285, 287–288, 291–292, 352, 374, 376, 378, 406, 409, 412, 423–427, 431–435, 440, 444–449, 458, 477–478, 484, 490, 493, 503, 508–509, 512, 515, 520, 531, 538

*anti-production* 431, 446, 458, 520

purposiveness 5, 26, 79–80, 82, 85, 122, 126, 128, 130, 148, 384

real, the 44, 53, 56, 71, 132, 150, 166, 195, 203, 210, 216, 224, 229, 247, 271, 283, 287, 337, 339–343, 346–347, 359, 363–364, 368–369, 371–372, 392, 399, 415–416, 418, 435, 444–445, 466, 482, 490, 533

repetition 26, 28, 40, 72, 86–87, 90, 93, 95, 136, 151, 159–160, 164, 170–173, 180–181, 187, 189–190, 194–195, 197, 199–201, 203–204, 206–211, 213, 216–217, 219, 221, 223, 225–226, 231–233, 237–238, 247, 253, 261–262, 267–268, 270, 272–273, 275, 277–282, 285–286, 291, 298, 313, 315, 324, 338, 350, 353, 355–356, 363, 374, 402–404, 416–417, 419–422, 434–436, 438, 452, 454, 456–458, 461–467, 470, 472–474, 479, 482, 491–492, 494–497, 499, 501–502, 509, 516

representation 106, 160–161, 207, 394, 444, 481

*organic representation* 5, 90–92, 141, 148, 192, 194, 481

Ricœur, Paul 159, 160

Ruyer, Raymond 384, 421

sadism 469, 470

Sartre, Jean-Paul 149, 160, 206, 229, 230, 232, 237, 251, 252, 254, 263

Schelling, Friedrich Wilhelm Joseph 20–21, 98, 116, 132–136, 139, 142, 164, 198–199, 216, 236, 247, 255, 305, 349, 398, 404, 493, 495–497, 500–501, 508

Schopenhauer, Arthur 127, 164, 265, 266, 444, 454, 456, 468, 484

self-organization 15, 80, 135, 303, 406, 427, 508
sensation 14, 39, 63–65, 74–75, 84, 106–108, 157, 168, 180, 186, 190–191, 193–196, 207, 291, 485–486, 522
sensible, the being of the 181, 186, 194–195, 207, 209, 262
singularity 233, 396, 400, 510–511
somatism 131, 133, 134–138, 142, 191
soul 19, 51, 64–65, 76, 81–82, 138, 154, 168, 175, 180, 224, 231, 266, 300, 305, 360, 422, 499
speculative realism 22, 24, 261, 278, 364, 368, 475
Spengler, Oswald 212
Spinoza, Baruch de 51–55, 60–61, 82, 213–214, 216, 218–219, 237, 250, 268, 312, 336, 358, 389, 407, 425, 428, 437, 440–441, 448, 451, 484–489, 522, 525, 534
stoicism 302, 436, 439–441
stones 11, 13, 15, 23, 47, 78, 145, 309, 381, 420, 505, 507, 530, 535
structure 32, 39–41, 43–44, 52–53, 62, 73, 75, 88, 92, 101, 104, 107–109, 111, 115–116, 132, 156, 169, 172, 177, 188, 195–199, 207, 218, 222–223, 230, 232, 248, 254, 256, 263, 269–272, 275–276, 278, 285–287, 299, 303, 315, 317–318, 320, 327, 338, 341, 346, 348, 350, 352, 359–360, 366–367, 392, 408, 412, 416–417, 421, 434, 436, 446, 457, 477–479, 491, 510–511, 519, 526, 530
stupidity 7, 37, 43, 45, 313, 363, 390, 481, 491–503, 507, 512
sub specie aeternitatis 437, 451, 534
sub-representational 26–27, 37, 383, 423
subjectivity 27, 166, 177, 226, 252, 258, 261, 307, 388, 391, 403, 409, 412, 417, 419–421, 423, 445, 454–455, 487
sublation 67, 191, 455, 457, 516–520
synthesis 6, 19, 33, 40, 43, 90–91, 105–107, 125, 141, 150–151, 153–159, 164–165, 186–187, 189, 194, 199–204, 206, 208–210, 216, 220, 223–224, 234, 247–249, 257, 268–269, 272–273, 291, 302, 318, 335, 339, 347–349, 399, 413, 415, 422, 427, 436, 444–445, 460, 463, 471–477, 480, 484, 490, 503, 508, 512, 515, 527
*failed synthesis* 272–273, 503
*passive synthesis* 6, 43, 107, 150, 155–156, 158–159, 164, 199–200, 204, 268–269, 422, 460, 473–474, 480, 508
*synthesis of time* 40, 247, 268, 272–273, 422, 427, 436, 460, 471, 474, 477, 480, 512
teleology 5, 15, 16, 19–20, 26, 43, 80–81, 83, 85, 92, 94, 96, 109, 113–115, 117, 120–122, 125, 127–129, 131, 133, 135, 138–139, 141, 148, 166, 213, 231, 241, 244, 274, 275, 288, 298, 299, 305, 313, 384, 405, 413, 448, 452, 454, 463, 478, 479, 508, 515
*dysteleological* 458, 463, 474
teratology 294, 295, 298
territorialization 188, 246, 301, 325
*deterritorialization* 188, 246, 301, 325
*reterritorialization* 246
theory 18, 24, 26–27, 40, 57, 59, 62, 79, 81, 89, 105, 107, 110–117, 126, 155, 160–162, 172, 176, 181, 203, 210–211, 216–218, 221, 223–224, 226–227, 231, 242, 265, 267, 275, 277, 299, 317–318, 326–327, 337, 351–352, 368, 374–378, 392, 394, 400, 408, 412, 414, 416, 418, 421, 447, 452, 456, 471, 501, 517, 524–525, 530
thought 5, 13–18, 21–23, 26–27, 40–44, 49–55, 57, 60–62, 66–68, 72–74, 78, 85–93, 96–97, 108, 115, 118–119, 123, 128, 130–131, 133–134, 136, 140–141, 143, 150–151, 156, 164, 167, 172–173, 177–178, 182, 185, 187–188, 192, 194–195, 197, 199, 202, 204–210, 212–214, 218, 220, 223, 227–231, 236, 238, 241–242, 246, 248–251, 255, 257, 269, 271–274, 300, 312, 317, 319–320, 322–325, 327–328, 331, 337–344, 346, 349–350, 356–360, 362–363, 368, 370, 372–376, 378, 385–387, 390, 394, 398, 407, 411, 413, 415, 417, 419, 423–427, 434–435, 442, 444–447, 456, 466–468, 470, 474–476, 478, 480–483, 487, 491–499, 501–503, 507, 509–510, 519, 521, 529–530
*involuntary thought* 50, 69–70, 474, 503

time 6, 13–14, 22–23, 25, 29, 31–32, 35, 38–40, 44, 49–51, 62, 65, 70–72, 75–77, 83, 90, 92, 94, 98, 103, 107, 110–111, 113–114, 117, 151, 156–157, 165–169, 175–177, 179, 181, 185, 188, 191, 196–206, 208–211, 213–214, 217, 219, 229–234, 238, 241–243, 246–254, 256–257, 259–263, 267–268, 270, 272–274, 278, 283, 285, 292, 294, 306, 317–318, 324, 327–328, 339, 341, 343, 345, 348, 350, 353, 360–362, 364, 386, 397, 399–400, 410, 413–414, 422, 426–427, 429–430, 434–436, 438–439, 442, 448–455, 458, 460, 462, 465, 468, 470–478, 480–481, 483–484, 489–490, 494–496, 499, 503, 507, 509, 512, 514–515, 518, 523–525, 530, 532, 535

totality 123, 124, 148, 149, 192, 196, 220, 270, 284, 384, 396, 401, 426, 429, 430, 456, 472–474, 530

trace 13, 17, 23, 432, 452–455, 518

transcendence 31, 143, 153, 214, 224, 227, 230, 234, 237, 249, 251, 283, 304, 340, 341, 343, 347, 350, 360, 367, 372, 386, 389, 391, 415, 431, 479

*transcendental arguments* 325, 330

*transcendental field* 6, 160, 227, 229–231, 233, 236–238, 304

trauma *294, 451–454, 457–460, 462, 463, 475, 511, 519*

unconscious *32, 50, 154, 166, 263, 265, 337, 445–447, 452*

unity 5, 15, 18–20, 26, 49–50, 52, 63, 71, 80–81, 83–84, 89–91, 93–94, 96, 99–100, 102–106, 109, 117, 122–124, 126–131, 139, 141–142, 152, 154, 157–158, 161, 163, 172, 175, 180, 185, 189, 191–194, 196, 206, 210–211, 224, 229, 231, 242–243, 246, 251–252, 284–287, 290, 298, 305–307, 338–340, 347–349, 360, 384, 391, 401, 406, 413, 415, 444, 446, 475, 478–480, 507–508, 514, 517–518, 533

univocity *29, 52, 177, 234, 236, 335, 340, 369, 372, 376, 391, 392, 399, 402, 418, 419, 465*

unilateral *44, 458, 510*

virtual 22, 26, 150, 195–196, 208, 210, 223, 231, 234, 247, 253, 272–274, 276, 282, 286, 298, 306, 311, 316, 318, 360–364, 369, 374–376, 392–394, 401, 417, 424, 426, 459, 477–478, 510

virtualism 364, 370

vision-in-One 368

vitalism 5–7, 16, 21–22, 25–28, 30, 34, 36–37, 43–45, 50, 57, 59–60, 203, 211–213, 233, 249, 252, 258, 265, 273, 283–287, 298, 301, 304, 306–307, 314–316, 318, 320, 325, 329, 333, 342, 344, 350–352, 363, 370, 374–377, 379, 383–387, 390–391, 395, 401–403, 406, 413, 416, 435, 438–439, 442, 448, 460, 463, 467–468, 472, 475, 479, 490, 507, 510–512, 515, 519, 521, 524

*active vitalism* 307, 375–376, 385–387, 413, 435, 438–439, 448, 460, 468, 507, 511, 515, 519, 521

*anti-vitalism* 319, 515

*biological vitalism* 213

*passive vitalism* 7, 307, 376–377, 379, 390, 460, 490, 507, 511, 521, 524

Whitehead, Alfred North 125, 198, 225, 230, 231, 419

will to Power 16, 55–56, 266–267, 269, 315, 319–320, 352–358, 360–361, 420, 428, 435, 514

Worringer, Wilhelm 30–34

Žižek, Slavoj 302–306, 389–391, 402, 510

Veröffentlicht mit Unterstützung des Austrian Science Fund (FWF):
[PUB-1045G]

DIAPHANES, Zurich 2024

Cover-Photo by Shaghayegh Talebian
Printed in Germany

ISBN 978-3-0358-0700-4